Late Capitalism is the first major synthesis to ha[ve] contemporary revival of Marxist economics. It [is the] only systematic attempt so far ever made to com[bine] of the 'laws of motion' of the capitalist mode of p[roduction of] Marx, with the concrete history of capitalism in the 20th century.

Mandel's book starts with a challenging discussion of the appropriate methods for studying the capitalist economies. He seeks to show why the classical approaches of Luxemburg, Bukharin, Bauer and Grossman failed to accomplish the further development of Marxist theory whose urgency became evident after Marx's death. He then sketches the structure of the world market and the variant types of surplus-profit that have characterised its successive stages. On these foundations, **Late Capitalism** proceeds to advance an extremely bold schema of the 'long-waves' of expansion and contraction in the history of capitalism, from the Napoleonic Wars to the present. Mandel criticises and refines Kondratieff's famous use of this notion.

Mandel's book surveys in turn the main economic characteristics of late capitalism as it has emerged in the contemporary period. The last expansionary long-wave, it argues, started with the victory of fascism on the European continent and the advent of the war economies in the USA and UK during the 1940s, and produced the record world boom of 1947-1972. Mandel discusses the reasons why the dynamic upswing of growth in this period was bound to reach its limits at the turn of the 70s, and why a long wave of economic stagnation and intensified class struggle has set in today.

Late Capitalism is a landmark in Marxist economic literature. Specifically designed to explain the international recession of the seventies, it is a central guide to understanding the nature of the world economic crisis today.

Ernest Mandel

Verso

Late Capitalism

Translated by Joris De Bres

First published as *Der Spätkapitalismus*, Suhrkamp Verlag, 1972
© Suhrkamp Verlag, 1972

English-language copyright NLB, 1975

Verso Edition, 1978

Verso, 7 Carlisle Street, London W1

Printed by Unwin Brothers Limited,
The Gresham Press,
Old Woking, Surrey

ISBN 86091 703 7

Contents

Introduction

One of the central purposes of this book is to provide a Marxist explanation of the causes of the long post-war wave of rapid growth in the international capitalist economy, which took both non-Marxist and Marxist economists by surprise; and at the same time to establish the inherent limits of this period, which ensured that it would be followed by another long wave of increasing social and economic crisis for world capitalism, characterized by a far lower rate of overall growth. When this work was first written and published in German in 1970-72, its basic theses still appeared to many readers empirically unproven or dubious, and were greeted with widespread scepticism — despite the premonitory signs of the breakdown of the international monetary system from 1967 onwards, and the mass explosion in France in May 1968. Today, few can doubt that the critical turning-point in post-war economic development is behind us and not in front of us, and that the 'long boom' is now a thing of the past. Belief in the permanence of rapid growth and full employment within the 'mixed economy' has proved a myth. This book tries to explain why this was necessarily so, and what the consequences of the actual dynamics of post-war capitalism are likely to be, within the framework of classical Marxist categories.

In revising *Late Capitalism* for the English-language edition, we have sought to resist the temptation to incorporate extensive new materials in it, to demonstrate the corroboration by events of our original arguments. We have instead corrected or clarified subsidiary formulations, and brought relevant statistics up to date. All further comments will be reserved for the international debate now under way on the general contradictions and long-term trends of world capitalism in its present phase, for an understanding of which *Late Capitalism* advances certain new hypotheses. Whether they are sufficient and coherent or not, only history will judge. We have no reason to fear its verdict.

For the fundamental aim of the present work is to provide an explanation of the history of the capitalist mode of production in the 20th century, capable of mediating the laws of motion of 'capital in general' with the concrete phenomenal forms of 'many capitals'. All attempts, either to confine analysis merely to the latter, or to deduce them directly from the former, are without methodological justification or hope of practical success. For a Marxist, it should be plain that the class struggle between capital and labour, the role of the bourgeois State and late capitalist ideology, the concrete and mutable structure of world trade, and the predominant forms of surplus-profit, all need to be incorporated into any account of the successive historical stages of capitalist development, and of the contemporary phase of late capitalism itself. In seeking to fulfil these objectives, the present work has assumed a structure not unrelated to the plan that Marx originally projected for *Capital* — that is to say, it deals with capital in general; competition; credit; share capital; landed property; wage-labour; state; foreign trade; and world market (in which final part Marx wanted to include world economic crises). I have not, however, followed every section of this plan, from which the final version of Marx's *Capital* itself, of course, deviated widely.

The first four chapters of *Late Capitalism* set the overall framework for the book. They deal respectively with the preliminary problem of method (Chapter 1); the relation between the development of the capitalist mode of production, with its inner contradictions, and the creation of a socio-geographic milieu adequate to its needs — i.e., the world market (Chapters 2 and 3); and the connection between the development of capitalist technology and the valorization of capital itself (Chapters 3 and 4). Readers who are less versed or interested in theory can omit the first chapter or leave it till the end of the book.

The nine analytic chapters which follow deal with the main features of late capitalism in logico-historical order: its original *point of departure* — the radical improvement in the conditions for the valorization of capital which resulted from the historic defeats of the working-class by fascism and war (Chapter 5); its *subsequent development* through the Third Technological Revolution (Chapter 6); its *specific traits* as a new phase in the development of capital — the abbreviation of the life-cycle of fixed capital, the acceleration of technological innovation (rents from which become the main form of monopolistic surplus-profits under late capitalism), and the absorption of surplus-capital by permanent rearmament (Chapters 7, 8 and 9); its *particular interconnexion with the world market* — the international concentration and centralization of capital that generates the multinational corporation as the main phenomenal form of capital, and the uneven exchange between nations producing commodities at different levels of average productivity of labour, that dominates world trade (Chapters 10 and 11); and its *new forms and 'solutions' of the problem of realization* — permanent inflation and the typical late-capitalist trade-cycle, which combines a classical industrial cycle with a credit-expansion and credit-contraction 'counter-cycle' under the sign of inflation (Chapters 12 and 13).

The last five chapters are by contrast synthesizing in character. They seek to bring together the results of the preceding analysis, and try to show the ways in which the fundamental laws of motion and the inherent contradictions of capital not merely continue to operate, but actually find their most extreme expression in late capitalism (Chapters 14 to 18).

Two warnings are needed here. Firstly, the term 'late capitalism' in no way suggests that capitalism has changed in essence, rendering the analytic findings of Marx's *Capital* and Lenin's *Imperialism* out of date. Just as Lenin was only able to develop his account of imperialism on the basis of *Capital*, as confirmation of the general laws governing the whole course of the capitalist mode of production discovered by Marx, so today we can only attempt to provide a Marxist analysis of late capitalism on the basis of Lenin's study of *Imperialism*. The era of late capitalism is not a new epoch of capitalist development. It is merely a further development of the imperialist, monopoly-capitalist epoch. By implication, the characteristics of the imperialist epoch enumerated by Lenin thus remain fully valid for late capitalism.

Secondly, we must express our regret at not being able to propose a better term for this historical era than 'late capitalism' — a term that is unsatisfactory because it is one of chronology, not of synthesis. In Chapter 16 of this book we explain why it remains preferable to the notion of 'state monopoly capitalism'. Its superiority over the term 'neo-capitalism' is obvious — given the ambiguity of the latter, which can be interpreted to imply either a radical continuity or discontinuity with traditional capitalism. In the near future, perhaps, discussion will yield us a better term of synthesis. In the meantime, we have retained the notion of 'late capitalism', judging it to be the most serviceable term available, and above all believing that what is really important is not to name, but to explain the historical development that has occurred in our age.

Late Capitalism tries to explain the post-war history of the capitalist mode of production in terms of the basic laws of motion of capitalism discovered by Marx in *Capital.* In other words, it attempts to demonstrate that the 'abstract' laws of motion of this mode of production remain operative and verifiable in and through the unfolding 'concrete' history of contemporary capitalism. It thereby runs directly counter to two basic trends in current socio-economic thought. It does not accept the assumption of those — in either academic or Marxist circles — who believe that Neo-Keynesian techniques, state intervention, monopoly power, private and public 'planning', or whatever combination of them each particular author or school prefers, are capable of neutralizing or cancelling the long-term laws of motion of capital. Nor, on the other hand, does it accept the opposite (but in reality converse) thesis that these economic laws of motion are so 'abstract' that they cannot manifest themselves in 'real history' at all, and that therefore the only function of an economist is to show how and why they become distorted or deviated by accidental factors in its actual development — not to show how they are manifested and confirmed in concrete and visible processes.

The recent revival of Marxist economics (which we predicted some time ago) has been a particularly gratifying phenomenon of the last few years. However, it must be conceded that the present reappropriation of the past history of Marxist theory by a younger generation of socialist scholars and workers, is a difficult and exacting task. This is especially true for readers in the Anglo-Saxon world, to whom some of the classical authorities discussed in this book — for example, in Chapters 1 and 4 — may still be largely unknown. Reference to these 'older' debates of the pre-1939 epoch is, however, in no way a mere matter of piety or erudition. For the great controversies of that time were directly concerned with the *pivotal problems* posed by the basic contradictions and long-term trends of bourgeois society, for Marxist theory. These problems are still very much with us today. Fascism and Stalinism eventually silenced nearly all the theorists of the earlier heyday of Marxist economic debate. But they could not suppress their intellectual legacy. It would be much harder to solve the central problems of capitalism today, without a due recovery of this heritage.

In the last decade, the revival of Marxist economic theory has coincided with a Neo-Ricardian assault upon 'neo-classical' marginalism, led by the so-called Cambridge School inspired by Piero Sraffa. While any rehabilitation of the labour theory of value, even in a pre-Marxist version, can only be welcomed, we ourselves remain convinced that no real synthesis is possible between Neo-Ricardianism and Marxism. Contemporary Marxists have a duty to defend all those decisive advances accomplished by Marx over Ricardo, which Neo-Ricardian theorists are now seeking to rescind. The present work is not concerned with the problem of the relationship between the two systems, except at one point: the specific issue of the role of arms production in the formation of the average rate of profit — in other words, the question of the transformation of values into prices of production, which is briefly discussed in Chapter 9.

The most serious difficulty for me in writing this book was the fact that Roman Rosdolsky, the political economist who was closest to me theoretically and politically in our time, died before I could start work on it. Memories of our common discussions and study of his great posthumous work, *Zur Entstehungsgeschichte des Marx' schen 'Kapital'*, had therefore, so far as possible, to be a substitute for the constructive criticisms of this gifted theorist.

The socialist students and assistant lecturers of the Faculty of Political Sciences at the Free University of West Berlin, who invited me to be visiting professor in the Winter Semester of 1970-71, provided the 'external pressure' — so often necessary for an author — to induce me to formulate my theoretical views on late capitalism in the systematic form in which they are presented here. They also gave me the leisure needed for this purpose.

I therefore dedicate this work to my late friend and comrade Roman Rosdolsky, who helped to found the Communist Party of the Western Ukraine and was a member of its Central Committee, who helped to create the Trotskyist movement in the Western Ukraine, and who during his whole life remained true to the cause of the emancipation of the working-class and the international socialist revolution, and in the darkest years of our turbulent century ensured the continuity of the theoretical tradition of revolutionary Marxism; and to the socialist students and assistant lecturers of the Free University of West Berlin, whose critical and creative intelligence will preserve and extend this tradition.

1

The Laws of Motion and the History of Capital

The relationship between the general laws of motion of capital — as discovered by Marx — and the history of the capitalist mode of production is one of the most complex problems of Marxist theory. Its difficulty can be measured by the fact that there has never yet been a satisfactory clarification of this relationship.

It has become a commonplace to repeat that Marx's discovery of the laws of development of capitalism was the outcome of a dialectical analysis which advanced from the abstract to the concrete: 'The economists of the seventeenth century, for example, always start out with the living whole, with population, nation, state, several states, and so on; but they always conclude by discovering through analysis a small number of determinant, abstract, general relations such as division of labour, money, value and so on. As soon as these individual moments had been more or less established and abstracted, there began the economic systems which ascended from the simple relations such as labour, division of labour, need, exchange value, to the level of the state, exchange between nations and the world market. The latter is obviously the scientifically correct method. The concrete is concrete because it is the concentration of many determinations, hence the unity of the diverse. It appears in the process of thinking, therefore, as a process of concentration, as a result, not as a point of departure, even if it is the point of departure in reality and hence also the point of departure for observation and conception. Along the first path, the full conception was evaporated to yield an abstract determination; along the second, the abstract determinations lead towards a reproduction of the concrete by way of thought. In this way Hegel fell into the illusion of conceiving the real as the product of thought concentrating itself, probing its own depths, and unfolding itself out of itself, by itself, whereas the method of rising from the abstract to the concrete is only the way in which thought appropriates the concrete, reproduces it as the concrete in mind.'[1]

To *reduce* Marx's method to a 'progression from the abstract to the concrete', however, is to ignore its full richness. In the first place, this misunderstanding overlooks the fact that, for Marx, the concrete was both the 'real starting point' and the final goal of knowledge, which he saw as an active and practical process; the 'reproduction of the concrete in the course of thought'. Secondly, it forgets that a progression from the abstract to the concrete is necessarily preceded, as Lenin put it, by a progression from the concrete to the abstract.[2] For the abstract itself is already the result of a previous work of analysis, which has sought to separate the concrete into its 'determinant relations'. Thirdly, this error destroys the unity of the two processes of analysis and synthesis. The abstract result is only true if it succeeds in reproducing the 'unity of the diverse elements' present in the concrete. Only the whole is true, says Hegel, and the whole is the unity of the abstract and the concrete — a unity of opposites, not their identity. Fourthly, the successful reproduction of the concrete totality only becomes conclusive by application in practice. This means, among other things, that — as Lenin expressly emphasized — each stage of the analysis must be subject to 'control either by facts, or by practice'.[3]

In their turn, however, the 'simplest abstract concepts' (categories) are not merely the products of 'pure understanding', but mirror the beginnings of actual historical development: 'Thus in this respect, it may be said that the simpler category can express the domi-' nant relations of a less developed whole, or else those subordinate relations of a more developed whole which already had a historic existence before this whole developed in the direction expressed by a more concrete category. To that extent, the path of abstract thought, rising from the simple to the combined, would correspond

[1] Karl Marx, *Grundrisse*, London, 1973, pp. 100-1.
[2] Lenin, *Collected Works*, Vol. 38, p. 171.
[3] Lenin, *Collected Works*, Vol. 38, p. 320.

to the real historical process.'[4] Marx's dialectic, therefore, to quote Lenin once more, implies 'a twofold analysis, deductive and inductive, logical and historical'.[5] It represents the *unity* of these two methods. An 'inductive' analysis can here be only a 'historical induction', for Marx regarded every relationship as determined by history, and his dialectic thus involved a unity of theory and empirical historical fact.[6]

It is well known that Marx stated that science was necessary precisely because essence and appearance never directly coincide.[7] He did not see the task of science solely as the discovery of the essence of relations obscured by their superficial appearances, but also as the explanation of these appearances themselves, in other words as the discovery of the intermediate links, or mediations, which enable essence and appearance to be reintegrated in a unity once again.[8] Where this integration fails to occur, theory is reduced to the speculative construction of abstract 'models' which bear no relation to empirical reality, and the dialectic regresses from materialism to idealism: 'A materialist analysis does not coincide with an idealistic dialectic, but with a materialist one; it deals with factors that are empirically verifiable.'[9] Otto Morf has rightly remarked: 'The process whereby the mediation between essence and appearance emerges in this unity of an identical and opposite duality, is necessarily a dialectical one.'[10]

Furthermore, there is no doubt that Marx considered that the *empirical appropriation of the material* should precede the analytical process of cognition, just as practical empirical verification should provisionally conclude it — that is, raise it to a higher level. Thus, in his Afterword to the Second Edition of *Capital*, he wrote: 'Of course

[4] Marx, *Grundrisse*, p. 102.   [5] Lenin, *Collected Works*, Vol. 38, p. 320.

[6] Otto Morf, *Geschichte und Dialektik in der politischen Ökonomie*, Frankfurt, 1970, p. 146. Karl Marx: 'This organic system itself, as a totality, has its presuppositions, and its development to its totality consists precisely in subordinating all elements of society to itself, or in creating out of it the organs which it still lacks. *This is historically how it becomes a totality*. The process of becoming this totality forms a moment of its process, of its development.' *Grundrisse*, p. 278 (Our italics).

[7] 'All science would be superfluous if the outward appearance and the essence of things directly coincided.' Marx, *Capital*, Vol. 3, London, 1972, p. 797.

[8] Marx: 'The various forms of capital, as evolved in this book, thus approach step by step the form which they assume on the surface of society, in the action of different capitals upon one another, in competition, and in the ordinary consciousness of the agents of production themselves.' *Capital*, Vol. 3, p. 25.

[9] Max Raphael, *Zur Erkenntnistheorie der konkreten Dialektik*, Frankfurt, 1962, p. 243.   [10] Morf, op. cit., p. 111.

the method of presentation must differ in form from that of inquiry. The latter has to appropriate the material in detail, to analyse its different forms of development, to trace out their inner connection. *Only after this work is done*, can the actual movement be adequately described. If this is done successfully, if the life of the subject matter is ideally reflected as in a mirror, then it may appear as if we had before us a mere *a priori* construction.'[11] A few years earlier, Engels had said much the same when he wrote: 'It is evident that mere empty talk can achieve nothing in this context and that only an abundance of critically examined historical material which has been completely mastered can make it possible to solve such a problem.'[12] Marx himself repeated this point again in a letter to Kugelmann: 'Lange is naive enough to say that I move with rare freedom in empirical matter. He hasn't the least idea that this "free movement in matter" is nothing but a paraphrase for the *method* of dealing with matter — that is, the *dialectical method*.'[13]

Karel Kosik thus rightly stresses that: 'The progression from the abstract to the concrete is always initially an abstract movement: its dialectic consists in *overcoming this abstraction*. In very broad terms, therefore, it is a movement from the parts to the whole and from the whole to the parts, from the appearance to the essence and from the essence to the appearance, from the totality to the contradiction and from the contradiction to the totality, from the object to the subject and from the subject to the object.'[14] In sum, we can suggest a six-fold articulation of Marx's dialectical method, which can be defined approximately thus:

1. Comprehensive appropriation of the empirical material, and mastery of this material (superficial appearances) in all its historically relevant detail.

2. Analytical division of this material into its constituent abstract elements (progression from the concrete to the abstract).[15]

[11]Marx, *Capital*, Vol. 1, London, 1970, p. 19 (Our italics).

[12]Friedrich Engels, 'Review of Karl Marx, *Contribution*', in Maurice Dobb (ed.), *A Contribution to the Critique of Political Economy*, London, 1971, p. 221.

[13]'Marx to Kugelmann in Hanover', in Marx and Engels, *Selected Correspondence* (revised edition), Moscow, 1965, p. 240.

[14]Karel Kosik, *Die Dialektik des Konkreten*, Frankfurt, 1967, p. 31. The Soviet author Ilyenkov has devoted an interesting book to the relationship between (and the unity of) the abstract and the concrete in Marx's *Capital*. See E.I. Ilyenkov, *La dialettica dell' astratto e del concreto nel Capitale di Marx*, Milan, 1961.

[15]Following on from the Soviet theorist Ilyenkov, Erich Hahn has emphasized that 'the division of the real concrete subject into abstract determinations must under no

3. Exploration of the decisive general connections between these elements, which explain the abstract laws of motion of the material, in other words its essence.

4. Discovery of the decisive intermediate links which effect the mediation between the essence and the superficial appearances of the material (progression from the abstract to the concrete, or the reproduction of the concrete in thought as a combination of multiple determinations).

5. Practical empirical verification of the analysis (2, 3, 4) in the developing movement of concrete history.

6. Discovery of new and empirically relevant data, and of new connections — often even of new abstract elementary determinations — through the application of the results of knowledge, and practice based on it, in the infinite complexity of reality.[16]

We are here not dealing with strictly separate stages of the cognitive process, for some of these moments are interlinked and there is an inevitable traffic between them. We can thus see that Marx's method is much richer than the procedures of 'successive concretization' or 'approximation' typical of academic science. 'Since the individual and particular features are (here) only superficially eliminated and reintroduced, in other words without any dialectical mediations, the illusion can easily arise that no qualitative bridge exists between the abstract and the concrete. It thus becomes perfectly logical to believe that the theoretical model does in fact (although in a simplified form) contain all the essential elements of the concrete object under investigation — as in the case, for example, of a photograph taken from a great height, which shows all the fundamental elements of a landscape, although all that is visible are mountain ranges, large rivers, or woods.'[17] The difference between

---

circumstances be equated with the movement from empirical matter to theory. The empirical stage of cognition merely serves to prepare for this process of division.' *Historischer Materialismus und marxistische Soziologie*, Berlin, 1968, pp. 199-200.

[16]Hahn (op. cit., pp. 185-7) refers to a seven-step scheme of scientific cognition proposed by the Soviet theorist V.A. Smirnov. At the outset Smirnov separates 'observations' from the 'analysis of the recorded observations', but thus fails to take into account the crucial mediation between essence and appearance and reduces the problem to a confrontation of theory and empirical matter.

[17]Roman Rosdolsky, *Zur Entstehungsgeschichte des Marxschen Kapitals*, Frankfurt, 1968, Vol. II, p. 533. See also Hegel: 'In thinking about the gradualness of the coming-to-be of something, it is ordinarily assumed that what comes to be is already sensibly or *actually in existence*; it is not yet perceptible only because of its smallness. Similarly with the gradual disappearance of something, the *non-being* or the other which takes

the reductionist method of vulgar materialism, in which the concrete specificity of individual objects disappears, and the materialist dialectic proper, becomes by the same stroke evident.[18] Jindřich Zelený rightly emphasizes that the intellectual reproduction of reality, or in Althusser's language, 'theoretical practice', must remain in constant contact with the actual movement of history: 'The whole of Marx's *Capital* is pervaded by an incessant oscillation between the abstract dialectical development and the material concrete reality of history. At the same time, however, it must be emphasized that Marx's analysis repeatedly *detaches* itself from the superficial course of the historical reality, to give *ideal* expression to the necessary inner relations of this reality. Marx was able to *grasp* historical reality only because he produced a scientific reflection of it in the form of a somewhat idealized and typified inner organization of real capitalist relations. He did not detach himself from them in order to achieve distance from historical reality, nor was he making an idealistic escape from it. The purpose of his detachment was a close and rational appropriation of reality.'[19]

There is a clear contrast with the views of Althusser and his school here. The principles set out above do not transform Marxism by 'historicizing' it, or dispute that the specific object of *Capital* is the structure and laws of development of the capitalist mode of production — and in no sense 'general laws of the economic activity of humanity'. They do, however, assert that the dialectic of the abstract and the concrete is also a dialectic between real history and the intellectual reproduction of this historical process, and that this dialectic must not be limited exclusively to the level of 'theoretical production'. The difference between Marx's and Althusser's conception comes out most clearly in Marx's *Marginal Notes to Wagner*, where he states explicitly: 'At the very outset *I do not start from "concepts"*. Therefore I do not start from the concept of value either, and hence I do not have to "introduce" it in any way. What I start from is the *simplest social form of the product of labour in present day society*, and that is the "commodity". That is what I analyse, and I analyse it initially in the form in which it appears.'[20] Althusser, on the other

its place is likewise assumed to be *really there*, but not yet observable . . . . In this way coming-to-be and ceasing-to-be lose all meaning.' *Science of Logic*, London, 1969, p. 370.   [18]Karel Kosik, op. cit., p. 27.

[19]Jindřich Zelený, *Die Wissenschaftslogik und das Kapital*, Frankfurt, 1969, p. 59.
[20]Marx, 'Marginal Notes to A. Wagner's *Lehrbuch der politischen Oekonomie*', *Werke*, Bd 19, p. 369 (Our italics).

hand, says: 'This is where we are led by ignoring the basic distinction Marx was careful to draw between the *"development of forms" of the concept in knowledge* and the development of the real categories in concrete history: to an empiricist ideology of knowledge and to the identification of the *logical* and *historical* in *Capital* itself. It should hardly surprise us that so many interpreters go round in circles in the question that hangs on this definition, if it is true that all problems concerned with the relation between the logical and the historical in *Capital* presuppose a *non-existent relation*.'[21]

Althusser thus sanctions only a relationship between economic theory and historical theory; the relationship between economic theory and concrete history is by contrast declared a 'false problem', 'non-existent' and 'imaginary'. What he does not seem to realize is that this is not only in contradiction to Marx's own explanation of his method, but that the attempt to escape the spectre of empiricism and its theory of knowledge — a spectre of his own making — by establishing a basic dualism between 'objects of knowledge' and 'real objects', inevitably runs the danger of idealism. [22]

The need for such a reintegration of theory and history has sometimes been disputed on the grounds that the specificity of the laws of motion of any mode of production, and of the capitalist mode of production in particular, precisely excludes any such unity with mere empirical facts. The laws of motion, it is argued, are only 'tendencies' in the very broad historical sense. They are therefore supposed to exclude the possibility of any causal connections with temporal events in the short or medium term, and even in the long term are deemed not to be demonstrable in a materially identifiable, empirical way. It is further often claimed that each of these tendencies may provoke counter-tendencies which can neutralize their own effect for a considerable period.[23] Marx's treatment of

[21] Louis Althusser, 'The Object of Capital', in Louis Althusser and Etienne Balibar, *Reading Capital*, London, 1970, p. 115.

[22] The spectre of 'empiricism' which Althusser conjures up on pp. 35-7 of *Reading Capital* is reduced by him to the danger of 'splitting' the object of knowledge, since the 'illusion' of the 'theoretical appropriation of reality' is accompanied by an unavoidable process of abstraction which can only partly grasp this reality. We have already indicated above how the active intellectual *reproduction* of reality can be characterized precisely as a process in which the abstract and the concrete, the universal and the particular, are increasingly reintegrated — in other words, a process in which this 'split' is progressively overcome. Naturally, it is impossible for thought and being to achieve any *complete* identity; the materialist dialectic can only try to reproduce reality with ever-increasing precision.

[23] See for example, Paul Mattick, 'Werttheorie und Kapitalismus', in *Kapitalismus und Krise, Eine Kontroverse um das Gesetz des tendenziellen Falls der Profitrate*,

the tendency of the rate of profit to fall in Chapters 13, 14 and 15 of the Third Volume of *Capital* has been endlessly cited as the classic example of a tendency and counter-tendency which allegedly enable nothing to be said of the final outcome.

From this, the conclusion is then drawn that it is scarcely possible to find empirical 'confirmation' for Marx's laws of development. Indeed, it is maintained that attempts to track down such 'empirical confirmations' reveal a fundamental 'positivist' misunderstanding of Marx's method and intentions, since the two different levels of abstraction, that of the 'pure' mode of production and that of the 'concrete' historical process are so far removed from one another that there is virtually nowhere that they could come into contact.

It would not be difficult to prove that Marx himself, at any rate, categorically and resolutely rejected this quasi-total rift between theoretical analysis and empirical data. For the real implication of this separation is a significant retreat from the materialist dialectic to the dialectic of idealism. From the standpoint of historical materialism, 'tendencies' which do not manifest themselves materially and empirically are not tendencies at all. They are products of false consciousness, or for those who dislike that phrase, of scientific errors. Moreover, they cannot lead to any scientific, materialist intervention in the historical process. As soon as 'laws of development' come to be regarded as so abstract that they can no longer explain the actual process of concrete history, then the discovery of such tendencies of development ceases to be an instrument for the revolutionary transformation of this process. All that remains is a degenerate form of speculative socio-economic philosophy, in which the 'laws of development' have the same shadowy existence as Hegel's 'world spirit' — always, as it were, beyond the reach of one's fingertips. In such constructed systems, the abstractions are truly 'empty', or in Engels's sharper language — a mere phrase. For this reason, the rejection of a mediated unity between theory and history, or theory and empirical data, has always been connected in the history of Marxism with a revision of Marxist principles — either with a mechanical-fatalistic determinism, or a pure voluntarism. Inability to re-unite theory and history inevitably leads to inability to re-unite theory and practice.

Thus Peter Jeffries has accused us of trying to verify Marx's categories empirically, while he claims that such categories as capital,

Frankfurt, 1970; Tom Kemp, *Theories of Imperialism*, London, 1967, pp. 27-8, etc. Note also Althusser's thesis that surplus-value is not measurable . . .

socially necessary labour-time, and so forth, do not appear empirically in the capitalist system. But are there no mediations which permit us to connect surface phenomena (profits, prices of production, average prices of commodities over a certain period of time) with Marx's basic categories by quantitative relationships? Marx and Engels themselves certainly thought so, at any rate.[24] Jeffries' relapse into the idealist dialectic is due to the fact *that he reduces the concrete to the appearance only,*[25] failing to understand that the essence, together with its mediations to the appearance, forms a unity of abstract and concrete elements, and that the object of the dialectic represents, to quote Hegel, 'not merely an abstract universal, but a universal which embraces within itself the wealth of the particular.'[26] He thus also fails to understand the following

[24]'Marx and Classical Political Economy', II, *Workers Press*, May 30, 1972. We shall give only one example here. In the First Volume of *Capital* Marx calculated the mass and rate of surplus-value for an English spinning mill, basing himself on exact data (declarations) from a Manchester manufacturer, as they had been given him by Engels: *Capital*, Vol. I, p. 219. In the 4th Chapter of the Third Volume of *Capital*, which he edited, Engels cites this example once more, and added: 'For that matter we have here an illustration of the actual composition of capital in modern large-scale industry. The total capital is broken up into £12,182 constant and £318 variable capital, a sum of £12,500.' Ibid., p. 76. For Engels, the problem was not that capital 'never appears empirically' or 'is not measurable', but that capitalists obstruct public access to their accounts, and so conceal the necessary and sufficient elements for measuring it. 'Since very few capitalists ever think of making calculations of this sort with reference to their own business, statistics is almost completely silent about the relation of the constant portion of the total social capital to its variable portion. Only the American census gives what is possible under modern conditions, namely the sum of wages paid in each line of business and the profits realized. Questionable as they may be, being based on the capitalist's own uncontrolled statements, they are nevertheless very valuable and the only records available to us on this subject.' *Capital*, III, p. 76.

[25]'Here Marx explains that the process of movement from abstract to concrete, from essence to appearance, cannot be an immediate one.' Peter Jeffries, 'Marx and Classical Political Economy', III, *Workers Press*, May 31, 1972. In the passage from *Capital* (Vol. 3, p. 25) to which Jeffries's interpretation refers, Marx manifestly made no such reduction of the concrete to the 'appearance' (as less 'real' than the abstract 'essence'). On the contrary, Marx there stated: 'In their *actual* movement capitals confront each other in such concrete shape, for which the form of capital in the immediate process of production, just as its form in the process of circulation, appear only as *special* instances' (Our italics). Marx's intention was precisely to *explain this actual movement*. For him, as for Hegel, the truth lay in the whole, that is, in the mediated unity of essence and appearance.

[26]*Science of Logic*, London, p. 58. Lucien Goldmann (*Immanuel Kant*, London, 1971, p. 134) has rightly pointed out that underlying Kant's *Critique of Pure Reason* was the notion of the unbridgeable contradiction between empirical matter and 'essence' (thing in itself). Jeffries is therefore, regressing from Hegel (not to mention Marx!) back to Kant when he reduces the essence to the abstract and shows his failure to understand the dialectical *unity* of the abstract and the concrete.

remark by Engels: 'When commodity exchange began, when products gradually turned into commodities, they were exchanged approximately *according* to their value. It was the amount of labour expended on two objects which provided the only standard for their quantitative comparison. Thus value had a *direct and real existence* at that time. We know that this direct realization of value in exchange ceased and that now it no longer happens. I believe that it won't be particularly difficult for you to trace the intermediate links, at least in general outline, that lead from directly real value to the value of the capitalist mode of production, which is so thoroughly hidden that our economists can calmly deny its existence. A genuinely historical exposition of these processes, which does indeed require thorough research but in return promises amply rewarding results, would be a very valuable supplement to *Capital.*'[27]

The two-fold problem to be solved, therefore, can be defined more precisely as follows:

1. How can the real history of the capitalist mode of production over the past hundred years be shown as the history of the unfolding development of the internal contradictions of this mode of production, in other words, as determined in the last resort by its 'abstract' laws of motion? What 'intermediate links' operate the unity between the abstract and the concrete elements of the analysis here?

2. How can the real history of the past hundred years be traced back to that of the capitalist mode of production, in other words, how can the combinations of expanding capital and the pre-capitalist (or semi-capitalist) spheres which it has conquered, be analysed in their appearance and explained in their essence?

The capitalist mode of production has not developed in a vacuum but within a specific socio-economic framework characterized by very important differences, for example, in Western Europe, Eastern Europe, Continental Asia, North America, Latin America and Japan.[28] The specific socio-economic formations — 'bourgeois societies' and capitalist economies — which arose in these different areas in the course of the 18th, 19th and 20th centuries and which

[27]'Engels to W. Sombart', in Marx and Engels, *Selected Correspondence*, p. 481.

[28]'This does not prevent the same economic basis — the same from the standpoint of its main conditions — due to the innumerable different empirical circumstances, natural environment, racial relations, external historical influences, and so on from showing infinite variations and gradations in appearance, which can be ascertained only by analysis of the empirically given circumstances.' (Karl Marx, *Capital*, Vol. 3, pp. 791-2.)

in their complex unity (together with the societies of Africa and Oceania) comprise 'concrete' capitalism, reproduce in varying forms and proportions a *combination* of past and present modes of production, or more precisely, of varying past and successive stages of the present mode of production.[29] The organic unity of the capitalist world system by no means reduces this combination, which is specific in each case, to a factor of only secondary importance in face of the primacy of the capitalist features common to the whole system. On the contrary: the capitalist world system is to a significant degree precisely a *function* of the universal validity of the law of unequal and combined development.[30] A more thorough analysis of the phenomenon of imperialism later in the book will confirm this: we are merely anticipating here.

Without the role that non-capitalist or only semi-capitalist societies and economies have played and still are playing in the world it would hardly be possible to comprehend specific features of every successive step of the capitalist mode of production — such as the British capitalism of free competition from Waterloo to Sedan, the classic epoch of imperialism before and between the two World Wars and the late capitalism of today.

Why is it that the integration of theory and history which Marx applied with such mastery in the *Grundrisse* and *Capital* has never since been repeated successfully, to explain these successive stages of the capitalist mode of production? Why is there still no satisfactory history of capitalism as a function of the inner laws of capital — with all the qualifications suggested above — and still less a satisfactory explanation of the new stage in the history of capitalism which clearly began after the Second World War?

[29] 'Colonial and semi-colonial countries are backward countries by their very essence. But backward countries are part of a world dominated by imperialism. Their development, therefore, has a *combined* character: the most primitive economic forms are combined with the last word in capitalist technique and culture. . . . The relative weight of the individual democratic and transitional demands in the proletariat's struggle, their mutual ties and their order of presentation, is determined by the peculiarities and specific conditions of each backward country and to a considerable extent — by the *degree* of its backwardness.' Leon Trotsky, 'The Death Agony of Capitalism and the Tasks of the Fourth International', pp. 40-1, in *The Founding Conference of the Fourth International*, New York, 1939.

[30] 'Capitalism finds various sections of mankind at different stages of development, each with its own profound internal contradictions. The extreme diversity in the levels attained and the extraordinary unevenness in the rate of development of the different sections of mankind during the various epochs, serve as the *starting point* of capitalism. Capitalism gains mastery only gradually over the inherited unevenness, breaking

The manifest lag of consciousness behind reality is at least partly to be explained by the temporary paralysis of theory that resulted from the apologetic perversion of Marxism by the Stalinist bureaucracy, which for a quarter of a century reduced the area in which the Marxist method could develop freely to the barest minimum. The long-term effects of this vulgarization of Marxism have still far from disappeared even today. Beyond the immediately social pressures which have prevented any satisfactory development of Marx's economic theory in the 20th century, however, there is also an inner logic in the development of Marxism which in our opinion at least partly explains why so many important attempts have fallen short of their goal. Two aspects of this inner logic of the history of Marxism deserve particular emphasis in this respect. One concerns the analytical tools of Marx's economic theory, the other the analytical method of the most important Marxist scholars.

Nearly all the attempts that have been made to explain specific phases of the capitalist mode of production — or specific problems arising from these phases — from the laws of motion of this mode of production, as revealed in *Capital*, have taken as their starting point the reproduction schemes used by Marx in the Second Volume of *Capital*. In our opinion, the reproduction schemes that Marx developed are unsuited to this purpose and cannot be used in the investigation of the laws of motion of capital or the history of capitalism. Hence any attempt to deduce either the impossibility of a 'pure' capitalist economy or the fatal collapse of the capitalist mode of production, the inevitable development towards monopoly capita-

---

and altering it, employing therein its own means and methods.... Thereby it brings about their *rapprochement* and equalizes the economic and cultural levels of the most progressive and the most backward countries.... By drawing the countries economically closer to one another and levelling out their stages of development, capitalism however operates by methods *of its own*, this is to say by anarchistic methods which constantly undermine its own work, set one country against another, and one branch of industry against another, developing some parts of the world economy while hampering and throwing back the development of others. Only the correlation of these two fundamental tendencies — both of which arise from the nature of capitalism — explains to us the living texture of the historical process': Trotsky, *The Third International after Lenin*, pp. 19-20, New York, 1970. See also Rosa Luxemburg, *The Accumulation of Capital*, London, 1971, p. 438: 'European capital has largely swallowed up the Egyptian peasant economy. Enormous tracts of land, labour, and labour products without number, accruing to the state as taxes, have ultimately been converted into European capital and have been accumulated. Evidently... it was just the primitive nature of Egyptian conditions which proved such fertile soil for the accumulation of capital.'

lism or the essence of late capitalism, from these schemes is doomed to failure.

Roman Rosdolsky has already provided a convincing foundation for this view in his important book *Zur Entstehungsgeschichte des Marx'schen 'Kapital'*. We can therefore limit ourselves to a short summary of his argument.[31] It explains why four of the most brilliant attempts by pupils of Karl Marx to reintegrate theory and history — those of Rudolf Hilferding, Rosa Luxemburg, Henryk Grossmann and Nikolai Bukharin — did not meet with success. The same is also true of the successive efforts of Otto Bauer, who for most of his life experimented with the same problem without arriving at any satisfactory answer to it.

Marx's reproduction schemes play a closely defined and specific role in his analysis of capitalism and they are designed to solve a single problem and no other. Their function is to explain why and how an economic system based on 'pure' market anarchy in which economic life seems to be determined by millions of unrelated decisions to buy and sell does not lead to continuous chaos and constant interruptions of the social and economic process of reproduction, but instead on the whole functions 'normally' — that is with a big crash in the form of an economic crisis breaking out (in Marx's time) once every seven or ten years. Or to put it differently: how can a system based on exchange value, that only functions for the sake of profit and regards the specific use values of the commodities it produces as a matter of indifference to it, nonetheless assure the material elements of the reproduction process which are determined precisely by their specific use value — in other words, how can it at least for a time 'spontaneously' overcome the antinomy between exchange value and use value? The function of the reproduction schemes is thus to prove *that it is possible for the capitalist mode* of production to exist at all.

Marx uses a number of familiar abstractions for this purpose. He groups all the firms into two categories, those that produce means of production (Department I) and those that produce consumer goods (Department II). All the producers at society's disposal who are forced to sell their labour power are similarly divided into these two spheres. The same division is applied to the mass of means of production at the disposal of society, whether fixed (machines, buildings,)

---

[31] Rosdolsky, op. cit., pp. 534-7, 583-6.

or circulating (raw materials, sources of power, auxiliary elements). With these analytical tools, Marx reaches the conclusion that social production is in a state of *equilibrium*, i.e., that social and economic reproduction can proceed undisturbed as long and in so far as the formula for equilibrium which he has discovered is observed. In the system of simple reproduction this formula is Iv + Is = IIc. This means that economic equilibrium depends on whether the production of commodities in Department I can evoke a monetarily effective demand for commodities in Department II corresponding in value to the commodities which it must itself deliver to Department II and vice versa. A similar formula for equilibrium can easily be deduced from Marx's schemes of expanded production; as far as we know this was first formulated by Otto Bauer.[32]

To make the structure of his argument as rigorous as possible, Marx deliberately left out of his schemes the non-capitalist sector of the economy. Nothing is said, therefore, of the simple commodity-producing peasants or artisans. It is not difficult, however, to construct a scheme in which these groups appear as a separate sector, and in which, for example, they themselves buy fixed means of production from Department I while at the same time they sell to this Department raw materials and consumer goods. In order to reconstruct Marx's formula for equilibrium, one would then have to reduce the volume of production in Department II by the value of the consumer goods produced by the simple commodity producers.

It is obvious, however, that the overall development of the capitalist mode of production *cannot* be subsumed under the notion of 'equilibrium'. It is rather a dialectical unity of periods of equilibrium and periods of disequilibrium, each of the two elements engendering its own negation. Each equilibrium inevitably leads to a disequilibrium, and after a certain period of time this in turn makes possible a new provisional equilibrium. Even more: it is one of the characteristics of the capitalist economy that not only crises but also accelerated growth of production, not only *interrupted* reproduction but also *extended* reproduction, are governed by ruptures of equilibrium. There is equally little doubt that the laws of motion of the

---

[32] Otto Bauer, 'Marx' Theorie der Wirtschaftskrisen' in *Die Neue Zeit*, Vol. 23/1, p. 167. Bukharin put the same formula into simpler and more elegant language: *Der Imperialismus und die Akkumulation des Kapitals*, Vienna, 1926, p. 11. For an English translation of the latter, see Rosa Luxemburg and Nikolai Bukharin, *Imperialism and the Accumulation of Capital*, London, 1972, p. 157.

capitalist mode of production lead to such constant disequilibria. An increase in the organic composition of capital — to give only one example — determines, among other things, a more rapid growth in Department I than Department II. One can even go further and say that ruptures of equilibrium, i.e., uneven development, pertain to the very essence of capital in so far as it is based on competition, or to use Marx's words, on the existence of 'many capitals'. Given the fact of competition, 'the incessant urge for enrichment' which is a feature of capital is really the search for surplus-profit, for profit above the average profit. This search leads to constant attempts to revolutionize technology, to achieve lower production costs than those of competitors, to obtain surplus-profits together with a greater organic composition of capital while at the same time increasing the rate of surplus value. All the characteristics of capitalism as an economic form are contained in this description and they are based on its inherent tendency towards ruptures of equilibrium. This same tendency also lies at the root of all the laws of motion of the capitalist mode of production.

It is obvious that schemes designed to prove the possibility of *periodical* equilibrium in the economy, despite the anarchical organization of production and the segmentation of capital into competing individual firms, will be inadequate for use as analytical tools to prove that the capitalist mode of production *must*, by its very essence, lead to periodic ruptures of equilibrium, and that under capitalism economic growth must *always* lead to disequilibrium just as it is itself always the result of it. Therefore, what is needed are other schemes which incorporate from the very start this tendency for the two Departments and all that corresponds to them to develop unevenly. These more general schemes ought to be constructed in such a way that Marx's reproduction schemes will only constitute a special case — just as economic equilibrium is only a special case of the tendency, characteristic of the capitalist mode of production, for the various sectors, departments and elements of the system to develop unevenly.

An uneven rate of growth in the two Departments ought to correspond to an uneven rate of profit in the two Departments. Uneven growth in the two Departments ought to find expression in an uneven rate of accumulation and an uneven tempo of growth for the organic composition of capital, which is in turn periodically and partially suspended by the uneven impact of crisis on the two Departments. These could be the factors that would enable us, as it were, to 'dynamicize' Marx's schemes. (His schemes remain important tools for the study of the possibilities and variants of periodical equilibrium or temporary supersession of disequilibrium.) The theoretical efforts of Rudolf Hilferding, Rosa Luxemburg, Henryk Grossmann, Nikolai Bukharin, Otto Bauer and many other were bound to fail because they attempted to *investigate the problems of the laws of development of capitalism, i.e., the problems of ruptured equilibrium, with tools designed for the analysis of equilibrium.*

In *Finanzkapital* Rudolf Hilferding claims that Marx's reproduction schemes demonstrate 'that in capitalist production, reproduction on both a simple and an extended scale can proceed undisturbed as long as these proportions are preserved. . . . It does not follow at all, therefore, that capitalist crisis must have its roots in underconsumption of the masses as an inherent feature of capitalist production. . . . Nor does it follow from the schemes themselves that there is a possibility of a general overproduction of commodities. On the contrary, what the schemes show is that any expansion of production is possible that is consonant with the potential of the available forces of production'.[33]

In actual fact, Marx in no way intended his reproduction schemes to justify statements about the alleged possibility of 'undisturbed production' under capitalism: on the contrary, he was profoundly convinced of the inherent susceptibility of capitalism to crises. He by no means ascribed this solely to the *anarchy of production*; he also attributed it to the discrepancy between the development of the forces of production and the development of mass consumption, that he believed to be integral to the very nature of capitalism. 'The conditions of direct exploitation, and those of realizing it, are not identical. They diverge not only in place and time, but also logically. The first are only limited by the productive power of society, the latter *by the proportional relation of the various branches of production and the consumer power of society.* But this last-named is not determined either by the absolute productive power, or by the absolute consumer power, but by the consumer power based on antagonistic conditions of distribution, which reduce the consumption of the bulk of society to a minimum varying within more or less narrow

[33] Rudolf Hilferding, *Das Finanzkapital*, Vienna, 1923, p. 310.

limits. It is furthermore restricted by the tendency to accumulate, the drive to expand capital and produce surplus value on an extended scale.'[34]

Marx thus says *exactly the opposite* of what Hilferding sought to read out of the reproduction schemes. This is all the more amazing in the light of Hilferding's own words at the beginning of his reflections on crises and reproduction schemes: 'In the capitalist mode of production too, there remains a general connection between production and consumption, which is a natural condition common to all social formations.' He goes on even more clearly: 'The narrow basis offered by the relations of consumption in capitalist production, however, is the general root of economic crisis because the impossibility of expanding consumption is a general precondition for the stagnation of sales. If consumption could be extended at will, overproduction would not be possible. But under capitalist conditions the extension of consumption means a reduction in the rate of profit. For an extension of the consumption of the broad masses is tied to a rise in wages.'[35] Despite these correct insights, Hilferding is later misled by the reproduction schemes into a theory of crises based on 'pure' disproportionality.

In *The Accumulation of Capital* Rosa Luxemburg accuses Marx of devising his schemes in such a way that 'it is downright impossible to achieve a faster expansion of Department I as against Department II.' A few pages later she declares that the scheme excludes 'the expansion of production by leaps and bounds'.[36] However, she attributes these apparent contradictions in the reproduction schemes solely to the consumer goods produced by Department II which cannot be sold, i.e., to the absence of a 'non-capitalist market outlet' which would be indispensible for the realization of the entire surplus-value produced. In actual fact, her criticism here corresponds to the misunderstanding outlined earlier over the purpose and function of the schemes. It is by no means their purpose to express the more rapid rate of growth in Department I as against Department II, which is inevitable under capitalism, or the 'expansion of production by leaps and bounds', which under capitalism inevitably leads to ruptures of equilibrium. On the contrary, the purpose of the schemes is to prove that despite this 'expansion by leaps and bounds' and despite the

[34]Marx, *Capital,* Vol. 3, p. 244. (Our italics.)
[35]Hilferding, *Finanzkapital,* p. 299.
[36]Rosa Luxemburg, *Accumulation of Capital,* pp. 340-1.

periodic ruptures of equilibrium, it is also possible to achieve periodic equilibria under capitalism.

This makes it clear why Marx did not make provision for 'reproduction by leaps and bounds'. It is equally plain that if we disregard the hypothesis of equilibrium we do not by any means have to look for the solution to the 'inner contradictions' of the reproduction schemes in 'non-capitalist buyers'; this is rather to be found in the transfer of surplus-value from Department II to Department I in the course of the equalization of the rate of profit made necessary by the lesser organic composition of capital in Department II. Rosa Luxemburg herself initially sees this as both the logical and the normal historical solution,[37] but she immediately rejects it on the grounds of the 'inner coherence' of the reproduction schemes, claiming that this solution does not conform to the conditions established by Marx for the working-out of the schemes (for instance, the sale of commodities at their value). She thereby fails to notice that the whole process of the growth of capitalist production, and the increasing unevenness of its development, are not even *meant* to conform to these conditions.

What is true of Rosa Luxemburg is even more true of Henryk Grossmann. At first glance this author seems to understand the function of the reproduction schemes better than Rosa Luxemburg. In his book *Das Akkumulations- und Zusammerbruchsgesetz des kapitalistischen Systems*, he explicitly underlines the fact that the schemes are calculated on the basis of a hypothetical state of equilibrium. It immediately transpires, however, that he is referring only to the equilibrium between the supply and demand of commodities, which leads to the absence of market *price-fluctuations*. In actual fact, however, such fluctuations in market prices are not merely excluded from the context of the reproduction schemes in Volume Two of *Capital*. Throughout Marx's analysis of capitalism they play no role whatsoever and are dealt with only in passing in Chapter 10 of Volume Three of *Capital*.

It is quite a different matter when we come to fluctuations in the· prices of production or rates of profit. These play a central role in Marx's system. In them, i.e., in the drive for surplus-profit, we have the basic explanation for the whole of the investing and accumulating activity of the capitalist. This in turn immediately brings us to competition. While Marx understandably ignores competition in

[37]Luxemburg, *Accumulation of Capital*, p. 340.

his attempt to prove that equilibrium is possible in the capitalist mode of production and presupposes not only the equilibrium of supply and demand but also the *even* development of both sectors, i.e., of all capitals, Grossmann carries the same presuppositions over into his investigation of the tendencies in capitalism towards accumulation, growth and collapse. He does not understand that such presuppositions are quite absurd for the analysis of these tendencies, for they in fact negate what he intends to analyse.

Incidentally, Grossmann's treatment of the reproduction schemes reveals, by contrast with Rosa Luxemburg's, a fundamental misunderstanding of the central role played by competition in Marx's system. Grossmann cites a passage from Marx about the appearance of competition out of its context — i.e., its relation to the problems of value — and concludes that it plays no important role in Marx's explanation of the inner logic of the capitalist mode of production. He does this despite the fact that he himself quotes the following passage from Volume Three of *Capital*,[38] which ought to have taught him better and shown him that capitalism without competition is capitalism without growth: 'As soon as formation of capital were to fall into the hands of a few established big capitals, for which the mass of profit compensates for the falling rate of profit, the vital flame of production would be altogether extinguished. It would die out.'[39]

In his argument Grossmann employs Otto Bauer's scheme, which the latter constructed in 1913 as a counter to Rosa Luxemburg's *The Accumulation of Capital*. Otto Bauer's schemes appear to take the laws of development of capital into account; for in them the organic composition of capital and with it the rate of accumulation grows, while the rate of profit conversely falls. But Bauer's schemes immediately negate their own assumptions, for together with a growing organic composition of capital they contain an identical rate of surplus-value and an identical rate of accumulation for both Departments, which is untenable logically and historically.[40] These schemes thus provide Grossmann with his 'mathematical proof' that accumulation must stagnate for lack of surplus-value, because otherwise not

[38] Henryk Grossmann, *Das Akkumulations — und Zusammenbruchsgesetz des kapitalistischen Systems*, Frankfurt, 1967, pp. 90-2.
[39] Marx, *Capital*, Vol. 3, p. 254.
[40] Otto Bauer, 'Die Akkumulation des Kapitals', p. 83, in *Die Neue Zeit*, Vol. 31/1, 1913.

enough will accrue to the capitalist for consumption. Admittedly it will only 'stagnate' in the 34th cycle. If we remember that the aim of the reproduction schemes is to formulate states of equilibrium purified by periodic crises every 5, 7 or 10 years, it is obvious that Grossmann — contrary to his own intentions — has in fact proved the opposite of what he set out to demonstrate. For the upshot of this argument is that capitalism could survive for many decades, if not for several centuries, before suffering economic collapse.

Bukharin also based his critique of Luxemburg on Marx's schemes. In the process he tried to conceive a 'general theory of the market and of crises' which once again starts from the conditions of equilibrium and at most arrives at disproportionality by way of 'contradictory tendencies in capitalism' (efforts to increase production but bring down wages) — not the immanent tendencies of development of capital or the laws of motion of the capitalist mode of production itself. In the process Bukharin appears to become so fascinated by the 'conditions of equilibrium' revealed in Marx's schemes that he argues, just like Hilferding, the thesis that there would be no more crises of reproduction if the 'anarchy of production' was eliminated, as in the case of 'state capitalism' with a planned economy.[41] In this he has the misfortune to take as the basis for his argument a passage in Marx's *Theories of Surplus Value* which says exactly the opposite. Bukharin quotes the following passage: 'Here, therefore, is presupposed 1.*capitalist production*, in which the production of each particular industry and its increase are not *directly* regulated and *controlled* by the wants of society, but by the productive forces at the disposal of each individual capitalist, independent of the wants of society. 2.It is assumed that nevertheless production is *proportional* (to the requirements) as though capital were employed in the different spheres of production directly by society in accordance with its needs. On this assumption, if capitalist production were entirely socialist production — a contradiction in terms — no overproduction could, in fact, occur.'[42]

Bukharin triumphantly adds: 'If there were a planned economy, there could be no crisis of overproduction. Marx's thoughts are very clear here: the conquest of anarchy, i.e., planning, is not *opposed* to the liquidation of the contradiction between production and consumption as a *particular* factor; it is portrayed as containing this

[41]Bukharin, *Imperialism and the Accumulation of Capital*, p. 226.
[42]Marx, *Theories of Surplus Value*, Vol. 3, London, 1972, p. 118.

liquidation'.[43] Bukharin has here overlooked that among the conditions in which capitalist production would be 'entirely socialist
production' Marx expressly includes not merely proportionality
between the individual spheres of production but also the employment of 'capital' *directly by society, in accordance with its needs*
(i.e., no production of commodities or exchange-values, but rather
production of use-values). Both the paragraph before the passage
quoted by Bukharin and the paragraphs following it show quite
clearly that for Marx proportional growth of the *creation of value*
in the various branches of industry is *not* the answer to the problem
of the realization of surplus-value, because this problem can only
be resolved under conditions of 'entirely socialist production'
*through the adaptation of the production of use-values to the needs
of society*: 'If all other capitals have accumulated at the same rate, it
does not follow at all that their production has increased at the same
rate. But if it has, it does not follow that they want one per cent more
of cutlery, as their demand for cutlery is not at all connected, either
with the increase in their own produce, or with their increased power
of buying cutlery.' Further: 'By the way, in the various branches of
industry in which *the same accumulation* of capital takes place (and
this too is an unfortunate assumption that capital is accumulated
at an *equal rate* in different spheres), the amount of products corresponding to the increased capital may vary greatly, since the
productive forces in the different industries or the total use values
produced in relation to the labour employed differ considerably.
The same value is produced in both cases, but the quantity of commodities in which it is represented is very different. It is quite incomprehensible, therefore, why industry *A*, because the value of
its output has increased by one per cent while the mass of its products
has grown by twenty per cent, must find a market in *B* where the
value has likewise increased by one per cent, but the quantity of
its output by five per cent. Here, the author has failed to take into
consideration the difference between use-value and exchange-
value.'[44]

In other words, crises, for Marx, are not caused solely by a disproportionality of value among the various branches of industry but
also by a disproportionality between the development of exchange
value and use value, i.e., by disproportionality between valorization

[43]Bukharin, *op.cit.*, pp. 228-9.
[44]Marx, *Theories of Surplus Value*, Vol. 3, pp. 118-9.

of capital and consumption. Bukharin's state capitalism, in which crises no longer occur, would have to eliminate this second type of 'disproportionality' as well, — in other words, it would no longer be capitalism at all, for it would no longer be based on the pressure for the valorization of capital. It would have overcome the antinomy of use value and exchange value.

If we now move from the inadequacy of Marx's reproduction schemes as tools for the analysis of the laws of development of capitalism, to the inadequacy of the methods of economic analysis employed after Marx, we are struck by one fact above all else. Discussions of the problem of the long-term tendencies of development and the inevitable collapse of the capitalist mode of production have been dominated for more than half a century by every author's attempts to reduce this problem *to a single factor*. [45]

For Rosa Luxemburg this factor is, of course, the difficulty of realizing surplus-value, and the consequent necessity of absorbing more and more spheres of the non-capitalist world into the capitalist circulation of commodities; the latter is seen as the only possible way to market the inevitable residue of consumer goods which cannot otherwise be sold. This basic mechanism is used to explain both the development of capitalism from free competition to imperialism and the predicted inevitability of the system's economic collapse. [46]

In Hilferding's *Finanzkapital*, competition — the anarchy of production — is the Achilles heel of capital. But Hilferding took this undoubtedly crucial feature of the capitalist mode of production out

[45] The most extreme — and naive — version to date of a 'monocausal' explanation of capitalist development can be found in Natalie Moszkowska: 'The same factor (!) that determines the conjunctural curve also determines the overall curve of the capitalist economy. If we disregard secondary factors and causes and only consider the main cause we can distinguish two diametrically opposed tendencies in economics. The representatives of one tendency see the cause of disruptions in the economy in excessive consumption and insufficient saving (under-accumulation), those of the other tendency conversely in insufficient consumption and excessive saving (over-accumulation).' She adds the following footnote: 'It is true that many economists reject monocausal theories of crises because of the "complexity of ways in which crises manifest themselves" and speak of a "multiplicity of sources for these events". But a closer examination shows that even in the theories of these researchers a single cause mostly predominates.' N. Moszkowska, *Zur Dynamik des Spätkapitalismus*, Zurich, 1943, p. 9.

[46] The first writers to develop these ideas systematically were: Heinrich Cunow, in 'Die Zusammenbruchstheorie' in *Die Neue Zeit*, 1898, pp. 424-30; Alexander Parvus *Die Handelskrisis und die Gewerkschaften*, Munich, 1901; Karl Kautsky 'Krisentheorien' in *Die Neue Zeit*, Vol. 20/2, 1902, p. 80; and the American Marxist Louis B. Boudin *The Theoretical System of Karl Marx*, 1907, pp. 163-9, 243-4.

of its overall context and identified it as the sole cause of capitalist crises and disequilibria. This inevitably led him to his later concept of 'organized capitalism' in which a 'general cartel' eliminates crises, and to his rejection of the notion of the ultimate economic collapse of capitalism.[47]

In Otto Bauer there is a continuous struggle to find the 'single' most crucial, internal economic contradiction of the capitalist mode of production, which leads him successively to a number of different positions. He gradually develops from his orginal view that the periodic release of non-accumulated money capital is the most important factor in the rupture of capitalist equilibrium, to a more ingenious version of Rosa Luxemburg's theory of under-consumption.[48] This finds expression in his last work of economic analysis, *Zwischen zwei Weltkriegen?*, in which he puts forward the thesis that the basic contradiction in capitalism is the fact that the production of constant capital (in Department I) grows more rapidly than the need for constant capital in the production of consumer goods. This is said to be an inevitable consequence in the rise of surplus-value.[49] Fritz Sternberg, Leon Sartre and Paul Sweezy have taken over Bauer's thesis with minor alterations, or have developed the same thesis independently,[50] with the result that in the end they all come to the same conclusion as Rosa Luxemburg: capitalism suffers inherently, if not from a residue of unsaleable consumer goods, then at least from unutilized capacity for the output of consumer goods (or, which amounts to the same thing, from a mass of means of production which cannot be sold because, although marketed for Department II, they cannot be bought by the latter).

[47]See Grossmann, op. cit., pp. 57-9.

[48]Otto Bauer's successive views on the subject are to be found mainly in his article entitled 'Marx' Theorie der Wirtschaftskrisen' in *Die Neue Zeit*, 1904; in his book *Die Nationalitätenfrage und die Sozialdemokratie*, Vienna, 1907, pp. 461-74; in his article 'Die Akkumulation des Kapitals' in *Die Neue Zeit*, 1913; and in his book *Zwischen zwei Weltkriegen?*, which was published in Bratislava in 1936. The crucial elements he singled out were, in chronological order, the fluctuations in the reconstitution of fixed capital (1904), the pressure of idle capital for investment abroad (1907), the discrepancy between capital accumulation and population growth (1913), and finally the discrepancy between the development of Department I and the demand for means of production in Department II (1936).

[49]Otto Bauer, *Zwischen zwei Weltkriegen?*, pp. 351-3.

[50]Paul M. Sweezy, *The Theory of Capitalist Development*, New York, 1942, pp. 180-4, Leon Sartre, *Esquisse d'une Théorie marxiste des Crises Périodiques*, Paris, 1937, pp. 28-40, 62-7; Fritz Sternberg, *Der Imperialismus und Seine Kritiker*, Berlin, 1929, pp. 163f.

In *Marxist Economic Theory*, I have already exposed the basic misunderstanding — an obvious *petitio principii* — which underlies this type of argument. All these authors work on the basic assumption that there is no change in the proportion of the value of production or productive capacity between the two Departments, while the demand for commodities from Department II, because of the rising rate of surplus-value and the growing organic composition of capital, naturally grows more slowly than the demand for commodities from Department I. Thereby crisis naturally becomes inevitable. But the constancy of this '*technical proportion*' (Otto Bauer speaks of a 'technical coefficient') between the growth of production in Department I, and the productive capacity of Department II (Sweezy) or the means of production required for the production of additional consumer goods (Bauer), has by no means been proved.

The fact that accelerated development in Department I must, by raising the organic composition of capital in the economy as a whole, ultimately also raise the productive capacity of Department II, by no means proves that the productive capacity of both Departments must rise *in the same proportion*. If there is a change in the proportion of the two capacities to each other, however, and given a large increase in the total production of commodities, an increased demand for commodities from Department I can certainly be accompanied by an absolute, if relatively smaller, increase in the productive capacity of Department II and by the full utilization of this capacity, without this necessarily leading to over-production or over-capacity.

Henryk Grossmann sees the main weakness of the capitalist mode of production in the growing problems of valorization of capital, which must necessarily lead to 'over-accumulation', i.e., to a state in which all the surplus-value available no longer suffices for the profitable valorization of the available capital. His argument, which relies too heavily on the quite arbitrary figures from which he starts, wavers between two main approaches. On the one hand he states that the difficulties of valorizing capital would become an absolute barrier if they actually led to a fall in the surplus-value unproductively consumed by the capitalist. On the other hand, he argues that the inability to valorize *all* the accumulated capital 'profitably' would bring the *entire* process of expansion to a halt.[51] The first argument does not hold water, for it disregards the fact that the part of the surplus-value marked for consumption could be divided

[51]Grossmann, op. cit., pp. 118-23, 129-35, 137-41.

among a *constantly decreasing* number of capitalists (even more so in Grossmann's scheme than in reality, for the difficulties of valorization which he presupposes would greatly intensify capitalist competition). A fall in consumption as a *share* of the surplus-value produced is quite compatible with a rise in the consumption of each capitalist family (we shall not consider here to what extent Grossmann is correct in regarding the consumer needs of the capitalist as the 'ultimate goal' of capitalist production). The second argument contains an obvious fallacy: for if the entire mass of the surplus-value available no longer suffices to valorize *all* the accumulated capital, the result would not be the collapse of the entire economy but only the devalorization (*Entwertung*) of the 'superfluous' capital through competition and crisis. All that Grossmann proves by this is that the inherent tendency towards over-accumulation, which is undoubtedly a feature of capitalism, must be neutralized by the tendency, which is similarly inherent in the system, towards the periodic devalorization of capital in order to avoid a longer stagnation of the process of valorization. This is precisely the function of crises of over-production, as Marx himself emphasized. Grossmann has not proved, therefore, that this process would make the valorization of capital generally impossible in the long run.[52]

The Polish-American economist Michal Kalecki has made the most advanced attempt hitherto to combine the research methods of Marxism with those of modern econometrics — his work anticipated many of Keynes's findings. His conclusion is a variant of Grossmann's thesis: namely, that the rate of accumulation of newly created surplus-value, i.e., the division of this surplus-value between nonproductive consumption and accumulation, is the 'strategic variable' in Marx's system. But the isolation of this factor out of the overall context of the system does not answer the question *why* the capitalists display a lower rate of accumulation over quite long periods, followed by a higher rate (or conversely, a higher rate of unproductive consumption followed by a lower rate again).[53]

Yet another variant of the same position is advanced by the theorists of the so-called 'permanent war economy', represented principally by the British Marxist Michael Kidron.[54] Accumulation can continue beyond its inner limits if more and more surplus-value

[52] A sharp critique of Grossmann's thesis is given by Fritz Sternberg, *Eine Umwäl-zung der Wissenschaft*, Berlin, 1930.
[53] Michal Kalecki, *Theory of Economic Dynamics*, London, 1954.
[54] Michael Kidron, *Western Capitalism Since the War*, London 1962.

is moved 'out of the system' through unproductive consumption. We will discuss the basic contradictions of this theory in Chapter 9: the postponement of the collapse of capitalism is explained by the unproductive use, i.e., waste, of surplus-value. It remains obscure, however, how the *production* of weapons, i.e., the production of commodities, i.e., the *production of value*, can be equated with the *waste of surplus value*; and how the waste of surplus value can lead to accelerated economic growth.

Bukharin is the only Marxist[55] who, in his critique of Rosa Luxemburg, has pointed out, in passing as it were, that several basic contradictions of the system would have to be taken into account in order to be able to foresee its inevitable collapse.[56] At the same time Grossmann is right when he accuses Bukharin of not devoting a single line to an analysis of the dynamics of these contradictions and of not explaining how far and why these — or some of them — should possess a tendency to become intensified.[57]

We thus find that all these theories (with the exception of a comment of Bukharin, who himself precisely failed to develop a systematic theory in this direction) suffer the basic ailment of wanting to deduce the whole dynamic of the capitalist mode of production from a single variable in the system. All the other laws of development that Marx discovered act more or less automatically only as functions of this single variable. But Marx himself flatly contradicts this assumption in several places, for example: 'The world trade crises must be regarded as the real concentration and forcible adjustment of all the contradictions of bourgeois economy. The individual factors which are condensed in these crises must therefore emerge and must be described in each sphere of the bourgeois economy and the further we advance in our examination of the latter, the more aspects of this conflict must be traced on the one hand, and on the other hand it must

[55] We are not taking Lenin into consideration here, because he does not provide a systematic theory of the contradictions of capitalist development. But his brochure *Imperialism, the Highest Stage of Capitalism* certainly does *not* suffer from the disease of 'monocausality'.

[56] Bukharin, pp. 229-30, 264-68.

[57] Henryk Grossmann, op cit., pp. 44-8. It is true that in one sentence Bukharin (op. cit., p. 264) does seek to deduce the collapse of capitalism from the destruction of the forces of production and the impossibility of reproducing labour-power, exactly following the scheme of his book *Zur Oekonomie der Transformationsperiode*. In the further course of this study, we shall have occasion to undertake a more thorough critical examination of these views.

be shown that its more abstract forms are recurring and are contained in the more concrete forms.'[58]

In fact, any single-factor assumption is clearly opposed to the notion of the capitalist mode of production as a dynamic totality in which the interplay of *all* the basic laws of development is necessary in order to produce any particular outcome. This notion means that up to a certain point *all* the basic variables of this mode of production can partially and periodically perform the role of autonomous variables — naturally not to the point of complete independence, but in an interplay constantly articulated through the laws of development of the whole capitalist mode of production. These variables include the following central items: the organic composition of capital in general and in the most important departments in particular (which also includes, among other things, the volume of capital and its distribution between the departments); distribution of constant capital between fixed and circulating capital (again in general and in each of the main departments; we will henceforth omit this self-evident addition to the formula); the development of the rate of surplus-value; the development of the rate of accumulation (the relation between productive surplus-value and surplus-value which is unproductively consumed); the development of the turnover-time of capital; and the relations of exchange between the two Departments (which are mainly but not exclusively a function of the given organic composition of capital in these Departments).

A major part of the present study will be devoted to an investigation of the development and correlation of these six basic variables of the capitalist mode of production. Our thesis is that the history of capitalism, and at the same time the history of its inner regularities and unfolding contradictions, can only be explained and understood as a function of the interplay of these six variables. Fluctuations in the rate of profit are the seismograph of this history, since they express most clearly the result of this interplay in accordance with the logic of a mode of production based on profit, in other words, the valorization of capital. But they are only *results* which must themselves be explained by the interplay of the variables.

Here — in anticipation of our later findings — we shall give a few examples which in our opinion show that this thesis is correct. The

[58] Marx, *Theories of Surplus Value*, Vol. 2, p. 510; ibid., p. 534: 'In world market crises, all the contradictions of bourgeois production erupt collectively'.

rate of surplus-value — i.e., the rate of exploitation of the working class — is a function of the class struggle[59] and its provisional outcome in each specific period of time, among other things. To see it as a mechanical function of the rate of accumulation, say in the simplified form — higher rate of accumulation = less unemployment = stabilization or even reduction of the rate of surplus-value — is to confuse objective conditions which *can* lead to a particular result, or can attenuate this result, with the result itself. Whether or not the rate of surplus-value does in actual fact rise depends among other things on the degree of resistance displayed by the working class to capital's efforts to increase it. How numerous are the variations which are possible in this respect and how diverse are their outcomes can readily be seen from the history of the working class and the labour movement over the past 150 years. An even more incorrect example of a mechanical relation can be found in Grossmann's formula: low productivity of labour = low rate of surplus-value; high productivity of labour = high rate of profit. Marx often pointed to the situation in the United States, where wages were high from the very beginning, not as a function of the high productivity of labour but of the chronic *shortage of labour-power* caused by the *frontier*; high productivity of labour in North America was thus not the *cause* but the *result* of high wages and was therefore accompanied for a very long time by a lower rate of profit than in Europe.

The degree of resistance of the proletariat, i.e., the unfolding of the class struggle, is not the only determinant that causes the rate of surplus-value to develop into a variable partially independent of the rate of accumulation. The *original historical position* of the industrial reserve army also plays a crucial role. Depending on the size of this reserve army, it is possible for a rising rate of accumulation to be accompanied by a rising, stationary or falling rate of surplus-value. When there is a massive reserve army the growing rate of accumulation has no significant influence on the relation between the demand and supply of the commodity of labour-power (except, possibly, in some highly qualified professions). This explains the rapid increase

[59] 'The maximum of profit is, therefore, limited by the physical minimum of wages and the physical maximum of the working day. It is evident that between the two limits of this *maximum rate of profit* an immense scale of variations is possible. The fixation of its actual degree is only settled by the continuous struggle between capital and labour.' Karl Marx, *Wages, Price and Profit*, in Marx/Engels, *Selected Works*, London, 1968, p. 226

in the rate of surplus-value despite the rapid increase in the rate of accumulation in England, for example, between 1750 and 1830, or in India after the First World War. Conversely: when there is a tendency for the industrial reserve army to decrease, due — among other things — to the massive emigration of 'superfluous' labour-power abroad, a rapid increase in the rate of accumulation can perfectly well be accompanied by a plateau or a fall in the rate of surplus value. This scheme would fit Western Europe, for instance, between 1880 and 1900, or Italy at the start of the 1960's.

Similarly, the rate of growth of the organic composition of capital cannot be regarded simply as a function of technological progress arising from competition. This technological progress does admittedly cause living capital to be replaced by dead capital in order to reduce costs, in other words it causes a more rapid rise in the outlay on *fixed capital* than wages. We can easily find empirical evidence for this in the history of capitalism. But as we know, constant capital is comprised of two parts: a fixed part (machines, buildings, and so on) and a circulating part (raw materials, sources of power, auxiliary elements, and so on). The rapid growth of fixed capital and the rapid increase in the social productivity of labour that results from it, still tell us nothing definite about the tendencies of development of the organic composition of capital. For if the productivity of labour in the sector that produces raw materials grows more rapidly than in the sector producing consumer goods, then circulating constant capital will become relatively cheaper than variable capital, and this will ultimately lead to a situation in which *the organic composition of capital, despite accelerated technological progress and despite accelerated accumulation of surplus-value in fixed capital, will grow more slowly and not more rapidly than before.*

We have anticipated these results of our later investigations here in order to illustrate the method that will be used in them. This method treats all the basic proportions of the capitalist mode of production simultaneously as partially independent variables, in order to be able to formulate long-term laws of development for this mode of production. The key task will be to analyze the effect that these partially independent variables have in concrete historical situations, in order to be able to interpret and explain the successive phases of the history of capitalism.

It will emerge that the interplay of these different variables and laws of development can be *summed up in a tendency for the various spheres of production and the various component parts of the value of capital to develop unevenly.* The uneven development of Department I and Department II is only the beginning of this process, which is by no means reducible to this single movement. At the same time, we will have to investigate the extent to which the inner logic of the capitalist mode of production leads not only to an uneven development in the two Departments, but also to an uneven development in the rate of accumulation and the rate of surplus-value in the two Departments and in the economy as a whole, an uneven development between fixed and circulating constant capital, an uneven development between the rate of accumulation and the industrial reserve army, and an uneven development between the unproductive waste of surplus-value and the increasing organic composition of capital.

The *combination* of all these uneven tendencies of development of the fundamental proportions of the capitalist mode of production — the combination of these partially independent variations of the major variables of Marx's system — will enable us to explain the history of the capitalist mode of production and above all the third phase of this mode of production, which we shall call 'late capitalism', by means of the laws of motion of capital itself, without resort to exogenous factors alien to the core of Marx's analysis of capital. In this way the 'life of the subject matter' should emerge in the interplay of all the laws of motion of capital: in other words, it is their totality which yields the mediation between the surface appearances and the essence of capital, and between 'many capitals' and 'capital in general'.

In his recent polemic with Arghiri Emmanuel, Charles Bettelheim has questioned the validity of the notion of 'independent variables' in the context of Marxist analysis. Although on the whole we concur with the direction of this polemic, we cannot concede this point without reservation. Bettelheim writes: 'When we are dealing with Marx's formulas and are using them in full awareness of their function, we have no right to alter the "magnitudes" given in these formulas unless such alterations are justified by variations that affect, in accordance with laws, the different elements making up the structure to which these formulas refer. Only such theoretically justified changes are capable of altering these magnitudes, not arbitrarily but in a way that conforms precisely to the actual laws of the structure.'[60] Here

⁶⁰Charles Bettelheim, in A. Emmanuel, *Unequal Exchange*, London, 1972, pp. 283-4.

Bettelheim overlooks two basic difficulties. Firstly, the fact that the reproduction schemes are not tools for the analysis of problems of growth and ruptures of equilibrium, and that it is therefore *impossible* for 'laws' of any sort to regulate the variations of their component parts. (An even growth of the two Departments or an even rate of accumulation of these two Departments are not 'laws' of the capitalist mode of production, but only methodological abstractions to fulfil the purpose of the schemes, which is to prove that periodic equilibrium in the economy is possible.) Secondly, the fact that although the laws of development of capitalism discovered by Marx reveal *long-term end-results* (the increasing organic composition of capital, the increasing rate of surplus-value, the falling rate of profit) they do not reveal any exact and regular proportions between these tendencies of development. It is therefore not only legitimate but imperative to treat the variables listed above as *partially* independent and partially interdependent in function. Obviously this independence is not arbitrary but exists within the framework of the inner logic of the specific mode of production and its general long-term tendencies of development [61]. But it is precisely the integration of the general long-term tendencies of development with the short and medium-term fluctuations of these variables which makes possible a mediation between abstract 'capital in general' and the concrete 'many capitals'. In other words, it is this which makes it possible to reproduce the actual historical process of the development of the capitalist mode of production through its successive stages. Thus the history of this mode of production becomes the history of the developing antagonism between capital and pre-capitalist and semi-capitalist economic relations, which the capitalist world market perpetually incorporates into itself. We shall therefore start with an account of the structural changes which the spread of the capitalist mode of production wrought in the world market in the epoch from Waterloo to Sarajevo, and then of the subsequent transformations of this world market in the epoch of capitalist decline inaugurated by the First World War.

---

[61] Bettelheim himself later admits that there is a 'relative indeterminacy' in the particular relations that Marx discovered: *Unequal Exchange*, p. 288.

2

The Structure of the Capitalist
World Market

The actual movement of capital obviously starts from non-capitalist
relations and proceeds within the framework of a constant, exploita-
tive, metabolic exchange with this non-capitalist milieu. This is by no
means merely one of Rosa Luxemburg's theses or discoveries: Marx
himself explicitly spelt out and underlined it on several occasions.
Thus, for example: 'The sudden expansion of the world market, the
multiplication of circulating commodities, the competitive zeal of the
European nations to possess themselves of the products of Asia and
the treasures of America, and the colonial system — all contributed
materially toward destroying the feudal fetters on production. *However, in its first period — the manufacturing period — the modern
mode of production developed only where the conditions for it had
taken shape within the Middle Ages.*[1] Compare, for instance, Holland
with Portugal. . . . The obstacles presented by the internal solidity
and organization of pre-capitalistic, national modes of production to
the corrosive influence of commerce are strikingly illustrated in the
intercourse of the English with India and China. . . . English commerce exerted a revolutionary influence on these communities and
tore them apart only in so far as the low prices of its goods served to
destroy the spinning and weaving industries, which were an ancient
integrating element of this unity of industrial and agricultural production. *Even so this work of dissolution proceeds very gradually.* . . .

[1] In this connection see our comments in *Marxist Economic Theory*, pp. 119-25.

Unlike the English, Russian commerce, on the other hand, leaves the economic groundwork of Asiatic production untouched[2] (Our italics).

Twenty years after Karl Marx wrote these words, Friedrich Engels stated soberly in a letter to Conrad Schmidt: 'It is exactly the same with the law of value and the distribution of the surplus-value by means of the rate of profit. . . . Both attain their most complete approximate realisation only *on the presupposition that capitalist production has been everywhere completely established*, i.e., that society has been reduced to the modern classes of landowners, capitalists (industrialists and merchants) and workers — all intermediate stages having been got rid of. *This condition does not exist even in England and never will exist* — we shall not let it get that far'[3] (Our italics).

Marx, moreover, worked out the simple theoretical axiom that the *genesis* of capital must not be equated with its *self-development*: 'The conditions and presuppositions of the *becoming*, of the *arising*, of capital presuppose precisely that it is not yet in being but merely in *becoming*; they therefore disappear as real capital arises, capital which itself, on the basis of its own reality, posits the conditions for its realization. Thus, for example, while the process in which money or value for-itself originally becomes capital presupposes on the part of the capitalist an accumulation — perhaps means of savings garnered from products and values created by his own labour, which he has undertaken as a *not-capitalist*, i.e., while the presuppositions under which money becomes capital appear as given, external presuppositions for the arising of capital — [nevertheless], as soon as capital has become capital as such, it creates its own presuppositions, i.e., the possession of the real conditions of the creation of new values *without exchange* — by means of its own production process'[4] (Marx's own italics).

We are thus dealing with a double process, and the two sides of this

[2] *Capital*, Vol. 3, pp. 332-4.

[3] Engels to Conrad Schmidt, letter of 12 March 1895, in Marx and Engels, *Selected Correspondence*, Moscow, 1965, p. 483. See also Marx: 'We take it (England) as an example, because the capitalist mode of production is at a developed stage there, *and no longer operates, as is the case in continental Europe, for the most part on the basis of a peasant economy which does not correspond to it* . . .' 'Resultate des unmittelbaren Produktionsprozesses' (the original 6th chapter of the first volume of *Capital*), *Arkhiv Marksa i Engelsa*, Vol. II (VI), Moscow, 1933, p. 258 (Our italics).

[4] Marx, *Grundrisse*, pp. 459-60.

process have to be combined if we are to understand both the genesis and subsequent self-development of capital. Primitive accumulation of capital and capital accumulation through the production of surplus-value are, in other words, not merely *successive* phases of economic history but also *concurrent* economic processes. Throughout the entire history of capitalism up to the present, processes of primitive accumulation of capital have constantly coexisted with the predominant form of capital accumulation through the creation of value in the process of production. Peasants, shopkeepers, artisans, sometimes even employees, civil servants and highly qualified workers try to become capitalists and themselves exploit labour power by managing in one way or another (exceptionally limited consumption; usury; theft; fraud; inheritance; lottery prizes) to secure an initial amount of capital. Although this process of primitive accumulation already presupposes the existence of the capitalist mode of production (as distinct from the historical process of primitive accumulation of capital described by Marx), and although its role in those capitalist countries which are already industrialized is insignificant, it is nonetheless of considerable importance in the colonial and semi-colonial countries — the so-called 'developing' countries. For these it generally still remains both quantitatively and qualitatively more decisive for social structure and economic development than the creation of surplus-value in the process of production itself.

These two separate moments must be brought into a structural connection with each other. Primitive accumulation of capital, whose historical origins go back to the genesis of the capitalist mode of production, derived its particular dynamic precisely from its *monopolistic character*; apart from the few points on the earth's surface where the first modern factories operating with machines sprang up, there was no large-scale capitalist industry in the world at all (although there was creation of value in capitalist manufacturing enterprises). Since, however, all of these had a more or less analogous level of productivity, whether they were in Western Europe or Latin America, in Russia, China or Japan, there was hardly any international gradient in their profits to stimulate a dynamic growth.[5]

The situation that defines processes of primitive accumulation

[5] André Gunder Frank quotes a former Chilean President as stating that in the 18th century manufacturing production in Brazil was more significant than in the USA; *Capitalism and Underdevelopment in Latin America*, New York, 1967, p. 60.

today is obviously very different. These occur within the framework of an already established capitalist mode of production and capitalist world market; they are thus in constant competition, or permanent metabolic exchange, with already established capitalist production. The international growth and spread of the capitalist mode of production for the past two centuries thus constitutes *a dialectical unity of three moments:*

(a) Ongoing capital accumulation in the domain of already capitalist processes of production;

(b) Ongoing primitive accumulation of capital outside the domain of already capitalist processes of production;

(c) Determination and limitation of the second moment by the first, i.e., struggle and competition between the second and the first moment.

What, then, is the inner logic of this third moment, the determination and limitation of ongoing primitive accumulation of capital by capital accumulation occurring in the domain of already capitalist processes of production?

Both in each individual country and internationally, capital presses outwards from the centre — in other words, its historic birth-places — towards the periphery. It constantly tries to extend itself to new domains, to convert new sectors of simple reproduction of commodities into spheres of capitalist production of commodities, and to replace sectors which have hitherto only produced use values by the production of commodities.[6] The extent to which this process continues to take place even today, before our eyes, in the highly industrialized countries, is exemplified by the expansion in the last two decades of the industries producing ready-to-eat meals, drink dispensing machines, and so forth.

[6] See Marx: 'Precisely the productivity of labour, the mass of production, the mass of population, the mass of surplus population, which are developed by this mode of production continually create, through the release of capital and labour, new branches of business in which capital can once again work on a small scale and once again go through the various developments, until these new branches of business are also carried on on a wide social scale. This process occurs continually. At the same time capitalist production tends to conquer all those branches of industry over which it has not yet gained mastery, which it has only formally subsumed. As soon as it has gained mastery over agriculture, the mining industry, the manufacture of the main materials for clothing, and so on, it takes hold of still further spheres, where its control is still only formal and where there are still even independent artisans.' *Resultate des unmittelbaren Produktionsprozesses*, pp. 120-2.

But the penetration of the capitalist mode of production into these spheres is limited by two crucial factors. Firstly, this mode of production must be competitive, i.e., the selling price must be less than the cost price of the same goods produced in the sphere of simple commodity production or family production, or at least low enough for the original producers to consider that their own cheaper production is no longer profitable in view of the time and labour saved by purchase of the new products.[7] Secondly, excess capital must be available, whose investment in these spheres will produce a higher rate of profit than its investment in already existing spheres (not necessarily an absolutely higher rate, but in any event higher than the *marginal* rate, yielded by additional capital investment in the spheres which are already capitalist).

To the precise extent that these two conditions are not realized, or only partly realized, or realized under too heavy limitations, the accumulation of self-reproducing capital still leaves room for the primitive accumulation of capital. Small and medium-sized capital penetrates this unoccupied space, carries out the 'dirty work' of destroying the indigenous and traditional relations of production[8] and in the process either founders in ruin or prepares the ground for the 'normal' production of surplus-value, in which it can then itself also participate. In the latter case, it is converted into 'normal' industrial, agricultural, financial or commercial capital.

Bukharin correctly defined the world economy as 'a system of relations of production and corresponding relations of exchange on an international scale'.[9] But in his book *Imperialism and World Economy* he failed to emphasize a crucial aspect of this system: namely that the capitalist world economy is an *articulated system of capitalist, semi-capitalist and pre-capitalist relations of production,*

[7] We are not discussing here the 'more normal' case in which the violent intervention of capital (expropriation of the original owners, expulsion of peasants from their land and homes, blockage of access to traditionally available reserves of land, means of subsistence and labour) *prevents* the production of use-values by the indigenous producers and transforms these into sellers of the commodity of labour-power and hence into buyers of industrially produced goods.

[8] See Rosa Luxemburg: 'According to Marxist theory, small capitalists play in the course of capitalist development the role of pioneers of technical change. They possess that role in a double sense. They initiate new methods of production in well established branches of industry, they are instrumental in the creation of new branches of production not yet exploited by the big capitalist.' *Social Reform or Revolution*, New York, 1970, p. 15.

[9] N. Bukharin, *Imperialism and World Economy*, London, 1972, pp. 25-6.

linked to each other by capitalist relations of exchange and dominated by the capitalist world market. It is only in this way that the formation of this world market can be understood as the product of the development of the capitalist mode of production — not to be confused with the world market created by mercantile capital, which was a precondition for this capitalist mode of production [10] — and as a combination of capitalistically developed and capitalistically under-developed economies and nations into a multilaterally self-conditioning system. We shall explore this problem more deeply both in the course of this chapter and when we come to deal with problems of unequal exchange and neo-colonialism.

The historian Oliver Cox has an inkling of this kind of articulated system. But he is too strongly influenced by his previous work on Venetian merchant capital to see this 'hierarchy of economies and nations' as determined by anything more than 'differentiated situations on the world market'. He thus completely disregards the existence of differing relations of production.[11] This is an error which other authors, such as Arrighi Emmanuel, Samir Amin and André Gunder Frank share to a greater or lesser degree with Cox, and we shall return to it in Chapter 11.

If we look at the history of the capitalist world economy since the Industrial Revolution, over the last two hundred years, we can distinguish the following stages in this specific articulation of capitalist, semi-capitalist and pre-capitalist relations of production. In the age of freely competitive capitalism, the direct production of surplus-value by large-scale industry was limited exclusively to Western Europe and North America. The process of primitive accumulation of capital, however, was taking place in many other parts of the world at the same time — even if its rhythm was uneven. Therewith, textile production by artisans and native peasants was gradually destroyed in these countries while rising domestic industry was often combined with actual factory industry. Foreign capital did, of course, flow into

---

[10]Marx: 'The world market itself forms the basis for this mode of production. On the other hand, the immanent necessity of this mode of production to produce on an ever-enlarged scale tends to extend the world market continually, so that it is not commerce in this case which revolutionizes commerce.' *Capital*, Vol. 3, p. 333. See also the footnote inserted by Engels in the Third Volume of *Capital*: 'The colossal expansion of the means of transportation and communication — ocean liners, railways, electrical telegraphy, the Suez Canal — has made a real world-market a fact.' Ibid., p. 489.

[11]Oliver C. Cox, *Capitalism as a System*, New York, 1964, pp. 1, 6, 10.

countries which were beginning to industrialize, but it was unable to dominate the processes of accumulation there.[12] Two of the most important obstacles to the domination of foreign capital over these nascent capitalist economies should be singled out. Firstly, the extent of capital accumulation in Great Britain, France or Belgium, was not sufficient to allow this capital to engage in the establishment of factories in other parts of the world. In Great Britain, annual capital investments abroad averaged only £29 million between 1860 and 1869; they then increased in the decade from 1870-79 by 75% to £51 million a year, and then to £68 million a year in the decade from 1880-89.[13] The second obstacle was the inadequacy of the means of communication — the uneven development of the Industrial Revolution in the manufacturing industry and in the transport industry.[14] This effectively blocked the penetration of the cheap goods mass-

[12]A.C. Carter estimates that Dutch capital comprised about a quarter of the total share-capital in Great Britain towards 1760 (see the discussion of this in Charles Wilson, 'Dutch Investment in 18th Century England', *Economic History Review*, April 1960). The role of English capital in the industrialization of Belgium is symbolized by the founders of the modern machine-building industry, the Cockerill Brothers. Belgian and English capital likewise played an important role in the first wave of French industrialization (see W.O. Henderson, *The Industrial Revolution on the Continent*, London, 1961; J. Dhont, 'The Cotton Industry at Ghent during the French Regime', in F. Crouzet, W.H. Chaloner and W.M. Stern (eds.) *Essays in European Economic History 1789-1914*, London, 1969). The same is true of Dutch capital with respect to the German textile industry on the left bank of the Rhine (see Gerhard Adelmann, 'Structural Changes in the Rhenish Linen and Cotton Trades at the Outset of Industrialization', in *Essays in European Economic History 1789-1914*). For the role of French capital in the first wave of industrialization in Italy, see A.B. Gille, *Les Investissements Français en Italie 1815-1940*, Turin, 1968, and Aldo Alessandro Mola (ed.), *L'Economia Italiana dopo l'Unità*, Turin, 1971, p. 130 ff. For the central role of foreign, mainly British capital in the construction of the US railway system (especially in the 1866-73 period), see L.H. Jenks' 'Railroads as an Economic Force in American Development', *Journal of Economic History*, IV, 1944.

[13]Phyllis Deane and W.A. Cole, *British Economic Growth 1688-1959*, Cambridge, 1967, pp. 36, 266. See also Marx: 'Ever more extended mass production floods the existing market and thereby works continually for a still greater expansion of this market, for breaking out of its limits. What restricts this mass production is not commerce (in so far as it expresses the existing demand) but the magnitude of employed capital and the level of development of the productivity of labour.' *Capital*, Vol. 3, p. 336. Further, Leland Hamilton Jenks, *The Migration of British Capital to 1875*, London, 1927. See also the well-known Foreign Office Circular dated 15 January 1848 to diplomatic missions abroad, which expressly underlined that domestic investments should have precedence over holdings abroad. (*Foreign Office Archives*, F.O. 16, Vol. 63, Circular dated 15.1.1848.)

[14] 'The chief means of reducing the time of circulation is improved communications. The last fifty years have brought about a revolution in this field, comparable only with the industrial revolution of the latter half of the 18th century.' Marx, *Capital*, Vol. 3, p. 71.

produced by large-scale industry in Western Europe, not merely into the farthest villages and small towns of Asia and Latin America, but even those of Southern and Eastern Europe. Indeed, the inadequacy of transport and communications systems hindered the formation of national markets proper in Western Europe itself. Before the spread of railways, the price of a ton of coal in France varied in 1838 from 6.90 francs in the mining region of St Etienne south of the Loire, to 36-45 francs in Paris, and even 50 francs in Bayonne and remoter Brittany.[15]

It is thus no accident that the slowly increasing impact of the foreign capital investments of Great Britain, France, Belgium and Holland was chiefly concentrated in *foreign railway construction*, for the extension of this world-wide communications network was a precondition for the gradual extension of their domination over the internal markets of the less developed countries which had been dragged into the maelstrom of the capitalist world economy.[16]

But precisely this concentration on the construction of railways led to a significant *time-lag* — lasting approximately from the 1848 Revolution to the 1860's — during which those economies which were themselves pressing towards a capitalist mode of production, were on the whole left unlimited scope for primitive accumulation of indigenous national capital. International wage differentials facilitated the same process.[17] The fact that even this first transport revolution did not achieve a decisive reduction in the costs of conveying cheap and easily perishable commodities over long distances, meant that the local capital of less developed countries continued to enjoy unthreatened markets in the food industry, brewing, haberdashery (excluding luxury goods in each case), and so on. Italy, Russia, Japan and Spain are the most striking examples of this phenomenon. There, if we disregard foreign investments in railway construction and public loans, it was local capital that dominated

---

[15]See Maurice Lévy-Leboyer, *Les Banques Européennes et l'Industrialisation Internationale dans la Première Moitié du 19e Siècle*, Paris, 1964, p. 320.

[16]'On the other hand, the cheapness of the articles produced by machinery, and the improved means of transport and communication furnish the weapons for conquering foreign markets.' Marx, *Capital*, Vol. I, p. 451. For the significance of railway construction for British exports of both capital and commodities in the pre-imperialist epoch, see among others, Maurice Dobb, *Studies in the Development of Capitalism*, London, 1963, pp. 297-8.

[17]In 1833, a male worker spinning a given type of yarn received a weekly wage equivalent to 37 francs for 69 hours of work in Britain, 19 francs for 72-84 hours of work in France, and 9-12 francs for a similar number of hours in Switzerland: Lévy-Leboyer, op. cit., p. 65.

the steady expansion of the internal market and the unchecked advance of primitive accumulation.

In Italy for example, the textile industry was still mainly composed of peasant and domestic-industrial artisans in the 1850's: about 300,000 peasant women were engaged, for approximately 150 working days a year, in the spinning of flax and hemp. Of the 1.2 million quintals of these raw materials, 300,000 were exported and 900,000 consumed in Italy itself. Little more than 1/9 of the latter was used by already mechanized industry, 8/9 by domestic production. Even in 1880 domestic weaving exceeded industrial weaving in flax and linen production. In the silk industry the industrial breakthrough began about 1870 and only came to completion at the end of the century. In cotton production, domestic industry predominated in the 1850's and 1860's; large-scale industry achieved a breakthrough in spinning about 1870, and in weaving not for another ten years after that.[18] In this entire process of industrialization foreign capital played no role.

The same is true of Russia, where although the first wave of industrialization from 1840-70 was carried through with imported machinery — Russia bought 26% of the machines exported by England in 1848 — there was no participation of foreign capital worth mentioning.[19] In 1845 the total imports and domestic production of machinery in Russia were worth scarcely more than 1 million roubles; in 1870 they had reached 65 million roubles. The total value of the industrial machinery used in Russia amounted to 100 million roubles in 1861, and 350 million roubles in 1870. The annual value of production in the most important industries (outside Poland and Finland) rose from approximately 100 million roubles in 1847 to over 280 million roubles in 1870. The capital that underlay this movement was almost exclusively national.[20] We find an analogous development in Japan. Its total bank capital grew from 2.5 million yen in 1875 to 43 million in 1880. In the latter year domestic industry still dominated cotton weaving and

[18]Emilio Sereni, *Il Capitalismo nelle Campagne*, 1968, pp. 18, 19, 22-3.

[19]S. Strumilin, 'Industrial Crises in Russia 1847-1867', in F. Crouzet, W.H. Chaloner and W.M. Stern (eds.), *Essays in European Economic History 1789-1914*, London, 1969, p. 158.

[20]The companies formed in Russia had a capital of 750,000 roubles in 1855 and of 51 million roubles in 1858(ibid., p. 68). See also Roger Portal, 'The Industrialization of Russia', in *Cambridge Economic History of Europe*, Vol. VI, Part 2, Cambridge, 1966, who quotes figures of 350 million roubles in 1860 and 700 million roubles for the share capital of the railway companies floated between 1860 and 1870.

spinning, but in 1890 large-scale industry had already consolidated its domination over these spheres.[21]

The concrete articulation between these countries, which were at that time capitalist 'developing nations', and the capitalist world market was two-fold. On the one hand, the import of cheap machine goods from abroad with the accompanying 'artillery of cheap prices' was the great destroyer of traditional domestic production. In Italy, at the beginning of the 1880's, half the imports still consisted of products of the manufacturing industry or semi-finished products, and in Japan the unrestricted import of cheap cotton yarn (average price about 29.6 yen per *Kin* in 1874 and 25.5 yen in 1878) had a devastating effect on peasant domestic industry (average price 42.7 yen in 1874, 45 yen in 1878).[22] But in both cases *local machine industry* was able to take the place of local domestic industry in about ten years, i.e., the foreign products simply cleared the ground for the development of 'national' capitalism.

On the other hand, the rapid specialization in their foreign trade (agricultural products, later also oil, in the case of Russia; raw silk and yarn in the case of Japan) was able to secure important sectors of the world market as outlets for these rising capitalist economies. The profits thus realized became, in their turn, the main source for the local accumulation of capital.

It is also true, of course, that integration into the world market and conditions of relative underdevelopment in this phase had very negative effects on primitive accumulation of capital in these countries. The exchange of commodities produced in conditions of a higher productivity of labour against commodities produced in conditions of a lower productivity of labour was an unequal one; it was an exchange of less against more labour, which inevitably led to a *drain*, an outward flow of value and capital from these countries to the advantage of Western Europe.[23] The presence of large reserves of cheap labour and land in these countries logically

[21]W. W. Lockwood, *The Economic Development of Japan*, Princeton, 1954, p. 113. The production of cotton yarn rose from 13,000 balls in 1884 to 292,000 in 1894 and 757,000 in 1899: Thomas C. Smith, *Political Change and Industrial Development in Japan: Government Enterprise 1868-1880*, Stanford, 1965, pp. 37, 63.

[22]Sereni, op. cit., pp. 32-3. Smith, op. cit., pp. 26-7.

[23]Strumilin estimates that between 1855 and 1860, 80 million roubles worth of gold flowed out of Russia, and 143 million roubles worth between 1861 and 1866 (pp. 167, 174). Admittedly, a large proportion of this second sum can be explained by the action of those Russian aristocrats who responded to the abolition of serfdom by the sale of their estates and a parasitical existence abroad.

resulted in a capital accumulation with a lower organic composition of capital than in the first industrialized countries.[24] But the extent of this drain and of this lower organic composition were not sufficient to pose a serious threat to the indigenous and independent accumulation of capital — at least not in those countries where social and political class forces were already capable of replacing the destruction of an artisanate by the development of national large-scale industry. In regions like Turkey, where these conditions either did not exist at all or only inadequately — because the state was unwilling or unable to perform its role as the midwife of modern capitalism (for example, where it was dominated by external merchant capital like the East India Company), or because foreigners, instead of a native bourgeoisie, already controlled primitive accumulation of money capital, and so on — attempts to engender domestic industrialization were bound to fail, although from a purely economic point of view the existing preconditions for them were no less propitious than in Russia, Spain or Japan.[25]

In the age of imperialism there was a radical change in this whole structure. The process of primitive accumulation of capital in previously uncapitalized economies was now also subjected to the reproduction of the Western big capital itself. From this point on, the capital export of the imperialist countries, and not the process of primary accumulation of the local ruling classes, determined the economic development of what later came to be called the 'Third World'. The latter was now forced to complement the needs of capitalist production in the metropolitan countries. This was not only an

[24] 'If wages and price of land are low in one country, while interest on capital is high, because the capitalist mode of production has not been developed generally, whereas in another country wages and price of land are nominally high, while interest on capital is low, then the capitalist employs more labour and land in the one country, and in the other relatively more capital.' 'Marx, *Capital*, Vol. 3. p. 852.

[25] See the excerpts from work by Omer Celal Sarç ('The Tanzimat and our Industry' and I. M. Smilianskaya, 'The Disintegration of Feudal Relations in Syria and Lebanon in the Middle of the 19th Century') in the anthology edited by Charles Issawi, *The Economic History of the Middle East*, Chicago 1966, pp. 48-51, 241-5. It is interesting to note that the lack of a 'return effect' ('cumulative industrialization') is actually determined by the complex we have described, and not by the *use-value* of the first commodities produced by capitalist means. In China's case these were not raw materials but textile products (see Jürgen Kuczynski, *Die Geschichte der Lage der Arbeiter unter dem Kapitalismus*, Berlin, 1964, pp. 16-41, 106-7, for the considerable extent of the Chinese textile industry in the period 1894-1913, and the renewed and significant growth of this industry during and after the First World War). Despite this, no process of cumulative industrialization took place. We will discuss this problem more thoroughly in Chapter 11.

indirect consequence of the competition of cheaper commodities from these metropolitan countries, it was above all a direct result of the fact that capital investment itself came from these metropolitan countries and established only such enterprises as corresponded to the interests of the imperialist bourgeoisie.

The process of the imperialist export of capital accordingly suffocated the economic development of the so-called 'Third World'. For, firstly, it absorbed the available local resources for primitive accumulation of capital by a qualitatively increased 'drain'. From the standpoint of the national economy, this drain now assumed the form of a continuous expropriation of the local social surplus product by foreign capital, which obviously entailed a significant reduction in the resources available for national accumulation of capital.[26] Secondly, it concentrated the remaining resources in those sectors which were to become characteristic of the 'development of underdevelopment' — to cite Gunder Frank — or the 'development of dependence', in the terminology of Theotonio Dos Santos[27]: foreign trade, agency services for the imperialist firms, speculation in land and real estate construction, usury, lumpen-bourgeois and petty-bourgeois 'service' enterprises (lotteries, corruption, gangsterism, gambling, to some extent tourism). Thirdly and finally, it restricted primitive accumulation of capital by consolidating the old ruling classes in their position in the countryside and keeping a significant part of the village population outside the sphere of the actual production of commodities and the money economy.[28]

At first glance, the result seems paradoxical: the extended reproduction of capital which, in the metropolitan countries, furthered the process of the concurrent primitive accumulation of capital, simultaneously impeded the same process in the non-industrialized countries. Precisely where it was 'most abundant', capital was accumulated more rapidly; where it was 'most scarce', mobilization and accumulation of capital was much slower and more contradictory. This picture, which seems to contradict the rules of the market

---

[26] See Paul A. Baran, *The Political Economy of Growth*, New York, 1957.

[27] André Gunder Frank, op. cit.; Theotonio Dos Santos, *Economica y Cambio Revolucionario en America Latina*, Caracas, 1970.

[28] Ernesto Laclau suggests that in the case of Argentina this was at least partially due to the fact that the differential land rent accruing to the local landowning class absorbed a large part of the surplus-value incorporated into agricultural export products in the 19th and early 20th centuries; see *Modos de Producción, Sistemas Economicos y Población Excedente*, Buenos Aires, 1970.

economy and liberal economic theory, nevertheless becomes immediately comprehensible, once we consider the question of the relative rate of profit. What determined the unilateral 'underdevelopment' of the so-called 'Third World' was neither the ill-will of the imperialists nor the social — let alone 'racial' — inability of its indigenous ruling classes, but rather a complex of economic and social conditions which, while promoting the primitive accumulation of money capital, made the accumulation of industrial capital less profitable — and in any case less secure — than the fields of investment listed above, not to speak of collaboration with imperialism in the extended reproduction of metropolitan capital. [29]

Accordingly, what changed in the transition from freely competitive capitalism to classical imperialism was the specific articulation of the relations of production and exchange between the metropolitan countries and the underdeveloped nations. The domination of foreign capital over the local accumulation of capital (mostly combined with political domination) now subjected local economic development to the interests of the bourgeoisie in the metropolitan countries. It was no longer the 'light artillery' of cheap commodities which now bombarded the underdeveloped countries, but the 'heavy artillery' of the control of capital resources. In the pre-imperialist epoch, on the other hand, concentration on the production and export of raw materials *under the control of the indigenous bourgeoisie* had only been a prelude to the replacement of pre-capitalist relations of production on the land in the interests of this bourgeoisie. In the classical imperialist epoch, however, a long-term social and political alliance between imperialism and local oligarchies came into being which froze pre-capitalist relations of production in the village. This decisively limited the extension of the 'internal market'[30] and thereby

[29]See, among other things, our essay, 'Die Marxsche Theorie der ursprünglichen Akkumulation und die Industrialisierung der Dritten Welt', in *Folgen einer Theorie, Essays über 'Das Kapital' von Karl Marx*, Frankfurt, 1967. Note also the recent book by Geoffrey Kay, *Development and Under-development: A Marxist Analysis*, London, 1974, which emphasises the specific weight and role of merchant capital in the colonies and semi-colonies, for any explanation of underdevelopment.

[30]For the crucial role played by the division of labour and the introduction of the money economy into the village, in the creation of an 'internal market' for the developing capitalist system, see Marx, *Capital*, Vol. 1, pp. 747-9; Lenin, *The Development of Capitalism in Russia*. A fine example of the contemporary social alliances which block this process is provided by the relations between oil companies and native landowners in Venezuela. See Federico Brito, *Venezuela, Siglo XX*, Havana, 1967, pp. 17-60, 181-221.

again impeded the cumulative industrialization of the country, or forced those processes of primitive accumulation which did none-theless occur into non-industrial channels.

We have an almost classical example of this transformation in the structure of the world economy, which took place between the epoch of freely competitive capitalism and the epoch of classical imperial-ism, in the case of Chile. The first wave of Chile's integration into the capitalist world market in the 19th century occurred in copper mining, which, however, was largely in Chilean hands.[31] The second wave, which began with the development of saltpetre extraction after Chile's victorious war with Peru, led to the complete domina-tion of British capital over Chilean mining. In 1880 the total amount of British capital invested in Chile was approximately £7.5 million sterling, more than £6 million of this in the form of public bonds. In 1890 this sum had risen to £24 million, £16 millions of which were privately invested (especially in the saltpetre pits and mines).[32] Characteristically, there had been no change in the nature of the decisive export product (first copper, then saltpetre). What had changed were the predominant processes of capital accumulation and the predominant relations of production.[33]

The domination of foreign capital over the processes of capital accumulation in the underdeveloped countries led to an economic development which, as we have said, made these countries comple-mentary to the development of the economy of the imperialist metro-politan countries. As is known, this meant especially that they had to concentrate on the production of vegetable and mineral raw materials. The hunt for raw materials went hand in hand, so to speak, with imperialist capital export and was to a considerable extent a causal determinant of it. In this way, the growth of a relative excess

[31] Hernan Ramirez Necochea, 'Englands wirtschaftliche Vorherrschaft in Chile 1810-1914', in *Lateinamerika zwischen Emanzipation und Imperialismus,* Berlin, 1961, pp. 131, 137. By the same author, *Historia del Imperialismo en Chile*, Havana, 1966, p. 62. The share of British capital in the copper mines was not higher than 20-30%. See also André Gunder Frank's synthetic treatment of this epoch (op. cit., pp. 57-63), in which he quotes a number of Chilean sources. It is interesting to note that in the first fifty years of its independence Chile built up a merchant fleet of 276 vessels, which reached its peak in 1860 and then fell back to 75 ships by the end of the 1870's.

[32] H. R. Necochea, 'Englands wirtschaftliche Vorherrschaft in Chile', p. 147.

[33] The domination of British capital in the North Chilean saltpetre industry, in which it invested more than £9 million in the space of two years, was accompani-ed — as always in the period of classical imperialism — by the domination of the whole of the public life of the province in question (Tarapaca): railways, water-works, and banks, Necochea, op. cit., pp. 146-7.

of capital in the metropolitan countries and the search for higher rates of profit and cheaper raw materials form an integrated complex.

The search for raw materials, however, is in its turn not accidental. It corresponds to the inner logic of the capitalist mode of production. This leads, through rising productivity of labour, to a steady increase in the mass of commodities that can be produced by a given quantity of machines and labour. This in turn leads to a tendency for the share of the fixed — constant and variable capital in the average value of the commodity to fall, i.e., to a tendency for the share of the costs of raw materials in the production of the average commodity to rise: 'The value of raw material, therefore, forms an ever-growing component of the value of the commodity-product in proportion to the development of the productivity of labour . . . because in every aliquot part of the aggregate product of the portion representing depreciation of machinery and the portion formed by the newly added labour — both continually decrease. Owing to this falling tendency, the other portion of the value representing raw material increases proportionally, *unless this increase is counterbalanced by a proportionate decrease in the value of raw material arising from the growing productivity of the labour employed in its own production*'[34] (Our italics).

The production of raw materials by primitive, pre-capitalist means in the overseas countries — symbolized by the slave economy in the Southern States of the USA — reinforced this tendency for raw materials to become relatively more expensive, and hence led to attempts by metropolitan capital to transform its initial hunt for raw materials into cheaper, i.e., *capitalist*, production of these raw materials.[35]

The increase in the price of cotton caused by the American Civil War was one of the determinant factors in this development, but by no means the only one. The general upward drift of not only the relative but also the absolute prices of raw materials, which was a distinctive feature of the mid-19th century, is quite sufficient to explain the universalization of this tendency.[36] *The direct intervention of Western capital in the process of primitive accumulation of capital*

---

[34] Marx, *Capital*, Vol. 3, p. 108 (pp. 108-9)

[35] Eugene Genovese, *The Political Economy of Slavery*, New York, 1965, pp. 43-69, furnishes a convincing mass of data concerning the low productivity of labour in the cotton plantations of the Southern States of the USA under the slave system.

[36] In the 60's and early 70's of the 19th century, the prices of raw materials imported by Great Britain had reached their highest point since the Napoleonic Wars. The sudden downward plunge began in 1873 and by about 1895 it had reduced the

in the underdeveloped countries was thus determined to a significant degree by the compulsive pressure on this capital to organize large-scale capitalist production of raw materials.

The capitalist production of raw materials in underdeveloped countries meant, however, capitalist production under very specific socio-economic conditions of production. The huge mass of cheap labour-power available in the underdeveloped countries made it unprofitable to employ fixed capital on a large scale. The modern machine could not compete with this cheap labour. In the realm of agriculture, therefore, this led essentially to a plantation economy, i.e., *a pre-industrial capitalism* – the capitalism of the period of manufactures. The advantages of the new plantation compared with a pre-capitalist plantation economy lay above all in the introduction of an elementary division of labour between manual labourers, greater work discipline and more rational organization and accounting.[37] In the sphere of mining, it is true, the capitalist mode of production of raw materials in the underdeveloped countries did mean the introduction of capitalist machinery and the beginning of industrial capitalism. But here too, the low price of the commodity of labour-power, the gigantic proportions of the industiral reserve army and the relative helplessness of the proletariat in these conditions, shifted the centre of gravity of capital from the production of *relative* surplus value, already predominant in the West, to the production of *absolute* surplus value.[38]

---

average index of import prices by half! See B. R. Mitchell and P. Deane, *Abstract of British Historical Statistics*, Cambridge, 1962; C. P. Kindleberger and others, *The Terms of Trade: A European Case Study*, Cambridge, USA, 1956; Potter and Christie, *Trends in Natural Resource Commodities*, Baltimore 1962. In the same period there was also an actual decline in the price of raw materials produced in England itself: between 1873 and 1886 the price of Bessemer steel fell to a quarter of its former level per ton (Maurice Dobb, op. cit., p. 306).

[37]There are numerous descriptions of the specific nature of pre-industrial plantation capitalism in the centres set up by foreign capital in the 'Third World' for the production of cotton, rubber, tea, coffee and other products. See, for example, the account of the plantations of Ceylon in S. J. Tambia, *The Role of Savings and Wealth in South East Asia and the West*, Paris, 1963, pp. 75-80 and 84ff. It is interesting to note that even at a later date there were several cases of the introduction of pre-capitalist production (as for example in the Egyptian cotton boom 1860-66) which made it possible to keep prices up, but thereby subsequently led to terrible ruin of the peasantry and a subsequent adapation to modern methods of production (E. R. J. Owen, 'Cotton Production and the Development of the Cotton Economy in 19th Century Egypt', in Charles Issawi (ed.), *The Economic History of the Middle East 1800-1914*, Chicago, 1965, p. 410.)

[38]In the Chinese textile industry the 12-hour working day remained in operation until the Second World War, even for children. In the cotton weaving mills in Shanghai

The picture which thus emerges is of an imperialist world system built up on a world-wide uneven development of capital accumulation, organic composition of capital, rate of surplus-value and productivity of labour. The reason the Industrial Revolution began in the West was that international money capital and bullion had been concentrated there for the preceding 300 years — as a result of the systematic plundering of the rest of the world by means of colonial conquests and colonial trade.[39] This led to the international concentration of capital at only a few points of the globe, the predominant industrial areas of Western Europe (and shortly afterwards North America). The industrial capital which emerged in the West, however, could not prevent the internal process of primitive accumulation of capital by the ruling classes of more backward countries. At best it could slow down this process. With certain differences in time and productivity, due to the British monopoly of the highest levels of industrial productivity, the process of industrialization gradually extended in the age of freely competitive capitalism to more and more countries.

With the massive export of capital to the underdeveloped countries for the organization of the capitalist production of raw materials there, the quantitative difference in the accumulation of capital and the level of productivity between the metropolitan countries and the economically backward ones was suddenly transformed into a qualitative difference. These countries now became dependent as well as backward. Foreign capital's domination over the accumulation of capital stifled the process of the primitive accumulation of capital in these countries. The industrial gap steadily widened. Moreover, because the production of raw materials was still pre-industrial or only rudimentarily industrial, since the low costs of labour-power provided no incentive for constant modernization of machinery, this industrial gap created a growing gulf in respective levels of productivity, which both expressed and perpetuated actual *under-development. From the Marxist point of view, i.e., from the standpoint of a consistent labour theory of value, underdevelopment is ultimately always underemployment, both quantitatively*

---

there were only 1.7 days of rest a month in 1930, and a document from the English General Consul in the city reported 14 hour working days without any breaks: see the documents in Jürgen Kuczynski, op. cit., pp. 170-3.

[39] Ernest Mandel, *Marxist Economic Theory*, pp. 443-7.

(massive unemployment) *and qualitatively* (low productivity of labour).[40]

In the last resort, this basic fact, which forms such a decisive aspect of the capitalist world economy in the past hundred years, can only be explained by an even more fundamental aspect of the international expansion of capital. It is true that capitalist commodities created and conquered the capitalist *world market*, i.e., carried the domination of the capitalist circulation of commodities, and the predominance of commodities produced in modern capitalist large-scale industry, to the utmost limits of the globe. But at the same time it did not everywhere universalize the capitalist *mode of production*. On the contrary, in the so-called Third World it created and consolidated a specific mixture of pre-capitalist and capitalist relations of production which *prevents* the universalization of the capitalist mode of production, and especially of capitalist large-scale industry, in these countries. Therein lies the chief cause of the permanent pre-revolutionary crisis in the dependent countries for over half a century, the basic reason why these countries have so far proved to be the weakest links in the imperialist world system.

The massive penetration of capital into the production of raw materials made it possible to put a radical stop after 1873 to the secular trend for the price of raw materials to rise. There followed not only the notorious slump in the price of agricultural goods — and the great crisis of European agriculture — but also a rapid fall in the relative price of minerals as compared to the price of products of the capitalist finished-goods industry.[41] But in the long run this trend was bound to be reversed by the low costs of reproducing labour-power in the underdeveloped countries due to the massive scale of underemployment and the low degree of labour productivity, which constantly increased the difference in the level of productivity between these and the metropolitan countries. With the stagnation of labour productivity in the dependent countries and simultaneously a rapid

[40] Fritz Sternberg *(Imperialismus,* Chapter 1 and p. 456ff) was the first to make a thorough investigation of the connection between the development of wages and the surplus population (i.e., industrial reserve army). For a further discussion of this problem see Chapter 5 of the present work.

[41] See United Nations, *Prix Relatifs des Exportations et Importations des Pays sous-développés,* New York, 1949. For Britain, the typical imperialist country of that epoch, the terms of trade became notably more advantageous, increasing from index 100-99 in 1880-83 to index 113-115 in 1905-07, and index 134-136 in 1919-20 (all high years in successive trade cycles).

increase in the labour productivity of the industrialized countries, it was only a question of time before the relative price of raw materials began to rise.

This began to manifest itself in the First World War and for some raw materials it continued through the 20's, up to the time of the world economic crisis of 1929-32. The consequences of this crisis caused a sudden interruption of the process, but it broke through again with the international armaments boom in the 40's and reached its height at the start of the Korean War in 1950.[42] The specific structure that the end of the 19th century had stamped on the world economy now became an obstacle to the valorization of capital, or more precisely, an additional factor in the fall of the average rate of profit.

The inner logic of capital thus brought about a repetition of the process that had already occurred in the 50's and 60's of the previous century. Just as at that time, when the relative price of raw materials began to rise rapidly, the production of these raw materials with pre-capitalist methods of labour and relations of production ceased to be a source of surplus-profits through the exploitation of cheap labour-power and became instead an obstacle to the further expansion of capital, so now the production of raw materials with methods dating from the period of manufacturing capitalism or early industry ceased to be a source of colonial surplus-profits and became a brake on the accumulation of capital on a world scale. Thus, just as at the time of the transition from freely competitive capitalism to the epoch of imperialism, the capital of the metropolitan countries replied to this challenge with a massive penetration of the sphere of raw materials, so when 'classical imperialism' gave way to late capitalism, capital responded with a further massive penetration of this sphere.

Starting from the 30's, and particularly in the 40's of the present century, this massive penetration of capital into the sphere of raw materials led (just as it had in the final quarter of the 19th century) to a fundamental upheaval in technology, organization of labour and relations of production. In the late 19th century it had been a question

---

[42] According to the United Nations publication *Etudes sur l'Economie mondiale*, Vol. 1, *Les Pays en voie de Développement dans le Commerce Mondial*, New York, 1963, the overall index of the export price of raw materials in the period 1950-52 rose to more than three times the average for 1934-38 and was 14% higher than the average level for 1924-28. In many cases the increase compared with 1924-28 was much greater: 31% for cotton, wool, jute and sisal; 29% for coffee, tea and cocoa; 23% for non-ferrous metals. In this period 1950-52 the export price index of processed goods was 10% lower than the average for 1924-28.

of replacing primitive, pre-capitalist organization of labour with organizational methods along the lines of manufacturing capitalism or early industry. Now these in turn had to be transformed into an advanced industrial organization of labour, by a major growth in the productivity of labour. This meant the disappearance, however, of one of the most important motives for the traditional concentration of raw material production in the underdeveloped countries. It was now less of a risk to use expensive machinery in the metropolitan centres than overseas, and the declining share of wage-costs in the total value of raw material commodities made it less attractive than before to utilize the cheap labour-power of the colonies instead of its dearer counterpart in the metropolitan countries. The production of raw materials was therefore shifted on a massive scale to the metropolitan lands (synthetic rubber, synthetic fibres), and in cases where for physical reasons this was not immediately possible (e.g., the oil industry), there was growing pressure for the preparation of this shift in the long term. This is, of course, already beginning to bear fruit (the massive outlay on oil-drilling in Western Europe and the North Sea and the search for European natural gas) and is accompanied by the continual refinement of production techniques.

The results of this reshuffle in the structure of the world economy in the transitional period between 'classical' imperialism and late capitalism were manifold, but of a very contradictory nature. The differences between the capital accumulation and national income of the metropolitan and underdeveloped countries were further widened, since now even the classical market for the raw materials exported by the countries of the so-called Third World suffered a relative decline, and their production was consequently unable to keep pace with the rhythm of increase in the industrialized countries.[43] By the same stroke, the internal socio-economic crisis of these countries was further exacerbated and under the favourable

[43] Here are some figures for the increase in the production of synthetic as compared to natural raw materials. The share of the production of synthetic fibres in the world production of textiles rose from 9.5% in 1938 and 11.5% in 1948 to 27.6% in 1965. The share of the production of synthetic rubber in total world production of natural and synthetic rubber rose from 6.4% in 1938 to 25.9% in 1948 and 56% in 1965. See Paul Bairoch. *Diagnostic de l' Evolution Economique du Tiers-Monde, 1900-1966,* Paris, 1967, p. 165. The production of plastics in the capitalist world rose from 2 million tons in 1953 to 13 million tons in 1965 — more than the total world production of non-ferrous metals. Bairoch also reports greatly increased economy in the consumption of raw materials (lower input of raw materials for the same quantity of the final product) as a result of technical progress: ibid., p. 162.

conditions of an ulterior political weakening of imperialism during and after the Second World War, this led to endemic movements of rebellion and liberation among the peoples of the so-called Third World. These spreading revolts considerably increased the risk of losing capital invested in these countries. This danger, together with the rise of new branches of industry in the metropolitan countries, then determined an abrupt change in the pattern of long-term capital export. In contrast to the period from 1880-1940, capital now no longer mainly moved from the metropolitan countries to the underdeveloped ones. Instead, it chiefly went from some metropolitan countries to other imperialist countries.[44]

The decline in the relative and absolute price of raw materials which occurred after the Korean War, because of competition from the goods produced by the more productive labour of modern large-scale industry, led to the acceleration of the relative and in some cases absolute impoverishment of the underdeveloped countries. At the same time, however, it meant that the imperialist capital invested in the sphere of raw materials, which had in the past been able to appropriate not only colonial but also monopoly profits, increasingly lost interest in limiting itself to the production of raw materials in the semi-colonies. International monopoly capital now became interested not only in producing cheap raw materials by advanced industrial methods, instead of using colonial slaves to produce them, but also in producing in the underdeveloped countries themselves finished goods which could be sold there at monopoly prices, instead of raw materials which had now become unduly cheap.[45] *Thus the reproduction of the division of labour created in*

---

[44] Of the £ 4 billion of English foreign capital investments in the period 1927-9 only 13.5% were invested in industrialized countries, while 86.5% went to developing countries (37.5% of this to the white dominions). In 1959 the share of the industrialized countries in the total foreign investment of £ 6.6 billion had risen to 33% (plus 24% for the white dominions): See Michael Barratt-Brown, *After Imperialism*, London, 1963, pp. 110, 282. The USA is currently the leading exporter of capital, and the change is even more emphatic here: of the $ 50 billion exported since the Second World War, 2/3 went to the industrialized countries up to 1960, and 3/4 in the period after 1960. See also Pierre Jalée, *L'Impérialisme en 1970.* pp. 77-8.

[45] The clearest example of this is provided by Latin America, where OECD sources show that foreign investments in 1966 amounted to $ 5.3 billion in manufacturing industry, as against $ 4.9 billions in the oil industry (including refineries and the distribution system), $1.7 billions in mining and $3.8 billions in banks, insurance companies, public services and plantations.

the 19th century is slowly but surely collapsing in face of the sudden extension of the production of raw materials and an alteration in the differential rates of profit from the production of raw materials and the production of finished goods.

This process has been reinforced, meanwhile, by a change in the structure of monopoly capital in the imperialist countries. In the 19th and early 20th centuries, the exports of the metropolitan countries were concentrated mainly in consumer goods, coal and steel. After the World Depression of 1929, however, and especially after the Second World War, the pattern of imperialist export industries shifted more and more towards machines, vehicles and equipment goods. The weight of this group of commodities in the export package of a country has become virtually an index of its degree of industrial development.[46] The growing export of elements of fixed capital, however, leads to a growing interest by the largest monopoly groups in an incipient industrialization of the Third World. After all, it is not possible to sell machines to the semi-colonial countries, if they are not allowed to use them. In the final analysis it is this — and not any philanthropic or political consideration — which constitutes the main root of the whole 'development ideology' which has been fostered in the 'Third World' by the ruling classes of the metropolitan countries.

Does this new turn in the structure of the world economy signify at last a tendency towards a thorough industrialization of the Third World, a universalization of the capitalist mode of production and eventual homogenisation of the world economy? Not at all. It simply means a change in the forms of juxtaposition of development and underdevelopment, or more correctly: new differential levels of capital accumulation, productivity, and surplus extraction are emerging, which although not of the same nature, are still more pronounced than those of the 'classical' imperialist epoch.

It must be pointed out, firstly, that so far as differences in the level of capital accumulation are concerned, the bulk of imperialist capital investment in the underdeveloped world does not come from the export of capital but from the re-investment of realized profits

[46]The share of the group of commodities comprising 'machines and means of transport' in the export of the imperialist powers rose from 6.5% in 1890 and 10.6% in 1910 for Great Britain to more than 40% for the USA, Great Britain and Japan in 1968 and 46% in West Germany in 1969.

there, the growing domination of the local capital market and the increasing absorption of the surplus-value and the agricultural surplus product produced in the underdeveloped countries themselves. In the case of Latin America, above all, we possess very accurate figures for this process.[47] Furthermore, the 'drain' or net outflow of value towards the metropolitan countries at the expense of the countries economically dependent on them, continues to operate unabatedly. Moreover, it can be claimed without exaggeration that this net transfer of value is even larger today than in the past, not only because of the transfer of the dividends, interest and directors' salaries of the imperialist *corporations* and the increasing *debts* of the underdeveloped countries[48] but also because of the aggravation of *unequal exchange*.

This brings us on to the problem of differences in levels of productivity. Unequal exchange on the world market, as Marx makes clear in the 22nd chapter of the First Volume of *Capital*[49] is always the result of a difference in the average productivity of labour between two nations. In itself, this has nothing to do with the material nature of the commodities which these nations produce — whether they be raw materials or finished goods, agrarian or industrial products. Indeed, the difference in the level of productivity embodied in consumer goods produced by modern industry and that embodied in machines and vehicles produced by semi-automated processes is to some extent as great as that embodied in raw materials produced by manufacturing capitalism or early industrial processes on the one hand, and that embodied in industrial finished goods on the other. For the organic compositions of capital in the first comparison are as discrepant as those in the second.

At the same time there is also an increasing accentuation of dif-

[47] Theotonio Dos Santos (op. cit., pp. 75-8) calculates that for the period 1946-68 there was an outflow of $15 billion from Latin America to the USA in the form of dividends, interest, etc., on foreign capital investments. The actual new capital exported from the USA to Latin America amounted to only $5.5 billion net and was thus much less than the drain of surplus-value.

[48] The Pearson Report on the 'Development Decade', *Partners in Development*, *Report of the Commission on International Development*, London, 1969, gives a striking picture of the huge increase in the debts of the semi-colonial countries. Between 1961 and 1968 these rose from $21.5 billion to $47.5 billion (p. 371). The annual payments for interest on these debts and for profits from foreign investments already exceed export income by 25% in Brazil, Mexico, Argentina, Columbia, and Chile, and by 20% in India and Tunisia (p. 374).

[49] Marx, *Capital*, Vol. 1, pp. 559-60.

ferences in the rate of surplus-value. In the imperialist countries it has become practically impossible to increase the production of absolute surplus-value because of the secular trend for the industrial reserve army to diminish. Capital now merely concentrates its efforts on increasing the creation of relative surplus-value, and even this it can only do in the degree to which it is able to neutralize the contradictory effect of increased productivity on the rate of surplus-value.

Quite the reverse is true in the underdeveloped countries. There, the beginnings of industrialization and the ensuing increase in the average social productivity of labour allows the costs of reproducing labour-power to fall significantly, even if this fall in value is not always expressed in its money-price as a result, among other things, of continuing inflation. At the same time, however, this increase in the average social productivity of labour does not lead to a growth in the moral and historical cost of reproducing labour-power; in other words, new needs are not incorporated in wages, or only to a very limited extent.

This phenomenon can in the first instance be attributed to the fact that the secular trend in the semi-colonies is for the industrial reserve army to increase because the slow beginnings of industrialization cannot keep pace with the accelerating separation of poor peasants from the land. The gradual switch of foreign capital to the production of finished goods further reinforces this trend, for the latter are capital-intensive while the production of raw materials was relatively labour-intensive. Thus the share of wage-labour in the working population of Latin America remained constant at 14% between 1925 and 1963, while the share of industrial production in the gross national product doubled from 11% to 23%.[50]

Secondly, an unfavourable relationship of forces on the labour market, due to a growing industrial reserve army, may make it impossible effectively to organize the mass of the industrial and mining proletariat in trade unions. As a result, the commodity of labour-power

[50] André Gunder Frank, *Lumpenburguesia: Lumpendesarrollo*, Caracas, 1970, p. 110. The sources are official publications of the United Nations (CEPAL and the International Labour Office). Likewise in India, the annual average rate of growth of industrial output was 6.6% from 1950 to 1972, whereas the annual average rate of growth of employment was a mere 3.3%, and even fell to 1.8% in 1966-73, when it was lower than the annual rate of growth of the population. See *Basic Statistics Relating to the Indian Economy*, published by the Commerce Research Bureau, Bombay, November 1973.

is in its turn not only sold at its declining value, but even *below* this value. In this way it becomes possible for capital, given reasonably favourable political conditions, to compensate any tendency for the rate of profit to fall by achieving a further increase in the rate of surplus-value through a significant reduction in real wages. This happened in Argentina in 1956-60, Brazil in 1964-66 and Indonesia in 1966-67.[51]

The existence of a much lower price for labour-power in the dependent, semi-colonial countries than in the imperialist countries undoubtedly allows a higher world average rate of profit — which ultimately explains why foreign capital flows into these countries at all. But at the same time it acts as a limit on the further accumulation of capital, for the extension of the market is kept within extremely narrow confines by the low level of real wages and the modest needs of the workers in the Third World. The familiar state of affairs already described in our short analysis of the heyday of imperialism, is consequently once again reproduced: it becomes more profitable for local capital to invest outside rather than inside industry. This tendency is further reinforced by the fact that those industries in the underdeveloped countries which are equipped with modern technology — even if often with only the 'discarded' equipment of the West — mostly suffer from a very high degree of unutilized capacity, as well as a lack of 'economies of scale'.[52] The effect is to brake the concentration of capital, impede the extension of production, promote the drain of capital into non-industrial and non-productive spheres and increase the army of unemployed and underemployed proletarians and semi-proletarians. Therein lies the real 'vicious circle of underdevelopment' and not in the alleged insufficiency of national income, causing an insufficient savings ratio.[53]

Accordingly, the structure of the world economy in the first phase

[51]Ruy Mauro Marini estimates the fall in real wages of industrial workers in São Paulo — the most highly industrialized centre in Brazil — at 15.6% in the two years following the military putsch in 1964. He bases this on the official cost of living index, which certainly underestimated the rate of inflation. *Subdesarrollo y Revolución*, Mexico, 1969, p. 134. In the longer-term, the purchasing power of the minimum wage in Brazil dropped by 62% between 1958 and 1968. See Emile Sader, 'Sur La Politique Economique Brésilienne', in *Critiques de l' Economie Politique*, Nos. 3, April-June, 1971

[52]See also Urs Müller-Plantenberg, 'Technologie et Dépendance'. in *Critiques de l'Economie Politique*, No. 3, April-June, 1971.

[53]Paul A. Baran, in *The Political Economy of Growth*, has subjected this thesis of academic economics to a thorough and convincing critique.

of late capitalism is distinguished by several important character-istics from its structure in the age of classical imperialism. But it reproduces and even reinforces the differences in levels of produc-tivity, income and prosperity between the imperialist and the under-developed countries. The share of the underdeveloped countries in world trade declines — instead of growing or remaining con-stant — and the decline is rapid. All private and public transfers of capital from the metropolitan countries cannot keep pace with the flow of values in the opposite direction, and the countries of the so-called Third World consequently suffer relative impoverishment in their transactions with the imperialist countries. Obviously this impoverishment cannot be accompanied by a growing share in world trade, i.e., by a growing share in international purchasing power.

The Third World's rapidly declining share in world trade — from approximately 32% in 1950 to approximately 17% in 1970 — naturally does not in any way imply that there has been an absolute decline in the dependence of imperialist countries on certain stra-tegic raw materials (such as uranium, iron ore, oil, nickel, bauxite, chromium, manganese, and others) exported by the semi-colonial countries: on the contrary, there has been an absolute increase in this dependence.[54] But within the framework of the capitalist world economy the contradiction between the use value and exchange value of commodities is expressed in the fact that the increased dependence of imperialism on the raw materials exported by the colonial countries is accompanied by a relative decline in the prices paid for these raw materials and a relative decline in their value.

However, the long-run decline in the terms of trade at the expense of countries exporting primary commodities, also results in a *relative* decline in the rate of profit of the monopolies producing these com-modities, as compared with those producing manufactured goods.[55]

[54] Pierre Jalée analyzes this increased dependence in great detail (op. cit., pp. 25-6). Bairoch (op. cit., p. 76) found that between 1928 and 1965 the share of the develop-ing countries in the world production of iron ore rose from 7% to 37%, their share in the world production of bauxite from 21% to 69% and their share in the production of oil from 25% to 65%.

[55] The successful efforts by European oil companies to break the world oil cartel's control of petroleum prices in the 60's led to an actual fall in these prices, and in the profits of the 'oil majors', which produced an — in part deliberately engineered — oil shortage and temporary reestablishment of price control by the cartel. This whole story of competition and monopoly, of a break-up and reinstitution of administered prices, together with the underlying operation of the law of value in the oil market, is recounted by H. Elsenhaus and G. Junne, 'Zu den Hintergründen der gegenwär-tigen Oelkrise', in *Blätter für deutsche und internationale Politik*, Cologne, 1973, No. 12.

This in turn necessarily leads to a much greater inflow of capital into manufacturing industry than into primary production. In the long-run, the growing disproportion between these two sectors inevitably ended in a sharp change in their relative prices — hence the great boom in primary commodity prices in 1972-74, in which speculation played a not insignificant secondary role. The conjunctural and speculative elements in this boom will ensure a new fall in these prices again — but not back to pre-1972 levels. The present abrupt modification of the relative prices of manufactured and primary products thus inaugurates a new phase — the third since the early 19th century — in which raw materials have suddenly become more expensive compared to manufactured goods.[56] Such a shift in relative prices will inevitably unleash new trends of uneven development in capital accumulation across the world.

Underlying the whole uneven and combined development of capitalist, semi-capitalist and pre-capitalist relations of production, linked together by capitalist relations of exchange, is the problem of the concrete effect of the law of value on the international level — in other words, the problem of the formation of world market prices and their repercussions on national economies. There is no doubt that only one law of value exists[57]; it has the function of regulating, through the exchange of medium-term equivalent quantities of labour, the distribution of the economic resources at the disposal of society into the various spheres of production, according to the fluctuations of socially effective demand — in other words the structure of consumption, or structure of income determined by capitalist relations of production and distribution. But this general fact

[56]See Angus Hone, 'The Primary Commodities Boom', *New Left Review*, No 81, September-October 1973.

[57]Pierre Naville is not on the virgin soil he believes when he presents this fact as a great discovery in *Le Salaire Socialiste*, Paris, 1970, pp 14-30. Moreover, he draws the mistaken conclusion from it that a 'single law of value' *regulates* all economic relations in the entire world, including the USSR (pp. 24-5). The law of value was already the 'single' law on the world market in the middle of the 19th century; but at that time it by no means regulated the distribution of economic resources over various branches of production in China. This necessitated a revolution in Chinese relations of production. Nor does the law of value regulate economic relations today in China or the USSR. Naville forgets that in the age of capitalism this regulation is determined not by the movement of commodities but by the movement of capital (we left simple commodity production behind a long time ago). It just so happens that the free movement of capital is not permitted either in China or the USSR, where investments are by no means determined by the laws of the market (hence ultimately by the law of value).

does not yet in anyway tell us *how* the law of value operates on the world market.

Although Marx discussed this problem on several occasions[58] he did not analyze it systematically in *Capital*. But on the basis of his remarks, the logic of his theory and an analysis of the development of the capitalist world market over the last 150 years, it is possible to formulate the following principles:

1. Under the conditions of capitalist relations of production, uniform prices of production (i.e., a wide-ranging equalization of rates of profit) only emerge within national markets (in pre-capitalist commodity production, different commodity values can even exist alongside each other in regional markets within a single country, based on the differing productivity of labour in the various areas, where there are impediments to the national circulation of commodities.)[59] The law of value would only lead to uniform prices all over the world if there had been a general international equalization of the rate of profit as a result of the complete international mobility of capital and the distribution of capital over all parts of the world, irrespective of the nationality or origin of its owners; in other words, in practice only if there were a homogenized capitalist world economy with a single capitalist world state.[60]

2. The restriction of uniform prices of production to 'national' markets necessarily determines a variation in the value of commodities in different nations. Marx expressly emphasized this specific effect of the law of value on the international level on several occasions. It is based on nationally differentiated levels of the productivity or intensity of labour (and hence of commodity values), nationally differentiated organic compositions of capital, nationally differentiated rates of surplus-value, and so on. On the world market, the labour of a country with a higher productivity of labour is valued as more intensive, so that the product of one day's work in such a

---

[58]For instance: *Capital*, Vol. 1, Chapter 22; *Capital*, Vol. 3, pp. 214-5; *Capital*, Vol. 3, Chapter 14, Section 5; *Capital*, Vol. 3, end of Chapter 20; *Capital*, Vol. 3, end of Chapter 39; *Capital*, Vol. 3, pp. 803-13; *Capital*, Vol. 3, Chapter 50, pp. 874-5; *Theories of Surplus Value*, Vol. 2, pp. 16-20; *Theories of Surplus Value*, Vol. 3, pp. 252-7; *Grundrisse*, p. 872; etc.

[59]See the example of contemporary India, where the prices of basic foodstuffs in the various states are still fundamentally different, where there can be a famine in one state and normal food prices in the neighbouring state. Complete freedom in the circulation of commodities and capital is obviously a precondition for the formation of a uniform value for commodities. *Capital*, Vol. 3, p. 196.

[60]See the development of this analysis in Chapter 10 of the present work.

nation is exchanged for the product of more than a day's work in an underdeveloped country.

3. By the export of commodities from a country with a higher level of labour productivity to a country with a lower one, the owners of the exported goods make a surplus-profit, because they are able to sell their commodities at a price above the price of production on their own internal market but below their 'national' value in the importing country.

4. If the volume of this export is sufficiently large to dominate the entire market of the importing country, then the 'national' value of the commodity in the latter will in time adjust to the value of the commodity in the exporting country under the pressure of competition from the imported goods, i.e., the extra profit will disappear. If the demand for this commodity subsequently continues to increase by leaps and bounds, and cannot be met by imports, room will become available for a national industry with a higher level of labour productivity to replace the ruined backward industry (as in the case of the textile industry in Russia, Italy, Japan and Spain after 1860-70, and even partly in India and China after 1890-1900), even if the labour productivity of this 'national' industry falls somewhat below that of the exporting country.

5. If the volume of this export remains too limited to be able to determine the amount of socially necessary labour contained in the given commodity within the importing country, then the value of the commodity in this market remains above that of the exporting country, and the commodities of the exporting country will continue to make a surplus-profit (this is partly the case with the pharmaceutical products exported by the imperialist countries to India, South-East Asia and Africa).

6. If a country possesses a virtual world monopoly of the production of a commodity, then its conditions of production form the preconditions for the world market price (and this naturally entails a monopoly surplus-profit over and above the ordinary average profit of the producing country). The same law is valid, *mutatis mutandis*, when the country does not have a monopoly on the production of the commodity, but does have a monopoly on its export.

7. If no country possesses a monopoly of the production or export of a commodity, its world market value will be determined by the average international level of the commodity values needed to satisfy the entire international, monetarily effective demand. This

average value may then exceed that of the most productive country just as much as it may remain far below that of the most backward country.[61]

8. If a country with an average level of labour productivity below the world average is caused to produce certain goods exclusively for export, then the value of these exported goods is not determined by the actual specific quantities of labour expended in their production, but by a hypothetical average (i.e., by the quantities of labour which would have been expended in their production had it been carried out with the average international level of labour productivity). In this case the country in question suffers a loss of substance through its export — in other words, in exchange for the quantities of labour expended in the production of these goods, it receives back the equivalent of a smaller quantity of labour. Even in this case it can make an absolute profit from this export transaction if mineral resources and labour power which would not otherwise be utilized are employed for these exports. But it will nonetheless suffer relative impoverishment in comparison to the countries which import these export goods.[62]

9. All the preceding principles to a greater or lesser extent presuppose extensive capitalist relations of production in the various nations trading with one another (see the quotation from Engels' letter to Conrad Schmidt at the beginning of this chapter). If, however, the relations of production in a country are only marginally capitalist, and if the exported commodities are produced in precapitalist or semi-capitalist conditions, then the tendency for commodities to be exported below their 'national' value may become significantly stronger — among other things because the 'wages' which enter into the commodity value may fall far below the value of the commodity of labour power, if the producers are only semi-proletarians who still possess their own means of producing the necessities of life or if they are small peasants who carry on

---

[61]This explains the sometimes significant fluctuations in the world market price of foodstuffs within relatively short spaces of time. For as soon as there is a sudden, even if only marginal food shortage on the world market, the products of the relatively least fertile areas in the least productive countries, which would normally not even be exported at all, can now all at once determine the world market price. Since world trade in grain, for example, forms only a very small percentage of world production of grain, a marginal increase in the demand in a large country can raise the price suddenly by 25% or 50%.

[62]Marx, *Capital*, Vol. 3, p. 238.

subsistence agriculture and whose consumption is limited to the physiological minimum for life.[63]

10. Precisely because of these *differences* in the value of commodities and the productivity of labour between each country integrated into the capitalist world market, the law of value inexorably compels the backward countries with a low level of labour productivity to specialize on the world market in a manner disadvantageous to themselves. If they wish, despite this fact, to embark on the production of high-value industrial goods (in small series and with colossal costs) they are condemned to sell these at a loss on their internal market, because the difference in production costs compared with those of the industrialized nations is too large, and exceeds the normal margin of profit on the domestic market. Russia and China escaped this fate after their socialist revolutions only by a protective monopoly of foreign trade.

[63]Marx, *Capital*, Vol. 3, pp. 805-6.

3

The Three Main Sources of Surplus Profit in the Development of Modern Capitalism

In the second chapter we argued that the problem of imperialism must be construed historically as a qualitative change in the structure of the world capitalist economy. We are thus dealing with the reproduction on a world-wide scale of one of the basic problems in Marx's analysis of capital, namely the relationship between uneven development and competition, which tends to suppress uneven development and yet is obstructed by it. We will discuss therewith the problem of the equalization of the rate of profit. Above all, we will be concerned with the role which the quest for surplus-profits plays in the process of capital accumulation and capitalist growth.

We have already pointed out that the growth of the capitalist mode of production by its nature always leads to disequilibrium. We must also bear in mind that the problem of the extension of capital to new realms of production — whether technical or geographical — is ultimately determined by a difference in the level of profit, which means that there must at the same time be a relative excess of capital, a relative immobility of capital and relative limits to equalization of different rates of profit set by monopoly. It follows that the actual growth process of the capitalist mode of production is not accompanied by any *effective equalization of the rates of profit.*[1]

___

[1]Marx: 'The industrial rates of profit in various spheres of production are themselves more or less uncertain; but in so far as they appear, it is not their uniformity but their differences which are perceptible. The general rate of profit, however, appears only as the lowest limit of profit, not as an empirical, directly visible form

If the accumulation of capital is said to be a means of extending the production of relative surplus-value, or of reproducing the industrial reserve army on an expanded scale in order to achieve an absolute or relative reduction in wages, then this all comes down to the same process of the redistribution of socially produced surplus-value to the advantage of those capitals which have achieved the greatest accumulation and possess the highest organic composition. If the accumulation of capital is said to be a response to the decline of the average rate of profit, then it is obvious that the strongest capitals will not be content merely to augment the *mass of profit* but will also attempt to increase their *rate of profit*. If the accumulation of capital is said to depend on the realization of surplus-value, then once again, in the context of 'many capitals' — i.e., of capitalist competition — the latter must ultimately be a problem of the quest for surplus profits. For the capitals that can only partially realize their surplus-value, or realize it only below or just at the average rate of profit, are at an obvious disadvantage compared to those that succeed in realizing the full value of their commodities, with so to speak a second helping—i.e., with a part of the surplus-value produced in other spheres added to it, or in other words with surplus-profits: 'The surplus-profit which some individual capital . . . realizes in a particular sphere of production . . . is due, aside from fortuitous deviations, to a reduction in cost-price, in production costs. This reduction arises either from the fact that capital is used in greater than average quantities, so that the *faux frais* of production are reduced, while the general causes increasing the productiveness of labour (co-operation, division of labour) can become effective to a higher degree, with more intensity, because their field of activity has become larger; or it may arise from the fact that, aside from the amount of functioning capital, better methods of labour, new inventions, improved machinery, chemical manufacturing secrets, etc., in short, new and improved, better than average means of production and methods of production are used.'[2]

---

of the actual rate of profit.' *Capital*, Vol. 3, p. 367. See also p. 369: 'The rate of profit, on the other hand, may vary even within the same sphere for commodities with the same price, depending on different conditions under which different capitals produce the same commodity, because the rate of profit of an individual capital is not determined by the market-price of a commodity, but rather by the difference between market-price and cost-price. These different rates of profit can strike a balance — first within the same sphere and then between different spheres — only through continual fluctuation.'   [2] Marx, *Capital*, Vol. 3, p. 644.

But is it not true to say that this double process, involving the expansion of the *mass* of capital and the reduction of the cost-price of commodities through improved machinery and a higher organic composition of capital, contains the whole meaning and purpose of capital accumulation under the pressure of competition? Are we not justified, therefore, in describing this process as dominated by the indefatigable search for surplus-profits?

As soon as it is acknowledged, however, that the process of extended reproduction is determined by the quest for surplus-profits, a new question arises: How can surplus-profits be made in a 'normal' capitalist economy? Here once again we find confirmation of a thesis already argued in the first chapter. It is impossible to reduce the conditions for making a surplus-profit to a single factor. *All* the laws of motion of the capitalist mode of production must be taken into account. In capitalism, surplus-profits arise:

1. When the organic composition of a specific capital is *smaller* than the social average, but institutional or structural factors at the same time prevent the above-average surplus-value produced in these sectors from entering the process of the equalization of the rate of profit.[3] This is, for example, the source of the surplus-profit called absolute ground rent, created by a monopoly of property in land under the capitalist mode of production. It is, more generally, the source of all monopolistic surplus-profits.

2. When the organic composition is above the social average, i.e., when a particular capital is able to exploit an advantage in productivity in a given sector and thus appropriate a part of the surplus-value produced by other firms in that sector. 'Our analysis has revealed how the market value (and everything said concerning it applies with appropriate modifications to the price of production) embraces a surplus-profit for those who produce in any particular sphere of production under the most favourable conditions.'[4]

3. When it is possible to force down the price paid for labour-power to a level below its social value, i.e., below its average social price, or what is the same thing, when it is possible to buy labour-power in countries where its value (average price) is lower than its value (average price) in the country where the commodities are

---

[3] 'A surplus profit may also arise if certain spheres of production are in a position to evade the conversion of the values of their commodities into prices of production, and thus the reduction of their profits to the average profit.' *Capital*, Vol. 3, p. 199. See also *Capital*, Vol. 3, p. 743.   [4] Ibid., p. 198.

sold.[5] In such cases surplus-profit arises from a rate of surplus-value which is higher than the social average.

4. When it is possible to force down the price paid for the various component parts of constant capital to a level below the social average (the price of production). In practice, this is normally only possible in the case of circulating, and not of fixed, constant capital — in other words, when the capital of a firm, an industry or a country has access to raw materials that are cheaper than those with which other capitals have to operate.

5. When the reproduction of circulating capital (and hence of variable capital) is accelerated, i.e., when the turnover-time of a specific circulating capital is shorter than that of the socially average circulating capital, without a medium-term generalization of this shorter period. Surplus-profit emerges here only when the rate of profit is calculated on total capital stock, not on annual capital flow, since it originates from additional production of surplus-value within the firm itself. This variant is in effect a special instance of the first case cited above: it amounts to a monopoly of techniques for shortening the turnover-time of circulating capital. An example is the difficulty of European auto firms in financing the high costs of conveyor belt and assembly line output in the motor industry during the 20s, which gave US firms a much shorter turnover-time for their circulating capital.

In all these cases we are dealing with surplus-profits which do *not* enter the process of equalization in the short term, and so do not lead simply to a growth in the average social rate of profit. They can indeed be accompanied by a drop in the average rate of profit, and in fact they mostly are. The classical case of monopoly capitalism, in which a surplus-profit arises in many sectors under monopoly protection, shows how surplus-profits can, if their volume is considerable, even sharply intensify the fall of the average rate of profit, for these surplus-profits have after all been taken out of the mass of surplus-value to be divided among the non-monopolized sectors.

[5] 'In fact, the direct interest taken by the capitalist, or the capital, of any particular sphere of production in the exploitation of the labourers who are directly employed is confined to making an extra gain, a profit exceeding the average, either through exceptional overwork, or reduction of the wage below the average, or through the exceptional productivity of the labour employed.' (K. Marx, *Capital*, Vol. 3, p. 197.)

Why is it that there were no major international movements of capital (and hence no significant disruption of the elementary pro- cesses of primitive accumulation of capital in the relatively back- ward countries either) in the period of freely competitive capitalism, while these emerged on a wide scale in the age of imperialism? The following factors impeded the rise of an international difference in the rate of profit or limited it to a minimum:

1. The structural importance of the industrial reserve army in the first countries to industrialize. In the long term this led to the stagnation or regression of real wages (with only occasional in- creases), so that there was relatively little incentive to exploit the cheap labour-power of the backward countries.[6]

2. The early institutional weakness of proletarian class struggle and permanent working-class organizations for this struggle, in the first instance trade unions, which must be attributed to the size of this industrial reserve army.[7]

3. The significant difference in the level of productivity be- tween agriculture and young, modern large-scale industry, was a source of 'unequal exchange' and surplus-profit for industrial capital

[6] This problem has been the object of considerable dispute between Marxist and non-Marxist historians. The issue is complicated by the fact the industrial revolution and its large-scale urbanization drastically altered the structure of consumption among the labouring population (for example, by the introduction of rent for lodgings), making comparison of real wages between say 1740 and 1840 hazard- ous. It should be noted, however, that two non-Marxist historians, E. H. Phelps- Brown and S. V. Hopkins, estimate that the real wages of English building-workers dropped from an index of 77 in the year 1744 (taking their level in 1451-75 as 100!) downwards until the years 1834-35, and again in 1836-42 and 1845-48: it was only from 1849 onwards that the 1744 level was definitively surpassed. See 'Seven Centuries of the Prices of Consumables, Compared with Builders' Wages', in *Eco- nomica,* 1956. Likewise, per capita consumption of sugar — a 'high-quality' consumer good — declined in England from 16.86 kg in 1811 to 7.9 kg in 1841. For the whole controversy, see among others: Eric Hobsbawm, 'The British Standard of Living', *Economic History Review,* 1957; T. S. Ashton, 'The Standard of Life of Workers in England 1790-1830', *Journal of Economic History,* Supplement XI, 1949; A. Taylor, 'Progress and Poverty in Britain 1780-1850' in *History,* XLV (1960).

[7] Fritz Sternberg, who was the first to make a thorough investigation of the signi- ficance of long-term fluctuations in the industrial reserve army for the development of capitalism, was wrong on this point. He claimed that the American case proves that trade unions are not a major determinant of wages, for wages are much higher in the USA than in Western Europe while the unions are much weaker: *Der Impe- rialismus,* p. 579. (Sternberg's book was written before the rise of the CIO, and his remark was quite correct at the time.) Sternberg, however, forgot Marx's emphasis on the historical and traditional element in the value of the commodity of labour- power which, in the USA, took the form of a shortage of labour-power and the fron- tier. Both of these facts *were given from the very outset of capitalism there,* and

in so far as the penetration of capital into agriculture and the appearance of capitalist ground rent were still only marginal phenomena.[8]

4. The abundance of freely accessible areas of investment in Western Europe (and North America) as a result, among other things, of the uninterrupted extension of railway construction, the industrialization of a number of spheres of production such as mining, textiles, machine construction, shoes, iron and steel, brickmaking, cement and so on.

But the same factors that led in the first century of the capitalist mode of production to the predominant immobility of capital on the international level (or to the predominant restriction of its mobility to Western Europe) began to have the opposite effect from the 1870s:

1. There was a rapid and uninterrupted emigration of labour-power from Western Europe overseas, first and foremost to North America, which absorbed 22.5 million immigrants between 1851 and 1909, of whom 9 million arrived in the three decades from 1861 to 1890, compared with 2 million from 1821 to 1850. Western and Central Europe were increasingly transformed into an industrial workshop for the entire world, so that it was no longer so much in the West that artisans and peasants were ruined and the industrial reserve army increased as in Eastern and Southern Europe and especially in other continents. There was consequently a long term decline in the industrial reserve army in the West, and a long term reinforcement of workers' organizations, which led to a slow but continuous increase in real wages.[9] There thus developed a new interest in the exploitation of cheap labour-power outside Western Europe and North America.

2. The difference in the level of productivity between agriculture and mining on the one hand and the processing industry on the other led to the opposite result. A growing and unsatisfied demand

---

for a long time *hindered* any rapid expansion of it. In Europe and elsewhere the secular fluctuations of the industrial reserve army certainly do determine the long-term *possibilities* of an increase in real wages; but even where these possibilities exist, their realization is dependent on the *struggle* of the working class and hence also on the strength of the trade unions. Compare the relative development of real wages in Germany and France, for example, before the First World War, which certainly cannot be explained by differences in the industrial reserve armies of the two countries.

[8] In France, Belgium and Germany, for example.

[9] On the connection between the long-term trend for the industrial reserve army to decline and the other developments here described, see the thorough analysis in Fritz Sternberg, *Der Imperialismus*.

arose for a number of important raw materials, reinforced by the catastrophic consequences of the American Civil War for the British cotton industry. In many cases there was an absolute increase in the price of raw materials, but there was at least a relative rise in all cases (the price of cotton continued to climb without interruption from 1849 to 1870).

3. The thorough industrialization of the countries of Western Europe reached an initial ceiling, especially after the French boom in the 1860s and the founding phase of the new German Empire: the steam technology of the first Industrial Revolution was now in universal use, and there was an abundance of excess capital in several Western European countries. The growing concentration of capital and the rising costs of new investments in spheres that had already been industrialized — and later the growth of trusts and monopolies — inevitably meant a rapid increase in the volume of capital pressing for new fields of investment.

4. In the long term a fall in the rate of profit became apparent, caused by the significant rise in the organic composition of capital.[10]

The rapid export of capital to less developed countries, which began on a massive scale in the 1880s, was hence an answer to all these problems. Exported imperialist capital now achieved surplus-profits by the following means:

1. Capital was invested in countries and spheres where the average organic composition of capital was significantly lower than in the manufacturing industries of the West, and hence it was possible to achieve a much higher rate of profit.

2. This rate of profit rose all the more because the rate of surplus-value was sometimes much higher in the dependent hands than in the metropolitan countries, due to the fact that the long term expansion of the reserve army caused the price of the commodity of labour-power to fall below its value and that the value of this commodity was far lower than that in the West.[11]

---

[10] The calculations of Phyllis Deane and W. A. Cole, which must be treated with great reserve, also reveal a fall in the share of profits, interest and 'mixed income' in the national income of Great Britain from an average of 39.4% in the decade 1865-74 to 38.2% in the decade 1870-79 and 37.8% for the decade 1885-94: *British Economic Growth*, p. 247. For Italy, Emilio Sereni cites a slump which is much sharper even than this: the average yield of capital (*rendimento medio del capitale*) is said to have fallen from 24.2% in the half decade from 1871-75 to 14.1% in the half decade from 1886-90: *Capitalismo e Mercato Nazionale in Italia*, Rome, 1968, pp. 246-7.

[11] Marx expressly points out that the rate of surplus-value can frequently be lower in the underdeveloped countries than in the developed ones. This continues to be

3. The concentration of capital exports on the realms of agriculture and mining, in other words on the production of raw materials, at first permitted this capital to make large surplus-profits at a given price for raw materials (in competition with traditional methods of production and a lower productivity of labour). It then led to a general decline in the price of raw materials altogether and consequently to an increase in the rate of profit (or reduction in the organic composition of capital) in the metropolitan countries.

4. These capital investments were entirely comprised of capital that was idle in the metropolitan countries and could no longer achieve the average *profit*, but only the average *interest*. The massive export of this capital therefore likewise caused a general increase in the average rate of profit. [12]

Seen in this light, the beginnings of the first two successive stages in the history of industrial capitalism — the stage of free competition and the stage of imperialism or classical monopoly capitalism as described by Lenin — appear as two phases of accelerated accumulation. *The movement of capital exports unleashed by the quest for surplus-profits, and the cheapening of circulating constant capital, led to a temporary rise in the average rate of profit in the*

---

the case in so far as capitalist technology is not used in production there, the productivity of labour is much lower, and the part of the working day in which the labourer merely reproduces his own wages is accordingly much greater, than in the metropolitan countries. But this is by no means a general law. For if capitalist technology is introduced into the colonies and semi-colonies without an increase in the consumption of labourers (among other things because of the presence of the industrial reserve army), then there can be a rapid decrease in the value of labour power and hence an increase in the rate of surplus-value to a level above that in the metropolitan countries, despite the fact that the average productivity of labour is still much lower than in the latter. *The rate of surplus-value is not a direct function of the productivity of labour.* It merely expresses the relation between the time needed by the labourer to reproduce the equivalent of his means of subsistence and the remaining labour-time left to the capitalist at no cost. If the total number of unemployed increases in the colonies while it decreases in the metropolitan countries, and if the reduction of the labour-time needed to reproduce the labourer's means of subsistence in the metropolitan countries is partially neutralized by an increase in the volume of commodities consumed by the labourer, while this volume remains constant (or even decreases) in the colonies, then a smaller increase in the productivity of labour in the colonies can by all means be accompanied by a comparatively greater increase in the rate of surplus-value than in the metropolitan countries. In Vol. 3 of *Capital* Marx at any rate says: 'Different national rates of profit are mostly based on different national rates of surplus-value.' (p. 151).

[12] Of late, several objections have been advanced against Lenin's theory of imperialism, which attributed key importance to the export of capital in search of surplus-profits. We shall discuss these objections at length in Chapter Eleven.

*metropolitan countries, which in turn explains the colossal increase
in the accumulation of capital in the period 1893-1914,* after the
long period of stagnation from 1873-93 which was dominated
by a falling rate of profit.[13] This increase in the average rate of
profit made it possible for capital to experience a second period of
tempestuous expansion before the First World War.

When capitalist commodity production conquered and unified
the world market, it did not create a uniform system of production prices, but a differentiated system of varying national prices
of production and unified world market prices. This allowed the
capital of the most developed capitalist countries to achieve surplus-
profits, for its commodities could be sold above their 'own' national
price of production and yet below the 'national price of production'
of the buying country. In the final analysis, this internationally
hierarchized and differentiated system of varying commodity
values is explained by an internationally hierarchized and differentiated system of varying levels of labour productivity. Imperialism, far from equalizing the organic composition of capital on an
international level — or leading to an international equalization of
rates of profit, *arrested and intensified* international differences
in the organic composition of capital and the level of the rates of
profit.

Marx envisaged the possibility of this when he wrote: 'Capital
succeeds in the equalization, to a greater or lesser degree, *depending on the extent of capitalist development in the given nation,* i.e.,
on the extent the conditions in the country in question are adapted
for the capitalist mode of production . . . The incessant equilibration of constant divergences is accomplished so much more quickly
1) the more mobile the capital, i.e., the more easily it can be shifted
from one sphere and from one place to another; 2) the more quickly labour-power can be transferred from one sphere to another
and from one production locality to another. The first condition
implies complete freedom of trade within the society and the
removal of all monopolies with the exception of the natural ones,
those, that is, which naturally arise out of the capitalist mode of

---

[13]The share of profits, interest and 'mixed income' in the national income of Great
Britain, which, according to the calculations of Phyllis Deane and W. A. Cole — see
footnote 10 — declined from 1865 to 1894, then rose once again to as much as 42%
in the decade 1905-14. Naturally these figures are by no means congruent with
the Marxist concept of the rate of profit. But they do clearly indicate a tendency.

production. It implies, furthermore, the development of the credit-system. . . . *Finally it implies the subordination of the various spheres of production to the control of the capitalists.* . . . But this equilibration itself *runs into greater obstacles, whenever numerous and large spheres of production not operated on a capitalist basis* (such as soil cultivation by small farmers) *filter in between the capitalist enterprises* and become linked with them.'[14]

It is clear that the obstacles which, for the reasons outlined above, hinder the equalization of the rate of profit on a national scale, acquire an even greater weight on the international level. The greater relative immobility of capital; the prevalent immobility of labour-power; and above all the existence on a massive scale of non-capitalist spheres of production, in other words, the generalized combination of capitalist with semi-capitalist and pre-capitalist relations of production: these are the factors which have rendered possible the differences in the level of profit between the colonies and the metropolitan countries since the inception of the age of imperialism, and which have made the investment of capital in the colonies and semi-colonies a permanent source of surplus profits.

In the final resort the difference in the level of development between the metropolitan countries on the one hand, and the colonies and semi-colonies on the other, must be ascribed to the fact that the capitalist world market universalizes the capitalist *circulation* of commodities, but not the capitalist *production* of commodities. To put it even more abstractly: in the final analysis the manifestations of imperialism are to be explained by the *lack of homogeneity* of the capitalist world economy.

From what does this lack of homogeneity stem? Does it come from the nature of capital itself, or is it the result of an initial historical structure—that of colonialism—which was certainly a concrete accompaniment of the triumphal march of capital across the globe, but which does not represent an essential precondition for the advance of capital accumulation? The answer to this question returns us to the problem of the differences in the level of profit, an expression of the restless search for surplus-profits, which derives from the uneven movement of capital accumulation itself. In the 'pure' case of continual increases in the organic composition of

[14]Marx, *Capital*, Vol. 3, p. 196 (Our italics).

capital and the incessant development of new techniques and technology, which Marx foresaw but which has emerged in its fully developed form only in late capitalism today, the differences in the level of profit arise out of the competition of capitals and the inexorable condemnation of all the firms, branches and areas which fall behind in this race and are thus forced to surrender a part of their 'own' surplus-value to those in the lead. What is this process, other than the continual production of underdeveloped firms, branches, areas and regions?

Thus even in the 'ideal case' of a homogeneous beginning, capitalist economic growth, extended reproduction and accumulation of capital are still synonymous with the juxtaposition and constant combination of development and underdevelopment. *The accumulation of capital itself produces development and underdevelopment as mutually determining moments of the uneven and combined movement of capital.* The lack of homogeneity in the capitalist economy is a necessary outcome of the unfolding laws of motion of capitalism itself.

We saw earlier that technological innovation and increases in the productivity of labour were by no means the only way of achieving surplus-profits. The discovery of cheap labour-power and its incorporation into the capitalist labour process, and the production of cheap raw materials, also served this goal. Cheap labour-power was discovered and reproduced under conditions in which there was not yet any widespread division of labour, while at the same time the reduction of the value of labour-power to the physical cost of its reproduction prevented any expansion of effective demand and hence any extension of the internal market. In these conditions, *capital itself created an insuperable limit to its own extension.* Ultimately even the cheapest commodities from Manchester, Solingen or Detroit were helpless against the lack of demand of Indian, Amerindian or Chinese peasant communities which were to a large extent imprisoned within a natural economy.

The differences in the level of productivity which resulted from these differences in the level of wages, tended to harden and become permanent. Capital accumulation crystallized internationally as the development, on the one hand, of large-scale industry in the metropolitan countries, proceeding towards complete industrialization through an advanced division of labour and technical innovation, and as the implantation, on the other hand, of the production of raw materials in the colonies, defined by an arrested or stagnant division of labour, laggard technology and pre-capitalist agricultural economy, blocking any thorough-going industrialization, and reinforcing and perpetuating underdevelopment.[15]

This process is not a mere exception to the more general tendencies of capital, for we can discover the same process at work in the industrialized countries themselves, in the so-called 'internal colonies'. It is not difficult to discern in the regional structure of the industrial countries of the 19th and early 20th centuries the same elements of unequal exchange, different levels of productivity, underindustrialization, blockage of capital accumulation, in other words *the juxtaposition of development and underdevelopment* which is the hallmark of the structure of the world economy in the age of imperalism.

In all these countries the emergence and development of industrial capital was localized and concentrated in a relatively small number of complexes, surrounded by a ring of agrarian regions which functioned as sources for the supply of raw materials and foodstuffs, as markets for industrial consumer goods and as reserves of cheap labour-power.

The classical case of an agrarian 'subsidiary country' within the large-scale industrial economy of Western Europe, which Marx himself investigated, is that of *Ireland:* 'Ireland is at present only an agricultural district of England, marked off by a wide channel from the country to which it yields corn, wool, cattle, industrial and military recruits.'[16] Obviously, this agricultural district also experienced an accumulation of capital, but a significant portion of this capital was drained off to the 'industrial districts', i.e., to England.[17] Thus there was a reciprocal determination of development and underdevelopment, for the drain of capital intensified

[15] We draw attention once more to the works by André Gunder Frank, Theotonio Dos Santos and Samir Amin already mentioned above, which contain similar ideas. Andre Gunder Frank's as yet unpublished book, *Towards a Theory of Underdevelopment*, is particularly noteworthy in this connection.

[16] Marx, *Capital*, Vol. 1, pp. 702-3.

[17] See Marx-Engels, *Werke*, Vol. 16, p. 452. The fact that this steady concentration of capital within agricultural districts and its drain to industrial districts occurred not only in Ireland but also in England itself, and in Scotland and Wales, has been expressly emphasized by historians of the English banking system. See, among others, W.T.C. King, *History of the London Discount Market*, London, 1936, pp. xii-xiii, 6ff.

the situation of relative underemployment in Ireland which under purely agricultural conditions only led to further impoverishment and parcellization.[18] Marx therefore expressly stated that at the dawn of capitalism the development of industry in the industrial strongholds is accompanied by the *destruction* of industry in the 'dependent countries'.[19]

Ireland was, however, by no means an exception in the history of capitalism in the 19th century. We can list at least three other cases of 'subsidiary countries' or 'internal colonies' in industrialized nations which were just as exemplary. First, there is the case of Flanders within Belgium. Belgium, which had become independent in 1830, was the second country in Europe to industrialize, after Great Britain. The destruction of Flemish cottage industry (linen and flax) by the advent of the modern large-scale factory led to processes of absolute impoverishment, mass unemployment, emigration and de-industrialization which broadly coincide with those described by Marx in Ireland. For more than half a century Flanders became a reservoir of cheap foodstuffs, cheap agricultural raw materials, cheap labour-power and obedient recruits for the whole of Belgian industry.[20] The percentage of industrial employees among the working population of West and East Flanders only increased from 22.3% to 26.4% between 1846 and 1890, while in the two Walloon provinces of Liège and Hainaut it rose in the same period from 18.3% to 48.4% and in the whole of Belgium from 15.2% to 33.6%.[21] As late as 1895 the average wage of agricultural labourers in the four Walloon provinces was 50% above that of the four Flemish provinces, and at 20 Belgian francs the lowest monthly wage in Flanders, in the infertile Kempen region, was three times lower than that of the least fertile region of Wallonia, the Ardennes, where it amounted to 60 francs.[22]

Secondly, there is the case of the Southern States of the USA,

[18] See also Francois Perroux: 'Growth is *disequilibrium.* Development *is* disequilibrium. The implantation of one pole of development *leads to a succession of social and economic imbalances.' L'Economie du XXe Siècle*, Paris, 1964, p. 169.

[19] Marx, *Capital*, Vol. 1, p. 757.

[20] For the devastating consequences of this destruction and the subsequent famine see A. G. Jacqemyns, *Histoire de la Crise Economique des Flandres, 1845-1850*, Brussels, 1929.

[21] Benoît Verhaegen, *Contribution à l'Histoire Economique des Flandres*, Vol. II, Louvain, 1961, pp. 57, 165.

[22] Laurent Dechesne, *Histoire Economique et Sociale de la Belgique*, Paris, 1932, p. 482.

both before and after the abolition of slavery. They functioned as a reservoir of agricultural raw materials and as an 'internal colony' in the sense that they formed a steady market for the industrial products of the North and did not develop any large-scale industry within their own territory (this was to change only with the Second World War).[23]

Thirdly, there is the case of the Mezzogiorno in Italy, where Italian unification was followed by a pronounced process of *de-industrialization*, which led to a steady *drain* of capital to the North, with a long term reservoir of cheap labour-power, cheap agricultural products and a docile clientele in the South.[24] Sylos-Labini notes that industrial employment in Southern Italy (even if this was mostly in domestic and small-scale industry) fell back from 1,956,000 persons in 1881 to 1,270,000 in 1911. The difference in the level of wages between Northern and Southern Italy rose from 12% in 1870 to 25% in 1920 and 27% in 1929. In 1916, some 13% of Italian share-capital was invested in the South, in 1947, a mere 8%. Between 1928 and 1954 the share of the Mezzogiorno in Italian national income dropped from 24.3% to 21.1%.[25]

In a more restricted sense the same fate was true of broad regions of the Austro-Hungarian Empire between the 1848 Revolution and the First World War; of zones like Bavaria, Silesia, Pomerania-Mecklenburg and Prussia in the German Empire (i.e., the East and South);[26] and of the agrarian West and Centre

----

[23]See Eugene D. Genovese, op. cit., pp. 19-26 and 280-5. Melvin M. Leiman, *Jacob N. Cardozo — Economic Thought in the Antebellum South*, New York, 1966, pp. 175-203, 238-43.

[24] There is a very considerable literature on the economic development of Southern Italy after Italian unification. See among others: Emilio Sereni, *Il Capitalismo nelle Campagne (1860-1900)*; Aldo Alessandro Mola, *L'Economia Italiana dopo l'Unità*, Turin, 1971; Luigi Dal Pane, *Lo Sviluppo Economico dell' Italia negli Ultimi Cento Anni*, Bologna, 1962; A. Caracciolo, *La Formazione dell' Italia Industriale*, Bari, 1970; Rosario Romeo, *Risorgimento e Capitalismo*, Bari, 1963. Antonio Gramsci dealt with this problem in a number of the texts he wrote in prison: *Quaderni del Carcere*, Vol. II, Turin, 1964, pp.97-8 and elsewhere. See also the volume edited by Rosario Villari, *Il Sud nella Storia d'Italia*, Bari, 1971.

[25] Paolo Sylos-Labini, *Problemi dello Sviluppo Economico*, Bari, 1970, pp. 130, 128.

[26]Thus, for example, minimum wages in the building trade in 1906 were twice as high in the large cities of Berlin, Hamburg, Kiel, Düsseldorf, Dortmund, and Essen as in the rural districts of East and West Prussia (Gumbinnen, Zoppot), Brandenburg and Silesia and some of the poorer regions of Bavaria, Saxony and the Eifel. R. Kuczynski, *Arbeitslohn und Arbeitszeit in Europa und Amerika 1870-1909*, Berlin, 1913, p. 689f.

(partly also the rural East) of France before the First World War. In Spain, during both the 19th and 20th century, the South fulfilled a completely comparable function not only as an 'internal colony' in the sense of the constant reproduction of underdevelopment, but above all as a catchment area for additional capital, which was squeezed out of agriculture after the Second World War to accelerate the process of industrialization in old and new industrial centres in other parts of the country.[27] An interesting special case of the same phenomenon was the so-called 'dual structure' of Japanese industry, which developed from the 20s onwards in two contrasted sectors — 'modern' and 'traditional' — the latter based on archaic domestic and putting-out systems.[28] This dual structure unquestionably yielded a massive transfer of surplus-value from the 'traditional' to the 'modern' sector, such that the former could be regarded virtually as an 'internal colony' of the latter. It was only after the reserve army of labour in the countryside sharply dwindled in the mid-60s, as a result of rapid industrialization and massive rural exodus, that this dual structure started to decline, and with it the characteristic 'semi-regional' source of surplus-value within Japan.

The relationship between these developed and underdeveloped regions inside the industrialized capitalist states bears more than a formal resemblance to the relationship between imperialist and underdeveloped countries, for its economic function is the same in both cases. The difference in the level of productivity between agriculture and industry — which resembles that between the production of raw materials and finished goods in the epoch of freely competitive capitalism and classical imperialism — creates unequal

[27]See among others, Alfonso C.Comin, *España del Sur*, Madrid, 1965.
[28]See among others, Miyohei Shinohara, *Structural Changes in Japan's Economic Development*, Tokyo, 1970, Chapter Eight; Seymour Broadbridge, *Industrial Dualism in Japan*, Chicago, 1966; K. Bieda, *The Structure and Operation of the Japanese Economy*, Sydney, 1970, pp. 186-99. In 1955 there were still 26.5% self-employed in the non-agricultural sector of the Japanese economy, as against 11.8% in Australia, 10% in the USA and 6.2% in Britain (in 1951). Wage differentials by size of manufacturing establishment covered a span of 30 to 100 in 1958, compared with 64/100 in the USA and 79/100 in Britain (in 1954). Japanese differentials were much higher before the First World War, when wages in the 'traditional' sector (mainly textiles and light industry) were 'tied to the low remuneration on the land': see G. Ranis, 'Factor Proportions in Japanese Economic Development', in *American Economic Review*, September 1957, p. 595.

exchange, or a *steady transfer of value* from the underdeveloped to the industrialized regions of the same capitalist state. The exchange of agricultural products against industrial goods is an unequal exchange.[29] The exchange of raw materials produced in the underdeveloped regions (e.g., cotton in the Southern States of the USA) against industrial finished goods is an unequal exchange. The role played by underdeveloped agricultural regions in the industrialized countries as reserves of underemployed or unemployed labour-power is one of the main functions of these regions, because it ensures the secular maintenance of the industrial reserve army (in addition to the periodic reproduction of the same industrial reserve army by the displacement of labour-power already in a wage-relationship, by machines).[30] The underdeveloped regions within capitalist countries, just like the 'external colonies', thus function as *sources of surplus-profits.* Here is Marx's description of the surplus-profits that industrial capital makes through exchange with the production of small peasants and artisans in its first great period of *Sturm und Drang:* 'So long as, in a given branch of industry, the factory system extends itself at the expense of the old handicrafts or of manufacture,[31] the result is as sure as is the result of an encounter between an army furnished with breech-loaders, and one armed with bows and arrows. This first period, during which machinery conquers its field of action, is of decisive importance owing to *the extraordinary profits* that it helps to produce. These profits not only form a source of accelerated accumulation, but also attract into the favoured sphere of production a large part of the additional social capital that is being constantly created, and is ever on the lookout for new investments. *The special advantages*

---

[29] Always with the reservation that we are speaking of agricultural production by small peasants, which is not yet conducted by capitalist methods and does not yet lead to the rise of capitalist ground rent. As soon as agriculture becomes fully capitalized, such unequal exchange disappears.

[30] See material on this problem in Sternberg, *Der Imperialismus.*

[31] A further parallel to the relationship between industrial nations and underdeveloped countries emerges here. For the economic source of this surplus-profit lies in the fact that in the whole period of the incipient development of large-scale industry, the market price of the commodity produced by machines, but which the large factory cannot yet supply in a sufficient quantity, will certainly lie *below* the individual value of the products of handicrafts and manufactures, but significantly *above* the individual value of the machine-made product. In the sale of the latter a considerable surplus-profit can thus be made, which is exactly what happens in the export of cheap, mass produced industrial goods to countries which are still at a pre-industrial stage.

of this first period of fast and furious activity are felt in every branch of production that machinery invades.' [32]

But now we come up against two theoretical difficulties which need to be solved. On the one hand, the lack of homogeneity in *production* on a world scale has been explained by a certain immobility of capital, in other words by the lack of a unified worldwide capital market. But a unified capital market certainly does exist within the industrialized nations; indeed, its creation mostly preceded, and partly even determined, the advent of modern large-scale industry. Why is it then, that this unitary national capital market does not lead to a unitary national industrial structure?

On the other hand, we know that large-scale capital exports began in the 1880s, or long before the agricultural regions inside the industrialized countries themselves had disappeared. Why was capital then exported from the imperialist countries to the 'external colonies' instead of first being used to industrialize these 'internal colonies'?

The answer to these questions will enable us to grasp more precisely a phenomenon peculiar to the capitalist production of commodities, namely the formation of capitalist prices of production and the specific application of the law of value on the world market. The creation of a unified capital market inside the industrialized states prior to, or at the inception of, the process of industrialization [33] created a uniform national rate of interest and profit. It permitted only marginal differences in the level of wages; differences in the level of industrial wages in different geographical areas of the same country could hardly exceed a certain limit. Thus when the first wave of industrialization was over and had filled and even over-filled the 'internal market', and when the first relative over-production of capital had occurred as a consequence, there was no longer any pressing interest in the thorough industrialization of the agricultural regions within the industrial country. Production there contributed to the equalization of the national rate of profit. No surplus-profits could be achieved there, *for the very reason that a uniform system of prices of production was in operation.* There could at most be a slight increase in the

---

[32] Marx, *Capital*, Vol. 1, p. 450.
[33] See among others, E. Lipson, *The Economic History of England*, London, 1931, pp. 244-6.

average rate of profit. But greater transport costs, a worse infra-structure and the lack of qualified labour power would very quickly have neutralized the rather small difference that existed in the level of wages.[34]

By contrast, capital exports to the backward countries could profit precisely from the fact that there was no uniform capital market on a world scale, no uniform prices of production and no uniform rate of profit. The difference in the level of wages was so great, and the likelihood of achieving surplus-profits merely by introducing manufacturing or early capitalist methods into agricul-ture and mining therefore so significant, that the rates of profit (surplus-profits) which imperialist capital could achieve in the 'external colonies' were initially much greater than those which the same capital could hope to achieve in the 'internal colonies'. These 'internal colonies' were victims of the fact that although they were certainly under-developed they were at the same time bunched together with the industrialized areas in a system of uniform production prices, profits and wages.

Up to now we have restricted ourselves only to cases of geogra-phical differences in the level of productivity, to 'external' and 'internal' colonies. Now, however, we must investigate the more general case of a difference in the level of productivity between different branches of industry in the same, already industrialized country. This type of difference arises principally through technical progress, the improvement of production techniques, the raising of the organic composition of capital and above all the extended reproduction of fixed capital. We must distinguish here between two variants. If, besides a unified capital market, a unified system of interest and unified prices of production, there are also no restrictions on the mobility of capital, then after a certain period the competition of capitals will lead once again to the disap-pearance of surplus-profits temporarily accruing from the intro-duction of modern technology. Capital will relinquish the branches with lower rates of profit and flow into the branches with a higher rate. There, over-production and over-accumulation will take place, lowering market prices and suppressing surplus-profits,

---

[34]Francois Perroux points out that when a region with a growth firm (*firme motrice*) is coupled with a region without such a firm (i.e., an underdeveloped region) within the same country, this can undoubtedly lead to a growing difference in their levels of development: *L'Economie du XXe Siècle*, p. 225ff.

while the branches which have suffered a drain of capital will no longer be able wholly to supply socially effective demand at current output. Market prices in the latter sectors will thus rise again. Equalization of the rate of profit will be the result.

In the analysis of this process, however, it should be recalled once more that even with complete mobility of capital there is no immediate equalization of the rate of profit. A significant period of time separates the first moment that a technological discovery is given a productive application (i.e., the moment of technological *innovation*) from the moment that there is an equalization of the rate of profit. The cheaper commodity, manufactured with more modern technology, is first produced and sold at the average social price of production. It thus yields the owner a surplus-profit. This only gradually — through information in business reports and so forth — penetrates the consciousness of the generality of the owners of capital. Production in this branch then increases and the competitive struggle intensifies, so that the commodity produced with more modern technology begins to lower the average social cost price (market value). Despite this, however, it continues to make a surplus-profit, because its individual value is still below the average market value. Competitors then attempt to apply the same more modern technology, or new owners of capital enter the branch of production in question with a view to achieving the same surplus-profits. Only when this intensified competition has lowered the profit of the innovating firm once more to the social average by a reduction in market value proportionate to the saving of social labour (for this is what any genuine technological progress amounts to in the end) and consequent diminution in the value of the commodity, can one say that equalization of the rate of profit has been achieved. *In the entire intermediate period technical innovation does actually permit the realization of a surplus-profit.*

It should further be pointed out that the whole process of the appearance and disappearance of surplus-profits unleashed by technical innovation is simultaneously a process of the accumulation and devalorization of capital, in which many capitals operating with an insufficient productivity of labour are ruined *before* the equalization of the rates of profit takes place. Devalorization of capital — reduction or destruction of values — implies, however, a decrease in the total mass of capital with which the total surplus-value produced has to be compared, and hence a temporary increase in the social rate of profit or a temporary halt of the tendency for the rate of profit to fall. All these points explain why it is highly profitable for a firm or a branch of industry to introduce technological innovations despite the (subsequent) equalization of the rate of profit.

We now come to the second variant, however, in which surplus-profits can be realized by the introduction of technical innovation even in the absence of perfect mobility of capital. This is the classical case of *monopolies,* where there are decisive restrictions on the mobility of capital because of a combination of operative agreements between the most important owners of capital and massive installation costs (*frais de premier établissement*) — in other words a qualitatively higher level of concentration and centralization of capital. This combination results not only in temporary surplus-profits, but also in the *lasting surplus-profits* which are a characteristic feature of the epoch of monopoly capitalism.

There are, of course, no absolute monopolies in the long-run, and the growth of the surplus-profits of monopolistic or oligopolistic concerns is not without its limits. For one thing, the annual mass of surplus-value is a *given magnitude,* which is limited in the final resort by the number of hours worked by the productive wage-labourers and which cannot be increased by phenomena of any kind in the sphere of circulation. Once the total mass of surplus-value, and hence the total mass of profit, is given, the surplus-profits of a few concerns or monopolized branches of industry can only be increased by the transfer of surplus-value from other enterprises or other branches of industry. For every surplus-profit there will be a corresponding drop in the profits of other firms. If there is an increase in monopolistic surplus-profits, then there will be a fall in the rate of profit in the non-monopolized spheres and general competition will be intensified to such a degree that ultimately a drop in the production prices (and the surplus-profits) of the monopolies will also become inevitable.[35] On the other hand, individual monopolistic or oligopolistic concerns cannot allow themselves excessive surplus-profits either, for as we have said no monopolies are absolute. The difficulty of breaking into monopolized spheres is always only relative; in other words, it involves a capital outlay which is relatively difficult to achieve. If, however, a concern allows

[35] Which certainly does not mean, of course, that through this the transfer of value from the non-monopolized sectors to the monopolized sectors ceases to occur.

itself an 'exaggerated' surplus-profit, then there will be growing attempts by other monopoly capitalist groups to obtain a share of this surplus-profit, i.e., to break into this sphere. Since in most cases the necessary capital is certainly available in all the capitalist countries — with a few characteristic exceptions to which we shall later return — and since the existent monopolists must constantly reckon with this possibility (which would involve a sharp competitive struggle with slumps in prices and profits on all sides), they mostly avoid such 'exaggerations' in the 'mutual interest' of all monopolies. They are *forced* to do this all the more because in a *system* in which most monopolies are also related to each other as mutual suppliers, the quantity of marketable commodities of one monopoly depends on the (monopoly) prices of the other monopolies.[36] A tendency equivalent to the *equalization of surplus-profits* thus arises, i.e., *two* average rates of profit come into existence side by side, one on the monopolized and the other in the non-monopolized sector of the imperialist countries.[37] This juxtaposition of two average rates of profit is none other than the juxtaposition of two different levels of productivity, or in other words the same discrepancy in productivity which we first discovered at the root of the transfer of value between the industrialized and the non-industrialized regions of the same imperialist state.[38]

This analysis has been accused of infringing the fundamental principles of Marx's theory of value, and indeed any form of the labour theory of value at all. According to this charge, the transfer

---

[36] Robert Triffin, *Monopolistic Competition and General Equilibrium Theory*, Cambridge, USA, 1940.

[37] Ernest Mandel, *Marxist Economic Theory*, pp. 423-6. The practical mechanisms for equalizing monopolistic surplus-profits in this way include not only the factors briefly outlined here, but also the limitation of the market and hence the rate of surplus-profit by the selling price, and the compulsion to restrict or prevent the spread of diversified or substitute products. For this, see the important literature on the theme of 'monopolistic competition' which we partly cite in *Marxist Economic Theory* and which begins with E.M. Chamberlin's book, *The Theory of Monopolistic Competition*, Cambridge, USA, 1933.

[38] In N. D. Kondratieff's essay, 'Die Preisdynamik der industriellen und landwirtschaftlichen Waren', in *Archiv für Sozialwissenschaft und Sozialpolitik*, Vol. 60/1, 1928, pp. 50-8, there is an eclectic confusion between the analysis of labour value and the analysis of marginal utility. This leads to peculiar results. On the one hand Kondratieff rightly acknowledges that long-term reductions in the price of commodities (expressed in constant monetary values) can only derive from an increase in the productivity of labour, i.e., from a reduction in the value of commodities. On the other hand, however, he speaks of the 'purchasing power' of agricultural goods and the 'purchasing power' of industrial goods without taking into account the fact that he is here comparing not labour values but relative market

of value under the conditions of 'normal' competition (i.e., excluding violence, fraud, swindles and monopolies) is impossible in the framework of Marx's theory of value, since commodities are exchanged at their value. It is incomprehensible that an increase in the productivity of labour could lead to the achievement of surplus-profits, since such an increase should surely find expression in a fall, and not a rise, in the value of commodities. If the production of one branch falls below the total average then the value of its commodities would rise, not fall, in comparison to a branch operating with an above-average productivity of labour. Finally, enterprises revealing a technical advantage would certainly make a surplus-profit, but this would be the result, not of a transfer of value, but simply of the fact that the labour expended by their labourers is calculated as more intensive because the level of its productivity is above-average — in other words, because the total production of values has increased, thanks to this more productive labour, by more hours of labour than the 'mere' figure of the hours of labour expended in these enterprises suggests.[39]

We would reply that these objections are mainly based on a confusion between simple commodity production and capitalist commodity production.[40] Under conditions of a stable productivity of labour, where the latter can be regarded as given, the categories of 'socially necessary labour-time' and 'socially squandered labour-time' are clear and transparent. Here the phenomena of the market, 'on the surface' of economic life, correspond on the whole to the deeper

---

prices. Furthermore: if in a given year the production of 1 ton of wheat demands 50 working hours and that of 3 suits demands 20, then 50 years later the relation may have sunk to 30 working hours in the former case and 10 in the latter, so that the 'purchasing power' of wheat has risen in comparison with that of textiles. But cloth production may still have been expanded at the cost of wheat output, and the exchange of wheat with cloth may still involve a transfer of value to the advantage of textile production. In order to find out whether the development of prices has altered the proportions between the production of wheat and of cloth, we must consider not only the elasticity of demand for the two products but also above all the different *rates of profit* in the two sectors. An increase in 'purchasing power' by no means implies an increase in the rate of profit — and only the latter would redirect capital from industry back into agriculture.

[39] See for example, Busch, Schöller and Seelow, *Weltmarkt und Weltwährungskrise*, Bremen, 1971, pp. 21-4.

[40] It is typical that the quotations on which these authors base their argument come from the First and not the Third Volume of *Capital*. In the First Volume of *Capital* Marx is concerned with 'capital in general', and the problem of capitalist competition and the transformation of value into prices of production which underlies the transfer of value is not considered at all.

essence of these phenomena, at least as far as the quantitative determination of value is concerned.[41] (The origin and essence of the value-form has, however, already ceased to be transparent in this epoch of simple commodity production.) But under the capitalist mode of production, which is characterized by the continual upheaval of technology, things cease to be so simple and transparent, even where the quantitative determination of value is concerned. It is *impossible to ascertain a priori* what constitutes socially necessary and what socially squandered labour-time in each commodity, for this after all can only be revealed *a posteriori* by establishing whether a certain capital has obtained the average profit, more than the average profit, or less than the average profit: 'Demand and supply imply the conversion of value into market-value, and so far as they proceed on a capitalist basis, so far as the commodities are products of capital, they are based on capitalist production processes, i.e., *on quite different relationships than the mere purchase and sale of goods.* Here it is not a question of the formal conversion of the value of commodities into prices, i.e., not of a mere change of form. It is a question of definitive deviations in quantity of the market prices from the market-values, and further, from the prices of production.... Under capitalist production it is not merely a matter of obtaining an equal mass of value in another form — be it that of money or some other commodity — for a mass of values thrown into circulation in the form of a commodity, but it is rather a matter of realizing *as much surplus-value, or profit,* on capital advanced for production, as any other capital of the same magnitude, or *pro rata* to its magnitude in whichever line it is applied. It is, therefore, *a matter, at least as a minimum, of selling the commodities at prices which yield the average profit, i.e., at prices of production.*'[42]

The process of the equalization of the rates of profit necessarily results in a transfer of value, since the sum of production prices is equal to the sum of values (since equalization, that is, competition, i.e., movements in the sphere of circulation, cannot in themselves 'create' a single atom of additional value). Accordingly, if one branch appropriates part of the surplus-value produced in other branches, then this can only mean that these other branches must sell the commodities they produce below their value. Marx expressly emphasized

[41] See Friedrich Engels, 'Supplement' to *Capital*, Vol. 3, p. 897.
[42] Marx, *Capital*, Vol. 3, pp. 194-5 (Our italics).

this.[43] The whole transformation of values into prices of production is based on such a transfer of surplus-value, i.e., of value.[44] In other words, it is based on the fact that commodities produced under capitalist conditions are generally *not* sold at their values.

Although there is a methodological problem involved in extending the 'technical' determination of value — socially necessary labour-time as determined by the average productivity of labour in each branch — to include the social needs for each specific use-value,[45] this problem does not lie in the necessary connexion between exchange value and use-value. Rosdolsky has shown that we must see this two-fold determination of value as 'two different stages of the investigation' — in order to determine, from relations of supply and demand, the *market values* of firms operating with an average, below-average, or above-average productivity of labour. The real difficulty is to determine the total *mass of surplus-value* which is available for distribution among the capitalists. If, for example, the market value of a particular commodity is determined by the price of production of the firms with the lowest productivity of labour — because demand exceeds supply over a long period — then most of the firms in this branch will obtain a surplus-profit, i.e., an above-average profit. Where does the surplus-profit come from? In the only case where Marx makes a specific investigation of this question, the case of ground rent, he says: it derives from the lower organic com-

[43] See for example *Capital*, Vol. 3, p. 758: 'It has been shown that the price of production of a commodity may lie above or below its value, and coincides with its value only by way of exception.' See also *Theories of Surplus Value*, Vol. 2, Part 1, p. 30: 'It is therefore wrong to say that competition among capitals brings about a general rate of profit by equalizing the prices of commodities to their values. On the contrary it does so by converting the values of the commodities into average prices, in which a part of the surplus-value is transferred from one commodity to another.' The same is said in *Grundrisse*, pp. 435-6, *Theories of Surplus Value*, II, Part I, p. 35, *Capital*, Vol. 3, pp. 178-9.

[44] Marx, *Capital*, Vol. 3, pp. 156, 163-4, and many other passages.

[45] Busch, Schöller and Seelow claim that I adhere to a 'reified' determination of socially necessary labour-time, seeing it as determined in a purely technical manner, i.e., independent of social needs or use-value. This is not true. As early as my *Traité d'Economie Marxiste* (Paris, 1962), I included precisely this aspect of social needs (relationship of demand and supply) in the determination of the prices of production (Vol. 1, pp. 193-4). See also my *Einführung in die marxistische Wirtschaftstheorie*, Frankfurt, 1967, p. 15: 'For a commodity which would not satisfy anyone's need, since it had no use-value . . . would be unsaleable from the very start; it would have no exchange value . . . . This balance therefore implies that the sum of social production, the sum of the productive forces, the sum of the working hours over which this society disposes, have been distributed over the various branches of industry in the same proportions as the consumers distribute their purchasing power over their various needs.'

position of capital in agriculture, where it is engendered in the sphere of production, and where the private ownership of the land prevents it from entering into the general redistribution of the overall social surplus-value. But the various branches of industry — with the exception of monopolies, which we cannot explore here — are unable to prevent the surplus-value being redistributed in this manner, so that Marx's solution does not apply. It is all the less applicable because the firms (or branches) with above-average productivity of labour are normally the very ones with a higher, rather than a lower, organic composition of capital. If this extra surplus-value is not engendered directly in the specific sphere of production, then it can only come from two sources: either it comes from the redistribution of surplus-value previously produced elsewhere, and is the result of a transfer of surplus-value, i.e., of value; or it 'comes into being' in the sphere of circulation. Obviously, only the first of these possibilities is compatible with Marx's labour theory of value and surplus-value.

Busch, Schöller and Seelow try to explain this surplus-profit by saying that enterprises operating with above-average productivity of labour are such that their labour is more intensive than that of those producing with average productivity — and accordingly that the labour which ultimately yields less than the average profit on the market was in part not value-creating. This is a pseudo-solution, however. All it really does is to shift the creation of value from the sphere of production into the sphere of circulation. For precisely under the capitalist relations of production the question as to whether an enterprise will obtain the average profit, less than the average profit or more than the average profit is by no means a foregone conclusion at the time of completion of the process of production. Only in the process of circulation does the transformation of values into prices of production take place.

'Monetarily effective demand' as the measure of the 'social needs' to be satisfied,[46] can by its very nature only appear on the market, and must fluctuate widely. According to Busch, Schöller and

---

[46] It must not be forgotten that (1) immediately following the passage in Chapter 10 in the third volume of *Capital*, in which Marx defines the case where supply exceeds demand as one in which social labour-time has been squandered, he goes on to say that 'the mass of the commodity (then) comes to *represent* a much smaller quantity of labour in the market *than is actually incorporated in it.*' (p. 187) (our italics); (2) a whole discussion precedes and follows this passage in which the volume of the social demand for a specific use-value is itself relativized and declared to be dependent on the volume of the market value.

Seelow, therefore, the total volume of surplus-value would be determined by these fluctuations. It was precisely this contradiction of his theory of surplus-value that Marx sought to avoid by posing the law that the total mass of surplus-value is already given by the process of production, and that the total sum of the prices of production must accord with the total sum of this surplus-value. This means, however, that any surplus-profits must be accompanied by below-average profits on the part of other owners of commodities.

The Marxist theory of value starts out from the axiom that the total mass of surplus-value is equal to the total mass of social *surplus labour*, or in other words is determined by the total number of manhours worked less the total amount of necessary labour (i.e., less the number of working hours needed to produce the equivalent of the total sum of the wages of the productive workers). On the whole, this is *independent* of the specific productivity of labour in each enterprise and, given constant wages, can only be modified by the productivity of labour in the consumer goods industry. To regard the total mass as given at the end of the process of production means, in reality, to regard as given an average labour intensity, an average wage, and an average rate of surplus-value. *This is the framework* in which surplus-profits normally arise.[47] Only in exceptional cases does the surplus-profit arise out of an above-average *rate of surplus-value* in the individual firm.[48]

Marx found a positive solution to this difficulty by starting out from the proposition that the production of surplus-value is determined by the physical expenditure of *living, abstract,* and — since equalization of the intensity of labour and the rate of surplus-value

[47]Marx: 'The fact that capitals employing unequal amounts of living labour produce unequal amounts of surplus-value, presupposes at least to a certain extent that the degree of exploitation or the rate of surplus-value are the same, or that any existing differences in them are equalized by real or imaginary (conventional) grounds of compensation. This would assume competition among labourers and equalization through their continual migration from one sphere of production to another. *Such a general rate of surplus-value* — viewed as a tendency, like all other economic laws — has been assumed by us for the sake of simplification. But in reality it *is an actual premise of the capitalist mode of production*, although it is more or less obstructed by practical frictions.' *Capital*, Vol. 3, p. 175 (Our italics).

[48]Marx: 'In fact, the direct interest taken by the capitalist, or the capital, of any individual sphere of production in the exploitation of the labourers who are directly employed is confined to making an extra gain, a profit exceeding the average, either through *exceptional* overwork, or reduction of the wage below the average, or through the *exceptional* productivity of the labour involved.' *Capital*, Vol. 3, p. 197 (Our italics).

is assumed — *homogeneous labour* in the sphere of production. All the phenomena evoked by the competition of capitals and the relationships of supply and demand on the market are only able to effect a redistribution of this quantity; they cannot augment or reduce it.

When Marx states that enterprises operating with below-average productivity obtain less than the average profit, and that ultimately this corresponds to the fact that they have squandered social labour, all this formula means is that the *value or surplus-value actually produced* by their workers is appropriated on the market by firms that function better. It does not at all mean that they have created less value or surplus-value than is indicated by the number of hours worked in them.[49] This is the only interpretation of *Capital*, Volume 3, Chapter 10, that can be reconciled with the text as a whole and with the spirit of Marx's theory of value; and it clearly simplifies the notion of the transfer of value.

We should add that Marx explicitly records the phenomenon of the transfer of value, not only between branches of industry — through the equalization of the rates of profit — but also within the same branch of industry.[50] He does this in precisely the manner that elegantly reconciles the 'technical' and 'use-value' ways of determining socially necessary labour time. If social demand is exactly met by production, and the productivity of labour in 'average' enterprises therefore determines commodity value, this means that the total quantity of labour expended in this branch of industry represents in a double sense socially necessary labour. For, on the assumption of an identical rate of surplus-value, the entire mass of surplus-value produced in this branch of production will be equal to the entire mass of profit. The surplus-profit of the firms operating with above-average productivity of labour can then only be explained by a transfer of value at the expense of the firms operating

---

[49] 'They may, for example, be sold exactly or approximately at their individual value, in which case the commodities produced under the least favourable conditions may not even realize their cost price, while those produced under average conditions realize *only a portion of the value contained in them.*' Marx, *Capital*, Vol. 3, p. 179 (Our italics.)

[50] 'If the ordinary demand is satisfied by the supply of commodities of average value, hence of a value midway between the two extremes, then the commodities whose individual value is below the market value realize an extra surplus-value, or surplus-profit, while those, whose individual value exceeds the market value, are unable to realize a portion of the surplus-value contained in them'. Marx, *Capital*, Vol. 3, p. 178.

with below-average productivity of labour. In this case—the 'normal case' under conditions of free competition and equalization of the rates of profit — the transfer of value is the solution proposed by Marx himself. In the case — exceptional under conditions of free competition — where firms with the lowest productivity of labour determine market values (where demand is much greater than supply), or where those with the highest do so (where supply is much greater than demand), the problem of the creation of value and the determination of the quantum of value is not so self-evident. But in this case we prefer our own solution to that of Busch, Schöller and Seelow for the reasons outlined above.

Busch, Schöller and Seelow have evidently been misled into their pseudo-solution by an analogy with the problems of international trade.[51] Thereby they have failed to note that precisely in the context of international trade the preconditions posed by Marx for the formation of prices of production and uniform market values — i.e., average and universally valid intensity of labour, wide-ranging mobility of capital and labour-power, and equalization of rates of profit — do not, or only rarely obtain.

The entire capitalist system thus appears as a hierarchical structure of different levels of productivity, and as the outcome of the uneven and combined development of states, regions, branches of industry and firms, unleashed by the quest for surplus-profit. It forms an integrated unity, but it is an integrated unity of non-homogeneous parts, and it is precisely the unity that here determines the lack of homogeneity. In this whole system development and underdevelopment reciprocally determine each other, for while the quest for surplus-profits constitutes the prime motive power behind the mechanisms of growth, surplus-profit can only be achieved at the expense of less productive countries, regions and branches of production. Hence development takes place only in juxtaposition with underdevelopment; it perpetuates the latter and itself develops thanks to this perpetuation.

Without underdeveloped regions, there can be no transfer of surplus to the industrialized regions and hence no acceleration of capital accumulation there. Over the span of a whole historical

---

[51]Busch, Schöller and Seelow, op. cit., pp. 32-3. The extent to which international 'unequal exchange' is a matter of the transfer of value will be clarified in Chapter 11. Here we shall merely mention the fact that Marx speaks in this connection not only of unequal quantities of labour, but also of unequal labour-time.

epoch no transfer of surplus to the imperialist countries could have occurred without the existence of under-developed countries, and there could have been no acceleration of capital accumulation in the former. Without the existence of underdeveloped branches of industry there would have been no transfer of surplus to the so-called growth sectors and no corresponding acceleration of the accumulation of capital in the past 25 years.

For although the capitalist world system is an integrated and hierarchized whole of development and underdevelopment on the international, regional and sectoral level,[52] the main weight of this ramified uneven and combined development takes different forms in different epochs. In the age of freely competitive capitalism its predominant weight lay in the regional juxtaposition of development and underdevelopment. In the age of classical imperialism it lay in the international juxtaposition of development in the imperialist states and underdevelopment in the colonial and semi-colonial countries. In the age of late capitalism it lies in the overall industrial juxtaposition of development in growth sectors and underdevelopment in others, primarily in the imperialist countries but also in the semi-colonies in a secondary way. This does not mean, of course, that 'technological rents' — surplus-profits originating from advances in productivity based on technical improvements, discoveries and patents — did not exist in the 19th century, or were exceptional even then. It only means that, in the absence of a high level of centralization of capital, they were of relatively short duration, and therefore had a lesser weight in *overall surplus-profits* than 'regional' surplus-profits, and later colonial surplus-profits. But technological innovation in itself played a key role in the growth of capital and the quest for surplus-profits from the outset of the industrial revolution.

If we understand the nature of the process of growth under the capitalist mode of production — i.e., the nature of the accumulation of capital — in this manner, we can see the source of Rosa Luxemburg's error when she thought she had discovered the 'inherent limit' of the capitalist mode of production in the complete industrialization of the world or in the extension of the capitalist mode of production to the whole world. What seems clear when we start from the

[52] 'The unevenness of development as between industries was one of the leading features of the period' (of the Industrial Revolution in Great Britain). Maurice Dobb, op. cit., p. 258.

abstraction of 'capital in general' proves meaningless as soon as we proceed to 'concrete capitalism', that is, to the 'many capitals' — in other words, to capitalist competition. For since the problem can-be reduced to the question of value or the transfer of value, there is no limit whatsoever in purely economic terms to this *process of the growth of capital accumulation at the expense of other capitals, the expansion of capital through conjoint accumulation and devalorization of capitals, through the dialectical unity and contradiction of competition and concentration.* Limits to the process of capitalist growth are — from a purely economic point of view — in this sense always merely temporary, because while they proceed out of the very conditions of a difference in the level of productivity, they can reverse these conditions. Industrial zones flourish at the expense of agricultural regions, but their expansion is limited by the very fact that their most important 'internal colony' is condemned to relative stagnation and sooner or later they therefore seek to overcome this limit by resorting to an 'external colony'. At the same time, however, the relationship 'industrial zone-agricultural region' does not remain eternally frozen under capitalism. If it provides a new stimulus to the process of growth (the possible source of such a stimulus has already been described in the second chapter, and we will come back to it in the further course of this book), then there is no reason why a zone which was industrialized early on should not be transformed into a relatively backward area, or a former agricultural district be transformed into an area of industrial concentration. Marx had already seen this possibility in his own time, when it was still at most a marginal phenomenon or manifest only in its earliest beginnings. He pointed to the re-orientation of production brought about by changes in communications and the costs of transport:[53] 'The improvement of the means of communication and transportation cuts down absolutely the wandering period of the commodities but does not eliminate the relative difference in the time of circulation of different commodity-capitals arising from their peregrinations, nor

---

[53] In his article 'International Trade and the Rate of Economic Growth', in *Economic History Review*, Second Series, Vol. XII, No. 3, April 1960, p. 352, Kenneth Berrill rightly points out that in some underdeveloped countries the preference for exporting goods overseas rather than producing for the internal market *may* be explained by the fact that sea transport is much cheaper there than transportation over land. Obviously this is only an additional reason to those listed above for the fact that *commodity* production in these countries develops first and foremost for the world market.

that of different portions of the same commodity-capital which migrate in different markets. For instance, the improved sailing vessels and steamships, which shorten travelling, do so equally for near and distant ports. The relative difference remains, although often diminished. But the relative differences may be shifted about by the development of the means of transportation and communication in a way that does not correspond to the geographical distances. For instance a railway which leads from a place of production to an inland centre of population may relatively or absolutely lengthen the distance to a nearer inland point not connected by rail, as compared to the one which geographically is more remote. In the same way the same circumstances may alter the relative distance of places of production from the larger markets, which explains the deterioration of old and the rise of new centres of production because of changes in communication and transportation facilities. (To this must be added the circumstances that long hauls are relatively cheaper than short ones.)' [54]

The effect of railways and steamships in the 19th century has been matched by. the effect of air transport, motorways and the container system after the Second World War: frequent upheavals in the relative costs of transport lead to the rise of certain centres of production and the decline of others.[55] In exactly the same way, leading branches of industry which obtain a transfer of value at the expense of other branches through their above-average organic composition of capital may gradually decline below the average social level of labour productivity if, in the course of a technological upheaval in industrial methods or energy supplies, they prove less capable of rapid adaptation to the new technology.

Examples of this role reversal of regions [56] can be found in the

[54]Marx, *Capital*, Vol. 2, p. 253.

[55]Western Europe's so-called 'maritime steel industry', for example, became profitable, i.e., possible, only because giant tankers and carriers were able to transport oil and iron-ore so cheaply over long distances that the former could compete with every cost advantage possessed by steel centres located in the vicinity of domestic coal deposits, as soon as coal became more expensive than oil.

[56]Walter Izard and John H. Cumberland applied Leontief's input-output calculation to interregional relations in 1958 and thereby provided us with the necessary tools for a formal exposition of the inequalities of regional development. In themselves, of course, these tools cannot reveal the causal and structural basis for the underdevelopment of certain regions, nor can they fully calculate the volume of the value transferred. Walter Izard and John H. Cumberland, 'Regional Input-Output Analysis', *Bulletin de l'Institut International de Statistique*, Stockholm, 1958.

relative decline of old industrialized zones such as New England in the USA, Scotland, Wales and the North in Great Britain, Nord/Pas-de-Calais and Haute-Loire in France, and Wallonia in Belgium. The Ruhr region in West Germany is partially threatened by a similar development. Examples of the role changes of branches of industry may be found in the relative decline of those sections of the textile industry engaged in processing natural fibres, the coal industry and potentially the steel industry.[57] There is no doubt that such regional role reversals occurred at the outset of the industrial revolution itself. An investigation of the causes of these shifts — which were never merely reducible to problems of mineral resources — would be a rewarding theme for Marxist economic history. Crouzet and Woronoff have published an interesting analysis of the origins of the decline of Bordeaux — the metropolis of mercantile and manufacturing capitalism in pre-revolutionary France. In addition to the factors mentioned by Marx — changes in transport and communication systems and modifications of markets — there above all occurred in this case changes in the main sources of rates of surplus-profit (previously: trade in West Indian colonial commodities; now: technological growth industries, above all textile factories) and the over-specialization of a regional bourgeoisie in an old-established business and entrepreneurial world, which made a rapid reconversion of it impossible. The geographically unpropitious position of

---

[57] There has been a rapid growth in the literature on the subject of 'regional differences in levels of income and prosperity' in the various European states. We shall limit ourselves here to a mention of the 'Regional Statistics' published by the EEC in 1971. These reveal that in Italy in 1968, for example, industrial employment in Sardinia, the far South and the Abruzzi lay below 30% of the work-force, while the average for the whole of Italy was already more than 41% (p. 47). In the same year, in West Germany, Rhineland-Palatinate, with 6% of the population, received only 3.9% of the bank credits, and in France the West and the East, with a total of 22.4% of the population, received 14% of bank credits (pp. 202-03). The gross internal product per capita in the 'wealthiest' state of the Federal Republic of West Germany (Hamburg) was more than twice as high as that in the 'poorest' (Schleswig-Holstein). The same is true in Belgium of the difference between the province of Luxemburg and the Brussels district, while in Italy the difference between the Molise district and Lombardy was nearly one to three (pp. 211-14). In the South of the Netherlands there were barely half as many doctors per 1,000 inhabitants as in the Amsterdam and Utrecht districts. In the Drenthe region private power consumption per family was less than half that in the Utrecht district. In the Nord/Pas-de-Calais there were only half as many hospital beds per 1,000 inhabitants as in Provence and the Cote d'Azur. Even in Bavaria the private consumption of electricity per inhabitant was only half that of Hamburg (pp. 215-18), and so on. In Spain these discrepancies are of course much greater.

the South-West, and the effects of the British blockade and the Continental System during the Napoleonic Wars, also played a role in the decline of the city.[58]

A crucial element, however, in the whole process of growth based on the uneven development of countries, regions and branches of industry, is the mechanism that sets it in motion. What sort of impetus is needed to upset a particular form of the juxtaposition of development and under-development, to guide it in a different direction or to revolutionize it? What factors would cause an abrupt modification of differences in levels of productivity? What sudden new impulse causes a phase of relative over-accumulation, relative excess of capital and hence slow-down of accumulation and growing difficulties in the valorization of total accumulated capital, to switch over into a phase of accelerated valorization and hence accelerated accumulation and accelerated economic growth?

These problems, too, cannot be answered with a single formula, any more than can the question of the sources of surplus-profit in the capitalist mode of production. Here too, all the basic variables of this mode of production must be considered. It must constantly be borne in mind that the exploitation of agricultural regions, the exploitation of colonies and semi-colonies and the exploitation of technologically less developed branches of production, do not merely follow each other in succession as the main sources of surplus-profit, but that they also co-exist side by side in each of the three phases of the capitalist mode of production. A clarification of these combinations is indispensable for an understanding of late capitalism.

[58]See A. D. Woronoff, 'Les Bourgeoisies Immobiles du Sud-Ouest', *Politique Aujourd'hui,* January 1971.

4

"Long Waves"
in the History of Capitalism

The cyclical course of the capitalist mode of production induced by
competition takes the form of the successive expansion and contraction of commodity production and hence of the production of surplus-
value. There corresponds to this a further cyclical movement of
expansion and contraction in the realization of surplus-value and the
accumulation of capital. In their timing, their volume and their
proportions, the realization of surplus-value and the accumulation
of capital are neither wholly identical with each other nor with the
production of surplus-value itself. The discrepancy between the third
and the first, and between the first and the second, provides the
explanation of capitalist crises of over-production. The fact that these
discrepancies cannot in any way be ascribed to coincidence, but spring
from the inner laws of the capitalist mode of production, is the reason
for the inevitability of conjunctural oscillations in capitalism.[1]

The upward and downward movements of capital accumulation
in the course of the industrial cycle can be characterized in the
following manner. In a period of the upswing, there is an increase in
the mass and the rate of profit, and a rise both in the volume and the
rhythm of accumulation. Conversely, in a crisis and subsequent

[1]We have attempted to summarize the various academic and Marxist theories of
the industrial cycle in the eleventh chapter of *Marxist Economic Theory*, in which
we set out the reasons why this cycle is inevitable within the framework of the capitalist
mode of production.

period of depression, both the mass and the rate of profit will decline, and both the volume and the rhythm of capital accumulation will decrease. The industrial cycle thus consists of the *successive acceleration and deceleration of accumulation.*

We shall leave out of our investigation at this point the extent to which the growth and decline of the *mass of profit* and of the *rate* of profit are identical with each other or merely congruent during the successive phases of the cycle. This question will be dealt with in the context of our treatment of the industrial cycle in late capitalism (see Chapter 14).

During the phase of upswing the accumulation of capital accelerates. But when this movement has reached a certain point it becomes difficult for the total mass of accumulated capital to achieve valorization. The fall of the rate of profit is the clearest sign of this watershed. The notion of over-accumulation indicates a situation in which a portion of the accumulated capital can only be invested at an inadequate *rate of profit* and increasingly only at a diminishing rate of interest. [2] The concept of over-accumulation is never absolute but always only relative: there is never 'absolutely' too much capital, but there is too much available to attain the expected social average rate of profit. [3]

Conversely, in the phase of the crisis and the ensuing depression, capital is devalorized and partially destroyed in value. Underinvestment now occurs, or in other words, less capital is invested than could be expanded at the given level of production of surplus-value and the given (rising) average rate of profit. As we know, these periods when capital is devalorized and under-invested precisely have the function of once again raising the average rate of profit of the entire mass of accumulated capital, which in turn allows the intensification of production and capital accumulation. The entire capitalist industrial cycle thus appears to be the consequence of accelerated capital accumulation, over-accumulation, decelerated capital accumulation

---

[2] Henryk Grossmann, op. cit., p. 118ff., uses the notion of 'over-accumulation' in this sense, although not directly in connection with the industrial cycle. Marx uses it in this way in *Capital*, Vol.3, p. 251.

[3] 'However, even under the extreme conditions assumed by us this absolute overproduction of capital is not absolute overproduction of means of production. It is overproduction of means of production only in so far as the latter *serve as capital*, and consequently include a self-expansion of value, must produce an additional value in proportion to the increased mass.' Marx, *Capital*, Vol.3, p. 255.

and under-investment.[4] The rise, fall and revitalization of the rate of profit both correspond to, and command, the successive movements of capital accumulation.

The question now poses itself: is this cyclical movement simply repeated every 10, 7 or even 5 years? Or is there a peculiar inner dynamic to the succession of industrial cycles over longer periods of time? Before we answer this question in the light of empirical data, we should examine it from a theoretical point of view.

Marx determined the length of the industrial cycle by the duration of the turnover-time necessary for the reconstruction of all fixed capital.[5] In each production cycle or in each year only a portion of the value of the fixed element of constant capital, i.e., principally of machines, is renewed. It takes several successive production cycles or years to complete this reconstruction of the value of fixed capital. In practice, machines are not renewed by 1/7 or 1/10 every year, which would mean that they would be completely reconstructed after 7 or 10 years. The actual process of the reproduction of fixed capital rather takes the form of mere repairs to these machines during the 7 or 10 years, after which they are replaced by new machines at a single stroke.[6]

In Marx's theory of cycles and crises, this renewal of fixed capital explains not only the length of the business cycle but also the decisive moment underlying *extended reproduction* as a whole, the upswing and acceleration of capital accumulation.[7] For it is the renewal of fixed capital that determines the feverish activity of the boom. In making this crucial point, incidentally, Marx anticipated the entire modern academic theory of cycles which, as we know, sees in the investment activity of the entrepreneurs the main stimulus for the upward movement of the cycle.

The characteristic element in the capitalist mode of production, however, is the fact that each new cycle of extended reproduction begins with different machines than the previous one. In capitalism,

[4] Cf. Paul Boccara, 'La crise du capitalisme monopoliste d'Etat et les luttes des travailleurs' in *Economie et Politique*, No. 185, December 1969, pp. 53-7, where he speaks of a cycle of over-accumulation and devalorization of capital.
[5] Marx, *Capital*, Vol.2, p. 185.
[6] Ibid., p. 170ff.
[7] Marx: 'But a crisis always forms the starting-point for large new investments. Therefore, from the point of view of society as a whole, it is more or less a new material basis for the next turnover cycle.' *Capital*, Vol.2, p. 186. See also *Capital*, Vol. 1, pp. 632-3.

under the whip of competition and the constant quest for surplus-profits, efforts are continually made to lower the costs of production and cheapen the value of commodities by means of technical improvements: 'Production for value and surplus-value implies, as has been shown in the course of our analysis, the constantly operating tendency to reduce the labour-time necessary for the production of a commodity, i.e., its value, below the actually prevailing social average. The pressure to reduce the cost price to its minimum becomes the strongest lever for raising the social productiveness of labour, which, however, appears here only as a continual increase in the productiveness of capital.'[8] The renewal of fixed capital thus implies *renewal at a higher level of technology*, and this in a triple sense.

Firstly, the value of the newer machines will form a greater component part of the total capital invested, i.e., the law of the increasing organic composition of capital will here prevail. Secondly, the newer machines will only be purchased if the cost of their acquisition and the values they will impart to ongoing output do not contradict the efforts of 'the capitalist to make a profit, i.e., if the saving on *paid* living labour exceeds the additional costs of the fixed capital, or more precisely, the total constant capital'.[9] Thirdly, the machines will only be bought if they not only save labour but also push down the total costs of production to a level below the social average, i.e., only if they constitute a source of surplus-profits for the entire period of transition — until these new machines determine the *average* productivity of labour in the given branch of production.

The problem of the increase in the organic composition of capital, i.e., the process of extended reproduction at a higher technical level, must not, however, be reduced merely to the problem of the value-composition of capital out of constant and variable capital. As Grossmann correctly explains with reference to Marx,[10] the notion of the organic composition of capital includes a technological element as well as a value element, and more particularly a correlation between these two elements (the value-composition is *determined* by the technological composition).[11] This means, therefore, that a certain *mass* of machinery requires a certain *mass* of raw and auxiliary materials, as well as a certain *mass* of labour-power, to set it in motion,

[8]K. Marx, *Capital,* Vol. 3, p. 859.   [9]Marx, *Capital,* Vol. 3, p. 262.
[10]Marx, *Capital,* Vol. 1, p. 612.   [11]Grossmann, op. cit., pp. 326-34.

independent of the immanent values of these masses.[12] These proportions depend not on the value of the machinery, but on its technical nature. On the other hand, however, the mass of the machinery employed depends on the basic technology which is used and not merely on the increased volume of fixed capital. For the purposes of a transition from a less productive to a more productive technical process, it is often sufficient to introduce minor improvements to the machinery, better labour organization, an accelerated work rhythm or better and cheaper raw materials. But in order *completely to reorganize* the technical process new machines are needed, which must previously have been designed; often new materials are needed, without which new branches of production cannot come into being; qualitative leaps forward are necessary in the organization of labour and forms of energy, such as the introduction of the conveyor belt, for example, or of automatic transfer machines. In other words, a distinction must be made between two different forms of the extended reproduction of fixed capital. There is the form in which there is certainly an extension of the scale of production, additional constant and variable capital is expended and the organic composition of capital indeed does increase, but in which all this occurs without a *revolution in technology* which affects the whole social apparatus of production; and the form in which there is not only an extension but a *fundamental renewal* of productive technology, or of fixed capital, which induces a qualitative change in the productivity of labour.[13]

Under normal conditions of the realization of surplus-value and the accumulation of capital, the extended reproduction of fixed capital every 7 or 10 years will be characterized by the fact that the capital set free in the course of the successive production cycles for the purchase or ordering of new machinery increases by a portion of value $M\beta$. If the total mass of surplus-value over the whole 10-year cycle is expressed as $M=M\alpha+M\beta+M\gamma$, then $M\alpha$ represents the surplus-value consumed unproductively by the capitalists and their clients, $M\gamma$ the additional circulating capital set free by the ten successive annual production cycles — which in turn divides into additional variable capital for the purchase of additional labour-power, and additional circulating constant capital for the continual

[12]Marx, *Capital*, Vol. 3, p. 243.
[13]Marx, *Capital*, Vol. 1, p. 629; 'The intermediate pauses are shortened, in which accumulation works as simple extension of production, on a given technical basis.'

injection of additional raw materials into production. The third component part of M, $M\beta$, is then the additional fixed capital which has progressively been set free and which can be used both for the purchase of *more*, and for the purchase of *more expensive*, more modern machines.

The relation of $M\beta$ to Cf, the additional to the existing fixed capital, forms the rate of increase of the fixed capital, $\triangle Cf$, or the rate *of increase in the value of the social stock of machinery*. The level of this rate of increase enables us to define periods of slow or rapid technological renewal.[14] These magnitudes must, of course, always be understood in *terms of value*. Obviously, the amortization fund of already existent fixed capital Cf can also be used for the purchase of machinery, but (at least in so far as we are dealing with a real amortization fund and not with concealed profits) never to a higher value than that of the machinery previously purchased.

Let us start from the fact that a basic change in productive technology determines a significant additional expenditure of fixed capital — among other things for the creation of new production sites and new instruments of production, besides the additional instruments of production which existing production processes can engender in cases of 'normal' accumulation. In other words, it determines a very high rate of $\frac{M\beta}{Cf}$. Every period of radical technical innovation thus appears as a period of *sudden acceleration of capital accumulation*.[15]

Against this background, the periodical under-investment of capital in the cyclical course of the capitalist mode of production henceforth embodies a double function. It not only serves to give expression to the inevitable periodical slump in the average rate of profit, but in doing so it also begins to brake the decline. It further

[14]Nonetheless, with a major acceleration of technological innovation, the *ongoing* improvement of productive technology through partial replacements of machinery may play an increasing role, diminishing the importance of $M\beta$ in raising the productivity of labour. Nick even regards this as one of the hallmarks of a 'technological-scientific revolution': Harry Nick, *Technische Revolution und Ökonomie der Produktionsfonds*, Berlin, 1967, pp. 17-18. We shall be returning to this complex of questions in Chapter 7.

[15]'A flow of new knowledge leads to continuous change in the production function for each commodity. This may take a variety of forms. Some advances, particularly those which originate in basic science, affect the whole nature of the production function as the basic processes of an industry undergo a radical change. Other advances lead to improvements in existing basic methods.' W.E.G. Salter, *Productivity and Technical Change*, Cambridge, 1960, p. 21.

creates a historical *reserve fund of capital*, from which can be drawn the means for *additional* accumulation needed over and above 'normal' extended reproduction to allow a fundamental renewal of productive technology. This can be expressed even more clearly: under 'normal' conditions of capitalist production the values set free at the end of *one* 7- or 10- year cycle are certainly sufficient for the acquisition of more and more expensive machines than were in use at the outset of this cycle. But they do not suffice for the acquisition of a fundamentally renewed productive technology, particularly in Department I, where such a renewal is generally linked to the creation of completely new productive installations. Only the values set free for the purchase of additional fixed capital in *several* successive cycles enable the accumulation process to make a qualitative forward leap of this kind. The cyclical recurrence of periods of under-investment fulfils the objective function of setting free the necessary capital for this kind of technological revolution. But this in itself does not explain the reasons for the occurrence of radical technological revolutions in some periods and not in others. The existence of a long period of under-investment is precisely the expression of the fact that additional capital was certainly available, but was not in fact invested or expended. The real problem is hence to explain why at a particular point in time this additional capital is expended on a massive scale, after lying idle for a long period. The answer is obvious: only a *sudden increase in the rate of profit* can explain the massive investment of surplus capitals — just as a prolonged fall in the rate of profit (or the fear that it will decline even more precipitously) can explain the idleness of the same capital over many years.[16] On the eve of a new spring tide of capital accumulation we should be able to record the appearance of the following factors, which render possible a sudden increase in the average rate of profit *beyond the periodic results of the devalorization of capital occurring in the course of the crisis.*

[16]Kondratieff also enumerated the preconditions which he thought were necessary for a sudden extension of capital accumulation. They were: '1. High intensity of savings activity; 2. A relatively abundant and cheap supply of loan capital; 3. Its accumulation in the hands of powerful enterprises and centres of finance; 4. A low level of commodity prices, stimulating savings activity and longterm capital investment.' *(Die Preisdynamik,* p. 37). The weakness of this explanation is obvious: all these phenomena occur, precisely in phases of under-investment (e.g., between 1933 and 1938 in the USA) without this leading to rapid technological renewal. Kondratieff completely overlooked the strategically crucial role of the rate of profit.

The relevant factors are these:

1. A sudden fall in the average organic composition of capital, for example as a result of the massive penetration of capital into spheres (or countries) with a very low organic composition.

2. A sudden increase in the rate of surplus-value, as a result, for example, of a rise in the intensity of labour due to a radical defeat and atomization of the working class which disables it from using advantageous conditions on the labour market to raise the price of the commodity of labour-power and forces it to sell this commodity below its value even in a period of economic prosperity.

3. A sudden fall in the price of elements of constant capital, especially of raw materials, which is comparable in effect to a sudden decline of the organic composition of capital, or a sudden fall in the price of fixed capital due to a revolutionary advance in the productivity of labour in Department I.

4. A sudden abbreviation of the turnover-time of circulating capital due to perfection of new systems of transport and communications, improved methods of distribution, accelerated rotation of stock, and so on.

Two processes must here be separated out temporally and conceptually. On the one hand, there is the process which permits the average rate of profit to rise and as it were sets this rise in motion, leading to a massive investment of previously idle capital; on the other, there is the process that springs from this massive investment of previously idle capital.

If the triggering factors are by their nature and volume such that their effect can quickly be neutralized by the increase in the mass of accumulated capital, then the average rate of profit will rise only briefly. In this case the quickening of the rhythm of capital accumulation will be braked abruptly and give way, after a short interruption, to renewed under-investment. This occurred, for example, in various imperialist countries during and immediately following the First World War. If, on the contrary, the triggering factors are by their nature and volume such that their effect cannot be neutralized by the immediate consequences of the sudden increase in the accumulation of capital, then the whole mass of capital previously not invested will progressively be drawn into the maelstrom of accumulation. It then becomes possible to achieve not only a partial and moderate, but a massive and universal revolution in production technology. This will ensue particularly if *several factors are simultaneously and cumulatively* contributing to a rise in the average rate of profit. In the preceding chapters we have already briefly emphasized the causes which led to such a persistent increase in the average rate of profit in the 90s of the last century: the sudden massive investment in the colonies of excess capital exported from the metropolitan countries, leading simultaneously to a considerable fall in the organic composition of world capital and a sudden decrease in the price of circulating constant capital, which combined to affect the average rate of profit.[17]

At least two other periods in the history of capitalism can be recorded, in which a comparably abrupt rise in the rate of profit also occurred. The first took place in the middle of the 19th century, immediately following the outbreak of the 1848 Revolution. The decisive triggering factor seems to have been, in this case, a radical increase in the rate of surplus-profit due to a radical rise in the average productivity of labour in the consumer goods industry, i.e., due to a radical increase in the production of relative surplus-value. The second occurred on the eve or at the start of the Second World War; it was likewise determined by a radical rise in the rate of surplus-value, which was rendered possible on this occasion, however, by a radical change in the relationship of class forces, prolonged by a radical increase in the intensity of labour and combined with a fall in the price, first of circulating constant capital due to the penetration of the most modern technology into spheres producing raw materials, then also of fixed constant capital due to a sudden rise in the productivity of labour in the machine-building industry. We shall return to the concrete causes and effects of this increase in the rate of surplus-value immediately preceding and during the Second World War in the next chapter.

What, then, are these 'revolutions in technology as a whole' which we have described as phases of the re-entry of idle capital into the process of valorization, determined by a sudden rise in the average rate of profit? In Chapter 15 of the first volume of *Capital*, Marx distinguishes three essentially different parts of all developed machinery: motive machinery, transmission machinery and tool or labour machines.[18] The evolution and transformation of the latter

---

[17] See, among other things, Footnote 13 of Chapter 3.
[18] Usher criticizes this definition of machines, which Marx took from Ure and Babbage. He claims that such a characterization omits the crucial criterion of progress in machinery, which is the creation of ever 'more elegant' (presumably

two, of course depend after a certain point on the development of the motive machines, which embody the decisively dynamic element of the whole: 'Increase in the size of the machine, and in the number of the working tools, calls for a more massive mechanism to drive it, and this mechanism requires, in order to overcome its resistance, a mightier moving power than that of man, apart from the fact that man is a very imperfect instrument for producing uniform, continued motion.'[19] Further: 'A system of machinery, whether it reposes on the mere cooperation of similar machines, as in weaving, or on a combination of different machines, as in spinning, constitutes in itself a huge automaton, whenever it is driven by a self-acting prime mover.'[20] The production of 'motive machines', i.e., the mechanical producers of energy, by machinery instead of by handicrafts, is the determinant movement in the formation of an 'organized system of machines', as Marx puts it. This production of machines, and first and foremost of motive machines, by other machines is the historical precondition for a radical change in technology: 'At a certain stage of its development, Modern Industry became technologically incompatible with the basis furnished for it by handicraft and Manufacture', i.e., with the production by handicraft or manufacture of the machines themselves. 'Modern Industry had therefore itself to take in hand the machine, its characteristic instrument of production, and to construct machines by machines. It was not till it did this, that it built up for itself a fitting technical foundation, and stood on its own feet. Machinery, simultaneously with the growing use of it, in the first decades of this century, appropriated, by degrees, the fabrication of machines proper. But it was only during the decade preceding 1866, that the construction of railways and ocean steamers on a

---

meaning 'more labour-saving') *combinations* of different elements into a unitary self-moving 'train': A. P. Usher, *A History of Mechanical Inventions*, Harvard, 1954, pp. 116-17. Usher here seems to have overlooked that Marx first described the historical genesis and development of the machine (*Capital*, Vol. 1, p. 378f.), so that he could then quite definitely place the emphasis on the mutual *combination* of machine parts or of different machines: 'An organized system of machines, to which motion is communicated by the transmitting mechanism from a central automaton, is the most developed form of production by machinery.' (ibid., p. 381). Babbage himself was no less aware of this, for his brilliant mind was engaged, a hundred years before the real beginnings of automation, in the design of an automatic calculating machine which was to take this notion of the articulated combination of all component parts to its highest level of development.

[19] K. Marx, *Capital*, Vol. 1, p. 376.
[20] Ibid., p. 381.

stupendous scale *called into existence the cyclopean machines* now employed in the construction of prime movers.'[21]

The fundamental revolutions in power technology — the technology of the production of motive machines by machines — thus appears as the determinant moment in revolutions of technology as a whole. Machine production of steam-driven motors since 1848; machine production of electric and combustion motors since the 90's of the 19th century; machine production of electronic and nuclear-powered apparatuses since the 40's of the 20th century — these are the three general revolutions in technology engendered by the capitalist mode of production since the 'original' industrial revolution of the later 18th century.

Once a revolution in the technology of productive motive machines by machinery has occurred, the whole system of machines is progressively transformed. For as Marx explains: 'A radical change in the mode of production in one sphere of industry involves a similar change in other spheres. This happens at first in such branches of industry as are connected together by being separate phases of a process, and yet are isolated by the social division of labour, in such a way that each of them produces an independent commodity. Thus spinning by machinery made weaving by machinery a necessity, and both together made the mechanical and chemical revolution that took place in bleaching, printing and dyeing, imperative. So too, on the other hand, the revolution in cotton spinning called forth the invention of the gin, for separating the seeds from the cotton fibre; it was only by means of this invention, that the production of cotton became possible on the enormous scale at present required. But more especially, the revolution in the modes of production of industry and agriculture made necessary a revolution in the general conditions of the social process of production, i.e., in the means of communication and of transport. In a society whose pivot, to use an expression of Fourier, was agriculture on a small scale, with its subsidiary domestic industries, and the urban handicrafts, the means of communication and transport were so utterly inadequate to the productive requirements of the manufacturing period, with its extended division of social labour, its concentration of the instruments of labour, and of the workmen, and its colonial markets, that they became in fact revolutionized. In the same way, the means of communication and transport handed down from the manufacturing

21 Ibid., pp. 384-5 (Our italics).

period soon became unbearable trammels on Modern Industry, with its feverish haste of production, its enormous extent, its constant flinging of capital and labour from one sphere of production into another, and its newly-created connexions with the markets of the whole world. Hence, apart from the radical changes introduced in the construction of sailing vessels, the means of communication and transport became gradually adapted to the modes of production of mechanical industry, by the creation of a system of river steamers, railways, ocean steamers, and telegraphs.'[22]

It is not difficult to provide evidence to show that each of the three fundamental revolutions in the machine production of energy sources and motive machines progressively transformed the whole productive technology of the entire economy, including the technology of the communications and transport systems.[23] Think, for example, of the ocean steamers and diesel locomotives, automobiles and radio communications in the epoch of the electric and combustion engines; and the jet transport planes, television, telex, radar and satellite communication networks, and atom-powered container freighters of the electronic and nuclear age.[24] The technological transformation arising from the revolution of the basic productive technology of motive machines and sources of energy thus leads to a new valorization of the excess capitals which have gradually been piling up from cycle to cycle within the capitalist mode of production. By exactly the same process, however, the gradual generalization of the new sources of energy and new motive machines must lead, after a longish phase of accelerated accumulation, to a longish phase of decelerating accumulation, i.e., renewed under-investment and reappearance of idle capital.

The production sites of the new motive machines imply long-term possibilities for the expansion of *newly* accumulated capitals. As long as the capitals invested over successive periods in the industries making steam-driven or electric motors or electronic apparatuses continue to dominate the market, only small and adventurous capitals condemned to experiment — in other words, to fall short of full valorization, will dare to venture into 'new realms' of energy and motive machinery. As the application of the new motors becomes more and more general, the growth rate of the industries making these motors gradually declines further and further, and it becomes

[22]Ibid., pp. 383-4.
[23]David Landes, op. cit., pp. 153-4, 423f.
[24]See an essay by Wolfgang Pfeifer in the *Neue Zürcher Zeitung*, 24.8.1972.

increasingly difficult for the capitals feverishly accumulated in the first phase of growth to continue their valorization.

A general transformation of productive technology also generates a significant rise in the organic composition of capital and, depending on concrete conditions, this will lead sooner or later to a fall in the average rate of profit. The decline of the average rate of profit in turn becomes the greatest impediment to the next technological revolution. The increasing difficulties of valorization in the second phase of the introduction of any new basic technology lead to growing under-investment and increasing creation of idle capital. Only if a combination of specific conditions generates a sudden rise in the average rate of profit will this idle capital, which has slowly gathered over several decades, be drawn on a massive scale into the new spheres of production capable of developing the new basic technology.

The history of capitalism on the international plane thus appears not only as a succession of cyclical movements every 7 or 10 years, but also as a succession of longer periods, of approximately 50 years, of which we have experienced four up till now:

— the long period from the end of the 18th century up to the crisis of 1847, characterized basically by the gradual spread of the *handicraft-made or manufacture-made steam engine* to all the most important branches of industry and industrial countries; this was the long wave of the industrial revolution itself.

— the long period, lasting from the crisis of 1847 until the beginning of the 1890s, characterized by the generalization of the *machine-made steam engine* as the principal motive machine. This was the long wave of the first technological revolution.[25]

— the long period, lasting from the 1890s to the Second World War, characterized by the generalized application of electric and

---

[25] In our opinion Oskar Lange is right to object to the use of the term 'industrial revolution' for great technological upheavals such as the automation of production processes since the Second World War. 'This usage obscures the historical specificity of the industrial revolution which formed the basis of industrialization. It must also be emphasized that the original industrial revolution which led to the rise of large-scale industry was closely connected with the genesis of the capitalist mode of production and hence with a new social formation.' Oskar Lange, *Entwicklungstendenzen der modernen Wirtschaft und Gesellschaft,* Vienna, 1964, p. 160. Accordingly, we here use the terms 'first, second and third technological revolutions' (instead of the widely-used formula 'second and third industrial revolution'). In doing so, we are correcting an error which we have ourselves committed in the past.

combustion engines in all branches of industry. This was the long wave of the second technological revolution.[26]

— the long period, beginning in North America in 1940 and in the other imperialist countries in 1945-48, characterized by the generalized control of machines by means of *electronic apparatuses* (as well as by the gradual introduction of nuclear energy). This is the long wave of the third technological revolution.

Each of these long periods can be subdivided into two parts: an initial phase, in which the technology actually undergoes a revolution, and when such things as the production sites for the new means of production have first to be created. This phase is distinguished by an increased rate of profit, *accelerated accumulation,* accelerated growth, accelerated self-expansion of previously idle capital and the accelerated devalorization of capital previously invested in Department I but now technically obsolescent. This first phase is followed by a second, in which the actual transformation in productive technology has already taken place, i.e., the new production sites for new means of production are for the most part already in existence and can only be further extended or improved in a quantitative sense. It is now a matter of getting the means of production made in these new production sites generally adopted in all branches of industry and economy. The force that determined the sudden extension by leaps and bounds of capital accumulation in Department I thus falls away, and accordingly this phase becomes one of retreating profits, *gradually decelerating accumulation,* decelerating economic growth, gradually increasing difficulties in the valorization of the total accumulated capital, and particularly of new additionally accumulated capital, and the gradual, self-reproducing increase in capital being laid idle.[27]

[26]Friedmann speaks in this connection of the 'second industrial revolution': George Friedmann, *'Sociologie du Travail et Science sociales,'* in G. Friedmann and Pierre Naville, *Traité de Sociologie du Travail,* Paris, 1961, p. 68.

[27]Between 1900 and 1912 the value of fixed capital in American non-agricultural enterprises doubled; it rose, at fixed prices (1947-49 dollars), from $16.8 billion to $31.4 billion. Between 1912 and 1929 it increased again, although at a slower rhythm, from $31.4 billion to $53.6 billion. It then remained almost constant for 18 years, after the Great Depression the figure $53 billion was not reached again until 1945, followed by a slight fall in 1946. In 1947 the figure was still only $54.9 billion and the peak of 1929 was finally surpassed only in 1948, with $63.3 billion. In the same period, however, bank assets increased from $72 billion in 1929 to $162 billion in 1945, and the assets of life insurance companies went up

According to this scheme, which covers the successive phases of accelerated growth until 1823, of decelerated growth 1824-47, of accelerated growth 1848-73, of decelerated growth 1874-93, of accelerated growth 1894-1913, of decelerated growth 1914-39,[28] of accelerated growth 1940-45 and 1948-66, we should today have entered into the second phase of the 'long wave' which began with the Second World War, characterized by decelerated capital accumulation. The more rapid succession of recessions in the most important imperialist economies (France 1962; Italy 1963; Japan 1964; West Germany 1966-67; USA 1969-71; Great Britain 1970-71; Italy 1971 and the world-wide recession of 1974-75) seems to confirm this hypothesis.

Obviously these 'long waves' do not assert themselves in a mechanical fashion, but function through the articulation of the 'classical cycles'.[29] In a phase of expansion the cyclical periods of boom will be longer and more intensive, the cyclical crises of over-production shorter and more superficial. Conversely, in those phases of the long wave where a tendency to stagnation is prevalent the periods of boom will prove less feverish and more transitory, while the periods of cyclical crisis of over-production will, by contrast, be longer and profounder. The 'long wave' is conceivable only as the result of these cyclical fluctuations and never as some kind of metaphysical superimposition upon them.

The first writer who seems to have discerned these 'long waves' in the history of capitalism was the Russian Marxist, Alexander Helphand (Parvus).[30] Through a study of agricultural crises he came to the conclusion, in the mid-1890s, that the long depression

from $17.5 billion to nearly $45 billion, i.e., with a dollar devaluation of approximately 30%, the increase was still 70% in the case of bank assets, and 100% in that of the insurance companies. US Department of Commerce, *Long-Term Economic Growth 1860-1965*, Washington, 1966, pp. 186, 200-2, 209.

[28] In principle we start every long period with the year after the crisis which has just ended a 'classical cycle', and end the long period with a crisis-year. Since crisis-years are not completely identical in all the capitalist countries, we have chosen those of the most important capitalist country, which sets the tone for the world market, i.e., Great Britain up to the First World War and thenceforth the USA.

[29] The Russian Marxist Bogdanov tried to call the possibility of this into question. Many opponents of 'long waves' have followed in his path. See our reply further below.

[30] This may be incorrect in the strict sense. Schumpeter reports that Jevons quotes an article by Hyde Clark entitled 'Political Economy', which allegedly records the existence of 'long waves' in cyclical economic development. The article appeared in the periodical *Railway Register*, 1874, but it had no influence on the further discussion of the problem: Joseph Schumpeter, *History of Economic Analysis*, New York, 1954.

which began in 1873 and to which Friedrich Engels had attached such great importance[31] ought soon to be replaced by a new long-term upswing. He expressed this idea for the first time in an article which appeared in the *Sächsische Arbeiterzeitung* in 1896, and then further elaborated it in his 1901 brochure, *Die Handelskrise und die Gewerkschaften*.[32] Basing himself on a well-known passage from Marx,[33] Parvus used the notion of a *Sturm und Drang* period of capital to provide a conceptual framework for 'long waves' of expansion followed by long waves of 'economic depression'. The determinant of this long-term wave-movement was for Parvus the extension of the world market by changes which were 'under way in all areas of the capitalist economy — in technology, the money market, trade, the colonies' — and were lifting 'the whole of world production onto a new and much more comprehensive basis'.[34] He did not give statistical data in support of his thesis; and he committed grave errors in his periodization.[35] Despite this, however, his sketch remains the brilliant attempt of a Marxist thinker possessed of a mind which was uncommonly acute, even if also undisciplined and inconsequent.[36]

More than ten years were to pass before this fertile idea of Parvus — which had won the immediate praise of Kautsky[37] — was taken up once more, this time by the Dutch Marxist J. Van Gelderen.[38] In 1913, under the pseudonym of J. Fedder, Van Gelderen published a series of three articles in the periodical of the Dutch 'left', *De Nieuwe Tijd*, in which, taking as his starting

[31] See, among other things, Engel's footnote in *Capital*, Vol.3, p. 489.

[32] Parvus, *Die Handelskrise und die Gewerkschaften*, Munich, 1901, pp. 26-7.

[33] We quote it in Chapter 3 of this book. See footnote 32 of the third chapter.

[34] Parvus, op. cit., p. 26.

[35] Thus he says that the *Sturm und Drang* period began in the 1860's and ended at the start of the 1870's, while it is now generally accepted that there was a 'long wave' of expansion from the 1847 crisis until 1873.

[36] Parvus was, among other things, together with Trotsky the originator of the theory of permanent revolution applied to Russia which, in contrast to the views of all other Russian Marxists, foresaw a workers' government as the outcome of the coming Russian revolution. But while Parvus envisaged a social-democratic government on the Australian pattern (i.e., a government which would remain within the framework of the capitalist mode of production), Trotsky was of the opinion as early as 1906 that the Russian revolution would lead to the dictatorship of the proletariat based on the support of the poor peasants.

[37] Karl Kautsky, 'Krisentheorien', in *Die Neue Zeit*, Vol.XX, 1901-1902, p. 137.

[38] Simultaneously with Van Gelderen — and independently of him — Albert Aftalion (*Les Crises Périodiques de Surproduction*), M. Tugan—Baranovsky (in the French edition of his *Studien zur Theorie und Geschichte der Handelskrisen in England*), J. Lescure, (*Des Crises Générales et Périodiques de Surproduction*), and

point the price rises everywhere discernible in the capitalist countries, he constructed a hypothesis of 'long waves' for the history of capitalism since the middle of the 19th century. These articles, which have received far too little attention in Marxist literature up till now, raised the whole problem onto a level which was qualitatively much higher than that on which it had been placed by Parvus or Kautsky. Van Gelderen not only attempted to assemble empirical evidence for his thesis and to follow in detail the movement of prices, foreign trade, output and productive capacity in many spheres, as well as movements of the bank rate, capital accumulation and the foundation of businesses, and so on.[39] He also tried to *explain* the long-term wave-movement of the capitalist mode of production, and in so doing he started out, in contrast to Parvus, not from the extension of the market, but from the extension of production: 'The precondition for the genesis of a spring tide in the capitalist economy[40] is an extension of production, whether spontaneous or gradual. This creates a demand for other products, indirectly always products of the industry making means of production, and raw materials. The nature of the demand generated by the extension of production ... can take the following two main forms:

1. Through the reclamation of sparsely inhabited regions. In these areas agriculture or animal husbandry provide the population with export products with which to pay for the wares it needs. The latter are of two kinds: mass-consumption goods, mostly manufactures, and materials for production: machines, elements for railways and other types of communication, building materials. The rise in prices which is the consequence of this demand spreads from one branch of production to another.

2. Through the quite sudden rise of a branch of production which is in a stronger position than was the case previously to satisfy a particular human need (automobile and electric industry). The effect

W. Pareto (in 1913) marginally noted the problem of 'long waves'. but only in a fragmentary way and without coming anywhere near the scope of Van Gelderen's analysis. See in this connection, Ulrich Weinstock, *Das Problem der Kondratieff-Zyklen*, Berlin and Munich, 1964, pp. 20-2. It is therefore not necessary to consider them here.

[39] J. Fedder, 'Springvloed-Beschouwingen over industrieele ontwikkeling en prijsbeweging', in *De Nieuwe Tijd*, Nos. 4, 5, 6, April, May, June, Vol.18, 1913.

[40] Van Gelderen calls the expansive 'long wave' the *springvloed* (spring tide) and the recessive 'long wave' the ebb.

of this is the same, on a smaller scale, as that of the first form.[41]

The conclusion that Van Gelderen drew from this analysis — independently of Kautsky, who formulated something similar at this time[42] — was that an expanding 'long wave' is typically preceded by a major increase in gold production.[43] Admittedly, his explanation suffered from a pronounced dualism, for 'spring-tides' were attributed either to the extension of the world market or to the development of new branches of production. Moreover, he failed to realize that the question of additional capital investments cannot be reduced to the production of money *material* (i.e., gold production) but constitutes a problem of the additional production and accumulation of *surplus-value*. One cannot demand of a pioneer, however, that he should straightaway provide satisfactory answers to all the aspects of a newly discovered complex of problems. For there can be no doubt that Van Gelderen's work was of a pioneering kind. Of the further elaborations of the theory of 'long waves' in the 1920s and 1930s—from Kondratieff to Schumpeter and Dupriez — hardly one went beyond the ideas developed by Van Gelderen. The inadequacy of the statistical material at his disposal does not detract from the pioneering quality of his contribution. Ulrich Weinstock is wrong to accuse him of arriving at 'the establishment of a peculiar change of tempo in all spheres of economic activity' on the basis of evidence embracing a mere 60 years, and to state that this should be 'rejected out of hand'.[44] What is at stake is not the formal question of the adequacy or inadequacy of Van Gelderen's evidence. The real point is the correctness or otherwise of Van Gelderen's working hypothesis in the light of the data at our disposal today. Weinstock omits to apply this test and cannot therefore appreciate the anticipatory quality of Van Gelderen's work.

The First World War was barely over when thinkers in the young Soviet State began to concern themselves in depth with the question

[41]J. Fedder, op. cit., pp. 447-8.

[42]Karl Kautsky, 'Die Wandlungen der Goldproduktion und der wechselnde Charakter der Teuerung', Supplement to *Die Neue Zeit*, No. 16, 1912-1913, Stuttgart, 24 January 1913. On page 20 of this essay, Kautsky explains the long-term downswing and upswing of prices, in the periods 1818-49, 1850-73, 1874-96 and 1897-1910, by the long-term fluctuations of gold production.

[43]J. Fedder, op. cit., pp. 448-9. This is also at least partially the explanation for 'long waves' advanced today by the Belgian professor Léon Dupriez (see further below).   [44]Weinstock, op. cit., p. 28.

of 'long waves'. N. D. Kondratieff, a former Deputy Minister of Food in Kerensky's Provisional Government, had been interested in the problem since 1919, and in 1920 he founded the Moscow Institute for Conjunctural Research (*Koniunkturny Institut*), which proceeded to collect material for his own 'theory of long waves'.[45] Leon Trotsky, who was working on the question of the post-war development of capitalism as compared to its development before 1914, also explored this complex of problems — although probably without an acquaintance with Van Gelderen's work,[46] which suffered the disadvantage of being written in a language accessible to few Marxists or economists. In his famous report on the world situation at the Third Congress of the Communist International, Trotsky declared on the question of long waves: 'In January of this year, the London *Times* published a table covering a period of 138 years — from the war of the thirteen American colonies for independence to our own day. In this interval there have been 16 cycles, i.e., 16 crises and 16 phases of prosperity . . . . If we analyze the curve of development more closely, we shall find that it falls into five segments, five different and distinct periods. From 1781 to 1851 the development is "very slow", there is scarcely any movement observable. We find that in the course of 70 years foreign trade rises only from £2 to £5 per capita. After the Revolution of 1848 which acted to extend the framework of the European market, there comes a breaking point. From 1851 to 1873, the curve of development rises steeply. In 22 years foreign trade climbs from £5 to £21 while the quantity of iron rises in the same period from 4.5 kg. to 13 kg. per capita. Then from 1873 on there follows an epoch of depression. From 1873 till approximately 1894 we notice stagnation in English trade . . . there is a drop from £21 to £17.4 — in the course of 22 years. Then comes another boom, lasting till the year 1913 — foreign trade rises from £17 to £30. Then finally with the year 1914, the fifth period begins — the period of the destruction of capitalist economy. How are the cyclical fluctuations blended with the primary movement of the capitalist curve of development? Very simply. In periods of capitalist development the crises are brief

[45] See the article on N. D. Kondratieff written by George Garvy for the Sixth Volume of the *International Encyclopedia of Social Sciences*, London, 1968.
[46] Kondratieff says, at any rate, that he was unacquainted with Van Gelderen's work when he wrote his Russian articles in 1922-25 and his famous 1926 German essay, 'Die langen Wellen der Konjunktur', in *Archiv für Sozialwissenschaft und Socialpolitik*, Vol. 56, No. 3, December 1926, p. 599ff. There is no reason to doubt the truth of this statement.

and superficial in character, while the booms are long-lasting and far-reaching. In periods of capitalist decline, the crises are of a prolonged character while the booms are fleeting, superficial and speculative.'[47]

Trotsky went on to speak of the *Sturm und Drang* period of capital after 1850 — in obvious reference to his former associate Parvus[48] — and concluded with two predictions: first, that in the short term a certain upswing of capitalism was not only economically possible but inevitable, although this upswing would be short and in no way precluded the historical chance of a socialist revolution in Europe. Second, that in the long term, 'after two or three decades', if the revolutionary activity of the European working class were to suffer a lasting setback, there was the possibility of a new expansion of capitalism.[49] In the following months Trotsky returned to the same problem in passing on several occasions,[50] but upon the appearance of Kondratieff's first work he dealt with the subject once more in the context of a letter to the editorial board of *Viestnik Sotsialisticheskoi Akademii*. In this letter he reaffirmed his conviction that besides the 'normal' industrial cycles there were longer periods in the history of capitalism which were of great importance for the understanding of the long-term development of the capitalist mode of production: 'This is the schema in the rough. We observe in history that homogeneous cycles are grouped in series. Entire epochs of capitalist development exist when a number of cycles is characterized by sharply delineated booms and weak, short-lived crises. As a result, we have a sharply rising movement of the basic curve of capitalist development. There obtain epochs of stagnation when this curve, while passing through partial cyclical oscillations, remains on approximately the same level for decades. Finally, during certain historical periods the basic curve, while passing as always through cyclical oscillations, dips downward as a whole, signalizing the decline of the productive

[47]Trotsky, 'Report on the World Economic Crisis and the New Tasks of the Communist International', Second Session, June 23, 1921, of the Third Congress of the Communist International, in Leon Trotsky, *The First Five Years of the Communist International,* Vol. 1, New York, 1945, p. 201.

[48]Ibid., p. 207.

[49]Ibid., p. 211.

[50]Trotsky: 'Flood-tide — the Economic Conjuncture and the World Labour Movement', *Pravda,* 25 December 1921, republished in Trotsky, *The First Five Years of the Comintern,* New York, 1953, pp. 79-84; Trotsky, 'Report on the Fifth Anniversary of the October Revolution and the Fourth World Congress of the Communist International', (20 October 1922), ibid., pp. 198-200.

forces.'[51] Trotsky even gave concrete specifications as to how a study of the 'long-term curve of capitalist development' should be under-taken, emphasizing that empirical investigations along these lines would be of exceptional importance in the enrichment of the theory of historical materialism.[52] What is most striking in this context is Trotsky's emphasis on the need to go beyond the limitations of 'purely' economic data and to integrate into any serious investiga-tion a whole series of social and political developments. This was in the tenor of his sharp criticism of Kondratieff's first study,[53] whose proof of the existence of 'long cycles' was based on purely statistical evidence: 'Following the Third World Congress of the Comintern, Professor Kondratieff approached this problem — as usual pain-stakingly evading the formulation of the question adopted by the Congress itself — and attempted to set up alongside of the "minor cycle", covering a period of ten years, the concept of a "major cycle", embracing approximately fifty years. According to this symmetrical-ly stylized construction a major economic cycle consists of some five minor cycles, and furthermore, half of them have the character of boom, while the other half is that of crises, with all the necessary transitional stages. The statistical determinations of major cycles compiled by Kondratieff should be subjected to careful and not overcredulous verification, both in respect to individual countries as well as the world market as a whole. It is already possible to refute in advance Professor Kondratieff's attempt to invest epochs labelled by him "major cycles" with the selfsame "rigidly lawful rhythm" that is observable in minor cycles; it is an obviously false generalization from a formal analogy. The periodic recurrence of minor cycles is conditioned by the internal dynamics of capitalist forces, and manifests itself always and everywhere, once the market comes into existence. As regards the large segments of the capitalist curve of development (50 years) which Professor Kondratieff incautiously proposes to designate also as cycles, their character and duration is determined not by the internal interplay of capita-list forces but by those external conditions through whose channel

[51] Trotsky, 'The Curve of Capitalist Development', first published as a letter to the editorial board of *Viestnik Sotsialisticheskoi Akademii* dated 21 April 1923, and pub-lished in the fourth number of this periodical, April-July 1923. We cite here the English translation, which appeared in *Fourth International*, May 1941, p. 112.
[52] Ibid., p. 114.
[53] The work in question is N. D. Kondratieff, *Die Weltwirtschaft und ihre Bedingungen während und nach dem Krieg*, Moscow, 1922.

capitalist development flows. The acquisition by capitalism of new countries and continents, the discovery of new natural resources, and, in the wake of these, such major facts of a "superstructural" order as wars and revolutions, determine the character and the replacement of ascending, stagnating or declining epoch of capitalist development.'[54]

George Garvy has interpreted this text to mean that although Trotsky accepted the existence of long-term fluctuations, he denied that they had a cyclical character.[55] This view is not quite accurate, unless we are to reduce the whole pattern to a pointless dispute as to the semantic differences between cycles, 'long waves', 'long periods' and 'large segments of the capitalist curve of development'. Trotsky put forward two central arguments against Kondratieff's thesis: first, that the *analogy* between 'long waves' and classical 'cycles' is false, i.e., that long waves are not possessed of the same 'natural necessity' as classical cycles. Second, that while classical cycles can be explained exclusively in terms of the internal dynamics of the capitalist mode of production, the explanation of long waves demands 'a more concrete study of the capitalist curve and the interrelationship between the latter and all the aspects of social life'.[56] In other words, Trotsky objected to a monocausal theory of 'long waves' constructed by analogy with Marx's explanation of classical cycles by the renewal of fixed capital.

These two criticisms — which were shared by many Soviet economists in the 1920s[57] — can be fully endorsed. If we have defined the 'long waves' as long waves of accelerated and decelerated accumulation determined by long waves in the rise and decline of the rate of profit, then it is plain that this ascent and decline is not determined by one single factor but must be explained by a series of social changes, in which the factors listed by Trotsky play a major role. The following table will help to make this clear:

[54]Trotsky, op. cit., pp. 112-14.
[55]Garvy, 'Kondratieff's Theory of Long Cycles', in *The Review of Economic Statistics*, Vol. XXV, No. 4, November 1943, pp. 203-20.
[56]Trotsky, op. cit., p. 114.
[57]Garvy quotes in this context the views of Bogdanov, Oparin, Studensky, Novozhilov, Granovsky and Guberman. See also Herzenstein. 'Gibt es grosse Konjunkturzyklen?', *Unter dem Banner des Marxismus*, 1929, Nos. 1-2: 'Basing himself on the deceptively cyclical appearance of long-term price waves, (Kondratieff explains) the uneven dynamic of the material forces of production by a rhythmical mechanism of conjunctural changes' (p. 123).

Long Wave	Main Tonality	Movement of the Value Components of Industrial Commodities	Origins of this Movement
1 1793-1825	expansive, rising rate of profit	Cf : rising steeply Cc: rising steeply, then falling v : falling s/v: rising	Artisan-produced machines, agriculture lags behind industry – rising prices for raw materials. Fall in real wages with a slow expansion of the industrial proletariat and mass unemployment. Vigorous expansion of the world market (South America).
2 1826-1847	slackening, stagnant rate of profit	Cf : rising Cc: falling s/v: stabilizes	Dwindling of profits made from competition with pre-capitalist production in England and Western Europe. Growing value of C neutralizes the higher rate of surplus-value. Expansion of the world market decelerates.
3 1848-1873	expansive, rising rate of profit	Cf : falling Cc: stable, then rising v : falling s/v: rising	Transition to machine-made machines lowers the value of Cf. Cc rises; but rise cannot keep pace with fall of Cf. Massive expansion of the world market following the growing industrialization and extension of railway construction in the whole of Europe and North America, as a result of the 1848 Revolution.
4 1874-1893	slackening, rate of profit falls, then stagnates, then rises slightly	Cf : rising Cc: falling v : slowly rising s/v: first falling then rising again	Machine-made machines are generalized. The commodities produced with them no longer produce a surplus-profit. The increased organic composition of capital leads to a decline in the average rate of profit. In Western Europe real wages rise. The results of the growing export of capital and the fall in the prices of raw materials only gradually permit an increase in capital accumulation. Relative stagnation of the world market.

Long Wave	Main Tonality	Movement of the Value Components of Industrial Commodities		Origins of this Movement
5 1894-1913	expansive, rate of profit rising, then stagnant	Cf : Cc : v : s/v:	falling rising, but slowly slowly rising, then stable rising steeply, then stable	The capital investments in the colonies, the breakthrough of imperialism, the generalization of monopolies, profiting even further from the notably slow rise in the price of raw materials, and promoted by the second technological revolution with its accompanying steep rise in the productivity of labour and the rate of surplus-value, permit a general increase in the rate of profit, which explains the rapid growth of capital accumulation. Vigorous expansion of the world market (Asia, Africa, Oceania).
6 1914-1939	regressive, rate of profit falling sharply	Cf : Cc : v : s/v:	stable falling falling, then stable, then falling falling, then stable (in Germany, rising from 1934)	The outbreak of the War, the disruption of world trade, the regression of material production, determine growing difficulties in the valorization of capital, reinforced by the victory of the Russian Revolution and the narrowing of the world market which it provoked.
7 1940/45-1966	expansive, rate of profit first rising, then slowly starting to fall	Cf : Cc : v : · s/v:	rising falls first stable or falling, then slowly rising steeply rising, then stable	The weakening (and partial atomization) of the working class determined by fascism and the Second World War permit a massive rise in the rate of profit, which promotes the accumulation of capital. This is first thrown into armaments production, then into the innovations of the third technological revolution, which significantly cheapens constant capital and thus promotes a long-term rise in the rate of profit. The world market shrinks through autarky, world war and the extension of non-capitalist zones (Eastern Europe, China, North Korea, North Vietnam, Cuba), but

Long Wave	Main Tonality	Movement of the Value Components of Industrial Commodities	Origins of this Movement
8 1967–...	slackening, rate of profit falling	Cf : stable and rising Cc: falling, then abruptly rising v : slowly rising, then stable s/v: stabilized	is then significantly extended by the intensification of the international division of labour in the imperialist countries and the beginnings of industrialization in the semi-colonies. The slow absorption of the 'industrial reserve army' in the imperialist countries acts as a block to a further rise in the rate of surplus-value despite increasing automation. The class struggle attacks the rate of profit. The intensification of international competition and the world currency crisis work in the same direction. Slow-down in the expansion of world trade.

Once it has been established that the upward and downward curves of a 'long wave' are determined by the criss-crossing of very different factors, and it is emphasized that these 'long waves' do not possess the same built-in periodicity as the classical cycles in the capitalist mode of production, then there is no reason to deny their close connection with the central mechanism, which is by its very nature a synthetic expression of *all* the changes to which capital is permanently subject: the fluctuations in the rate of profit.[58]

At the same time as Kondratieff, but independently of him, the Dutch Marxist Sam De Wolff attempted to refine Van Gelderen's thesis statistically, among other things by working out 'decycled' figure-series. In the process, however, he carried Kondratieff's error of a formal analogy with the classical cycles, already pointed out by Trotsky, to an even greater extreme by postulating an 'absolute regularity' for the 'long cycles'—2½ 'classical cycles per long cycle'. De Wolff attributed a rigid length to the one and the other, although he thought that the duration of the 'classical cycle' would gradually decrease from 10 to 9, then to 8 and even to 7 years.[59] De Wolff's analysis of 1924 was dominated by the development of prices and gold production and in this sense provided no explanation for the 'long waves', thus regressing behind Van Gelderen's account. In a work which appeared in 1929,[60] he did admittedly offer such an explanation, which was very similar to that of Kondratieff and was based on the reconstitution of very durable fixed capital such as buildings, gas factories, rolling-stock, pipes, cables, and so on. A rigid analogy with Marx's explanation of 'classical cycles' was postulated once again; its validity has never been verified empirically.[61]

---

[58] See in this context the importance that Tinbergen and Kalecki attribute to profit and the rate of profit — although obviously not defined in the Marxist sense of the terms — in the industrial cycle. Tinbergen and Polak, *The Dynamics of Business Cycles*, London, 1950, p. 167, 170f. etc. Michael Kalecki, *Theory of Economic Dynamics*.

[59] Sam de Wolff: 'Prosperitats- und Depressionsperioden', in Otto Jenssen (ed.), *Der Lebendige Marxismus*, Jena, 1924, pp. 30, 38-9.

[60] Sam de Wolff: *Het Economisch getij*, Amsterdam, 1929, pp. 416-19.

[61] Thus the building or building-and-transport cycles discerned by Isard, Riggleman, Alvin Hansen and others in the USA have an average length of only 17-18 years, and not 38 as de Wolff assumed. See Walter Isard, 'A neglected cycle: the transport-building cycle', in *Review of Economic Statistics*, Vol. 34, 1942, republished in Hansen and Clemence, *Readings in Business Cycles and National Income*, London, 1953, p. 467, 479. For the building cycle — often called the 'Kuznets cycle' — in the USA, see Simon Kuznets, *Long Term Changes in National Income of the United States*

Kondratieff's famous attempt to isolate and define 'long waves'[62] was later elevated into 'the' explanation of long periods *par excellence* by Schumpeter. In its first mature form,[63] however, Kondratieff still wavered to and fro between different types of the explanation. He retained the notion that the 'ebb-periods' of long waves were characterized by severe agricultural depressions, while typical features of 'long periods of upswing' included the application of many discoveries and inventions dating from the previous phase, an acceleration of gold extraction, and great social upheavals, including wars. In direct (but unacknowledged) reference to Trotsky's criticism, Kondratieff polemicized against the 'essential' but not 'watertight' consideration that 'long waves', in contrast to those of medium length, were 'determined by contingent circumstances and external events', 'for example by changes in technology, wars and revolutions, the integration of new countries into the world economy and fluctuations in the extraction of gold'.[64] These factors, which he himself emphasized, were said to be *effects* and not *causes*; the rhythmic movement of these factors, whose influence he did not deny in the least, were said to be explicable only by the long-term fluctuations of economic development. Thus, for example, he argued that it is 'not the incorporation of new regions (which gives) impetus to the ascent of long waves in the economy, but on the contrary, a new upswing which, by accelerating the tempo of the economic dynamic of the capitalist countries, makes it possible and necessary to exploit new countries and new markets for sales and raw materials.'[65]

This in itself did not yet provide an explanation of the 'long waves', which was to follow two years later in Kondratieff's second German essay.[66] His explanation was mainly based on the longevity of 'large investments', the fluctuations of savings activity, the idleness of money capital (loan capital) and the consequences of a low

---

since 1869, Cambridge, USA, 1952. For both the connection and (in part) contrary course of the American and English building cycles, see the essays collected in Derek Aldcroft and Peter Fearon (eds.), *British Economic Fluctuations 1790-1939*, London, 1972.

[62] N. D. Kondratieff, 'Die langen Wellen der Konjunktur'.

[63] Probably influenced by the criticisms of Trotsky and other Russian Marxists, Kondratieff replaced the notion of 'long cycles' with that of 'long waves' in 1926. But in substance his 'waves' are identical with cycles.

[64] Kondratieff, op. cit., p. 593.   [65] Ibid., p. 593.

[66] Kondratieff, *Die Preisdynamik der industriellen und landwirtschaftlichen Waren (Zum Problem der relativen Dynamik und Konjunktur),* referred to earlier.

price level continuing over a long period: 'These goods (large invest-ments, ameliorations, cadres of qualified labour, and so on) have a capacity for long-term use. Their construction or production requires longish periods, extending beyond the span of the ordinary commercial and industrial cycles. The process of extending the fund of such capital goods is neither continuous nor regular. The existence of long economic waves is connected precisely with the mechanism of the extension of this fund; the period of its accelerated expansion coincides with the ascending wave, while the period in which the production of these capital goods slackens or stagnates coincides with the descending wave of the large cycle. The production of the kind of capital goods in question necessitates a vast outlay of capital, over a relatively long time-span. The occurrence of such periods of increased production of capital goods, i.e., periods of long ascending waves, is hence dependent on a series of pre-conditions. These preconditions are: 1. A high intensity of saving activity. 2. A relatively abundant and cheap supply of loan capital. 3. Its accumulation in the hands of powerful enterprises and centres of finance. 4. A low level of commodity prices, which acts as a stimulant to savings activity and long-term capital investments. The presence of these preconditions creates a situation which will lead sooner or later to an increase in the production of the kind of basic capital goods mentioned above and hence to the emergence of a long ascendant economic wave.'[67] After he seems to have given a closed explanation of 'long waves' in this way, Kondratieff shifts to an investigation of the different rhythms with which the average productivity of labour develops in agriculture and in industry, coming to the conclusion that the 'increase in the purchas-ing power of agricultural goods' determined by the retardation of the productivity of agrarian labour ultimately sets in motion the 'long waves', because thereby the demand for all commodities is quickened.[68]

[67] Ibid., p. 37.
[68] Ibid., p. 58-59. Probably without having read Kondratieff's article, De Wolff formulated a not dissimilar explanation for classical cycles, which he related to sun spot cycles. Years with minimum sunspots would determine bad harvests, hence advantageous exchange relations for agriculture, and years with maximum sun spots a rich harvest and hence good exchange relations for industry, hence increased profits and increased investment of fixed capital. De Wolff however expressly re-stricted this argument, which relied on Jevons, to the launching period of industrial capitalism. Sam de Wolff, *Het economisch getij*, pp. 286-7.

Kondratieff's own retort to his critics applies equally well to the five causal relations listed by him: he has by no means proved that these are causes and not effects. The increased gap between supply and demand for agricultural goods in the expansive .'long waves' up to the First World War might well be regarded more as an effect than as a cause of general expansion: growing employment and increasing industrial output in fact create a demand of this kind, while agrarian production is less elastic than industrial.[69] If there is a rise in the prices of agricultural raw materials and foodstuffs, however, then the effects not only on the demand for industrial goods but also on the rate of profit ought to be investigated, and this Kondratieff failed to do. He was thus unable to answer the question as to why the 'falling purchasing power of industrial commodities' does not rapidly stifle expansion.

Idle money capital (loan-capital) is a characteristic of every crisis; why does this capital remain idle for long periods — despite the low rate of interest — instead of being invested productively? The same question applies to an increase in savings activity and growing concentration of capital, which could rather be described as constants of capitalist development (with brief interruptions at the peak of successive 'booms') than as variables.[70] Moreover, as far as 'long-lived capital goods' are concerned,[71] the same objection applies as to the similar thesis of De Wolff: 'capital goods' with a productive life of forty to fifty years play only a marginal role in capitalism. If the means of production in question have a shorter life-span than this, then no 'echo effect' can evoke a forty to fifty year cycle. The upward and downward movements of capital laid idle and capital productively invested would then be restricted largely to the ten year cycle. By excluding from his argument two crucial determinants — long-term fluctuations in the average rate of profit and the influence of technological revolutions on the volume and value of renewed fixed capital — Kondratieff himself barred the way to the solution of the question he had raised. The methodological basis of the errors made by Kondratieff in working out an

[69] Kondratieff himself emphasized this, op. cit., p. 60.

[70] It is true that periods of accelerated capital accumulation are also characterized by an increased mobilization of capital. The period 1849-73 witnessed the expansion of stock exchanges and joint-stock companies; the period 1893-1913 that of trusts, investment banks and holding companies; the period 1945-67 that of common investment funds, convertible bonds, eurocheques, and so on.

[71] In his reflections on this subject, Kondratieff was clearly influenced by Professor Spiethoff's article, 'Krisen', in *Handwörterbuch der Staatswissenschaften*, Vol. 4,

explanation of 'long waves' can be attributed to his exaggerated *fixation on price fluctuations* and *insufficient analysis of fluctuations in industrial production and the growth of productivity*. In the final resort this can be traced back to his rejection, or revision, of Marx's theory of value and money.

Joseph Schumpeter, who was responsible for the most thorough treatment of 'long waves in the economy',[72] tried to avoid these mistakes. Starting from his general theory of capitalist development, which he had already completed[73] when Kondratieff drew his attention to 'long waves', he worked out a concept of 'long waves' which was based on the 'innovatory activity of entrepreneurs', i.e., remained in harmony with his overall theory of capitalism. He also sought to give greater importance to production-series than to price-series, although he appears to have failed empirically in this respect.[74] Moreover, the problem as to why innovation is introduced on a massive scale ('in clusters') in certain periods cannot be satisfactorily resolved without a more thorough treatment of 1) the role of productive technology; and 2) the long-term fluctuations in the *rate of profit*. Precisely these two factors are inadequately explored in Schumpeter's *magnum opus*. This is all the more astonishing in that Schumpeter fully acknowledged the central importance of the problem of profit.[75]

The most systematic critiques so far of Schumpeter's and Kondratieff's theories of 'long waves' have been made by Herzenstein and Garvy (for Kondratieff), Kuznets (for Schumpeter) and Weinstock.[76] They are not very convincing. The technical inadequacies of Kondratieff's statistical methods, the arbitrary selection of starting and finishing points for the 'long waves' and the unconvincing nature of Schumpeter's series except as regards price levels, can all be granted. The fact still remains that economic historians are practically unanimous in distinguishing major expansion in the years 1848-73, pronounced long-term depression in the years 1873-93,

---

1923. A revised edition of this article can be found in Arthur Spiethoff, *Die wirtschaftlichen Wechsellagen,*Tubingen, 1955.

[72]Joseph Schumpeter, *Business Cycles,* 2 Vols., New York, 1939.

[73]Joseph Schumpeter, *Die Theorie der wirtschaftlichen Entwicklung,* 1911. (English: *The Theory of Economic Development,* New York, 1961).

[74]Weinstock, op, cit., pp. 87-90.

[75]For example, Schumpeter, *Business Cycles,* pp. 15-17, 105-6, etc.

[76]Garvy, op. cit., Weinstock, op. cit.; Kuznets, 'Schumpeter's Business Cycles', in *Economic Change,* New York, 1953, pp. 105-24. Weinstock relies heavily on Garvy's critique of Kondratieff and Kuznets's critique of Schumpeter.

a tempestuous increase in economic activity in the years 1893-1913, strongly decelerated, if not stagnant and regressive development between the two World Wars, and a renewed major increase in growth after the Second World War.[77] Only with regard to the 'first Kondratieff'— i.e., the alleged alternation of faster growth 1793-1823 and of slower growth 1824-47 — is there any, partly justified, doubt.[78] Such a succession of at least five 'long waves' cannot be attributed either to pure accident or to various exogenous factors.

Herzenstein's critique of Kondratieff exposed most of the errors in his theoretical explanation. But he bent the stick too far in the other direction, when he sought to refute the very existence of 'long waves' empirically. He improperly extrapolated trends from the economic development of the USA and thereby tried to confine the long upswing of 1849-73, as well as the protracted depression of 1873-93, to Great Britain alone. The statistical material assembled at the end of this chapter, however, proves beyond any doubt that these two long waves manifestly swept the entire *world* production and *world* market of 19th-century capitalism. Herzenstein,

[77] It would extend too far to list bibliographical references for the feverish expansion of the world economy from 1848-73, in the period between the 1890's and the First World War, and the period following the Second World War, or for the major world depressions. There is an extensive bibliography on the 'long depression' of the period 1873-1896 in Hans Rosenberg, 'Political and Social Consequences of the Great Depression of 1873-1896', in *The Economic History Review*, Nos. 1-2, 1943, pp. 58-61.

[78] The reason for this was already explained by Marx a century ago, in a passage added to the French translation of the First Volume of *Capital:* 'But only when mechanical industry had struck its roots so deep that it exercised an overwhelming influence over the whole of national production; when the world market had successively mastered widespread areas of the New World, Asia and Australia; and when, finally, a sufficient number of industrial nations had entered the arena — only from this time on do there occur those constantly self-generating cycles, embracing years in their successive phases, which always end in a general crisis, constituting the conclusion of one cycle and the starting point of the next'. (This passage is not included in the English edition of *Capital*; it should appear before the last sentence on p. 633 — *translator.*) The fact that many historians and economists nevertheless assert the existence of a long wave 1793-1847 is due, not only to successive price movements, but to the feverish expansion of world trade (especially British commerce) from the outbreak of the industrial revolution to the aftermath of the Napoleonic Wars, which was then followed by the stagnation or even contraction of international trade. English exports, which had reached an annual average value of £43.5 million in 1815-19, declined to £36.8 million in 1820-24, then to £36 million in 1825-29 and £38·7 million in 1830-34. The 1815-19 level was not attained again in absolute figures until 1835-39, and in per capita terms until the end of the 1840's.

in fact, went so far as to reject even the increased growth of the 1893-1913 period, on the basis of one insubstantial article in a single journal. His theoretical arguments against Kondratieff were more interesting. He objected to the latter's attempt to 'classify historical epochs as periodic cycles', because — he wrote — Kondratieff's series of 'unique historical constellations . . . leading to fundamental changes in the general conditions of the world market and the inter-relations between the territorial sectors of this market', was logically incapable of explaining 'repeated fluctuations of fixed regularity'.[79] But he overlooked the fact that 'unique historical constellations' on the capitalist world market can indeed be classified into two basic categories; those which cause the average rate of profit to rise, and those which cause it to decline over the long-run. Herzenstein fails to establish that these constellations will have only random and irrelevant effects on the rate of profit. In the absence of such a proof (one that in our view is theoretically and empirically impossible to furnish), there is no reason why 'unique constellations' cannot indeed be regarded as successively promoting long-term upswings and downswings of the average rate of profit — in other words, of capital accumulation and rates of economic growth.

The attempt to interpret 'long waves' out of existence as simple expressions of 'stronger' or 'weaker' classical cycles is equally unconvincing.[80] The fact that long-term economic development is influenced, in rhythmical alternation, more strongly by phases of economic prosperity at one time and phases of crisis and stagnation at another, ought at least to present a problem. As soon as it is acknowledged as such and not as a self-evident fact, an explanation for it must be sought, and we thus come back once more to the problematic of the 'long waves'. Following Kuznets it has become fashionable to replace 'long waves' by 'trends' and arbitrary 'decennial averages'. But here too, a genuine problem is conjured away by its dissolution into very long periods of time. Even the Great Depression of 1929-32 disappears in some of these 'trend calculations'.[81] No one can doubt the existence of that particular crisis, however.

[79] Herzenstein, op. cit., p. 125.

[80] Bogdanov appears to have been the first to make such an attempt. 'The long waves are not independent of the conjunctural cycles, but simply (!) the result of the summation of individual conjunctural cycles of different lengths which happen to (!) fall within each phase of the long cycles.' Garvy quotes this passage with approval, and Weinstock repeats it. (op. cit., p. 50).

[81] Thus Kuznets operates with 'averages' of the 10-year growth of world trade in the

Weinstock argues that the theory of long waves is Marxist in inspiration and therefore unutilizable,[82] basing himself on Popper's polemic against 'historicism'; it is he, of course, and not any Marxist, who thereby reveals unscientific bias. The real issue is ultimately whether or not the existence of 'long waves' has been established, and if so, how they are to be explained. Weinstock further objects that: 'The time-series for output and income, which would be needed for a proof of long waves, cannot be reconstructed for a sufficient number of relatively advanced countries with the necessary reliability for the period since the French Revolution.'[83] In other words, the 'long waves' are not demonstrable statistically. We, on the contrary, regard the main problem *not* as one of statistical verification, but of theoretical explanation,[84] although it goes without saying that, if the theory of 'long waves' could not be confirmed empirically, it would be an unfounded working hypothesis, and ultimately a mystification. Methods of empirical verification must themselves, however, be appropriate to the specific problem to be explained. Price movements, which may be provoked by inflationary development — including, in the context of a gold standard, a greater reduction in the commodity value of precious metals than in the

---

period 1928-63 or even 1913-63 which completely obliterate the specific fact of a marked contraction of world trade in the period 1929-39: Simon Kuznets, 'Quantitative Aspects of the Economic Growth of Nations, M-X Level and Structure of Foreign Trade: Long Term Trends', in *Economic Development and Cultural Change*, Vol.XV, Part II, No. 2, January 1967. This is reminiscent of those notorious 'statistical averages' which would calculate the 'per capita income' of a backward country as $1,000 and use this to determine its 'relative standard of living', without taking into account that this average is the result, say, of a situation in which 75% of the population receive only $100, 24% receive $2,000 and 1% receives $45,000.

[82] Weinstock, op. cit., pp. 62-6. Weinstock comes to the conclusion that long waves must be regarded more as 'historical epochs' than as 'true cycles' (ibid. p. 201), apparently without realizing that the same idea had been formulated forty years before by the Marxist Trotsky. (For the relevant sources, see above, footnotes 51 and 54.)

[83] Weinstock, op. cit., p. 101.

[84] In a posthumous work Lange commented: 'Even though the historical facts cited above (the alternating phases of capitalist production since the year 1825) are not subject to any serious reservations, they are not sufficient proof of the existence of long-range cycles. To prove this theory it would be necessary to show that there exists a causal relation between two consecutive phases of the cycle and nobody has succeeded in showing this.' (Oskar Lange, *Theory of Reproduction and Accumulation*, Warsaw, 1969, pp. 76-7). Although we likewise reject the concept of the 'long cycle' and do not, therefore, accept the mechanical determination of the 'ebb' by the 'flow' and vice versa, we have nevertheless attempted to show that the inner logic of the long wave is determined by long-term oscillations in the rate of profit.

average value of other commodities — are definitely not a reliable indicator.[85] Output figures for individual commodities, which may be heavily influenced in certain periods by the role of particular branches of production as 'growth sectors', should likewise be treated with caution. Income curves, which may be co-determined by inflationary price movements, are also derivative indices and can only be used after fundamental historical analysis. The most convincing indicators consequently appear to be those of industrial output as a whole and the development of the volume of world trade (or of per capita world trade); the former will express the long-term tendency of capitalist *production* and the latter the rhythm of expansion of the *world market*. Precisely where these two indicators are concerned, it is quite possible to provide empirical verification for 'long waves' after the crisis of the year 1847:

Annual cumulative rate of growth of the industrial output of Great Britain[86]

Deane and Cole, *British Economic Growth 1688-1959*, p. 170 (includes the building trade).

1827-1847 : 3.2% [87]
1848-1875 : 4.55%
1876-1893 : 1.2%
1894-1913 : 2.2%
1914-1938 : 2%
1939-1967 : 3%

Annual cumulative rate of growth of the industrial output of Germany[88]
(after 1945: Federal Republic of Germany)

1850 — 1874 : 4.5%
1875 — 1892 : 2.5%
1893 — 1913 : 4.3%
1914 — 1938 : 2.2%
1939 — 1967 : 3.9%

[85]The theses of Gaston Imbert, which are based exclusively on price movements, must therefore be rejected. Gaston Imbert, *Des Mouvements de Longue Durée Kondratieff*, Aix-en-Provence, 1959. David Landes refuses the notion of 'long waves' for the evolution of prices; but he has not thereby in any way refuted their existence. Landes, op. cit., pp. 233-4.

[86]B. R. Mitchell and Phyllis Deane, *Abstract of British Historical Statistics*; the Hoffmann index until 1913; the Lomax index 1914-38 (both without the building trade). Calculations for the period after the Second World War are taken from EEC Office of Statistics and include the building trade.

[87]Average 1801-1811 until average 1831-1841: 4.7%

[88]For the figures until 1938, Walther G. Hoffmann, *Das Wachstum der deutschen Wirtschaft seit der Mitte des 19. Jahrhunderts*, Berlin, 1965. The figures after the Second World War come from the *Statistisches Jahrbuch für die Bundesrepublik*.

Annual cumulative rate of growth of the industrial output of the USA[89]

1849 — 1873	: 5.4%
1874 — 1893	: 4.9%[90]
1894 — 1913	: 5.9%
1914 — 1938	: 2%
1939 — 1967	: 5.2%

Annual cumulative rate of growth of physical per capita output on a world scale[91]

1865 — 1882	: 2.58%
1880 — 1894	: 0.89%
1895 — 1913	: 1.75%
1913 — 1938	: 0.66%

Annual cumulative rate of growth in the volume of world trade[92]

1820 — 1840	: 2.7%
1840 — 1870	: 5.5%
1870 — 1890	: 2.2%
1891 — 1913	: 3.7%
1913 — 1937	: 0.4%
1938 — 1967	: 4.8%

The switch since 1967 from a long wave of expansion to a long wage of much slower growth is statistically confirmed by the respective trends of world industrial production for each period:

Annual Compound Percentage Growth of Industrial Output [93]

	1947-1966	1966-1975
USA	5.0%*	1.9%
Original EEC 'Six'	8.9%	4.6%
Japan	9.6%	7.9%
UK	2.9%	2.0%

*   For the USA, 1940-1966

[89] For the figures 1849-1873, Robert E. Gallmann, 'Commodity-Output 1839-1899, in *Trends in the American Economy in the 19th Century*, Vol. XXIV of *Studies in Income and Wealth*, Princeton, 1960. The later figures are from *Long-Term Economic Growth 1860-1965*, Bureau of the Census, US Department of Commerce.

[90] This figure is much higher than average, because a certain postponement of the 'long wave' was brought about by the Civil War, so that production increased more steeply in the USA than in Europe in the 1880's.

[91] Léon H. Dupriez, *Des Mouvements Economiques Généraux*, Vol. II, Louvain, 1947, p. 567.

[92] Calculated by us from Mulhall, *Dictionary of Statistics*, London 1889; Mulhall and Harper, *Comparative Statistical Tables and Charts of the World*, Philadelphia, 1899; Simon Kuznets, 'Quantitative Growth of the Economic Wealth of Nations'; Ingvar Svennilson, *Growth and Stagnation in the European Economy*, Geneva, 1954; *Statistisches Jahrbuch für die Bundesrepublik Deutschland*, 1969.

[93] Calculations based upon United Nations and OECD statistics. We assume the following rates of decline during the present recession: for 1974: USA -3%, Japan

Dupriez, for his part, published his theory of long waves in economic development in its final form after the Second World War.[94] This theory attributed the decisive role in the explanation of Kondratieff's waves to the deviations of the value of money index from the value of goods index: 'The fundamental connection between the bundle of essential economic processes and contingent historical facts must be sought in the deviation of the value of money index: failing any stabilization of the relation between money and goods, such deviations are virtually inevitable. This is the basic economic reality governing the Kondratieff waves, which determines all the processes linked to price changes. It is the new fact we introduce into the explanation of the secular progress which extends beneath the Kondratieff waves, where it proves to be a much more decisive and straightforward determinant than in business cycles themselves.'[95] The basis of Dupriez's argument rests on the great variability in the demand for capital (Marxists would say: the demand of the industrial capitalists for additional money capital). In the ascendant phase of the long wave, the rising prices which result from a fall in the value of money index, stimulate this demand for capital. Then there occurs a turning point, mostly after wars or revolutions, at which 'the desire for a reorganization of public finances' becomes predominant, the money-value index rises because of the diminished volume of money for credit, and the corresponding deflation and fall in prices act as a damper on the growth of the economy.[96]

The decisive turning point in this whole schema is thus occasioned by a purely psychological factor — which, in exactly the same way as Schumpeter's outstanding entrepreneurial personalities with a proclivity for epoch-making innovations, performs the role of an arbitrary *deus ex machina* in it.[97] Quite apart from this weakness,

---

-3%, EEC -1%, UK -2%; for 1975: USA -2%, Japan -1%, EEC -2%. UK -1%. These assessments probably underestimate the scale of the general recession of 1974-75. Since the rate of growth during the rest of the 70's will certainly be below that of the 60's, especially in Japan, the long-term trend will tend to accentuate rather than to reduce the contrast between the growth rates of the 1947-66 period and the 1967-198? period.

[94] Dupriez, op. cit., and *Konjunkturphilosophie*, Berlin, 1963.

[95] Ibid, pp. 201-2.

[96] Dupriez, *Des Mouvements Economiques Généraux*, pp. 92, 96.

[97] Schumpeter had already worked out this thesis in his *Theory of Economic Development*, where he expressly stated that the appearance of a few 'innovatory personalities' would inevitably provoke a whole wave of innovations. In his *Business Cycles* he further clung to this theory. Kuznets is therefore right to accuse him of having worked out a thesis of the cycle of entrepreneurial *capability*. Simon Kuznets, 'Schumpeter's Business Cycles', p. 112.

however, Dupriez's argument represents a peculiar new version of that dualism of commodities and money which Marx had already criticized so severely in Ricardo, and which fails to understand that money can only perform its role as a medium of exchange because it is itself a commodity. Once, however, the commodity value (production price) of the money material, i.e., of precious metal, as determined by its own conditions of production, is eliminated from the argument, then the factor declared by Dupriez to be the crucial motor behind long waves is reduced to fluctuations in paper money, i.e., the inflation of paper money. Since, however, the initial impetus of long waves was attributed to demand for capital — real capital capable of valorization and not paper money — the argument collapses of its own accord. It is not clear why a lack of circulating paper money should in certain periods throttle the *demand* for money capital and hence be accompanied by a *falling* rate of interest, while in other periods, precisely when there is an expansion of credit, the demand for money rises even more steeply and thus boosts the rate of interest. Indeed Dupriez himself has published a table showing cyclical fluctuations in the long-term rate of interest in Great Britain, which demonstrates the opposite of what he sets out to prove. For precisely in phases of 'reorganization of money' and 'money scarcity', the interest rate is lower than in phases of 'money inflation':

Average long-term rate of interest in Great Britain [98]

1825 – 1847	:	3.99%
1852 – 1870	:	4.24%
1874 – 1896	:	3.11%
1897 – 1913	:	3.25%

As in the case of Kondratieff and Schumpeter, so in that of Dupriez, what should be the crucial connecting link in the whole argument is missing — the rate of profit. The ebb and flow of long waves of economic development are not the result of the 'scarcity' or 'super-abundance' of money, depending on whether there is an 'inflationary' generation at the helm or one which is inspired by the 'desire for a reorganization of public finances'. On the contrary: the demand for money capital and hence the rate of interest undergo a relative decline when the falling average rate of profit puts a brake on the investment activity of the capitalists. Only when specific

[98] Dupriez, *Des Mouvements Economiques Généraux*, Vol. II, p. 54.

conditions permit a steep rise in the average rate of profit and a significant extension of the market will this investment activity take possession of the technical discoveries capable of revolutionizing the whole of industry and thus bring about a long-term expansionary tendency in the accumulation of capital and the demand for money capital (at a relatively high rate of interest).

The specific contribution of our own analysis to a solution of the problem of 'long waves' has been to relate the diverse combinations of factors that may influence the rate of profit (such as a radical fall in the cost of raw materials; a sudden expansion of the world market or of new fields for investment for capital; a rapid increase or decline in the rate of surplus-value; wars and revolutions) to the inner logic of the process of long-term accumulation and valorization of capital, based upon spurts of radical renewal or reproduction of fundamental productive technology. It explains these movements by the inner logic of the process of accumulation and self-expansion of capital itself. Even if we assume that the activity of invention and discovery is continuous, the long-term development of capital accumulation must still remain discontinuous, for conditions promoting the valorization of capital (and resulting in a rise or stabilization at a high level of the rate of profit) must in time turn into conditions determining a deterioration in this valorization (in other words, a fall in the average rate of profit). The concrete mechanisms of this conversion must be analysed by reference to the concrete historical conditions of the development of the capitalist mode of production at the time of these major turning points (i.e., the start of the 20's and the 70's of the 19th century; immediately preceding the First World War; the mid-60's of the 20th century). That is what we have tried to demonstrate in this chapter. We have shown that a *different* combination of triggering factors was responsible for the successive and sudden increases in the average rate of profit after 1848, after 1893, and after 1940 (USA) and 1948 (Western Europe and Japan). After the Revolutions of 1848, the rise in the rate of profit was essentially due to the rapid expansion of the world market, itself partially a result of these revolutions, and to the sudden expansion of gold production in California and Australia, which created propitious conditions for the first technological revolution. This in turn led to a radical cheapening of fixed constant capital and a steep upswing in the rate of surplus-value — with a massive increase in the productivity of labour in Department II, and thereby a massive increase in the production of relative surplus-value. All these determinants released a sharp upward shift of both the average rate of profit and therefore of capital accumulation as such.

In the early 90's of the last century, the triggering factors of the new long wave of expansion were the momentous drive of capital exports to the colonies and semi-colonies, and resultant cheapening of raw materials and foodstuffs, which similarly led to a sharp increase in the rate of profit in the imperialist countries. This permitted the second technological revolution, a fall in the costs of fixed capital and a pronounced acceleration of the turnover-time of industrial capital in general — in other words, to another major increase in the mass and rate of surplus-value and of profit. The central problem posed by the most recent past is why, after the long recession or stagnation of capital accumulation after 1913, which was intensified by the Great Depression of 1929-32, it was possible for a new rise in the average rate of profit and a new acceleration of capital accumulation to take place immediately before, during and after the Second World War (depending on the particular imperialist country in question). This raises the further question of whether a new long wave can be predicted from the second half of the 1960's onwards — the ebb after the flow. We shall try to answer these questions in the following chapters.

5

Valorization of Capital, Class Struggle and the Rate of Surplus Value in Late Capitalism

An increase in the organic composition of capital means a fall in the rate of profit, all other factors being equal. In the 14th Chapter of the Third Volume of *Capital*, Marx shows that two of the most important factors which can halt the fall of the average rate of profit are the cheapening of elements of constant capital and the raising of the rate of surplus-value (either by an increase in the degree of the exploitation of labour or by a depression of wages to a level below the value of the commodity of labour-power).[1] In the preceding chapters we have already investigated the development of the value of the circulating portion of constant capital since the 1920's. In the following chapters we shall consider the development of the value of fixed constant capital. We must first, however, examine the fluctuations in the rate of surplus-value in the 20th century.

If the length of the working day remains the same — and this has largely been the case since the general introduction of the eight-hour day following the First World War, with the exception of the epoch of Fascism and the Second World War (if we leave aside fluctuations in overtime and part-time work) — then the rate of surplus-value will rise under the following conditions. 1) If the productivity of labour in Department II increases more rapidly than wages, i.e., if the worker uses up less of an unaltered working day to produce the

[1]Marx, *Capital*, Vol. 3, p. 232ff.

equivalent of his wages; 2) if an increase in the intensity of labour leads to the same result, i.e., the labourer produces the value-equivalent of his wages in less working hours than before, so that there is an increase in the duration of surplus labour; 3) if, with no alteration in the productivity or intensity of labour (and *a fortiori* with a growth in the productivity and intensity of labour) there is a fall in real wages, i.e., the value-equivalent of wages can once more be produced in a smaller fraction of the working day.

The increase in the rate of surplus-value will be all the more significant if two or all three of these factors are in operation simultaneously. Under normal conditions, i.e., as long as the price of the commodity of labour-power is regulated by the laws of the market, this is a rare occurrence. With a rise in the productivity of labour real wages will only fall absolutely if the secular tendency is for the industrial reserve army to increase, and in the industrialized or imperialist countries this has not been the case since the last third of the 19th century. If, in the long-term, the industrial reserve army remains stable or diminishes, then a rise in the productivity of labour will have a two-fold and contradictory effect on the level of wages. On the one hand the value of the commodity of labour-power will be reduced, because the commodities traditionally needed for the reproduction of labour-power now lose some of their value. On the other, the value of the commodity of labour-power will be raised through the incorporation of new commodities into the necessary minimum for life (for example, the so-called durable consumer goods, the purchasing price of which has gradually found its way into the average wage). This happened in the USA in the 20's, 30's and 40's, in Western Europe in the 50's and 60's, while in Japan the process is currently in full swing.[2]

We can also note that under normal conditions it is difficult to unite unaltered working time, falling real wages and increased intensity of labour, because a fall in real wages makes the worker more passive and indifferent, as well as in part objectively weakening

---

[2] Failure to understand that what Marx called the 'historical or social element' in the value of the commodity of labour-power is not static and traditional, but at least potentially dynamic, is the greatest weakness of Arghiri Emmanuel's theory of wages: Emmanuel, *Unequal Exchange*, pp. 116-20. It leads him to the idealist thesis that 'what society regards, in a certain place and at a certain moment, as the standard of wages' is the determinant of wages; ibid., p. 119.

him psychologically and physically,[3] and thus creates a material limit which cannot be broken down by the intensity of labour. Admittedly, growing unemployment here has the opposite effect, for the fear of losing one's job reduces fluctuations and encourages greater 'labour discipline', i.e., greater attention and effort, as employers in West Germany discovered in the 1966-67 recession.[4]

Fascism and World War are not 'normal' conditions, however. One of their chief objective functions was precisely to permit all the sources for an increase in the rate of surplus-value to flow simultaneously, as it were, to combine an increase in the productivity and intensity of labour at least partially with a decline in real wages.

One of Marx's greatest achievements was to point out that no such thing existed as a clearly defined 'wages fund', nor any other sort of 'iron law of wages' determining the level of wages with the force of natural necessity. Although in the final analysis the determination of the value of the commodity of labour-power in a commodity-producing society is governed by objective laws just like every determination of any kind of commodity value, there is nonetheless something special about this particular commodity value, because it is influenced to a large extent by conflicts between capital and labour — in other words, by class struggle. In *Wages, Price and Profit,* Marx says: 'Besides this mere physical element, the value of labour is in every country determined by a *traditional standard of life.* It is not mere physical life, but it is the satisfaction of certain wants springing from the social conditions in which people are placed and reared up. The English standard of life may be reduced to the Irish standard; the standard of life of a German peasant to that of a Livonian peasant. The important part which historical tradition and social habitude play in this respect, you may learn from Mr. Thornton's work on *Over-population....* This historical or social element, entering into the value of labour, may be expanded, or contracted, or altogether extinguished, so that nothing remains but the physical

[3] See in this connection Jacquemyns' investigation of the development of the state of health and labour capacity of Belgian workers during the Second World War: J. Jacquemyns, *La Société Belge sous l'Occupation Allemande,* Brussels, 1950, Vol. I, pp. 135-8, 463-5, Vol. II, pp. 149-64.

[4] See among other things *Zweites Weissbuch zur Unternehmemoral,* published by the I. G. Metall (the West German Metalworkers Union), Frankfurt, 1967, and Ernest Mandel, *Die deutsche Wirtschaftskrise — Lehren der Rezession 1966-7,* Frankfurt, 1969, p. 25.

limit. . . . By comparing the standard of wages or values of labour in different countries, and by comparing them in different historical epochs of the same country, you will find that the *value of labour* itself is not a fixed but a variable magnitude, even supposing the values of all other commodities to remain constant.'[5] Marx added, even more specifically: 'But as to *profits,* there exists no law which determines their *minimum.* We cannot say what is the ultimate limit of their decrease. Why cannot we fix that limit? Because, although we can fix the *minimum* of wages, we cannot fix their *maximum.* We can only say that, the limits of the working day being given, the *maximum* of profit corresponds to the *physical minimum of wages;* and that wages being given, the *maximum of profit* corresponds to such a prolongation of the working day as is compatible with the physical forces of the labourer. The maximum of profit is, therefore, limited by the physical minimum of wages and the physical maximum of the working day. It is evident that between the two limits of this *maximum rate of profit* an immense scale of variations is possible. The fixation of its actual degree is only settled by the continuous struggle between capital and labour, the capitalist constantly tending to reduce wages to their physical minimum, and to extend the working day to its physical maximum, while the working man constantly presses in the opposite direction. *The matter resolves itself into a question of the respective powers of the combatants.'*[6]

Since the 'respective powers of the combatants' determine the distribution of the newly created value between capital and labour, they likewise determine the rate of surplus-value. This must be understood in a double sense. First, when the political and social relationship of forces is propitious, the working class can succeed in incorporating new needs, determined by historical and social conditions and to be satisfied by wages, into the value of labour-power,[7]

[5] Marx, *Wages, Price and Profit*, in Marx and Engels, *Selected Works*, London, 1968, pp. 225-6.

[6] Ibid, p. 226(Our italics).

[7] "The main function of trade unions is that, by raising the needs of the workers, by raising their customary standards above the physical minimum for existence, they create a cultural and social subsistence minimum, i.e., a particular cultural standard of living of the working-class, below which wages cannot fall without immediately provoking united struggle and resistance. The great economic significance of Social Democracy particularly lies in the fact that, by arousing the broad masses of workers intellectually and politically, it raises their cultural level and therewith their economic needs. When, for example, it becomes habitual for workers to subscribe to a

i.e., it can succeed in raising this value. If economic conditions are advantageous, however, namely when there is an acute shortage of labour-power due to an abnormal rhythm of the accumulation of capital, then the price of the commodity of labour-power (wages) can also periodically rise above its value. Conversely, when the political and social relationship of forces is disadvantageous to the working class, capital can successfully lower the value of labour-power by annihilating a series of workers' historical or social achievements, i.e., by partially eliminating commodities which cover their needs from the 'standard of life' regarded as normal. Similarly, capital can successfully force the price of the commodity of labour-power down to a level below its value, when the economic relationship of forces is particularly disadvantageous to the working class.

The mechanism inherent in the capitalist mode of production which normally keeps the increase in the value and the price of wages within bounds is the expansion or reconstruction of the industrial reserve army induced by the accumulation of capital itself, i.e., by the inevitable appearance, in periods of rising wages, of attempts to replace living labour-power by machines on a vast scale.[8] The fall in the average rate of profit resulting from an increase in the organic composition of capital and rising wages has the same effect. If the rate of profit sinks below the level necessary to promote a further accumulation of capital, then the latter will fall back abruptly; in the resulting depression the demand for the commodity of labour-power falls rapidly and the industrial reserve army is reconstructed, thus checking the rise of wages or causing them to fall.

In *Der Imperialismus,* his main work, Sternberg made the first attempt to investigate, with reference to the history of the capitalist mode of production in the first decades of the 20th century, the role

---

newspaper or to buy pamphlets, the worker's economic standard of living rises correspondingly, and so, consequently, do his wages.' Rosa Luxemburg, *Einführung in die Nationalökonomie*, Berlin, 1925, p. 275.

[8] 'The stagnation of production would have laid off a part of the working class and would thereby have placed the employed part in a situation, where it would have to submit to a reduction of wages even below the average. This has the very same effect on capital as an increase of the relative or absolute surplus-value at average wages would have had. . . . The fall in prices and the competitive struggle would have driven every individual capitalist to lower the individual value of his total product below its general value by means of new machines, new and improved working methods, new combinations, i.e., to increase the productivity of a given quantity of labour, to lower the proportion of variable to constant capital, and thereby to release some labourers; in short to create an artificial over-population.' Marx, *Capital*, Vol. 3, pp. 254-5.

of the industrial reserve army as the most important regulator of fluctuations in wages, a role which was expressly emphasized by Marx.[9] This service cannot be denied him,[10] even if his work reveals many methodological and theoretical errors, criticized by Grossmann and others.[11]

In his critique of Sternberg, Grossmann rightly refuted the frivolous formulations in which Sternberg felt himself obliged to show up the 'shortcomings' of Marx's *Capital*.[12] But his criticisms overlooked the essence of Sternberg's thesis, missing the import of Marx's definitions of wages (which were much more complex than Grossmann chooses to admit),[13] and so were unable to provide a mediation between the abstract and the concrete — in other words, a mediation between the general laws determining the value of the commodity of labour-power and the concrete development of wages in Western Europe since the second half of the 19th century.

It must also be expressly emphasized that, as soon as the workers succeed in largely eliminating competition amongst one another by means of a strong trade union organization — itself determined by a long-term contraction of the industrial reserve army — a renewed

[9] See Marx, *Capital*, Vol. 1, p. 637: 'Taking them as a whole, the general movements of wages are exclusively regulated by the expansion and contraction of the industrial reserve army, and these again correspond to the periodic changes of the industrial cycle.'

[10] Sternberg, *Der Imperialismus*, especially the first two chapters. It is true that occasionally, under the influence of the theories of Franz Oppenheimer to which he adhered in his pre-Marxist youth, he slips from a correct understanding of the regulative role of the industrial reserve army of labour in *wage-fluctuations*, to an over-estimation of it as the decisive determinant of the *manifestation* of surplus-value — i.e., of the *value of labour-power* itself.

[11] Henryk Grossmann, 'Eine neue Theorie über Imperialismus und soziale Revolution', originally published in Grünberg's *Archiv für die Geschichte des Sozialismus und der Arbeiterbewegung*, Vol. XIII, Leipzig, 1928. Our references here are to the reprint in Henryk Grossmann, *Aufsätze zur Krisentheorie*, Frankfurt, 1971, pp. 111-64.

[12] Among other things, Sternberg's claim that Marx under-estimated the importance of the petty bourgeois middle strata; that he failed to realize that a postponement of the socialist revolution could undo the European and American economy's 'ripeness for socialization'; that Marx's theory of wages was one of absolute immiseration, and so on.

[13] Thus Grossmann completely forgets (op. cit., p. 137ff) the importance of the 'historical and social element' in the determination of the value of the commodity of labour-power, and speaks of the 'exactly fixed' costs of reproduction of the latter, without taking the fact into account that these costs in turn depend on the particular needs they must satisfy. On p. 142 we even find a formula which is truly astonishing for a writer so familiar with Marx's *Capital*: 'wages, i.e., the value of labour power', where it should be 'the price of labour power'.

rise in unemployment (short of catastrophic proportions) need not lead automatically to a fall in the price of the commodity of labour-power. Unemployment can then only have this effect indirectly, firstly through the fact that the real wages of the unorganized strata of the working-class begin to fall as a result of the disadvantageous development of the relationship between the demand and the supply of labour-power, and secondly when the trade-union combativity of the organized layers of the proletariat is weakened. This second condition is, however, a necessary mediation between rising unemployment and falling real wages. If it does not materialize, or does not do so immediately or sufficiently, then rising unemployment can actually be accompanied by rising real wages, as is shown by the example of the USA in 1936-39 or of Great Britain in 1968-70. Capital will then seek to extend the volume of unemployment in such a way that this mediation will prevail all the same—i.e., it will try to undermine class solidarity between employed and unemployed workers to such an extent that massive unemployment ultimately does impair the fighting strength of organized and still-employed wage earners.[14] The struggle against the extension of unemployment then becomes a question of life and death for organized workers.

[14]The social origin and composition of the industrial reserve army, or the relative proportion of its different components, is of major significance in this respect. Rosa Luxemburg, among others, summed up these components as follows: 'The industrial reserve army of the unemployed, however, puts what might be called a spatial restriction on the effect of the trade unions: only the upper stratum of better placed workers, for whom unemployment is only periodical and, as Marx put it, "fluid", has access to trade-union organization and its effect. The lower strata of the proletariat, consisting of unskilled builder's labourers constantly pouring off the land into the city, and of all those in semi-rural, irregular occupations such as brick-making and earth-works, are already significantly less suited to trade union organization because of the spatial and temporal conditions inherent in the nature of their employment and because of its social milieu. Finally, the lowest strata of the industrial reserve army, the unemployed who find occasional work, domestic labourers, and further the casually employed poor, lie completely beyond the reach of organization. Generally speaking: the greater the misery and pressure in a given layer of the proletariat, the smaller the possibility of effective trade unionism. The efficacy of trade unions within the proletariat is thus only shallow on the vertical plane, while it is, in contrast, broad on the horizontal plane. In other words, even if trade unions only include a part of the uppermost stratum of the proletariat their effect will extend to the whole of this stratum, because their achivements will benefit the whole mass of the workers employed in the occupations in question'. Rosa Luxemburg, *Einführung in die Nationalökonomie*, pp. 276-7. A striking confirmation of this analysis in our own day can be found as regards the USA in Michael Harrington. *The Other America,* Harmondsworth, 1963, pp. 36-9, 48-52, 88ff.

It thus becomes comprehensible why the so-called Phillips Curve does not possess the *mechanical and automatic* significance attributed to it by its author.[15] As opposed to the shallow liberal-reformist thesis that 'full employment' has become a lasting and normal element in the 'social market economy' or the 'mixed economy' of 'neo-capitalist society', Phillips was quite right to demonstrate that there is a definite correlation between the rate of change of money-wages on the one hand, and the level of unemployment, or rate of change of unemployment, on the other hand. This means that capitalism, today as yesterday, needs the industrial reserve army in order to prevent an 'excessive' rise in real wages, or to keep the rate of surplus-value and the rate of profit at a level which will stimulate the accumulation of capital. But Phillips was wrong to construct a mechanical and automatic relationship between the level of unemployment (or rate of change of unemployment) and the rate of growth rate of nominal wages, without taking the 'respective powers of the combatants' into account. The latter, however, include not only the relationship between demand and supply on the 'labour market', but also the degree of organization, fighting strength, and class consciousness of the working class.

Following on from an essay by Lewis, which located the main cause of accelerated capital accumulation in the early phase of industrialization in the existence of an abundant supply of labour-power (i.e., of a permanent real or potential industrial reserve army)—thereby effectively rehabilitating the classical theses of Ricardo and Marx (although explicitly denying their validity for the 'more mature' industrial states)—[16] Kindleberger has attempted, in a somewhat less mechanical way than Phillips, to make the heavily increased inflow of labour-power[17] the chief factor in the accelerated economic growth of Western Europe and Japan after the Second World War, while at the same time taking into account technological progress.[18]

[15] Phillips, 'The Relation between Unemployment and the Rate of Change of Money Wages in the United Kingdom', in *Economica*, Vol. XXV, November 1958.
[16] W. Arthur Lewis, 'Development with Unlimited Supplies of Labour', in *The Manchester School of Economic and Social Studies*, Vol. XXII, May 1954.
[17] Before Kindleberger, and independently of him, we ourselves pointed out the great importance of the reconstruction of the industrial reserve army for the accelerated growth of capitalism in Western Europe and Japan after the Second World War: see 'The Economics of Neo-Capitalism', in *Socialist Register 1964*, London, 1964, p. 60.
[18] Charles P. Kindleberger, *Europe's Postwar Growth — The Role of Labour Supply*, Cambridge, USA, 1967.

However, since he excludes both the rate of profit and the rate of sur-plus-value from his model (only the negative moment of a prevention of 'wage inflation' plays a dynamic role in it) it becomes incomprehensible why the mass release of peasants, artisans, or small traders, which played a crucial role in the genesis of the industrial reserve army in such countries as Italy, Japan, France, or the Netherlands, should not have had the same effect at an earlier stage, before the Second World War.

This whole complex of questions has also, of course, played an important role in Marxist literature — and not only in the three best known controversies on the subject: Marx versus Lassalle and Weston; Rosa Luxemburg versus Bernstein; and Sternberg versus Grossmann. The thesis of 'absolute immiseration', which has been falsely attributed to Marx over and over again,[19] is in complete contradiction with his theory, set out in the passages quoted above, that *two* elements — physiological and moral or historical — determine the value of the commodity of labour-power. As the physiological minimum by its very nature hardly permits of compression, it is logical that for Marx the 'variable' or 'flexible' element in the value of the commodity of labour-power was precisely the historical or moral element. The fluctuation of the industrial reserve army and the stage reached by the class struggle at any given time are accordingly the determinant factors in the expansion or contraction of the needs to be satisfied by wages. From the point of view of the capitalist class, the struggle over the rate of surplus-value is a struggle to restrict wages to such needs as are compatible with a fall in the value of labour-power (given a major increase in the productivity of labour, there is of course no reason why this *fall in value* should not be combined with a *rise in the mass* of consumer goods), while conversely the working-class strives to have a constantly growing number of needs satisfied by wages.

In opposition to the persistent legend that Marx took the view that the worker was condemned to stagnating or even falling wages, many passages from his works can be cited which explicitly reject this hypothesis.[20] In the Second Volume of *Capital* we read: 'The reverse takes place in periods of prosperity, particularly during the

---

[19] For example, Kindleberger once again, op. cit., p. 20; John Strachey, *Contemporary Capitalism*, London, 1956, pp. 93-5.

[20] Roman Rosdolsky performed a great service in combatting this simplification: Rosdolsky, *Zur Entstehungsgeschichte des Marx'schen 'Kapital'*, Vol. I, p. 330f.

times of bogus prosperity. . . . It is not alone the consumption of necessities of life which increased. The working-class (*now actively reinforced by its entire reserve army*) also enjoys momentarily *articles of luxury ordinarily beyond its reach*, and those articles which at other times constitute for the great part consumer "necessities" only for the capitalist class.' [21]

Several passages in the *Grundrisse* refer to the same complex of questions. Only three of these need to be quoted here. In the first, Marx remarks: 'To each capitalist, the total mass of all workers, with the exception of his own workers, appear not as workers, but as consumers, possessors of exchange values (wages), money, which they exchange for his commodity. They are so many centres of circulation with whom the act of exchange starts and by whom the exchange value of the capital is maintained. *They form a proportionally very great part* — although not quite so great as is generally imagined, if one focuses on the industrial worker proper — *of all consumers.* The greater their number — the number of the industrial population — and the mass of money at their disposal, the greater the sphere of exchange for capital. We have seen that it is the tendency of capital to increase the industrial population as much as possible.'[22] In another passage, Marx wrote: 'This much, however, can even now be mentioned in passing, namely that the relative restriction on the sphere of workers' consumption (which is only quantitative, not qualitative, or rather, only qualitative as posited through the quantitative) gives them as consumers (in the further development of capital the relation between consumption and production must, in general, be more closely examined) an entirely different importance as agents of production from that which they possessed, e.g., in antiquity or the Middle ages, or now possess in Asia.' Marx went on to say: 'The worker's participation in the higher, even cultural, satisfactions, the agitation for his own interests, newspaper subscriptions, attending lectures, educating his children, developing his taste, and so on, his only share in civilization which distinguishes him from the slave, is economically only possible *by widening the sphere of his pleasures at the times when business is good.* . . . In spite of all "pious" speeches, (the capitalist) therefore searches for means

---

[21]Marx, *Capital,* Vol. 2, p. 414(Our italics).
[22]Marx, *Grundrisse,* pp. 419-20(Our italics).

to spur them on to consumption, to give his wares new charms, to *inspire them with new needs* by constant chatter, and so on. It is precisely this side of the relation of capital and labour which is an essential civilizing moment, and on which the historic justification, but also the contemporary power of capital rests.'[23]

In his questionable book, *Die Theorie der Lage der Arbeiter*, which dogmatically expounded the Stalinist thesis of the 'absolute immiseration of the working class' — a notion highly rated at the time — Kuczynski formally took into account the importance of increased needs for any evaluation of the development of wages: 'Now if one looks at the history of capitalism over the past 150 years it can certainly be said that the historical element in the value of labour-power has had a tendency to rise.'[24] However, Kuczynski tried to combine acceptance of an increase in new historical needs, to be satisfied by wages, with assertion of a fall in the satisfaction of physiological needs below the minimum level for existence, with the help of dubious statistics based on particular tendencies in the development of nutrition. There is, however, no serious foundation for such a peculiar combination, which contradicts the very essence of the concept of a 'physiological minimum for existence'. It would be much more correct to comment that 1) an uninterrupted rise in the intensity of labour simultaneous with the advance of technology *must* lead to a tendency for this minimum for existence to rise — for without an increase in real wages the labourer's capacity for work will itself be threatened; 2) capitalism tends to increase the needs of the working class more than it raises real wages, so that even with rising real wages, it is possible for wage-levels to remain below the value of labour-power. Kuczynski himself indicates both these moments.[25]

Once again: if the fighting strength and degree of organization of the working-class are high, even a fall in real wages as a result of heavy unemployment will only be transient in nature and will be made good once again by a rapid rise in wages in the subsequent phase of industrial upswing. It is enough to study the development of wages in the USA from 1929 to 1937, or France between the years

[23] Ibid., pp. 283 and 287.

[24] Jurgen Kuczynski, *Die Theorie der Lage der Arbeiter*, Berlin, 1948, p. 88.

[25] Lenin unequivocally stated that capitalism has a tendency to intensify the needs of the proletariat, and therewith the historical-social element that enters into the value of the commodity of labour-power: *Collected Works*, Vol. I, p. 106.

1932 and 1937, to find that in the long-term even increasing or widespread unemployment cannot automatically lower real wages or raise the rate of surplus-value.

In this way, the category of the 'value of the commodity of labour-power' acquires its full significance, without in any way contradicting the determination of wages through the 'respective powers of the combatants'. *In the short run* these wages fluctuate about the value of labour-power which can be regarded as given, or corresponding to an average living standard accepted by both capital and labour. *In the long run* the value of the commodity of labour-power, disregarding fluctuations in the value of commodities needed to satisfy the 'normal' vital needs of the workers, can rise or decline, depending on whether the proletariat, in the process of bitter class struggle, successfully incorporates new needs in the living standards accepted as normal, or the bourgeoisie manages to eliminate needs previously regarded as normal from them.

If, on the other hand, capital succeeds in decisively weakening, or even smashing, the trade unions and all other organizations of the working-class — including their political organization; if it succeeds in atomizing and intimidating the proletariat to such an extent that any form of collective defence becomes impossible and workers are once more relegated to the point from which they started — in other words, the 'ideal' situation, from the point of view of capital, of universal competition of worker against worker, then it is quite possible 1) to use the pressure of unemployment to bring about a significant reduction in real wages; 2) to prevent wages returning to their previous level even in the phase of upswing following a crisis, i.e., to lower the value of the commodity of labour-power in the long term; 3) to force the price of the commodity of labour-power down, by means of manipulations, deductions and various swindles, even below this already diminished value; 4) simultaneously to achieve a significant increase in the average social intensity of labour and even to attempt, in tendency, to prolong the working day. The outcome of all these changes can only be a rapid and massive rise in the rate of surplus-value.

This is exactly what occurred in Germany following the victory of Fascism under Hitler. The pressure of mass unemployment had forced German workers to bear with significant wage reductions in the years 1929-1932. These were less catastrophic in *real* than in *nominal* terms, for there was a simultaneous fall in the price of consumer goods — but they were nonetheless considerable. The average gross hourly wage fell from the index figure of 129.5 in 1929 to 94.6 in 1932, i.e., by more than 35%. The average hourly wage of skilled workers in 17 branches of industry dropped from 95.9 pfennigs in 1929 to 70.5 pfennigs, i.e., by 27%; in the case of unskilled workers the drop was less severe: from 75.2 to 62.3 pfennigs, or only 17%. These percentages must be multiplied by the fall-back in the hours worked. However, since the price of foodstuffs declined by nearly 20% in the same period, and the price of industrial goods fell by a similarly high percentage, the decline in real wages was not as steep as would appear from the abrupt plunge of nominal wages. At any rate, it was not as grave as might have been assumed with unemployment near the 6,000,000 mark and a catastrophic collapse in profits.[26] The rate of surplus-value fell — as it mostly does in severe economic crises — partly because of the devalorization of the commodities embodying surplus-value, and partly because a portion of the surplus-value produced could not be realized, but most of all because the production of surplus-value was itself declining due to part-time work and the decrease in the number of hours worked, since it is not possible to reduce the number of working hours necessary to reproduce labour-power exactly as much as the length of the total working day.[27]

What, then, occurred after the Nazis' seizure of power? The average gross hourly wage increased from the index figure of 94.6 in the year 1933 to 100 in 1936 and 108.6 in 1939. Despite full employment, therefore, the average gross hourly wage in 1939 was far below the level of 1929, when it had reached 129.5. The total mass of wages and salaries paid out in 1938 was still less than in 1929 (RM 42.7 billion as against RM 43 billion in 1929), while at the same time the total number of wage-earners had risen from 17.6 million in 1929 to 20.4 million in 1938.[28] Taking into account the

[26]Charles Bettelheim, *L'Economie Allemande Sous le Nazisme*, Paris, 1946, pp. 210, 211, 152.

[27]Kuczynski calculates that gross money wages in the metal industry plunged from an index figure of 184 in 1929 to 150 in 1930, in the chemical industry from 247 to 203, and in the whole of industry from 215 to 177. By contrast, the index of wages actually paid out is said to have fallen by half, and the index of net real wages from 100 in 1928 to 64 in 1932, hence by a full third. This last figure ought to be examined critically. Jurgen Kuczynski, *Die Geschichte der Lage der Arbeiter in Deutschland*, Berlin, 1949, Vol. I, pp. 325-6, 329-30.

[28]Bettelheim, op. cit., pp. 210-222.

vast increase in wage deduction (which rose from less than 10% to more than 20% of the total mass of wages) it can be estimated that the annual income actually at the disposal of the wage earners fell back from RM 2215 in 1929 to RM 1700 in 1938. This constitutes a drop of approximately 23%. The cost of living was approximately 7% higher in 1938 than in 1933 and hence probably about 10% lower than in 1929. Before the Second World War, therefore, the real wages of the German worker under National Socialism had already fallen by more than 10% as compared with the pre-crisis period, despite the considerable increase in production (in 1938 it was 25% above the 1929 level) and the rise in the average productivity of labour (in 1938 it was approximately 10% higher than in 1939) achieved under Nazi rule.[29] It is little wonder that under such conditions the mass of profit shot upwards: from RM 15.4 billion in 1929 and RM 8 billion in 1932 to RM 20 billion in 1938 (these figures refer to all forms of profit, including commercial and bank profits and undistributed company profits).[30]

The rise in the rate of surplus-value was thus on a vast scale. The share of wages and salaries in the national income fell from 68.8% in 1929 to 63.1% in 1938; the share of capital rose from 21.0% to 26.6%. This rise in the rate of surplus-value can be calculated with even greater accuracy by comparison with the worst year of the crisis, 1932. From 1932 to 1938 the total nominal wages at the disposal of the wage earners rose by 69%, the number of those employed by 56%, the level of output by 112% and the number of hours worked by 117%. It is scarcely surprising that under such conditions the mass of surplus-value directly accuring to capital increased by 146%.[31]

What were the economic springs, from which this vast increase in the rate of surplus-value flowed? (It seems virtually to have doubled, as can be seen from the ratio 8/26 and 20/35).[32] In the first place, it sprang from a significant prolongation of the working

[29] Ibid., p. 212.
[30] Franz Neumann, *Behemoth*, New York, 1963, pp. 435-6.
[31] Ibid., pp. 435-6.
[32] 8 billion Reichsmarks profits as against 26 billion Reichsmarks in disposable wages and salaries in 1932; 20 billion Reichsmarks profits as against a disposable income of wage and salary earners of 35 billion Reichsmarks in 1938. These figures do not correspond exactly to Marx's categories of surplus-value and variable capital, but they serve as indicators. A further clarification of this problem follows further below.

day without any considerable rise in real wages. In the period 1932-38 the nominal wage per wage-earner rose by less than 10% while the cost of living increased by 7%. Simultaneously, however, the number of hours worked per wage-earner increased by nearly 40%. The mass of absolute surplus-value thus rose significantly. Therein lies the most important secret of the exceedingly rapid increase in the mass of surplus-value and the rate of surplus-value under the Nazis.

Secondly, however, the value of the commodity of labour-power revealed a tendency to fall; for one thing, because the needs which wages had to meet were less numerous than before, and for the other, because there was a significant decline in the quality of the commodities available to satisfy these needs. For example, there was an abrupt decline in civilian building, i.e., a deterioration in the housing conditions of the workers (RM 2.8 billion expended in 1928, RM 2.5 billion ten years later, with a much larger working population, a change equivalent to a decrease of 20% in home-building per wage-earner). There was also a significant increase in the price of textiles: on average, textile prices rose by 26% between 1932 and 1938.[33] There was a visible rise in the share of expenditure on food and necessities in the average worker's budget, which in the history of capitalism has always been a typical sign of a fall in the value of the commodity of labour-power.[34] The deterioration in the quality of consumer goods was expressed both in industrial consumer goods (clothes made from substitute materials) and in foodstuffs.

Thirdly, the sellers of the commodity of labour-power were prevented from taking advantage of more advantageous conditions on the labour market after the disappearance of unemployment to raise the price of the commodity for sale. Once this price had fallen below its current value under the pressure of the great crash, it remained at this level in the succeeding boom. The Nazis thus successfully achieved the first 'German Economic Miracle' by durably

[33] Between April 1933 and April 1941 the rise in the cost of clothing for the average consumer rose nearly 50%: Neumann, op. cit., p. 506. Kuczynski states that the net increase in homes in 1938 — some 285, 269 — was even below the level of 317, 682, in 1929. Kuczynski, *Die Geschichte der Lage der Arbeiter in Deutschland*, Berlin 1949, Vol. II, pp. 210-11.

[34] The prices of foodstuffs rose less than all other components of the cost of living, with the exception of rents — especially less than textiles and industrial consumer goods. On the eve of the Second World War the per-capita production of consumer goods remained exactly at the pre-crisis level of 1928: Bettelheim, op. cit., pp. 207-8.

lowering the value of the commodity of labour-power, while simultaneously forcing the price of labour-power down even below its value in spite of full employment.

It is not difficult to locate the social and political secret behind this 'success'. The smashing of trade unions and all other workers' organizations, and the resultant atomization, intimidation and demoralization, condemned a whole generation of workers to loss of their capacity for self-defence. In the 'incessant struggle between capital and labour' one of the contending parties had its hands tied and its head stunned. The 'respective powers of the combatants' had been tilted decisively towards capital.

Even under conditions where the working-class is completely atomized, however, the laws of the market which determine short-term fluctuations in the price of the commodity of labour-power do not disappear. As soon as the industrial reserve army contracted in the Third Reich, workers were able to try, by means of rapid job mobility — for instance into the spheres of heavy industry and armaments which paid higher wage-rates and overtime — to achieve at least a modest improvement in their wages, even without trade union action. Only a violent intervention by the Nazi State to sustain the rate of surplus-value and the rate of profit, in the form of the legal *prohibition* of job changes, and the *compulsory tying* of workers to their jobs, was able to prevent the working-class from utilizing more propitious conditions on the labour market.[35] This abolition of the freedom of movement of the German proletariat was one of the most striking demonstrations of the capitalist class nature of the National Socialist State.[36]

In the other imperialist countries of key importance for the fate of the capitalist world economy, a similar process took place on the eve of and during the Second World War: this was especially so in Italy, France, Japan and Spain. In Italy, Sylos-Labini suggests that the real wages of the working-class fell from index 56 in 1922 to index 46 in 1938.[37] After the Liberation, wages were frozen at fascist levels, and reached the 1922 index only in 1948. Thereafter they

[35] On the restriction of the freedom of movement of wage-earners in the Third Reich as from 1936, see, among others, Kuczynski, op. cit., Vol. II, pp. 119-21, 195-8; Neumann, op. cit., pp. 341-2, 619.
[36] See Neumann, op. cit., pp. 344-8, for cases in which wage-earners reacted to the some of the most severe coercive measures of the Third Reich by slowing down their work and met with partial success; for example, such action led to the reversal of the decision to abolish special pay for overtime or work on Sundays.
[37] See Paulo Sylos-Labini, *Saggio sulle Classi Sociali*, Bari, 1974, p. 185.

rose above that level very slowly up to 1960, when they had attained index 70. In Spain, official sources indicate a decline of per capita real income from 8,500 pesetas in 1935 to 5,400 pesetas in 1945 — at 1953 money values, which of course involved a much greater fall in real wages.[38] Between 1945 and 1950, the cost of living increased again by 60%, while wages remained blocked. It was only after 1950 that there was a gradual recovery of real wages, which nevertheless probably reached their 1935 levels only towards the end of the 50's. In the meantime, Spanish industrial output had doubled.

The case of Japan is the clearest of all. There is some dispute about the pattern of wages during the installation of the fascist military dictatorship before the Second World War. However, the sharp increase in the percentage of wages spent on food — from 34.4% in 1933-34 to 43.5% in 1940-41, and the concomitant decline in the percentage spent on clothes, recreation, health and personal services — from 25.4% in 1933-34 to 21.75% in 1940-41, is unmistakeable evidence of a fall in the real standard of living of the masses. This naturally suffered a further catastrophic blow during the Second World War itself. Wages were then blocked at a very low level during the American occupation. They increased slowly with the onset of the post-war boom, but overall remained extremely modest, so long as there subsisted a massive industrial reserve army of labour in the countryside, which supplied Japanese industry with a constant influx of cheap manpower. In 1957-59, the annual per capita consumption of sugar in Japan was 13 kg, against 50 in Britain, 40 in Finland and 18 in Ceylon; the consumption of proteins per day was 67 gr against 86 in Britain, 78 in Syria and 68 in Mexico. Wages increased so slowly compared with output and productivity that throughout the 50's, the share of wages and salaries in the gross value of manufacturing industry (establishments with 4 employees or more) actually declined even in the official statistics, from 39.6% in 1953 to 33.7% in 1960.[39] Shinohara comments bluntly: 'Generally speaking, an economy with an excess labour force has a strong possibility of realizing a higher rate of growth (i.e., a higher rate of capital accumulation because of a higher rate of profit — EM) than one lacking such a condition, if other circumstances are equal. It is not only because the labour force will constitute no bottleneck there,

---

[38] Juan Clavera, Joan Esteban, Antonio Mones, Antoni Monserrat, Ros Rombravella, *Capitalismo Español: De La Autarquía a La Establización (1939-1959)*, Madrid, 1973, Vol. I, p. 51; Vol. II, pp. 30, 27, 26.
[39] Shinohara, op. cit., p. 273; Bieda, op. cit., pp. 4-5.

but because relatively low wages combined with high levels of technology introduced from abroad will result in lower prices and expansion of exports.'[40] In these circumstances, there is no mystery about the exceptionally high level of 'savings' — i.e., surplus-value, capital accumulation and investment — achieved during the remarkable post-war boom in Japan.

It is also instructive to consider more closely the example of the US economy. An examination of the American case is made more difficult by the fact that the development was much less straightforward in the USA than in Nazi Germany. During the Second World War, both the expenditure of workers' wages and the real accumulation of capital were held in check. A mass of frustrated demand was therefore built up, which only led to a clearly expressed rise in the rate of surplus-value in the period immediately following the War. T. N. Vance calculates this development [41] as follows:

Year	Variable Capital (in $ billions)	Surplus-Value	Rate of Surplus-Value
1939	43.3	39.9	92%
1940	46.7	46.3	99%
1944	98.8	103.0	104%
1945	98.1	104.7	107%
1946	92.6	106.3	115%
1947	98.9	119.6	121%
1948	105.4	136.3	129%

An indirect confirmation of this trend can be found in the rapid decline of the share of private consumption in the American net social product. While the latter rose from an index figure of 100 in the year 1939 to 178 in 1945 and 158 in 1953, private consumption only rose from 100 in 1939 to 118 in 1945 and 135 in 1953. At fixed prices, per capita private consumption in 1953 was only 11.5% higher than in 1939, despite a massive increase in production, and this does not even take into account the class stratification of this private consumption.[42] The Polish Marxist Kalecki came to a similar conclusion: according to him the share of private consumption in the total national product of the USA fell from 78.7% in 1937 to 72.5% in

---

[40] Shinohara, op. cit., pp. 64, 13.
[41] T. N. Vance, *The Permanent War Economy*, Berkeley, 1970, p. 23.
[42] Ibid., pp. 15, 16.

1955, while in the same period the share of private capital accumulation rose from 16.4% to 21.4%.[43] Baran and Sweezy, for their part, calculate that the share of 'property income' (surplus-value) in the total national income of the USA ($26.6 billion in 1945 and $58.5 billion in 1955, out of a national income of $181.5 billion in 1945 and $331 billion in 1955) rose from 14.7% to 17.7%.[44]

A number of similar indications for Japan confirm this general trend. According to official statistics, private consumption fell from 60.4% of the Gross National Product in 1951, to 54.9% in 1960 and 51.1% in 1970. At the same time expenditure on the private purchase of fixed capital rose sharply from 12.1% of the GNP in 1951 to 20.3% in 1960. In the 1960's this percentage fell, under the influence of the recession, growing amortisations and investment in stocks. The formation of capital continued to rise, however, and had reached more than 35% of the GNP (compared with 27% in the year 1951) in 1966.

The application of Marx's categories to these series of figures must, of course, be handled with extreme caution. The official calculations of aggregates can be reduced to these categories only by means of very complicated calculations. From the standpoint of Marx's theory of value they contain numerous overlapping quantities.[45] According to this theory, part of the sum of wages and salaries belongs neither to the variable capital paid out each year nor to the annual quantities of surplus-value; this applies above all to the wages of employees in commerce and in all spheres where capital is certainly invested in order to reap some of the surplus-value created elsewhere, but which themselves produce no surplus-value. Part of this sum of wages and salaries obviously further belongs to surplus-value and not to variable capital — the income of managers, higher employees in industry and the state apparatus, and so on. Yet another part of the sum of wages and salaries (and of the social product) represents revenue which has been spent two or three times over (including the

[43]Michal Kalecki, 'Economic Situation in the USA as compared with Pre-war', manuscript of the English translation of an article published in the Polish periodical *Ekonomista* in 1956 and kindly made available to us by the editors of Monthly Review Press.

[44]Baran and Sweezy, *Monopoly Capital*, pp. 385-7. To these figures they add a part of the surplus-value supposedly 'concealed' in depreciation allowances. We have resubtracted this.

[45]These overlapping quantities are further discussed in Chapter 13 of the present work.

wages of employees in the service sectors). These would have to be subtracted in order to calculate the rate of surplus-value.[46]

However that may be, a comparison between the official calculations of the share of the sum of wages and salaries and the share of the mass of profits in the national product certainly provides a reliable *indication* of the medium-term development of the rate of surplus-value, for the necessary correction of these aggregates to align them with Marxist categories is unlikely to alter in any decisive way the proportions between them in these periods of time.

It must, however, be emphasized that there is a major distinction between the 'economic miracle' of the 50's in West Germany, Japan, and Italy and of the 60's in the USA on the one hand, and the pre-war development of Nazi Germany and Japan on the other: for in spite of a steep rise in the rate of surplus-value in Nazi Germany and fascist Japan, there did *not* occur a significant increase in private civilian investments. Virtually the entire increase in investments can be traced back to the initiative of the State or the armaments industry. It is therefore not possible to discover the elements of a long-term cumulative process of growth in the Nazi economy. The same is also true, *mutatis mutandis*, of the war economy in the USA of 1941-44. By contrast, the climb of the rate of surplus-value in the post-war period in West Germany, Japan, Italy, France and the USA, both in the first half of the 50's and the first half of the 60's did in fact lead to a mighty extension of private civilian investments, in other words, to a cumulative growth of the economy outside the sphere of armaments.

In 1938 private investments in German industry were only about 25% higher than in 1928, while in 1937 they were still lower than the pre-crisis level even in absolute figures. It is interesting to compare these figures with the overall production index of industry which, if we take the year 1928 = 100, reached 117 in 1937 and 125 in 1938.[47]

---

[46] Both Vance and Baran and Sweezy try to make such corrections, but do so only very inadequately. Vance calculates the income of wage-earners (including agriculture) by deducting higher salaries (over $1,000 a year), but then subtracts this sum from the net social product in order to determine surplus-value. He thus retains both overlapping quantities and inclusion of a part of the social *capital* in the calculation of the new value created each year (op. cit., p. 23). Baran and Sweezy proceed in a similar way, and further add a part of the annual *retained value* of fixed capital to the surplus-value produced, i.e., to the *new value*.

[47] Bettelheim, op. cit., p. 225.

In other words: it was only after five years of the Nazi economy, when rearmament was in full swing and the outbreak of the Second World War was at hand, that private investments hoisted themselves back up to the proportion of industrial production that they had attained before the outbreak of the Great Depression.

In the USA gross private investments remained below the 1929 level for the whole period 1939-45, with the single exception of the year 1941. In 1946-1947 the 1929 level was surpassed, but the average for the period 1940-47 yields an annual gross private investment sum which is 21% *below* the 1929 level (calculations at fixed prices).[48] Even the average for the period 1945-47 fell slightly short of the level of gross investments in 1929, while the output of the manufacturing industry in these three years *exceeded* the 1929 level by an average of 78% and the total private gross social product was 54% higher. The lag in private investments is to be explained by three main causes:

1) Before the introduction of the actual war economy (in Germany) or immediately following its cessation (in the USA), the relative stagnation of real wages and private consumption constituted a limit which restrained an increase in investment activity in Department II. This inevitably affected market expectations, and hence also the investments in Department. I.[49]

2) After the war economy had reached full development, the volume of the means of destruction produced (Department III) grew so rapidly that material conditions only sufficed for a very modest extension of reproduction, or permitted no further extension of reproduction at all. Since the goods of Department III do not enter into the process of reproduction, a growing rift developed between the increase of absolute industrial production and the possibilities of further growth, If, for example, the production index rose from 100 to 150 in the course of 4 years, but 35 of these points represented goods of Department III, only 115 (150-35) would be available to Departments I and II for reproduction. Moreover, of these 115, say 20 points in Department I and 15 points in Department II would have

[48] Bureau of the Census, US Department of Commerce, *Long Term Economic Growth*, p. 171. These figures represent the gross investments of the whole economy, hence also of home-building, and so on.
[49] For Germany, Bettelheim, op. cit., pp. 233, 235, 274, where there is an analysis, among other things, of the significant over-capacity of light industry in 1929.

had to be deflected into the production of Department III, so that in actual fact, in comparison to the base year (let us say 1940), re-production in Departments I and II would have receded rather than advanced (for only 80 points remain at the disposal of the two produc-tive Departments for reproduction, as compared to 100 at the start of the four-year period).[50] In other words: *in the long-run an arms economy is functional for the accumulation of capital only if it absorbs surplus capitals, without also deflecting into the armaments industry capitals needed for the extended reproduction of Departments I and II.* An arms and war economy carried beyond this point increasingly annihilates the material conditions for extended reproduction and thus in the long-term hampers the accumulation of capital instead of promoting it.

3) As Kuczynski has calculated on the basis of official data,[51] the average productivity of labour in the German consumer goods industry actually fell *below* the 1932 level in 1937. On the whole, therefore, the Nazi dictatorship was unable to achieve an increase in *relative* surplus value, and could only raise the rate of surplus-value by increasing *absolute* surplus-value through a reduction in the value of the commodity of labour-power. The possibilities for doing this were naturally limited. By contrast, the characteristic method of extraction of surplus labour under late capitalism is to increase *relative* surplus-value.

The importance of these considerations is that they show that increased expenditure on armaments cannot in itself generate a long-term acceleration of accumulation, and that a continual increase in arms expenditure cannot ultimately overcome the limits of the valori-zation of capital. Two additional factors were necessary for the major increase in the rate of surplus-value in Germany after 1933 and again after 1948, and in most of the other imperialist countries after 1945, actually to lead to a long-term acceleration of the accumu-lation of capital, i.e., to a 'long wave with a basically expansionary tone'. These were *a constantly expanding market, and conditions in which this expansion did not itself rapidly lower the rate of surplus-value, or did not cause a rapid decline in the rate of profit.* In the con-crete situation after the Second World War, this combination could not be created by a geographical expansion of the market, but only by

[50] See further on this in Chapter 9 of the present work.
[51] Kuczysnski, *Die Geschichte der Lage der Arbeiter — Deutschland*, Vol. 2, p. 143.

a technological transformation in Department I. Only an upheaval as fundamental as this could lead simultaneously to a cumulative growth in all branches of industry and to a significant rise in the productivity of labour, to a major increase in the production of relative surplus-value together with an expansion of the selling market for consumer goods (therefore also a rise in the real income of wage-earners). A precondition of this constellation was that the above-average level of the rate of surplus-value due to the ongoing reconstruction of the industrial reserve army (and due further to the relative weakening of the workers' fighting strength as a result of subjective factors) should remain in force.

It was precisely this configuration which formed the essence of the 'German Economic Miracle' after the currency reform of 1948 and, with minor variations, of all 'economic miracles' in imperialist countries after the Second World War. For ten years, from 1949 to 1959, the share of the wage and salary earners in the German national income remained below its levels in 1929 and 1932.[52]

Year	National Income (billions of RM & DM)	Gross income from employed labour	II as % of I
1929	42.9	26.5	61.9%
1932	25.3	15.6	61.8%
1938	47.3	26.0	54.9%
1950	75.2	44.1	59.1%
1959	194.0	116.8	60.2%

If we calculate the *relative share of wages*, by dividing the income per wage-earner by the social product per inhabitant (i.e., by taking into account the fact that since 1929 there has been a significant rise, from approximately 62% to more than 80%, in the share of wage-earners in the whole employed population), we arrive at the result that from an index figure of 150 in the year 1929, it fell to 140 in 1950, 128 in 1952, 121 in 1955 and a mere 117 in 1959. By then the relative share of wages had sunk below its level even under the

[52] For the years 1929, 1932, 1938: figures from the Office of Statistics, recalculated for the area of the Federal Republic (excluding the Saarland and Berlin), by H. O. Draker, 'Internationale Wirtschaftsstatistiken I', in *WISO — Korrespondenz fur Wirtschafts-und Sozialwissenschaften,* No. 22, 15 Nov. 1960, p. 1054. For the years 1950 and 1959, *Jahresgutachten des Sachverständigenrates zur Begutachtung der gesamtwirtschaftlichen Entwicklung,* Drucksache VI/100 des Deutschen Bundestages, 6th electoral period, 1 Dec. 1969.

Nazis in 1938; in that year it was 125.[53] This time, however, the rise in the rate of surplus-value was accompanied not by a relative stagnation in the productivity of labour as in the years 1933-38, but by an extremely rapid rise in the productivity of labour as a result of accelerated technological innovation. Moreover, the canalization of millions of refugees, peasants, small traders and housewives into the production process guaranteed an ongoing reconstruction of the industrial reserve army which kept the share of wages in newly created value below certain limits. Only with the advent of full employment in 1960, when the number of vacant posts exceeded the number of unemployed (despite the introduction of further millions of workers, this time from abroad), did the relative share of wages cease to fall. At the same time, a decline in the rate of surplus-value and the average rate of profit set in, which the capitalist class then attempted to check by accelerating automation, which in turn led to the recession of 1966-67.[54]

The importance of international migration of labour must be emphasized in this context. It climbed spectacularly from the moment when the internal reserve army of labour had virtually disappeared in West Germany. In July 1958, there were only 127,000 foreign workers in the Federal Republic and only 167,000 in July 1959. Their numbers then rose to 279,000 in mid-1960, 507,000 in mid-1961, 811,000 in mid-1963, 933,000 in mid-1964, passed the 1,000,000 mark in mid-1965, reached 1,300,000 in mid-1966, and overtook the 2,000,000 mark in 1971.[55] Without this exodus of labour from Southern Europe, which allowed it to reconstruct a reserve army at home, West German capitalism would have been unable to achieve its formidable expansion of output in the 60's without a catastrophic decline in the rate of profit. The same is true, *mutatis mutandis,* of France, Switzerland and the Benelux countries, which in the 1958-71 period together absorbed another 2,000,000 foreign workers into their proletariat.

A long-term increase in the rate of surplus-value on the one hand; a long-term expansion of the market through accelerated technological innovation on the other hand — in other words, a long-term

---

[53] Our own calculation, on the basis of official figures for the gross internal product, population and gross income from dependent labour per average employed wage-earner.

[54] Calculated by the method used above, the ratio of gross income per wage-earner/ gross internal product per inhabitant rose once more to 137 in 1966.

[55] Marios Nikolinakos, *Politische Ökonomie der Gastarbeiterfrage*, Hamburg, 1973, p. 38.

increase in the rate of surplus-value with a simultaneous rise in real wages: this was the specific combination which made possible the long-term cumulative growth of the economy of the imperialist states in the period 1945-65, by contrast with the Nazi period or the Second World War. But the Nazi dictatorship and the Second World War created the decisive preconditions for this development so advantageous to capital, in that they made possible a radical increase in the rate of surplus-value and a radical erosion of the value of labour-power which had proved impossible to achieve in 'normal' and 'peaceful' conditions after the First World War, because of the great increase in the fighting strength of the proletariat under the influence of the Russian Revolution and the international wave of revolutionary eruptions.

The absorption of over 10 million refugees and millions of foreign workers in post-war West Germany had its equivalent in Italy in the incorporation of millions of peasants and rural inhabitants from Southern Italy into North Italian industry, in Japan in the absorption of yet more millions of peasants and labourers occupied in traditional sectors of the economy by modern Japanese large industry with similar effects, and in the USA by the absorption into the urban labour force of over 10 million married women, together with more than 4 million farmers, share-croppers and agricultural labourers. In Japan, too, when the reserve army of labour in the countryside and in the 'traditional' sector of industry started to dry up, an exceptional influx of women into wage-labour occurred during the long post-war boom: in fact, the number of Japanese women gainfully employed increased from 3 million in 1950 and 6.5 million in 1960 to 12 million in 1970. These movements were the necessary and sufficient precondition for the long-term persistence of an above-average rate of surplus-value—in other words, for a long-term blockage of the fall of the average rate of profit, and hence for a long-term above-average growth in the accumulation of capital. Thus, between 1950 and 1965, approximately 7 million labourers emigrated from the agricultural sector in Japan.[56] In the same period the number of wage-earners in manufacturing industry doubled (rising from 4.5 to 9 millions). The total sum of wages and salaries paid out by manufacturing industry (including those of highly-remunerated employees, which must be reckoned as part of surplus-value rather than variable

[56]Masayoshi Namiki, *The Farm Population in Japan 1872-1965*, Agricultural Development Series, No. 17, Tokyo (no date), pp. 42-3.

capital) rose from 744 billion yen in 1955 to 2,733.5 billion yen in 1963, while the value-added in manufacturing industry rose from approximately 1.99 billion yen to 7.459 billion yen in the same period, and the annual investments in new fixed capital in the same industry increased from 288 billion yen to 1,750 billion yen.[57] The secret of this imposing growth is easy to see: between 1960 and 1965 real wages per wage-earner in manufacturing industry rose by only 20%, while the physical productivity of labour per employee increased by 48%:[58] hence a vast increase in the production of relative surplus-value.

This decline in the relative share of wages can also be demonstrated in the Netherlands, since the share of wages, salaries and social contributions in the national income remained virtually unaltered between 1938 and 1960 (1938: 55.9%; 1956: 55.3%; 1960: 56.6%) while in the same period the share of wage-earners in the working population rose from 70% in 1938 to 78.8% in 1960.

The long-term development of the relation between the income of labour and the income of capital in industry and handicrafts, as shown for Germany by Hoffmann, and the long-term relation between the income of labour and the income of capital in manufacturing industry, as revealed in the official statistics of the USA, are clear indicators of the long-waves in the self-expansion of capital. Once again: they are only indicators and not series of figures which correspond exactly to Marx's categories. Hoffmann deducted the income of higher employees from the income of labour, but was unable to include in the income of capital in industry and handicrafts that part of surplus-value which, although it is certainly produced there, is appropriated outside this sector. Despite this, there is clear evidence of a long-term rise and fall of the rate of surplus-value, which belies the reiterated thesis of 'a constant share of labour in the net product'[59] which the Cambridge School in particular, and academic economists in general, treat virtually as an axiom.

[57]Ministry of International Trade and Industry, *Statistics on Japanese Industries 1966*, Tokyo, 1966; pp. 26-7, 87.

[58]Ibid., pp. 88-9.

[59]See, for example, Arthur Lewis, 'Unlimited Labour: Further Notes', in *The Manchester School of Economics and Social Studies*, Vol., XXVI, No. 1, January 1958, p. 12. Strachey repeats the same thesis with the reservation that the working class can only retain its 'stable share' by an ongoing struggle. John Strachey, *Contemporary Capitalism*, pp. 133-49; Joan Robinson, *An Essay on Marxian Economics*, 2nd Ed., London, 1966, p. 93; Nicholas Kaldor, 'Capital Accumulation and Economic Growth', in F. A. Lutz and D. C. Hague (eds.), *The Theory of Capital*, London, 1961.

Year	Income of capital (I) in German industry and handicrafts	Income of labour (II) in German industry and handicrafts	I/II in %
1870	736	3,716	
1871	900	3,930	
1872	1,178	4,461	
1873	1,316	5,099	
1874	1,174	5,310	
1875	1,082	5,405	
1876	998	5,356	
Average 1870-1876			22.2%
1907	4,995	16,086	
1908	4,554	16,035	
1909	4,536	16,248	
1910	4,890	17,164	
1911	5,198	18,291	
1912	5,910	19,374	
1913	6,242	20,138	
Average 1907-1913			29.4%
1925	2,617	31,232	
1926	2,295	30,078	
1927	5,900	36,635	
1928	5,333	40,839	
1929	5,489	42,915	
1930	3,044	39,169	
Average 1925-1930			11.2%
1935	7,088	30,485	
1936	7,565	33,336	
1937	13,488	36,590	
1938	17,049	39,494	
Average 1935-1938			32.3%
1950	15,462	38,943	39.7%
1953	24,919	56,884	
1954	30,257	62,319	
1955	32,976	70,733	
1956	34,352	79,083	
1957	37,482	85,767	
1958	37,130	92,038	
1959	46,643	98,357	
Average 1953-1959			44.7% [60]

The extent to which the year 1950 saw a reproduction of the massive increase in the rate of surplus-value achieved under the

[60] Walther G. Hoffmann, op. cit., pp. 508-9.

Third Reich can be seen at a glance by comparing the figures for that year with those of the years 1927-28: while the income of labour is the same (at that time the average was RM 38·7 billion; in 1950 it was DM 38.9 billion) the surplus-value appropriated by industry and handicrafts themselves has *nearly tripled* (it rose from an average RM 5.6 billion to DM 15.5 billion!). Not until the 60's was there a renewed decline in the rate of surplus-value.

The figures for manufacturing industry in the USA show major discrepancies from Vance's estimates quoted above. The main reason for this may lie in the increasing mass of surplus-value appropriated *outside* industry. Calculation of the long-term development of the rate of surplus-value in manufacturing industry in the USA is further complicated by the fact that the statistics in the official *Census of Manufactures* include depreciation allowances in the category of 'value-added' and furthermore do not give the precise volume of these allowances. We have calculated the rate of surplus-value according to the method used by Gillman.[61] Yet another problem is whether the wages of productive workers alone should count as variable capital or whether at least a section of white-collar workers—those who are indispensable for the production and realization of surplus-value, as Marx puts it—should not also be included among the recipients of variable capital; and if this is accepted, the extent of this section remains to be determined.

Below we give four series of figures, all of which are based on official data:

Series   I: Surplus-value = value added, minus wages.
Series II: Surplus-value = value added, minus depreciation allowances and wages.
Series III: Surplus-value = value added, minus wages and 50% of salaries.
Series IV: Surplus-value = value added, minus depreciation allowances, wages and 50% of salaries.

Accordingly, in Series III and IV 50% of salaries are also counted as variable capital (*see* table on following page).

The astonishing parallellism between the four series makes it relatively simple to interpret these figures, even if one point remains questionable. From the start of the century until after the First World War, the rate of surplus-value slowly fell, because of the

---

[61]Joseph Gillman, *The Falling Rate of Profit*, London, 1967, pp. 46-7, 60-1.

Year	Rate of surplus value = surplus value / variable capital			
	I	II	III	IV
1904	146%	134%	117%	97%
1914	149%	127%	108%	94%
1919	146%	125%	108%	94%
1923	142%	127%	106%	84%
1929	180%	163%	135%	113%
1935	153%	135%	124%	97%
1939	182%	154%	. . .	. . . [62]
1947	146%	129%	113%	98%
1950	159%	140%	118%	102%
1954	151%	143%	112%	96%
1958	185%	165%	121%	106%
1963	209%	192%	137%	124%
1966	219%	200%	146%	131% [63]

long-term decline of unemployment and the growth of trade-union organization. It then rose steeply during the 'period of prosperity' 1923-29, as a result of the rapid growth in productivity (production of relative surplus-value) and the reconstitution of the industrial reserve army. During the Great Depression it fell (but not as much as is generally assumed) because of part-time work (decline in absolute surplus-value and a relative increase in fixed costs). It underwent irregular fluctuations during and after the Second World War (first suspension, then reproduction of the industrial reserve army) and as from the mid-50's it registered a major upswing (massive increase in the productivity of labour and the production of relative surplus-value).

The third and fourth series of figures — which deviate somewhat from the estimates by Vance cited earlier in this chapter, but probably correspond more closely to the actual development — enable us to explain more accurately both the acceleration and the economic function of automation in the USA in the 50's (and West Germany in the 60's). The first effects of the third technological revolution made themselves felt in a relative fall in the share of raw materials and often even machines in average commodity values, and hence led to a rise in the share of wages in costs per unit.[64] For the

[62] The figures for the salaries of white collar workers in 1939 are not given in the *Statistical Abstracts of the United States* at our disposal.

[63] Data on value added, the sum of wages and salaries in manufacturing industry of the USA, in *Statistical Abstract of the United States*, No. 60, Washington 1938, p. 749; No. 69, Washington, 1948, p. 825; No. 89, Washington, 1968, pp. 717-19.

[64] W. E. G. Salter, *Productivity and Technical Change*, Cambridge, 1960, p. 25. See Chapter 6 of the present work.

individual capitalist the struggle to raise the rate of surplus-value found empirical expression in the struggle to force down the share of wages. The purpose of automation was to achieve this reduction, and simultaneously to reconstruct the industrial reserve army.

In an extremely interesting, and hitherto unpublished, doctoral thesis, Shane Mage comes to opposite conclusions. He claims that the long-term development of the rate of surplus-value from the start of this century to the end of the Second World War was sharply downward in the USA. Even so, according to him the rate of surplus-value ceased to fall after 1946 and started — if only modestly — to rise again. Mage has tried, with greater accuracy than Vance or Baran and Sweezy, to reduce official US statistics to the categories employed by Marx. Thus, under 'variable capital' he includes only the wages of productive workers, while on the other hand, all business profits are designated surplus-value. These two corrections are perfectly in line with the import of Marx's analysis. Mage makes a two-fold error, however, which falsifies his findings.[65] Firstly, he takes only the *net profits* (and the *net* interest and annuities) of capitalist firms as surplus-value, although for Marx taxes represent part of the social surplus-value.[66] Secondly, he adds the wages of ·workers employed in service firms into variable capital, although if the labour theory of value is rigorously applied, services in the real sense of the word — i.e., all except those producing commodity transportation, gas, electricity and water — do not produce commodities, and hence do not create any new value. However, if Mage's tables are dually corrected in this way, then the long-term fall of the rate of surplus-value disappears altogether. Mage himself makes a partial — if inexact — correction, but only in the form of a working hypothesis in an appendix to his work, in which he calculates surplus-value from gross wages and gross profits (taxes paid by workers — as distinct from deductions for social security — cannot normally be included in variable capital in Marx's sense of the term, since they have nothing to do with the reproduction of the commodity of labour-

---

[65]Shane Mage, *The 'Law of the Falling Tendency of the Rate of Profit': Its Place in the Marxian System and Relevance to the US Economy*, Columbia University Ph.D., 1963, University Microfilms Inc., Ann Arbor, Michigan, pp. 174-5, 164-7, 161, 164, 225f.

[66]In Marx's theory all revenues are traced back to wages or surplus-value. Since state revenues can hardly be regarded as variable capital — unless they are used to buy productive labour-power, for instance in state industrial enterprises — they can only be regarded as a redistribution of social surplus-value or an increase of it by deduc-

power). Even when this unsatisfactory correction has been made, however, we find that there was an increase in the rate of surplus-value from 45.1% in the period 1930-40 to 57.1% in the period 1940-1960.[67] If the full correction is made, then an increase is obtained which is perfectly congruent with the series advanced by us.

The example of the USA from the close of the Second World War till the end of the 50's is all the more significant, in that it contradicts Lewis's thesis that it is not possible to speak of a durable reproduction of the industrial reserve army after the disappearance of the pre-capitalist sectors of the economy, and that Marx was consequently mistaken in his assumption that *in the course of the accumulation of capital* living labour would be replaced by 'dead labour'.[68] This period saw precisely such a replacement of workers by machines — in other words, an annual growth rate of labour productivity exceeding the annual growth rate of production.[69] The result was the very rapid reappearance of the industrial reserve army which had disappeared in the course of the Second World War — with all the ensuing implications for the rate of surplus-value.[70]

---

tions from wages. Their function becomes even clearer in cases where taxes are directly capital-forming, so that their character as part of the social surplus-value cannot be disputed without throwing the whole of Marx's theory of capital into question. See for example *Capital*, Vol. 1, p. 756.

[67] Shane Mage, op. cit., pp. 272-3. Calculations by Phelps-Brown and Browne suggest a rapid rise in the rate of surplus-value as early as the period from 1933 to 1940, and then again markedly between 1946 and 1951: *A Century of Pay*, London. 1968, pp. 450-2.

[68] W. Arthur Lewis, *'Unlimited Labour — Further Notes'*, p. 25.

[69] In the years 1945-61 the total American proletariat, defined as the mass of the wage and salary earners — i.e., the mass of those who are forced to sell their labour power-rose by 14 million or 35% (there was an increase of only 1 million in actual manufacturing industry, however, and only 2.5 million in manufacturing industry plus construction plus transport, gas, electricity and other public services excluding the actual state apparatus). Physical output per wage-earner (i.e. the productivity of labour) rose by 50% in the manufacturing industry from 1947-61 and by 42% in non-manufacturing industry. The sum total of hours worked rose by 15% in industry, physical output by nearly 70%. By contrast, weekly real wages only rose by 29%, and the per capita real consumption by only 20%. No wonder that in the same period investments in fixed capital climbed by 70% and investments in Department I by as much as 100%, while unemployment (except for the three years of the Korean boom) fluctuated about 4.5% of total employed, or even 5-6% if partial unemployment is taken into account, although at the same time several million wage-earners were serving in the army. *Economic Report of the President — Transmitted to Congress, January 1962*, Washington,1962, pp. 236, 244-5, 242, 227, 248.

[70] In West Germany, too, massive numbers of workers were laid off in many branches of industry in 1958-60, but they found new employment in the more expansionary branches. The IFO Economic Research Institute calculated that in the

This reproduction of the industrial reserve army in the USA after the Second World War, just like the combination of growing rates of surplus-value and rising real wages[71] in Western Europe and Japan after 1945 or 1948, was only rendered possible by a significant and long-term increase in the productivity of labour — in other words, it corresponded to a 'Great Leap Forward' in the production of relative surplus-value. It is precisely in this sense that the third technological revolution must be seen as an essential part of our understanding of late capitalism. As long as the industrial reserve army enables the rate of surplus-value to grow — a condition created in turn by a significant increase in the productivity of labour in Department II — there are no particular problems here. Hence the years 1949-60 in such countries as West Germany and Italy, 1950-65 in Japan, and 1951-65 in the USA formed genuine halcyon periods for late capitalism, in which all factors appeared to promote expansion: a high rate of investment; a rapid growth of labour productivity; a rising rate of surplus-value facilitated by the industrial reserve army, hence a slower growth of real wages as compared to the productivity of labour, with a simultaneous dampening of social tensions.

We can now summarize the general mechanism of the long wave of expansion from 1940/1948 to 1966, together with the particular differences in its operation in the various imperialist states. Rearmament and the Second World War enabled capital accumulation to take off again, after the Great Depression, by bringing large volumes of surplus capital back into surplus-value production.[72] This reinjection of capital was accompanied by a significant increase in the rate of surplus-value, first of all in Germany, Japan, Italy, France and Spain — i.e., those countries where the working-class had suffered grave defeats through fascism and war; and then in the USA, where the no-strike pledge of the trade-union bureaucracy during the Second World War, the imposition of the Taft-Hartley

---

period 1950-61 4.33% of the employed work force was annually made redundant by capital intensification and technical progress. In 1958-65 there was a significant decrease in the number of people employed in the textile industry, the leather industry, the fine ceramics industry, the wood processing industry and other branches. Kruse, Kunz and Uhlmann, *Wirtschaftliche Auswirkungen der Automatisierung*, pp. 79, 65.

[71] Marx expressly took into account the possibility of such a development. See *Grundrisse*, p. 757.

[72] We shall study the theoretical problems posed by the revival of capital accumulation after the Great Depression by means of rearmament expenditure and arms production, in Chapter 11.

Act after two years of post-war industrial militancy, and the capitulation of the AFL-CIO apparatus to the 'Cold War' and MacCarthyism, led to a more gradual erosion of working-class combativity.

Increasing rates of surplus-value and of profit now facilitated the birth of the third technological revolution. After a phase of 'extensive industrialization', capital investment henceforward took the form of semi-automation and automation, especially in the USA, West Germany and Japan. There occurred a massive increase in the productivity of labour in Department II, and therewith a corresponding increase in the output of relative surplus-value and hence in the rate of surplus-value. A reverse movement only became evident when the very dynamic of this expansionary long wave started to reach the limits of the reserve army of labour and conditions on the 'labour market' consequently turned to the advantage of the working-class, and a pronounced increase in real wages started to roll back the rate of surplus-value.

Britain constitutes the exception which proves the rule. There, the working-class suffered an epochal defeat earlier than in the other major European countries (with the exception of Italy), with the debacle of the General Strike in 1926 and the disintegration of the Labour Government in 1931. Throughout the 30's, unemployment then remained at a high level in England. The combined result was a slow but steady increase in the rate of surplus-value.[73] At the end of the decade, however, the situation of the British working-class had improved objectively, with a decline in the industrial reserve army of labour. Thereafter it was subjectively the only major proletariat in the world which suffered no serious defeat for the thirty years from 1936 to 1966 — an experience which profoundly modified the relationship of class forces in England. Thus Britain became the only imperialist power which proved unable to increase the rate of exploitation of its working-class significantly during or after the Second World War; the rate in the UK was now stablized at the lower pre-war levels in the new epoch.[74] From a capitalist point of view the result was evident: an erosion of the rate of profit, and a much slower rate of economic growth and accumulation than in the other imperialist countries (and the stimulating influence of international expansion on the British economy was responsible for a significant part even of this growth).

[73]Phelps Brown and Browne, op. cit., pp. 248-50, 446-7.   [74]Ibid., p. 458.

As soon as expansion led to the dismantling and disappearance of the industrial reserve army, however, and simultaneously generational changes began to diminish subjective scepticism and resignation in the working-class, the golden years of late capitalism were internationally over. There was now no longer any chance of an automatic increase in the rate of profit or its maintenance at a high level. *The struggle over the rate of surplus-value now flared up anew.* Moreover, in this struggle it was precisely the high level of employment which contributed to a significant increase in the strength of wage-earners, to whom extra-economic pressures were now applied in order to prevent them from diminishing the rate of surplus-value. This, of course, was the common purpose of the wide variety of state interventions, proclaiming 'social programming', 'concerted action', an 'incomes policy', if not even a 'state wages policy' or 'wage freeze'. Since genuine bargaining autonomy on the part of the trade unions, real trade union freedom and the unrestricted right to strike constitute obstacles along this road, various forms of 'strong state' legislation have been drafted or passed to eliminate them.

The transition from a 'long wave with a basically expansionary tone' to a 'long wave with a basically stagnant tone' about the years 1966-67 was thus closely related to this struggle for the rate of surplus-value. Late capitalism cannot avoid a period of relatively decelerated economic expansion if it fails to break the resistance of wage-earners and so to achieve a new radical increase in the rate of surplus-value. This is unthinkable, however, without stagnation, and indeed even without a temporary fall in real wages. In the mid-60's, therefore, a new phase of intensified class struggle set in within all the imperialist countries. Starting from Great Britain, Italy and France, this wave gradually spread to West Germany and the rest of capitalist Europe, and later also to Japan and the USA. The intensification of inter-imperialist rivalry at the same time has reduced the possibilities of displacing this struggle by the export of social tensions and in particular the export of unemployment.

In this intensification of class struggle, capital has no chance of achieving an effective increase in the rate of surplus-value comparable to that under the Nazi dictatorship or in the Second World War, so long as conditions on the labour market themselves tilt the 'respective powers of the combatants' to the advantage of the proletariat. The extension of the industrial reserve army has consequently today become a conscious instrument of economic policy in the service of capital.[75] In this context, it is necessary to recall the passage from Rosa Luxemburg cited above (see footnote 14), and to analyze the various components of the industrial reserve army. Among other things, the considerable fluctuations in the employment of women and young people under 21, together with foreign workers, which act as shock absorbers in the reconstitution of this reserve army, must be considered. Thus in the USA for example, the number of adult women employed rose by 71% between 1950 and 1970, and that of employable teenagers by 65%, while the increase in the employment of adult males was only 16% in the same two decades. For this reason, in February 1972 the unemployment rate for teenagers was 18.8%, and for adult women 10.5%, as compared with a rate of only 2.7% for married men. The same shock absorbers, however, mean that official unemployment figures by no means correspond to the actual amount of people excluded from the labour process, for a significant number of women and young people do not offer their labour-power if the chances of selling it are not very high. In the case of the Italian labour market, Luca Meldolesi has arrived at frighteningly high figures of *concealed*

---

[75]The use of foreign workers as a deliberate cushion against excessive 'internal fluctuations of employment' became clear during the West German recession of 1966-67, when more than 400,000 foreign workers lost their jobs between June 1966 and June 1968 (Nikolinakos, op. cit., pp. 38, 66-70). The same phenomenon can be noted in the USA, with its Puerto Rican, Mexican and (of late) Central American immigrant labour. There is no space here to analyze the complex effects of the fluctuations in this *internationalized industrial reserve army of labour* on the economic development of the poorer ancillary countries neighbouring on the wealthy imperialist States. It is notorious, however, that a large proportion of immigrant workers are unskilled labourers, confined to the dirtiest, hardest and worst paid jobs in the metropolitan economies. A new stratification within the proletariat is thereby deliberately created by capital, between 'indigenous' and 'foreign' workers. This allows employers at one and the same time to keep wages of unskilled labour down, to brake the development of proletarian class consciousness by stimulating ethnic and sectional particularisms, and to exploit these artificial antagonisms to propagate xenophobia and racism in the working-class. The Schwarzenbach campaign in Switzerland, Powellism in Britain and the anti-Arab pogroms in France are all examples of the latter. The cause of international proletarian solidarity therewith becomes an elementary duty even from the point of view 'trade-union' consciousness, not to speak of political class consciousness proper. For the discriminations to which foreign workers are subject in Western Europe, see the documentation in S. Castles and G. Kossack, *Immigrant Workers and the Class Structure in Western Europe*, Oxford, 1973.

unemployment, which must be included in the industrial reserve army.[76] It is important to emphasize the *dual role* of the additional pool of labour-power comprised by married women and youth, as well as immigrant workers (including racial and national minorities in the USA: Blacks, Chicanos and Puerto Ricans), in the preservation or reconstruction of an industrial reserve army of labour. On the one hand, the fluctuations in their employment are much greater than those of 'stable' workers who are 'heads of families'. On the other hand, they are paid much less for their labour-power, as the bourgeoisie cynically assumes that their income is only a 'supplement' to the 'family budget'. Their wages are often inadequate even for the physical reconstruction of their labour-power, so that they are obliged to have recourse to welfare, social security, 'illegal' quests for income and so on, to eke out their existence. Part of the costs of the reproduction of their labour-power thus becomes 'socialized'.[77]

Capital today has two ways available to it of reconstructing the industrial army: on the one hand, the intensification of capital exports and the systematic suffocation of investments at home, i.e., sending capital where there is still excess labour-power, instead of bringing labour-power to excess capital; on the other, the intensification of automation, or in other words the concentration of investments to set free as much living labour as possible (industrialization 'in depth' rather than 'in breadth').

In the long-run, both tactics can achieve only a limited success, and both will reproduce even more acute social contradictions. On the one hand, the suffocation of investments at home diminishes the rate of growth and thus intensifies social antagonisms. On

[76] *Wall Street Journal*, 25 October 1971; *Survey of Current Business*, February 1972; Luca Meldolesi, *Disoccupazione ed Esercito Industriale di Riserva in Italia*, Bari, 1972. While in 1940, only 27.4% of American women above the age of 16 were gainfully employed, this percentage had risen to 42.6% by 1970. Among married women, the increase was even greater — from 16.7% to 41.4%. In the same year, 1970, the percentage of women between the ages of 15 and 64 who were gainfully employed was 59.4% in Sweden, 55.5% in Japan, 52.1% in Britain, and 48.6% in West Germany, but only 29.1% in Italy, where the real industrial reserve army of labour is still to be found in the underdeveloped regions of the Centre and South of the country.

[77] James O'Connor, op. cit., pp. 14-15, 33-4. In 1968, 10 million wage-earners in the USA earned less than 1.6 dollars an hour and 3.5 million less than 1 dollar an hour, while the average wage in manufacturing industry was over 3 dollars an hour, and in construction reached 4.4 dollars. There now exists an extensive literature on the super-exploitation of the 'sub-proletariat' of the imperialist countries.

the other hand, after a certain time-lag — and the time-lag is a question of crucial importance — the differences in the level of wages between the country exporting capital and the country importing capital will also start to dwindle. To a considerable extent, of course, the rate of this process will be determined by the internal economic and social structure of the country importing capital (if the country in question is already industrialized, this process will not be postponable; if the country is an under-developed semi-colony, it can be held in check for a longer period). At the same time, as is shown in the next chapter, labour-saving automation must in the long-run tend to limit the mass of surplus-value produced, and thereby necessarily make a further rise in the rate of surplus-value more difficult. But more important than these long-term contradictions in the tactical response of capital to the fall in the average rate of profit is the immediate effect of this response on the class struggle. Late capitalism is a great school for the proletariat, teaching it to concern itself not only with the immediate apportionment of newly created value between wages and profits, but with all questions of economic policy and development, and particularly with all questions revolving on the organization of labour, the process of production and the exercise of political power.

6

The Specific Nature of the Third Technological Revolution

We shall now attempt to combine the two analyses pursued in the preceding chapters: analysis of the successively predominant forms of differences in levels of productivity, together with the main directions of the quest for surplus profits which correspond to them; and analysis of the successively predominant types of motive machines and sources of energy that determine the overall structure of production in Department I.

In the age of freely competitive capitalism the mainspring of extended reproduction seems to have been the uneven and combined development of different regions within the most important capitalist countries. The resultant release of money capital via the progressive pentration of agriculture by capitalist commodity circulation, and of producers separated from land and soil, led to the continuous drain of money capital to the major industrial districts, where evicted ex-peasants now formed an industrial reserve army.

Two intermediate phases can here be distinguished. The first saw the advent of production of motive machines and machines which in their turn produced these machines, mostly on the basis of handicrafts or manufactures. A significant portion of the production of Department I was not exchanged against commodities from Department II and did not serve for mechanized output of consumer goods, but remained within Department I itself. The production of raw materials in agriculture was also still substantially carried on by cottage industry. In this epoch only the iron and coal industry was characterized by a significant mechanization of certain production processes. But even in the coal industry there was still such a prevalence of manual labour that pure wage costs accounted for more than 66%, and sometimes even more than 75% of the cost price of the product. This manifestly corresponded to a very low organic composition of capital, which in agricultural production of industrial raw materials was probably lower still.

During the second phase of the period of freely competitive capitalism, machine production now also penetrated the sphere of motive machines, of steam-driven motors. The point was reached where machines produced machines to construct other machines. But in this phase, too, artisanal production of raw materials continued to predominate, It is characteristic, for example, that before the application of the Bessemer and Siemens-Martin patents, the steel industry was composed of only medium-scale enterprises and did not reveal any form of mass production.[1]

During these first two phases of the epoch of freely competitive capitalism, therefore, machine-operated large industry predominated only in the consumer goods industry (with the main emphasis on the textile industry). Even the large industrial producers of means of transport — especially railways — only made their appearance in the second phase of this period, and were among the determinant factors of the emergence of a 'long wave with an undertone of expansion' from 1847-73.

Surprisingly, we thus discover that in the first century after the Industrial Revolution the organic composition of capital in Department II was generally speaking higher than in Department I. The genesis of industrial capitalism, as it is depicted by Karl Marx in Chapter 15 of the First Volume of *Capital*, must in fact be described as the *machine-industrial production of consumer goods by means of hand-made machines.*

[1] David S. Landes, *The Unbound Prometheus,* Cambridge, 1970, pp. 254-9. Bessemer's invention was closely linked to military needs in the wake of the Crimean War: see W. H. Armytage, *A Social History of Engineering,* London, 1969, pp. 153-5. 'The repercussions on industrial organization, especially in the ship-building industry, were decisive. The age of metal and machinery inevitably ripened the growth of large-scale industrial units. Share-holders in the Great Eastern . . . went through the kind of traumatic experience that their predecessors had suffered in the railway mania of a decade before.' p. 155.

Once this state of affairs has been grasped, it becomes possible to explain why it took such a long time to introduce machine-production in Department I. The equalization of the rate of profit between Department I, where productivity of labour was lower, and Department II, where productivity was higher, led to a constant transfer of surplus-value from Department I to Department II. The process of unequal exchange disbursing surplus-profits was in this period an exchange between agricultural goods and products of Department II; the mass introduction of machines and artificial fertilizers into agriculture had hardly occurred anywhere. In Western Europe (and the USA) the whole inner dynamic of the capitalist mode of production in this epoch was concentrated on *accelerating accumulation in Department II at the cost of accumulation in Department I.*

The same configuration also explains:

(a) why the main international direction of the penetration of capitalist commodity production into non-industrialized countries in this phase took the form of the export of commodities, namely *the export of consumer goods;* for throughout this phase it was this sector which dominated the capitalist economy of the metropolitan countries and every time that there was cyclical overproduction it took the form above all of the overproduction of industrial consumer goods.

(b) why capitalism was in this epoch in actual fact freely competitive because the modest character of the minimum capital needed to penetrate the consumer goods sector prevented the rise of monopolies and oligopolies.

The turning point which occurred at the start of the imperialist epoch was the result of two concurrent and combined changes in the operation of the capitalist mode of production. On the one hand, Department I went over from the machine production of steam-driven motors to the machine production of electric motors. The consequent transformation of the entire production process in Department I caused a vast increase in the organic composition of capital in the sub-department of Department I producing *fixed* constant capital. But a transformation also occurred in the technology of the sub-department of Department I producing *circulating* constant capital — the production of raw materials. We characterized this transformation as 'the transition from the production of raw materials by handicrafts to their production on the lines of manufactures or early industry'. Taken together, the two processes thus determined — to a varying degree — a significant increase in the organic composition of capital in Department I. It is obvious that the rise in the organic composition of capital in Department II could not be on a comparable scale to that in Department I. On the whole, the revolutionization of productive technology in Department II was limited to the replacement of the steam-driven motor by the electric motor, which could hardly lead to a fundamental change in the organic composition of capital.[2]

On the other hand, the progressive introduction of machine-made steam-driven machines in the period 1847-73, combined with the growing generalization of railway construction in this period, absorbed colossal amounts of capital.[3] This large transfer of capital began to consolidate the predominance of Department I over Department II. The organic composition of capital in Department I gradually approached that of Department II, and then rapidly overtook it. The fundamental transfer of surplus-value from Department I to Department II, accompanying the equalization of the rate of profit, thereupon ceased; the transfer was now inversely from Department II to Department I.

The specific nature of fixed capital produced in Department I, however, meant that it was produced mainly on order and not for sale on an anonymous market. Production sites were accordingly adjusted to maximum orders. As soon as the most important branches of industry in the capitalist countries had been equipped with machine-made steam-driven motors — which was probably the case at the beginning of the 1870's — the production capacity of Department I could no longer be utilized at full load. This was one of the main causes of the long wave with an undertone of stagnation, 1873-93. It meant, however, that an important part of the surplus-value realized by Department I, and a not insignificant part of the surplus-value produced in Department II but appropriated by Department I through the equalization of the rate of profit, could now no longer be valorized. Just as, in the preceding fifty years, the limits to the further development of the capitalist mode of production took the form of overproduction in Department II, so in the final quarter

---

[2]Landes speaks of the 'exhaustion of the technological possibilities of the Industrial Revolution' and, with the exception of the transformation of the steel industry, the dwindling of the 'gains implicit in the original cluster of innovations that had constituted the Industrial Revolution'. Ibid., pp. 234-5, 237.

[3]*Ibid.*, pp. 153-5, 541.

of the 19th Century it took the form of *over-capitalization in Department I*. The logical outcome was a change in the main thrust of the capitalist drive for expansion: no longer export of consumer goods to pre-capitalist areas, but export of capitals (and of goods bought with these capitals, principally railway lines, locomotives, and port facilities, i.e., infrastructural facilities to simplify and cheapen the export of raw materials produced with metropolitan capital). Together with the growing concentration of capital, this was the decisive reason for the emergence of the new, imperialist structure of the capitalist world economy.

This change in the operation of the capitalist mode of production, or in the proportions between the major independent variables of this mode of production, also explains the transition from freely competitive to monopoly capitalism. The massive penetration of capital into Department I created production plants there which, as Marx put it, had to operate with cyclopean instruments of production and hence also cyclopean amounts of capital. There was a massive growth in the minimum capital needed to be able to compete in this field. Increasingly, competition led to concentration; only a limited number of independent enterprises and joint stock companies were able to survive. The fact that the long-term phase of stagnation from 1873-93 coincided with the emergence of the second technological revolution — above all in the technology of electric motors — was a compelling reason for the formation of trusts and monopolies. Lenin already emphasized the decisive role played by these two factors in the formation of monopoly capitalism.[4] It is not surprising this monopolization occurred more rapidly in the 'new' branches of industry (steel,[5] electric machines, oil) and in the 'new' industrial nations (USA, Germany) than in the 'old' branches of industry (textiles, coal) and the 'old' industrial states (England, France).

How then does the development of the past fifty years appear in the light of this schema? The accelerated accumulation of capital engendered by the second technological revolution 1893-1914 was followed by a long period of braked accumulation and relative economic stagnation, lasting from the end of the First World War until the

---

[4] See Lenin, *Imperialism, the Highest Stage of Capitalism*, in *Selected Works*, London, 1969, p. 177.

[5] This preponderance is so self-evident that Landes calls the phase of development of the European economy beginning in the 1870s 'The Age of Steel'. Landes, op. cit., p. 249f.

beginning of the Second World War. We have already explained the main cause of this stagnation in Chapters 4 and 5: the significant rise in the organic composition of capital as a result of general electrification produced a tendency for the average rate of profit to fall, which could have been neutralized only by a correspondingly significant increase in the rate of surplus-value. In the great post-revolutionary wave after the First World War, however, the capitalist class had to make concessions to the working-class in order to preserve its political domination, which were more likely to stabilize or even to lower the rate of surplus-value than to increase it. After a brief economic upswing in 1924-29, the fall in the rate of profit led to the Great Depression of 1929-32, and to stagnation in activities promoting valorization and accumulation. Only the victory of Hitler's fascism — and in other countries the Second World War — enabled capital to achieve a rise in the rate of surplus-value sufficiently large to allow the average rate of profit to soar for a time, despite the higher organic composition of capital.

In the meantime, however, other important changes in the overall conditions of capital's existence had occurred. In the first place, Soviet Russia had broken out of the capitalist world market, and so for the first time since the genesis of the capitalist mode of production, the capitalist world market had undergone a contraction rather than an expansion. For a short time it seemed as if recent rises in the price of raw materials and intensified colonization of England's 'Third Empire' in Africa[6] might boost export of capital again. But soon after the outbreak of the Great Depression it became clear that there was a long-term tendency for the export of capital to the colonies and semi-colonies to decline, primarily as a result of the monopolistic character of the imperialist concerns dominating the colonial production of raw materials. Under-accumulation in the metropolitan countries and the decline of capital exports to the colonies thus merely reinforced the emergence of excess capital and the fall of the rate of profit. As we know, excess capital only obtains the average interest and not the average profit. Since, however, it does not itself participate in the immediate valorization of capital, and this interest must therefore be paid for out of the total social surplus-value, it forces the average rate of profit down even further.

In the second place, this excess capital now began to penetrate

[6] See George Padmore, *Africa, Britain's Third Empire*, London, 1948.

into Department II. A new sector of consumer goods was created, producing so-called *durable consumer goods,* which represented the application of the second technological revolution to the consumer goods sector: automobile production and the beginning of the output of electrical apparatuses (vacuum cleaners, radios, electric sewing machines, and so on). Although, in the form of mass production, this transformation was mainly limited to the USA, it nonetheless led to a substantial increase in the organic composition of capital which, especially in the USA, began to decrease the advantage of Department I in the redistribution of surplus-value between the two Departments. Since this coincided in time with a phase in which the average rate of profit in Department I was anyway falling sharply, and then with the great crisis which shook the whole of Department I, the pressure to raise the rate of profit in this Department became positively explosive. This pressure took four forms:

1) Towards an immediate increase in the rate of surplus value (fascism, war economy).

2) Towards an immediate valorization of excess capital by means of rearmament.

3) Towards a new attempt to lower the cost of constant capital, i.e., renewed massive penetration of capital into the production of raw materials (both minerals and agriculture), but this time with advanced industrial technology, and hence to bring down the cost of fixed constant capital. The pressure to shorten the turnover time of capital was related to this attempt.

4) Towards a radical reduction in the share of wage costs in the cost price of commodities, accompanied by experiments in semi-automation and automation. The reason for this temporary tendency was the trend for the relative share of wage costs to increase, concomitant with the radical reduction in the price of raw materials and the share of value represented by fixed capital.

As soon as the first crucial objective had been achieved, i.e., the rate of profit had moved up once again, capital expansion was able to rocket through the use of the additional capital accumulated but not valorized, in the period 1929-39, and the simultaneous exploitation of the other three tendencies listed above. The result was the shift into the third 'long wave with an undertone of expansion', from 1940 (1945) to 1965.

This new period was characterized, among other things, by the fact that alongside machine-made industrial consumer goods (as from the early 19th century) and machine-made machines (as from the mid-19th century), we now find machine-produced raw materials and foodstuffs. *Late capitalism, far from representing a 'post-industrial society',* [7] *thus appears as the period in which all branches of the economy are fully industrialized for the first time;* to which one could further add the increasing mechanization of the sphere of circulation (with the exception of pure repair services) and the increasing mechanization of the superstructure.

This development, however, simultaneously determined a general equalization of the average productivity of labour in the most important realms of production. Indeed, in some branches producing agricultural goods or raw materials (e.g., in oil refineries and the synthetic fibres industry) and in some branches making consumer goods (e.g., fully automated food industries) labour productivity has in the last 25 years registered a higher average increase than in branches producing fixed capital. In the USA, agricultural production per man-hour worked rose from 100 to 377 from 1929 to 1964, while in the same period it rose to only 229 in manufacturing industry. [8] In West Germany in the years 1958-65 there was an annual increase of 7.7% in the productivity of employees in the textile industry, of 7% in wood processing, 6.9% in the glass industry and 5.1% in the food industry, as opposed to 4.2% in the metal industry, 4.6% in the electrotechnical industry, 4% in the iron industry, 3.8% in vehicle production, 3.2% in iron and steel construction and 2.8% in machine production. Altogether the average annual rate of growth of labour productivity in this period was 6.1% in the consumer goods industry as opposed to 4.2% in the investments goods industry. [9]

This equalization of the average productivity of the two large Departments, i.e., of the average organic composition of capital, is part of the very essence of automation. For once it becomes possible to apply the principle of fully automated processes to mass production, it can be applied with equal success both to the mass

[7] This notion—later discussed and criticized in Chapter 12—is used by, among others, Daniel Bell in *The Reforming of General Education*, New York, 1966, Hermann Kahn in *The Year 2000*, New York, 1967, and Jean Jacques Servan-Schreiber in *The American Challenge*, London, 1970.

[8] U.S. Department of Commerce, Bureau of the Census, *Long-Term Economic Growth 1860-1965*, Washington, 1966.

[9] Kruse, Kunz and Uhlmann, *Wirtschaftliche Auswirkungen der Automation*, pp. 68-9. The synthetic fibres industry registered an annual growth rate of 9% in the productivity of labour in the period 1950-65.

production of raw materials and 'light' consumer goods and to that of transistorized gadgets or to synthetic fibres.

The age of late capitalism thus confronts capital once again with a situation not dissimilar to that of the mid-19th century: a growing equalization of the average productivity of labour. From this two conclusions can be drawn:

1) In the first place, regional or international differences in levels of productivity no longer provide the main source for the realization of surplus-profits. This role is now assumed by such differences between sectors and enterprises,[10] as can be deduced logically from the situation described above. We must not forget that while the previous historical period of the 19th century was characterized by diminishing differences in the productivity of labour as between the two Departments, capital had greater opportunities of evading the consequences of this diminution by moving into agriculture and especially into the colonies and semi-colonies. For the reasons already described, such opportunities either no longer exist, or are only very limited today.

2) There thus develops a permanent pressure to *accelerate technological innovation*. For the dwindling of other sources of surplus-profits inevitably leads to a constant hunt for 'technological rents' which can only be obtained through permanent technological renewal.[11] Technological rents are surplus-profits derived from a monopolization of technical progress — i.e., from discoveries and inventions which lower the cost-price of commodities but cannot (at least in the medium-run) become generalized throughout a given branch of production and applied by all competitors, because of the structure of monopoly capital itself: difficulties of entry, size of minimum investment, control of patents, cartel arrangements, and so on. In this sense the latent overproduction of consumer goods of the age of freely competitive capitalism and the latent capital surplus of the age of imperialism give way, in the phase of late capitalism, to

[10] Examples of these differences are given by, among others, the American trade union leader Charles Levinson in his recent book, *Capital, Inflation and the Multinationals*, London, 1971, p. 28f. The European Economic Commission of the United Nations gives the annual growth rate of labour productivity per branch in Western Europe as fluctuating between 1.3% in the leather industry, and 9% in the oil industry. This is a variation of 1 to 7. *Economic Survey of Europe in 1970*, Geneva, 1971.

[11] A more extensive treatment of this problem follows in the next two chapters of this book.

the *latent overproduction of means of production* as the *predominant* form of the economic contradictions of the capitalist economy, although obviously combined with these other two forms.[12]

The basic features of late capitalism can thus already be derived from the laws of motion of capital. In the further course of this analysis we will integrate several other factors, essentially based on those just elaborated. The immediate origin of the third technological revolution can be traced back to the four main objectives of capital in the 30's and 40's of the 20th century listed above. The technical possibility of automation springs from the arms economy, or from the technical necessities corresponding to the particular degree of development reached by the arms economy. This applies to the general principle of automatic, continuous processes of production, completely emancipated from direct contact by human hands (which becomes a physiological necessity with the use of nuclear energy). It also applies to the compulsion to construct automatic calculators, produced by direct derivation from cybernetic principles, which can collect data at lightning speed, and draw conclusion from them for the determination of decisions — for example, the precise guidance of automatic air defence missiles to knock out bomber planes.[13]

The productive application of this new technology began in those realms of the chemical industry where the decisive driving force is the cheapening of circulating constant capital. From the beginning of the 50's, it gradually spread to an increasing number of realms where the main objective was radically to reduce direct wage costs — i.e., to eliminate living labour from the process of production. In the USA this objective undoubtedly corresponded to the need to make good the sometimes substantial increases in wages which had occurred in the immediate post-war period.[14] The compulsion felt by 'many capitals' to reduce wage-costs had its counterpart for 'capital in general' in the tendency for the industrial reserve army to be reconstructed through the release of unemployed labour power.

Rezler distinguishes four types of automation, or more precisely, semi-automated and automated production processes, which define the field of the third technological revolution:

— Transfer of parts between successive production processes,

[12] This latent overproduction of instruments of production takes the form, above all, of a permanent over-capacity in the branches of Department I.
[13] Friedrich Pollock, *Automation*, Frankfurt, 1964, pp. 46-7.
[14] See the fourth column in the table on p. 175 of the present work.

based on automatic devices — for example, in the Detroit automobile industry.

— Continuous flow processes, based on automatic control of the flow and its quality — for example, in the chemical industry, oil refineries, gas and electricity utilities.

— Computer-controlled processes, in any manufacturing plant.

— Various combinations of the above systems — for example, the super-imposition of computers on Detroit-style semi-automation created numerically-controlled machine-tool complexes; the combination of continuous flow processes with computers has nearly realized the goal of completely automatic production units in oil-refining and public-utility plants.[15]

The extent of the third technological revolution can be assessed from the fact that 'a survey conducted by McGraw-Hill Company in the middle 60's . . . indicated that some automatic control and measurement devices and data-handling systems were used by 21,000 out of 32,000 (US) manufacturing establishments employing over 100 persons. Nearly 9 out of 10 petroleum, instrument, computer and control equipment plants reported using these devices. Two-thirds of equipment machinery and metal-working plants also were using control systems . . . In 1963, this survey indicated that nearly 7 billion dollars, or 18% of the gross investment in manufacturing (and roughly one-third of investment in machinery) was being spent on equipment that respondents considered either automatic or advanced.'[16]

The inception of the use of electronic data-processing machines in the private sector of the American economy in 1954 finally opened up, for numerous if not all branches of production, the field of accelerated technological innovation and the hunt for technological surplus-profits which characterizes late capitalism. Incidentally, we can thus date the end of the reconstruction period after the Second World War and the start of the boom unleashed by the third technological revolution from that year. The distinction between these two sub-periods in the 'long wave with an undertone of expansion' from 1945 to 1965 is of significance both in economic — historical and in social-political terms.

Economically, the following ten main characteristics of the third technological revolution can be discerned:

[15] Julius Rezler, *Automation and Industrial Labor,* New York, 1969, pp. 7-8.
[16] Joseph Froomkin, 'Automation', in *International Encyclopaedia of Social Sciences,* New York, 1968, Vol. I., p. 180.

1) A qualitative acceleration of the increase in the organic composition of capital, i.e., the displacement of living by dead labour.
In those enterprises which are fully automated this displacement is
virtually total.[17]

2) A shift of living labour power still engaged in the process of
production from the actual treatment of raw materials to preparatory
or supervisory functions. It must be emphasized that these functions
nevertheless constitute value-creating activities as defined by Marx,
i.e., activities essential in determining the form of the specific use-
values produced. The scientists, laboratory workers, projectors and
draughtsmen who work in the forecourt of the actual production
process also perform productive, value — and surplus value-creating
labour. Indeed, precisely the age of the third technological revolution, under late capitalism, is generally characterized by that *process
of integration of social labour capacity*, which was so accurately
analysed by Marx in his original version of the 6th Chapter of the First
Volume of *Capital*: 'Since, with the development of the *real subsumption of labour under capital*, or of the *specific capitalist mode of production*, the real *functionary* of the total labour process becomes, not
the individual labourer, but increasingly a *socially unified labour
capacity*, and since the various labour capacities competing within
the form of total productive machines, participate in very different
ways in the immediate process of the formation of commodities, or
what is better in this context, the formation of products, one working
more with his hands, the other more with his head, one as a manager,
engineer, technologist, another as a supervisor, and a third as a direct
manual labourer or even merely as an odd-jobber, the *functions of
labour capacity* are ranged beneath the direct concept of *productive
labour* and its agents beneath the concept of *productive labourers*,
directly exploited by capital and *subordinated* to its valorization
and to the production process as a whole. If we consider the *total
labourer* who makes up this workshop, then his *combined activity*
is directly realized materially in a *total product*, which is simultaneously a *total mass of commodities*, and it is a matter of complete indifference whether the function of the individual labourer, who represents only a limb of the total labourer, is more or less distant from
the immediate labour done by hand.'[18]

[17]Levinson, op. cit., pp. 228-9, cites the example of petro-chemical works in
Britain, in which the proportion of production costs representing wages and salaries
has sunk to 0.02, 0.03, and 0.01%.
[18]Marx, *Resultate des unmittelbaren Produktionsprozesses*, pp. 128-30.

3) A radical change in the proportion between the two functions of the commodity of labour-power in automated enterprises. As we know, labour-power both creates and preserves value. In the history of the capitalist mode of production, the creation of value has hitherto obviously been the crucial function. In fully automated enterprises, by contrast, the preservation of value now becomes critical.[19] This is so not only in the banal sense of the automatic transfer of a portion of the machinery set in motion and of the raw materials processed to the value of the finished commodity, but also in the much more specific sense of the economies of means of labour, or savings of value, which correspond to the colossal growth in value and the increase in applicability of cybernetically-controlled automatic machine aggregates.[20]

4) A radical change in the proportion between the creation of surplus-value within the enterprise itself and the appropriation of surplus-value produced in other enterprises, within fully automated enterprises or branches. This is a necessary outcome of the three preceding characteristics of automation.

5) A change in the proportion between construction costs and the outlay on the purchase of new machines in the structure of fixed capital, and hence also in industrial investments. In the USA, the proportions of basic capital changed as follows[21]:

	1929	1960
Share of construction	59%	32%
Share of equipment	32%	52%
Share of means of circulation	9%	16%

6) A shortening of the production period, achieved by means of continuous output and radical acceleration of preparation and installation work (and transition to ongoing repairs).[22] Pressure to

[19] Nick, *Technische Revolution und Ökonomie der Produktionsfonds*, p. 13: 'A qualitatively new situation arises if the main economies in labour occur in the field of objectified labour.'
[20] Pollock, op. cit., pp. 256, 284-5. Pollock speaks of the 'massive damage' which can result from the mishandling of controls.
[21] Nick, op. cit., p. 21. This is related to the reduction in the size of automated machines. Cf. Helmut Ludwig, *Die Grössendegression der technischen Produktionsmittel*, Cologne, 1962. In the Belgian metal-working industry, 3.8 billion francs were invested in 1973 in buildings, and 13.5 billion in equipment: *Bulletin Fabrimetal*, 3/12/1973.
[22] Reuss, op. cit., pp. 27-8; Kruse, Kunz and Uhlmann, op. cit., pp. 28-9. See also ibid., p. 49, for the reduction of reject-quotas and economies in material costs: 'The

abbreviate the circulation period — hence a shorter turnover-time for capital — through planning of stocks, market research, and so forth.[23]

7) A compulsion to accelerate technological innovation, and a steep increase in the costs of 'research and development'. This is the logical outcome of the three preceding forces.

8) A shorter life-span of fixed capital, especially machines. Increasing compulsion to introduce exact planning of production within each enterprise and programming of the economy as a whole.

9) A higher organic composition of capital leads to a rise in the share of constant capital in the average commodity value. Depending on each individual case, this increase may be limited to the share of circulating constant capital (the cost of raw materials, energy, auxiliary substances); or may extend to fixed constant capital (amortization of the machines); or may affect both. In the example of the petro-chemical industry already cited above, Levinson gives the following proportions for raw materials and energy costs: ethylbenzol:87%; vinylchloride:78%; acetylene-athelene:59.6%. The share of fixed capital costs amounts respectively to 12%, 21% and 40% in these cases.[24] Nick and Pollock rightly emphasize that the increase in the *relative* share of constant capital in the average commodity value is inevitably accompanied by a decrease in the *absolute* expenditure of constant capital per commodity if automation is to be at all competitive in capitalism.[25]

10) The combined upshot of these main economic characteristics of the third technological revolution is a tendency for all the contradictions of the capitalist mode of production to be intensified: the contradiction between the growing socialization of labour and private appropriation; the contradiction between the production of use-values (which rises to the immeasurable) and the realization of exchange values (which continues to be tied to the purchasing power

introduction of an analogy calculator on a cold-belt rolling-train for the regulation of thickness led to a drop of 35% in wasted material. In one generating plant the introduction of automatically regulated supply and pressure reduced the consumption of primary energy by 42% in kilowatt hours.'

[23] The magnitude of individual investment projects has risen so much that even purely in cost terms it represents a compelling pressure for optimal utilization.

[24] Levinson, op. cit., pp. 228-9.

[25] Nick, op. cit., pp. 46-54; Pollock, op. cit., p. 166. In the long run, with the spread of the automated production of raw materials, the fixed constant share of value would become the most important part in relative terms. Cf. Kruse, Kunz and Uhlmann, op. cit., p. 113.

of the population); the contradiction between the process of labour and the process of valorization; the contradiction between the accumulation of capital and its valorization, and so on and so forth.

The proportion between partial automation and total automation is a crucial problem of the third technological revolution, in the phase of late capitalism, which must be investigated in the light of this general tendency towards the intensification of all the contradictions of the capitalist mode of production. If semi-automatic processes of production are introduced into certain branches of production on a massive scale, this merely reproduces at a higher level the inherent tendency for capital to increase its organic composition and does not raise any important theoretical issues. However, in so far as semi-automation, particularly in sectors making light industrial goods, leads to a substantial reduction in the value of the consumer goods needed to realize real wages, it can easily lead to a no less substantial increase in the production of relative surplus-value. According to figures quoted by Otto Brenner, the industries producing food and drink and the textile industry in West Germany registered a decline in the number of working hours needed to produce commodities to the value DM 1,000, from 77 to 37 and 210 to 89 hours respectively, between 1950 and 1964. [26] This significant increase in relative surplus-value was accompanied only to a limited extent by a rise in real wages, i.e., by the inclusion of additional commodities in the determination of the value of the commodity of labour power.

If, however, fully automated production processes are introduced on a mass scale into certain realms of production, the whole picture alters. In these realms, the production of absolute or relative surplus-value ceases to rise and the entire underlying tendency of capitalism turns into its own negation: *in these realms surplus-value hardly continues to be produced at all.* The total profit appropriated by firms engaged in these realms is taken from the remaining non- or semi-automated branches. In these latter branches, therefore, there arises severe pressure for substantial measures of rationalization and intensification of production at least partially to bridge the growing differences in levels of productivity separating them from automated branches, since otherwise they stand to lose an increasing portion of the mass of surplus-value produced by 'their' workers to their more productive competitors. Hence the phenomena, so characteristic of the past ten years, of speeding up the conveyor belts and

[26] In *Automation, Risiko und Chance*, Frankfurt, 1966, Vol. I, p. 23.

squeezing the last second of surplus labour out of the worker (in M-T-M or Motion-Time-Measurement, not unjustly called 'the minimum time process' in West Germany, the basic unit is set at 1/16 of a second).

But whatever is available for distribution first has to be produced. So long as fully automated enterprises and branches of production still constitute only a small minority,[27] so long as the semi-automated enterprises and branches do not show any substantial reduction in man-hours worked, and so long as the total quantity of labour expended in industry hence still continues to rise, late capitalism is necessarily defined by intensified competition among large concerns and between these and the non-monopolized sectors of industry. But on the whole, of course, this process is not qualitatively different from that of 'classical' monopoly capitalism.

Whilst on this subject, let us briefly consider the objection advanced by many critics of Marx's economic theory, according to which there is no empirical proof or theoretical evidence for his notion of the increasing organic composition of capital. These critics argue that a reduction in the cost of machines and raw materials, and economies in their use, could lead to 'neutral' technical progress, whereby the value of constant capital entering into the ongoing output of commodities would only grow at the same rate as the value of the variable capital, despite growth in the productivity of labour.[28] Empirically, it is easy to demonstrate that there has been a more rapid growth in the branches of production making fixed capital than in the branches of industry producing consumer goods; since the increase in the production of raw materials and intermediate goods is certainly not lower than the increase in Department II, and since the rise in the production of energy is clearly even higher than the latter, it should not be difficult

[27]Although Pollock, op. cit., p. 109, notes that fully automated processes of production, extending from the raw materials to the final product, are already in use in the manufacture of steel tubes, oil distillation and refinery, glass-ware and paper, biscuits and ice creams, cigarettes and military shells, and flour milling, he comments that overall fully automated plants form only a small minority. He points to the technical obstacles hindering generalized automation: the need to render production homogeneous and continuous, to divide the process of production into standardized individual actions, and so on. Added to these technical difficulties are the obvious economic difficulties which we have outlined briefly above.

[28]See among others Joan Robinson, *The Accumulation of Capital*, London, 1956; J. R. Hicks, *The Theory of Wages*, 2nd Edition, London, 1966, Chapter 6; Rolf Güsten, *Die langfristige Tendenz der Profitrate bei Karl Marx und Joan Robinson*, Doctoral Dissertation, Munich, 1960.

to provide empirical evidence of a long-term growth in the organic composition of capital. Such a demonstration already exists for shorter periods, for example in the case of the USA for the years 1939-61. Using the tools of Leontief's input-output calculations, Carter has investigated the structural changes in the American economy in this period. Her conclusions are eminently clear: 'Most labour coefficients fell more than the corresponding capital coefficients and thus the capital-to-labour ratio increased in most sectors'. Carter goes on even more unequivocally: 'Of all the structural changes reviewed thus far, the declines in direct labour coefficients are most pronounced. . . . The economy behaves as if labour-saving were the goal of technical progress and most changes in intermediate and capital structure can be justified by reduced direct, and to a lesser extent, indirect labour requirements.' There is no doubt that the emergence of automated production must empirically confirm this general economic trend. In individual branches of industry the same tendency is equally clear. We have already cited the fact that in steel production the transition from the Thomas process to the acid process has lowered the share of labour costs in the total costs of production from 25% to 17%, while the share of fixed capital costs rose from 16% to 25%. In oil refineries, the proportion of fixed capital costs rose, for four successive cracking procedures between 1913 and 1955, from 0.21 to 10; while the number of living labour hours needed for producing 10,000 tons of gasoline dropped from 56 in 1913 to 0.4 in 1955. In a specific British factory, the transition from traditional machine-tools to numerically-controlled equipment halved production costs and changed the relation between annual depreciation costs and the wage-salary bill from 15/91 to 21/35. The replacement of universal production machines by fully automated transfer machines in the French Renault auto plants similarly altered the relation between labour costs and equipment costs per vehicle from 640/131 to 53/200. In the West German plastics industry, gross fixed investment per wage- and salary-earner rose from 2,110 DM in 1960 to 3,905 DM in 1966, or 85%, while wages and salaries per employee increased only 68.5% (wages alone, 65.8%) in the same period. In the cotton-spinning industry of the Federal Republic, the value of equipment per employee rose from 30,000 DM in 1950 to 324,000 DM in 1971 for a model plant incorporating the latest machinery, while the number of employees working in three shifts declined over the same period from 274 to 62, and the total wage-and-salary bill (based on the average for the textile industry) increased only from 601,200 DM to 785,000 DM a year. Such examples could be multiplied indefinitely.[29] Virtually no commodity can be found for which living labour costs represent a growing share of total production costs, in the strict sense of the word.[30]

The impression of a long-term 'stability of factor shares' or even of an increase in the 'labour share' given by official statistics, does not contradict this basic trend towards a long-term rise in the organic composition of capital. 'Factor costs' include not only fixed constant and variable capital, but surplus-value; while they exclude the value of circulating constant capital. They are therefore not comparable to c/v. Hence in this type of statistical material, a decline in the rate of surplus-value would conceal any rise in the organic composition of capital. Moreover, 'labour share' includes higher salary costs which represent, at least in part, surplus-value and not variable capital. Calculated on a macro-economic basis, 'factor costs' deviate still further from the Marxist concept of the organic composition of capital, for they include compensation for unproductive labour in the notion of 'labour share', which cannot properly be included in the category of variable capital.[31]

[29] See Anne P. Carter, *Structural Changes in the American Economy*, Harvard, 1970, pp. 143, 152. Levinson, op. cit., p. 129; John L. Enos, 'Invention and Innovation in the Petroleum Industry', in Richard Nelson (ed.), *The Rate and Direction of Inventive Activity*, Princeton, 1962, p. 318; Gerald W. Smith, *Engineering Economy: Analysis of Capital Expenditures*, Iowa, 1968, p. 427; Pollock, op. cit., p. 101; Marius Hammer, *Vergleichende Morphologie der europäische Automobilindustrie*, Basle, 1959, pp. 69-70; *Wirtschaftskonjunktur*, December 1967, p. 27; Ammann, Einhoff, Helmstadter and Isselhorst, (*Entwicklungsstrategie und Faktorintensität*), *Zeitschrift fur allgemeine und Textile Marktwirtschaft*, 1972, Heft II; *Statistisches Jahrbuch für die BRD 1952, 1972*.

[30] In the above examples, raw material costs are not included. Theoretically, it would be possible to conceive a situation in which a radical reduction in the price of raw materials compensated the increase in fixed capital costs per unit of output, and therefore left the relation between constant capital and variable capital stable. But in the period since the Second World War, this has hardly been a practical proposition. While there have been constant economies in the physical consumption of raw materials, there has been no long-term absolute decline in the costs of primary products used in the main branches of industry, while fixed capital costs have increased relative to wage costs. This obviously implies a rise in the organic composition of capital.

[31] Over shorter periods, specific delays or advances in technical progress, which cheapen machinery more than consumer goods, can of course lead to a stagnation or even a regression in the organic composition of capital. Bela Gold cites the example of the US steel industry, where wage costs fell as part of 'total costs' (including profits) in blast furnaces from 8.9% in 1899 to 5.1% in 1939, while they increased in

Curiously enough, even Paul Sweezy has joined the ranks of those writers who deny any long-term tendency for the organic composition of capital to rise in the 20th century, or indeed argue that it has tended to decline.[32] We can only add to the arguments and facts marshalled above the well-known difference in the proportion of labour-costs to value added for the same branch of industry in less and more technically-advanced countries, which reflects this increase in the organic composition of capital (although it must be re-emphasised that the notion of 'value-added' includes profits and excludes raw material costs, and is therefore in no way identical to c/v):

Labour Costs as % of Value Added

	Knitting Mills	Basic Chemicals and Fertilizers
USA (1954)	23.06%	8.14%
Canada (1954)	27.79%	9.73%
Australia (1955-56)	38.37%	23.41%
New Zealand (1955-56)	39.85%	16.03%
Denmark (1954)	50.04%	24.77%
Norway (1954)	50.46%	20.28%
Colombia (1953)	53.02%	30.50%
Mexico (1951)	79.68%	35.09%[33]

Mage, in his polemic against Güsten, has sought to prove theoretically that there *must* be an increase in the organic composition of capital as a result of the laws of development of capital.[34] Much of his proof is convincing, but his demonstration would have been simpler if he had not excluded the *functional* role of the increase in the organic composition of capital in Marx's analysis. According to Marx, technical progress is induced under the constraint of

rolling mills from 17.1% to 21.4% during the same period: *Explorations in Managerial Economics—Productivity, Costs, Technology and Growth*, London, 1971, p. 102. Setting aside the fact that fluctuations in profit-margins may have influenced these results, it should be pointed out that major technological revolutions occurred in rolling mills in the 50's and 60's with the introduction of large-scale automation. Fixed investment costs per labour-hour stood only 17% above the level of 1899 in 1939, but had increased to 25% of the 1939 level by 1958.

[32] Paul Sweezy, 'Some Problems in the Theory of Capital Accumulation', *Monthly Review*, May 1974, especially pp. 46-7.

[33] Bagicha Singh Minas, *An International Comparison of Factor Costs and Factor Use*, Amsterdam, pp. 102-3.

[34] Mage, op. cit., pp. 151-9.

competition, by the constant pressure to economise on production costs, whose macro-economic outcome cannot be different from its micro-economic results. Cost economies without an increase in the organic composition of capital would presuppose either that living labour could profitably replace more and more complex machinery, or that Department I could produce modern machinery which saves labour and value without an increase in the intrinsic value of such machine complexes, or a decrease in the value of new materials greater than the decrease in the value of wage-goods. This, however, would necessitate a more rapid growth in the productivity of labour in Department I than in the economy as a whole. Since new equipment must be constructed with pre-existent machinery and pre-given techniques, and *its own value* is thus determined by present labour productivity, and not by the future productivity it helps to increase; and since this equipment cannot be mass-produced in the initial stages, such an assumption is unrealistic over the long-run. Consequently, economies in unit costs will have a long-term tendency towards economies in labour-costs, as Carter correctly stresses. Economy in costs will thus always be accompanied in the long-run by a relative decrease in the share of wage costs in the value of the commodity, and hence also by the relative decline of the variable component of total capital.

Although the conventional critique of Marx's thesis of the increasing organic composition of capital is inadequate when taken as a whole, it does contain a grain of truth, in that this increase is effected less automatically and radically than has been assumed in many vulgarizations.[35] It is perfectly possible to achieve extended reproduction without any radical alteration in the organic composition of capital, over limited periods. Indeed, there may periodically occur sudden increases in the productivity of labour in Department I which are far greater than the social average and thus permit substantial cost economies in manufacturing industry without an increase in the constant value incorporated into their commodities.

[35]Marx: 'The reason is simply that, with the increasing productivity of labour, not only does the mass of the means of production consumed by it increase, but their value compared with their mass diminishes. Their value therefore rises absolutely, but not in proportion to their mass. The increase of the difference between constant and variable capital is, therefore, much less than that of the difference between the mass of the means of production into which the constant, and the mass of the labour-power into which the variable, capital is converted. The former difference increases with the latter, but in a smaller degree.' *Capital*, Vol. I. p. 623.

But in the long-run these tendencies cannot be sustained on an over-all social scale. The confrontation between partially automated and fully automated production precisely offers an insight into the nature of the general development today. For if fully automated enterprises and branches, and semi-automated concerns, grow so numerous that they become decisive for the structure of the whole of industry, reducing 'classical' industrial enterprises to only a relatively small share of total production, then the contradictions of late capitalism assume an explosive character: *the total mass of surplus-value,* in other words, the total number of hours of surplus labour, *is then tendentially condemned to diminish.*

In an otherwise excellent study, Roth and Kanzow overlook the connection between partial automation and total automation, between the case in which the rise by leaps and bounds of labour productivity (decrease in costs of production) of some enterprises is an *exception,* and the case where these leaps forward in labour pro-ductivity are generalized. They also overlook the resultant qualitative differences in difficulties of realization (or difficulties of valorizing *total* capital). They write: 'Their technologically determined advance into new branches of industry permits the combined capitals constantly to extend their possibilities of compensating for the tendency of their rates of profit to decline, by counteracting measures.' Clearly, however, this is only true of a *minority* of capitals. For how, with the spread of automation — in other words, with a radical reduction in the mass of surplus-value and a steep rise in the organic composition of capital — can all capitals increase their rate of profit? In the numerical example given by Roth and Kanzow,[36] they consider four successive stages — from conveyor belt production to wide-scale automation, or from the use of 31 units of labour power to 9 units[37] — and draw the conclusion that production doubles, the gross product increases six-fold, and the rate of profit rises from 12% to 55.6%. But Roth and Kanzow ignore the *overall economic* implica-tions of the three conditions which precede this process, and what

[36] Karl-Heinz Roth and Eckhard Kanzow, *Unwissen als Ohnmacht — Zum Wechsel-verhältnis von Kapital und Wissenschaft,* Berlin, 1970, p. 17.

[37] The following instance shows that this numerical example, far from being an overstatement, is rather an understatement: 'A transfer belt introduced, together with an inductive hardening machine, into a car factory, performed 24 basic or partial technical operations which had previously been carried out by 18 individual aggregates of 15 workers; the new plant was serviced by one worker.' Kruse, Kunz and Uhlmann, op. cit., p. 21.

would become of the latter in the event of generalized partial automation (not to speak of full automation): a constant selling price; a doubled volume of physical output; a drop of wage and salary costs by half. It is obvious that the combination of these three conditions becomes untenable with the extension of semi-automation. Who is supposed to buy a doubled volume of durable consumer goods if, with a constant selling price, the nominal income of the population is reduced by half? In the *special case* dealt with by Roth and Kanzow the following premises must be accepted:

(1) that the decline in nominal wages in the enterprise concerned is accompanied by an increase in overall consumer income;

(2) that certain automatically produced durable consumer goods have been substituted for ones produced by non-automatic processes. It is enough to formulate these implicit conditions to see that they are doomed to dwindle or disappear with the growing extension of semi-automation. A massive problem of marketing or realization must then arise.

A similar mistake, albeit of an opposite kind (pessimistic rather than optimistic) has been made by Pollock in a study of the connection between employment and automation. He writes: 'One of the main motives behind the introduction of automation is admittedly higher productivity, but this means a *net* saving of wages and salaries. If the workers thereby set free were to find new jobs in servicing or manufacturing the control apparatuses themselves, no net savings on wage costs (given a constant quantity of products) would be possible at all. These would merely have been transferred to different activities, which are, however, just as much an element in costs, so that while it is certainly possible to speak of a change in methods of production, there is no increase in productivity.'[38] The catch in this argument lies in the words in brackets: 'given a constant quantity of products'. As we have just seen, however, automation will never mean a constant quantity of products. Pollock's argument is hence only correct if there is homogeneous automation in all realms of production (with an unaltered structure of consumption). If, however, automation has reached different stages in different realms of production, it is quite possible for an increase in the productivity and the marketed output of the automated branches to be accompanied by an absorption of released workers into sectors producing control

[38] Pollock, op. cit., p. 202.

apparatuses. The whole process then develops at the expense of the non-automated (or less automated) branches. This is, in fact, just what has actually happened in the history of late capitalism over the past twenty years.

Once the late capitalist sphere of production is grasped as a contradictory unity of non-, semi- and fully-automated enterprises (in industry and agriculture, hence in all realms of commodity production together), it becomes evident that capital *must* by its very nature put up growing resistance to automation beyond a certain point.[39] The forms of this resistance include the use of cheap labour in the semi-automated branches of industry (such as female and apprentice labour in the textile, food and drink industries), which shifts the profitability threshold for the introduction of fully automated complexes; constant changes and mutual competition in the production of automated machine complexes, which impede the cheapening of these complexes and hence their swifter introduction into further branches of industry; the incessant search for new use-values, which are first produced in non-automated or semi-automated enterprises, and so on. The most important point is that, just as in the first phase of machine-operated large industry, the large machines were themselves produced not by machine but by hand, so in the first phase of automation currently in progress the automatic machine aggregates are not constructed automatically but on the conveyor belt. In fact, the industry which produces electronic means of production has a *notably low* organic composition of capital. In the mid-60's the share of wage and salary costs in the gross annual turnover of this branch of industry in the USA and Western Europe fluctuated between 45% and 50%.[40] This explains why the massive amount of capital which has streamed into it since the beginning of the 50's has lowered rather than raised the average social composition of capital and, correspondingly, has raised rather than lowered the average rate of profit. *The automatic production of automatic machines would hence be a new qualitative turning point,* equal in significance to the appearance of the machine-production of machines in

[39] Kruse, Kunz and Uhlmann establish empirically that 'for rotary machines (there is) a threshold value of about 75%, up to which point increasing automation produces an output disproportionately higher than the capital outlay. Beyond this threshold value it becomes uneconomic to raise the degree of automation.' op. cit., p. 113.
[40] C. Freeman, 'Research and Development in Electronic Capital Goods', in *National Institute Economic Review*, No. 34, November 1965, p. 51.

the mid-19th century,[41] stressed by Marx: 'A development of productive forces which would diminish the absolute number of labourers, i.e., which would enable the entire nation to accomplish its total production in a shorter time span, would cause a revolution, because it would put the bulk of the population out of the running. This is another manifestation of the specific barrier of capitalist production, showing also that capitalist production is by no means an absolute form for the development of the productive forces and for the creation of wealth, but rather that at a certain point it comes into collision with this development.'[42]

For we have here arrived at the absolute inner limit of the capitalist mode of production. This absolute limit lies neither in the complete capitalist penetration of the world market (i.e., the elimination of non-capitalist realms of production) — as Rosa Luxemburg believed — nor in the ultimate impossibility of valorizing total accumulated capital, even with a rising mass of surplus-value — as Henryk Grossman believed. It lies in the fact that the *mass of surplus-value itself necessarily diminishes as a result of the elimination of living labour from the production process in the course of the final stage of mechanization-automation.* Capitalism is incompatible with fully automated production in the whole of industry and agriculture, because this no longer allows the creation of surplus-value or valorization of capital. It is hence impossible for automation to spread to the entire realm of production in the age of late capitalism:[43] 'As soon as labour in the direct form has ceased to be the great well-spring of wealth, labour time ceases and must cease to be its measure, and hence exchange value [must cease to be the measure] of use-value. *The surplus-labour of the mass* has ceased to be the condition for the development of general wealth, just as the *non-labour of the few*, for the development of the general powers of the human mind. With that, *production based on exchange value breaks down*, and the

[41] Nick, op. cit., p. 52, comes to the same conclusion. He here follows Pollock (op. cit., p. 95) who, however, sees that automated assembly apparatuses (AUTOFAB) contain in themselves the possibility of a paradox, in that 'the very industry which delivers apparatuses for automation is itself dependent in the main on manual labour.'

[42] Marx, *Capital*, Vol. 3, p. 258.

[43] This is, of course, only true on an international scale. Theoretically, it is conceivable that a fully automated industry in the USA or West Germany could corner the surplus-value necessary for the valorization of its capital through exchange with non-automatically produced commodities from other countries. In practice, the social and political consequences of such a situation would be immeasurably explosive.

direct, material production process is stripped of the form of penury and antithesis.[44]

It may be objected that automation eliminates living labour only in the production plant; it increases it in all those spheres which precede direct output (laboratories, research and experimental departments) where labour is employed that unquestionably forms an integral part of the 'collective productive labourer' in the Marxist sense of the term. Setting aside the fact that a transformation of the totality of productive labour into scientifically trained producers would create explosive difficulties for the valorization of capital, and without even considering the question how far it would be compatible with the preservation of commodity production as such, it is clear that a transformation of this kind would imply a radical suppression of the social division between manual and intellectual labour. Such a radical modification of the whole social formation and culture of the proletariat would undermine the entire hierarchical structure of factory and economy, without which the extortion of surplus-value from productive labour would be impossible. Capitalist relations of production, in other words, would collapse. The first *signs* of such a *trend* are already visible by-products of late capitalism, as we shall demonstrate in the last chapters of this book. But under capitalism, they are inevitably condemned to remain embryonic. For reasons of its own self-preservation, capital could never afford to transform all workers into scientists, just as it could never afford to transform all material production into full automation.

The following numerical examples show how serious are the consequences of this tendency for the quantity of value-creating labour to diminish as a result of automation. As will be seen, it profoundly affects the ability of late capitalism to halt the fall in the rate of profit by raising the rate of surplus-value and its ability to prevent the intensification of social tensions by increasing real wages. Let four successive cyclical peak years be called A, B, C and D, and the distance between them be approximately 10 years. In the starting year of our comparison let the total number of man-hours worked by the productive labourers in both Departments together be 10 billion (approximately 5 million productive workers working 2,000 hours annually, or 6 million working 1,666 hours annually). Let the rate

[44]Marx, *Grundrisse*, pp. 705-6.

of surplus-value be 100%, i.e., 5 billion hours are devoted to the production of surplus-value. As a result of increased employment despite growing automation, in the year B 12 billion instead of 10 billion hours of productive labour are expended. We assume that the rate of surplus-value now rises from 100% to 150% (instead of using half of their labour time for the production of the equivalent of their real wages, the productive workers now use only 2/5 for this purpose). The mass of surplus-value rises from the product of 5 billion to the product of 7.2 billion working hours, i.e., it rises by 44%. Since the productive workers henceforth produce the equivalent of their wages in 4.8 instead of 5 billion working hours, a total increase of 30% in real wages of all workers (a modest annual growth rate of 2.6%) would necessitate a 35% increase in the productivity of labour in Department II. This remains within the framework of the possible; it indeed accords with the development of the last 25 years.

In year C of our comparison automation has already halted the rise in the mass of employment or of the man-hours worked. It remains constant at 12 billion. For example, in order to make up for the increase in the organic composition of capital (which has risen by 50% between A and B and between B and C) the rate of surplus-value would have to rise once more from 150% to 233.33%, i.e., instead of disposing of 4 working hours in 10 to produce the equivalent of his real wages, the productive worker now has a mere 3 out of 10 at his disposal for this purpose. The total mass of surplus-value has now risen to a product of 8.4 billion hours, i.e., by a whole 16.6%. If the workers, however, are to be able to achieve a further 30% increase in real consumption (in the mass of products or use values) in the 3.6 billion working hours still available to them for the production of the equivalent of their consumer goods, as compared to the 4.8 billion working hours of ten years previously, the productivity of labour in Department II would have to be increased by 70%, i.e., an annual growth rate of 5.4%. This is still just on the edge of the possible.

Let us now consider the fourth year, D. In order to neutralize the rise in the organic composition of capital (approximately 70% since the year C), the rate of surplus-value would now have to go up from 233.33% to 400%, i.e., the productive worker would now be left with only 1 working hour in 5 to produce the equivalent of his wage. Let us say, however, that automation has reduced the total number of man-hours worked from 12 billion to 10 billion. The *absolute mass of surplus-value* is now equivalent to 8 billion working hours, or in other words, *despite a massive increase in the rate of surplus-value,* from 233.33% to 400%, *the mass has declined.*[45] For the mass of surplus-value to remain at least the same, the rate of surplus-value would have to be 525% instead of 400%, so that a mere 1.6 billion working hours would remain for the production of the equivalent of real wages. But even if the rate of surplus-value 'only' rose to 400%, a further 30% increase in real wages over ten years would necessitate that the mass of products made in the 2 billion working hours in the year D increase by 30% over the mass of products produced in 3.6 billion working hours in the year C, i.e., an increase of 140% in the productivity of labour in Department II: the realization of an average growth rate of 9.1% needed to achieve this goal would seem to be impossible. This would still be much less than the annual average necessary to guarantee a 30% increase in real wages by the year D with only 1.6 billion available man-hours, i.e., where the mass of surplus-value remains constant. In this case, the productivity of labour would have to rise, in the course of the decade, by as much as 192.5%, i.e., an absolutely unattainable growth rate of 11.4%.

The conclusion is obvious: with increasing automation, increasing organic composition of capital and the onset of a fall in the total man-hours worked by productive labourers, it is impossible in the long run seriously to continue to increase real wages and at the same time maintain a constant mass of surplus-value. One of the two quantities will diminish. Since under normal conditions, i.e., without fascism or war, a significant decline in real wages can be excluded, there emerges *an historical crisis of the valorization of capital* and an inevitable decline, first in the mass of surplus-value and then also in the rate of surplus-value, and hence there follows an abrupt fall in the average rate of profit. In our numerical example, even if real wages were to stagnate in the year D while the mass of surplus-value fell from 8.4 to 8 billion working hours, this would still mean that the productivity of labour would have increased by 80% (an annual

[45] Marx, *Grundrisse*, p. 335ff, had already demonstrated that surplus-value cannot rise in the same proportion as the productivity of labour, and that the increase of surplus labour is proportional to the diminution of necessary labour and not to the increase of the productivity of labour. This diminution of necessary labour itself has limits, even given the hypothesis, used by Marx in these calculations, of stagnating proletarian consumption. If there is a modest increase in working-class consumption, this limit is naturally still narrower.

rate of increase of 6%). If the mass of surplus-value remained constant as well as real wages, labour productivity would have increased by 125%, i.e., an unattainable growth rate of 8.4% annually.[46]

Even more clearly than in Chapter 5, therefore, we can here see the reasons why it is of the very essence of automation to intensify the struggle over the rate of surplus-value in late capitalism, and to make it increasingly difficult to overcome the obstacles to the valorization of capital as soon as the mass of man-hours spent in the creation of value begins to decline. The following table shows that this hypothesis is by no means unreal:

Number of man-hours worked in
manufacturing industry in the USA[47]

1947:	24.3 billion
1950:	23.7 billion
1954:	24.3 billion
1958:	22.7 billion
1963:	24.5 billion
1966:	28.2 billion
1970:	27.6 billion

The index of total hours performed by production workers in manufacturing industry declined from 100 in 1967 to 97.5 in 1972. In West Germany the same trend is even more evident. Since 1961 there has been an absolute regression in the number of man-hours worked in industry:

[46] It could be objected that with a declining number of working hours, i.e., a declining rate of employment, real wages per capita of the employed producers do not need such a high rate of growth in the productivity of labour in order to remain constant or to register a modest growth. The answer to this is: 1. the reduction of working hours is greater than the decline in the number of those employed, or even compatible with a constant or slightly rising number of employed, because in the long run a further increase in the intensity of labour caused by automation makes a decrease in the normal working day inevitable: 2. the real consumption of the productive labourers must be conceived as covering the mass of the class, in other words it also includes old age pensions for producers retired earlier than normal, unemployment relief, payment of young people not employed after completion of their studies or apprenticeship, and hence, with a declining number of working hours in which to create its equivalent, it really does presuppose the high rates of increase of productivity for its realization, postulated above.

[47] *Statistical Abstract of the United States, 1968,* pp. 717-19, for the years up to and including 1966. For 1970, calculated by us on the basis of US figures published in the official *Monthly Labour Review* of the USA, published by the Department of Labour (issue of May 1971); for West Germany, see Sachverständigenrat, *Jahresgutachten 1974,* Bonn, 1974.

Number of man-hours worked in
manufacturing industry in
West Germany [47]

1950:	8.1	billion
1956:	11.7	billion
1958:	11.2	billion
1960:	12.37	billion
1961:	12.44	billion
1962:	12.11	billion
1964:	11.81	billion
1966:	11.57	billion
1968:	10.83	billion
1969:	11.48	billion
1970:	11.80	billion
1971:	11.3	billion
1972:	10.8	billion
1973:	10.8	billion

Predictably, the rise in the organic composition of capital combined with the stagnation in the rate of surplus-value since the 60's, has led to a decline in the average rate of profit. These are the figures for Britain, calculated by two socialist economists on the basis of official capitalist statistics rather than strictly Marxist categories — but indicating a *trend* indubitably similar to that of the rate of profit in the Marxist sense of the word:[48]

Rate of Profit (after deducting appreciation) on
Net Assets of Industrial and Commercial Companies

	Pre-Tax	Post-Tax
1950-1954	16.5%	6.7%
1955-1959	14.7%	7.0%
1960-1964	13.0%	7.0%
1965-1969	11.7%	5.3%
1968	11.6%	5.2%
1969	11.1%	4.7%
1970	9.7%	4.1%

In the USA, two enquiries have yielded similar results, independently of each other. Nell has estimated a fall in the rate of surplus-value from 22.9% in 1965 to 17.5% in 1970 (i.e., the share of

[47] *Statistical Abstract of the United States, 1968*, pp. 717-719, for the years up to and including 1966. For 1970, calculated by us on the basis of US figures published in the official *Monthly Labour Review* of the USA, published by the Department of Labour (issue of May 1971); for West Germany, see Sachverständigenrat, *Jahresgutachten 1974*, Bonn, 1974.

[48] Andrew Glyn and Bob Sutcliffe, *British Capitalism, Workers and the Profit Squeeze*, London, 1972. p. 66. These calculations have been subjected to various

profit and interest in net value added of non-financial joint-stock companies).[49] Nordhaus has established the following table, after careful correction for fictious 'inventory' profits due merely to inflation:[50]

Genuine Rates of Return on Non-Financial Corporate Capital

	Before Taxes	After Taxes
1948-1950	16.2%	8.6%
1951-1955	14.3%	6.4%
1956-1960	12.2%	6.2%
1961-1965	14.1%	8.3%
1966-1970	12.9%	7.7%
1970	9.1%	5.3%
1971	9.6%	5.7%
1972	9.9%	5.6%
1973	10.5%	5.4%

In France, the journal *Entreprise* reports a gradual decline of the rate of profit between 1950 and 1963, a certain stabilization in the period 1964-67, a significant drop in 1967-68, a sharp shift upwards in 1969-70 and a further decline again since then. In French manufacturing industry, the net rate of profit towards 1970 on propertied assets was reckoned to be one-third lower than in the early 60's. Correcting for inflationary revaluations of stock, the ratio of self-financing in French enterprises seems to have fallen from 79.5% in the 1961-64 period and 83% in the 1965-68 period to 75.1% in 1971, 76.6% in 1972, 73% in 1973 and 65% in 1974 (provisional figures). Templé calculates that the net rate of profit dropped from 5.3% in the 1954-64 period to 4.3% in the 1964-67 period and 3.8% in the 1969-73 period.[51] In West Germany, the official economic consultants of the Federal Republic compute a precipitous decline of the gross income of companies (minus fictitious entrepreneurial salaries and divided by net assets of the same firms) of some 20% between 1960 and 1968 (a year in which profits registered a sharp increase,

---

criticisms, but have since been largely confirmed by the independent analysis of G. Burgess and A. Webb, 'The Profits of British Industry', *Lloyd's Bank Review*, April 1974.

[49] Edward Nell, 'Profit Erosion in the United States', introduction to the US edition of the book by Glyn and Sutcliffe, entitled *Capitalism in Crisis*, New York, 1972.

[50] William Nordhaus, 'The Falling Share of Profits', in A. Okun and L. Perry (eds.), *Brookings Papers on Economic Activity*, No. 1, 1974, p. 180.

[51] *Entreprise*, 13/10/1972; Philippe Templé, 'Repartition des Gains de Productivite et Hausses des Prix de 1959 à 1973', *Economie et Statistique*, No. 59, 1974.

after the decline of the recession years of 1966 and 1967), and by a further 25% between 1968 and 1973.[52]

The concept of late capitalism as a new phase of imperialism or of the age of monopoly capitalism, characterized by a structural crisis of the capitalist mode of production, can thus be defined more precisely. This structural crisis does *not* find expression in an *absolute* cessation of the growth of the forces of production. In the conclusions to his analysis of imperialism, Lenin clearly warned against any interpretation of this kind. He even wrote that on a global scale imperialism was marked by an acceleration of growth: 'It would be a mistake to believe that this tendency to decay precludes the rapid growth of capitalism. It does not. In the epoch of imperialism, certain branches of industry, certain strata of the bourgeoisie and certain countries betray, to a greater or lesser degree, now one and now another of these tendencies. *On the whole, capitalism is growing far more rapidly than before;* but this growth is not only becoming more and more uneven in general, its unevenness also manifests itself, in particular, in the decay of the countries which are richest in capital (Britain).'[53]

The hallmark of imperialism, therefore, and of its second phase, late capitalism, is not a decline in the forces of production but an increase in the parasitism and waste accompanying or overlaying this growth. The inherent inability of late capitalism to generalize the vast possibilities of the third technological revolution or of automation constitutes as potent an expression of this tendency as its squandering of forces of production by turning them into forces of destruction:[54] permanent arms build-up, hunger in the semi-colonies (whose average labour productivity has been restricted to a level entirely unrelated to what is technically and scientifically feasible today), contamination of the atmosphere and waters, disruption of the ecological equilibrium, and so on — the features of imperialism or late capitalism traditionally most denounced by socialists.

In absolute terms, there has been a more rapid increase in the

[52] Sachverständigenrat, *Jahresgutachten 1974*, p. 71.

[53] V. I. Lenin, *Imperialism, the Highest State of Capitalism*, in *Selected Works*, London, 1969, p. 260 (Our italics).

[54] Cf. Marx: 'In the development of productive forces there comes a stage at which productive forces and means of intercourse are called into existence, which, under the existing relationships, only cause mischief, and which are no longer productive but destructive forces (machinery and money)': Marx and Engels, *The German Ideology*, New York, 1960, p. 68.

forces of production in the age of late capitalism than ever before. This growth can be measured over the last 25 years by the figures for physical output or productive capacity, and for the size of the industrial proletariat.[55] Both sets of figures have risen substantially for the world capitalist economy as a whole. But compared with possibilities of the third technological revolution, the potential of automation, and their capacity radically to reduce the surplus labour worked by the mass of producers in the industrialized countries, the result is pitiful. In this sense — but only on the basis of this definition — Lenin's definition of imperialism as a phase of 'the increasing decay of the capitalist mode of production' continues to be fully justified.

The squandering of real and potential forces of production by capital applies not only to material, but also to human productive forces. The age of the third technological revolution is necessarily an epoch of unprecedented fusion of science, technology and production. Science could genuinely become a direct productive force. In increasingly automated production there is no further place for unskilled workers or office workers. A massive and generalized transformation of manual into intellectual work is not only made possible, but economically and socially essential by automation. The prophetic vision outlined by Marx and Engels of a society in which 'the free development of each is the condition for the free development of all'[56] and in which real wealth comes to be found in 'the developed productive force of all individuals' could now come true nearly word for word: 'The free development of individualities [is now the goal] and

---

[55] For Marx, the concept of the forces of production was in the last analysis reducible to the material forces of production and the physical productivity of labour. See *Grundrisse*, p. 694: 'The productive force of society is measured in *fixed capital*, exists there in its objective form . . .' See also *Capital*, Vol. I, pp. 329, 621. To give any foundation to the claim that the forces of production have ceased to grow, it is necessary to detach the concept of 'productive forces' from its materialist basis and give it an idealistic content. This is the procedure, for example, of the editors of the French periodical *La Vérité*, (No. 551, pp. 2-3), who identify it with the 'development of the social individual', without noticing that this definition is not only incompatible with the views of Marx, but retrospectively embellishes the capitalism of the 19th century – which, according to them, did develop the forces of production and hence also the 'social individual'. (See Marx's views by contrast, *Grundrisse*, p. 750, and many other passages.) The thesis becomes even more grotesque, if 'the development of the social individual' is replaced by the correct Marxist formula, 'material possibilities for the development of the social individual'. For how can anyone seriously deny that automation enlarges these possibilities on a far vaster scale than the machines of the 19th century?

[56] Marx and Engels, *The Communist Manifesto*, in *Selected Works*, London, 1960, p. 53. Marx, *Grundrisse*, p. 708.

hence not the reduction of necessary labour time so as to posit surplus labour, but rather the general reduction of the necessary labour of society to a minimum, which then corresponds to the artistic or scientific development of the individuals in the time set free, and with the means created, for all of them.'[57]

The worst form of waste, inherent in late capitalism, lies in the *misuse* of existing material and human forces of production; instead of being used for the development of free men and women, they are increasingly employed in the production of useless and harmful things. All the historical contradictions of capitalism are concentrated in the twofold character of automation. On the one hand, it represents the perfected development of material forces of production, which could in themselves potentially liberate mankind from the compulsion to perform mechanical, repetitive, dull and alienating labour. On the other hand, it represents a new threat to job and income, a new intensification of anxiety, insecurity, return to chronic mass unemployment, periodic losses of consumption and income, and intellectual and moral impoverishment. Capitalist automation as the mighty development of both the *productive forces of labour and the alienating and destructive forces of commodity and capital* thus becomes the objectified quintessence of the antinomies inherent in the capitalist mode of production.

The idea that the epoch of the structural crisis of capitalism — i.e., the age that from an historical point of view is ripe for the socialist world revolution — should somehow be characterized by an absolute decline or at least an absolute stagnation of the forces of production goes back to a false and mechanical interpretation of a sentence from Marx's famous preface to the *Contribution to the Critique of Political Economy*, in which he gave the most summary sketch of the theory of historical materialism. Marx characterized an epoch of social revolution in the following manner: 'At a certain stage of development, the material productive forces of society come into conflict with the existing relations of production or — this merely expresses the same thing in legal terms — with the property relations within the framework of which they have operated hitherto. From forms of development of the productive forces these relations turn into their fetters. Then begins an era of social revolution. . . . No social order is ever destroyed before all the productive forces for which it

[57]Marx, *Grundrisse*, p. 706.

is sufficient have been developed, and new superior relations of production never replace older once before the material conditions for their existence have matured within the framework of the older society.'[58] It seems obvious enough that the phrase — 'all the productive forces for which it is sufficient' is in effect nothing more than a repetition of the first sentence; in other words, it is based on the statement that there comes a point when the development of the forces of production comes into conflict with the existing relations of production. From this point onwards, capitalist society has developed all the productive forces 'for which it is sufficient'. But this does not imply by any means that from then on, any further development would be quite impossible without the overthrow of this mode of production. It means only that from this epoch on, the forces of production which are further developed will conflict ever more intensely with the existing mode of production and tend towards its overthrow.[59]

Mechanical interpretations of this famous paragraph were undoubtedly reinforced by the experience of the October Revolution in Russia, and especially by Bukharin's theoretical generalization of this experience in his *Ökonomik der Transformationsperiode*.[60] In this work, Bukharin actually laid it down as a rule that the socialist revolution would be either preceded or accompanied by a decline of the forces of production. The specifically Russian configuration of the years 1917-20 — Revolution after a World War, combined with

[58] Marx, *A Contribution to the Critique of Political Economy*, London, 1971, p. 21.

[59] This is all the more obvious as Marx is not referring here to the specific overthrow of capitalism but to the overthrow of all class societies in general. It would certainly never have occurred to him to characterize the period preceding the history of the bourgeois revolutions (for example, the victory of the Dutch revolution in the 16th, the English revolution in the 17th, and the American and great French Revolution in the 18th centuries) as a phase of stagnating or even regressing productive forces.

[60] N. Bukharin, *Ökonomik der Transformationsperiode*, Hamburg, 1922, p. 67. In his later book, *Theorie des Historischen Materialismus*, Hamburg, 1922, Bukharin wavered between three positions on this question. On p. 289 he wrote: 'The revolution therefore takes place when there is a flagrant conflict between *growing* productive forces, which can no longer be contained within the husk of the relations of production' (Our italics). On p. 290 he went on: 'These relations of production hinder the development of the productive forces to such an extent that they must unconditionally be cast off if society is to develop further. If they cannot be, then they will hamper and choke the development of the forces of production, and the whole society will stagnate or regress.' But on p. 298 he cited his earlier book, *Ökonomik der Transformationsperiode*, in which he had declared: 'Its (i.e., the World War's) shattering force is a fairly accurate indicator of the degree of capitalist development and a tragic expression of the *complete incompatibility of a further growth of the forces of*

a long drawn-out Civil War which completely disrupted the whole economy of the country and caused a deep plunge in productive forces[61] — is an extremely unlikely variant for the highly industrialized capitalist states. There is no reason for it to be elevated to a norm.[62]

The theoreticians of the Communist International rightly recorded a decline in the forces of production in the first years after the Russian Revolution. They measured this fall materially in output, employment, and so on, and concluded that capitalism would find it very difficult to overcome the social and economic crisis in which it was gripped, even temporarily.[63] The Great Depression which set in with full force in 1929, after a brief boom period, confirmed the accuracy of this prognosis. But both Lenin and Trotsky remained much more cautious in their judgments of long-term development. Thus Trotsky declared at the 3rd Congress of the Communist International: 'If we grant — and let us grant it for the moment — that the working class fails to rise in revolutionary struggle, but allows the bourgeoisie to rule the world's destiny for a long number of years, say, two or three decades, then assuredly some sort of new equilibrium will be established. Europe will be thrown violently into

---

production within the husk of capitalist relations of production' (Our italics). If there is no essential contradiction between the first and the second of these passages (the second doubtless refers to an entire historical epoch which, *to an increasing extent*, hampers the development of the forces of production, which does not mean that they will *immediately* cease to grow, but only *ultimately*), the contradiction between the first and the third is patent. Lenin adopted a position corresponding to a combination of the first and the second, but not to the third of these passages from Bukharin.

[61] For a realistic analysis of the plunge of the productive forces in Russia at the time of the Civil War and War Communism, see among others, Leo N. Kritzman, *Die heroische Periode der grossen russischen Revolution,* Frankfurt, 1971, chapters 9-12.

[62] The future typology of socialist revolutions in the highly industrialized countries will probably follow the pattern of the revolutionary crises already experienced in Spain (1931-37), France (1936), Italy (1948), Belgium (1960-61), France (May 1968), Italy (Autumn 1969-70), more closely than that of the crises of 'collapse' after the First World War.

[63] See for example Trotsky's description of the decline of the forces of production in England in his Report to the Third Congress of the Communist International: 'England is poorer. The productivity of labour has fallen. Her world trade for 1920 has, in comparison to the last pre-war year, declined by at least one third, and in some of the most important branches, even more. . . . In 1913 England's coal industry supplied 287 million tons of coal; in 1920, 233 million tons, i.e., 20% less. In 1913, the production of iron amounted to 10.4 million tons; in 1920 — a little more than 8 million tons, i.e., again 20% less.' *Report on the World Economic Crisis and the New Tasks of the Communist International,* in Leon Trotsky, *The First Five Years of the Communist International,* p. 191.

reverse gear. Millions of European workers will die from unemployment and malnutrition. The United States will be compelled to reorient itself on the world market, reconvert its industry, and suffer curtailment for a considerable period. Afterwards, after a new world division of labour is thus established in agony for 15 or 20 or 25 years, a new epoch of capitalist upswing might perhaps ensue. But this entire conception is exceedingly abstract and one-sided. Matters are pictured here as if the proletariat had ceased to struggle. Meanwhile, there cannot even be talk of this if only for the reason that the class contradictions have become aggravated in the extreme precisely during the recent years.'[64]

As is so often the case with Trotsky, the first paragraph of this quotation is of prophetic power. It was written in the year 1921. Exactly 25 years later, in the year 1946, millions of European workers had died from unemployment, malnutrition, war and fascism. The USA had been compelled to reconvert its industry and for a considerable period (1929-39) substantially to curtail production and employment. It had reoriented itself on the world market — naturally both the commodity market and the capital market, ultimately generating a new international division of labour and a new phase of capitalist expansion of material production.

The second paragraph of the same quotation, on the other hand, is clearly limited by the conditions of its time.[65] Trotsky was absolutely right to state in 1921 that it was abstract and formal to predict a new upswing of productive forces: for at that point in time the fighting strength of the European working class was still in the ascendant. Under such conditions, a substantial increase in the rate of surplus-value — and consequently in the rate of profit — was unthinkable. What was on the agenda was not speculation about the possibility of a new stage of capitalist growth, but preparation of the working class to transform the structural crisis of capitalism into a victory of the proletarian revolution in the most important continental countries. The theories of a new upswing of capitalism advanced by the leaders of the Social Democrats were designed to justify their refusal to

[64] Trotsky, *The First Five Years of the Communist International*, Vol. 1, p. 211.
[65] The same is true of the sentence in the *Transitional Programme of the Fourth International* which Trotsky wrote in 1938: 'The productive forces of humanity have ceased to grow.' Trotsky immediately added: 'New discoveries already no longer raise the level of material wealth.' It would never have occurred to him to deny the growth of the forces of production when — as in the past twenty years — 'new discoveries and improvements' have actually and manifestly raised the overall level of material wealth.

lead this revolutionary struggle.[66] Their harvest was not a long period of upswing but, after the brief interlude of 1924-29, the Great Depression, mass unemployment, fascism and the horrors of the Second World War. Trotsky's analysis and prognosis had proved to be quite right.

What Trotsky could not have meant in 1921, however, was this: that in the long run it would be enough for the working class to *struggle* in order to prevent a new period of long-term upswing for capitalist forces of production. For this, it was necessary for it to *win*. Historical fatalism is no less shortsighted in questions of economic perspectives than in questions of great political class struggles. Trotsky was quite unequivocal on this point when, seven years later, he criticized Bukharin and Stalin's Programme for the Comintern: 'Will the bourgeoisie be able to secure for itself a new epoch of capitalist growth and power? Merely to deny such a possibility counting on the "hopeless position" in which capitalism finds itself would be mere revolutionary verbiage. "There are no absolutely hopeless situations" (Lenin). The present unstable class equilibrium in the European countries cannot continue indefinitely precisely because of its instability. . . . A situation so unstable that the proletariat cannot take power, while the bourgeoisie does not feel firmly enough the master of its own home, must sooner or later be abruptly resolved one way or another, either in favour of the proletarian dictatorship or in favour of a serious and prolonged capitalist stabilization on the backs of the popular masses, on the bones of the colonial people and . . . perhaps on our own bones. "There are no absolutely hopeless situations!" The European bourgeoisie can find a lasting way out of its grave contradictions only through the defeats of the proletariat and the mistakes of the revolutionary leadership. But the converse is equally true. There will be no new boom of world capitalism (of course, with the prospect of a new epoch of great upheavals) only in the event that the proletariat will be able to find a way out of the present unstable equilibrium on the revolutionary road.'[67] This prophetic vision was substantiated in every point. The phase of unstable equilibrium, which began with the history of the Russian Revolution and the defeat of the German Revolution, came to an end in the year 1929. Because of the incapacity of its leadership, the European working class was not in a position to resolve the acute

[66]See, for example, the essays of Rudolf Hilferding and Karl Kautsky in the Social Democratic periodical *Die Gesellschaft*, Vol. 1, No. 1, April 1924.
[67]Trotsky, *The Third International after Lenin*, New York, 1970, pp. 64-5.

social crisis to its own advantage. Fascism and the Second World War created the preconditions for this crisis to be resolved temporarily in favour of capital. Once again, at the end of the Second World War, the helm could have been swung over in France, Italy and Great Britain. Once again, the traditional parties of the working class not only proved themselves totally incapable of fulfilling their historical task but also showed themselves to be the perfect accomplices for European big capital in the stabilization of the late capitalist economy and the late capitalist state.[68]

This was the historical basis for the third technological revolution, for the third 'long wave with an undertone of expansion', and for late capitalism. It was by no means 'purely' the product of economic developments, proof of the alleged vitality of the capitalist mode of production or a justification for its existence. All it proved was that in the imperialist countries, given existing technology and forces of production, there are no 'absolutely hopeless situations' in a purely economic sense for capital, and that the long-term failure to accomplish a socialist revolution can ultimately give the capitalist mode of production a new lease of life, which the latter will then exploit in accordance with its inherent logic: as soon as the rate of profit rises again, it will accelerate the accumulation of capital, renovate technology, resume the incessant quest for surplus-value, average profit and surplus-profit, and develop further forces of production.

This is, in effect, the meaning of the third technological revolution. It is also what determines its historical limits. Offspring of the capitalist mode of production, it reproduces all the inner contradictions of this social and economic form. Engendered within the capitalist mode of production in the epoch of imperialism and monopoly capitalism, the age of structural crisis and gradual disintegration of this mode of production, this renewed upswing of the forces of production must add to the classical contradictions of capitalism a whole series of further contradictions, which we shall examine in the next chapters and which create the possibility of even broader and deeper revolutionary crises than those of the period 1917-37.

It should be remembered that Marx saw the historical mission of the capitalist mode of production not in a quantitatively unlimited development of the forces of production, but in determinate qualitative results of this development: 'The great historic quality of capital

[68] It is sufficient in this connection to cite General de Gaulle's comments on the role played by Maurice Thorez and the leadership of the French Communist Party after September 1944: See *Mémoires de Guerre*, Vol. 3, Paris, 1959, pp. 118-19.

is to *create* this *surplus labour*, superfluous labour from the standpoint of mere use value, mere subsistence; and its historic destiny is
fulfilled as soon as, on the one side, there has been such a development
of needs that surplus labour above and beyond necessity has itself
become a general need arising out of individual needs themselves —
and, on the other side, where the severe discipline of capital, acting
on succeeding generations, has developed general industriousness as
the general property of the new species — and, finally, when the
development of the productive powers of labour, which capital
incessantly whips forward with its unlimited mania for wealth, and
of the sole conditions in which this mania can be realized, have
flourished to the stage where the possession and preservation of
general wealth require a lesser labour time of society as a whole, and
where the labouring society relates scientifically to the process of
its progressive reproduction; hence where labour in which a human
being does what a thing could do has ceased.'[69] Once these qualitative
results have been achieved, capitalism has fulfilled its historical role,
and social relations are ready for socialism. There then commences
the epoch of the decline of bourgeois society. Although the forces of
production may still develop yet further, this does not alter the fact
that the real historical mission of capital has been completed. Indeed
such a further quantitative development may in certain circumstances actually endanger its qualitative achievements. Lenin's thesis
that there are no absolutely hopeless situations for the imperialist
bourgeoisie, does not imply that, so long as a socialist revolution has
not occurred, the capitalist mode of production can survive indefinitely at the price of lengthening periods of economic stagnation and
social crisis. For not merely does generalized automation, which
betokens a faster decrease in the mass of surplus-value, pose an
absolute barrier to the valorization of capital, which cannot be overcome by any increase in the rate of surplus-value. The dynamic of
the wastage and destruction of potential development that is henceforward involved in the actual development of the forces of production, is so great that the sole alternative to the self-destruction of
the system, or even of all civilization, is a higher form of society.
Despite all the international growth of the forces of production in
the capitalist world during the last twenty years, the option between
'socialism or barbarism' thus acquires its full relevance today.

[69] Marx, *Grundrisse*, p. 325.

7

The Reduction of the Turnover-Time of Fixed Capital and the Pressure towards Company Planning and Economic Programming

The reduction of the turnover-time of the fixed capital is one of the fundamental characteristics of late capitalism. The immediate origin of the reduction lies in the acceleration of technological innovation,[1] which is in turn a result of the reallocation of industrial capital, that is invested not only in the direct activity of production but increasingly also in pre-productive spheres (Research and Development).[2] The compulsion to engage in an arms race with non-capitalist states, whose development of technology is not restricted by conditions of valorization in their productive activity, and the inner logic of scientific development, are contributing factors in this process.

In the context of the history of capitalism, however, the decisive force behind the reduction of the turnover-time of fixed capital is undoubtedly the fact that the principal source of surplus-profits is now to be found in 'technological rents' or the productivity differential between firms and branches of industry. *The continuous and systematic hunt for technological innovations and the corresponding surplus-profits* becomes the standard hallmark of late capitalist enterprises

---

[1] This subject is dealt with in the next chapter.

[2] The amount of expenditure on Research and Development by industrial capital itself rose in the USA from less than $100 million before the Second World War to $2.24 billion in 1953 and $5.57 billion in 1963. This excludes State expenditure. See Edwin Mansfield, *The Economics of Technological Change*, London, 1969, p. 55. Levinson states that the total private outlay on Research and Development (hence not merely in industry) was $17 billion in 1968 and $20.7 billion in 1970.

and especially of the late capitalist large corporations. [3] This hunt for surplus-profit by 'different capitals', takes the form for 'capital in general' of pressure to reduce the cost of constant capital and to increase the rate of surplus-value through additional production of relative surplus-value.

The third technological revolution, which is itself both the origin and the outcome of accelerated technological innovation and the reduction of the turnover-time of fixed capital, has adverse physical and technical repercussions on the length of life of fixed capital, both because it increases the speed at which machines are used and because it accelerates their obsolescence. [4]

The reduction of the turnover-time of fixed capital is twofold in character. On the one hand, it is the sum of the accelerated replacement of old plants by completely new ones, i.e., a process of the accelerated obsolescence of fixed capital. At the same time, it also represents the transition from the classical practice of rotating repairs of existing plant, that is fundamentally renewed only every ten years, to the modern practice of general repairs, which involves *ongoing* and sometimes important technological innovations. [5] In terms of value this can be expressed as follows: while previously the process of simple reproduction of fixed capital and the process of accumulation of additional fixed capital were kept strictly separate and led to extended reproduction — with only minor alterations in productive technology — at the start of every new ten-year cycle, these two processes are now increasingly combined. Simple reproduction proceeds continuously, accompanied by constant technological

[3] The Vice-President of the Budd Concern is very clear on this point. 'Any innovation worth undertaking should have dramatically greater than "normal" profit margins associated with it': Aaron J. Gellman, 'Market Analysis and Marketing', in Maurice Goldsmith (ed.), *Technological Innovation and the Economy*, London, 1970, p. 131.

[4] For the increased speed of machines since the end of the Second World War see, for instance, Hansjörg Reuker, 'Einfluss der Automatisierung auf Werkstück und Werkzeugmaschine', *Fortschrittberichte des Vereins Deutscher Ingenieure*, Series I, No. 8, October 1966, pp. 29-30; Salter, op. cit., p. 44; Kruse, Kunz and Uhlmann, op. cit., pp. 59-60, etc. This increased speed is one of the main forces behind the trend towards automation, which in its turn leads to a massive increase in the speed of the production process by making it independent of the rhythm of the *slowest* operation, which had hitherto determined labour on the conveyor belt. See Pierre Naville, 'Division du Travail et Repartition des Tâches', in Georges Friedmann and Pierre Naville (eds.). *Traité de Sociologie du Travail*, Vol. 1, Paris, 1961, pp. 380-1. Marx dealt with the question of machine labour in, for example, *Capital*, Vol. I, p. 412f., and Vol. III, p. 233.   [5] Nick, op. cit., p. 17.

renewal, and thus flows into extended reproduction, which leads in shorter periods than previously — a five-year cycle can currently be assumed — to a complete renewal of production technology.

The acceleration of the turnover-time of fixed capital also has repercussions on the turnover-time of circulating capital. On the one hand, it increases the demand for ongoing investment activity. This leads to an ongoing reconversion of circulating capital into fixed capital and increases the tendency, which is anyway inherent in monopoly capitalism, for companies to convert their total capital into fixed capital and to draw most, if not all of their circulating capital from bank credits. This has repercussions on the self-financing of companies, which is one of the most important characteristics distinguishing late capitalism from the classical imperialism described by Lenin, which was dominated by finance capital. It also has effects on the whole activity of the banks in creating money and credit, which we shall analyse later.[6] On the other hand, it increases the interest of capital in a further acceleration of the turnover-time of circulating capital, as a source of additional production of surplus-value that becomes all the more important as the acceleration of the turnover-time of fixed capital increases the organic composition of capital and thereby creates an additional pressure towards a compensating increase in the mass and the rate of surplus-value. The result is a tendency towards an 'acceleration' of all capitalist processes, which expresses itself among other ways in the parallel phenomena of a more acute intensification of the labour process and a faster 'acceleration' (quantitative differentitation and qualitative deterioration) of workers' consumption — i.e., of the reproduction of labour-power itself.[7]

The reduction of the turnover-time of fixed capital can be corroborated by a great deal of empirical evidence, and has been much discussed by both capitalists and economists. Thus, for example, Alan C. Mattison, Chairman of the Mattison Machine Works, declared before the US Congressional Committee on Automation: 'The cycle of obsolescence of machine tools is in the process of diminishing rapidly from 8 or 10 years to 5 years.'[8] In the American automobile industry, it has become customary to write off *within one*

[6] See Chapter 13 of this volume.
[7] See Chapter 12 of this volume.
[8] Cited in *L'Automation — Méthodologie de la Recherche*, ILO, Geneva, 1964, p. 27.

year the costs of the specific tools and dies manufactured for the production of each new auto model, if and when a firm manufactures and sells at least 400,000 cars of that model. (The costs of such tools and dies typically amount to about one third of total fixed capital of a large US auto plant).[9] Freeman reports that in the electronic capital goods industry the 'life of products' is between 3 and 10 years, i.e., an average of 6½ years, as compared with a span of 13 years which Engels gave as the average life of machines in his epoch in a letter to Marx.[10] The average life of computers is as little as 5 years, and of nautical radar, 7 years.[11] In 1971, West German weaving mills were using completely different machines (double-broad Sulzer models with shaft-machines) from the most modern equipment employed in 1965 (conventional automatic shaft-machines without unifil).[12] The American tax authorities estimate that there has been a general reduction of approximately 33% in the physical life of machines since the 30's.[13] This figure has been sharply criticized both by those who consider the corresponding amortization allowance too high (i.e., regard it as a means by which enterprises camouflage their profits) and by those who regard it as too low. Using practical examples, Terborgh has estimated that the life of screw machines has been reduced from 39 to 18 years, that of 'gear shapers' from 35-42 to 20 years, and that of steam generators from 30 to 20 years.[14] He uses cases of concrete enterprises, not averages for the industry or for all manufacturing industry. In the most modern petro-chemical works producing ethylene, fixed capital is amortized in 4 to 8 years, depending on its size.[15] General comments

[9] Lawrence White, *The Automobile Industry since 1945*, Harvard, 1971, pp. 39, 57-8.
[10] *Werke*, Vol. 31, Berlin, 1965, p. 329f. The letter is dated 27 August 1867.
[11] C. Freeman, 'Research and Development in Electronic Capital Goods', *National Institute Economic Review*, No. 34, November 1965, p. 68.
[12] Anmann-Einhoff-Helmstädter-Isselhorst, op. cit., p. 30.
[13] 'Equipment service life' in manufacturing industry was estimated to be 34% shorter in 1961 than in 1942. Allan H. Young, 'Alternative Estimates of Corporate Depreciation of Profits', Part I, in *Survey of Current Business*, Vol. 48,No. 4, April 1968, p. 20. See also the Second Part of the same article, *Survey of Current Business,* Vol. 48, No. 5, May 1968, pp. 18-19, 22. George Jaszi calculates that the actual average age of fixed capital (including buildings) in US manufacturing industry declined from 12 years in 1945 to 10.3 in 1950, 9.4 in 1953 and 8.5 in 1961: *Survey of Current Business*, November 1962.
[14] George Terborgh, *Business Investment Policy*, Washington 1962, pp. 158, 179.
[15] *National Institute Economic Review*, No. 45, August 1968, p. 39. Nick, op. cit., p. 59, states that in the chemical industry fixed capital is renewed every 5-6 years.

on the reduced life-span of fixed capital are too numerous to list. The following table of depreciation norms in the early 1920's and 1960's — i.e., some forty-five years later — provides graphic evidence of the acceleration of the turnover-time of fixed capital:

Estimates of Productive Life Expectation of Fixed Equipment[16]

	A	B	C	D
	+ 1922	+ 1942	+ 1957	+ 1965
steel tubes	30-60 years		15 years	
steam boilers	15-20		15	
water gauges	20		15	
turbines	50		22	
brewery machines	25	15-20 years		16 years
factory buildings	50-100	40-50		35
mechanical saws	14	10		
machine tools	20			16
printing machines	40			16
woodworking machines	33			20

This reduction of the turnover-time of fixed capital gives rise to a twofold contradiction. On the one hand, it involves an increase in the period of preparation and experimentation for specific processes of production, and in the time it takes to construct plants.[17] This contradiction is so great that sometimes a particular production process or a particular plant may already be considered technologically out of date before it is even applied to mass production.[18] On the other hand, the production plants called into being by the third technological revolution demand capital investments far in excess of those necessitated by the first and second technological revolutions. The commitment of these colossal amounts of capital, combined with

[16] Series A: P. Wojtiechow, *Amortisationsnormen und Eigentumsbewertung*, cited in A. Herzenstein, 'Gibt es grosse Konjunkturzyklen?', *Unter dem Banner des Marxismus*, 1929, Heft II, p. 307. Series B: Bulletin F of US Bureau of Internal Revenue (1942), basis of fiscal depreciation charges. Series C: decision of the West German Ministry of Finance, August 15, 1957, establishing depreciation norms. Series D: Jacques Mairesse, *L'Evaluation du Capital Fixe Productif*, Collections de I'INSEE, Series C, No. 18-19, November 1972.

[17] Many writers estimate that there is a ten to fifteen year period between an actual discovery and its profitable production. Edwin Mansfield, op. cit., p. 102, cites estimates compiled by Frank Lynn, which suggests that in the period 1945-64 the gap between discovery and commercialization can be estimated at 14 years, compared with 24 years in the period 1920-44.

[18] Nick, op. cit., p. 20.

the accelerated obsolescence of plants and ranges of products, thus make the whole of capitalist production much more hazardous under late capitalism than it was in the age of freely competitive capitalism or 'classical' monopoly capitalism.

These increased risks are further multiplied by the particular technical rigidity of automated production, which no longer permits fluctuations in ongoing production or employment, which may now endanger the whole minimum profitability of the enterprise.[19] The volume of the means committed to research and development moreover, makes it urgently necessary to calculate and pre-plan this expenditure as exactly as possible — including the indirect expenses which may arise from the creation and sale of new products.[20] A four-fold pressure thus arises for ever more exact planning within the late capitalist enterprise:

— pressure arising from the very nature of automation for exact planning of the process of production within the enterprise;

— pressure to plan investments in research and development, combined with pressure for planned technological innovation;[21]

— pressure to plan general investments derived from the previous trend;

— pressure towards cost planning for all the elements of production.

The instruments of automation — above all the electronic computer — make the exact planning of details in all these spheres poss-

[19] 'The rising capital outlay involved in growing automation implies an increase in time-dependent costs, and a decrease in the elasticity of enterprises. With a constant life-span, i.e., a constant annual rate of depreciation, the more capital that is invested in means of production, the more capital will be immobilized if the latter are laid idle and production capacity is prematurely restricted. The rise in the demand for capital as a result of automation thus dictates all-out utilization of the means of production. The increase in time-dependent capital costs involved in automation can only be covered by the utmost intensity of utilization.' Kruse, Kunz and Uhlmann, op. cit., p. 46.

[20] K. G. H. Binning, 'The Uncertainties of Planning Major Research and Development', in B. W. Denning (ed.), *Corporate Long Range Planning*, London, 1969, pp. 172-3.

[21] An investigation by the IFO in Munich showed that in the mid-60s 75% of large firms questioned in West Germany drew up an investment plan for every two or three years, and 33% of large firms for four or more years. 'Investments' take first place in all long-range plans. R. Bemerl, F. O. Bonhoeffer and W. Strigel, 'Wie plant die Industrie?' in *Wirtschaftskonjunktur*, Vol. 19, No. 1, April 1966, p. 31. See also, 'For all these reasons we at Merck have felt it necessary to plan our growth and operations with a 5-year perspective.' Antonie T. Knoppers, 'A Management View of Innovation', in B. W. Denning (ed.), *Corporate Long-Range Planning*, p. 172.

ible through the rapid processing of colossal quantities and complexes of data. In other words, they make it possible to calculate optimal variants of the various possible modes of operation. The techniques of PERT and C.P.M. thus come into use — which, like the electronic processors themselves are by-products of military research.[22]

The exact planning of investments, financing and costs, naturally loses its meaning as soon as there is no guarantee of sale. The logic of the third technological revolution therefore drives late capitalist companies to plan their sales, with the familiar result of colossal outlays on market research and market analysis,[23] advertisements and customer manipulation, planned obsolescence of commodities (which very often brings with it a fall in the quality of the commodities)[24] and so on. This whole process culminates in concentrated pressure on the State to limit oscillations in the economy, at the cost of permanent inflation. It generates the growing trend towards *State guarantee of profits,* firstly through increasing government contracts, especially in the military sphere, then through underwriting of technologically advanced companies. This trend towards State guarantees of the profits of the large companies, which has spread from the sphere of production and research into that of the export of commodities and capital, is another of the crucial hallmarks of late capitalism.[25]

Besides the trend for the State to guarantee the profits of large companies, late capitalism reveals a second characteristic response to the increased risks attached to colossal investment projects in conditions of accelerated technological innovation and the reduced turnover-time of fixed capital: the attempt to create a continuous *differentiation* of products, projects and markets,[26] which finds expression both in the formation of giant *conglomerates* and in the

---

[22] Spacecraft tracking by NASA has produced similar progress in computer techniques for civilian industry and transport, for example the use of IBM 41800 computers for analysis of solvents in chemical plants or 'quality-audit' testing of cars coming off the assembly line in the automobile industry. See *The Times*, June 28, 1968.

[23] 'Market research approaches a market which already exists; market analysis determines whether or not there is a market.' Aaron J. Gellman, op. cit., p. 137.

[24] See for instance the discussion of planned obsolescence in Vance Packard, *The Waste Makers,* London, 1963, Chapter 6.

[25] See Ernest Mandel, *Marxist Economic Theory,* pp. 501-7.

[26] On the corporation strategy of diversification, see among others, Heckmann, op. cit., pp. 71-6; H. I. Ansoff, T. A. Anderson, F. Norton and J. F. Weston, 'Planning for Diversification Through Merger', in H. Igor Ansoff (ed.), *Business Strategy,* London 1969, p. 290f.

establishment of multinational companies.[27] The extent to which these processes are related to the reduction in the turnover-time of fixed capital is shown by the volume of amortizations and their weight in the total mass of gross investments. The reduction of the turnover-time of fixed capital creates for each enterprise a geometrically proportionate risk of being left behind in the competitive struggle, for the tempo of competition increases with the tempo of reproduction of fixed capital. At the same time, the function of this competition — the reallocation of the total surplus-value created in the production process — becomes much more vital than before, as a result of the pressure of emerging tendencies towards full automation. The increasing reunification of simple reproduction with the accumulation of fixed capital, together with the reduction of the turnover-time of fixed capital, creates a *compulsion towards regular and regulated amortization*, i.e., a tendency towards *planned amortization*. This is symbolized by the fact that financial analysts now increasingly employ the concept of *cash-flow* to judge the solidity of a corporation — a notion which refers to the sum of profits and depreciation charges.

In the case where the fixed capital is renewed every ten years, there is only an annual burden of amortization of 10% of the machine value on the annual product of the enterprise or company. If, as a result of a bad business situation and a fall in the gross income of the company this 10% of the machine value cannot be made good, this does not endanger the entire reproduction of its fixed capital. This 10% of the machine value must then be spread over the nine remaining years of the cycle, or the annual burden of amortization must be raised from 10 to 11.1%, i.e., by only 1.1% of the machine value. It is a different matter when the turnover-time of fixed capital is 5 or even only 4 years. In this case, the failure to achieve the reproduction allowance for the renewal of the machine stock even for a single year already fundamentally undermines the whole investment calculation, if it does not mean the outright impossibility of renewing the fixed capital in the cycle envisaged. The annual burden of amortization has thus now increased from 10 to 20 or 25% of the machine value, and the failure to make good the allowance even for a single year means the necessity of reallocating this 20% in a five-year cycle to four years, in other words, of raising the annual amortiza-

---

[27] For this complex of questions see Chapter 10 of the present work.

tion allowance from 20% to 25% of the machine value or by 25% (as opposed to only 10% in a ten-year cycle). Where the turnover-time of fixed capital is only four years the loss of the amortization allowance for only one year means in effect the compulsion to reallocate 25% of the value of the machine-stock over the other three years of the cycle, i.e., to raise the annual amortization allowance to 33.3% of the value of the machines and by 33.3% (instead of by 10% in a ten-year cycle and 25% in a five-year cycle). This is virtually impossible in a normal conjuncture, without exceptional boom conditions. In the US automobile industry, the rate of profit (calculated on an 'official' and not on a marxist basis) would fall from 15.4% to 11.4% or 8.7%, if the depreciation of 'tooling costs' for new models was realized in two or three years rather than one year.[28]

Hence the inherent pressure in late capitalism for planned, long-range amortization or long-range investment planning. But long-range investment planning means long-range planning of gross income and hence also of costs. Long-range planning of costs, however, cannot of itself achieve the goal at which it aims. For in order actually to realize the gross income projected by a concern, it is not sufficient to plan costs and selling prices. Sales must also be guaranteed. *The spreading tendency towards economic programming in the most important imperialist states* thus corresponds in the age of late capitalism to the *constraint on companies to plan long-range investments.* This tendency is simply an attempt to bridge over, at least partially, the contradiction between the anarchy of capitalist production inherent in the private ownership of the means of production and this growing objective pressure to plan amortization and investments. Planning *within* capitalist enterprises is as old as the formal subsumption of labour under capital, in other words, the elementary division of labour under the command of capital in the capitalist mode of production, beginning with the period of manufactures. The more complicated the actual process of production becomes, and the more it integrates dozen of simultaneous processes — including processes in the spheres of circulation and reproduction — the more complex and exact such planning also inevitably becomes. The first serious book on internal planning in enterprises was written shortly after the First World War.[29] Once the necessary set of instruments

---

[28] Lawrence White, op. cit., p. 39.
[29] M. Lohmann, *Der Wirtschftsplan des Betriebes und der Unternehmung*, Berlin, 1928.

(conceptual and mechanical) had been perfected with the onset of the third technological revolution, this planning within the enterprise could move onto a qualitatively higher plane.

Clausewitz once made a comparison between war and trade and saw in victorious battle an analogy to successful exchange. In late capitalism, or at least in its vocabulary and ideology, the relationship between military science and economic practice is inverted: one now speaks of big companies planning their strategy.[30] It is a fact that in the age of monopoly capitalism there can no longer be any question of selling the available range of commodities produced at top speed with maximum profit. In conditions of monopolistic competition short-term profit maximization is a completely senseless goal. [31] Company strategy aims at *long-term profit maximization,* in which factors such as domination of the market, share of the market, brand familiarity, future ability to meet demand, safeguarding of opportunities for innovation, i.e., for growth, become more important than the selling price which can be obtained immediately or the profit margin which this represents.[32] The decisive factor here is not by any means disposal over all the relevant information. On the contrary: the necessity of making strategic decisions — in the final analysis the *compulsion* for internal planning in the enterprise — expresses precisely the *uncertainty* which is inherent in every economic decision in a market economy of commodity production. What makes planning possible is thus not the fact that today it is easier than ever before to collect a maximum quantity of data on matters outside the enterprise. What makes planning possible is the *actual control* that the capitalist has over the means of production and the labourers in his enterprise, and over the capital which in the event may be accumulated outside the enterprise.[33]

Inside the enterprise or company there is no exchange of com-

---

[30] Heckmann, op. cit., p. 42. Bemerl, Bonhoeffer and Strigel, op. cit., p. 30. See also such titles as H. Igor Ansoff (ed.), *Business Strategy,* Alfred D. Chandler, *Strategy and Structure,* and the like.

[31] One of the basic errors in Galbraith's *The New Industrial State,* (London, 1969) is that he ignores the distinction between short-and long-term maximization of profits. We shall return to this question in Chapter 17 of this book.

[32] Gordon Yewdall (ed.), *Management Decision Making,* London, 1969, p. 91f., Bemerl, Bonhoeffer and Strigel, op. cit., p. 34: 'Market expectations and considerations of profitability (exercise) the greatest influence on the long-term planning of enterprises'.

[33] 'Part of the information needed refers to processes and conditions within the enterprise. The extent to which these are available and the enterprise thereby becomes transparent is largely determinable by the management of the enterprise

modities. Profitability considerations in no way determine whether a larger or smaller number of bodies, as opposed to engines or chassis, are produced within an automobile corporation.[34] Within the company labour is directly socialized in the sense that the overall plan of the company — the production of x cars per week, per month or per year — directly determines the output of the various factories, workshops and conveyor belts. The investment activity in these various factories or workshops of the same company is determined centrally and not by the directors of the individual plants. Within the company, therefore, planning is genuine.

Such planning can, of course, fail to achieve its strategic objectives; it is nevertheless real planning. There is a difference between a situation in which 5% of an output of one million cars cannot be sold because of a sudden slump in demand, and a situation where with an output of one million car bodies and engines, 50,000 cars cannot be assembled because production of chassis has been inadequate. In the first case, circumstances outside the enterprise — whether or not these were foreseeable is another question — have an adverse effect on a planned objective. The second case is one of bad planning. The precise coordination of all the factors under the actual control of the individual company is objectively possible and only a matter of good planning. The precise coordination of all the factors inside and outside the enterprise, on which long-term profit maximization ultimately depends, is by contrast impossible, because the company cannot — or cannot fully — control the factors outside the enterprise. There is thus a clear distinction between *planning* within the enterprise (or company) and *programming* of the economy as a whole.

In the overall economy of a capitalist country — or still more: in the total capitalist world economy — *no planning centres or authorities possess any control whatsoever* over the available means of production, the accumulated capital and the existing economic resources, with the possible exceptions of nationalized industries. The

itself.' Bemerl, Bonhoeffer and Strigel, op. cit., p. 32. The availability of the data depends of course on the control over the means of production, and not the other way round.

[34] It may occur that 'profitability calculations' are made within the corporation or within the factory for individual departments. These are then used to measure the relative efficiency of the management of this department. See for instance A. J. Merrett, 'Incomes, Taxation, Managerial Effectiveness and Planning', in B. W. Denning, (ed.) *Corporate Long Range Planning*, pp. 90-1. It is a matter, however, of fictitious or simulated profitability, since these departments do not possess independent capital, and the investments in them do not depend on 'profitability' but on the overall strategic plan of the corporation.

various companies or branches of industry can in no way deploy their resources independently of calculations or expectations of profitability. In the final resort, the law of value in its capitalist form — the compulsion for capital to obtain at least the average profit and to seek surplus-profits beyond this average — here determines the inflow and outflow of capital, hence of the economic resources and means of production, from one branch into another or from one company into another. There is thus no overall plan which stipulates that, given a production of x number of car bodies, technical-economic co-efficients require the production of x number of chassis. Here the competition of capital, the expectation of profit and the actual realization of surplus-value create a situation in which private and industrial demand for coal equivalents may be z millions tons, but what is in actual fact produced is x million tons of coal, y million tons of coal-equivalent oil and w million tons of coal-equivalent natural gas, where $(x+y+w)$ may turn out to be significantly less or significantly more than the demand z. For while the production of car bodies, chassis and engines is determined within a company from *one* centre and by *one* owner, the production of coal, oil and natural gas is determined by various owners on the basis of calculations of their private or particular interests. In contrast to the industrial company, there is here no central control over the means of production.

Economic programming in late capitalism, therefore, in contrast to economic planning within industrial companies today (or within society tomorrow after the overthrow of the capitalist mode of production) cannot do more than merely co-ordinate the independent production prospects of the companies,[35] which are based in the final analysis on the commodity character of production — that is, on the private ownership of the means of production and the private character of the labour expended in the different companies. Such programming is thus irrevocably beset by two crucial elements of uncertainty.

[35]'The guiding principle of planning (in France) is to integrate the sum of these interdependent effects by extending the typical behaviour of the iron and steel producer as regards his supplies and outlets, to the whole economy. The instrument for market research on a national scale is the *Tableau économique* devised by François Quesnay, revised by Leontief and adapted for France by Gruson. The procedure is that of concerted consultation within modernization commissions . . . . A co-ordination of this kind can operate indirectly through the influence of the dominant industrial groups . . . . It is to their mutual advantage that a confrontation of the forecasts and decisions of the private sector should take place in a public context.' Pierre Massé, *Le Plan ou l'Anti-Hasard*, Paris, 1965, p. 173.

In the first place, it is based on investment plans and expectations which are mostly nothing more than projections, corrected with certain variables, of *past* tendencies of development. If there is a sudden alteration in the market situation or an unexpected change in the relation between demand and supply; if a new product unexpectedly comes onto the market and threatens the 'planned', i.e., expected demand for a certain product produced by a company; if there is a sudden recession or if the cycle unexpectedly moves to 'overstrain', then companies may be forced to make abrupt alterations in their investment plans either by reducing them radically (i.e., postponing them) or by increasing them suddenly, i.e., accelerating them. Moreover, these companies can err by making false appraisals of the market situation, sales trends or business cycle; they are then obliged to re-adapt their plans to economic reality all the more drastically because belatedly.

In the second place, different units of capital are nominally coordinated in economic programming, which in this context do not have common, but *different interests*. All large companies, of course, have a common interest in knowing the investment plans of their most important supply and customer companies. In the last resort, this is the objective basis for the exchange of information underlying late capitalist economic programming. But these companies do not want this information so that they can *adapt* themselves to it; on the contrary, they want it in order to calculate their own private profit maximization as effectively as possible, and so ultimately in order to *combat* the plans of their competitors as effectively as possible. Competition and private ownership therefore means that precisely *because* there has been an exchange of information, co-ordination between different investment projects is liable not to function, because of the temptation precisely to use the plans of a competing firm to outlap it and force it to retreat. The co-ordination of the plans of private companies therefore inevitably implies both actual co-ordination and the negation of any co-ordination.

The fundamental uncertainty of late capitalist economic programming — in reality, the projection of future overall economic developments by a co-ordination of the investment plans provided by individual companies[36] — is the basis of its *forecast*-character, as opposed

---

[36]'Individual firms, having made separate market studies may find that the state of the market in respect to both the supply of inputs and the demand for outputs does not warrant any expansion of the firm. This assessment may be fully correct within that framework, but if a respected planning body sets up a target for, say, 10%

to the *goal*-character of a socialist planned economy. Those who construct these forecasts do not possess the economic power, i.e., the control over the means of production, to see that these forecasts are realized. It is characteristic in this context that the only means at the disposal of late capitalist economic programmers for the correction of actual development when they deviate from predictions, is State intervention in the economy — a change in government policy on money, credit, taxes, foreign trade or public investment activity. The limits of such government policy will be dealt with in a later context.

One of the greatest weaknesses of Shonfield's interpretation of late capitalism lies in its confusion of the fundamental difference between capitalist economic programming and post-capitalist economic planning. Shonfield cites the exception of US agriculture, where government agencies lay down the areas to be cultivated and even the quantities to be produced — with what success is another matter. He does not seem to see the difference between such practices and a loose 'consensus' among companies, where private control over the means of production is predominant. Such a consensus is always limited by efforts to compete, in other words by the constraint towards the separate maximization of profit on the part of each competitor. It is at the very least surprising that Shonfield, who views the above-average growth of international trade as one of the main causes of the long post-war boom, can exclude international competition from his analysis of the trend towards economic programming which is specific to late capitalism, and overlook the fact that integration into the world economy and international competition create even more hurdles for effective national economic programming.[37]

There is undoubtedly a certain reciprocal effect, of a both technical and economic character between planning of production and

---

expansion, it may be easily attained both individually and collectively, except, of course, or the external sector . . . . The Japanese plan 'forecasts' how the private sector and the public sector *would behave* if each business and government department carried out extensive research studies at both micro- and macro-levels considering all important economic factors and potentialities both at home and abroad, and after that proceeded to optimize its behaviour. Thus the plans are forecasts of what the optimal behaviour of the Japanese economy as a whole and in parts would be. . . . Briefly, in Japan the execution or implementation of the plan rests solely on the 'announcement effect' of the plan, and the Economic Planning Agency acts as a consultant, and not as a director.' K. Bieda, op. cit., pp. 57, 59-60.

[37] Andrew Shonfield, *Modern Capitalism*, Oxford, 1969, pp. 231-2, 255-7, 299-300.

accumulation within individual companies and programming of the economy as a whole. The need to plan and calculate exactly within the enterprise, determined by the reduction in the turnover-time of fixed capital, creates the technical tools and interest for a much more precise registration of economic data, which can also be applied to the overall economy. This progress vastly increases the technical potential of effective socialist planning, compared with the techniques at man's disposal, say, in the year 1918 or 1929.

On the other hand, however, the basic economic uncertainty inherent in late capitalist programming must also have profound effects on the application of exact planning techniques within companies. Years of calculations and experiments, gigantic outlays on research and development may have to be thrown overboard at a stroke because of vicissitudes on the market or decisions by rival firms over which a company has no control and about which it can do nothing. Major errors in forecasting belong to the same category. Public programming centres have up to now repeatedly made such mistakes, sometimes with substantial boomerang results, such as the intensification of cyclical disequilibrium instead of the anti-cyclical effect expected.[38] Wide annual fluctuations in the volume of private investments similarly fall into this category. Economic programming and increased State intervention in the economy have by no means caused these fluctuations to disappear; they continue to be a decisive feature of the capitalist mode of production and its cyclical development. In France, the very country which has an 'exemplary planned economy', these fluctuations have been particularly prominent:

Annual Rate of Increase of Gross Capital Formation in France[39]

1954:	12.4%	1959:	5.7%	1964:	9.6%
1955:	9.3%	1960:	16.2%	1965:	4.3%
1956:	21.0%	1961:	2.3%	1966:	9.3%
1957:	5.5%	1962:	11.6%	1967:	5.6%
1958:	7.3%	1963:	3.2%	1968:	7.4%
				1969:	10.3%

[38] "There was the plan in 1962 that the economy would grow at 4%, but what happened? The economy did not grow at 4% and this resulted in too much capital equipment in electric power, steel making and in many other industries'. Denning (ed.), op. cit., p. 197. For the mistaken forecasts of Swedish economic programmes, see Holger Heide, *Langfristige Wirtschaftsplanung in Schweden*, Tübingen, 1965.

[39] Data up to 1963; *Rapport sur les Comptes de la Nation de 1963*; from 1964 onwards, in productive branches only, Mairesse, op. cit., p. 52.

While the effect of economic programming is always uncertain and sometimes positively 'slap-dash', the calculations of so-called 'social programming' are of the utmost importance for late capitalism. The shortened turnover-time of fixed capital compels companies to plan and calculate costs with precision. But the exact planning of costs also implies the exact planning of wage costs. The exact planning of wage costs in turn presupposes the emancipation of the price of the commodity of labour-power from the fluctuations of demand and supply on the so-called labour market. It implies a tendency towards the long-range advance planning of these wage costs.

The simplest method of achieving this is a system of long-term binding collective agreements which eliminate all uncertainty concerning wage costs in ensuing years. But in a normal late-capitalist parliamentary democracy, in which there is a minimum freedom of development for the workers' movement and the class struggle, this solution cannot be enforced in the long run and has in practice proved a failure.[40] For one thing, during the 'long wave with an undertone of expansion' after the Second World War, the general tendency on the labour market was towards an increasing shortage of labour-power in a growing number of countries, so that agreements of this kind came to conflict with the laws of the market. They represented an attempt to cheat the workers of the chances of wage increases afforded by a relatively advantageous market situation. This inevitably became clear to a growing number of workers through experience (possibilities of changing jobs, payments above the agreements by employers, and sometimes enticements to other jobs). In the long run, even a trade-union movement which was only partially responsive to pressure from below could not escape the repercussions of these empirical discoveries by its membership. The impossibility of exact wage planning of a 'voluntary' nature between employers and trade unions thus became increasingly clear, and gave way to a tendency for state mediation. 'Government incomes policy' or 'concerted action', i.e., the proclamation of wage-growth rates binding on 'both sides of industry' has increasingly replaced purely contractual long-term agreements.

But the same laws and forces which doomed long-term collective agreements to failure, likewise condemn 'government incomes

---

[40] The tendency towards long-term wage agreements has been reversed in the USA, West Germany, Belgium and other countries.

policies'. Wage earners have not been slow to discover that a bourgeois state is fully capable of planning and controlling wages or
wage increases, but is incapable of keeping a similar rein on increases
in the price of commodities or in the income of other social classes,
first and foremost of capitalists and capitalist enterprises. 'Government incomes policies' have thus proved to be mere 'policing of
wages' — in other words, an attempt artificially to restrict wage
increases, and nothing more.[41] Wage-earners have consequently
defended themselves against this particular method of cheating them
just as they had against voluntary self-restraint by trade unions; they
have typically sought, by pressure on the trade unions and by 'unofficial strikes' or by a combination of both, at least to adjust the sale
of the commodity of labour-power to the conditions of the labour
market when these were relatively advantageous to the sellers, and
not only when they were disadvantageous to them.

The medium and long-term planning of wage costs needed by
large companies in the age of late capitalism thus calls for measures
by the bourgeois state going far beyond the voluntary self-restraint
of the trade unions or a 'government incomes policy' relying on the
co-operation of the trade union bureaucracy. For a minimum degree
of efficacy there must further be a legal restriction on the level of
wages and the bargaining freedom of the unions, and a legal limitation of the right to strike. If a shortage of labour-power, i.e., a situation
of actual full employment, which is not propitious to big capital, can
be avoided, and the industrial reserve army at the same time be
reconstituted, then the measures just mentioned will in actual fact
have a certain temporary effect, as was indeed the case in the USA
from the time of the passing of the Taft-Hartley Act until the mid-60's.

There would then be an intensification of the integration, already
incipient in the age of classical imperialism, of the trade-union
apparatuses into the state.[42] In this case, the wage-earners increasingly lose all interest in paying their dues to an apparatus which does

---

[41] Bauchet admits that French trade union leaders restricted wage increases, while
at the same time the official price-index was falsified; the government was not in a
position to control the rise in prices, and there was no mention either of controlling
undistributed company profits, so that there was by no means an 'equal sacrifice by
all', Pierre Bauchet, *La Planification Française*, Paris, 1966, pp. 320-1. We would
add: the result was May 1968.

[42] Trotsky analysed the growing tendency in capitalism for the unions to be integrated into the bourgeois state as early as 1940: see 'Trade Unions in the Epoch of
Imperialist Decay', in *Leon Trotsky on the Trade Unions*, New York, 1969.

continual damage to their everyday interests, and the mass basis of trade-unions declines. Since, however, the bourgeois class does not want to punish but to reward the trade-union apparatus for integrating itself in this way, loss of membership dues must be neutralized or compensated. The logical outcome of the whole process is thus ultimately compulsory collection of dues by the employer at the source, i.e., compulsory membership of the unions. We would then see the public transformation of free trade unions into state trade unions, the conversion of union dues into taxes and the transformation of the trade union apparatus into a specific department of the government bureaucracy, whose special job would be to 'administer' the commodity labour-power, just as other departments of the state machine administer buildings, planes or railways.[43] Since, however, wage-earners would by no means simply accept such a process and would interpose new private or 'illegal' mediators between the sellers and buyers of the commodity of labour-power in order to obtain the highest possible price for the sellers, such a system of state unions would be unthinkable without a major increase in passive and active repression — in other words, a substantial limitation, not only of the right to strike, but also of the freedom of association, assembly, demonstration and publication.[44] Hence the trend towards the elimination of the *struggle* between the buyer and the seller of the commodity of labour-power in the determination of the price of this commodity must ultimately culminate in a decisive limitation or abolition of basic democratic freedoms, i.e., the coercive system of a 'strong state'.

If, however, the trade unions, pressed by a membership increasingly acting on its own initiative and recreating union democracy, successfully escape further integration into the bourgeois state apparatus and revert to resolute defence of the direct interests of the wage-earners, they can shatter not only the exact planning of costs and wage costs within large companies but also any possibility of indicative economic planning by bourgeois governments. The trade unions must then increasingly come into collision not only with individual companies and enterprises, not only with employers' federations,

[43] The so-called 'vertical trade unions' in Spain are a classic example of such a function of the 'trade union apparatus'.

[44] The 'Industrial Relations Act' forced through the British Parliament by the conservative Government of 1970-74, made it illegal for unauthorized persons', which includes newspapers, to call for a strike.

but also with governments and the bourgeois state apparatus. For the growing extent to which the interests of large companies are intertwined with government policies on money, finance and trade is among the characteristics of late capitalism. This collision will then grow inexorably into a test of strength between the workers on the one hand and the bourgeois class and the bourgeois state on the other, for capital must again attempt as far as possible to restrict or suppress the activity of workers' organizations — this time also of the 'official' trade unions — which threaten its basic interests. In this scenario too, therefore, the whole process would end in a growing limitation of the right to strike and of the freedoms of association, assembly, demonstration and publication — *if* capital were to triumph.

Employers attempt on their part to turn to their own advantage the consequences of the temporary disappearance of the industrial reserve army, which is of such importance in the alteration of the relationship of forces between the seller and buyer of the commodity of labour-power. Techniques such as job-evaluation, Measured Time Work, Method-Time-Measurement and the like[45] are designed to reverse the *collective* sale of the commodity of labour-power (which is the justification for the existence of the trade unions) by individualizing wages, in other words by atomizing wage-earners once more and reintroducing competition into their ranks. The success or failure of such attempts, however, is in turn mainly dependent on the current relationship of forces between capital and labour.[46]

The combination of the trend towards the reduction of the turnover-time of fixed capital and the trend towards the limitation of the bargaining freedom of the trade unions clarifies a more general law: *the inherent constraint in late capitalism to increase systematic control over all elements of the processes of production, circulation and reproduction,* a systematic control which is impossible without growing regimentation of the economic and social life as a whole. This law has one of its mainsprings in the mighty concentration

[45] See for example *Leistungslohn-systeme*, Zurich, 1970; Bernard Meier, *Salaires, Systématique de Rendement*, Lucerne, 1968, and the contributions of Hans Mayr, Nat Weinberg and Hans Pornschlegel in *Automation — Risiko und Chance*, Vol. II, Frankfurt, 1965.

[46] See, among others, Tony Cliff, *The Employers' Offensive*, London, 1970. Antonio Lettieri analyses the conditions which led to the abolition of job evaluation in the most recent labour agreement (concluded in 1971) in the Italian state steel trust Italsider: Antonio Lettieri, in *Problemi del Socialismo*, No. 49.

of economic power in the hands of a few dozen large companies and financial groups in each country, and of a few hundred large companies and financial groups in the totality of all the capitalist states. The pressure of this gigantic concentration of economic power towards a similar concentration of social and political power was described by Rudolf Hilferding even before the First World War as a characteristic feature of the whole epoch of imperialism and monopoly capitalism. In the conclusion to his book *Das Finanzkapital* he wrote: 'Economic power simultaneously means political power. Domination over the economy at the same time assures control over the means of state coercion. The greater the concentration in the economic sphere, the more unlimited will be the domination of big capital over the state. The resultant tight integration of all the state's instruments of action appears as the highest development of its power, the state as the invincible instrument for the maintenance of economic domination. At the same time, however, the conquest of political power thereby appears as the precondition of economic liberation.'[47]

But in the late capitalist phase still further driving forces are associated with this general tendency. The trend towards exact planning of costs and indicative economic programming, which we have described above, necessitates much close control not only over the level of wages or wage costs but over all elements of the reproduction of capital: 'programmed' research and innovation; organized search for raw materials; planned design of new machines; remote-controlled and planned reproduction of skilled labour-power; guided workers' consumption; a pre-determined share for private consumption in the national income or the Gross National Product, and so on. Yet since this whole development is itself an objective education for the proletariat, teaching it to carry the class struggle beyond the enterprise to the overall economic and hence political level, care must be taken that the vast array of facts, which has been collected by empirical research for the specific purposes of the late capitalist bourgeoisie and the late capitalist state, either does not reach the workers at all or does so only in a fragmentary, ideological and mystified form, veiling the actual conditions of class domination and exploitation. For this reason, the late capitalist state's function of general organization, regimentation and standardization must be extended to the whole superstructure, and specifically to the sphere

[47] Rudolf Hilferding, *Das Finanzkapital*, p. 476.

of ideology, with the permanent aim of attenuating the class-consciousness of the proletariat.

The actual extent to which these tendencies prevail, the extent to which their success is limited by the ultimate inability of the system to cancel or conceal its objective contradictions, and the extent to which the objective relationship of forces between the contending classes — which partially depends, of course, on the objective liability of late capitalism to sharp crises — eventually also shapes subjective class relations, will be investigated later in this book.[48]

The tendency towards thorough planning and organization within the companies or enterprises of late capitalism necessarily repercusses on the structure of the bourgeois class and the nature of economic administration itself. The constraint to adopt exact planning and calculation within enterprises and companies and to make maximum economies in constant capital, leads to the introduction of more refined and scientific *methods of organization* by late capitalist monopolies.[49] A far more technicized division of labour now replaces the old factory hierarchy. This gives rise to the illusion that bureaucratization of the *administration* of a company is equivalent to an actual bureaucratization of the *function of capital* — in other words, to an ever-increasing delegation of control over the means of production to an expanding army of managers, directors, engineers and 'bosses' large and small.[50]

The reality by no means corresponds to this appearance. The radical technicization and rationalization of the administration of enterprises and companies represents a dialectical unity of two opposite processes — the growing *delegation* of the power to decide questions of detail on the one hand, and the growing *concentration* of the power to decide questions crucial for the expansion of capital on the other. Organizationally and technically, this finds expression in the 'multi-divisional' corporation[51] and in the compulsion to subordinate the delegation of authority more rigorously than ever

[48] See the final chapter of this book.

[49] Pollock, op. cit., p. 282f.; Reuss, op. cit., pp. 48-51; William H. Whyte, *The Organization Man*, London, 1960, and so on.

[50] This theory of the 'bureaucratization' of capital, which has remained fashionable for the past forty years, from the standard work by Berle and Means (*The Modern Corporation and Private Property*, New York, 1933) through Burnham's *The Managerial Revolution* to Galbraith's *The New Industrial State*, is dealt with in greater detail in Chapter 17 of the present work.

[51] See, among others, Alfred D. Chandler, *Strategy and Structure*, New York, 1961.

before to considerations of the overall profitability of the corpora-tion.[52] The tendency for the direction of the 'immediate process of production' to be technically separated from the process of the accu-mulation of capital, a tendency which first emerged with the appear-ance of joint-stock companies and was briefly described by Marx and further reviewed by Engels, becomes more widespread in the age of late capitalism.[53] Actual productive technology, or scientific research in the laboratory, market research, advertising and distribu-tion, can achieve a large degree of autonomy. But the ultimate deter-minant of decision in any company is profitability — in other words, the valorization of the total mass of accumulated capital. If this valorization is insufficient, then the whole of a corporation's prog-ramme of production, research, advertising and distribution may be thrown overboard, without the major shareholders who dominate the administrative board ever submitting themselves to the 'specialist knowledge' of the engineers, laboratory workers and market re-searchers. Indeed, the company may even be sold, temporarily closed down or finally dissolved without any of all these 'managers', technical experts, and controllers of detail ever being able to do anything about it. The unity of the delegation of power to decide questions of detail and the concentration of power to decide questions concerning the valorization of capital thus forms a unity of opposites, in which the defining relationship of capital, i.e., the capacity to dispose of the largest amounts of capital, is the ultimate arbiter. The mistake of those who argue the thesis of the 'bureaucratization' of corporations or the dominance of the 'technostructure' lies in the fact that they confuse the technical articulation of the exercise of power with its economic foundation — the actual sources of this power.

The questionable character of the whole notion of the 'manager' becomes evident when the problem of the relative financial inde-pendence of large corporations in a period of accelerated growth,

[52]'The fundamental problem of modern management is the control (effectively the planning) of profitability in large companies, given that such companies are, under modern conditions, subject to extremely powerful forces whose ultimate effect is towards the disintegration of central control over corporate profitability, with the result that the company becomes (or remains) a largely uncontrolled and inefficient confederation of conflicting power blocks and functional interests.' Merrett, op. cit., p. 89.

[53]Marx, *Capital*, Vol. 3, pp. 380, 514-26; Friedrich Engels, *Socialism, Utopian and Scientific*, in Marx and Engels, *Selected Works*, pp. 427-8.

with a high rate of self-financing, is confused with the problem of the alleged conflict of interests between the big bourgeois who own shares and company administrators. The increase in the rate of corporation self-financing as compared since the Second World War is a fact — as is the cyclical limitation of it. This has nothing to do with a conflict of interests between managers and large shareholders — who, after all, are much more interested in increasing the value of their shares than in raising dividends. It can hardly be denied today that these large shareholders further continue to dominate the American economy[54]— even if they do not normally need to interfere with the day-to-day running of companies. On the other hand, it is necessary to remember that in a capitalist social order, in which only property — the ownership of capital — guarantees income and power in the long run, managers themselves are extremely interested in acquiring property in shares. Indeed, this is precisely the way in which top managers climb up the social ladder into the ruling class of capital owners itself. The technique of purchasing optional shares, for example, is an important means to this end. When this device was called into question by fiscal technicalities in the USA, its function had to be fulfilled by other means.[55]

The real consequences of the reduced turnover-time of fixed capital, of the accelerated obsolescence of machinery and of the corresponding increase in the importance of intellectual labour in the capitalist mode of production is a shift in the emphasis of the activity of the major owners of capital. *In the age of freely competitive capitalism, this emphasis lay principally in the immediate sphere of production, and in the age of classical imperialism in the sphere of accumulation (the dominance of financial capital); today, in the age of late capitalism, it lies in the sphere of reproduction.*[56]

[54] Domhoff confirms that 1% of American adults owned more than 75% of all company shares in 1960 — a higher proportion than in 1922 or 1929 (when it was 61.5%). A Senate Commission has even reckoned that 0.2% of US households control 2/3 of all such shares: William Domhoff, *Who Rules America?*, New York, 1967, p. 45. In 1960, the boardroom directors of 141 out of 232 large corporations possessed enough shares to control their concerns (p. 49). See also Ferdinand Lundberg, *The Rich and the Super-Rich*, New York, 1968, who likewise sharply attacks the notion of any managerial supremacy.

[55] For this, see Arch Patton, 'Are Stock Options Dead?', *Harvard Business Review*, September-October 1970; and Shorey Peterson, in *The Quarterly Journal of Economics*, February 1965, p. 18.

[56] 'A recent report gave the observations of over forty of America's professional industrial managers on management in nine intensely industrialized countries of Europe.

The spheres of both production and accumulation have become largely technicized and self-regulating. Objective scientific rules enable these processes to run more or less 'smoothly'. During the 'long wave with an undertone of expansion' from 1940-65 it was customary for large monopolies to finance investments through prices, without the aid of bank credits. It is for this general reason that powers of detailed decision can be delegated to specialists, for they only need to ensure trouble-free operation of already predetermined processes.[57] The crucial area for the future and fortune of monopolistic and oligopolistic corporations lies in the *selection* and not in the running of these processes — in other words, *in the decision as to what, where and how production will take place,* or still more precisely, *where and how extended reproduction will proceed. Precisely because* accelerated technological innovation, accelerated obsolescence of the material means of production, and reduced turnover-time of fixed capital create *greater uncertainty* in the sphere of reproduction than was the case in the age of classical imperialism or classical monopoly capitalism, the options made in this sphere constitute the *really strategic* decisions which determine the life or death of corporations and also to a great extent the overall tendencies of the economy. The real masters of capital, the large shareholders of corporations, industrial magnates and financial groups, reserve such decisions for themselves without any delegation whatsoever.[58]

Ultimately, the impossibility of a genuine coordination between the economic plans of the different private companies is not due — as bourgeois economists claim [59] — to the uncertainty and discontinuity of technical progress, but to the fact that behaviour which is

---

They visited hundreds of industrial enterprises. . . . They found too many instances where top managers . . . failed to realize that their primary function is to plan for the future', OEEC, *Problems of Business Management,* Paris, 1954, cited in Goodman, op. cit., pp. 188-9.

[57]Heckmann, op. cit., pp. 85-8. See also Merrett: 'Incomes, Taxation, Management Effectiveness and Planning', in B. W. Denning (ed.), *Corporate Long-Range Planning,* pp. 89-90.

[58]Heckmann, op. cit., p. 63, distinguishes between the first two phases of long-term planning by enterprises (establishment of enterprise objectives and 'optimal competitive strategy') and the third and fourth phase (formulation of a programme of action and testing and revising the plans). The first two fall within the competence of 'top management'. The third and fourth can no longer be controlled by the top management of the firm alone, even if they take all final decisions.

[59]See our discussion of this thesis in *Marxist Economic Theory,* pp. 373-6.

rational for individual companies *can* lead and periodically *must* lead to irrational results for the economy as a whole. Maximization of the yield of the economy as a whole cannot be simply the sum of the profit maximization of industrial companies. It is not the discontinuity of technical progress as such, but the discontinuity of technical progress within private companies governed by private maximization of profits – i.e., private property and commodity production – which is responsible for the insuperable instability and discontinuity of economic development in the capitalist mode of production.

In this sense the contradiction characteristic of late capitalism, between the constraint to plan within the company and the incapacity to move beyond 'indicative' economic programming in the overall context of the economy, is only a more acute expression of the general contradiction, which Marx and Engels showed to be inherent in capitalism, between the planned organization of *parts* of the economic process (production within the factory, disposal within the company, and so on) and the anarchy of the economy as a whole, dominated by the law of value: 'The contradiction between socialized production and capitalistic appropriation now presents itself as an *antagonism between the organization of the production in the individual workshop and the anarchy of production in society generally.*'[60] *This contradiction between the rationality of the parts and the irrationality of the whole, which reaches its apogee in the epoch of late capitalism,* is the key to an understanding of late capitalist ideology, as we shall see in the course of our analysis.[61]

[60] Friedrich Engels, *Socialism, Utopian and Scientific*, in Marx and Engels, *Selected Works*, p. 423.
[61] See Chapter 16 of this book.

8

The Acceleration of Technological Innovation

The reduction of the turnover-time of fixed capital is closely related to the acceleration of technological innovation. The first is often merely the value expression of the second. The acceleration of technological innovation determines the acceleration of the obsolescence of machinery, which in turn compels the acceleration of the replacement of fixed capital in use, and hence reduces the turnover-time of fixed capital.[1]

The acceleration of technological innovation is a corollary of the systematic application of science to production. Although this application is rooted in the logic of the capitalist mode of production, it has by no means been continuously and evenly bound up with it in the history of this mode of production. On the contrary, Marx in the *Grundrisse* expressly pointed out that it initially penetrates very gradually into that mode of production, and *does not* constitute the basis of the historical development of machinery: 'In machinery, the appropriation of living labour by capital achieves a direct reality in this respect as well. It is, firstly, the analysis and application of mechanical and chemical laws, arising directly out of science, which enables the machine to perform the same labour as that previously performed by the worker. However, the development of machinery along this path occurs only when large industry has

---

[1] See Pollock's description of automation, along the same lines: Pollock, op. cit., p. 16.

already reached a higher stage, and all the sciences have been pressed into the service of capital; and when, secondly, the available machinery itself already provides great capabilities. *Invention then becomes a business, and the application of science to direct production itself becomes a prospect which determines and solicits it.* But this is not the road along which machinery, by and large, arose, and even less the road on which it progresses in detail. This road is, rather, analysis through the division of labour, which gradually transforms the worker's operations into more and more mechanical ones, so that at a certain point a mechanism can step into their places. Thus the specific mode of working here appears directly as becoming transferred from the worker to capital in the form of the machine, and his own labour capacity devalued thereby. Hence the workers' struggle against machinery. What was the living worker's activity becomes the activity of the machine.'[2]

This analysis is a brilliant anticipation by Marx of conditions which only developed much later, with the acceleration of technical and scientific discovery and inventions after the onset of the second technological revolution, but above all since the 40's of the 20th century, with the third technological revolution. *The situation in which 'all the sciences have been pressed into the service of capital' and in which 'invention becomes a branch of business, and the application of science to direct production itself becomes a prospect which determines and solicits it' only finds its specific application in the phase of late capitalism.* Obviously, this does not mean that no scientifically-determined inventions occurred during the 19th or early 20th centuries. Still less does it imply that inventive activity in that epoch proceeded 'independently' of capital. *However, the systematic organization of research and development as a specific business organized on a capitalist basis* — in other words, autonomous investment (in fixed capital and in wage-labour) into R and D, fully came into its own only under late capitalism.

Two problems must be distinguished here, which demand separate analysis: the tendencies of development inherent in intellectual

[2]*Grundrisse*, pp. 703-4. According to C. F. Carter and B. R. Williams it was not until the end of the 19th century, with the development of the chemical and electrical industry, that innovation became directly interlinked with scientific knowledge, and a scientific training became indispensible for inventors: *Investment in Innovation*, London, p. 12.

labour capable of leading to an acceleration of invention; and the specific conditions of valorization of capital capable of effecting an accelerated application of accelerated discoveries and inventions. The two categories of 'scientific and technical invention and discovery' and of 'technological innovation' are not identical.[3] The increasing acceleration of technical and scientific invention has been determined by a number of interacting factors in the history of science, labour and society.[4] The historical significance of the second scientific revolution, which began in the early 20th century and developed with quantum physics, Einstein's theory of relativity, atomic research and the basic advances of modern mathematics, is evident enough. The role of the computer in the acceleration of scientific activity, the exponential growth rate of this activity, and its increasing socialization and capitalist organization are no less obvious.[5] The second scientific revolution created a scientific substructure which gradually transformed all sciences, just as the scientific revolution brought about by Copernicus, Galileo and Newton inaugurated the whole of the classical mechanics and chemistry of the 18th and 19th centuries. Just as classical physics provided the basis for an unbroken series of technological applications, from the steam engine to the electric motor, so the second scientific revolution laid the foundations for an unbroken chain of technological applications from the 20's and 30's of the 20th century onwards, culminating in the release of nuclear energy, cybernetics and automation. It is self-evident that there is a direct causal rela-

[3] Obviously they cannot be regarded as exogenous factors, but as functions of economic development in its entirety (above all of the accumulation of capital, the rate of profit and the rate of surplus-value.) In this connection, see Joseph D. Phillips, 'Labour's Share and Wage Parity', in *Review of Economics and Statistics*, May 1960, p. 188.

[4] The volume *Die Wissenschaft von der Wissenschaft*, Berlin,1968, produced by an authorized collective at the Karl Marx University, Leipzig, contains an interesting analysis of the social foundations of science and its 'strategic' function in social development (p. 70f.). For the inner logic of the history of science, see Thomas S. Kuhn, *The Structure of Scientific Revolutions*, New York, 1964, who, however, unduly neglects its interaction with the development of labour and society. For the social determinations of the history of science see J. D. Bernal, *The Social Function of Science*, London, 1939, *Science in History*, London, 1969, and S. Lilley, 'Social Aspects of the History of Science', in *Archives Internationales d'Histoire des Sciences*, No. 2, p. 376f.

[5] John Diebold, *Man and the Computer*, New York, 1970; Thomas S. Kuhn, op. cit., pp. 72-4, 106-8, etc.; *Die Wissenschaft der Wissenschaft*, pp. 9-10, etc.

tionship linking Einstein's theory of relativity and atomic research to the technical application of nuclear energy and automation.

The objective conditions for the acceleration of invention were intimately connected with the Second World War and the subsequent post-war rearmament. Since the phase 1914-39 was one of decelerated economic growth — a 'long wave with an undertone of stagnation'— the inter-war period was characterized by a slowing down of technological innovation coincident with an incipient acceleration of discovery and invention as a result of the second scientific revolution.[6] The result was to create a reserve of unapplied technical discoveries or potential technological innovations. The arms build-up then began to absorb a substantial part of these inventions or even create their precondition. The example of the atomic bomb obviously springs to mind, but it was by no means the only significant case of this type.[7] Radar, miniaturization of electronic equipment, development of new electronic components, indeed even the first applications of mathematics to problems of economic organization — 'operational research' — all had their origins in the wartime or arms economy. The so-called synergetic model of company planning — in which the overall result of various programmes exceeds the sum of the partial results foreseen for each individual programme — is likewise parallel to, or derived from, military programmes.[8] The systematic and purposeful *organization* of scientific research, with the aim of accelerating technological innovation, was also pioneered in the context of the wartime or arms economy.[9] The

[6] 'Ever since the invention of the photo-electric cell in the early thirties, a crude form of automation has been possible. A large degree of automatic control had been achieved in power stations, oil refineries and some chemical processes before 1940, and it is probable that automation in the metal-fabricating industries was technically possible although, of course, it would have been an economic monstrosity. During the war and early post-war years, rapid advances in electronics enormously increased knowledge relevant to automation; whether or not this alone would have been sufficient to induce its use in industry is a matter of speculation. In any case . . . labour became substantially dearer relative to capital equipment, and this encouraged the use and development of automation.' Salter, op. cit., p. 25.

[7] The first fully automated factory in manufacturing industry was the Rockford Ordnance Plant, which was ready for production at the end of the Second World War. Goodman, op. cit., pp. 104-5.

[8] Frank G. Gilmore and Richard C. Brandenburg, 'Anatomy of Corporate Planning', *Harvard Business Review*, November-December 1962.

[9] For the role played by the First World War in this respect, see, for instance, Edwin Mansfield, *The Economics of Technological Change*, London, 1969, p. 45.

number of industrial research laboratories in the USA was less than 100 at the beginning of the First World War, but by 1920 it had risen to 220 remained at this level thereafter: 'Confidence in organized research was increased by wartime successess.'[10] During and after the Second World War these company-dominated laboratories increased greatly in number, and by 1960 they totalled 5,400. The sum total of scientists engaged in research was quadrupled, rising from 87,000 in 1941 to 387,000 in 1961.[11]

In the context of capitalist production of commodities, the steady growth in the volume of research inevitably led to specialization and 'autonomization'. First, research and development became a separate branch within the division of labour of large companies. Later they might take the form of an independent enterprise; privately-operated research laboratories came into being, which sold their discoveries and inventions to the highest bidder.[12] Marx's forecast was thus substantiated: invention had become a systematically organized capitalist business.

Like any other business, 'research' too has one single aim in capitalism: to maximize profit for the enterprise. The enormous expansion of research and development since the Second World War is itself already proof of its strictly capitalist 'profitability'.[13] Leontief, in fact, comments that: 'So far as the general conditions of production are concerned, organized research is not different from any other industry. One builds a laboratory, installs the necessary equipment, hires qualified personnel and waits for the results. These like any other product, either can be used directly by the same business in which they were made or can be sold to others — for a price; or as it often happens, both.'[14] Silk records that more and more capital is now flowing into research and development because there it 'earns a fabulously high average rate of return on the dollars spent'.[15] This is fully in accordance with the logic of late capitalism,

[10] Leonard S. Silk, *The Research Revolution*, New York, 1960, p. 54. Mansfield, op. cit., p. 45.

[11] Ibid., p. 54.

[12] Silk, op. cit., pp. 54-5, makes a distinction between 'organized investigators' and 'organized scientists.'

[13] We are speaking here of *private* expenditure on research and development, and not of state expenditure which is to some extent freed from the constraint of profitability.

[14] Leontief, *Introduction* to Silk, op. cit., pp. xii-xiv.

[15] Silk, op. cit., p. 3.

under which technological rents have become the main source of surplus-profits.

Even more significant than 'pure research' is actual industrial innovation, the development of new products or processes of production. The greater the acceleration of technological renewal and the reduction of the turnover-time of fixed capital, the more the installation of new processes of production, and indeed the construction of whole new production sites becomes a separate business in the division of labour. The supply of fully-equipped factories, complete with manufacturing process, technical 'know-how', patents and licences, as well as the most important specialists, thus becomes a new form of capital investment or capital export. In the chemical industry this is already the predominant form of the renewal of fixed capital. Organizationally, reproduction is completely separated from production; its technical realization is left to special firms.[16] It should be emphasized that the length of time involved in the planning and development of major investment projects, and the number of skilled personnel needed for them, lead to a discontinuous use of technicians, if employed by one corporation only. 'The doubling of the size of the Usinor steel plant at Dunkirk, increasing its capacity from 4 to 8 million tons a year, needed a study group of 1500 persons working for three years, without taking into account the equivalent services of the building firms. The Solmer steel factory built at Fos on open land confronted even larger problems and the research and planning teams were even more numerous for a similar production capacity. The sheer scale and irregularity of such teams makes it impossible for plant-construction firms to employ them on a continuous basis. . . . This is the first rationale for using special engineering firms, whose essential vocation is planning and projection, for these investments.'[17]

Capital directly invested in the sphere of production leads to a continuous production of commodities or an uninterrupted valorization. Capital invested in the sphere of research and development, which precedes or follows actual production,[18] achieves valorization

---

[16] C. Freeman, 'Chemical Process Plant: Innovation and World Market', in *National Institute Economic Review*, No. 45, August 1968, pp. 29-30.

[17] *Revue Economique de la Banque Nationale de Paris*, April 1974.

[18] The spheres of research and development referred to here are always those which are indispensable for the manufacture and consumption of *products*, not those which belong to so-called selling costs (for example, advertising research) and which correspond to the specific social conditions of the capitalist economy.

only in the degree to which the labour performed there is productive, i.e. leads to the production of new commodities. From the standpoint of the capitalist enterprise, any discoveries or inventions which do not find application are *faux frais* of production, overheads which ought to be reduced to a minimum. However, since in a market economy it is never sure from the outset that it will be possible to apply new discoveries and inventions, the profit risk of capital invested in the sphere of research is higher than average. This is one of the main reasons for the preponderance of large companies in this sphere.[19] The volume and the growth of expenditure on research and development can be seen from the following examples: it cost $1 million to develop nylon and $5 million to develop orlon. The development of penicillin demanded several million dollars, and that of catalytic 'oil-crackings' $11 million. The Pilkington Glass Company in Great Britain invested $20 million in the invention and development of the patent for Float Glass. American experts refer to television as a 'fifty million dollar gamble' because of the money spent on research and development before commercialization. In the aircraft industry research and development costs have soared to astronomic heights; up to 1965 alone the XB-70 project had cost $1.5 billion and Concorde $2 billion.[20] In the pharmaceutical industry, expenditure on research generally amounts to some 8-10% of total turnover, although only part of this sum is spent on basic research. Hoechst claims that it has spent as much as 25 million dollars on the research and development of a new drug; Hoffmann-La Roche spent sums equivalent to 11-16% of its turnover on R and D in 1973. The basic incentive for these enormous outlays of capital remains the commensurately higher than average surplus-profits to be won by companies which achieve a 'break-through'.[21]

[19] Paolo Sylos Labini, *Oligopolo e Progresso Tecnico*, Turin, 1967, p. 226 f. Jewkes, Sawers and Stillerman, *The Sources of Invention*, London, 1969, pp. 128, 152. In 1961 research and development investments were recorded for 11,000 firms in the USA. 86% of these outlays, however, were made by only 391 of these firms, and four giant companies alone accounted for more than 22% of the total expenditure on research and development: Richard R. Nelson, Merton J. Peck and Edward D. Kalachek, *Technology, Economic Growth and Public Policy*, Brookings Institution, 1967.

[20] Jewkes, Sawers and Stillerman, op. cit., p. 155; James R. Bright (ed.), *Technological Planning on the Corporate Level*, Boston, 1962, p. 61.

[21] For the pharmaceutical industry, see *Neue Zürcher Zeitung*, April 25, June 30, 1974; Charles Levinson, *The Multinational Pharmaceutical Industry*, Geneva, 1973: 'It is basic research alone that produces the medical breakthroughs by which the

Like any other productive capital, the capital invested in the sphere of research is made up of fixed and variable components. The fixed capital consists of the building and equipment of the laboratories, the variable capital of the wages and salaries of the staff employed in them. The fact that the labour of many of these employees is incorporated into the value of specific commodities only much later — or never — does not alter the nature of the *total labour* of those engaged in the research and development sector, which is productive labour in the sense that it is indispensable for the production of new use values and hence also of new exchange values. The same is true of workers who have to devote a part of their annual labour time to starting up the machines, finding and cleaning their apparatus and performing necessary repairs.[22] This in no way alters the nature of their labour time. For it would be just as impossible to maintain ongoing production without such procedures as it would be in the absence of models, formulae, drawings, preparations, and so on, from the laboratory and office. Marx, who often stressed that the nature of industrial capital was defined among other things by its ability to appropriate gratis the benefits of the division of labour or the productive application of science,[23] unequivocally stated that the labour of the research worker and engineer was productive in character. In the passage from the *Resultate des unmittelbaren Produktionsprozesses* which we have already cited in the preceding chapter, he explicitly included technologists among productive labourers; and in *Theories of Surplus Value* he wrote: 'Included among these productive workers, of course, are all those who contribute in one way or another to the production of a commodity, from the actual operative to the manager or engineer (as distinct from the capitalist).'[24]

The uncertainty whether capital invested in research will achieve valorization, represents — particularly in an epoch of accelerated technological innovation — an increasingly powerful incentive to *plan research*. As in any other sector engaged in the sale of commodities, such planning is beset — in this case even *within* the domain

industry glorifies and justifies its economics. The middle-ground of applied research produces specific products or improved versions. The area of development, however, is little more than tinkering with dosages, formulations and production processes to get round patents and to come up with a *new* marketable proposition'. pp. 25-6.

[22] Marx, *Capital*, Vol. 2, p. 174ff.
[23] *Grundrisse*, p. 694.
[24] Marx, *Theories of Surplus Value*, Vol. 1, pp 156-7.

of the company — by the buffeting of chance, arbitrariness and un-scientific extrapolation of current trends.[25] Precisely in this sector, however, the constraints of planning are unmistakeable.

Jewkes, Sawers and Stillerman have tried to disprove the thesis that the acceleration of technological innovation is due, among other things, to the systematic organization of research and development. All they have demonstrated, however, is that even in the 19th century inventions were more closely related to scientific knowledge and advances than is often assumed, and that even today individual inventors are responsible for a multitude of often revolutionary discoveries.[26] But their evidence in no way contradicts the fact that an increasing proportion of inventions, as can be seem among other things by patents, stems from the laboratories of industrial com-panies,[27] or that the rapid expansion in the number of scientifically trained personnel must result in an acceleration of the growth of scientific knowledge and technological innovation, even if the correlation between the two is not directly proportional.[28] These authors, who attach exaggerated importance to the 'inventive indi-vidual', are on firmer ground when they point to the disadvantages accruing to inventive activity from the pragmatic, goal-oriented nature of the research controlled by monopolies and from the sub-ordination of this research to the corporate drive for profit. It is obvious enough that knowledge and orginality cannot be produced in the same way and with the same automated regularity as consumer

[25] Fascinating analyses and examples of this are to be found in Gordon Wills, David Ashton and Bernard Taylor (eds.), *Technological Forecasting and Corporate Strategy*, Bradford, 1969. A recent example is provided by the British firm, Rio Tinto Zinc, supposedly famous for its exceptional efficiency, whose new giant smelter plant for lead and tin in Gloucestershire, heralded as the most modern in the world, turned out to be a spectacular example of defective planning. Because of the unexpected poisoning of the whole region by lead fumes, the plant had to be closed for several months and rebuilt. Many phenomena of environmental pollution can be traced back to bad technological planning of this sort.

[26] Jewkes, Sawers and Stillerman, op. cit., pp. 40-60 passim, p. 73.

[27] 80% of all patents taken out in the USA in the year 1900 were held by individuals; this percentage had dropped to 40% of the patents taken out in 1957 and to 36.5% for the years 1956-60. Klaus Schulz-Hanssen, *Die Stellung der Elektro-Industrie im Industrialisierungsprozess*, Berlin, 1970, p. 81.

[28] Charpie speaks of a 7% cumulative annual rate of growth of scientific activity. He also emphasizes the mushrooming of scientific publications, which possess a much higher rate of growth than the world's population or industrialization. Robert A. Charpie, 'Technological Innovation and the International Economy', in Maurice Goldsmith (ed.), *Technological Innovation and the Economy*, p. I. See also Diebold, op. cit., pp. 33-4.

goods. This is not an argument against teamwork in research — but it certainly is against teamwork subordinated to the quest for profit.

Another typical contradiction of late capitalism lies in the fact that the big monopolies (oligopolies) are never completely shielded from competition and hence always have an interest in perfecting and bringing a new product onto the market earlier and more massively than their competitors. In this sense, they are undoubtedly interested in expanding the research and development under their control. At the same time, however, in considering each expensive research project they must take into account the inherent risk not only that it may fail to result in any new marketable product at all, but also that a *simultaneous* innovation by a competitor may make it impossible to realize the anticipated surplus-profits, so that it may ultimately take a long time before the capital invested in the costs of research and development is valorized out of the 'normal' profit; a different product, which would have secured a temporary monopoly, would have yielded more. This is the explanation of the complex innovating strategy of the big companies, which compels them both to differentiate their research and at the same time, for pure reasons of valorization of capital, to narrow their development. In this sense, Jewkes, Sawers and Stillerman are undoubtedly right when they say that monopolies ultimately hamper technical progress, even if this must be understood in a relative rather than absolute way.[29]

There has been an enormous overall increase in expenditure on R and D in late capitalism: in the USA it rose from under $100 million in 1928 to $5 billion in 1953-54, $12 billion in 1959, $14 billion in 1965 and $20.7 billion in 1970.[30] These increases render a rise in the volume of innovations inevitable, even if it is quite probable that the return on these outlays, which was very high in the 50's

---

[29] Nelson, Peck and Kalachek note that the direction of R and D expenditure, determined by the profit goals of the large companies, is overwhelmingly oriented towards projects which offer a quick return instead of into fundamental research (which only accounts for about 4% of total private expenditure on R and D), thereby distorting and impeding technological progress. Op. cit., pp. 85, 87.

[30] Silk, op. cit., p. 158; Jewkes, Sawers and Stillerman, op. cit., p. 197. Levinson, op. cit., p. 44. The fact that these costs were met purely out of private sources before the Second World War, while today about 60% of them are covered by the state, makes no difference to the vast increase in their volume. The reasons for the growing socialization of research costs are discussed in Altvater's contribution to E. Altvater and F. Huisken (eds.), *Materialien zur politischen Ökonomie des Ausbildungssektors*, Erlangen, 1971, pp. 356-7.

and early 60's, will gradually diminish. US pharmaceutical firms have registered a reduction of the period during which they enjoy 'technological rents' from 17 to 10 years, together with an ensuing decline in the rate of surplus-profits.[31] Does this mean that with a permanent arms build-up, the acceleration of technological innovation in civilian industry — and especially in Department I — will likewise acquire a permanent character? Not at all. The conditions of valorization of capital remain the decisive determination of the dynamic of late capitalism. They cannot be outlapped by developments in the domain of science and technology. Accelerated technological innovation ultimately means accelerated growth of the average productivity of labour. Only in conditions of major market expansion, however, can accelerated growth of the productivity of labour be combined with a relatively high rate of growth of the social product, or a relatively high level of employment. In the preceding chapters we have seen the reasons for the market expansion of the age of late capitalism: the third technological revolution, and the transition from productive technology based on simple electric motors to electronics, automation and nuclear energy.

Once this upheaval has taken place and a new sector of Department I has been formed to manufacture automated machines and machine-complexes, the growth rate of Department I begins to fall, and with it the growth rate of the entire capitalist economy, for there is no longer any fundamental renewal of production in Department I, only a quantitative expansion of already existing productive techniques. We then enter a 'long wave with an undertone of stagnation'. On the other hand, the very special conditions which enabled the rate of surplus-value to rise suddenly after the Second World War also made possible the renewed influx of excess capital into production. With the cessation of the 'long wave with an undertone of expansion', however, the increasing organic composition of capital causes a deterioration in the conditions of valorization of capital. If this process persists, it must lead inexorably to a fall in investment activity. Simultaneous processes from the angle of valorization and the angle of realization therefore tend to brake the growth of innovative activity. Consequently the gap between invention and innovation will increase once more in the second phase of late capitalism. For this reason Bernal's thesis, repeated

---

[31]*Business Week*, November 23, 1974.

by a 'writers' collective' in Leipzig University and many other East German authors, that science in our age has become an 'immediate force of production', is untenable.[32] Scientific activity is only a productive force if it is directly incorporated into material production. In the capitalist mode of production this means: if it flows into the activity of commodity production. If this does not occur — as a result, among other things, of reservations or difficulties affecting the valorization of capital — then it remains only a *potential* and not a *real* force of production.[33]

The growth of research and development by leaps and bounds has created a vast increase in the demand for highly-skilled intellectual labour-power. Hence the 'university explosion'; which in turn is accompanied by a vast supply of candidates (apprentices) for intellectually trained labour-power, which can be explained by the higher standard of living and individual social promotion associated with it. Already at the end of the 50's, 32.2% of the 20-24 age group were enrolled in higher education in the USA, 16.2% in New Zealand, 13.1% in Australia and the Netherlands and 10% in Argentina; since then these percentages have increased rapidly. At the beginning of the 60's over 75% of 15-19 year olds completed a secondary education in the USA, Australia, New Zealand, Japan, Great Britain, Holland and Belgium.[34]

The most arresting result of the social transformation caused by

[32] J. D. Bernal, *Science in History*, p. 1248; *Die Wissenschaft von der Wissenschaft*, pp. 42, 102-5, 262-3. This is also the main error of the important study published by the Czechoslovak Academy of Sciences, the so-called Richta Report. Richta sees science as a 'residual factor' of economic progress; he regards it as a force of production which is not embodied in machines and tools. The knowledge and experience of human labour-power — not only its technical, but also its intellectual qualification in the general sense of the word — are undoubtedly an integral component of these forces of production. But they only have a productive 'effect' if they *produce* use-values (in a post-capitalist society) or use values and exchange values (in a capitalist society). Outside such production they remain merely a potential, rather than a real, productive force.

[33] Marx's formula for knowledge that has become an immediate productive force is to be found in a section of the *Grundrisse* dealing with the theme 'Contradiction between the Foundation of Bourgeois Production (Value as Measure) and its Development' (*Grundrisse*, p. 704). The passage allows for no ambiguity: 'The development of fixed capital indicates to what degree general social knowledge has become a direct form of production, and to what degree, hence, the conditions of the process of social life itself have come under the control of the general intellect, and been transformed in accordance with it.' (*Grundrisse*, p. 706.)

[34] F. H. Harbison and C. A. Myers, *Education, Manpower and Economic Growth*, cited in M. Blaug (ed.), *Economics of Education*, Vol. 2, Harmondsworth, 1969, p. 41.

Growth in Higher Education [35]

			1950	1965	1980 (Projection)
USA	(a)	in '000s	2297	5570	
	(b)	as % of age group	20%	41%	58%
Japan	(a)		400	1085	
	(b)		5%	12%	23%
UK	(a)		180	432	
	(b)		5%	12%	20%
France	(a)		187	524	
	(b)		6%	17%	31%
West Germany	(a)		135	368	
	(b)		4%	9%	24%
Italy	(a)		241	405	
	(b)		6%	11%	24%

this 'university explosion' is that at least in the USA, and probably also in several other capitalist countries, the number of academically-educated workers, if not also of students, exceeds that of farmers or peasants today.

The hallmark of this growth of scientific intellectual labour — elicited by the cumulative growth of scientific knowledge, research and development, and ultimately determined by accelerated technological innovation — is the massive reunification of intellectual and productive activity, and the entry of intellectual labour into the sphere of production. Since this reintroduction of intellectual labour into the process of production corresponds to the immediate needs of late capitalist technology, the education of intellectual workers must likewise be strictly subordinated to these needs. The result is the crisis of the classical humanist university, rendered anachronistic not only for *formal* reasons (excessive number of students, backwardness of material infrastructure, changes in social background of students, which demand an above-average social expenditure in the university sector, and so on) and not only for *overall social* reasons (attempts to avoid the emergence of an unemployed intelligentsia; attempts to restrain student revolt, and to step up the ideologization of science for the purposes of manipulating the masses) but also and above all for *directly economic* reasons specific to the nature of intellectual labour in late capitalism; the

[35]*OECD Report* (unpublished).

constraint to adapt the structure of the university, the selection of students and the choice of syllabuses to accelerated technological innovation under capitalist conditions.[36] The main task of the university is no longer to produce 'educated' men of judgment and property — an ideal which corresponded to the needs of freely competitive capitalism — but to produce intellectually skilled wage-earners for the production and circulation of commodities.

The new social phenomenon of the mass increase in intellectual labour generates in turn a new social contradiction. On the one hand, in a system of internalized commodity relations which leaves the individual with the illusion of free choice, the mass introduction of intellectual workers into the 'research and development' sector cannot be achieved merely by direct compulsion. The dominant ideology of late capitalism therefore seeks to steer youth into the relevant areas of science and technology (an important function is fulfilled in this respect by the mass media, from comic strips, children's books and television to scientific fiction). This development certainly also corresponds to objective overall social *needs* and not merely to the short-term orientation of large companies to competition and profitability. The cumulative development of science and technology, which has created a mighty potential for the liberation of humanity from the age-old curse of burdensome and mechanical manual labour impeding or crippling the development of the individual, has its own natural appeal for the youth of today which instinctively senses this emancipating function.

On the other hand, however, this generalized need for higher qualifications, university education and intellectual labour inevitably comes into collision with the attempt of the bourgeois class and the bourgeois state to subordinate the production of intellectual skills to the needs of the valorization of capital by means of technocratic reforms of higher education. What capital needs is not a large number of highly-qualified intellectual workers. It needs an increasing but limited quantity of intellectual producers equipped with specific qualifications and with specific tasks to fulfil in the process of production or circulation.[37] The greater the cumulative growth of science and the faster the acceleration of research and development, the

---

[36] Altvater, in Altvater and Huisken, op. cit., pp. 59-62, 358-63. See also Nelson, Peck and Kalachek, who have studied the inter-connections between education, training and economic activity (op. cit., p. 10). Janossy discusses these problems in detail in his book.

[37] Ibid., pp. 367-8.

more the specifically capitalist processes of increasing division of labour, rationalization and specialization in the interests of private profit—in other words, a constant fragmentation of labour—penetrate the spheres of intellectual labour and scientific instruction. A new branch of economics starts to develop, whose field is analysis of the 'material yield' of outlays on education.[38] Its adepts speak freely of 'productive investments' in the educational system and increasingly embark on calculations of its 'profitability'.[39] It goes without saying that the 'profitability' in question has no relation to the fulfilment of general social needs, i.e., the production of use values, any more than that of any other branch of political economy based on the production of commodities and exchange values. It refers merely to profitability within the framework of existing late capitalist society, based on profit-maximization by large industrial companies.[40] It is equally clear that such calculations are not of simply platonic pursuits of 'pure knowledge' but help to lay the financial-political groundwork for technocratic reforms of higher education designed to increase its profitability in this sense.

Applied science, specialized and subjected to the capitalist division of labour—fragmented science, subordinated to profit maximization by the monopolies: such is the battle-cry of late capitalism in higher education. Marx's words cited at the outset of this chapter have become a reality: when the application of science to immediate production both determines and solicits this production, invention becomes a branch of business and the various sciences become the prisoners of capital. But from an overall social standpoint, the standpoint of the interests of the wage-earners and the great majority of the population, it is the liberating potential of science and technology which lends a progressive significance to every 'Great Leap Forward' in this realm. A new and acute social contradiction

[38] This procedure mostly involves projections of the higher incomes yielded by intellectually qualified occupations; a given range of income is simply submitted to a long-term extrapolation. The whole of Dennison's ideological analysis of 'human capital' is thoroughly criticized in Altvater and Huisken, op. cit., pp. 298-300.

[39] See for example the characteristic title of an article by Blaug: 'The Rate of Return on Investment in Education', in M. Blaug (ed.), *Economics of Education*, Vol. 1, London 1968, p. 215f.

[40] The real calculation of interest to capital is naturally that of the additional value product which entrepreneurs can appropriate because of the availability of highly qualified labour-power, while they themselves do not have to bear the costs of producing the qualification involved, or do so only partially and indirectly through their taxes.

therefore develops between — on the one hand, the cumulative growth of science, the social need to appropriate and disseminate it to the maximum, the increasing individual need for fluency in contemporary science and technology[41] — and on the other hand, the inherent tendency of late capitalism to make science a captive of its profit transactions and profit calculations.

This conflict is essentially a new and specific form of the general contradiction characteristic of the capitalist mode of production: the contradiction between expanding social wealth and increasingly alienated and impoverished labour, so long as this social wealth is imprisoned by private appropriation. In late capitalism, this contradiction acquires a new dimension. The more higher education becomes a qualification for specific labour processes, the more intellectual labour becomes proletarianized, in other words transformed into a commodity, and the more the commodity of intellectual labour-power is sold on a specific 'labour market for intellectual and scientific qualifications',[42] and the more the price of this commodity tends to be forced down to its conditions of reproduction, oscillating about its value in response to supply and demand at any given moment. The further this process of proletarianization advances, the deeper the division of labour becomes entrenched within the sciences, accompanied inevitably by increasing overspecialization and 'expert idiocy', and the more students become prisoners of a blinkered education strictly subordinated to the conditions of the valorization of capital. The more fragmented intellectual qualification and labour become the, more alienating university education merges into alienated intellectual labour subsumed under capital, within the total production process of late capitalism. *This is the underlying socio-economic basis of the spreading student revolt in late capitalism*, and the mark of its objectively anti-capitalist drive.

In the epoch of late capitalism, the dominant monopolies seek to establish control over all phases of production and reproduction — whether through the agency of the State or of 'private initiative'. The State and the major monopolies are thus predictably now trying

---

[41] On this subject, see Janossy, op. cit., pp. 219-21.

[42] Cf. the activity of the so-called 'talent scouts' who recruit students on graduation by promising precise salaries in particular companies. There are already specialist studies of this 'labour-market', for example, Glen Cain, Richard Freeman and Lee Hansen, *Labor Market Analysis of Engineers and Technical Workers*, Baltimore, 1973.

to get an organizational 'grip' on the process of the subsumption of intellectual labour under capital, by 'programming' the number of universities, the range of their courses and the allocation of their students to the various disciplines. Some planners have already prepared schemes for future 'compulsory retraining', i.e., periodical disqualification of intellectually qualified workers: the projects for a so-called 'prefabricated comprehensive university' are an example. All these programmes involve a permanent *numerus clausus*, to ensure the necessary selection and distribution of students for the valorization of capital. Such programmes, of course, no more 'get a grip' on real cultural developments than capitalist economic programming provides accurate forecasting of the real economic developments. On the other hand, 'planning' of this sort naturally intesifies the alienation of student life and intellectual labour. In late capitalism, the increased demand for intellectually qualified labour is by no means confined to the needs of the production process. The development of intellectual labour today has a twofold character, which corresponds to two fundamental tendencies of development of late capitalism as a whole — on the one hand, the shorter turnover-time of fixed capital due to the acceleration of technological innovation; on the other, the resultant constraint to gain systematic control over all aspects of the social process of production and reproduction. The growing integration of intellectual labour into the production process corresponds to the former characteristic of late capitalism; the growing integration of intellectual labour into superstructural institutions and the administration of the force of production (including factory administration and the 'administration' of labour-power) corresponds to the latter.[43]

There are significant differences between the social position occupied by intellectually qualified labour incorporated into the process of production and by intellectually qualified labour integrated into administrative and superstructural institutions. These cannot be reduced to the distinction between those individuals or groups whose material existence is based on the creation of surplus-value and those who receive income from surplus-value, although this dividing line does undoubtedly play a role in determining the social interest of each specific section of the intellectually qualified work-force.

---

[43] In 1973, 77% of all 'leading managers' of continental European capitalist firms are said to have had academic training: *Neue Zürcher Zeitung*, October 4, 1973.

The decisive distinction, however, is rather the structural effect which the specific position of each specialized group in the sphere of production, administration or superstructure has on the formation of its consciousness.

The social position of all those groups that occupationally participate in supervising the extraction of surplus-value from the commodity of labour-power or the preservation of constant capital by labour-power, typically induces a general identification of their function with the class interests of the entrepreneurial bourgeoisie. It might even be said that such identification is a precondition of the performance of their specific function in factory or society. Time-and-motion experts who systematically sympathize and solidarize with the workers are no good at their job in a capitalist mode of production; they are not qualified to measure time or motion and will quickly find themselves out of work; in other words, they have to change either their attitude or their occupation. Officers of the law who assist political prisoners to escape have little chance of a career and will likewise lose their job. The same applies in the long run to factory doctors, factory sociologists and psychologists, the administrative personnel of the means of communication, commanders of the bourgeois police and all the senior functionaries of the state apparatus. By contrast, intellectually qualified workers engaged in the immediate process of production or reproduction, or those whose social function does not necessarily come into collision with the class interest of wage-earners — for example, health-insurance doctors or social workers employed by a local authority — are much less liable to identify subjectively with the class interests of capital, and are more likely to align themselves with the class interests of the proletariat. The increasing technicization, specialization and rationalization in the spheres of capital accumulation and the superstructure, including the division of labour in the realm of management itself, can lead to a growth of both groups of intellectually qualified labourers. Technocratic reformers of the university, of course, hope to use the material division between these two groups to split and reintegrate rebellious student bodies, and they are undoubtedly capable of partially achieving their aims. On the other hand, one of the hallmarks of the student revolt has been precisely its rejection of overspecialization and the unscientific and defective education that is dictated by it. To seek to overcome 'expert idiocy' is to strive towards an understanding of the totality of society as a whole. Should they acquire such an understanding in university, then qualified industrial doctors, sociologists and psychologists, administrative personnel in the media, indeed even judges, can expose, unsettle and threaten the system. For example, doctors can refuse to limit certificates of illness to the number suitable to the entrepreneur for reasons of profitability and concern themselves exclusively with protecting the health of the individual wage-earners — in other words, act as honest physicians and not as agents of capital.

So long as such 'revolutionary vocational practice' is limited to only a few industrial doctors, they will in the long run lose their jobs. On the other hand, if an increasing number of doctors were to attempt to free themselves from the grip of capital, the relationship of forces on this specific labour market might change to such an extent that summary dismissals could be prevented. The subjective precondition for such a development would be the maintenance of revolutionary social convictions acquired at university, and the refusal of any gradual integration into bourgeois society. The indispensable objective precondition for a professional militancy of this type is participation in a revolutionary organization, uniting revolutionary theory and revolutionary practice. For revolutionary *vocational practice* is necessarily a *partial* practice. It can only remain politically revolutionary if it is embedded in an *overall social* revolutionary practice.

It is interesting to extend this analysis to a specific stratum of intellectually qualified workers, namely those engaged in education. In general this stratum cannot be counted as part of the productive labour-force, even though it increases the potential of individual and social labour-capacity — in other words, makes a productive contribution to the formation of a specific commodity, that of qualified labour-power. But this does not alter the fact that objectively teachers constitute a part of the class of wage labourers [44] and are capable of coming to feel that they belong to this class and act accordingly. If growing unionization and increasing participation in the struggles of the whole working class lead to such a subjective adhesion to the cause of the proletariat, then here too 'revolutionary vocational

[44] Compare Marx: 'Every productive worker is a wage labourer, but this does not mean that every wage labourer is a productive worker. . . . The same work . . . can be done by the same working man in the service of an industrial capitalist or of a direct consumer. In both cases he is a wage labourer or a casual labourer, but in the one case he is a productive, in the other an unproductive worker, because in the one case he produces capital and in the other he does not.' *Resultate des unmittelbaren Produktionsprozesses*, pp. 130, 138-40.

practice' can contribute significantly to the weakening of capitalist exploitation and oppression. Education upholding the bourgeois state can be replaced by education critical of capitalist society. Instead of being trained to be obedient subjects and disciplined wage-earners dominated by the ideology of individual achievement, young people can be encouraged to think independently and to act in collective solidarity. It is self-evident that a practice of this kind must lead to serious conflicts with the ruling class and cannot in the long-run be reconciled with the normal workings of late capitalist society.

The contradiction between scientifically qualified labour and its subsumption under the interests of capital is thus potentially of a much more general nature than at first appears. In late capitalism, science is a potential force of production in a twofold sense. It increases the material possibility of man's liberation from enslavement to class exploitation, commodity production and the social division of labour. It also potentially facilitates the emancipation of workers from superstructural manipulation and ideological alienation. It becomes more and more difficult to separate science as a source of material wealth from science as a source of revolutionary consciousness, as all the sciences increasingly become the prisoners of capital in the age of late capitalism and more and more scientists rebel against their captivity.[45] This rebellion can be of a limited technocratic nature, expressed in the parallel attempts of a Galbraith in the West or a Löbl in the East to depict the scientist as the actual creator of material wealth and hence the natural administrator (i.e., objective ruler) of economy and state.[46] The same rebellion, however, can also acquire a radical and irreconcilable character once it is fused with the workers' movement, the revolutionary struggle to emancipate labour as a whole.

The age of late capitalism with its accelerated technological innovation and concomitant massive extension of intellectually qualified labour, drives the basic contradiction of the capitalist mode of production to its highest pitch. The socialization of labour is taken to its most extreme extent as the total accumulated result of

---

[45] In the final chapter of this work we shall discuss yet another aspect of this contradiction: namely the conflict between the inherent tendency in both automation and intellectually qualified labour, for individual responsibility in the *labour process* to increase, and the constraint inherent in late capitalism towards the further subsumption of intellectual labour under capital in the process of valorization.

[46] Eugen Löbl, *Geistige Arbeit, die wahre Quelle des Reichtums*, Vienna, 1968.

the scientific and technical development of the whole of society and humanity increasingly becomes the immediate precondition for each particular process of production in each particular sphere of production. With the achievement of full automation this would be realized in a literal sense. Private appropriation of this socialized production leads to the crying contradiction that this vast scientific and technical 'capital' at mankind's disposal is subordinated to the conditions of the valorization of actual capital, and is consequently withheld from millions of people or made available to them only in a deformed or fragmentary fashion. Only when the forces of production finally cast off the shell of private appropriation surrounding them, will the revolutionary powers which are still for the most part slumbering in contemporary science be able to be fully utilized to serve the liberation of labour and the liberation of man.

Does the increasing introduction of intellectually qualified labour into the actual process of production bring with it a growing disqualification of manual labour, so that the tendency for intellectual wage labour to be integrated into the proletariat paradoxically encounters the barrier of an increasing antagonism between manual and intellectual labour? It is very difficult to answer this question empirically, because several contradictory processes are at work side by side within the capitalist economy, because of the uneven development of its different branches; and occupational statistics only give the sum of these divergent processes. A breakdown of global results reveals that increasing industrialization causes an absolute growth in the number of wage-earners, while increasing automation causes it to diminish; that growing mechanization and semi-automation increases the number of semi-skilled workers at the expense of both skilled and unskilled workers,[47] while full automation reduces the number of semi-skilled workers and gives rise to a new and highly skilled polyvalent worker force.[48] In particular, those branches of production most affected by the advance of automation, such as the

[47] There is a mass of empirical evidence for this tendency. In West German industry as a whole, the percentage of semi-skilled workers rose from 28% in 1951 to 36.4% in 1960 and 37% in 1969, while that of skilled workers dropped from 47.6% in 1951 to 40.6% in 1960 and 42.8% in 1969. The percentage of unskilled workers dropped from 24.4% in 1951 to 23% in 1960 and 20.2% in 1969. See Wulf Hund, *Geistige Arbeit und Geselleschaftsformation*, Frankfurt,1973, p. 103. Siebricht reports an increase in the percentage of semi-skilled specialized workers in the period 1951-57 from 29% to 32.4%, a decline of skilled workers from 47.6% to 44.8%, and of the unskilled workers from 24.4% to 22.8%. *Automation—Risiko und Chance*, Vol. 1, p. 383.

[48] Pierre Naville, in Naville-Friedmann, op. cit., p. 381f.

chemical industry, already reveal a climb in the number of skilled workers in the total labour-force, against the average trend. The distinction between workers and office employees largely loses its meaning in fully automated factories, and comes to correspond more to formal conditions of contracts and status than to actual operational positions in the process of production.[49]

The most serious long-term projection in this field up to now has been made by Bright, who studied seventeen successive stages of mechanization and in the final stage (full automation with wage labourers only exercising control functions) found a tendency for knowledge and responsibility to diminish, although these remained on a higher plane than in semi-automated or non-automated industry.[50] This analysis, based exclusively on empirical data, confirms the theoretical assumption that late capitalist automation, as the captive of the valorization of capital, in the long-run generates a relative rather than an absolute disqualification of labour. In other words, the qualifications demanded by industry will tend to drop further and further *below* what is technically and scientifically *possible*, although they will remain on average *above* the previous levels demanded by capitalism. It should in any case be stressed that the radical transformation of the labour and production process implied in the third technological revolution, with the acceleration, of semi-automation and automation, involves not merely a change in the machines used by capitalism, but also a change in the skills and capacities of living labour—related both to modifications in equipment and to increased difficulties in the valorization of capital. At least in fully automated factories, the decline of traditional skills is accompanied by a greater mobility and plasticity of labour-power within the plant. In principle, this makes possible an intelligent comprehension and control of the overall production process by the producers, which had largely disappeared in factories based on conveyor belt and parcellized labour. But the increased average level of skill of the 'collective labourer' takes the form under capitalism of only a slight increase in the average skill of each worker, combined with a substantial increase in the skill of a small minority

[49] This leads among other things to increasing demands by workers for 'employee' status (including a month's notice of dismissal and monthly payment of wages) and successful achievement of them by trade union action.

[50] James R. Bright, 'Lohnfindung an modernen Arbeitsplätzen in den U.S.A., in *Automation und technischer Fortschritt in Deutschland und den U.S.A.*, Frankfurt, 1963, pp. 159-68.

of highly qualified producers (polyvalent technicians and repair-workers).

The conceptual analysis of the production and reproduction of qualified labour-power is one of the most difficult and controversial topics of Marxist theory.[51] We can share the view of Roth and Kanzow, who regard the *costs* of education as deductions from social revenue rather than as expenditure of social capital.[52] While the revenue spent on education undoubtedly increases social labour capacity, indeed forms certain necessary conditions of labour,[53] it does not itself immediately create value. It is thus not surprising that capital will only invest in education in selected sectors and by way of exception. However, there is no theoretical law here, for Marx expressly emphasized that it is possible for capital to be invested in these 'general social conditions of production'.[54] The claim, by contrast, that the costs of education do not 'directly' enter into the determination of the value of the commodity of 'qualified labour-power', is in complete contradiction to Marx's view of the matter. Altvater's criticism of this thesis is correct in this respect, although he in turn does not distinguish adequately between the value of the commodity of 'qualified labour power' and the 'advance of the production costs of this qualification'. Roth's fear of falling into Adam Smith's contradiction (determination of commodity value

[51] There is a summary of previous discussions on the relationship between qualified and unqualified labour, and the way in which the first can be reduced to the second, in Roman Rosdolsky, op. cit., Vol. II, pp. 597-614. See also Robert Rowthorn, *Komplizierte Arbeit in Marxschen System*, in H. Nutzinger and E. Wulstetter (ed.), *Die Marxsche Theorie und ihre Kritik*, Frankfurt, 1974, p. 129ff.

[52] Roth and Kanzow, op. cit., pp. 71-6.

[53] Cf. Marx, *Grundrisse*, p. 533: 'All *general, communal* conditions of production . . . are therefore paid for out of a part of the country's revenue — out of the government's treasury — and the workers do not appear as productive workers, even though they increase the productive force of capital.'

[54] Marx, *Grundrisse*, p. 532: 'The highest development of capital exists when the general conditions of the process of social production are not paid out of *deductions from the social revenue*, the State's taxes . . . but rather out of *capital as capital*.' Cf. also *Theories of Surplus Value*, Vol. I, pp. 410-11, where Marx speaks of teachers in private schools as productive workers when they enrich the capitalists who own these schools. But in the same volume, pp. 167-8 we also read: 'As to the purchase of such services as those which train labour-power, maintain or modify it, in a word, give it a specialized form or even only maintain it — thus for example the schoolmaster's service, in so far as it is "industrially" necessary or useful . . . these are services which yield in return a "vendible commodity", namely labour-power itself, into whose costs of production or reproduction these services enter. . . . The labour of the doctor or the schoolmaster does not directly create the fund out of which they are paid, although their labours enter into the production costs of the fund which creates all values whatsoever — namely, the production costs of labour-power.'

by wages and of wages by commodity value) becomes groundless if we do not read anything more into Marx's formula—'into whose costs of production and reproduction these services enter'—than actually appears there.[55] Obviously Marx does not say that the value of the commodity of 'qualified labour power' is simply *determined* by the costs of its qualification. Its value is determined by the costs of its reproduction as a whole, which include physiological and moral-historical elements as well as the costs of reproducing its qualification.[56]

Precisely because the costs of education are met by the State — via its redistribution of income — and the educational system does not constitute a field of investment for capital hatching surplus-value, a contradiction arises between the objective demand for a quantitative increase in this sector because of the need for accelerated technological innovation and the reluctance of the 'many capitals' to bear the necessary costs of this expansion by increasing the non-accumulated part of surplus-value (taxes). The socialization of the costs of education therefore represents capital's attempt to pass on these expenses as far as possible to wage-earners, by financing them via tax deductions from the income of workers and employees. This contradiction is reproduced within the capitalist class, where those sections of the bourgeoisie which are based on the exploitation of cheap labour-power (handicrafts, small enterprises, backward branches of industry) naturally resist major increases in expenditure on education, while the large companies and advanced industries are prepared to cover a part of the costs of education by so-called in-service training within the enterprise.[57]

The conclusion drawn by the Hungarian Marxist Janossy, that the inadequate development of highly qualified labour-power by capitalism is in the long-run a decisive brake on above-average rates of economic growth, is therefore doubly wrong.[58] For one thing, there is no reason why the *undeniable retardation* of late

[55]Altvater and Huisken, op. cit., pp. 256 f., 294-5.

[56]Rosdolsky, op. cit., pp. 612-14. See also Marx, *Capital*, Vol. I, p. 519: 'There are besides two other factors that enter into the determination of the value of labour-power. One, the expenses of developing that power, which vary with the mode of production; the other its natural diversity, the difference between the labour-power of men and women, children and adults.'

[57]For the attitude of capitalist industry to technical colleges and the apprentice system, see among others Altvater and Huisken, op. cit., pp. 162-5, 173 f.

[58]Franz Janossy, *Das Ende der Wirtschaftswunder*, Frankfurt, 1969, pp. 234-5, 250, 252-4, etc.

capitalism in adapting the occupational structure to the technological needs of its economy should mean that such adaptation is
impossible. In the end the exigencies of the valorization of monopoly capital will prevail in the educational system too; the only force
capable of preventing this in the long-run is the working class,
not middle strata or weaker capitalist circles.[59] The second point
is that precisely in late capitalism the long-term tendencies of the
rate of profit depend less and less on the specific needs of occupational distribution and labour qualification of the 'many capitals',
and more and more on the general relation of the supply and
demand for the commodity of labour-power as a whole — in other
words, on the *social average rate of surplus-value*[60] co-determined
partly by fluctuations in the industrial reserve army. The reproduction of the industrial reserve army is much more important
than the reproduction of special forms of qualification for the
long-term tendencies of growth of late capitalism. Indeed, it can
even be said that the typical late capitalist corporation is increasingly
indifferent to *specific* forms of labour qualification, for with accelerated technological innovation these must anyway be changed
several times in the life-span of a worker; it is interested above
all in comprehensive schooling which develops polytechnical
'talent' and adaptability. The experience of German engineering
schools and of higher technological education in Japan shows that

[59] The *main tendency* during the 'long wave with an undertone of expansion' in the
period 1945-65 was for wage increases in specific branches of the economy where
there was a shortage of labour, to spread to the whole work-force under conditions
of a dwindling industrial reserve army.

[60] We cannot develop here a critique of Janossy's very stimulating and valuable
book. We will merely point out that on pp. 246-7 — as in the whole conclusion of his
book — he confuses value calculations and price calculations, and so falls into inex-
tricable contradictions. If the number of workers employed in a branch of industry
A declines from 8,000 to 1,000, with labour-time remaining constant, then the newly
created value (variable capital plus surplus-value) will fall to 12.5% of its former level.
Conversely if in branch *B* of an enterprise the number of workers rises from 2,000
to 9,000, i.e. by 450%, then the mass of newly created value will also rise by 450%.
In this example, however, the *total* mass of new value (income) will remain constant,
namely 10,000 x in both cases (where x=the number of man-hours per worker),
since the increased productivity of labour finds expression in a fall in the value of
the commodities. Market fluctuations can *redistribute* this mass of value, but cannot
increase it. This is concealed by Janossy's inflationary calculation of prices, which
ultimately produces a twelve-fold increase in 'national income'. The commodity
prices here appear to be determined by wages and not by values, while the wages
in one branch double solely on the basis of the market, in other words completely
free themselves from the value of the commodity of labour-power.

late capitalism is quite capable of meeting its needs for intellectually qualified labour-power in a fairly short space of time. The most important contradictions of late capitalism do not lie in the structural underdevelopment of its education system but in its renewed crisis of valorization, and in the growing insurgency of wage-earners against capitalist relations of production, an insurgency which can increasingly spread to intellectual producers as well, not because of the underdevelopment of education but because of its subordination to needs of capital, which increasingly and frontally clash with the needs of free creative activity.

9

The Permanent Arms Economy and Late Capitalism

Since the end of the 30's the production of weapons has played a significant role in the imperialist economy. This latter has now experienced more than three decades of uninterrupted armament. There are no indications that this tendency towards a permanent arms economy will diminish in the foreseeable future. We are thus dealing with one of the hallmarks of late capitalism, which must be explained by the social and economic development of this mode of production itself. In particular, we must investigate the extent to which certain specific economic features of late capitalism, which distinguish it from earlier phases of bourgeois society, are connected with the phenomenon of permanent arms expenditure and whether, if the latter should persist, these features too will continue to condition the entire historical epoch of late capitalism.

There is certainly nothing peculiarly new about the production of weapons and military expenditure, as economic phenomena in the history of the capitalist mode of production. The production of weapons for the dynastic wars from the 15th to the 18th century was a major source of primitive accumulation and one of the most important midwives of early capitalism.[1] As a stimulus to accelerate industrialization or to extend the capitalist market, arms expenditure and war played a considerable role in the acceleration of industrial- .

[1] See for instance Marx, *Capital*, Vol. 1, p. 751; Josef Kulischer, *Allgemeine Wirtschaftsgeschichte*, Vol. 2, p. 361; *Histoire Economique et Sociale de la France*, Vol. 2, pp. 269-76, 310-21.

ization or extension of the capitalist market throughout modern history (compare, for example, the upswing of English industry after 1793; French war production during the Napoleonic conquests; the Crimean struggle between Great Britain, France and Russia; armaments as the main lever for industrialization in Meiji Japan, and so on).[2] After the onset of the age of imperialism proper, military expenditure likewise contributed substantially to the accelerated expansion of output in the twenty years preceding the First World War.[3] In none of these earlier epochs of the capitalist mode of production, however, did arms production show such a long and uninterrupted tendency to rise or to absorb such a significant portion of the total annual product (as a fraction of the national income or of the gross national product, in other words, of the new value annually created or of the annual value of commodity production). According to Vilmar's calculations, world-wide expenditure on armaments per year, expressed in billions of gold dollars, grew from 4 billion in the period 1901-14 to 13 billion in the epoch 1945-55.[4] We are therefore justified in speaking of a change from quantity to quality; the increased volume of arms expenditure has undoubtedly created a new quality in economic terms. We need only cite one figure to demonstrate this: in 1961 the production of weapons amounted to nearly half of gross investments the world over (gross capital formation or net investments plus ongoing amortization of fixed capital).[5]

The proportion of arms production and military spending in the gross national product of the USA has undergone the following development (taking account only of direct, not of indirect, military expenditure):[6]

[2] George W. F. Hallgarten, *Imperialismus vor 1914*, p. 53; K. Marx, F. Engels, *Werke*, XIV, p. 375; Thomas C. Smith, *Political Change and Industrial Development in Japan*, p. 4 f; Lockwood, op. cit., pp. 18-19.

[3] Ernest Kaemmel, *Finanzgeschichte*, Berlin, 1966, pp. 330-1, 335.

[4] Fritz Vilmar, *Rüstung und Abrüstung im Spätkapitalismus*, p. 28

[5] United Nations, *The Economic and Social Consequences of Disarmament*, New York, 1962, p. 3.

[6] Direct military spending excludes veterans' benefits as well as NASA expenditure. The figures for the years 1952-65 are taken from: US Department of Commerce, *The National Income and Products of the USA 1929-1965*. Those after 1965 come from the annual *Statistical Abstracts of the USA*. The figures before 1952 are from T. N. Vance, *The Permanent War Economy*, p. 8. Vance's series is not completely comparable with official estimates and from 1941 may lie about 1.5% annually above those later computed by the US Department of Commerce. After 1960 NASA outlays ought to be included, which from 1963 onwards would add approximately an annual 0.5 to 0.7% of the GNP to the figures mentioned.

1939 :	1.5 %	1950 :	5.7 %	1961 :	9.3 %
1940 :	2.7 %	1951 :	13.4 %	1962 :	9.4 %
1941 :	11.1 %	1952 :	13.5 %	1963 :	8.8 %
1942 :	31.5 %	1953 :	13.6 %	1964 :	8.1 %
1943 :	42.8 %	1954 :	11.5 %	1965 :	7.6 %
1944 :	42.5 %	1955 :	9.9 %	1966 :	7.9 %
1945 :	36.6 %	1956 :	9.8 %	1967 :	9.1 %
1946 :	11.4 %	1957 :	10.2 %	1968 :	9.7 %
1947 :	6.2 %	1958 :	10.4 %	1969 :	9.0 %
1948 :	4.3 %	1959 :	9.7 %	1970 :	8.3 %
1949 :	5·0%	1960 :	9.1 %	1971 :	7.5 %

Military expenditure in the other imperialist states in the period since the Second World War can be estimated as follows:

Currect Expenditure on Defence as % of G.D.P. at Current Prices[7]

	1950	1955	1960	1965	1970
U.K.	6.3 %	7.7 %	6.3 %	5.9 %	4.9 %
France	5.8 %	4.9 %	5.4 %	4.0 %	3.3 %
W. Germany	4.5 %	3.3 %	3.2 %	3.9 %	3.2 %
Italy	3.2 % (°)	2.8 %	2.5 %	2.5 %	3.6 %

(°) 1951

Average % Change p.a. 1950-70 Constant Prices Military Expenditure

U.S.A.	+6.2 %
Japan	+3.9 % (°)
U.K.	+1.3 %
France	+4.2 %
W. Germany	+5.8 %
Italy	+4.1 % (°) 1951-70

What we need to do now is to investigate the effects of this enormous military expenditure on the development of the late capitalist economy as a whole. The most reliable method is probably to analyse the dynamic of the most important internal contradictions or difficulties of development of the capitalist mode of production in the light of a permanent and substantial arms budget. For this purpose we must convert Marx's reproduction scheme, which operates with two sectors — Department I: means of production;

[7] OECD National Accounts, calculated from data in country tables on GDP and defense expenditure; *World Armaments and Disarmaments*, SIPRI Yearbook, 1972, Tables 4.4 and 4.9.

Department II: consumer goods — into a scheme with three sectors, adding to these two Departments a third Department producing means of destruction.[8] We are justified in making this distinction because Department III, unlike Departments I and II, produces commodities which do not enter into the process of *reproduction* of the material elements of production (replacing and extending the means of production and labour-power consumed) and are furthermore not interchangeable with these elements, as is certainly the case, for example, with the consumer goods absorbed unproductively by the capitalist class and those who serve it.

I. ARMS PRODUCTION AND THE DIFFICULTIES OF REALIZATION

The growing organic composition of capital in Departments I and II leads to difficulties of realization, for with technical progress the purchasing power (sum of wages) for consumer goods created in the production of means of production rises more slowly than the demand for means of production engendered in the production of consumer goods. The purchasing power for consumer goods created in Department I does not suffice to realize the total commodity value of the commodities produced by — and not in circulation within — Department II. Unless these consumer goods are sold at their value — in other words, unless surplus-value is redistributed towards Department I at the expense of Department II [9] — an unsaleable residue of consumer goods will remain, as is

[8] Michael Tugan-Baranovsky was the first to make use of Department III in his book *Studien zur Theorie und Geschichte der Handelskrisen in England*, published in 1901. He restricted its application, however, to the production of luxury goods (the unproductive consumption of capitalists) and to the case of simple reproduction. In our *Marxist Economic Theory* we used Department III as the armaments sector to show the possibility of regressive reproduction. For the sake of conceptual clarity we must stress that such a third Department is strictly limited to armaments (weapons and munitions) and does not include all military expenditure in an auditing sense. If the army buys blankets or barracks for its soldiers, then obviously it is buying commodities made by Departments I and II, and not commodities from Department III. If, by contrast, machines are bought for the production of weapons, and the workers employed in the armaments industry buy consumer goods out of their wages, then constant and variable capital from Department III is being exchanged for commodities from Departments I and II. Our analysis is concerned with the effects of this exchange on the overall social circulation, not the effects of the military budget in and for itself.

[9] Marx explicitly excluded these hypotheses in his treatment of reproduction: see *Capital*, Vol. 2, p. 368.

shown by the familiar schemes of Tugan-Baranovsky and Otto Bauer: 'This is a corollary of the fact that with a growing organic composition of capital less new workers are hired and hence social consumption cannot expand sufficiently to absorb the whole commodity product of Department II. Similar disequilibria will necessarily occur if there is a growth in the rate of surplus-value or if the accumulated part of the newly created surplus-value is greater than in the preceding production periods. In these cases, too, the smooth progress of extended reproduction foreseen by the schemes becomes impossible, for the disproportions in the relations of exchange between the two Departments caused by technical progress must destroy their earlier proportionality.'[10] Can the emergence of Department III, then, transcend these difficulties of realization or re-establish the proportionality between Departments I and II despite the growing organic composition of capital?

Department III could do this only if
$$IIc + IIs\beta + IIIc + IIIs\beta = Iv + Isa + Is\gamma + IIIv + IIIsa + IIIs\gamma,$$
(where surplus-value is divided into a portion a which is consumed unproductively, a portion β which is accumulated in constant capital and a portion γ which is accumulated in variable capital). We know, however, that with a growing organic composition of capital $IIc + IIs\beta$ will be greater that $Iv + Isa + Is\gamma$ (this is the very reason for the existence of an unsaleable residue of consumer goods at all). For the formula for equalization to work, $IIIv + IIIsa + IIIs\gamma$ would hence have to be greater than $IIIc + IIIs\beta$, in other words, *the arms sector would have to be characterized in the long-run by a declining organic composition of capital.* Obviously this is normally impossible (with the exception, perhaps, of the final phase of a destructive war). This proves that an arms industry cannot furnish a solution for the difficulties of realization caused by the increase in the organic composition of capital.

Let us take the numerical example in Bauer's schemes. For the first production cycle we get the following commodity value for the two Departments:

I: $120,000c + 50,000v + 50,000s = 220,000$ I
II: $80,000c + 50,000v + 50,000s = 160,000$ II

Bauer assumes that 75% of the surplus-value of each of the two Departments (37,500 units of value) is consumed unproductively by

[10]Rosdolsky, *Zur Entstehungsgeschichte*, p. 358.

the capitalists, that 10,000 units are accumulated in additional constant capital and 2,500 in additional variable capital.[11] The system is in equilibrium, for Department II buys $80,000c + 10,000s\beta$ $= 90,000$ from Department I, to which it simultaneously sells $50,000v + 37,500sa + 2,500s\gamma = 90,000$. If the rate of surplus-value and the unproductive consumption of the capitalists remain constant, then the commodity value of the second production cycle will have the following proportions:

$$\text{I}: \quad 130,000c + 52,500v + 52,500s = 235,000 \text{ I}$$
$$\text{II}: \quad 90,000c + 52,500v + 52,500s = 195,000 \text{ II}$$

The system has therefore now been thrown out of equilibrium, for although Department II would have to buy $90,000c + $ more than $12,000s\beta$ (i.e., more than 102,000 units of value altogether) from Department I to ensure a further growth in the organic composition of capital, it can only sell this Department $52,000v + 37,500sa$ $+$ less than $3,000s\gamma$, i.e., less than 93,000 units of value altogether. There thus comes into being an unsaleable residue of approximately 10,000 units of value in consumer goods. In Bauer's scheme, this residue disappears because a part of the surplus-value realized in Department II in the first cycle is accumulated in Department I in the second (in other words, the commodity value produced in Department II is realized fully only because it is kept considerably lower than it would be in the case of a normal process of accumulation in this Department).[12]

If we seek a solution to the difficulties of realization in the rise of a Department III (production of destructive goods) instead of in Bauer's schemes, which contradict the logic of Marx's schemes of reproduction, then we will find such a solution only if the productive value of the three Departments develops approximately as follows in the second production cycle:

$$\text{I}: \quad 126,000c + 51,500v + 51,500s = 229,000 \text{ I}$$
$$\text{II}: \quad 86,000c + 51,500v + 51,500s = 189,000 \text{ II}$$
$$\text{III}: \quad 4,000c + 1,000v + 7,000s = 12,000 \text{ III}$$

[11] Otto Bauer, 'Die Akkumulation des Kapitals', in *Die Neue Zeit,* Vol. 31/1, 1913, p. 836.

[12] "Such a hypertrophy of the production of means of production, without a corresponding increase in social consumption, is the inexorable outcome of Bauer's scheme, but is certainly not compatible with the spirit of Marx's theory. Marx emphasized after all that "the production of constant capital never occurs for its own sake but only because more of it is needed in the spheres of production whose products enter individual consumption".' Rosdolsky, *Zur Entstehungsgeschichte,* p. 592.

The conditions of a constant rate of surplus-value and a constant unproductive consumption by the capitalists are retained in this hypothesis for Departments I and II. Department II now sells Department I consumer goods to the value of $51,000v + 37,500sa + 4,000s\gamma$. Simultaneously it sells consumer goods to the value of $4,000v + 3,375sa + 125s\gamma$ to Department III. The total commodity value realized outside Department II thus amounts to 100,500 units of value. For these units of value Department II buys back the 86,000 units of value it needs to replace c, and the 10,000 it needs to accumulate additional means of production. 4,500 units of the surplus-value realized by Department II are siphoned off by the state in the form of taxes and serve to purchase 4,500 means of destruction in Department III. Department I sells $86,000 + 10,000$ units of value in means of production to Department II and $4,000 + 500$ units of value in means of production to Department III. For the 100,500 units of value realized through this sale, Department I buys 51,000 consumer goods from Department II to reproduce the labour-power expended in producing the means of production, 37,500 consumer goods for the unproductive consumption of the capitalists and 4,000 consumer goods as equivalent for the accumulation of additional variable capital. 7,500 units of the surplus-value realized in Department I are deducted by the state as taxes to purchase 7,500 means of destruction. The total value of the means of destruction produced in Department III is thus realized by means of this two-fold tax deduction of $4,500 + 7,500$.

This numerical example reveals that the rise of a 'permanent arms sector' can only solve the problem of the realization of the commodity value (surplus-value) produced in Department II on a further precondition: *that the total purchasing power needed to buy weapons and destructive goods is tapped from total surplus-value while leaving the real wages of the working class intact.*

From the standpoint of the logic of the capitalist mode of production, neither precondition makes any sense. In normal circumstances it is unthinkable that a lower organic composition of capital than in Departments I and II could permanently prevail in the weapons sector (moreover, as can be seen from the algebraic formula above, an organic composition which falls in the same proportion as that of Department II rises). It is even more unthinkable that capitalists would organize the production of weapons in order to increase the social sum of wages instead of attempting to bring it down.

Such an increase is, however, logically concealed within the idea of a 'solution' of the problem of realization through the arms industry. For if we compare the second production cycle without the arms sector with the second production cycle which includes it, we see that the total sum of wages has risen from 105,000 to 107,000 although the value of the products remains constant at 430,000. In order to produce the same value, the capitalists have paid out more wages, even though this runs counter to the whole logic of the capitalist mode of production. Nor should this surprise us, for after all, the difficulty of realization can ultimately be resolved only by increasing the monetarily effective demand for *consumer goods*. The fact that such a development does not correspond to historical reality any more than it does to analytical logic need not be demonstrated here. We have already shown at length in Chapter 5 that fascism, the war economy and the post-war economy were accompanied by a substantial reduction in the share of productive workers' consumption in the gross national product, i.e., by a considerable increase in the rate of surplus-value. Consequently, a permanent armament industry is incapable of solving the problem of realization inherent in the capitalist mode of production when technical progress is increasing. The customary debates as to whether arms expenditure is really equivalent to a 'tapping of wages' or to a 'tapping of surplus-value' have their origin in a methodologically incorrect way of formulating the problem: they attempt to comprehend a movement, a change, with static categories. From a formal point of view, any *durable* 'deduction' from wages constitutes an increase in surplus-value. Hence both wage deductions and direct alienation of surplus-value to fund arms expenditure indifferently mean that armaments are financed out of surplus-value. Such a formula consequently tells us nothing about the *dynamic* of the process, for it fails to answer the question whether the taxes which fund the arms budget have altered the total relation between surplus-value and sum of wages, and if they do, in what direction. The correct question to ask therefore concerns the *change in the relation* between wages and surplus-value, in other words, the *development of the rate of surplus-value* that follows from arms expenditure. If these outlays lead to a fall in the share of net wages (workers' consumption) in the national income, then military expenditure is undoubtedly financed 'at the expense of the working class', i.e., by a relative decline in wages. If increased military taxes on wages lead to a *durable* reduction of net wages as a proportion of gross wages, we can even speak of a decline in the value of the commodity of labour-power, since this value is after all represented only by the commodity package bought by wages for the reproduction of labour-power and not by the category of 'gross wages', which is irrelevant to the consumption of the workers.

In this sense Tsuru, Baran and Sweezy, and Kidron are wrong to see military expenditure simply as a 'tax on surplus-value' or as 'expenditure of the social surplus product'.[13] Rosa Luxemburg, by contrast, was quite right when in her analysis of arms expenditure she wrote: 'Some of the money circulating as variable capital breaks free of this cycle and in the state treasury it represents a new demand. For the technique of taxation, of course, the order of events is rather different, since the amount of the indirect taxes is actually advanced to the state by capital and is merely being refunded to the capitalists by the sale of their commodities, as part of their price. But economically speaking, it makes no difference. The crucial point is that the quantity of money with the function of variable capital should first mediate the exchange between capital and labour power. Later, when there is an exchange between workers and capitalists as buyers and sellers of commodities respectively, this money will change hands and accrue to the state as taxes. This money, which capital has set circulating, first fulfils its primary function in the exchange with labour-power, but subsequently, by mediation of the state, it begins an entirely new career. As a new purchasing power, belonging with neither labour nor capital, it becomes interested in new products, in a special branch of production which does not cater for either the capitalists or the working class, and thus it offers capital new opportunities for creating and realizing surplus-values. When we were formerly taking it for granted that the indirect taxes extorted from the workers are used for paying the officials and for provisioning the army, we found the 'saving' in the consumption of the working class to mean that the workers rather than the capitalists were made to pay for the personal consumption of the hangers-on of the capitalist class and the tools of their classrule. This change devolved from the surplus-value to the variable capital, and a corresponding amount of the surplus-

---

[13] Shigeto Tsuru, *Adonde va el capitalismo?*, Barcelona, 1967, p. 31. Paul A. Baran wnd Paul M. Sweezy, *Monopoly Capital*, p. 178 f. Michael Kidron, *Western Capitalism since the War*, London, 1968, p. 39.

value became available for purposes of capitalization. Now we see how the taxes extorted from the workers afford capital a new opportunity for accumulation when they are used for armament manufacture. On the basis of indirect taxation, militarism in practice works both ways. By lowering the normal standard of living for the working class, it ensures both that capital should be able to maintain a regular army, the organ of capitalist rule, and that it may tap an impressive field for further accumulation.' [14]

If this is true and we simultaneously accept Rosdolsky's view, based on the schemes of Tugan-Baranovsky and Bauer (and on the inner logic of the capitalist mode of production) that the problem of realization ultimately always lies in the difficulty of realizing the surplus-value frozen in the commodities of Department II, then a permanent armaments industry clearly cannot solve *this* difficulty.

II. ARMS PRODUCTION AND THE TENDENCY FOR THE RATE OF PROFIT TO FALL

The difficulty of accumulation inherent in the development of the capitalist mode of production ultimately lies in the tendency for the average rate of profit to fall because of the increased organic composition of capital. Can a permanent arms industry solve this difficulty? Obviously only if the following two conditions are met.

In the first place, if Department III has a lower organic composition of capital than Departments I and II and hence if a permanent arms industry reduces the socially average organic composition of capital. In normal capitalist conditions this hypothesis is completely unrealistic; on the contrary, the organic composition of capital in

[14]Rosa Luxemburg, *The Accumulation of Capital,* pp. 463-4. The assumption that state fiscal revenue comes *exclusively* from wage deductions must of course be rejected as unrealistic. Taxes hit both wages and surplus-value, and only the concrete way *how* they diminish these gross incomes—in other words, how they modify the relationship between surplus-value and wages—can tell us whether or not arms expenditure has reduced the relative wage. Marx expressly stated that state expenditure through taxes is met by the sum of wages *and* surplus-value. Cf. *Theories of Surplus Value,* Vol. 1, p. 406; *Capital,* Vol. 1, p. 756. Heininger comments that 'the state appropriates various sources of income (namely profits, wages and the surplus product of simple commodity producers)' and uses these 'for a particular form of parasitic state consumption . . . in the exclusive class interest of the financial oligarchy.' Horst Heininger, *Zur Theorie des staatsmonopolistischen Kapitalismus,* p. 119 f.

Department III is normally higher than the social average. It is equivalent to the composition of the heavy industrial sectors of Department I which operate with the most expensive machines. Nor can one say that permanent arms expenditure would reduce the price of constant capital.

The second condition is if the emergence of Department III leads to a permanent increase in the rate of surplus-value as compared to its normal level before this Department came into existence. Here, in turn, we need to distinguish two cases:

a) *The rate of surplus-value in Department III rises so far above the social average that it contributes to an increase in this average.* This would happen, for instance, if the second production cycle in the value schemes used above took the following form:

$$\text{I}: \quad 126{,}000c + 51{,}500v + 51{,}500s = 229{,}000 \text{ II}$$
$$\text{II}: \quad 86{,}000c + 51{,}500v + 51{,}500s = 189{,}000 \text{ II}$$
$$\text{III}: \quad 4{,}000c + 1{,}000v + 7{,}000s = 12{,}000 \text{ III}$$

In other words, if there was a change in the original form of Department III: $4{,}000c + 4{,}000v + 4{,}000s = 12{,}000$. The social rate of profit would then have risen from 33.3% to 34.4%, i.e., the fall in the rate of profit from the first to the second cycle without the armaments industry (from 33.3% to 32.3%) would have been converted into a rise in the rate of profit thanks to Department III from 33.3% to 34.4%. The relatively small volume of this increase is due only to the fact that the armaments sector still represents only a very small portion of the social product (less than 3% in our example). If the size of the 'permanent arms budget' is significantly increased (say to 10% or 15% of the gross national product) the rise in the social rate of profit deriving from the increase in the rate of surplus-value in Department III would be far more pronounced.

Obviously, such an extraordinary increase in the rate of surplus in Department III could not be the result of a rise in relative surplus-value. The latter flows from an increase in the productivity of labour in Department II, in other words, from a reduction in the *value* of the commodity of labour-power (not to be confused with real wages) because a particular packet of consumer goods can now be produced in a smaller fraction of the working day, thus adding to the duration of surplus labour. An increase in relative surplus-value could thus never be a feature specific to Department III but would determine the value of the commodity of labour-power for the whole of industry.

What we are thus dealing with in our numerical example is an increase in the rate of surplus-value in Department III because the labour-power engaged in this Department has been paid or 'bought' *far below its value*. Again, under 'normal' capitalist conditions such a discrepancy is impossible. It obtains only in an exceptional case: namely, when the production of Department III is carried out *not* by 'free' workers but by slave labour (prisoners of all kinds), as in the final phase of Hitler's war economy. The consequence of 'paying' for labour-power far below its value can only be a rapid fall in the intensity and productivity of labour.[15] The outcome is a logic which is completely alien to normal capital accumulation and extended reproduction — a logic of *declining reproduction*, in which ruinous predation of the commodity of labour-power and then ruinous predation of social fixed capital, because of a hypertrophy of Department III, leads to *destruction* of the material elements of extended reproduction.

b) The very rise of Department III or of permanent arms production raises the overall social average rate of surplus-value (hence not the rate of surplus-value of Department III in particular). Since the establishment of Department III cannot in itself augment the production of relative surplus-value, this condition can be realized only if permanent arms production is financed by a relative decrease in the value of the commodity of labour-power (if, therefore, real wages and the physical consumption of workers are lower than they would be without the taxes paid by workers to finance armaments manufacture). This is the normal case of capitalist arms expenditure, if this is financed to a considerable extent by taxes on wages and by indirect taxation (an increase in the price of consumer goods).

But there is an immediate catch here. The arms economy, as we have already stressed, has by its very nature a higher organic composition of capital than the social average in Departments I and II. Consequently the permanent arms budget normally has a *contradictory effect* on the social average rate of profit. By raising the average organic composition of capital, it *accelerates* the tendency for the rate of profit to fall. But by determining an increase in the rate of surplus-value through rising taxation of wages and rising price-levels of consumer goods, it *brakes* this same tendency for the rate of profit to fall. The two effects can neutralize each other, so that in the end — once again under 'normal' capitalist conditions — the

[15]Rosa Luxemburg understood and predicted this. See her footnote on p. 464 of *The Accumulation of Capital.*

development of a permanent arms industry will tend to be neutral in its effect on fluctuations of the average rate of profit. Only under the 'abnormal' conditions of a war economy and (or) fascism, or atomization of the working class, can the development of Department III cause so marked a rise in the rate of surplus-value (with relative or absolute *downward pressure on wages* despite a high level of employment) that it more than keeps pace with the increase in the social organic composition of capital which its own existence has created.[16]

If, instead of the second production cycle:

$$\left.\begin{array}{l} \text{I}: \ 130,000c + 52,500v + 52,500s = 235,000 \ \text{I} \\ \text{II}: \ \ 90,000c + 52,500v + 52,500s = 195,000 \ \text{II} \end{array}\right\} 430,000$$

we suppose the following second production cycle including Department III:

$$\left.\begin{array}{l} \text{I}: \ 126,000c + 50,000v + 52,000s = 228,000 \ \text{I} \\ \text{II}: \ \ 84,000c + 50,000v + 52,000s = 186,000 \ \text{II} \\ \text{III}: \ \ 10,000c + \ \ 2,500v + \ \ 3,500s = \ \ 16,000 \ \text{III} \end{array}\right\} 430,000$$

to succeed a first production cycle with the following value product:

$$\left.\begin{array}{l} \text{I}: \ 120,000c + 50,000v + 50,000s = 220,000 \ \text{I} \\ \text{II}: \ \ 80,000c + 50,000v + 50,000s = 180,000 \ \text{II} \end{array}\right\} 400,000$$

then although the social organic composition of capital has risen from 2 to 2.14, the average rate of profit has simultaneously remained constant at 33.3%.

$$\frac{100,000s}{200,000c + 100,000v} \text{ in the first production cycle.}$$

$$\frac{107,500s}{220,000c + 102,500v} \text{ in the second.}$$

This results from the fact that the rate of surplus-value has risen from 100% to 104% because nominal wages have been cut by the equivalent of 5,000 units of value through taxation to finance the purchase of military goods by the State, instead of consumer goods by the workers. The greater the volume of Department III and the faster the growth of the average social organic composition of capital, the steeper must be this increase in the rate of surplus-value without a rise in relative surplus-value, in order to counteract the otherwise inevitable plunge of the average rate of profit. This would very quickly mean an *absolute* fall in the sum of wages, which can be

[16] It can admittedly achieve this *indirectly* through the acceleration of technological innovation in general, which also results in an accelerated increase in the productivity of labour in Department II. See Chapters 5, 7 and 8.

regarded as improbable, if not impossible, with *rising* employment under 'normal' conditions. For example, if the total social constant capital increases by 15% from the second to the third production cycle, or from 220,000 units of value to 253,000, while the value of the total social product rises by 7.5% from 430,000 to 462,250, then the total variable capital will have to *fall* from 102,500 to 93,755 if the average rate of profit is to be kept constant at 33.3%. The commodity value produced would have to assume something like the following form:

$$\begin{array}{llll}
\text{I}: & 138,000c + 44,387.5v + 54,737.5s = 237,125 \text{ I} & \\
\text{II}: & 90,000c + 44,387.5v + 54,737.5s = 189,125 \text{ II} & \left.\vphantom{\begin{array}{l}1\\2\\3\end{array}}\right\} \ 462,250 \\
\text{III}: & 25,000c + \ \ 5,000v \ \ + \ \ 6,000s \ \ = \ \ 36,000 \text{ III} &
\end{array}$$

Here there would not have occurred an absolute decline in the total sum of wages in value terms, but the portion of nominal wages siphoned from the workers through taxes and price increases would have risen to 21,700 units of value, i.e., to approximately 20% of the sum of wages achieved without this extortion. It is obvious that such a state of affairs is scarcely attainable, short of outright fascism and complete atomization of the working class.

What, then, are we to make of the claim made by the British economist Kidron, that arms expenditure does in the long-run facilitate the process of accumulation by arresting the tendency for the average rate of profit to fall? Kidron's argument runs as follows: 'The model (of Marx) is a closed system, in which all output flows back as inputs in the form of investment goods or wage goods. There are no leaks. Yet in principle a leak could insulate the compulsion to grow from its most important consequences. . . . If 'capital intensive' goods were drawn off, the rise would be slower and — depending on the volume and composition of the leak — could even stop or be reversed. In such a case there would be no decline in the average rate of profit, no reason to expect increasingly severe slumps and so on. Capitalism has never formed a closed system in practice. Wars and slumps have destroyed immense quantities of output. Capital exports have diverted and frozen other quantities for long stretches of time. A lot, since World War II, filtered out in the production of arms. Each of these leaks has acted to slow the rise in the overall organic composition and the fall in the rate of profit.'[17]

The vague category of 'leaks' confuses various different

---

[17]Michael Kidron, 'Maginot Marxism', in *International Socialism*, No. 36, p. 33.

phenomena. Slumps destroy capital by means of *devalorization* and devalorized capital obviously means (with a constant rate of surplus-value) increased rates of profit. Generally speaking wars in no way devalorize capital (except lost wars, and even then only as a result of the effects of defeat). They can only be regarded as 'leaks' which slow the tendency of the rate of profit to fall if they destroy capital (i.e., *destroy it physically*). Capital exports only brake the fall of the average rate of profit, if they are invested in countries with a lower average organic composition of capital. In other words, in all these cases, there is no mysterious 'leak', but merely the classical increase in the rate of profit as a result of a reduction in the organic composition of capital, including the destruction of capital (the destruction of value, with or without physical destruction).

When Kidron applies the notion of a 'leak' to armaments, he is patently confusing the *process of production* (as the combined process of labour and of valorization) and the *process of reproduction* (which does *not* constitute a unity of the processes of the realization of surplus-value, capital accumulation and the return of all the commodities produced into the process of production). When the capital invested in the various branches of production has been valorized and the commodities in its possession have been sold at their price of production, the surplus-value from this capital has been realized *irrespective* of whether or not the commodities sold enter into the process of reproduction. In this case there is no question of any 'devalorization'. The surplus labour (mass of surplus-value) generated by the proletariat in the production of 'luxury goods' or weapons enters into the distribution of the total social surplus-value just as much as the surplus labour expended in the production of means of production or consumer goods for the reconstitution of labour-power.

For Kidron's comparison of the production of weapons with crises or wars, or with capital exports to underdeveloped countries, to have any validity, it would be necessary to show that this production represents an investment of capital at a lower organic composition than is the case in Departments I and II.[18] Kidron naturally cannot

---

[18] This would be the meaning of Kidron's remark that 'in so far as capital is taxed to sustain expenditure on arms it is deprived of resources that might otherwise go towards further investment. . . . Since one obvious result of such expenditure is high employment and, as a direct consequence of that, rates of growth amongst the highest ever, the dampening (?) effect of such taxation is not readily apparent. But it is not

prove any such thesis. For this reason his assertion that permanent arms manufacture slows the rise of the organic composition of capital, and thus the fall of the rate of profit, is quite empty.[19] In his book *Western Capitalism Since the War*, Kidron appeals to authority in lieu of proof: Ladislaus Von Bortkiewicz is said to have demonstrated that the organic composition of capital in Department III ('luxury production' in Von Bortkiewicz) has no influence on the social average rate of profit.[20] Von Bortkiewicz did in fact make such a claim.[21] It was based, however, on a misunderstanding of the nature of production prices, which Von Bortkiewicz confused with 'gold prices'. In reality, prices of production are for Marx by no means 'prices' in the ordinary sense of the word (expressions of commodity value in quantities of gold, and fluctuating about that value under the influence of the law of supply and demand, i.e., market prices); they are rather merely results of the redistribution of the social

---

absent. Were capital left alone to invest its entire pre-tax profit, the state creating demand (?) as and when necessary, growth rates would be very much higher (!)' (p. 39). We can leave to Kidron the truly astounding discovery that the arms economy is a factor that *slows down* late capitalist growth. In this general discussion he forgets the element of *relation*. Only if the rate of profit is higher in the arms industry than in Departments I and II can the removal of economic resources to Department III brake the fall of the average rate of profit. Only if the accumulation of capital in Department III proceeds *at a slower pace* than in Departments I and II, does this removal mean a slowing down of the average rate of accumulation or growth. The production of military goods is capitalist commodity production carried out for the sake of profit and in no way a form of the destruction of values or capital.

[19] Harman claims that the drain of capital into Department III takes capital away from Departments I and II which would have increased the organic composition if it had been invested there. (Paul Sweezy made a similar assertion in *The Theory of Capitalist Development*, p. 233.) He is quite right. But he forgets that the investment of this capital in Department III likewise raises the organic composition there. How this can then stop the average rate of profit from falling remains a mystery: Chris Harman, 'The Inconsistencies of Ernest Mandel', in *International Socialism*, No. 41, p. 39. His fellow-thinker Cliff claims that a war economy smoothes out the obstacles to capitalist production and staves off crises of over-production, by its devalorization or destruction of capital, and deceleration of accumulation (T. Cliff, *Russia—A Marxist Analysis*, p. 174). Other representatives of the same trend argue that surplus-value used to *purchase* weapons is not accumulated surplus-value. That is, of course, correct. But surplus-value used to build arms factories and to produce weapons certainly is accumulated surplus-value. The *purchase* of weapons must after all have been preceded by the *production* of weapons *as commodities*. This elementary fact has escaped adherents of the notion of the 'permanent arms economy' as a mechanism for suppressing the internal contradictions of the capitalist mode of production.

[20] M. Kidron, *Western Capitalism since the War*, pp. 46-7.

[21] L. Von Bortkiewicz, 'Zur Berichtigung der Grundlagen der theoretischen Konstruktion von Marx im Dritten Band des 'Kapital', in *Jahrbücher für Nationalökonomie und Statistik*, July 1907, p. 327.

surplus-value among the various branches of production. In effect, Von Bortkiewicz had to discard Marx's thesis that the sum of the production prices is equal to the sum of values; in other words, his construction made value (socially necessary quantities of expended labour) 'disappear' or 'arise' arbitrarily and mysteriously in the process of commodity circulation and equalization of the rate of profit. He was in fact regressing to an inconsistency which Marx corrected in Ricardo's labour theory of value. This inconsistency was related to the inadequacy of Ricardo's analysis of commodity value and his failure to comprehend the nature of abstract, value-creating labour. Ricardo was thereby led to the false conclusion that only a cheapening of *workers' means of subsistence* could produce an increase in the rate of profit.[22] Sraffa, the second authority on whom Kidron relies, has fallen into the same error as Ricardo.

In *Theories of Surplus-Value* Marx explicitly criticized the passage from Ricardo cited by Von Bortkiewicz in support of his hypothesis. Marx first quotes the following paragraph from the 7th chapter of Ricardo's *Principles:* 'It has been my endeavour to show throughout this work, that the rate of profit can never be increased but by a fall in wages, and that there can be no permanent fall of wages but in consequence of a fall in the necessaries on which wages are expended. If, therefore, by the extension of foreign trade, or by improvements in machinery, the food and necessaries of the labourer can be brought to market at a reduced price, profits will rise. If, instead of growing our own corn, or manufacturing the clothing and other necessaries of the labourer, we discover a new market from which we can supply ourselves with these commodities at a cheaper price, wages will fall and profits rise; *but if the commodities obtained at a cheaper rate, by the extension of foreign commerce, or by the improvement of machinery, be exclusively the commodities consumed by the rich, no alteration will take place in the rate of profits. The rate of wages would not be affected, although wine, velvets,*

<hr/>

[22] Ricardo did not understand the twofold character of labour-power as a *preserver of value* and a *creator of value*. This is why he, like Adam Smith, was unable to grasp the problem of the distinction between the rate of surplus-value and the rate of profit. This leads him — as it was later to do Sraffa — to the consistent conclusion that only an increase in the value of labour-power (but not a rise in the organic composition of capital) could lower the rate of profit (which for him was the same as the rate of surplus-value). The rate of surplus-value, of course, only rises and falls as a function of the development of Department II (which produces consumer goods for workers, which serve the reproduction of the commodity of labour-power), if the working-day and the value of the commodity of labour-power remain constant. The rate of profit, by contrast, also depends on the development of the organic composition of capital.

silks and other expensive commodities should fall 50%, and consequently profits would continue unaltered. '[23] Marx then comments: 'It is evident that this passage is rather loosely worded. But apart from this formal aspect, the statements are only true if one reads 'rate of surplus-value' for rate of profit, and this applies to the whole of this investigation into relative surplus-value. Even in the case of luxury articles, such improvements can raise the general rate of profit, *since the rate of profit in these spheres of production, as in all others, bears a share in the levelling out of all particular rates of profit into the average rate of profit.* If in such cases, as a result of the above-mentioned influences, the value of the constant capital falls proportionately to the variable, or the period of turnover is reduced (i.e., change takes place in the circulation process) then the rate of profit rises. Furthermore, the influence of foreign trade is expounded in an entirely one-sided way. The development of the product into a commodity is fundamental to capitalist production and this is intrinsically bound up with the expansion of the market, the creation of the world market, and therefore foreign trade.' [24]

Thereafter Marx goes to the root of Ricardo's errors, which were later to be repeated by Von Bortkiewicz and then copied by Kidron: 'If the working day is given . . . then the general rate of surplus-value, i.e., of surplus labour, is given since wages are on the average the same. Ricardo is preoccupied with this idea, and he confuses the general rate of surplus-value with the general rate of profit. [Von Bortkiewicz did not even understand the general rate of surplus-value, and altered the rate of surplus-value by transformation of values into prices in the circulation process.   E.M.] I have shown that with the same general rate of surplus-value, the rates of profit in different branches of production must be very different, if the commodities are to be sold at their respective values. The general rate of profit is formed through the total surplus-value produced being calculated on the total capital of society (of the class of capitalists). Each capital, therefore, in each particular branch, represents a portion of a total capital of the same organic composition, both as regards constant and variable capital, and circulating and fixed capital . . . . It is evident that the emergence, realization, creation of the general rate of profit necessitates the transformation of values into cost prices that are different from these

---

[23] Karl Marx, *Theories of Surplus Value*, Vol. 2. p. 422. (Our italics.)
[24] Ibid., p. 423. (Our italics.)

values. Ricardo on the contrary assumes the identity of values and cost prices, because he confuses the rate of profit with the rate of surplus-value. Hence he has not the faintest notion of the general change which takes place in the prices of commodities, in the course of the establishment of a general rate of profit, before there can be any talk of a general rate of profit. He accepts this rate of profit as something pre-existent which, therefore, even plays a part in his determination of value.'[25] Marx goes on: 'Because of his completely wrong conception of the rate of profit, Ricardo misunderstands entirely the influence of foreign trade, when it does not directly lower the price of the labourers' food. He does not see how enormously important it is for England, for example, to secure cheaper raw materials for industry, and that in this case I have shown previously, the rate of profit rises although prices fall, whereas in the reverse case, with rising prices, the rate of profit can fall, even if wages remain the same in both cases. . . . The rate of profit does not depend on the price of the individual commodity but on the amount of surplus labour which can be realized with a given capital. Elsewhere Ricardo also fails to recognize the importance of the market because he does not understand the nature of money.'[26]

For Marx, it is abstract labour that creates value. This labour is part of the total social labour capacity, and produces a commodity which, irrespective of its use-value, finds its equivalent on the market because it fulfills a social need. It is a matter of complete indifference from the standpoint of the formation of value whether this need is traced to workers or capitalists, or the state or non-capitalist producers. Consequently the total volume of value output, irrespective of the specific use-value of individual commodities (and hence irrespective also of their specific position within the process of reproduction), is determined by the total volume of commodity output. The social rate of profit thus depends on the total mass of unpaid labour — surplus labour — set in motion in the production of commodities by social capital, *irrespective of the sector in which this occurs*. If a rise in the organic composition of capital in one sector (that of weapons manufacture, for example) leads to a growth in the total sum of capital compared to a constant mass of surplus labour, this will result in a fall of the average rate of profit regardless of the relation between productive and unproductive consumption or consumption and accumulation. If a reduction in constant capital or an increase in the mass of surplus-value causes the proportions of the value of the aggregate social capital to fall in comparison to the total mass of surplus labour which it sets in motion, the social rate of profit will rise regardless of the changes which may in the event have taken place in the proportions of the various categories of use values produced. In this sense the expansion of Department III in the form of arms output can only increase (or slow the plunge of) the rate of profit, if it either possesses a lower organic composition of capital than the other branches of commodity production (which is obviously not the case) or directly or indirectly causes a steeper rise in the rate of surplus-value than would have been the case without its existence (which is only possible under very limited conditions, as was shown in the preceding pages).[27]

III. ARMS PRODUCTION AND THE DIFFICULTIES OF VALORIZATION OF CAPITAL

A third fundamental contradiction of the capitalist mode of production, which emerges when it has reached a certain level of maturity, is the increasing difficulty of valorization of capital, expressed in the phenomenon of *surplus capital* which can no longer be invested productively. This has been evident in the most developed capitalist countries since the start of the age of imperialism (monopoly capitalism) and became particularly prominent in the years 1913-40 (1945). By contrast with theories which view permanent arms expenditure essentially as a device to solve difficulties of realization or to slow the fall of the average rate of profit, it is in this distinct context that the specific function of the armaments industry should be seen.

Suppose that the total social output in a particular period is represented in 400,000 units of value, while simultaneously there exist 60,000 units of value of idle capital. Production has the following value-structure:

$$\text{I: } 120{,}000c + 50{,}000v + 50{,}000s = 220{,}000 \text{ I}$$
$$\text{II: } 80{,}000c + 50{,}000v + 50{,}000s = 180{,}000 \text{ II}$$

$$\left.\right\} \ 400{,}000$$

Suppose likewise that of the 75,000s (37,500 in each Department)

---

[27] An able criticism of the Neo-Ricardian 'solution' of the so-called transformation problem (transformation of values into prices), advanced by Von Bortkiewicz and Sraffa, can be found in David Yaffe, 'Value and Price in Marx's Capital', *Revolutionary Communist*, No. 1, January 1975.

unproductively consumed by the capitalists, 3,000 represent the interest received by an idle capital of 60,000 as its share of the total surplus-value. [28] Now if these 60,000 are gradually invested in Department III so that they themselves receive the average profit of 33% (i.e., set so many workers in motion that the mass of surplus-value is increased by 20,000 units) there has been an obvious *economic expansion* as far as the capitalist class is concerned. The total capital invested has increased; the volume of commodity production and its value have increased; the mass of surplus-value produced has grown; employment has risen; and the national income is higher than before.

So long as there are unused reserves available in the economy — and this is the starting point of the 'permanent arms industry' — no particular problems are created by the specific use value of the additional 80,000 units of value (in other words, by the fact that the goods produced in Department III neither enter into the reconstruction and expansion of constant capital nor serve to reconstitute and expand living labour-power). There is then nothing inevitable about the equation $Ic + Iv + Is = Ic + IIc + IIIc + \triangle c$ $(I + II + III)$, for the additional capital used in Department III need not necessarily employ *newly created* means of production. It may simply absorb already existent production capacities not fully utilized (or lay claim to newly created means of production while allowing the ongoing output of means of production for Department II to proceed through a fuller utilization of existing production capacities or the absorption of existing stocks of raw materials). Thus a second production cycle:

$$\text{I: } 120,000c + 50,000v + 50,000s = 220,000 \quad \text{I}$$
$$\text{II: } 80,000c + 50,000v + 50,000s = 180,000 \quad \text{II}$$
$$\text{III: } 45,000c + 15,000v + 15,000s = 75,000 \quad \text{III}$$

is throughly possible and could even develop into a third production cycle:

$$\text{I: } 126,000c + 51,500v + 51,500s = 229,000 \quad \text{I}$$
$$\text{II: } 84,000c + 51,500v + 51,500s = 187,000 \quad \text{II}$$
$$\text{III: } 50,000c + 18,000v + 18,000s = 86,000 \quad \text{III}$$

without any need to replace the total value of the expended constant

[28] We cannot here study the question why the owners of productive capital can be forced to relinquish part of the surplus-value in their possession to the owners of idle capital. It is bound up with the complex nature of the division of labour within the capitalist class and the long term structural advantages derived by productive capital

capital (245,000 units of value in the second cycle, and 260,000 in the third cycle), plus the values needed for the accumulation of constant capital, exclusively out of the ongoing output of constant capital (220,000 in the second cycle, and 229,000 in the third cycle).

Equally little does the accumulation of capital have to be fully guaranteed by the ongoing production and realization of surplus-value, for the whole process of accelerated expansion has been due to the valorization of money capital already available but not previously valorized. If all surplus capital is switched into the prodution of Department III gradually rather than suddenly, it is possible for an acceleration of capital accumulation to take place which goes beyond the ongoing production and realization of surplus-value, until finally the entire surplus capital has been drawn into the process of valorization. This means that the total value of the constant capital currently consumed can partially be made good by the surplus capitals drawn into circulation and production once more, just as part of the machines and raw materials additionally used does not stem from current production but from unused stocks left over from a previous plan. The total commodity value is certainly realized, however, and no owner of commodities sells his goods below their value. As soon as the fiction is abandoned that there is only a single capitalist firm in each of the three Departments, and as soon as we imagine, for example, productions starting up again in previously existing factories that have temporarily been laid idle, then such a re-entry of surplus capitals into operation creates no theoretical problems for the logic of the reproduction scheme.

The surplus capital will only be invested productively once again if it is guaranteed a 'profitable' sale. The additional demand is initially engendered by the State, partly through taxes and partly through loans. Kozlik is right on this point.[29] Inflation, in so far as it leads to an extension of commodity production and the income generated by it, is in fact able to stimulate genuine capitalist economic growth (as long as sufficient reserves of machinery, raw materials and labour-power are available). Kozlik is thus, of course, wrong when he speaks of the 'destruction' or 'pulverization' of capital by the arms economy. For capital previously lying idle and now used

---

from it. Let us assume, for the sake of simplicity, that productive capitalists pay interest to idle capital because they treat it as a social reserve fund, which they can and must resort to in time of need.

[29] Adolf Kozlik, *Der Vergeudungskapitalismus*, pp. 339-40.

to create surplus-value, far from being 'destroyed', has thus been valorized.

There is equally little foundation for Heininger's assertion that 'not only Marxist, but recently also a growing number of bourgeois economists and politicians have demonstrated that the arms race does not promote economic growth but ultimately to a large extent undermines it.'[30] This notion does not even confront the *central* problem of surplus capital at all.[31]

When the available reserves of machinery, raw materials and labour-power have all been absorbed into the process of production, however, the fundamental difficulty of valorization of capital comes to the fore once again. For those formulae for proportionality now regain their validity, which start from the assumption that each Department can buy commodities from the others only to the value of the commodities which it has itself sold to the latter. The value of the commodities produced in Department III must now therefore be financed fully out of deductions from the total social surplus-value and the total social wage. If we suppose for the sake of simplicity, that the State imposes the same tax rate x (about 25%) on both wages and surplus-value, we obtain the following formula:

$III = Ivx + Isx + IIvx + IIsx + IIIvx + IIIsx$ We can also write the value of III out in full:

$IIIc + IIIv + IIIs = Ivx + Isx + IIvx + IIsx + IIIvx + IIIsx$, which gives us:

$IIIc + III v (1 - x) + IIIs (1 - x) = Ivx + Isx + II vx + IIsx$, or, if $x = 25\%$ $IIIc + 75\%$ of $IIIv + 75\%$ of $IIIs = 25\%$ of $Iv + 25\%$ of $Is + 25\%$ of $IIv + 25\%$ of IIs.

In other words: for the system to be in equilibrium, the volume of permanent arms production must be such that the sum of the value of the constant capital expended in the armaments sector, plus the net wages of the workers employed in this Department, plus the net profit of the arms manufacturers, is neither above nor below the taxes imposed on the incomes of the workers and the capitalists in the other two Departments. The classical equation for proportionality between the two Departments alone is thus altered as follows:

[30] Heininger, *Zur Theorie des staatsmonopolistischen Kapitalismus*, p. 107.
[31] Obviously this volte-face on the part of the official ideologues of the CP after the end of the 'Cold War' was *ideological* and not theoretical. Their objective is now to prove that disarmament is possible in monopoly capitalism, since such disarmament is desired by Soviet diplomacy.

$Ic + Iv + Is = Ic + IIc + IIIc + Is \ (1-x) \ \beta + IIs \ (1-x) \ \beta + IIIs \ (1-x) \ \beta,$
which gives us:
$Iv + Isx + Is \ (1-x) \ a, \ \gamma = IIc + IIIc + IIs \ (1-x) \ \beta + IIIs \ (1-x) \ \beta.$

This means that the gross wages of the workers employed in Department I plus the total surplus-value, not invested in new constant capital, created in this Department (including taxes, hence the gross surplus-value) must be equal to the demand for new means of production generated in the other two Departments. Since this demand derives both from Department II and Department III, this equation does in fact apply to gross wages and gross surplus-value, as opposed to net wages and net surplus-value (with the exception of the surplus value accumulated in c) which must be exchanged solely with the commodities from Department II and not with those from Department III.

The fact that increasing technical progress, growing organic composition of capital and a rising rate of surplus-value must destroy these conditions of equilibrium just as they do in a system consisting of two Departments is dictated by the inner logic of the system, as we have already shown in the first part of this chapter. The taxes imposed on wages and surplus-value are after all epiphenomena which presuppose that surplus-value has been fully realized and wages have been wholly paid — in other words, proportionate production in Departments I and II, with no unsaleable commodities left over. There is now even the additional difficulty of maintaining the exact proportionality between Department III on the one hand and Departments I and II on the other. Naturally this does not mean that permanent arms production will affect the economic cycle only as long as there is excess capital, idle instruments of labour and unemployed labour-power. Even after full employment has been achieved it can have a significant influence in a so-called war economy, when the change of proportions between the three Departments fails to ensure adequate material elements of extended reproduction and there may be a cycle of regressive reproduction, and in 'normal' peacetime conditions, when a permanent arms budget alters the relation between the overall social wage and the overall social surplus-value — by leading to a rise in the social rate of surplus-value. It is certainly possible for this to occur with rising employment and a growing sum of wages (not only gross sum of wages but also net sum), as can be seen from the following numerical examples:

First Cycle (gross income of the social classes):

$$I: 120,000c + 48,500v + 48,500s$$
$$II: \ \ 80,000c + 48,500v + 48,500s$$
$$III: \ \ 10,000c + \ \ 3,000v + \ \ 3,000s$$
$$\overline{\ \ \ \ 100,000 \ \ \ \ \ \ 100,000 \ \ \ }$$

The purchase of arms output to the total value of 16,000 units of value is financed by taxation, which takes 10% of the workers' income and 6% of surplus-value (the capitalists' income). The final picture of the first production cycle then looks like this:

First Cycle (net income of the social classes):

I: $120,000c + 43,650$ net $v + 45,590$ net $s + 7,760$ taxes for the purchase of III

II: $\ \ 80,000c + 43,650$ net $v + 45,590$ net $s + 7,760$ taxes for the purchase of III

III: $\ \ 10,000c + \ \ 2,700$ net $v + \ \ 2,820$ net $s + \ \ \ \ 480$ taxes for the purchase of III

$$\overline{\ \ 90,000 \ \ } \qquad \overline{\ \ 94,000 \ \ } \qquad \overline{\ \ 16,000 \ \ }$$

Second Cycle (gross income of the social classes):

$$I: 123,000c + 50,000v + 50,000s$$
$$II: \ \ 82,000c + 50,000v + 50,000s$$
$$III: \ \ 12,000c + \ \ 4,000v + \ \ 4,000s$$
$$\overline{\ \ \ \ 104,000 \ \ \ \ \ \ 104,000 \ \ \ }$$

The purchase of arms output to the total value of 20,000 units of value is financed by taxation, which takes 12% of the workers' income and only 7% of the capitalists' income. The final picture of the distribution of value and income thus has the following form in the second cycle:

Second Cycle (net income of the social classes):

I: $123,000c + 44,000$ net $v + 46,400$ net $s + 9,600$ taxes for the purchase of III

II: $82,000c + 44,000$ net $v + 46,400$ net $s + 9,600$ taxes for the
purchase of III
III: $12,000c + 3,500$ net $v + 3,700$ net $s + 800$ taxes for the
purchase of III

| 91,500 | 96,500 | 20,000 |

The gross sum of wages has risen by 4,000 units of value from one cycle to the next. The net sum of wages has risen by 2,500 units of value. Yet the social rate of surplus value has increased from 104.4% to 105.5%.

Permanent military expenditure also means a redistribution of profits towards the armaments companies, which are mostly, if not exclusively, companies in Department I, and at the expense of the companies in Department II. If we assume that all the companies engaged in the production of Department III can be reduced to those of Department I, the net surplus-value achieved by the latter in the first cycle (48,410 units of value) nearly equals the gross surplus-value of Department I, and in the second cycle (50,100 units of value) surpasses the gross surplus-value of Department I in the first and the second cycle.[32] From the second cycle onwards, therefore, the *capitalist* costs of armaments are met exclusively by the capitalists of Department II, while the arms costs paid by the working class are equivalent to an increase in surplus-value. Hence the capitalists of Department I make a double profit out of armaments — at the expense of the working class and at the expense of the capitalists of Department II.

We thus see how right Rosa Luxemburg was to write in the following passage: 'What would normally have been hoarded by the peasants and the lower middle classes until it has grown big enough to invest in savings banks and other banks, is now set free to constitute an effective demand and an opportunity for investment. Further the multitude of individual and insignificant demands for a whole range

[32]The extent to which this is a realistic assumption can be seen from the fact that according to official US sources the total deliveries to the Defence Department in the budget year 1958-59, which amounted to $ 22.7 billion, comprised only $ 2 billion of light industrial goods (including agricultural goods!) and $1.8 billion from the services sector, while all the rest came from firms in Department 1 (US Congress, *Background Material on Economic Aspects of Military Procurement and Supply*). According to the OECD study *Government and Technical Innovation* (p. 27) the 'government market' in the USA at the end of the 50's was the sole purchaser for 9/10 of the 'final demand' of the aviation industry, 3/5 of the non-ferrous metal industry, more than 50% of the electronic and chemical industry, and more than 35% of the industry for telecommunications and scientific apparatus.

of commodities, which will become effective at different times and which might often be met just as well by a comprehensive and homogeneous demand of the state. And the satisfaction of this demand presupposes a big industry of the highest order. It requires the most favourable conditions for the production of surplus-value and for accumulation. In the form of government contracts for army supplies the scattered purchasing power of the consumers is concentrated in large quantities and, free of the vagaries and subjective fluctuations of personal consumption, it achieves an almost automatic regularity and rhythmic growth. Capital itself ultimately controls this automatic and rhythmic movement of militarist production through the legislature and a press whose function is to mould so-called "public opinion". That is why this particular province of capitalist accumulation at first seems capable of infinite expansion. All other attempts to expand markets and set up operational bases for capital largely depend on historical, social and political factors beyond the control of capital, whereas production for militarism represents a province whose regular and progressive expansion seems primarily determined by capital itself.'[33]

IV. THE ARMS ECONOMY AND THE
LONG-TERM CHANCES OF GROWTH IN LATE CAPITALISM

The preceding analysis provides a partial explanation of the reasons why, in the whole post-war epoch since 1945, permanent arms production has not only been one of the most important

[33]Rosa Luxemburg, *The Accumulation of Capital*, pp. 465-6. Paul Mattick wavers to and fro between different interpretations. At one point he claims that 'production promoted by the state' (including arms production) merely increases consumption and not accumulation of capital (*Marx and Keynes*, pp. 117-18). Elsewhere, however, he states that war production is not simply 'squandered production', but helps to step up the process of accumulation again. (Ibid., pp. 137-8). In his criticism of Baran and Sweezy's *Monopoly Capital*, Mattick is even clearer: 'What is the real function of the State, when it combines labour and unused resources for the production of non-marketable (?) goods? Taxes are part of revenue realized as a result of market transactions. When these are deducted from capital, they depress profits, regardless of whether these profits would have been consumed or invested as additional capital. If used in neither of these ways, unemployed capital would still have existed in monetary form as private hoarding. As such, it cannot contribute to the development of capitalism. But nor can it do so when the State uses it to finance unprofitable output of public works and public waste. Instead of a monetary hoard that is senseless for capitalism, there appears a production of goods and services that is senseless for capi-

solutions to the problem of surplus capital, but has also and above all, been a powerful spur to the acceleration of technological innovation.[34] The arms race with a complex of non-capitalist states played an important role in this stimulus. But the question now arises whether a permanent arms industry can *in the long run* neutralize the tendencies of the capitalist mode of production towards crisis and collapse, and ensure it a relatively high degree of growth.

The first political economists basing themselves on Marx to give a positive answer to this question were Natalie Moszkowska (1943) and Walter J. Oakes (1944). Under the name of T.N. Vance, the latter subsequently dealt with this theme systematically and coined the concept of 'permanent war economy' — although the term was characteristically first used by the chief of General Motors and subsequent Secretary for Defence, Charles E. Wilson, in January 1944.

Moszkowska's argument runs as follows: 'The capacity of civilian industry and consumer goods production to expand depends on the standard of living of the population. If this is restricted, there will be similar limits on the producer and consumer goods industry. The possibilities of investing capital profitably in civilian industry thus become narrowly confined. Capital grows much more rapidly than its opportunities for valorization. The smaller volume of capital seeks for fields of activity which do not depend on the inadequate purchasing power of the masses; it desires spheres of production with unlimited possibilities for investment. Such a sphere, dreamt of by capital, emerges in the war industry. Since the production of consumer goods cannot develop adequately because of the restrictions on the purchasing power of the masses, capital must increasingly — even if it were otherwise pacific — transfer itself to the

---

talism. But there remains a difference: in the absence of taxation, capital would possess a monetary hoard, which as a result of taxation is expropriated from it.' (In Hermanin, Monte and Rolshausen (ed.), *Monopolkapital — Thesen zu dem Buch von Paul Baran and Paul Sweezy*, Frankfurt, 1969, pp. 54-5. Mattick fails to understand that his 'expropriated monetary hoard' has been replaced by arms *production*, which is commodity production absorbing *additional surplus labour and thereby creating additional surplus-value* — extracted from a labour-power which otherwise would not have yielded an atom of surplus-value. This is increased valorization of capital, leading to increased accumulation of capital, and therefore in no way 'senseless' from the point of view of capitalism, so long as surplus capital exists — in other words, so long as capital invested in arms production is not withdrawn from capital productively applied in Departments I and II.

[34] Tsuru, op. cit., p. 33; James O'Connor, *The Fiscal Crisis of the State*, New York, 1973, p. 113.

production of murderous weapons. In the circumstances, there is no other field in which it can invest. If ascendant capitalism developed the producer and consumer goods industries, declining capitalism is inevitably forced to develop first and foremost the arms industry. The development of civilian industry is increasingly cramped by the absence of monetarily effective demand and by stagnant sales. The development of the war industry knows no such restrictions. Based on the presupposition of war, the armaments industry can develop at a totally different rate and with an impetus never previously known or even suspected.'[35] Moszkowska goes on: 'The invasion of capitalism into the non-capitalist sphere, like the industrial application of technical inventions, can only retard the crisis. Once it has occurred, even more acute crises than hitherto may be expected. This is not so, however, when arms production lays claim to over-accumulated capital. Capital is there absorbed without any need to augment the capacity of civilian output in either the producer or consumer goods industry, or to increase social purchasing power. For there is neither demand nor supply on the market for products of the armaments industry. The arms industry does not supply the market nor depend on its capacity to absorb its goods. The state here both provides orders and takes delivery . . . . The expansion of the arms industry does not, however, abolish the dangers inherent in the capitalist economy. The danger of an explosion in the form of a crisis is replaced by the danger of an explosion in the form of a war'.[36] Moszkowska, in effect, sees only two limits to the growth of late capitalism under the stimulus of the permanent arms economy: the absolute immiseration of the population (i.e., the limit of regressive reproduction, at which the excessive fall in the production of Department II makes the physiological reconstitution of labour-power impossible and hence provokes a precipitous fall in the productivity and intensity of labour in Department III) and the more or less inevitable tendency for an arms economy to unleash actual imperialist wars.

For Vance the permanent arms economy represents above all a mechanism for achieving a higher level of employment. Growing capital accumulation, instead of leading to increasing unemployment, in this way determines a falling standard of living.[37] The

[35] Natalie Moszkowska, *Zur Dynamik des Spätkapitalismus*, p. 117-18.
[36] Ibid., pp. 179-80.
[37] Vance was clearly mistaken on this point, as also in his assumption of a permanent structural decline in private capital exports. See *Permanent War Economy*, p. 12.

permanent arms economy can also temporarily arrest the growth of the organic composition of capital, although not in the long-run.[38] The growth of the organic composition of capital and the corresponding tendency for the average rate of profit to fall remains, in Vance's view, the 'Damocles Sword' which hangs over the permanent war economy.

Vance is thus more cautious than Moszkowska, but they make one fundamental mistake in common: they both isolate Department III from its effects on Departments I and II and are hence incapable of analysing the long-term effects of a 'permanent arms economy' on the late capitalist *economy as a whole*. Leaving aside the marginal case of regressive reproduction (a war economy in its final phase) it is simply not true that a 'permanent arms economy' can develop without limit. In a capitalist mode of production the arms economy too is only a means to an end, and not an end in itself. For the capitalists the end remains the realization of profit, the accumulation of capital *for the purpose of profit* and not simply from a mythical delight in accumulation for the sake of accumulation. The more the development of the arms economy threatens to reduce the gross profit of the major corporations (in other words, the higher tax rate it determines), the stronger will be the resistance of these companies to any further extension of it.[39] In any event, since an expanding arms economy determines a redistribution of surplus-value towards a small number of companies at the expense of an increasing number of other capitalists, the further growth of Department III (and with it, the further growth of tax rates beyond a certain ceiling) would completely eclipse the profit of many capitalists and threaten a substantial section of their class with bankruptcy. Any growth of the arms economy beyond a certain point must therefore enormously intensify the political and social tensions and struggles within the capitalist class, just as it must intensify the conflict between capital and labour in 'market' conditions of relatively high employment which are precisely not disadvantageous to the working class. It is therefore safe to conclude that—with the exception of overt war

[38] Ibid., p. 32.
[39] No lesser man than the one-time Commander-in-Chief of US troops in the Pacific and the Korean War, General Douglas MacArthur, when he subsequently became a director of the Remington Rand company, complained in a speech to the share-holders of the Sperry Rand Corporation in 1957 that the only aim of the 'permanent anxiety psychosis' which the US Government had created in the American population was to demand 'excessive defence outlays' which imposed intolerable tax burdens on corporations.

and fascism — the extension of a permanent arms economy is necessarily beset by objective, internal social limits.

We can eliminate Moszkowska's and Vance's hypothesis that *growing* employment is combined with a *falling* standard of living in the 'permanent arms economy' — a hypothesis which runs completely counter to the logic of capitalism and its transformation of labour-power into a commodity whose price is influenced by market conditions, and which is not even confirmed by developments in the Third Reich. Both writers clearly confuse here a growing *rate of surplus-value* with falling *real wages*.[40] Once this hypothesis is dismissed, the automatic result is that an 'arms cycle' which temporarily limits the cyclical fluctuations of capitalism must also have a stimulating effect on capital accumulation in Departments II and I, which will then however more or less inevitably reproduce the classical features of every capitalist boom: over-accumulation, a falling rate of profit, a declining utilization of capacity and so on. In Chapter 13, we will explain how permanent inflation represents a response of late capitalism to these problems, how arms expenditure is however responsible only for part (and moreover a declining part) of the inflationary creation of money, and how in the long-run inflation inexorably hastens towards a catastrophe which no arms economy can halt.

In contrast to Vance we are of the opinion that historically the permanent arms economy *speeds up* rather than *brakes* intensive technological innovation, and hence the growth of the organic composition of capital (Vance elsewhere says the opposite, when he mistakenly confuses a war economy with an arms economy).[41] It is equally inevitable that this technological innovation will spread from Department III to Departments I and II with all the corresponding consequences.[42] It is likewise inevitable that in the sphere

[40] We have shown the steep increase in the rate of surplus-value in the Third Reich in Chapter 5. But the decline of unemployment in Germany led to an increase in nominal hourly wages of approximately 25% between 1933 and 1942, for the most part wiped out by the increase in the cost of living, the deterioration in the quality of consumer goods, increased wage deductions and so on. Bettelheim, *L'Economie Allemande sous le Nazisme*, pp. 210, 222-4.

[41] Vance, *The Permanent War Economy*, p. 32.

[42] 'Arms contracts in the first instance constitute an incentive for additional investments; but in view of the constant growth of productivity there must be a constant increase in outlays in order to ensure a given degree of utilization of new plant and even the mere stabilization of military outlays threatens to lead to overcapacity.' Theodor Prager, *Wirtschaftswunder oder keines?*, p. 133.

of the arms economy itself there will be a marked shift, precisely as the growth of arms expenditure slows down, from the purchase of materials and payment of salaries to outlays for research and development, which will substantially reduce the 'crisis-dampening' role of the arms economy in the overall economy of late capitalism. For the decelerated growth of this expenditure determines a quest for 'increasing (destruction) returns' on each additional outlay.[43] Heininger provides some interesting evidence in this respect:[44]

Military Expenditure in the USA (Without the Expenditure of Space Authority)		Share of the Expenditure Devoted to Military Research
1939/40	1.5 billion dollars	0.2%
1944/45	81.2 billion dollars	1.7%
1952/53	50.4 billion dollars	5.5%
1957/58	44.2 billion dollars	10.2%
1960/61	47.5 billion dollars	16.2%
1962/63	53.0 billion dollars	16.0%
1963/64	55.4 billion dollars	16.6% (22.4% including space research; the analogous percentage for 1960/61 would then be 17.6%)

The following two sets of figures are even more revealing:

Share of Arms Purchases in the Proceeds from the Sales of the Durable Goods Industry in the USA:

1955: 9%   1958: 9.1%   1960: 7.6%   1961: 7.8%   1962: 7.8%

Share of Arms Consumption in the Total Consumption of the USA

	1948	1952	1954	1955	1959	1960	1962
Steel:	?	?	9.7%	3.0%	1.8%	1.2%	1.5%
Copper:	?	17.8%	6.5%	2.3%	1.9%	?	?
Aluminium:	6%	30.0%	?	14.5%	13.6%	9.8%	43.0%

Kidron likewise finds, correctly, that: 'The existence of a ceiling

[43]See in this connection Malcolm W. Hoag's study for the Rand Corporation, 'Increasing Returns in Military Production Functions', in Roland N. McKean (ed.), *Issues in Defence Economics*, New York, 1967.
[44]*Zur Theorie des staatsmonopolistischen Kapitalismus*, pp. 139, 143-4.

on military outlay is important for another reason. It provides a massive incentive to increases in productivity (measured in potential deaths per dollar) and so leads to the arms industries becoming increasingly specialist and divorced from general engineering practice. . .Coupled with this specialization[45] and partly as a consequence, go a rising capital—and technological—intensity in the arms industries. On both counts they become less able to underpin full employment even at the same level of relative expenditure. At a declining one, and given the existence of some technological spin-off to civilian productivity, which makes the need more exacting, their potency as an offset becomes increasingly questionable.'[46]

We can thus draw the conclusion that in the long-run the 'permanent arms economy' cannot resolve any of the basic contradictions of the capitalist mode of production and cannot eliminate any of the pressure towards crisis inherent in it. Even its *temporary* buffering of these contradictions and pressures towards crisis only occurs at the expense of their transfer from one sphere into another—above all, from that of actual overproduction to that of inflation and overcapacity. In the long-run this transfer, too, becomes increasingly less successful, as we shall demonstrate in our chapter on permanent inflation. The 'permanent arms economy' contributed substantially to the accelerated accumulation of capital in the 'long wave' of 1945-65; but it was not the basic determinant of this wave.

Naturally, it is necessary not to go from one extreme to the other, and to underestimate the effects of a 'permanent arms sector' on the late capitalist economy. It is certainly not a *deus ex machina* in any way capable of achieving a qualitative change in the mechanisms of the capitalist mode of production. Its specific effects on the economy certainly resolve themselves ultimately into all the general features characteristic of late capitalism: the struggle to increase the rate of surplus-value, to cheapen the cost of constant capital, to reduce the turnover-time of capital, and to achieve the valorization of surplus capital. For in the end capital has no other ways of escaping its fate—the falling rate of profit. It is, however, un-

---

[45] Murray Weidenbaum states that 90% of military goods comprise specific products manufactured in specially constructed factories. 'Friedliche Nützung der Rüstungs-industrie', in *Atomzeitalter*, No. 5, 1964, p. 133.

[46] M. Kidron, *Western Capitalism Since the War*, p. 55. Baran and Sweezy (op. cit., pp. 214-15) earlier made the same comment.

doubtedly true that both for the reasons described by Luxemburg, and because arms production creates use values which do not reduce or threaten the market of any of the commodities produced by Departments I and II[47] (even ensuring a long-term sales expansion for some of them), big capital shows a particular predilection and preference for *this* form of state expenditure as compared to all others, especially so-called 'social' expenditure, which would lead sooner or later to an increase in the value of the commodity of labour-power.[48] Perroux makes some very apt comments in this respect on the specifically economic side of the production of Department III: 'The additional demand for armaments cannot be assimilated to an additional demand for investment goods. An additional demand for investment goods in a normal industrial economy engenders, if stocks are maintained at commercially optimum levels, supplementary products for the market or for the production of real capital goods. In the case of armaments, a greater portion of the additional production is stocked by virtue of the nature of the goods. Atomic bombs, artillery, munitions and equipment for troops do not come on to the market. . . . Apart from its effect on the consumer goods sector, the price level of armaments is not integrated into the forces restoring equilibrium on the market.'[49]

This in turn raises complex problems concerning the formation of prices in Department III, in other words, the equalization of the rate of profit (or of the monopoly rate of surplus-profit) between armaments companies and other monopolies.[50]

[47] Vilmar (op. cit., pp. 193-206)discusses the debates of the early 60's over the problems of possible reconversion of the armaments industry into 'peaceful' industry. He contrasts the optimistic and partially apologetic views of such writers as Baade with the more cautious utterances of Leontief. The real problem centres on the *shift of purchasing power* involved in any such reconversion: what type of shift is compatible with maintaining a high rate of surplus-value, without which capitalist investment activity and the level of employment dependent on it would immediately plummet? Seymour Melman therefore proposes the retention of the 'State' as customer and the electronics industry as producer, and the conversion of production to such apparatuses as would have practically *no* effect on the value of the commodity of labour-power: traffic control devices, electronic learning machines, medical equipment. Other projects speak of automatic systems for refuse disposal and for control of air and water pollution.

[48] Tsuru, op. cit., p. 39; Vilmar, op. cit., pp. 60f., 209-16, and many others.

[49] François Perroux, *La Coexistence Pacifique*, III, p. 500.

[50] See in this connection Oliver R. Williamson, 'The Economics of Defence Contracting: Incentives and Performances', in Roland N. McKean (ed.), *Issues in Defence Economics*; Merton J. Peck and Frederick M. Scherer, *The Weapons Acquisition Process: An Economic Analysis*, Boston, 1962, etc.

It is clear, in any case, how closely foreign and domestic policy, social and economic forces, mesh to generate the rise of the 'permanent arms economy'. This interlocking process makes attempts to prove that political and not economic elements were decisive in this development, somewhat questionable. An example of the interdependence of the two is, of course, the 'military-industrial complex' —the intimate fusion of arms companies, military commanders and bourgeois politicians.[51] Vilmar is then right to stress that it is 'not simply the particular profit interests of the armament industries but the imperialist and expansionary tendencies (and subsequently cyclical interests) of late capitalism as such which are responsible for the enormous growth of the arms economy.'[52] The growth of the 'permanent arms economy' after the Second World War also performed, among other things, the very concrete function of protecting the vast foreign capital investments of the US, of safeguarding the 'free world' for 'free capital investments' and 'free repatriation of profits', and of guaranteeing US monopoly capital 'free' access to a series of vital raw materials. In 1957, the chairman of the board of Texaco frankly stated that in his view the primary task of the American government was to create 'a political and financial climate both here and abroad . . . conducive to overseas investment'![53] Vilmar is likewise right to emphasize that the armaments companies have played a particularly active role in this whole process.

The growing significance of the arms traffic in world trade must also not be underestimated—a business which, incidentally, shows how nonsensical it is not to treat the production of weapons as commodity production and not to see the investments in this sector as accumulation of capital. In 1955 arms exports on the world market

[51] The term was initially coined by President Eisenhower in his valedictory speech to the American nation (17 January 1961). There has since been a vigorous growth in the literature on the 'military-industrial complex': for example, Cook's *The Warfare State*, which we have already cited on several occasions, and Galbraith's *How to Control the Military*. The US Senator Proxmire has likewise devoted a book to the subject: *Report from Wasteland*, New York, 1970. See also Seymour Melman, *Pentagon Capitalism*, New York, 1970, and R. Kaufman, *The War Profiteers*, Indianapolis. From 1959 to 1969, the number of former senior officers (with a rank of colonel or above) working for the 43 corporations which receive the main defense contracts, increased from 721 to 2072.

[52] Vilmar, *Rüstung und Abrüstung im Spätkapitalismus*, p. 47.

[53] This and many other similar quotations may be found in Richard Barnet, *Roots of War*, Baltimore, 1973, p. 200ff.

totalled approximately 2.2 billion dollars. In 1962-68 the average was already 5.8 billion dollars, of which the Soviet Union was responsible for 2 billion.[54]

The whole phenomenon of the permanent arms economy vividly highlights, of course, the parasitic nature of monopoly capitalism, already exposed over half a century ago by Lenin in his analysis of imperialism. For how else can one regard a system which for 25 years has constantly squandered such a substantial part of its available economic resources on the production of means of destruction?

[54] These estimates are taken from the *Stockholm International Peace Research Institute*. The whole subject is surveyed in a work published by this institute: *The Arms Trade with the Third World*, Stockholm, 1971; in J. Stanley and M. Pearton, *The International Trade in Arms*, London, 1972; and Ulrich Albrecht, *Der Handel mit Waffen*, Munich, 1971.

10

The International Concentration and Centralization of Capital

Capital by its very nature tolerates no geographical limits to its expansion.[1] Its historical ascent led to the levelling of regional boundaries and the formation of large national markets, which laid the foundation for the creation of the modern nation state. Hardly had capital penetrated into the sphere of production, however, before its expansion brushed aside these national limits as well. It sought to create a genuine world market for all its commodities instead of only for the luxury goods which were traded internationally in the pre-capitalist age. The cheap mass production made possible by capitalist large industry was the most important weapon in this process, but it was not the only one. The State, as the servant of the bourgeoisie, had to use political and often military force to remove the obstacles which pre-capitalist classes and states represented to the unrestricted expansion of the capitalist export of commodities. Even the most 'liberal' and 'pure' bourgeois states of the age of freely competitive capitalism never dispensed with this use of coercion to capture international markets: it is enough to recall the examples of the Opium Wars conducted by British capitalism in China and the English campaigns of conquest and

[1] 'The world market itself forms the basis for this (capitalist—E.M.) mode of production. On the other hand, the immanent necessity of this mode of production to produce on an ever-enlarged scale tends to extend the world market continually, so that it is not commerce in this case which revolutionized industry, but industry which constantly revolutionizes commerce.' Karl Marx, *Capital*, Vol. 3, p. 328.

consolidation in India, the expansionary war of the USA in Mexico, France's war in Algeria, and so on.

The relation between the national and international expansion of capital thus determined a combined structure from the start, and this was reflected in the contradictory attitudes of the bourgeoisie when it came to the use of force on the international plane. In the final analysis, this relation was an expression of the law of uneven and combined development which, as explained in Chapter 2, is inherent in the capitalist mode of production. Capital innately tends to combine international expansion with the formation and consolidation of national markets. Depending on the development of productive forces and social conditions, therefore, world-wide capitalist relations of exchange bind together capitalist, semi-capitalist and pre-capitalist relations of production in an organic unity.[2]

In the imperialist, monopoly capitalist phase of development of the capitalist mode of production, a new dimension was added both to the relationship between national and international expansion and to the relationship between capitalist laws of development and the deliberate use of state coercion for economic purposes. The *concentration* of capital on a national level—accelerated by the second technological revolution and the consequent substantial increase in the accumulation of capital needed for effective competition in the growth sectors of that time—increasingly led to the *centralization* of capital. This meant a radical reduction in the number of 'different capitals' competing with one another, until entire branches of industry were dominated by a handful of trusts, companies and monopolies, and common price agreements altered the economic behaviour of these monopolies. The resultant tendency for competition and hence also the expansion of the home market to be narrowed down then tended to generate overcapitalization, increasing export of capital and a growing capitalist interest not only in *periodic* gunboat expeditions to ensure a free path for commodity exports, but *permanent* military occupation and control of new fields of investment for capital exports. The universal division of the world by the big imperialist powers, itself a result of the

[2] Marx explicitly points out that the expansion of the British capitalist cotton industry 'pushed on with tropical luxuriance' the mode of production based on the slave trade and slave labour in the Southern States of the USA: *Capital*, Vol. 1, p. 443. In this connection see also Eric Williams, *Capitalism and Slavery*, London, 1964, pp. 169-77, 186-91, 194-6.

contraction of capitalist competition on the domestic market, led to an intensification of international capitalist competition on the world market, to inter-imperialist rivalry and to the tendency for the world market to be redistributed periodically, including by means of armed force—in a word, by imperialist wars.[3]

With the outbreak of the general structural crisis of capitalism[4] in the 20th century, however, a vast zone was subtracted from the capitalist world market by the victory of the October Revolution in Russia. The secular tendency was thereafter towards a further restriction of the geographical sphere of capital accumulation, which had come to the end of its victorious march around the globe with the incorporation of China at the close of the 19th century. International competition now increasingly rebounded from foreign markets back into the home countries of imperialism. These now gradually started to change from subjects into objects of the international competition of capital, as became clear especially during and after the Second World War. Simultaneously the coercive power of the bourgeois State intervened ever more directly in the economy, both to ensure the smooth collection of monopoly surplus-profits abroad and to guarantee conditions for smooth capital accumulation at home. This step marked the beginning of the late capitalist era.[5]

The early capitalist era of free competition had been characterized by a relative international immobility of capital. Concentration of capital remained predominantly national; centralization exclusively so. Even in this phase the main tendency was, of course, crossed by a counter-tendency towards international movements of capital, borne above all by a few large financial groups and finding expression in the importance of international state loans. The growing international mobility of labour-power too, above all to the so-called white settler colonies, was accompanied by a certain

[3] It is interesting that Lenin, in his notes on Hilferding's *Finanzkapital*, criticizes the latter's definition of finance capital as bank capital dominating industry, and makes internal developments *within the sphere of production* the starting point for his own analysis: *Collected Works*, Vol. 39, p. 338.

[4] Eugen Varga was the first to employ the notion of the 'period of capitalist decline' in his book of the same name: *Der Niedergangsperiode des Kapitalismus*, Hamburg, 1922.

[5] For state guarantees of late capitalist — and especially monopoly — profits, see Ernest Mandel, *Marxist Economic Theory*, pp. 501-7.

degree of international capital mobility, particularly in North America. In the Mediterranean, not only did Britain, France and Belgium export commodities, but West European capital increasingly penetrated indirectly into Egypt and the Ottoman Empire by means of state debts, thus laying the foundations for later imperialist capital investments in these countries.[6] But on the whole this international mobility of capital remained small in scale, above all because there were not as yet any critical limits to the expansion of capital accumulation on the home market, and in the pre-imperialist era the security of domestic capital investments was so much greater than that of investments abroad that any differences in the rate of profit overseas were more than cancelled out by the surrounding conditions of uncertainty.

In the classical era of imperialism the concentration of capital became increasingly international in character. Capital investments in colonial and semi-colonial countries became an important part of the accumulation process and there was a steady growth in the contributions made by colonial surplus-profits. The international mobility of capital forged ahead with giant strides, for the classical bourgeois state had already become a restriction on the growth of the forces of production. The difficulties of further expanding domestic markets because of monopolization of the major internal sales-fields, especially in heavy industry, increasingly forced capital accumulation to take an international course. But the classical era of imperialism was marked by an intensified competitive struggle between the big imperialist powers, in which military and political control over geographical zones (home market plus colonies) provided the basis for the defence or expansion of their share of the world market.[7] Precisely for this reason, the *international concentration* of capital did not mainly take the form of an *international centralization* of capital, but pitted national imperialist monopolies against each other as antagonists on the international market for

---

[6] For Egypt, see among others David Landes, *Bankers and Pashas*, London, 1958, and for Turkey, Bernard Lewis, *The Emergence of Modern Turkey*, Oxford, 1968, p. 452f.

[7] 'The causes of capitalist expansion lie both in the condition of buying as well as in the process of production itself, and finally in the conditions of selling. Three problems are generally related to that: the problem of the raw material markets and labour-power; the problem of new spheres for capital investment; lastly the problem of the market.' Bukharin, *Imperialism and the Accumulation of Capital*, p. 256.

commodities, raw materials and capital. Only very rarely was there any actual international fusion of capital.[8] *Classical monopoly merged on a national level while on the international level it was content with temporary agreements* (international cartels, and so on). National centralization was promoted and accelerated by crises and recessions, which mercilessly eliminated weaker companies, while state intervention was used increasingly to guarantee the surplus-profits of the monopolies. By contrast, international agreements periodically broke down, because they were unable in the long-run to withstand international crises, recessions and wars, or alternations in the relationship of inter-capitalist forces determined by the law of uneven development.[9] This does not mean that before the Second World War, there were no multinational corporations in the sense of monopolies an important part of whose commodity production was situated outside their home country. Imperialist concerns monopolizing raw materials were nearly all in this category. It is interesting to note that even such monopolies which did assure a large part of their output in the imperialist metropolis itself — like the Rockefeller group in the US oil industry — developed very early in the 20th century a strategy of control over foreign production sites rather than of foreign markets. This whole process occurred, however, in the framework of international concentration and national centralization of capital, without significant international interpenetration of capital, and without seriously affecting the manufacturing sector proper. From a purely quantitative point of view, furthermore, the weight of multinational corporations in the capital export process was marginal. In 1914, nearly 90% of all international capital movements took the form of portfolio investment, while today 75% of this flow is constituted by the direct investment of multinational corporations.[10]

Between 1890 and 1940 there were, of course, some exceptions to this main tendency. The two big Anglo-Dutch companies, Royal Dutch Shell and Unilever, were the outcome of an international

[8] When Bukharin first raised the problem of the centralization of capital he failed to make the fundamental distinction between national and international centralization (*Imperialism and World Economy*, pp. 41-5, 53-60). He became clearer on this point later, however.

[9] Cf. N. Bukharin, *Imperialism and World Economy*, p. 60. E. Varga and L. Mendelsohn (eds.), *New Data for Lenin's 'Imperialism'*, New York, 1940, p. 167.

[10] Raymond Vernon, *Sovereignty at Bay*, London, 1971, pp. 37, 40-1; Christopher Tugendhat, *The Multinationals*, London, 1973, p. 38.

fusion of capital. Major Swiss companies such as Hoffmann-La Roche and Nestles produced far more beyond their borders. The Swedish Kreuger company belonged to the same category before its collapse. Belgian and French capital had already co-operated before the First World War in the construction of the Russian iron industry, and in some spheres this cooperation was continued on a larger scale after the First World War as well. These exceptions, however, characteristically involved 1) countries of small specific weight but relatively substantial capital wealth, which were increasingly incapable of pursuing an *independent* imperialist world policy, although at the same time they needed to increase their international investments because of their relative excess capital (Holland, Belgium, to some extent Switzerland and Sweden); 2) spheres which were not vital to the economic strength of the big imperialist powers. It is significant, for instance, that when the big chemical companies were formed in Great Britain and Germany — ICI and IG-Farben — the major foreign shareholders, who were in some cases far from unimportant (in the case of ICI, Solvay was even the largest single shareholder),[11] were excluded from the control of this big capital rather than included in the leadership of the company.

Although Bukharin is sometimes a little shaky on this question, he nonetheless on the whole correctly grasped that in the age of imperialism before the First World War (we would add: and between the two World Wars), the significance of 'international organizations' (international companies and cartels) was 'by no means as great as would appear at first glance'.[12] In his view the trend towards the internationalization of economic life was still over-trumped by the process of the nationalization of capital.[13] 'The "national economy" is transformed into a single, vast combined trust, in which the participants are the financial groups and

---

[11] George W. Stocking and Myron W. Watkins, *Cartels in Action*, New York, 1946, p. 431.

[12] N. Bukharin, *Imperialism and World Economy*, p. 60. Bukharin also cites a characteristic sentence from the classical work on the world economy by Sartorius von Waltershausen, *Das volkswirtschaftliche System der Kapitalanlage im Auslande*, Berlin, 1907, p. 100: 'It seems unlikely that international companies with centralized (*einheitlicher*) management of production will be created.' Bernard Harms, by contrast, correctly identified the beginnings of the internationalization of production in *Volkswirtschaft und Weltwirtschaft*, June 1912.

[13] N. Bukharin, *Imperialism and World Economy*, pp. 61, 53ff.

the state. Such formations we call state capitalist trusts.'[14] According to Bukharin, the chief characteristic of the (classical) imperialist
epoch was competition between these 'state capitalist trusts', and
not international fusion of capital.

The third technological revolution and the formation of the late
capitalism marked a crucial turning point in this respect: *the international concentration of capital henceforward started to develop
into international centralization. In late capitalism, the multinational
company becomes the determinant organizational form of big
capital.* The forces which have played an exceptional role in this
process, and help us to grasp the quantitative differences between
the development of companies in the late capitalist era and their
development in the age of classical imperialism, are the following:

1. The new development of the forces of production unleashed
by the third technological revolution has reached a point at which in
a growing number of spheres it is no longer possible to produce at
a profit on a national scale, not only because of the limits of the
domestic market but also because of the enormous volume of capital
needed for production. The space industry or the manufacture of
supersonic transport aircraft, and tomorrow most probably also the
'anti-pollution industry', are the classical *absolute* examples of this
process in Western Europe. The production of integrated circuits,
which although begun in many European countries, can now be
developed profitably only by a single producer for the whole of
Western Europe, is a *relative* example of the same tendency. But
there is evidence in many other areas as well that contemporary
forces of production are bursting through the framework of the
nation state, for the minimum threshhold of profitability for the
production of certain commodities involves output series commensurate with the markets of several countries.[15] For example, there
exists a single machine today which, with rational speed and loading,
can produce matches for ten million consumers; another which can
produce glass bulbs for electric lights for twenty-five million; a single
oil refinery which can cover the petrol consumption of more than

[14] Ibid., pp. 117-20. See also N. Bukharin, *Okonomik der Transformationsperiode*,
pp. 10-13.
[15] Brown furnishes the following interesting figures: a modern furnace can produce
enough iron for an industrial society with 1 million inhabitants; a modern steel mill
can produce enough for a similar society of 2-3 million inhabitants; a modern continuous rolling mill for a community of 20 million inhabitants; a modern rolling mill
for special products such as wide-band and magnetized plates, for even greater
populations: A. J. Brown, *Introduction to the World Economy*, London, 1965, p. 125.

fifteen million users, and so on.[16] For a country like Sweden, the internal market (domestic consumption) only allows for 30% of the minimal optimum capacity of one factory producing cigarettes, 50% of one factory producing refrigerators, and 70% of a brewery. Even in Canada, the domestic market is too small to permit the utilization of the minimal optimum capacity of a single plant producing refrigerators.[17] The internationalization of forces of production thus creates the substructure for the internationalization of capital. This is expressed, among other things, by the fact that an increasing portion of international trade movements in actual fact take place within the same international company (among other things, the export of car parts to be assembled elsewhere, spare parts, and so on). The structural pressure exerted by the growth of the forces of production puts the cost of many giant research projects beyond the financial means of medium-sized States, forcing them increasingly in the direction of international coordination, cooperation and division of labour in publicly-financed research. An additional stimulant to the creation of multinational corporations is the *compulsion towards vertical integration* that is one of the motive forces of the centralization of capital. Such a vertical integration, however, increasingly involves a combination of production sites situated in disparate countries, corresponding to the uneven development of raw material sources, technological innovation and capital accumulation across the world.

2. Advancing accumulation and concentration of capital in the age of monopoly capitalism puts ever more capital at the disposal of the big oligopolistic and monopolistic companies, through the surplus-profits which they realize. The consequences are self-financing and over-capitalization.[18] Since, however, it is typical of monopoly capital to eliminate price competition, growth of sales and output

---

[16] Ibid., p 126-7. This is true not only of actual production, but also of the sphere of transport. Thus the introduction on a mass scale of the container system on the North Atlantic route has been taken over by the *Atlantic Container Line*, which was formed by six European shipping companies from four different countries (Compagnie Generale Transatlantique, the Cunard Line, the Holland-America Line, the Transatlantic Steamship Company of Sweden, the Swedish American Line, and the Wallenius Shipping Company). None of the national shipping companies would have been able to sustain the costs and risks involved in this technological transformation on their own.

[17] Minimal optimum capacity is a level below which unit costs of production start to increase. See F. M. Scherer, 'The Determinants of Industrial Plant Sizes', *Review of Economics and Statistics*, May 1973, p. 141.

[18] E. Mandel, *Marxist Economic Theory*, pp. 511-21.

becomes increasingly limited at home. The result is in turn a compulsion for large companies to expand beyond the national market to secure outlets for their products. This expansion follows two paths: differentiation and combination of sectors on the home market [19] and specialization and differentiation of products on the world market. For reasons of long-term profit maximization (the advantages of big series, internal and external economies of scale, and market controls), it is the second of these tendencies which predominates, leading big companies to produce and sell on a worldwide scale. The chemical industry offers a good example. The large Swiss concern, Ciba (today Ciba-Geigy), penetrated photo-chemistry (among other things, by absorbing the British Ilford Company), and thence moved into the sphere of audio-visual equipment, printing and the production of instruments for military aerial photography. The large pharmaceutical companies have invaded the food industry (Bristol Myers), the area of cosmetics (Roche, Eli-Lilly, Roussel-Uclaf), and of hospital and medical equipment (Johnson and Johnson, Roche).[20]

3. In late capitalism surplus-profits predominantly take the form of technological surplus-profits (technological rents). The reduced turnover-time of fixed capital and the acceleration of technological innovation determine a pursuit for new products and new production processes, which involve inherent risks to capital expansion because of the enormous outlays necessary on research and development, and demand maximum output and sales for the newly manufactured commodities.[21] A spokesman of the American chemical industry has stated unambiguously: 'In order to obtain above-average profit margins, new products and new specialities must be discovered continually which can give high profit margins, while the older products in the same category drop to being chemical goods with lower profit margins.'[22] This pressure in turn provides

[19] The most important form taken by this trend in late capitalism is the so-called 'conglomerates.' A thorough analysis of this phenomenon has been published in the *American Economic Review*, No. 2, Vol. XI, May 1971. See also W. F. Fueller, 'A Theory of Conglomerate Mergers', in *Quarterly Journal of Economics*, November 1969. In the years 1965-69 more than 80% of company mergers in the USA led to the creation of conglomerates, as compared with 52% in the years 1948-53. Anne-Marie Kumps and Michel Cardon de Lichtbuer, 'La concentration conglomérate', in *Reflets et Perspectives de la Vie Economique*, No. 2, 1971.

[20] *Neue Zürcher Zeitung*, 29 June 1969; *Entreprise*, 31 March 1972.

[21] Stephen H. Hymer, 'The Efficiency (Contradictions) of Multi-National Corporations', in *The American Economic Review*, May 1970, Vol. LX, No. 2, p. 445.

[22] J. Backman, *The Economics of the Chemical Industry*, Washington, 1970, p. 215.

a powerful incentive for international production, encouraged by relative facility of access to big markets (concentrations of population in the large urban areas).[23] *A new form of the international division of labour based on product specialization therefore now corresponds to the big multinational companies of late capitalism.*[24] They also try to profit from the international price differentials in the purchase of raw materials, equipment, land and buildings, as well as labour-power, and of differences in market prices for the commodities which are produced in their factories, in order to maximize their monopoly surplus-profits on a world-wide scale.[25] A striking example is furnished by the automobile industry, in which European and Japanese companies dominate the US market for small cars; certain firms (Mercedes, Volvo, BMW, Alfa-Romeo, Citroen, American companies) predominate on the European market for large cars and luxury models; particular firms specialize in the production of medium-class Sedans and others in lighter or heavier lorries, and so on.

4. Socio-political forces (constant revolutionary ferment in the colonies and semi-colonies ever since the Second World War) as well as economic forces (the conversion of the production of raw materials from early industrial to advanced industrial technology; the growing development of chemical rather than natural methods of producing these materials, and so on) have caused a relative decline in capital exports to underdeveloped regions. In consequence, excess capital now predominantly moves to and fro between the imperialist metropolitan countries, which further promotes the ascent of the multinational company. Although after the Second World War this flow of

[23]Charles P. Kindleberger, *American Business Abroad*, p. 14, stresses that two preconditions for a rapid development of the major corporations' radius of operations are a high degree of pre-existent national concentration of industry and broad international sales possibilities created by brand-name familiarity. This answers Heilbronner's question as to why there is widespread 'international production' of glass and cars, but not of machine-tools or ship building: Robert L. Heilbronner, 'The Multinational Corporation and the Nation State', in *The New York Review of Books*, February 11, 1971.

[24]Kindleberger, *Europe's Post-War Growth*, p. 114; Vernon, op. cit., pp. 71-82.

[25]'(By the late 1960s) Bendix was using the cheap labour of Taiwan to assemble automobile radios for world markets. Ford was making fender steel in Holland for car production in the rest of Europe and tractor components in Germany and motors for compact models in Britain to be used in US assembly plants. Singer was crosshauling its many makes and models of sewing machines between Scotland, Canada, Japan and the United States, concentrating the production of different types where market and factor costs suggested': Vernon, *Sovereignty at Bay*, p. 110. For other examples, see Tugendhat, *The Multinationals*, pp. 139, 142 and 149.

capital originated principally in America and Britain, Continental-European and Japanese capital plays a growing part in this movement of inter-imperialist export today. The uneven development of the various imperialist countries is itself an important stimulus for the international interlocking of capital; in Europe, for instance, the capacity of isolated 'national' European companies to resist the competition of their US rivals will be critically threatened if such interlocking does not occur.[26]

5. The uneven development of the various big imperialist powers (or regions), and the protectionist or partially protectionist policies which they pursue, reinforce the contemporary tendency to replace the export of commodities by the export of capital, in order to circumvent such tariff restrictions. Thus US and British companies have established numerous branches within the EEC in order to protect their share of the market from the effects of the common EEC tariff on exports from third countries. This factor already played a role in the earliest efforts to establish production units outside the homeland of large firms, practised by Lever Brothers, Bayer or Jurgens (one of the original constituents of Unilever) before the First World War. Today the recent protectionist trend in US trade policy — already evident for some years, but strident in Nixon's speech of 15 August 1971 — may similarly speed up European and Japanese capital exports to the USA. A comparable role is played by the increasing instability of the international currency system, which engenders growing fears of unpredictable fluctuations in rates of exchange and likewise represents a brake on the expansion of commodity exports, while at the same time stimulating the export of capital of the internationalization of production sites.[27]

6. The specialization and 'rationalization' of control over capital attendant on the growing centralization of capital on a national scale promotes direct investments abroad, to the extent that it

[26] For a thorough investigation of the problems involved here see our book, *Europe Versus America?*, London, 1970. The rapid growth of Japanese capital exports in recent years has been particularly impressive. Before 1967, these never averaged more than $100-200 million a year. Then they rose by leaps and bounds, to $400 million in 1968, $670 million in 1969, $913 million in 1970 and over $1 billion in 1971. The total value of Japanese foreign investments has now passed the $10 billion mark. European direct investment in the USA alone increased from $6 billion in 1966 to $10 billion in 1971; European long-term portfolio investment in the USA grew from $11.5 billion in 1966 to $26 billion in 1971.

[27] Kindleberger, *American Business Abroad*, pp. 188-9; Levinson, *Capital, Inflation and the Multinationals*, pp. 36, 54-5, etc.

allows capitalists to specialize more and more in the sphere of 'pure' reproductive activity and permits preferences for new investments to be determined by objective criteria irrespective of national or international considerations. The logic of oligopolistic competition and its bond with technical progress work in the same direction, for in the case of certain products there is no longer any question of a 'normal market' other than the world market. The self-development of a company from national to international status corresponds on the level of the 'many capitals' to the objective developmental tendencies of 'capital in general' already outlined.[28]

The Chairman of the Managerial Board of the big German company Robert Bosch GmbH recently summed up the economic considerations which determined the decision of his company to go international as follows:

1. Contemporary markets, which often necessitate production of a commodity in the zone of its consumption, for reasons which include transport costs, security of supply, adaptation of products to local needs, employment and structural problems of the sales region.

2. Factors of production, which include not only raw materials and energy, but especially labour-power, whose optimum combination is a precondition for the minimization of production costs;

3. World-wide development of technology, which comprises different sectors of advance in different regions, and demands international coordination;

4. Distribution of risks, an understandable goal when current tendencies are towards falling returns and growing hazards.

A few figures will be enough to indicate the scale of this internationalization of the *production*, as distinct from the *realization* of surplus-value. If we define an 'international company' as one at least 25% of whose total turnover, investment, production or employment lies outside its country of origin or central administration, then 75 to 85 of the 200 largest American corporations and 200 biggest European companies fall in this category.[29] In 71 of the 176

[28]For the origins of the multinational company in the inner development of the large capitalist enterprise see Hymer, op. cit., pp. 442-3; Chandler, *Strategy and Structure*, pp. 42-51, 324f. Both authors assign a crucial role to the multi-divisional corporation, which emerged in the 30's but only became general after the Second World War, as an intermediate stage between the 'national' and the 'international' company.

[29]Sidney E. Rolfe and Walter Danim (eds.), *The Multi-National Corporation in the World Economy*, New York, 1970, p. 17.

largest US concerns, an average of one third of the employees reside abroad.[30] In 1967 the exports of the ten leading capitalist industrial nations at $130 billion barely exceeded half the turnover of subsidiaries and foreign production centres of the companies of the same nations ($240 billion). In 1971, multinational corporations are said to have produced commodities worth 300 billion dollars outside their home territories, which is more than the total value of world trade.[31] According to Magdoff, in 1965 22% of US company profits came from their foreign holdings.[32] In early 1972, the total turnover of all companies which have been described as multinational was estimated to be between 300 and 450 billion dollars, according to the definitions used — in other words, approximately 15% to 20% of the gross social product of the whole capitalist world.[33] Since this turnover has grown at twice the rate of the gross social product over the past decade, its share in the latter would rise to some 28%-40% in the next ten years, if the current tendency were to continue, which appears improbable.

However, in speaking of a tendency towards the international centralization of capital, we must distinguish between its different forms and describe more exactly, or relativize, the concept of the 'multi-national company'. Centralization of capital implies central commanding power, or *centralization of control over the means of production* — in other words, centralized private ownership. It is of no importance in this context whether shares are widely scattered internationally over small or medium sized shareholders. For it is a notorious feature of the capitalist joint stock company, and monopoly capital as a whole, that the ownership of a large amount of capital within any major corporation affords power of command over even greater quantities of capital.

International centralization of capital thus means central command over capital with originally different national origins and controls. This centralization can accordingly take two forms: either companies and large enterprises with *different* national imperialist owners can come under the control of one *single* imperialist class

[30] Kenneth Simmonds in Courtney Brown, *World Business: Promise and Problems*, New York, 1969, p.49.

[31] Tugendhat, *The Multinationals*, p. 21.

[32] Heilbroner, op. cit., p. 21; Magdoff, op. cit., p. 159.

[33] The lower estimate is given by Norman MacRae, 'The Future of International Business', *the Economist*, 22 January 1972; the higher estimate is given by the American business magnate Arthur Ross, 'Trends bei multinationalen Konzernen', in *Gottlieb Duttweiler-Institute — Topics*, 3rd Year, No. 5, May 1972.

(as for instance when Machines Bull was absorbed by General Electric, the Phoenix works by Firestone, the Belgian ACEC company by Westinghouse, and so on); or, on the other hand, companies and large enterprises with *different* national owners can become interwoven within *one* international company *without* control falling to the owners of any single power, as, for instance, in the amalgamation of AGFA and Gevaert, the Ijmuiden-Hoesch-Dortmund-Horder-Hütten-Union merger, the Dunlop-Pirelli and AEG-Zanussi amalgamations, and the VFW-Fokker (German-Dutch aircraft trust) fusion.[34]

The huge US corporations which have created branches and subsidiaries in a large number of countries (for example General Motors, Ford, Esso Standard, Texaco, Westinghouse, General Electric, and I.B.M.) obviously fall outside the category of a real international fusion of capital, for both the origin and the control of their capital remain unequivocally national in character. Although these North American companies, like those of the classical English concerns of the British Empire, represent an international concentration of capital, because a growing proportion of the capital accumulated by them undoubtedly stems from the production and realization of surplus-value outside the home country,[35] they do not represent an international centralization of capital. Such international centralization only occurs when these companies absorb local firms and enterprises in various countries in the course of their international activity.

To clarify the long-term tendencies of development of the international centralization of capital and its relationship to the late capitalist State, it is essential to make a strict distinction between the internationalization of the *realization* of surplus-value (the sale of commodities), the internationalization of the *production* of surplus-value (the production of commodities), the internationalization of the

[34] A marginal case of international fusion of capital would be one in which the international sale of shares had 'diluted' the ownership pattern to such an extent that the original 'founder nationality' had lost control over the company. It is sometimes claimed that this is already the case with the big Swiss company Nestlé, and even the Dutch Company Phillips. We are sceptical as to whether this is really the case.

[35] Massive 'portfolio investments' in foreign securities unaccompanied by influence (or control) over the companies concerned is a specific late capitalist form of international capital concentration without international centralization (it was already present embryonically in the age of 'classical' imperialism). Thus European capitalists altogether owned a total of $26 billion worth of securities in US firms in which they have no share in the administration. Whereas European capital exports to the USA — hitherto — are predominantly portfolio investments. US capital exports to Western Europe are predominately direct investments in Europe.

purchase of the *commodity of labour-power* (or the specific market for this commodity) and the internationalization of the power of command over capital, which is ultimately always based on the internationalization of *capital ownership*.

The internationalization of the realization of surplus-value, i.e., the sale of commodities, is a tendency inherent in capitalism, but develops in very different ways in the history of this mode of production. Broadly speaking, this internationalization increased from the early 19th century up to the eve of the First World War (that is, exports accounted for a growing share of industrial output of the advanced capitalist countries); it then fell back from 1914 to 1945; with the advent of the late capitalist era it once again climbed upwards, although the relative level (in other words, relative per capita share of exports) reached before the First World War was not overtaken until the 1960's.[36]

In the past there was only marginal internationalization of the production of surplus-value in actual manufacturing industry, outside the domain of raw materials. Today it constitues the really new and specific aspect of the internationalization of capital in the late capitalist epoch. A majority of large companies now spend constant and variable capital in many countries of the earth, whether it be in branches under their direct control or in joint ventures with other companies, whether in enterprises founded by foreign companies in foreign countries and subsequently bought up, or in big multinational companies in which foreign concerns are interwoven. This development started immediately after the Second World War, especially in the US oil, automobile and electrical apparatus industries, and has today become a world-wide phenomenon which for the first time actually provides an *immediately* international framework for the competition of capital (an obvious example is the international field of competition between the most important US computer companies in the electronics industry).[37]

---

[36] According to the estimates of Lamartine Yates, per capita world trade was lower in 1937 than in 1913 (—7%), while the average ten year growth-rate of this per capita world trade over the period 1913-63 was 8%. But while the share of exports in world output rose for a whole century (it is said to have increased from 3% in 1800 to 33% in 1913), it went into a long decline between the two World Wars; even in 1963, when it was 22%, it had still not regained its 1913 level: Simon Kuznets, *Quantitative Aspects of the Economic Growth of Nations*, pp. 4-9.

[37] It is advisable to distinguish national companies operating internationally from international companies, according to the respective proportions of their domestic

The internationalization of the purchase of the commodity of labour-power is an inevitable consequence of the internationalization of the production of surplus-value, although the two do not necessarily coincide in a mechanical fashion. On the one hand, production abroad can take place without much foreign labour-power, especially in enterprises or branches of industry which are highly mechanized or automated. On the other, there can be large international movements of labour-power in search of work without this necessarily being accompanied by the internationalization of production sites or their ownership: witness the mass movements of Italian, Spanish, Portuguese, Greek, Yugoslav, Turkish and Moroccan labour-power to Western Europe and especially to the EEC countries, without any changes in the relations of ownership in West European industry. In one sense these two movements, the international mobility of capital and the international mobility of labour-power, are not parallel or complementary in the age of late capitalism (as opposed to their tendency in early capitalist era) but run counter to each other. Labour-power streams from the less developed marginal areas into the industrial centres of Western Europe for the very reason that capital does *not* (or does not sufficiently) flow out of these centres into those marginal areas.[38]

The internationalization of the power of command over capital, the actual centralization of capital, always means a *transfer of ownership,* either from one country to another or from one national group of capital owners to several. Here too the law of uneven and combined development prevails. The international centralization of capital is neither necessarily nor mechanically congruent with the internationalization either of production or of the producers, or of the sale of commodities. Only if the internationalization of production leads to the internationalization — in other words, an international

---

and foreign production, and also to distinguish between international companies (controlled by the capital of a single nationality) and those of a multinational type, according to their respective patterns of ownership. Kindleberger, *American Business Abroad*, pp. 180-4.

[38] In the case of the mass European emigration to the so-called white settler colonies in the 19th and early 20th centuries, labour-power and capital travelled in the same direction — even if their rhythm and volume differed. The same is (and was) true of the Chinese and Japanese emigration to the Pacific, of the Indian and Lebanese emigrations to East and West Africa respectively, and of the smaller movements of emigration in the Mediterranean (Greeks and Italians). In the case of contemporary emigration from Eastern and Southern Europe to the West of the continent, however, labour moves in the opposite direction to capital.

alteration — of capital ownership, can we really speak of an internationalization of the power of command over capital.[39] The material infrastructure which enables capital to exercise a real international power of command has only been created by the third technological revolution, with its telex equipment, jet aircraft and other facilities.

Three variant types of relationship between the bourgeois 'nation state and the international centralization of capital must be distinguished here. The international centralization of capital may be accompanied by the international extension of the power of *one single state*. This tendency was already observable in the First World War, and in the course of the Second World War and its aftermath it found spectacular expression in the world-wide political and military hegemony of US imperialism. It basically corresponds to the first of the two major forms of the international centralization of capital: decisive control over an increasing share of the international apparatus of production by the owners of a single national class of capitalists, with foreign capitalists participating at most as *junior partners*. The increasing international power of a single imperialist state is congruent with the growing international supremacy of a single national group of capital owners in the total field of international capital.

The international centralization of capital may also be accompanied by a gradual dismantling of the power of the various bourgeois national states and the rise of a *new, federal*, supranational *bourgeois state power*. This variant, which seems at least possible, if not even probable, for the West European EEC area, corresponds to the second major form of the international centralization of capital: the international fusion of capital without the predominance of any particular group of national capitalists. Just as no kind of hegemony is tolerated in these really multinational companies, the state form corresponding to this form of capital cannot in the long-run involve the supremacy of a single bourgeois nation state over others, nor a

[39] Capital ownership must here be understood as meaning control over capital, which can be based on holdings of relatively small minority percentages of total capital. According to Kindleberger, US companies on average own no more than 60% of their foreign branches: *American Business Abroad*, p. 31. This may be contrasted with the fact that foreigners occupied only 1.6% of the 1,851 top posts in the management of US companies with substantial operations abroad. Tugendhat rightly comments: 'The most striking characteristic of the modern multinational company is its central direction. However large it may be, and however many subsidiaries it may have scattered across the globe, all its operations are coordinated from the centre.' *The Multinationals*, p. 31.

loose confederation of sovereign nation states. It must rather take the form of a supranational federal state characterized by the transfer of crucial sovereign rights.

It would certainly be a grave mistake to treat purely economic forces as absolute in this respect and to divorce them from the overall historical context. It is not only the immediate economic interests of capital-owners — or of the decisive group of capitalists in each phase of the capitalist mode of production — that the bourgeois state functions to safeguard. To perform this role effectively, in fact, it must also extend its activity to all the spheres of the super-structure, a task which presents great difficulties if it is undertaken without careful consideration of the national and cultural peculiari-ties of each particular nationality.[40] In the late capitalist epoch, the direct or indirect economic functions of the bourgeois state apparatus are pushed so far into the foreground — by the constraint to gain increasing control over all the phases of the processes of production and reproduction — that under certain conditions monopoly capital may undoubtedly consider a certain division of labour between a supra-national federal state and cultural activity by nation states a lesser evil. It should not be forgotten that in the United States, for example, all questions concerning education, religion and culture have — ever since the foundation of the Union — remained in the hands of the individual states rather than those of the Federal Government. Moreover, regulation of educational and cultural questions in various languages is by no means impossible (witness the cantonal system of the Swiss Federation).

The overwhelming compulsion towards the creation of a supra-national imperialist state in Western Europe — if the international centralization of capital were in fact to take the predominant form of capital fusion on a European level without the hegemony of any one national bourgeois class — springs precisely from the immediate economic function of the State in late capitalism. Economic program-ming within the nation state is incompatible in the long-run with multinational fusion of capital.[41] The first will either force back the second, especially in periods of crisis or recession, or the second

[40] The particular emphasis on this non-economic superstructural factor explains why the French Gaullists hold fast to the axiom of European 'small states' and why they resist the 'supranationality' represented by 'soulless Eurocrats'.
[41] This is the reason why we have for several years expressed the view that the EEC is not yet finally 'irreversible' and could still fall victim to a severe general recession.

will have to create an international form of programming congruent with itself.[42]

The choice between these two alternatives will ultimately come to a head over the issue of anti-cyclical economic policy, for a successful struggle against crises and recessions, in harmony with the interests of multinational companies, cannot be conducted on a national level; it can only be international. Since the instruments of anti-cyclical policy consist of monetary, credit, budgetary, tax and tariff devices, such a policy must ultimately have at its disposal a uniform international currency, and a uniform international line on credit, budgeting and taxes (a common international trade policy is already a reality in the EEC). But it is impossible in the long-run to have a common currency, a common budget, a common system of taxes and a common public works programme[43] without a federal government with sovereignty in matters of taxation and finance, and with an executive power of repression to enforce its authority — in other words, without a common State. It should also be said that big multinational companies also create a multinational capital market which in any case makes the survival of national currencies, national credit policies and national budgets and taxes more and more problematic.[44]

The third possible variant of the relationship between the international centralization of capital and the development of the late capitalist State is that of a relative *indifference* of the former to the latter. The example of big British, Canadian and some Dutch companies, in particular, is often cited in this connection.[45] It is customary

---

[42]The latter must be understood in a two-fold sense: in the first place, quantitatively — in other words, a type of economic programming which could set in motion great enough masses of anti-cyclical resources by the State to cope with conjunctural difficulties of realization and sales experienced by huge companies such as Siemans, Phillips, FIAT, or ICI; in the second place, qualitatively — in other words, a type of economic programming capable of quelling particularist regional interests to the wider benefit of the largest multinational companies.

[43]Scitovsky pointed out as early as 1958 that structural and unemployment crises would inevitably result from the creation of the EEC, and argued that a common employment and infrastructural policy (or a policy of public works) would therefore in the long run prove equally inevitable in the EEC: *Economic Theory and Western European Integration*, London 1967, pp. 97-8.

[44]Several authors have already pointed out the role played by multinational companies in thwarting national attempts to stabilize interest and currency rates in recent years. See for instance, Levinson, op. cit., pp. 36-7, 70-1; Tugendhat, op. cit., p. 161. We shall deal with this problem in Chapters 13 and 14.

[45]Robert Rowthorn (with the collaboration of Stephen Hymer), *International Big Business 1957-1967*, Cambridge, 1971, pp. 62-3, 74.

to emphasize that these companies have internationalized their activities to such an extent, and produce and realize surplus-value in so many countries, that they have become largely indifferent to the development of the economic and social conjuncture of their mother country.[46]

Without denying the existence of this variant, we may, however, regard it as basically no more than an intermediate between the two main variants outlined above. For on closer analysis we must distinguish between two different cases in the operations of these 'state-indifferent' companies. There is the case in which they operate in countries where national state power is itself so weak that it offers no resistance to the quest for additional profits by expatriate concerns: this is ultimately only true of, say, semi-colonial countries controlled by British capital. Or there is the case in which they operate in countries where the national state power that intervenes in the economy is independent of them. With further intensification of international competition and the centralization of capital, the countries in the first group will tend to become increasingly liable to use what State power they have at their disposal to defend their own interests from possible competitors. In the countries of the second group, however, the position of 'state-indifferent' companies is liable to become increasingly threatened by those corporations that enjoy the real support of the local State apparatus. It is then only a question of time before such companies abandon their attitude of indifference to the State and seek to dominate either their home State or the local State within whose frontiers the bulk of their operations takes place. If they fail, these once 'indifferent' companies may have to pay a high price for having underestimated the role of the State in the epoch of late capitalism; they will ultimately fall to their competitors.[47]

Thus the only significant conclusion that can be drawn from a

[46]See among others Robert Rowthorn, 'Imperialism: Unity or Rivalry?', in *New Left Review*, No. 69 (September-October 1971), pp. 46-7. Robin Murray, 'Internationalization of Capital and the Nation State', in *New Left Review*, No. 67 (May-June 1971), pp. 104-8, acknowledges the contradiction and concludes that late capitalism is becoming increasingly unstable, without noting that the big companies *must* therefore seek a State power adequate to their needs.

[47]In the recession year of 1974, even very large corporations like British Leyland or Citroen could only be saved from bankruptcy by massive subsidies from their national governments. But these are corporations which are just below the limit of what national states in Western Europe can still sustain. Multinationals like Phillips, ICI, Siemens, Fiat or Rhône-Poulenc would need subventions on such a scale, in case of serious financial crisis, that no single national government in capitalist Europe could provide them.

consideration of this third variant is that even without internationalization of capital-ownership, the increasing internationalization of
the production of surplus-value can lead to the 'denationalization'
of a big company. In other words, if a company such as Phillips or
British Petroleum were to transfer a major part of its activities to
North America, it would be more interested in the economic conjuncture of Canada or the USA than that of Britain or Europe, and
would therefore have to make more use of the North American than
the British State apparatus to pursue its economic interests, and
might ultimately itself become a part of the US bourgeoisie, perhaps
via its amalgamation with 'purely' North American concerns. There
is no space here to investigate the probability of such a 'migration',
beyond establishing its theoretical possibility. But any such evolution
only leads us back by a detour to the first two variants.

All those writers who, like Charles Levinson, regard the multinational companies as sovereign colossi overriding the power of
the late capitalist State, tacitly assume a notion which was extremely
popular in the 50's and 60's namely that big capital no longer needs
to reckon with any serious difficulties in sales or realization, or with
major social crises,[48] and that even in times of so-called 'bad business'
their investment activity proceeds unscathed. In other words, they
simply presuppose that there is no further need for the State to
intervene in the economy in order to master acute cyclical and structural crises, or great eruptions of the class struggle. The recession in
West Germany in 1966-67; the French revolt of May 1968; the 'hot
autumn' in Italy in 1969-70; the US recession of 1969-71; and the
world-wide recession in all the imperialist countries in 1974-75,
have shown the unrealism of this assumption. In fact, the one certain
prediction that can now be made is that multinational companies
will not only need a State, but a State which is actually stronger than
the 'classical' nation state, to enable them, at least in part, to overcome the economic and social contradictions which periodically
threaten their gigantic capitals.

These three variants of the possible relationship between the
international centralization of capital and the late bourgeois State
provide three possible models for the international structure of the
metropolitan political system of imperialism in the coming years and
decades:

[48] For this question see Chapters 15 and 17.

1. The model of *super-imperialism*. In this model a single imperialist power possesses such hegemony that the other imperialist powers lose any real independence of it and sink to the status of semi-colonial small powers. In the long-run such a process cannot rest solely on the military supremacy of the super-imperialist power — a predominance which could only be possessed by US imperialism — but must drive towards direct ownership and control of the most important production sites and concentrations of capital, banks and other financial institutions elsewhere. Without such direct control, in other words, without the immediate power to dispose of capital, there is nothing to ensure that in the long-run the law of uneven development will not again so change the economic relationship of forces between the major capitalist states that the military supremacy of the foremost imperialist power is itself undermined.

The advocates of the notion of 'super-imperialism' accordingly see the major US international companies as the real — potential or virtual — rulers of the world market.[49] They doubt the ability of the big European and Japanese companies to provide effective competition to their US counterparts in the long-run, because the latter are deemed to be too technologically backward, possess too little capital strength, or lack 'managerial skills'.[50] Alternatively, they doubt the political will of European or Japanese companies, even if perhaps capable of 'purely economic' competition, to resist US competition, when such obstruction might deal a fatal blow to the military and political centre of contemporary world imperialism and hence in the final resort to themselves.[51] In this respect, Poulantzas's contention that we ourselves have been misled by 'territorial' statistics into under-estimating the supremacy of American capital (including European-based US corporations) is typical, but it has no foundation.[52] Our arguments on this score have always been based on the competition between various international corporations *owned* by different (US, European or Japanese) groups of national capitalists.

---

[49] See Baran and Sweezy, *Monopoly Capital*; Harry Magdoff, *The Age of Imperialism*.

[50] This is the warning contained in Servan-Schreiber's *Le Défi Americian*, if the amalgamation of European capital is postponed and the political unity of Western Europe fails to materialise.

[51] This thesis is advanced by Martin Nicolaus in his polemic against us: *Die Objectivität des Imperialismus*, Berlin, 1971.

[52] Nicos Poulantzas, *Classes in Contemporary Capitalism*, London, 1975, pp. 50-57.

Phillips, Fiat, ICI, Siemens or Rhône-Poulenc are owned by European capitalists, just as Mitsubishi, Hitachi, Matsushita or Sony are owned by their Japanese counterparts, and General Motors, Exxon, General Electric or US Steel are owned by American capitalists.

2. The model of *ultra-imperialism*. In this model the international fusion of capital has advanced so far that all critical differences of economic interest between the capital owners of the different nationalities disappear. All major capitalists have spread their capital ownership, production of surplus-value, realization of surplus-value and capital accumulation (new investments) so evenly over different countries and parts of the world that they have become completely indifferent to the particular conjuncture, the particular course of the class struggle and the 'national' peculiarities of political development in any particular country. Incidentally, it is obvious that such a complete internationalization of the world economy would also mean the general disappearance of national economic cycles. In this eventuality, all that would remain would be competition between big multinational companies; there would no longer be any inter-imperialist competition proper — in other words, competition would finally be freed from its starting point in the nation state. Naturally in such a case the imperialist state would not 'wither away'; all that would vanish is its role as an instrument of inter-imperialist competition. Its role as the central weapon for the defence of the common interests of all the imperialist owners of capital from the threat of economic crises, the insurgency of the proletariat within the imperialist countries, the revolt of the colonial peoples, and the power of non-imperialist states abroad, would be more pronounced than ever before. Only this state would no longer be an imperialist nation state but a supranational imperialist 'world state'. Many advocates of the thesis of the growing 'indifference' of multinational companies towards the power of the bourgeois State come very close to this notion of a nascent 'ultra-imperialism'; this is especially so in the case of Levinson.[53]

3. The model of continuing *inter-imperialist competition*, taking new historical forms. In this model, although the international fusion of capital has proceeded far enough to replace a larger number of independent big imperialist powers with a smaller number of imperialist super-powers, the counteracting force of the uneven develop-

---

[53] Levinson, op. cit., pp. 103-6.

ment of capital prevents the formation of an actual global comunity of interest for capital. *Capital fusion is achieved on a continental level, but thereby intercontinental imperialist competition is all the more intensified.* The novelty of this latter-day inter-imperialist competition, by comparison with the classical imperialism of Lenin's analysis, lies in the first instance in the fact that only three world powers confront each other in the international imperialist economy, namely US imperialism (which has largely pocketed Canada and Australia), Japanese imperialism [54] and West European imperialism. The further development of Japanese imperialism, in the direction of either independence or fusion with the big US companies, would here probably decide the final outcome of this competitive struggle. Secondly, of course, there is the fact that in the present socio-political world conjuncture, which is basically unpropitious to capital, global inter-imperialist world wars have become extremely unlikely, if not impossible. This does not, of course, exclude either local inter-imperialist wars (by proxy, so to speak), new colonial wars of pillage, or counter-revolutionary wars against national liberation movements—let alone the danger of a nuclear world war against the bureaucratized workers' states.

It is well-known that Karl Kautsky was the first to entertain the possibility of an 'ultra-imperialist understanding' between all the world powers. He did so first before the First World War. [55] It is also well-known how sharply Lenin refuted him. [56] Nicolaus has accused the author of the present work of treading 'in Kautsky's

---

[54] For the growing role of Japanese imperialism and large Japanese companies in the Pacific see Stephen Hymer, 'The United States Multinational Corporations and Japanese competition in the Pacific', (lecture prepared for Conferencia del Pacifico, Vina del Mar, Chile, Sept. 27 — Oct. 3, 1970), the manuscript of which was kindly sent to us by the author. Hermann Kahn, *The Emerging Japanese Super-state*, London, 1971, deals with the same subject, but this book is marked by the author's typical tendency towards unrestrained extrapolation. Japanese capital is the major foreign investor in South Korea (67%) and Thailand (37.3% against 16.2% for the USA), and the second largest in Singapore: see *Far Eastern Economic Review*, May 13, 1974.

[55] Karl Kautsky, 'Der Imperialismus', in *Die Neue Zeit*, 11 Sept. 1914: 'Hence from the purely economic standpoint it is not impossible that capitalism may still live through another phase, the translation of cartellization into foreign policy: a phase of *ultra-imperialism*, which of course we must struggle against as energetically as we do against imperialism, but whose perils lie in another direction, not in that of the arms race and the threat to world peace.' See the translation of Kautsky's article, published in *New Left Review*, No. 59, January-February 1970, p. 46.

[56] See Lenin, *Imperialism, the Highest Stage of Capitalism*, in *Selected Works*, Vol. I, pp. 764-72.

footsteps' by envisaging the possibility of various European powers fusing into one European imperialist super-power.[57] This analogy is purely formal and superficial. Kautsky's perspective was that of a gradual weakening of imperialist contradictions, leading to 'ultra-imperialism'. Our perspective is diametrically opposite. It envisages an *intensification* in the age of late capitalism of all the contradictions inherent in imperialism: the antagonism between capital and labour in the metropolitan countries and the semi-colonies; the antagonism between imperialist metropolitan states and colonial or semi-colonial nations; the intensification of inter-imperialist rivalry. Precisely such an *intensification* of inter-imperialist contradictions will necessarily bring in its wake a tendency for *certain* imperialist powers to amalgamate. They would otherwise be unable to continue the competitive struggle at all. Whereas Kautsky's analysis led inexorably to reformist and apologetic conclusions, ours by contrast logically culminates in even greater emphasis on the independent revolutionary tasks of the proletariat in the metropolitan countries.[58]

Lenin himself, of course, in no way excluded the possibility of further international concentration and centralization of capital — including that of the big imperialist powers: in fact, he expressly stated that the long-term historical tendency was 'logically' towards a single world trust. He was, however, convinced that long before this development could reach its conclusion, imperialism would have collapsed as a result both of its inner contradictions and of the revolutionary struggle of the proletariat and the oppressed peoples against it.[59] We share this conception and conclude that the postponement of the proletarian revolution in the imperialist metropolitan countries has rendered possible, if not actually probable, the simplification of the pattern of multiple imperialist powers into three 'super-powers'.

The last of the three models set out above is thus by far the most probable, at least in the visible future. In the final analysis, the re-

[57] Nicolaus, *Die Objectivität des Imperialismus*.
[58] See our reply to Martin Nicolaus, *Die Widersprüche des Imperialismus*, Berlin, 1971.
[59] 'There is doubt that the development is going *in the direction* of a single world trust that will swallow up all enterprises and all states without exception. But the development in this direction is proceeding under such stress, with such a tempo, with such contradictions, conflicts and convulsions — not only economical, but also political, national, and so on — that before a single world trust will be reached, before the respective national finance capitals will have formed a world union of "ultra-imperialism", imperialism will inevitably explode, capitalism will turn into its opposite.' Lenin, Introduction to Bukharin's *Imperialism and World Economy*, p. 14.

spective realization of each of these models depends on the predominant form taken by the international centralization of capital, however important may also be the temporarily autonomous weight of military or political forces.

Super-imperialism can only be realized if the monopoly capital of the hegemonic imperialist power acquires a decisive degree of *capital ownership* within its most important potential competitors. Hitherto US imperialism has failed to achieve this in either Western Europe or in Japan. The financial capital of these countries is largely independent of its US counterpart. US banks play only a marginal role in their economies. Although US ownership of industrial capital is of greater import, and especially in so-called growth sectors is sometimes well above the average, its current share can be estimated at little more than 10-15% of total capital investments. Nor is any tendency evident for this share to grow uninterruptedly; it seems rather to be levelling out. So far, therefore, it emphatically cannot be said that the West European or Japanese states have sunk to the status of semi-colonies. They pursue independent policies in trade, foreign and military affairs, even if this independence is exercised within the framework of a common alliance against common class enemies. It should be noted that this alliance fully accords with the common interests of all capitalists classes and by no means only with the particular interest of US imperialism. Indeed, it may be added that since the beginning of the 50's the relationship of forces between US imperialism and its West European and Japanese counterparts has continuously altered to the disadvantage of the former and the advantage of the latter.[60]

Evolution of Economic Relationship of Forces USA — Western Europe — Japan[61]

Percentage of Total Capitalist World Industrial Output

	1953	1963	1970
U.S.A.	52%	44%	40.5%
E.E.C.	16%	21.1%	22%
U.K.	10%	6.4%	5%
Japan	2%	5.3%	9.5%

[60] See the empirical evidence for this shift in our study, *Europe versus America?* While the data presented there refers principally to *production capacity*, more recent developments have highlighted different rhythms of *capital export*. Today West Germany and Japanese exports of capital are growing much faster than those of the USA.

[61] First three tables: Michael Barratt-Brown, *From Labourism to Socialism*,

Percentage of Total Capitalist World Exports

	1953	1963	1970
U.S.A.	21%	17%	15.5%
E.E.C.	19.3%	27.8%	32%
U.K.	9.7%	8.7%	7%
Japan	1.7%	4%	7%

Percentage of Total Capitalist World Gold and Foreign Reserves

U.S.A.	43%	25%	8.3%
E.E.C.	11.5%	29.5%	37.0%
U.K.	5%	4.3%	3.5%
Japan	1.5%	3.0%	11.2%

Percentage of Total Capitalist World Foreign Investment

	1960	1971
U.S.A.	59.1%	52.0%
U.K.	24.5%	14.5%
France	4.7%	5.8%
W.Germany	1.1%	4.4%
Japan	0.1%	2.7%
Switzerland		4.1%
Canada		3.6%
Netherlands		2.2%
Sweden		2.1%
Belgium		2.0%
Italy		2.0%

Developments in this field, however, have by no means yet reached their conclusion. The intensification of international capital competition has been gathering momentum for a number of years, and sooner or later must lead to a new and qualitatively higher stage of the international centralization of capital.[62] The number of important international companies is today estimated at approximately 800. Perlmutter has predicted that by about 1985 the capitalist world economy will be dominated by some 300 such companies. In

Nottingham, 1972, p. 110, except column for February 1973 gold and foreign currency holdings, from *National Institute Economic Review*, May 1973, p. 99. Fourth table: 1960 estimate from Magdoff, op. cit., p. 56; 1971 estimate from *Les Sociétés Multinationales et le Développement Mondial*, UN, New York, 1973, p. 144.

[62]Admittedly one cannot exclude the possibility that in some branches of heavy industry which suffer from permanent over-capacity and structural crisis, a 'world cartel' might be formed to prevent dumping and 'exaggerated' investments, and hence to stabilize prices on the world market. We have here in mind above all the steel industry.

a somewhat impressionistic work, Lattes foresees some sixty multi-national companies sharing the world market between them.[63] Will these be solely US companies, or US companies on the one hand, and European and Japanese, or European, Nippo-European and Nippo-American companies on the other? The answer to this question will doubtless settle the probability or improbability of the model of super-imperialism. In the end everything will depend on which of the two major forms of the international centralization of capital ultimately triumph, in the event of a further postponement of the proletarian revolution in the metropolitan countries.

It is plain that the so-called multinational companies of the USA enter this new phase of intensified competitive struggle with two critical advantages over their rivals: they at present possess on average much greater capital resources (three or four times that of their most important competitors) and a much more powerful State at their disposal. Their West European and Japanese counterparts will only be able to survive if they in turn undergo a rapid process of international mergers, attain a scale of capital ownership and productive capacity equal to that of their largest US rivals and, at least in Western Europe, establish a federal state on an equal political and military footing with the USA. The fate of the EEC in the next and next-but-one recessions will thus probably decide the possibility or impossibility of an independent West European super-power — and therewith the chances of realization of a US super-imperialism.

For the ultra-imperialist model to become a reality there must first be a much greater degree of international centralization of capital than appears to be in prospect today. Above all, it presupposes the massive participation of large European and Japanese shareholders in the running of the most important US companies, which implies a reduction in native US ownership of these companies to relative minority holdings. Today this seems even more unlikely than a parallel reduction in the ownership pattern of large European and Japanese companies.[64]

[63]See *Interplay*, November 1958, quoted by Heilbroner, op. cit., p. 22; Robert Lattes, *Mille Milliards de Dollars*, Paris, 1969, p. 10. Lattes cites a prediction made by the National Industrial Conference Board of the USA. according to which 20% of the US Gross National Product will be controlled by European and Japanese companies, and 25% of the West European and Japanese Gross National Products by US firms in 1975 (pp. 37-8).

[64] It should be emphasized that in the course of the growing 'planetization' of the business activity of international companies, European and particularly West German,

It is certainly true that the rapid extension of European and Japanese exports to the American market—which today plays the same central role on the world market as the British domestic market once did in the epoch 1780-1880—is accompanied by a tendency towards wider European and Japanese capital investment in the United States. Although this movement is not yet anything like as important as US capital investment in Western Europe, it nonetheless cannot be discounted as insignificant. Besides direct investments of European firms in the USA, some notable absorptions of US companies by European corporations should also be mentioned. British Petroleum has acquired *de facto* control over Standard Oil of Ohio, and a big stake in Alaskan oil. Fiat now possesses similar control over the road-building equipment division of Allis Chambers. Olivetti has bought up Underwood. It is also true that the World Bank and other international organizations have promoted common projects linking many of the most important industrial giants of the world. In addition, conscious efforts have been made by lobbies inspired by 'Atlantic' ideology to achieve an increasingly close community of interest and interlocking of capital between Europe and North America. But the merciless dictates of competition outweigh political insight or notions of world citizenship in the conduct of the imperialist bourgeoisies. *The main tendency of the intensifying international competitive struggle today is not for big capital to merge on a world scale, but for several imperialist formations to harden in their mutual antagonism.*

The model of continuing inter-imperialist rivalry consequently seems the most probable and realistic of the three, even with the proviso that an international fusion of capital must be achieved with some speed in Western Europe and Japan to safeguard the independence of the imperialist classes of these zones from US imperialism.[65] In the final analysis, the greater probability of this third model is

---

firms have for some time been transferring production sites to East Asia (for instance to Singapore, Hong Kong and South Korea) in order to exploit the advantages of local cheap labour-power in their competitive struggle with Japanese companies. See Levinson, op. cit., pp. 95-9.

[65]Bukharin fully acknowledged the importance of international fusion of capital, even though it was only a marginal phenomenon in his time: 'There is only one case in which we can say with assurance that solidarity of interests is created. This is the case of growing "participation" and financing, i.e., when, due to the common ownership of securities, the class of capitalists of various countries possesses collective property in one and the same object.' *Imperialism and World Economy*, p. 62.

linked to the question of whether the second major form of international centralization will effectively counter the first—in other words, *whether the international centralization of capital in the coming decades will take the form of a combination of US-dominated companies on the one hand, and internationally fused, multinational companies on the other.*

The trend towards a community of interest and reciprocal participation within European finance capital is particularly important in this respect. Hitherto it is this tendency which has predominated in Western Europe, and not, as Levinson thinks,[66] the emergence of a community of interest between European and American big banks and financial groups. Of the four most important multinational financial communities of interest, two are purely European:

—the *European Banks' International Company* (the British Midland Bank, the German Deutsche Bank, the Belgian Société Générale de Banque and the Dutch Amsterdam-Rotterdam Bank) which, among other things, has created the *Banque Européenne de Crédit Moyen*, as well as a common and financial company in the USA, the *European-American Banking Corporation*, and a joint enterprise in the Pacific, the *Euro-Pacific Finance Corporation* (Australia, Indonesia and South Africa);

—the *C.C.B. Group*, which combines the German Commerzbank, the French Crédit Lyonnais and the Italian Banco di Roma, together with the Spanish Banco Hispano-Americano, in a manner bordering on amalgamation, and which is reputed to be linked to Lloyd's Bank of London.

—the third group, the *Société Financiére Europeenne*, does have a US partner, the *Bank of America*, but the latter plays only a subsidiary role in the consortium. It is mainly European, and unites Barclay's Bank (Britain), the Algemene Bank Nederland (Holland), the Dresdner Bank (Germany), the Banque de Bruxelles (Belgium), the Banco Nazionale del Lavoro (Italy), and the Banque Nationale de Paris (France). The total balance-sheet of these banks exceeds 80 billion dollars — larger than that of any other banking or financial group in the world. This group—without the Bank of America!— has created, together with various partners in Latin America—a banking consortium for operations in that continent, called the Euro-Latinamerican Bank (Eulabank).

[66]Levinson, op. cit., pp. 111-12.

—Only the fourth combine, the so-called *Orion Group*, can be described as non-European. Besides the Chase Manhattan Bank of the USA, it includes the Royal Bank of Canada, the National Westminster Bank (Great Britain) and the Westdeutsche Landesbank (Germany).

In 1970, a fifth important banking group was created, the *United International Bank*, formed by the Banco di Roma, Mees and Hope, the Bank of Nova Scotia, the Bayerische Hypothek-und-Wechselbank, the Banque Française du Commerce Extérieur, and the Crédit du Nord. A US Bank, the Crocker-Citizens National Bank, participates in this consortium, but in a minority role (14.3%). European merchant bankers have likewise achieved considerable progress in cooperation—instanced by the recent agreement between the Companie Financière de Suez and Morgan Grenfell Holdings. In the spring of 1974, the Banque de Paris et des Pays-Bas, the Schweizerische Kreditanstalt and the French Société Générale founded a company for financing major new energy projects, called Finerg. The Belgian Société Générale de Banque, the British Midland Bank and the Dutch Amsterdam-Rotterdam Bank subsequently decided to join Finerg. The characteristic feature of all these multinational financial groups is their ability to grant giant credits to the giant multinational companies. They are thus simultaneously a product of the international centralization of capital and a product of the emergence of a genuinely international capital market.[67]

It is true that up to now, direct capital interpenetration inside the EEC has advanced rather slowly. Between 1961 and 1969, there were a total of 257 fusions between firms from several EEC member countries, as against 820 fusions between firms of member countries and firms of third countries, and 1861 fusions between firms of the same country. Juridical and organizational difficulties—which correspond in the final analysis to the absence of a West European federal State—have played an important role in slowing down capital interpenetration within the EEC. In these circumstances, cooperation between firms of different European countries has developed more rapidly than outright fusion. Examples are Unidata,

---

[67]See the interesting study by Michael Von Clemm, 'The Rise of Consortium Banking' in the *Harvard Business Review*, May-June 1971. This compilation lists some 50 consortia. Of these, European (including those with very small US participation) and mixed European-American are about equal in numbers. But among those with the highest consortium capital, European combinations are by far the most important.

the computer consortium created by Phillips (Netherlands), Siemens (West Germany) and CII (France); and Eurodif and Urenco for the construction of enriched uranium plants, the fuel for light nuclear reactors.

The more the rhythm of growth of the international imperialist economy slows down, the more acute will become the social contradictions within the most important capitalist states. The fiercer the international competition of capital, the more these social contradictions will be further sharpened, and with them the attempts of each individual imperialist class to resolve its particular contradictions and difficulties at the expense both of its own workers and its rivals—in other words, to export them to the countries of their competitors. The outcome of the intensifying class struggles of the coming years will in turn co-determine the rhythms and forms of the international centralization of capital. The more the class struggle swings upwards from campaigns over the distribution of the national income to attacks on the control of the means of production and assaults on capitalist relations of production, the more independent will be the stance of the working class towards *all* variants of the international centralization of capital, the more will it avoid the road of any policy of the 'lesser evil', and, in Western Europe, the less bemused it will be in the conflicts between US hegemony, projects for an 'Atlantic Community', a European federal state as a new imperialist super-power or a continuation of the plethora of small European states; and the more confidently and vigorously it will assert its own standpoint—for the United Socialist States of Europe!

In conditions of decelerated economic growth and intensified international competition, any temporary solution to the problem of the international centralization of capital can only be achieved at the expense of the working class. For every such solution is in the end determined by a sudden increase in the average rate of profit in the monopoly sector, and in the coming years an increase of this kind can only be secured by raising the rate of surplus-value, in other words, by intensified exploitation of the working class. The fact that the West European working class, and later the North American and Japanese proletariats, will resist such an intensification of exploitation can be seen from the practical experience of the past four years.

Above all, a more savage attack on real wages can be expected in the USA itself. American industry could sustain its substantial wage differential for decades because of its lead in productivity. Today this lead is disappearing in many branches of production. In the period from 1950 to 1965, the average productivity of labour in the USA grew by 2.6% a year against 4% in Western Europe and 6.8% in Japan. In the period from 1965 to 1969 these figures were respectively 1.7%, 4.5% and 10.6%.[68] In 1973-74, labour productivity stopped growing altogether in the USA. In these circumstances, US capital has an urgent interest in reducing wage differentials. Thus in 1968 output per employee in the steel industry was the same in the USA, Belgium and Japan, whereas wage-costs per hour in the USA were twice as high as in Belgium and four times as high as in Japan.[69]

The international centralization of capital must be understood as capital's attempt to break through the historical barriers of the nation-state, just as national (and tomorrow perhaps supra-national) economic programming represents an attempt partially to overcome the barriers of private ownership and private appropriation for the further development of the forces of production. Both, in Marx's words, are attempts to transcend capital within the limits of the capitalist mode of production itself.[70] Hence both merely reproduce on a higher plane the internal contradictions of this mode of production, above all the antagonism between use-value and exchange-value which lies at the root of all the contradictions of capitalist commodity production. The extent to which the pressure for an international capital and money market adequate to the needs of the increasing internationalization of capital *must* collide with economic programming on the national level, and thus—after a phase of extraordinary economic growth—intensify the susceptibility of the late capitalist economy to crises, will be explained in Chapters 13 and 14 of this book. First, however, we must analyse the effects of the new organizational forms of late capitalism upon the relations between the metropolitan and semi-colonial economies (Chapter 11), and then upon the relations between the sphere of production and the sphere of distribution (Chapter 12).

[68] Harvey Brooks, 'What's Happening to the US Lead in Technology?' *Harvard Business Review*, May-June 1972.

[69] International Metalworkers Federation, *Alljahrliche Erhebung über Lohn—und Arbeitsbedingungen, Produktion und Beschaftigte in der wichtigsten Zweigen der Metallindustrie*, 1968, pp. 12-13, 2.

[70] K. Marx, *Capital*, Vol. 3, p. 417.

11

Neo-Colonialism and Unequal Exchange

International movements of capital constantly reproduce and extend the international productivity differential which is characteristic of the history of modern capitalism, and are themselves in turn further determined by this differential. In the closing decades of the 19th Century there still existed large reserves of unutilized raw materials and labour-power not yet drawn into the production of surplus-value. These reserves combined with the availability of substantial excesses of capital in the earliest industrialized countries to create a growing export of capital from the metropolitan countries to the colonies and semi-colonies. In the classical imperialist period the main form of surplus-profits originated from the differences between the rates of profit in the metropolitan countries and the colonies.

Let us briefly recall the sources of the substantial differences in the rates of profit on capital invested in the metropolitan countries and the colonies which we discussed in Chapter 2.

1. The average organic composition of capital in colonial plantations producing raw materials, foodstuffs and luxury goods, as well as in colonial mines was substantially lower than that of the light and heavy industries of the metropolitan countries.

2. The average rate of surplus-value in the colonies likewise often exceeded that of the metropolitan countries, especially since the production of *absolute* surplus-value in colonial territories could

proceed beyond the limits possible in metropolitan countries. (Although, of course, the production of relative surplus value lagged far behind that of the metropolitan zones.) Furthermore, the value of labour-power in the colonies fell not only relatively, but even absolutely in the long-run, as had once been the case in the West between the middle of the 18th and the middle of the 19th centuries.

3. The presence of an enormous industrial reserve army allowed the price of the commodity of labour-power to fall even further below its value in the colonies. Whereas wages in the metropolitan countries have risen in periods of economic prosperity ever since the second half of the 19th Century, and even in periods of crisis have never fallen below their level in the previous crisis or the previous boom, wages in the colonies dropped systematically in every phase of crisis without recovering their pre-crisis levels again in the following boom period (often they did not rise at all in phases of upswing).[1]

4. The colonial system transferred a portion of the indirect costs of the overall social functioning of the capitalist mode of production, which have to be financed in the metropoles out of the mass of surplus-value produced and accordingly lower the average profit on productive capital, to the pre-capitalist surplus product in the colonies (the income of the native social classes, such as large land-owners, peasants, artisans and traders). Local taxes, for example, covered the costs of colonial administration and some of the expenditure on infrastructural works.[2] This made possible an often considerable increase in the net rate of profit on productively invested capital.

In the period of classical imperialism this substantial difference in the average rate of profit between the colonies and the metropolitan countries resulted not in the acceleration, but the deceleration of capital accumulation in the colonies, for a substantial part of the surplus-value capitalistically produced in these countries (not only of surplus-profits, but of all profits) was siphoned out of

[1] See the variety of sources confirming this thesis in our *Marxist Economic Theory*, pp. 457-8; also H. Myint, *The Economics of the Developing Countries*, London, 1964, p. 53 f. Note also Marx, *Capital*, vol. 3, pp. 786-93.

[2] Günther Kohlmey, 'Karl Marx' Theorie von den internationalen Werten, mit einigen Schlussfolgerungen für die Preisbildung im Aussenhandel zwischen den sozialistischen Staaten', in *Probleme der Politischen Ökonomie*, Vol. 5, Berlin.

them back to the metropolitan countries, where it was either used to boost accumulation or distributed as surplus revenue.

To these surplus-profits was added a further mechanism of exploitation of the colonies and semi-colonies by the metropolitan states, namely unequal exchange, which became the general rule after the start of the imperialist phase (interrupted by the two periods of the World Wars and the Korean War, 1914-18 and 1940-53). This unequal exchange meant that the colonies and semi-colonies tended to exchange increasing quantities of indigenous labour (or products of labour) for a constant amount of metropolitan labour (or products of labour). The long-term development of the *terms of trade* was a gauge of this tendency, although other determinants also influenced them: among other things, monopoly control over markets for raw materials and colonial output of these materials by large imperialist companies from the metropolitan countries, and so on.

Although it is difficult to make statistical calculations, it is nonetheless clear that both before the First World War and in the inter-war period unequal exchange was quantitatively less important than the direct production and transfer of colonial surplus-profits. Colonial surplus-profits were hence the *chief form* of the metropolitan exploitation of the Third World at that time, unequal exchange being only a *secondary form*. It is not easy to provide estimates here; at best these can only represent approximations. Let us start from the fact that on the eve of the First World War the world's biggest trading nation, Great Britain, drew an annual income of about £ 200 million sterling from foreign capital investments — admittedly not only in the colonies and semi-colonies but also in a number of industrialized countries, especially the USA. This figure can be compared with the following data. In 1910-13 Britain's foreign terms of trade were practically the same as in 1871-74. For a quarter of a century they had remained more advantageous for England than in the epoch before the 'Great Depression' of 1873-93, although the most important advantages accrued to the UK only in the 1880's; thereafter the development of the terms of trade ceased to be advantageous to Great Britain.[3]

[3] Michael Barratt Brown, *After Imperialism*, p. 76. Imlah, on the other hand, claims that the terms of trade improved about 20% to England's advantage between the 1880's and the eve of the First World War: 'The Terms of Trade in the United Kingdom', in *Journal of History*, November 1950.

Less than 50% of British foreign trade between 1880 and 1914 was conducted with the colonial and semi-colonial countries of the British Empire and Latin America (admittedly we would have to add to this the figures for Eastern Europe)[4] and the total volume of this foreign trade was £ 1.3 billion in 1913. We may assume that profits from unequal exchange at the terms of trade of the epoch could not have exceeded 20% (exports 10% above 'national' value and imports 10% below 'colonial' value). This supposition gives a profit of about £ 130 million as compared to a capital income of £ 200 million.

The proportions changed in the late capitalist epoch. Unequal exchange henceforth between the main form of colonial exploitation, the direct production of colonial surplus-profits playing a secondary role. Samir Amin has estimated that the volume of the losses incurred by the colonial and semi-colonial countries as a result of 'unequal exchange' was approximately $ 22 billion a year in the mid-60's.[5] This sum can be compared with a total gross income of $ 12 billion from private foreign capital investments in 1964.[6] The contrast with the situation before the First World War is manifest (it should not be forgotten that there has been a very substantial deterioration in the terms of trade for colonial and semi-colonial products since the 20's,[7] whereas this phenomenon was less significant in the heyday of imperialism before the First World War).

This change is closely connected with a series of structural transformations of the world capitalist economy and the international movement of capital, which we have already outlined. The main flow of capital exports is no longer from the metropolitan countries into the colonies but between the metropolitan states themselves. In the underdeveloped countries the emphasis of foreign investments has shifted from the pure production of raw materials to the

[4] Barratt Brown, op. cit., p. 110.

[5] Samir Amin, *L'Accumulation à l'Echelle Mondiale*, Paris, 1970, p. 76.

[6] *Britain's Invisible Earnings*, Report of the Committee on Invisible Exports, London, 1967, p. 27.

[7] Amin, op. cit., pp 90-1, summarizes a number of familiar sources. For the period 1954-65 the deterioration of the terms of trade in the 'Third World' has been estimated at 19%; for the period 1928-65 it is reckoned that it was 68% for Latin America (with the exception of Venezuela). According to UN calculations, the terms of trade deteriorated by 40% between 1876-80 and 1938, to the disadvantage of the 'Third World' countries. United Nations, *Relative Prices of Exports and Imports of Underdeveloped Countries*, New York, 1969, p. 22.

manufacture of consumer goods. Local anti-imperialist movements have induced colonies and semi-colonies to introduce measures designed to make it more difficult to transfer profits and dividends to the metropolitan countries. The colonial bourgeoisies have attempted, not unsuccessfully, to increase the proportion of the surplus-value produced by these workers and poor peasants which accrues to themselves rather than to the imperialist companies and states. The transition effected by imperialism from direct to indirect rule in the underdeveloped countries, with the generalization of political independence, has made it possible for the indigenous ruling classes to finance at least part of the indirect costs of the production of surplus-value, which previously had to be met from the non-capitalist surplus product appropriated by them, out of surplus-value itself—in other words, some of these costs have been transferred to imperialist capital.[8]

The development of multinational companies and the shift of emphasis within imperialism towards the export of machines, equipment and vehicles further reinforces this trend, which cannot therefore be regarded merely as a 'tactical' response to the liberation movements in the colonies and semi-colonies. It must be seen also as an 'organic' outcome of the development of late capitalism itself.[9] The world-wide strategy of the major multinational firms includes an undoubted interest in dominating the limited, but slowly growing internal markets of the semi-colonies, even if only in order to secure *future* mastery of these markets. This process tends to deprive the so-called 'national' bourgeoisie of its predominance in manufacturing industry, where the *joint venture*, combining indigenous, foreign, private and public capital, becomes one of the most important features of the late capitalist or neo-colonialist phase of imperialism.[10]

While from 1948 to March 1967, all foreign companies in India registered a growth in net assets of Rs 860 million (to make total assets of Rs 2.5 billion), in the manufacturing sector alone joint

[8] See Emmanuel, op. cit., p. 228-9.

[9] We predicted this trend in *Marxist Economic Theory* at the beginning of the 60's: pp. 480-1. It has been fully confirmed in the intervening decade.

[10] We have undertaken a close analysis of this tendency in our article, 'Imperialismo y burguesia nacional en America Latina', in *Cuarta Internacional*, No. 2, February 1971. It is based principally on material from Brazil, Chile, Columbia and Argentina. For a similar analysis of Peru, see Anibal Quijano, 'Nationalism and Capitalism in Peru', *Monthly Review*, Vol. 23, No. 3, July-August 1971.

ventures established between 1956 and 1964 represented more than Rs 2 billion initial capital, 800 million of which was foreign-controlled, together with much larger assets. In 1967, US multinational corporations participated in more than 550 joint ventures in Latin America. The real large-scale pioneers in this field, however, have been European multinational corporations in the automobile, chemical, electrical machinery and steel industries. In Africa, Unilever and its local subsidiary have increasingly established joint ventures in countries like Nigeria. The Japanese multinationals are now imitating this pattern widely in East and South-East Asia, the Middle East, Africa and Latin America. An example is the 200 billion yen petrochemical plant which Sumitomo is building as a joint venture with the Singapore government for the production of 300,000 tons of ethylene a year. A prominent instance of a complex *international* joint venture is the project for a giant 800 million dollar steel complex at Al Jubayl in Saudi Arabia, with the following capital structure: 50% Petromin (Saudi-Arabian state-owned company), 20% Marcona (controlled by Utah International, a US corporation), 12.5% Hoogovens Ijmuiden-Hoesch-Dortmund Hörder-Hutten Union (Dutch-German steel company), and 12.5% Nippon Steel and Nippon Kokan (Japanese company).[11]

For all these reasons, colonial surplus-profits directly produced in the underdeveloped countries, although they remain very substantial in absolute terms in the specific case of British imperialism[12], have steadily diminished in importance since the end of the Second World War relative to the total profits of the major imperialist companies. The figures customarily cited in this connection should, however, be qualified in three ways. Firstly, imperialist companies

[11] K. K. Subrahamaniam, *Import of Capital and Technology*, New Delhi, 1972, pp. 44-5, 64-5; Vernon, op. cit., p. 141; *Business Week*, August 3, 1974.

[12] Before the First World War the annual British income from foreign capital investments amounted to £151 million (the average for 1906-10), and £188 million (the average for 1911-13). In the years 1926-30 it increased further to £245 million, but then fell in 1934-38 to £170 million (devalued currency). In 1965 it had reached nearly £1,000 million gross and £450 million net (the enormous increase in the difference between gross and net earnings was due to the fact that large masses of foreign capital, especially from the USA, had meanwhile been invested in Britain): Report of the Committee on Invisible Exports, *Britain's Invisible Earnings*, London, 1967, pp. 21-3. If we estimate the purchasing power of the pound at about 25% of its purchasing power in 1914, the gross income of Britain's foreign capital investments increased from approximately £200 million in gold in 1914 to about £250 million in gold in 1965, whereas the net income, by contrast, declined from £188 million in gold to £125 million in gold.

frequently succeed in concealing a part of the profits directly produced in the semi-colonial or colonial countries by representing it as generated in the metropolitan states. The best-known examples of this type of operation are the oil industry, and the bauxite and non-ferrous metals industry, whose raw materials are exported from the under-developed countries in crude form to be processed for industrial use in the metropolitan zones. By artificially depressing the export price from the semi-colonies concerned, the imperialist companies in these fields conjure away in accounting terms a part of the surplus-value produced in them, which only turns up in the selling price of the refined oil, aluminium, copper, tin, and so on.[13] In so far as the companies in question are integrated monoplies which control all stages of production and distribution from the actual extraction of the raw materials to their sale to manufacturing industry, it makes no difference to them whether the profit is shown as that of their extracting firm, transport or shipping enterprise or refinery. A portion of the mass of value which the statistics of the imperialist countries show as profit produced by the big raw materials companies on the domestic market is thus in fact surplus-value created not by metropolitan workers but by producers in the semi-colonies.[14]

In so far as this concerns operations between subsidiaries of the same multinational corporation, 'transfer prices' independent of any separate 'profit maximization' obtain, which obviously facilitate concealment of profits. Cases have been cited in which, for example in Colombia, subsidiaries of multinational pharmaceutical firms have paid 155% more than the normal export-price for goods imported from the parent company. Transfer prices 40% above normal export prices in the rubber industry and 258% to 1100% higher in the electronic industry are also reported. Likewise, exports of semi-colonial subsidiaries of multinational corporations can be heavily "underpriced". A study of such practices in Mexico, Brazil, Argentina and Venezuela shows that some 75% of

[13] Pierre Jalee, *L'Imperialisme en 1970*, p. 33f. Magdoff, op. cit., pp. 145-7, emphasizes the use of protective tariffs by the US governments to block the processing of raw materials by the semi-colonies.
[14] What is involved in this case is *not* unequal exchange but an accounting 'redistribution' of published profits. The surplus-value in question, produced by workers in the colonies and semi-colonies, has in fact been realized. In the case of unequal exchange, in which commodities are sold below the 'national' price of production, a certain amount of the value, or a part of the surplus-value, is not realized.

the subsidiaries examined had underpriced their export products by 50% relative to prices received by local firms for similar products.[15]

Secondly, the surplus-profits derived from unequal exchange are often themselves only a disguised form of directly produced colonial surplus-profits. This is the case when vertically integrated trusts export raw materials from the colonies to the metropolitan countries and then send back from the metropolitan countries to the semi-colonies the finished goods which have been produced with these raw materials.[16] In addition, if a major international price differential for commodities produced by the same international company can be shown to exist between the semi-colonies and the metropolitan countries, there may well have been direct production of surplus-profit in the semi-colony disguised as an export profit in the metropolitan state.

Thirdly, the amounts of surplus-value newly accumulated in the semi-colonies which are disguised as reserves and thus not entered as profits in the balance sheets of imperialist companies must likewise be added to the total sum of colonial profits and surplus-profits.[17]

But even when all these qualifications are made, there is no doubt that the total volume of directly produced colonial surplus-profit is today less significant as a form of imperialist exploitation of the Third World than unequal exchange. Data for Latin America make this very clear: there, the continental loss on export returns far exceeded the drain of capital through the profits of foreign companies in the period 1951-66.[18]

Where then does the loss or gain of value underlying unequal

[15] Dale Weigel, 'Vues Multinationales sur les Societes Multinationales', *Finances et Développement*, Vol. 11, No. 3, September 1974; Ronald Muller, 'The Multinational Corporation and the Underdevelopment of the Third World', in C. K. Wilber (ed.), *The Political Economy of Development and Underdevelopment*, New York, 1974.

[16] The classical case is that of the aluminium companies and the re-export of aluminium finished goods (including aircraft) to countries producing bauxite.

[17] It should be emphasized that a significant part of the foreign capital 'invested' in the semi-colonies consists not of real capital exports but of non-distributed profits (i.e., produced by local wage-labour). For Latin America, Dos Santos, (op. cit., p. 77) estimates the total sum of reinvested profits of US companies as $4.4 billion in the period 1946-67, which compares with $5.4 billion newly exported capital. These $5.4 billion must then further be compared with the $14.8 billion which US capital repatriated from Latin America in the same period.

[18] Dos Santos (op. cit., pp. 75-6) cites a calculation published by ECLA, according to which the deterioriation of the terms of trade from 1951-66 brought a total loss of

exchange come from? Marx gave a clear answer to this question, which represents an application of the general labour theory of value to international trade.[19] In the epoch of capitalism,[20] unequal exchange ultimately derives from the exchange of *unequal* quantities of labour.

Within the framework of the capitalist world economy there are basically two sources of unequal exchange:

1. The fact that the labour of the industrialized countries counts as more intensive (hence more productive of value) on the world market than that of the underdeveloped lands (or, what amounts to the same thing, by contrast to the situation within a national market, less intensive and productive labour receives normal remuneration, hence more intensive and productive labour receives a higher remuneration).

2. The fact that *no* equalization of the rates of profit occurs on the world market, where different national prices of production (average rates of profit) exist side by side and are articulated with one another in a manner described in Chapter 2.[21]

Starting from theses originally advanced by Raul Prebisch[22], Arghiri Emmanuel and Samir Amin have sought to clarify this problem with the aid of an eclectic theory combining Marx and Ricardo and detouring through wage costs,[23] even though it can be resolved

---

$26.4 billion for Latin America (excluding Cuba), or twice as much as the drain in profits to the metropolitan countries. This sum is larger than the entire 'economic aid' received by Latin America in this period. It must further be remembered that according to ECLA less than half of this aid represented a genuine import of new economic resources for the continent. (op. cit., p. 65).

[19] Amin's assertion (op. cit., pp. 106, 157) that Marx was never concerned with the problem of 'accumulation on a world scale' in the 19th century is based exclusively on a quotation from a political essay on the future of India, and pays no heed to the numerous passages from *Capital*, the *Grundrisse* and *Theories of Surplus Value*, cited here in Chapter 2, dealing with the role of foreign trade as a means of transferring value from less developed to more developed countries.

[20] As distinct from 'unequal exchange of unequal value' in the age of usurers' and merchants' capital. See Ernest Mandel, 'Die Marxsche Theorie der ursprünglichen Akkumulation und die Industrialisierung der Dritten Welt', in *Folgen einer Theorie — Essays über 'Das Kapital' von Karl Marx*, Frankfurt, 1967.

[21] Kohlmey's summary of Marx's theory of international production prices (values) in the article cited above is on the whole correct, even though the second part, with its references to a 'socialist world market' and 'international price formations', contains views incompatible with classical Marxist theory.

[22] Raul Prebisch, *The Economic Development of Latin America and its Problems*, New York, 1950.

[23] Thus Amin, for example, (op. cit., p. 64) advances the typical Ricardian thesis that the general level of prices is proportionate to nominal wages. There is no empirical evidence for this assertion, which leads straight to the notorious illusion of

quite satisfactorily and directly within the context of Marx's theory of value and surplus-value. They thereby became entangled in numerous contradictions, some of which we shall discuss here. Both authors start from the hypothesis that there exists international immobility of labour-power and international mobility of capital. The logical corollary is international equalization of the rates of profit[24] – in other words, the formation of uniform prices of production on a world-wide scale. But under such conditions capital would normally stream into those countries with lowest wages. Far from explaining structural underdevelopment, this hypothesis implies – in the classical Ricardian sense – the *impossibility of underdevelopment*; it is incapable of showing why countries with high wages undergo industrialization while underdeveloped nations possess relatively little industry.[25]

The hypothesis of international equalization of the rates of profit cannot be sustained either theoretically or empirically. Theoretically, it presupposes perfect international mobility of capital – in effect, the equalization of all economic, social and political conditions propitious to the development of modern capitalism on a world scale. Such equalization, however, is completely contradicted by the law of uneven and combined development which dominates this development. Unequal conditions of development for the capitalist mode of production determine unequal sizes of internal markets and uneven rhythms of accumulation of capital.[26]

---

the 'wage-price spiral'. Nominal wages in the USA, which are more than twice as high as in the EEC, have by no means led to a price level twice as high as that of Western Europe.

[24] Christian Palloix, *Problèmes de la Croissance en économie ouverte*, Paris, 1969, p. 100, even claims that Marx supported this thesis. He refers to a passage in the Third Volume of *Capital* (pp. 232-3), which he has manifestly misunderstood. Marx merely says that higher colonial profits, to the extent 1. that they are repatriated and 2. that no monopolies exist, enter into the equalization of the rate of profit in the *mother country*, i.e., raise the average rate of profit there. This is obvious, but in no way proves that the rate of profit in the colony will therefore gradually be forced down to the level of that of the mother country. For this to happen there would have to be unrestricted free international movement of capital and this simply does not exist. Marx never said anything different, for otherwise capital export and capital investment in foreign trade could hardly be a way of arresting the fall of the average rate of profit.

[25] Admittedly Amin vacillates on this question, sometimes maintaining the notion of international equalization (op. cit., pp. 34, 136, for example) and then on the other hand denying it again (ibid., pp. 123-4, 156-7).

[26] Amin expressly emphasizes this (ibid., pp. 103, 171, 189, etc.), but thereby completely contradicts Emmanuel's thesis, which he nonetheless attempts to integrate into his own theory.

In this sense, the vast international differences in the value and the price of the commodity of labour-power, which Arghiri Emmanuel rightly underscores, are *not causes but results* of the uneven development of the capitalist *mode of production*, or of labour productivity in the world. For the logic of capital normally drives it to those zones where it has the greatest prospects of valorization.Thus the answer given by Emmanuel and Amin to the question of the origin and nature of underdevelopment in its turn poses a riddle: how does it come about that prospects for valorization of capital are *not* most advantageous where wages are lowest, and that for a hundred years capital has *not* decamped on a massive scale from countries with high wages to countries with low wages? The answer to this question takes us back to the problems of the 'domestic market', the alienation of capital accumulation, the transfer of surplus-value and the narrow limits imposed on 'internal' capital accumulation *by the existing social structure*. [27] The low wages which follow from a vast industrial reserve army and enormous underemployment are thus a function of the damming-up of capital accumulation, and can only be explained by the operation of the international capitalist system. [28] All of these phenomena, however, presuppose precisely restricted rather than general international mobility of capital. Empirically, it is easy to give evidence of the big differences in the rate of profit in the various provinces of the capitalist world economy. Calculations made by official American agencies of the rate of profit of the foreign capital investments of US companies provides a striking confirmation of Marx's classical thesis of different international rates of profit — principally as a function of different organic compositions of capital — even if the concept of the rate of profit underlying these calculations naturally does not coincide with Marx's own. In 1967 the return on these investments was 7.4% in Europe, 12.3% in Latin America, 14% in Asia and 19.7% in Africa.

In the years 1970, 1971 and 1972, the official rates of profit for US foreign investments were respectively 20.1%, 21.8% and 22.3% in the semi-colonies and 13%, 13.5% and 15% in the imperialist countries. [29] These statistics are based on declared profits; and since concealment of profits is much more developed in the semi-colonial

[27] See Chapters 2 and 3 of this book.
[28] Palloix (op. cit., p. 113) advances a similar thesis.
[29] E. L. Nelson and F. Cutler, 'The International Investment Position of the United States in 1967', in *Survey of Current Business*, Vol. 48, No. 10, October 1968, pp. 24-5; *Survey of Current Business*, September 1973. In the last years before in-

than in the imperialist countries, the former are certainly well below the real figures. Muller cites the case of the pharmaceutical firms in Colombia which declared 6.7% profits and whose real rate of profit was 136%.

The contradictions which result from Emmanuel's hypothesis emerge very clearly from his numerical examples, in which, with some exceptions,[30] he assumes that the organic composition of capital is higher in the colonies than in the metropolitan countries.[31] He does not even mention the one working assumption that is in keeping with the spirit of Marx's *Capital* — namely, that a far smaller mass of capital exists in underdeveloped countries, a much lower organic composition of capital and a lower rate of surplus-value[32] — the last of which by no means neutralizes the effect of the lower organic composition of capital. This hypothesis, moreover, corresponds fully to the actual development of international capital over the last century. It can be summarized in something like the following formula (where A is the developed, and B the underdeveloped country):

Value of the package of goods exported by A:

$5,000c + 4,000v + 4,000s = 13,000$; rate of profit 44%

Value of the package of goods exported by B:

$200c + 2,000v + 1,800s = 4,000$; rate of profit 82%

If there was an equalization of the rate of profit, a part of the surplus-value produced in B would in actual fact be transferred to A. The 'international prices of production' of the two export packages would then be structured as follows:

A: $5,000c + 4,000v + 4,680pr = 13,680$ production price
B: $\ \ \ 200c + 2,000v + 1,120pr = \ \ 3,320$ production price

---

dependence, Belgian colonial companies in the Congo achieved a rate of profit twice as high as that of companies active in Belgium. With only 16% of the total share capital of all Belgian companies, these colonial firms contributed a full third of their total profit.

[30] Emmanuel, op. cit., pp. 52-5. But in these cases the rate of surplus-value remains the same, and the author even equates constant wages with a constant rate of surplus-value, without noticing that with an increasing organic composition of capital a constant rate of surplus-value in effect means steeply rising real wages, because it implies a substantial increase in the social productivity of labour in Department II.

[31] Emmanuel, op. cit., pp. 55-63, 73-80, 161-3, 165, 170-1, 189-93, 203-5. On pp. 73, 80 and 205 the organic composition of capital is five times higher in the colonies than in the metropolitan countries.

[32] This is normally presupposed in Marx because he assumes that with much higher labour productivity in the metropolitan countries there will be an *increase* in the relation between surplus labour/necessary labour, or in other words, in the rate of

The 'international average profit' would be $+52\%$. There would be relatively little additional profit for the metropolitan capital, but the loss of surplus-value by the colonial capital would be very significant[33]; this, in fact, conforms to the empirical pattern. But the *precondition* for this equalization would be a constant and substantial *drain* of capital from A to B, a relative decline in the demand for the products exported by A and a rapid increase in the demand for the products produced by B. Failing such movements, there will be no 'international equalization of the rates of profit', relatively little capital will flow to B and the loss of value suffered by B to the benefit of A as a result of 'unequal exchange' will slow down the accumulation of productive capital in B. *Precisely this slower rhythm of the accumulation of productive capital then explains the growth of underemployment in B* — in other words, the low wages which Emmanuel takes as the starting point for his argument.[34]

Similarly, employing an eclectic theory of value and an uncritical manipulation of macro-economic aggregates, Emmanuel has since sought to question the whole Leninist theory of imperialism by refuting the very existence of an increasing export of capital in search of colonial surplus-profits from the imperialist countries to the colonies and semi-colonies before the First World War.[35] He calculates that there was no net export of capital at all, given the large-scale flow of income from the colonies to the metropolitan countries, and that even setting this aside, the actual growth of foreign investment, based on regular reinvestment of non-distributed profits, only shows an annual rate of profit of 3%. Emmanuel has here committed two analytical mistakes that are astonishing for such an intelligent economist. In the first place, he combines long-term capital flows with short-term revenue flows — while all serious balance-of-payments analyses separate these two accounts. When sons and

---

exploitation of labour-power, and that the worker will reproduce his real wage (even if it has risen) in a smaller part of the shorter working day than the worker in a backward country. This whole dimension of the question is completely absent in Emmanuel.

[33] Amin draws a similar conclusion from his empirical calculations of the results of 'unequal exchange'. (op. cit., p. 76)

[34] Franz Hinkelammert, 'Teoria de la Dialectica del Desarrollo Desigual', in *Cuadernos de la Realidad Nacional*, no. 6, December, 1970, agrees with our view that underemployment is the key to underdevelopment, and that lower wages are a consequence rather than a cause of underemployment.

[35] Arghiri Emmanuel, ' White-Settler Colonialism and the Myth of Investment Imperialism' , *New Left Review*, No. 73, May-June 1972.

grandsons of rentiers repatriated £100 million a year in interests and dividends on US railways stocks or Indian debt bonds, this figure may 'cancel out' £100 million newly invested by British entrepreneurs and financiers in Sough African goldmines, Malayan rubber plantations or Persian oil fields. But this equation does not conjure these new enterprises out of economic existence, even if they disappear from oversimplified statistics. The question remains: why do these capitalists invest in South Africa, Malaya or Persia, instead of in Britain? Instead of answering the question, Emmanuel makes it vanish by a sleight of hand.[36] In the second place, Emmanuel forgets that external revenue flows to Britain represented additional income from overseas investments, over and above reinvested profits. If we then add to these two categories the profits consumed in the colonies and semi-colonies by British capitalists and their retainers, and correct Emmanuel's slightly inaccurate figures by retaining the classical estimates of Imlah, the annual rate of profit from British foreign investments in the 1880-1914 epoch is nearer to 10% than to the meagre 3% mentioned by Emmanuel. This is what explains why these foreign investments occurred in the first instance, and what imperialism was all about.

Christian Palloix has correctly seen some of the weaknesses of Emmanuel's argument[37], but he too is unable to solve the problem of unequal exchange, among other things because of his eclectic theory of value[38]. In the course of examining the analyses of the

[36] Michael Barrat Brown, who also rejects Lenin's theory of imperialism (albeit on other empirical grounds) reproduces a table showing the capital and revenue flows to and from Britain in the pre-1914 period: *After Imperialism*, London, 1963. The *increasing* capital outflow is evident: annual capital exports rose from an average of 4.5% of the national income in the 1870-9 decade to 6% in the 1885-94 decade, 6.25% in the 1895-1904 decade, and more than 8% in 1905-13. In several periods, net overseas capital investment was higher than net home investment — for example, 1885-94 (6% of national income as against 4% for domestic investment) and 1905-13 (8.5% as against 4.5%). Revenue flows from these investments steadily increased, from an annual average of £50 million in the 70's to £100 million in the late 90's, £150 million in the 1906-10 period and £188 million in 1911-13: *Britain's Invisible Earnings*, Committee on Invisible Exports, pp. 20-1.

[37] See Palloix, op. cit., pp. 112-14.

[38] In our view this can be traced to Palloix's uncritical acceptance of Baran's notion of 'surplus'. The extent of his confusion is shown among other things by the fact that Palloix uses this notion to denote no less than five different things: 1) surplus = an excess of commodities unsaleable on the domestic market (pp. 36-40, 119 etc.); 2) the agricultural surplus product (pp. 40-2 and 71-2); 3) the industrial surplus product in the (unmarxist) sense of that part of the industrial product which cannot be realized by earnings — monetarily effective demand — arising out of industrial production

Czechoslavak Marxist Pavel[39] —which are largely an apologia for the foreign trade policy of the Soviet bureaucracy—he defines 'international values' as averages[40] of the 'lower values' of the industrialized countries and the 'higher values' of the colonies and semi-colonies, thus arriving at the following formula, in which v represents value, a an export, b an import, 1 an underdeveloped country, 2 an industrialized country and v' 'international value':

$$v_{1a} > v'_a > v_{2a}$$
$$v_{1b} > v'_b > v_{2b}$$

From this he concludes that 'What Pavel forgets is that the developed country, 2, having abandoned the production of a, loses in the import of that product (the difference $v'_a - v_{2a}$) exactly what it gains from the other (the difference $v'_b - v_{2b}$). One can apply the same reasoning to the underdeveloped country, 1. The distribution of gain, or surplus, arising out of international specialization is beneficial to all. There is no transfer.'[41]

In the first place, even mathematically speaking the conclusion drawn from this formula is incorrect: it would only be right if the difference $(v'_a - v_{2a})$ and $(v'_b - v_{2b})$ were *identical*, which is by no means automatically implied by this formula. In the second place, the conclusion suggests Ricardo's hypothesis of 'harmony', by which the capitals of the mother country 'work out' how they ought to redistribute the production already in existence in the metropolitan countries over the whole world for greater profit. The reverse, of course, occurs in the real historical process: these capitals attempt to spread internationally in line with the *needs* of the production of surplus-value and valorization of capital at home. The idea of the British cotton industry being 'transferred' to the USA, India or Egypt because cotton could be produced more 'profitably' there is absurd. Cotton production in these countries was

---

(e. g., pp. 47-8, 69-70); 4) surplus profits or profits which halt the fall of the average rate of profit (pp. 63, 65, 79-81, 99); 5) the sum of surplus-value and (!) unproductive selling costs and state expenditure (p. 222 f.), i. e., surplus in Baran and Sweezy's sense of 'monopoly capital'.

[39] T. Pavel, 'Pour un juste calcul de la rentabilité et l'efficacité du commerce extérieur socialiste, in *Etudes Economiques*, Nos. 106-7, 1957, p. 29.

[40] We have already discussed the question as to whether 'international values' always correspond to the 'average productivity of labour on the world market' (see Chapter 2). The notion itself is often meaningless: what is the 'average world market value' of a commodity which is produced only in one country or a handful of countries?

[41] Palloix, op. cit., p. 95.

created by the expansion of the British textile industry. Thereby, however, the alleged 'loss' of the mother country, which could have produced the commodities which it now imports just as cheaply as the ones it now exports, disappears. Thirdly, the 'relative advantage' which both countries can draw from foreign trade is offered as proof of the fact that there is no transfer of value; in his polemic against Ricardo, however, Marx stressed precisely that *both can exist simultaneously*: the 'relative advantage' of both countries plus a transfer of value.[42]

Hence if the content of Palloix's formula is corrected to read, as it should:

$v'_a = v'_b$ if

$v_{1a} > v'_a$ and

$v'_b > v_{2b}$

then it can be seen immediately that a transfer of value, i.e., an exchange of different quantities of labour, has in fact taken place.

With the aid of the numerical example which we used in our criticism of Emmanuel, we can now define more exactly the content of 'unequal exchange'. Let us suppose once again that the value structure of export production is $5,000c + 4,000v + 4,000s = 13,000$ in the imperialist country, and $200c + 2,000v + 1,800s = 4,000$ in the underdeveloped country. To avoid unnecessary complications in the argument, we shall introduce three additional simplifying hypotheses:

1. That these 'values' correspond exactly to international values, i.e., world market values.

2. that the underdeveloped country sends its entire export package to the imperialist country.

3. that the balance of trade between the two countries is in equilibrium, and that all items of the balance of payments which are additional to the transfer of value from the semi-colony to the metropolitan country remain outside our consideration.

The semi-colony hence exchanges commodities to the value of Fr 4,000 million for commodities to the same value from the imperialist metropolitan country. The *equivalence of international values* (world market values) will take the following form on the world market:

$$1,538cA + 1,231vA + 1,231sA = 200cB + 2,000vB + 1,800sB.$$

[42]Marx, *Grundrisse*, pp. 872-3.

Equal international values are exchanged for equal international values. Where then, does the 'unequal exchange' lie hidden behind this equivalence? It is to be found in the fact that these equal international values represent *unequal quantities of labour*. In the commodity package exported from the metroplitan country let us say that there are approximately 300 million hours of work; the commodity package exported from the semi-colony, by contrast, contains—let us say—some 1,200 million working hours.

The difference between these two quantities of labour does *not* merely reflect a difference in *wages* (such a theory would take us back past Marx and even Ricardo to the contradictions of Adam Smith's primitive labour theory of value). Let us suppose that the average working day is the same length in both countries, and that the 1,200 million working hours in the semi-colony are performed by four times as many workers (approximately 600,000) as are needed for the 300 million working hours in the metropolitan countries (in this case 150,000). The money wages (variable capital per worker) would then be Fr 8,207 in A and Fr 3,333 in B. This proportion of 1:2.5 would already differ greatly from the proportion between 300 million and 1,200 million working hours. But in itself this too would say nothing about the *real wages* in both cases.

The unequal exchange consists in the exchange of the product of 300 million for the product of 1,200 million working hours, in other words, in the fact that on the world market the working hour of the developed country counts as more productive and intensive than that of the backward nation. Does this exchange of equivalent international commodity values, consisting of unequal quantities of labour, imply an international transfer of value? At first glance the question might be dismissed as purely semantic. When seen statically and in isolation, it may seem largely inessential whether the world market or the national market is considered as the determinant of value. (Theoretically, for Marx, the second is the correct framework). In the former case, no transfer of *value* occurs in the real sense of the word, since labour not remunerated or acknowledged on the market, i.e., socially squandered labour, does not after all create value. In the second case it can be said that labour which is socially necessary on the national scale (performed under conditions of the social average productivity of labour) is less acknowledged internationally, but is still in fact fully creative of value.

If, however, we move from a static to a dynamic viewpoint—

the only one which accords with a rigorous application of the theory of value and surplus-value—the picture changes completely. The country A disposes over a labour potential which is subject to exact limits: production, consumption and accumulation (extended reproduction) are strictly determined by the total number of working hours performed. Suppose that the value of the total annual product in A is Fr 50,000 million and the newly created value Fr 30,800 million, so that the export package represents approximately 26% of the year's production, and the export package exchanged for commodities from the semi-colony contains about 11.55% of the newly created value (to avoid complicating the example, we assume that the annual product, export package and commodities exported to the semi-colony have an identical value structure). Let the total number of hours of living, value-creating labour at the disposal of country A be approximately 2.6 billion (1.3 million productive workers doing 50 weeks a year and 40 hours a week).

Now if there had not been any unequal exchange A would have had to pay, not 300 million, but 1,200 million working hours for the commodity package imported from the semi-colony. It would only have been capable of realizing a fraction of this import. At the very least there would have been a significant reduction in the resources for consumption and accumulation.[43] Economic growth would have slowed down. *In this sense* the formula of the 'international transfer of value' would certainly be of concrete significance. This 'unequal exchange' mediated through the international transfer of value (the transfer of quantities of labour) must be augmented even further by that part of the surplus-value accumulated in B but belonging to the capitalists of the metropolitan countries and drained off by them, as well as the substantial burdens imposed on B by underdevelopment in the form of payments for 'international services (transport and insurance costs, and so on).[44] *Unequal exchange hence leads to a transfer of value* (transfer of quantities of labour, i.e., economic resources) *not contrary to but in*

[43] André Gunder Frank, *Toward a Theory of Capitalist Underdevelopment*, p. 109, has pointed out the crucial role played by the export surplus of the colonies and semi-colonies in financing English investments in the 19th and the beginning of the 20th centuries.

[44] Frank, ibid., pp. 105-6, 100-1, stresses the importance of this factor in the age of 'classical' imperialism.

consequence of the law of value — not because of an international equalization of the rates of profit but despite the absence of such equalization.

In our opinion this analysis of the sources of unequal exchange is in accordance both with Marx's theory of value and with the actual historical process. It enables us to understand and explain the existence side-by-side of higher rates of profit and lower wages, capital accumulation and labour productivity in the underdeveloped countries, and the relative enrichment of the metropolitan countries at the expense of the colonies and semi-colonies, by transfers of value resulting from the exchange of unequal quantities of labour on the world market.

A critical treatment of the controversy with Bettelheim which appears as an appendix to Emmanuel's book throws further light on the elements of a comprehensive explanation, based on Marx's theory of value and surplus-value, of the difference in development between the metropolitan countries and the colonies and semi-colonies. Emmanuel sees wages as the 'independent variable' of economic development in capitalism.[45] In the underdeveloped countries low wages led to 'labour-intensive' investments which reinforced the difference between their productivity and that of the metropolitan countries.[46] In the metropolitan countries the growth of trade-union organization (monopolization of the supply of the commodity of labour-power) at the end of the 19th century made possible a secular increase in real wages.[47] This then generated a compulsion towards capital-intensive economic growth in the metropolitan countries. The differences in productivity were thus results rather than causes of the differences in wages.

Bettelheim is opposed to this thesis and considers it, as we do, a revision of the Marxist theory of value. In his opinion what lies at the basis of unequal exchange is an unequal development of

[45] Emmanuel, op. cit., pp. 64-7 ff.

[46] For Emmanuel (ibid., pp. 265-7), differences in the social productivity of labour in the imperialist metropolitan countries and the colonies or semi-colonies are inadequate to explain wage differences. Amin even claims that 75% of exports from semi-colonies consist of products manufactured by big companies under conditions of the 'highest productivity of labour'. It is patent, however, that there is a substantial difference in the level of productivity obtaining even in mines and plantations organized with modern technology in the semi-colonies, and factories in the manufacturing industry of the metropolitan countries.

[47] Emmanuel, op. cit., pp. 119-23.

labour productivity and the relations of production specific to the semi-colonies, where among other things many of the producers in the export branch are recruited from the stratum of the semi-proletariat who engage in wage labour only to obtain a supplementary income to eke out their means of subsistence in agriculture, so that wages can fall far below the minimum for existence without thereby necessarily determining the actual living conditions of this semi-proletariat. Bettelheim rejects Emmanuel's thesis of the relative autonomy of the development of wages and needs, and recalls Marx's insistence that development in the sphere of consumption and wages is ultimately always determined by development in the sphere of production.[48]

Both parties in this controversy make the mistake of trying artificially to break down the complex and integrated development of the capitalist world economy into various logical series independent of one another. It is undoubtedly a fact that since about the middle of the 19th century wages have been subject to different tendencies of development in the underdeveloped and the metropolitan countries, and this divergence has undoubtedly had a significant influence on international economic development. But wage differences are a long way from constituting a *deus ex machina* capable of determining the entire structure of the world economy independently of the laws of development of the capitalist mode of production. On the contrary, increasing divergences in wage levels are themselves a result rather than a cause of the general tendencies of development of the capitalist world economy. The long-term development of wages is dependent on the long-term trend of the industrial reserve army and the long-term trend in the productivity of labour in the consumer goods sector and agriculture. These, in turn, are determined by two factors: *the starting-point* for the demand and supply of labour-power, and the secular tendency of the *accumulation of capital*. The first explains why wages in the so-called 'empty' settlement colonies of the USA, Australia, Canada and New Zealand (empty among other things because of the systematic extermination of their original inhabitants) were higher from the very beginning. The second explains why wages in the countries of Western Europe revealed a long-term tendency to fall between the middle of the 18th and the middle of the 19th centuries,

---

[48] Bettelheim, in A. Emmanuel, op. cit., pp. 287-93.

and why this tendency was subsequently reversed from the second half of the 19th century onwards.

As long as the accumulation of capital proceeded principally by disruption of pre-capitalist processes of production and social classes on the domestic market, it destroyed more jobs than it created, so that the industrial reserve army tended to grow, and workers were consequently unable to build a strong trade union movement — in other words, to achieve a relative monopoly of supply on the market for the commodity of labour-power, and to integrate the satisfaction of new needs into a socially acknowledged standard of living (value of labour-power). Real wages therefore sank in the long run. As soon, however, as the accumulation of capital ceased to advance principally through the displacement of pre-capitalist classes on the internal market and turned instead to the expansion of the external market, it started to create more jobs than it destroyed in the metropolitan countries, *because the jobs it destroyed were henceforward located in the underdeveloped countries.*[49] It is this that explains why the secular trend now came to be a gradual reduction of the industrial reserve army in the metropolitan countries and a gradual swelling of the reserve army in the underdeveloped lands, which in turn explains the increasing discrepancy of real wages in the two parts of the world. Far from being independent variables, the two divergent trajectories of wages in the semi-colonies and the metropolitan countries were mutually determined. For they represented two complementary movements of a single, worldwide process of capital accumulation, or two fundamental aspects of the repercussions of this process on the social and economic development of mankind in the grip of capital. The formula, used by various authors, of the mutually determined development of the capitalist centre and underdevelopment of the capitalist periphery is perfectly apt.[50]

The divergence which Emmanuel cites as proof of his thesis, between countries specializing in agricultural production like Australia and New Zealand — with high wages — and countries like Algeria and Portugal, which despite their integration into the world market and similar specialization in agrarian exports have continued to remain underdeveloped countries with low wages,[51] can

---

[49] See chapters 2 and 3 of this book. For similar reflections, see Hinkelammert, op. cit., pp. 64-8. [50] Hinkelammert, op. cit., p. 37.
[51] Emmanuel, op. cit., pp. 124-5, 265.

be explained much more rationally by our thesis than by his tauto-
logically roundabout route through the 'blocking' of needs, and
hence of the value of the commodity of labour-power, at the physiological minimum for existence in the underdeveloped countries.
In the 'empty' countries of Australia and New Zealand the whole
population was incorporated from the outset into the capitalist
production of commodities. This population consisted principally
of independent commodity producers who were themselves owners
of their means of production (proprietors of the extremely cheap
or free land which was available in abundance) and who were
therefore guaranteed a high minimum level of existence from the
very start, with which the price of the commodity of labour-power
had to compete in order to allow wage-labour to come into being at
all. In Portugal or Algeria, by contrast, the mass of the population
existed outside the realm of capitalist commodity production. The
slow displacement of pre-capitalist relations of production led to
the increasing immiseration of the indigenous population, which
became willing to sell its labour-power at ever lower prices in order
to be able to bear at least part of the ever more oppressive burden
of ground-rent, usury and taxes. The destruction of native handicrafts and the separation of the indigenous peasants from their land
and soil was therefore accompanied in the long run by the secular
growth of an industrial reserve army, which *explains* the blocking
of wages and needs instead of simply proceeding from it axio-
matically.

In contrast to Emmanuel, Bettelheim is methodologically correct
in taking as his starting-point relations of production and relative
differences in productivity, as the origin of the fundamentally divergent trends of development in the semi-colonies and the metropolitan
countries. He does not, however, sufficiently consider the concrete
forms of the effects of the latter on the former, *which have arrested
or steadily widened the productivity gap*. It is not enough to quote
historical data which show why industrialization was first achieved
in Western Europe and not in China, India or Latin America. These
data — analysed more thoroughly in our *Marxist Economic Theory* —
only explain the initial difference. This difference could, however,
have narrowed down in the long run, as indeed happened in the
case of Japan, for example, which industrialized a century after
England: today the average productivity of labour in Japan has
reached the level of Great Britain, if it has not even already
surpassed it.

The initial productivity gap is thus inadequate to explain the *contemporary* gulf. To it must be added the way in which the world economy has functioned for 200 years to arrest or widen this difference. Bettelheim speaks in this connection of the uneven development of the productive forces of the centre and the periphery, which determines their unequal levels of labour productivity. Since, however, the development of the forces of production in capitalism is no more an independent variable than the level of subsistence, but ultimately only represents the outcome of a particular rhythm of accumulation of productive capital and a particular organic composition of capital, the central problem raised by Bettelheim's argument, the *productivity differential that does not precede capitalism but is produced by it*, takes us back to the problem of the accumulation of capital on a world scale. This problem cannot be solved without seeing that it was the specific structure of the capitalist economy, especially in the age of imperialism but also partly prior to it, which ensured that the accumulation of industrial capital in the metropolitan countries put a decisive brake on the accumulation of industrial capital in the so-called Third World.

The problem of 'unequal exchange' ultimately goes back to the problem of the different social structure of the underdeveloped countries. *In this respect* we are in complete agreement with Emmanuel, Palloix and Amin; well before these authors, we pointed out that disadvantageous conditions for the accumulation of capital in these countries must be ascribed to *social* causes which were hardened by the effects of imperialism.[52] We also concur with André Gunder Frank's basic thesis in this respect: the development of capitalism itself produces the juxtaposition of 'overdevelopment' in the metropolitan countries *and* 'underdevelopment' in the colonies and semi-colonies. Our differences with Frank stem from his analysis of the mechanisms which permit the dependence of the latter: he sees them in the capitalist nature of the economy of these colonies and semi-colonies (which he confuses with subordination to the capitalist world market); we see them in the specific combination of pre-capitalist, semi-capitalist and capitalist relations of production which characterizes the social structure of these countries.[53] In his later works, especially in his still unpublished

[52] See *Marxist Economic Theory*, pp. 472-6.
[53] There is a good critique of the weaknesses of Frank's theory in this respect in George Novack, 'Hybrid Formations and the Permanent Revolution in Latin America' in *Understanding History*, New York, 1972. Ernesto Laclau ('Feudalism and

Toward a Theory of Capitalist Underdevelopment, Frank makes
at least a partial attempt to take account of the justified criticisms
made of his earlier works. He now emphasizes the repercussions
of integration into the world market on the ruinous exploitation of
land and labour-power in certain regions of the colonies and semi-
colonies.[54] The examples given by Frank are undoubtedly convincing. But his use of the notion of 'mode of production' is inexact. What
he really understands by it is 'techniques' or 'organization' of production, and not *social* relations of production.[55] But it is precisely
the relations of production which would need to be included in his
analysis, to grasp the mechanisms of the 'development of underdevelopment' which *block* the disintegration of pre-capitalist and
semi-capitalist relations of production precisely by the specific
form of their integration into the world market.[56] Because he does
not take social relations of production into account, however, Frank
is unable to explain why the extension of commodity production
for export in the colonies and semi-colonies has not set in motion
the same cumulative process of capital accumulation and capitalist
production as occurred in the imperialist countries (including
Russia) and the 'White Dominions', which Lenin analysed in such
a masterly fashion in his *Development of Capitalism in Russia*.
The answer lies in the relations of production and social structure

Capitalism in Latin America', in *New Left Review*, No. 67, May-June 1971, p. 19 f)
argues a thesis which is similar to Novack's and our own. But he perhaps does not
sufficiently distinguish between feudal, semi-feudal and semi-capitalist conditions
of production; he thus fails to emphasize that the growing integration of underdeveloped countries into the capitalist world market, in successive phases of the development of the capitalist mode of production in the metropolitan countries, has variant
repercussions on the relations of production in the dependent countries.

[54] Frank, *Toward a Theory of Capitalist Underdevelopment*, pp. 30-2.

[55] Hinkelammert makes a similar mistake when he claims that the semi-colonies
become capitalist countries 'because their relations of production are determined
by their integration into the capitalist world market' (op. cit., p. 68). Capitalist relations of production are based on the specific relation of wage-labour and capital—
in other words, the conversion of labour-power into a commodity and of the means
of production into capital. Where this conversion is not generalized, there are no
generalized capitalist relations of production, in spite of the hegemony of capital
(which exploits the great majority of the population as merchant, usury and banking capital, and not as industrially or agriculturally productive capital employing
wage-labour and increasing the output of surplus-value), and in spite of integration
into the capitalist world market.

[56] An interesting analogy is the consolidation of feudal agricultural production in
Eastern Europe (and Eastern Germany) after the 16th century, precisely as a result
of extended production for the world market.

of the colonial and semi-colonial countries, which ensured that the major share of the social surplus product was not used for productive purposes. In other words, there was accumulation of capital, but it consisted of (1) foreign capital and (2) money capital (in general unproductively invested) rather than industrial capital.[57]

The same logic explains the contrasting development of North and South America in the 19th century, whose divergence has confounded many economic historians.[58] It naturally cannot be explained by either race or climate, but derives from the predominance of small, independent capitalist commodity enterprise in the North American economy as opposed to the predominance of large agricultural *hacienda* with or without a combination of natural-economic Indian *comunidades* in South America. In the first case the accumulation of capital was held up for a long time by the stubborn revival of the small farmer, which explains among other things why, despite enormous natural resources, the USA was not the world's predominant industrialized nation in the 19th century.[59] The high level of real wages, determined by the relatively high subsistence minimum of the North American farmer and the chronic shortage of labour-power, in turn led to a higher level of mechanization from the very beginning, and thus in the long-run to a higher potential for industrialization. This did not become a reality, however, until the disappearance of the frontier had prevented the small farmer class from escaping when threatened by competition to unoccupied territory, and until the mass emigration of the European industrial reserve army had created the supplementary labour power needed for this rapid industrialization.

The particular agrarian structure of Latin America, by contrast, from the outset determined a much lower level of wages and a much more limited domestic market. In the initial phase this structure may have been adequate for an early industrialization of products for the world market (e.g., the Cuban sugar industry) or luxury goods for the native ruling classes (e.g., the manufacture of certain

[57] See Amin's remarkable analysis (op. cit., p. 198f) of the three-fold distortion of capital accumulation in the underdeveloped countries, as a result of their subordination to the needs of the capitalist world market and the interests of the metropolitan countries in the valorization of their capital.

[58] Frank, *Toward a Theory of Underdevelopment*, pp. 37-48.

[59] For the dependence of the early development of the USA on the capitalist world market and the 'specialization' of the Northern and Western States of the Union in agriculture for precisely this reason, see George Novack, 'US Capitalism: National

textiles in South America) on a scale equivalent, say, to the early industrialization of Canada. But it could not then proceed to full industrialization, for the separation of agriculture and handicrafts in the *hacienda* occurred only very slowly if at all, while the mass of the native population was not drawn into the expanding process of commodity circulation. Neo-colonialism or neo-imperialism brings no change in this difference of development or productivity, just as it in no way eliminates 'unequal exchange'. On the contrary, the sources of metropolitan imperialist exploitation of the semi-colonies today flow more abundantly than ever. There has merely been a double change of form: in the first place the share of colonial surplus-profits has undergone a decline relative to the transfer of value via 'unequal exchange'; in the second place, the international division of labour is slowly moving towards the exchange of light industrial goods for machines, equipment and vehicles, in addition to the 'classical' unequal exchange of foodstuffs and raw materials for industrial consumer goods. Ultimately, however, the transfer of value is not tied to a particular type of material production, nor to a particular degree of industrialization, but to a difference in the respective levels of capital accumulation, labour productivity and the rate of surplus-value. Only if there were a *general homogenization* of capitalist production on a world scale would the sources of surplus-profit dry up. Failing such homogenization, all that shifts is the *form* of underdevelopment, not its *content*.

The increasing accumulation of capital which is visible in the semi-colonies today is accumulation of a specific kind. It is the accumulation of industrial capital moving from the sphere of raw materials into that of manufacturing industry, but on average remaining one or two stages behind the technology or type of industrialization predominating in the metropolitan countries. As we have already explained, this is a corollary of the narrow domestic market, the enormous industrial reserve army, and the trend towards industrialization with obsolescent machinery (i.e., with the 'cast-offs' of Western industry discarded because of the accelerated obsolescence of fixed capital) and even with obsolete equipment especially produced for this industry (itself in turn determined by

or International?', in *Essays in American History*, New York, 1969, pp. 15-6. Frank, *Toward a Theory of Underdevelopment*, pp. 37-40, 47.

the narrowness of the market, i.e., by small production series, which are unable to achieve the valorization of capital needed for the most modern equipment).[60]

Vernon remarks that 'some enterprises have been known to fall back on the use of a product or process that they had outgrown in their more advanced markets.' Citing various enquiries, he adds that 'the tendency of subsidiaries of US enterprises in Mexico and Puerto Rico to use second-hand equipment was quite strong during the early 60's.' Subrahamaniam asserts equally categorically: 'We came across instances wherein technology discarded in the foreign countries had been imported into India. The germanium instead of silicon technology for transistors was a case in point; Japan and Germany had given up germanium 10 to 15 years ago. . . . Similarly, foreign technicians of a foundry shop remarked that continuous casting was an accepted postwar development, vacuum-moulding and vacuum-casting methods were the modern techniques. Yet very few ventures had gone for these.'[61]

Using data from Congolese industry before independence, Jacques Gouverneur has shown both theoretically and empirically that the small size of the domestic market and the low level of local wages (determined by the industrial reserve army) *force* capitalist firms to use sub-optimal technology, even if it gradually improves with time.[62] Where optimal technology is notwithstanding employed (which only occurs exceptionally in the semi-colonies, for example, in Argentina), it leads to a very low utilization of capacity: in Argentina, the average utilization of capacity in the period 1961-64 was 50.1% in the metal-processing industry (excluding the

[60]See also the notorious examples in the automobile industry, which show that US companies in Latin America produce cars which are twice as expensive as in the USA itself, with obsolete 'new' machines specially built for small series. Leo Fenster, 'Mexican Auto Swindle', in *The Nation*, June 2, 1969. Bernard Munk, 'The Welfare costs of Content Protection: The Automative Industry in Latin America' in *Journal of Political Economy*.

[61]Vernon, op. cit., p. 180; Subrahamaniam, op. cit., pp. 170-1.

[62]J. Gouverneur, *Productivity and Factor Proportions in Less Developed Countries*, Oxford, 1971, pp. 20-1, 26, 119. A comparison between the capital/labour proportion of Belgian and Congolese cement companies gives C/L proportion for two Congolese companies in 1930 which represent no more than 23% and 41% respectively of the Belgian proportion; while in 1956-60 these figures were 50% and 32% respectively. (op. cit., p. 103). The C/L proportion is related to Marx's organic composition of capital, although they are by no means identical.

machine industry), and in the machine and electrical apparatus industry it was 47.7%.[63]

It might seem that contradictory accusations are often levelled against imperialist and international capital, so far as industrialization in the semi-colonies is concerned. For they are simultaneously condemned for using obsolete technology and hyper-modern, 'capital-intensive' plant which does not increase employment and involves massive monopolist overpricing because of sub-optimum capacity utilization. But the apparent contradiction disappears when economic analysis is substituted for moral indignation. There is no point in reproaching multinational corporations with disregarding the interests of balanced growth in the semi-colonial economies. For it is the compulsion of competition inherent in the capitalist mode of production that ensures the combination of both evils in the operations of foreign firms in the semi-colonies, given the prevalent socio-economic structures of the latter.

Two important conclusions follow. The first is that the industrial goods produced with obsolete technology remain incapable of providing serious competition on the world market to the industrial goods produced in the metropolitan countries. In the semi-colonies, therefore, exports continue to be concentrated in the raw materials sector more than indigenous production as a whole.[64] But since this raw materials sector has lost the position of relative monopoly on the world market which it once enjoyed in the age of 'classical' imperialism,[65] the prices of the raw materials exported by the semi-colonies and produced by manufactures or early industrial techniques have tended to fall towards the production price of raw materials produced with the most modern technology in the metropolitan countries. This obliges the semi-colonies to import a growing

[63] See Pierre Salama, *Le Procès du Sous-Développement*, Paris, 1972, p. 154.

[64] Of approximately $40 billion exports from the underdeveloped countries in 1965, only $4 billion (i.e., 10%) were industrial products (and of these again $600 million were processed agricultural goods): *Pearson Report*, p. 370, 367. At the same time, however, industrial production had already risen to more than 20% of the Gross National Product of the underdeveloped countries.

[65] In 1971, 80% of the raw materials imported by the USA, but only 60% of those imported by Japan, 50% of those imported by Britain and Italy, and 42% of those imported by Western Germany and Belgium, derived from the semi-colonies. The UNCTAD Secretarial Note of April 4, 1974 comments that the 1973 commodity boom 'resulted in much greater benefits to developed than to developing countries'. It earned an extra $29 billion for the advanced countries, compared to an extra $11 billion for the underdeveloped countries, apart from the oil exporters.

mass of expensive machinery and even more expensive spare parts from the metropolitan countries in order to be able to further their industrialization.[66] On the world market the metropolitan countries now operate as monopolist sellers of machines and equipment goods, while the semi-colonies have lost their position as monopolistic sellers of raw materials.[67] There is thus a steady transfer of value from one zone to the other via the deterioration of the terms of trade for the semi-colonies.

However, since 1972, a new rise in primary commodity prices has occurred—determined in part by short-term speculative and inflationary boom of 1972-73, but also partly reflecting real relative scarcities, caused by the slower rate of capital investment in the primary producing sectors than in the manufacturing sector during the previous long-term period.[68] This new upswing in prices will not be entirely cancelled by the 1974-75 world recession; it will enable the semi-colonial bourgeoisies to ameliorate their position as junior partners of imperialism, not only politically but also financially and economically. The increasing dependence of US imperialism on a whole series of raw material imports[69] makes the largest imperialist power more vulnerable to such changes than in the past (when the USA was itself the main world exporter of primary products) and could induce major new military conflicts.

In the second place, the world market also continues to function as a siphon, transferring from the semi-colonies to the metropolitan countries not only ongoing surplus-value, but also capitalized surplus-value, i.e., capital. Admittedly the chronic deficit in the balance of payments of the semi-colonies, which accompanies their

[66] Anibal Quijano, *Redefinición de la Dependencia y Proceso de Marginalización en America Latina'*, pp. 43-4.

[67] Kohlmey, op. cit., pp. 70-1. This means, among other things, that part of the surplus-profits accruing to the imperialist bourgeoisies from 'unequal exchange' correspond to 'technological rents'—in other words, to the typical form of surplus-profits in late capitalism.

[68] The annual GATT report *Le Commerce International 1973/1974*, Geneva, 1974, demonstrates this discrepancy between investment in the primary products sector and in the manufacturing industries of the USA: p. 32.

[69] Between 1950 and 1970, the import share of US domestic consumption of bauxite increased from 64% to 85%, of tin from 77% to 98%, of zinc from 38% to 59%, of potassium from 13% to 42%, of iron ore from 8% to 30%, of sulphur from 2% to 15%. Imports of chromium accounted for 100% of domestic consumption. Decreases were registered for nickel—from 94% to 90%, for vanadium—24% to 21%, and for copper—31% to 17%. See Richard Barnet and Ronald Muller, *Global Reach: The Power of the Multinational Corporations*, New York, 1974.

incipient industrialization, is compensated by so-called 'development aid', but this aid thereby merely reveals its character as state assistance to the monopolies exporting machines from the imperialist countries.[70] For such grants lead in turn to a growing burden of debt, so that an increasing portion of the total returns on exports of the semi-colonies must be converted into interest re-exported to the metropolitan states. At the end of 1972, the accumulated outstanding debts of the semi-colonies had grown to $100 billion. Debt service by now absorbed 31.5% of the export revenues of the United Arab Republic, 37.5% of those of Uruguay, 25% of those of Pakistan, 24.1% of those of India, 22.2% of those of Argentina, 20.4% of those of Afghanistan, and 18.8% of those of Turkey. At the same time the penetration of imperialist capital into the manufacturing industry of the semi-colonies and its growing fusion with the indigenous capital of the so-called 'national bourgeoisie' mean that an increasing proportion of capital ownership in these countries falls into the hands of the imperialist concerns (even if this is often camouflaged by local straw men or various forms of joint ventures, often combined with state, national or international institutions). This process is acompanied by a disguised capital outflow in such forms as high payment for international experts and technicians. The importance of such experts and technicians increases together with local industrialization, since manufacturing industry is after all much more dependent than raw materials production on foreign technology.[71]

The following statistics graphically reveal the extent of mass poverty and social inequality in the semi-colonies:[72] (*see* p. 373)

Real income differentials are much higher than these statistics

[70] This can be seen from the *bilateral* nature of a large proportion of development aid. Of the public loans described as aid, 66% were bilateral in 1961, as many as 85% in 1966, and 71% in 1971. Recently, however, there has occurred a new reversal in the proportion of public "development aid" compared to private capital exports to the semi-colonies. In 1973, for the first time, the former category was inferior to the latter — $9.4 billion dollars as against $10.9 billion. This, of course, was not unrelated to the new raw materials price boom of 1973-74.

[71] Hinkelammert, op. cit., pp. 93-5. The example of Chile shows the extent to which technological dependence has increased over time during the last decades. Whereas in 1937, 34.5% of all patents were still held by nationals, this percentage fell to 20% in 1947, 11% in 1958 and 5.5% in 1967: Muller, op. cit.

[72] See Montek Singh Ahluwalia, 'Inégalité des Revenus: Quelques Aspects du Problème', *Finances et Développement*, No. 3, 1974. See also Salama, op. cit., pp. 85-6.

	Annual Per capita G.N.P. in $U.S.	% of GNP received by Income of 40% Poorest Incomes	Annual Per capita Income of 40% Poorest Incomes	Annual Per capita Income of 20% Richest Incomes
Kenya (1969)	136	10 %	34	462.4
Sierra Leone (1968)	159	9,6%	38,8	540.6
Philippines (1971)	239	11,6%	65,1	642.6
Tunisia (1970)	239	11,4%	70,4	675.8
Equador (1970)	277	6,5%	46,2	1018.-
Malaysia (1970)	330	11,6%	91,2	924.-
Turkey (1968)	282	9,3%	70,0	857.3
Brazil (1970)	390	10,0%	97,5	1200.-
Peru (1971)	480	6,5%	79	1440.-
S. Africa (1965)	669	6,5%	104,8	1940.-

suggest, for the top 1% or 2% of the population will possess an income as much above that of the 'middle-class' 20% as that of the 'middle-class' itself is above that of the poor. The result is a system of compartmentalized 'internal markets' which tends to reproduce itself.

Admittedly it is necessary to emphasize that there is a counter-tendency in one sector: labour-intensive industries producing finished goods, which can operate with relatively cheap machine equipment. In such cases the availability of cheap labour-power in the semi-colonies, where it is accompanied by an adequate infra-structure and 'social normalization' in the interests of the owners of capital, permits the rise of an industry producing light industrial finished goods for export which can compete across the world market. The only limits on growth in the initial phase are set by costs of trans-port. This phenomenon has led to the production of transistor apparatuses for the US market in South Korea, Hong Kong and Formosa, of Asian textiles and African tinned foods for the markets of North America and Western Europe, and of the migration of the watch industry to the semi-colonies.[73] A new phenomenon appears, that of international sub-contracting: Singer has 120 plants in the Far East which manufacture or assemble parts for its products, while Swiss watch-makers commission work in Mauritius, and so on. In these cases, the wage differentials mean a surplus-profit for the capital invested in the semi-colonies rather than that invested in

[73] In mid-1973 there were 86 subsidiaries of foreign corporations in Singapore and some 250 in Hong Kong. Japanese corporations had established 400 subsidiaries in South Korea.

the metropolitan countries. There are, however, several limits to the extension of this tendency. The labour-intensive branches of industry are today declining in overall economic significance as compared to the capital-intensive, semi-automated or automated branches which monopoly capital has no incentive to transfer to the semi-colonies. Metropolitan monopoly capital has obtained partial or complete control over the modern, labour-intensive branches of production in the semicolonies. The surplus-profits achieved by certain semi-colonies on the world market because of wage advantages are thus anyway pocketed by the monopoly capital of the metropolitan countries. Hence, all that generally takes place is a compensatory transaction within the orbit of the imperialist companies themselves, i.e., a redistribution of surplus-value in favour of those monopolies participating in the new export business at the expense of those which do not, rather than any genuine redistribution towards the 'national bourgeoisie' of the underdeveloped countries. The more the tendency for branches of light industry to be transferred to countries with cheap labour-power develops, the sharper will become the corresponsing competitive struggle between the metropolitan capitalists involved in these branches or directly affected by them. This struggle will take the form of increasing rationalization and automation and will thus cancel out the temporary difference in production costs resulting from the difference in wage-levels that now gives an advantage to the underdeveloped countries — in other words, it will eliminate the surplus-profits hitherto achieved in these countries.

Relative progress in the industrialization of countries like Brazil (foreign capital-induced) and Iran (oil revenue-financed) is undeniable. Its momentum has ended by generating autonomous finance capital in these countries, active not only internally but even internationally, with a certain degree of independence from Western imperialism, however close its political and military association with it. This phenomenon is typically accompanied by a certain development of heavy industry (steel, petrochemicals). It is not, however, correct to speak in these cases of a 'sub-imperialism'. The emergence of finance-capital is only one of a number of characteristics which must all be present for an imperialist structure proper to exist. Most of these other elements are plainly absent from Brazil, not to mention Iran, and they will remain so as long as these countries remain capitalist, because of the constriction of the internal market, the backwardness of the indigenous agricultural sector, the intertwining of the interests of financiers, industrialists and technocrats with those of landowners, usurers, compradors and foreign corporations.[74]

The fate of the semi-colonies under the international imperialist system assumes its most tragic form in the growing under-nourishment of these nations. In the 30's they were still able to export 14 million tons of grain products annually. By the 60's they had to import 10 million tons of grain-products annually, and the volume of these imports risks becoming much large during the second half of the 70's. This is due neither to demographic explosion nor lack of foresight, but to the socio-economic structures imposed by imperialism. Increasing areas of land are being converted to export crops, catering to the needs of the metropolitan countries and not those of the local populations: in Africa alone, coffee output increased by 300% between 1959 and 1967. Increasing proletarianization in the village and increasing unemployment and underemployment create an increasing lag between potential and average productivity of labour on the land. Increasing class differentiation and a stagnant internal market below the 'middle-classes', result in a tremendous waste of productive resources. Increasing dependence on imported technology, often applied irresponsibly and heedlessly of its environmental consequences, cause social and ecological disasters.[75] Increasing dependence on imperialist food exports is monetized on the capitalist world market via higher prices, if necessary by artificially induced shortages. The famines of 1973-74 were directly related to decisions to *restrict* output by the major grain exporters in the late 60's and early 70's.

The decisive fact continues to be the impossibility of any thorough industrialization of the underdeveloped countries within

[74]For a good criticism of the notion of sub-imperialism' , see Pierre Salama, in *Critiques de l'Economie Politique*, No. 16-17, April-September 1974, pp. 77-9.

[75]See the monumental report of the 1968 conference on the ecological aspects of international development, M. Taghi Farvar and John Milton (eds.), *The Careless Technology*, Washington, 1971. Some of the papers presented at this conference anticipated the Sahel catastrophe. Disastrous mistakes in the new irrigation systems of Egypt's Aswan Dam and in South Asia are emphasized, and similar if not graver dangers in the Mekong Delta projects are denounced.

the framework of the world market, in the age of late capitalism and neocolonialism, just as much as in the age of 'classical' imperialism.[76] Inter-zonal differences of development, industrialization and productivity are steadily increasing. In such conditions all the mechanisms ensuring a situation of permanent social crisis in the semi-colonies will continue to function; the working strata of these countries will have to push the colonial revolution towards the point where liberation from the capitalist world market by socialization of the major means of production and the social surplus product makes it possible to solve the agrarian problem and to launch full-scale industrialization. The building of a socialist economy can itself, of course, only be completed on world scale.

[76] The annual FAO Report for 1972 indicates that between 1950 and 1970, the absolute figures of those 'employed' (under-employed would be a more correct term) in agriculture actually *increased* by 0.8% in Far Eastern Asia outside Japan and by 1.2% in Africa.

12

The Expansion of the Services Sector, the "Consumer Society" and the Realization of Surplus-Value

The capitalist mode of production as generalized production of commodities implies a constant development of the social division of
labour.[1] The outstanding historical phenomenon in this respect was
the progressive separation of agriculture and handicrafts, of country
and town, which ultimately evolved into the counterposition of consumer goods (Department II) and means of production (Department
I). But in the end the uninterrupted advance of the division of labour
also gradually dissolves this strict separation of the two basic
sectors of the economy. For just as the capitalist production of
commodities destroyed once and for all the unity of agriculture and
handicrafts, it also dissolved a whole series of other links

[1] 'Since the production and the circulation of commodities are the general pre-
requisites of the capitalist mode of production, division of labour in manufacture
demands, that division of labour in society at large should previously have attained
a certain degree of development. Inversely, the former division reacts upon and
develops and multiplies the latter. Simultaneously, with the differentiation of the
instruments of labour, the industries that produce these instruments, become more
and more differentiated. If the manufacturing system seizes upon an industry, which,
previously, was carried on in connection with others, either as a chief or as a subordinate industry, and by one producer, these industries immediately separate their
connection, and become independent. If it seizes upon a particular stage in the
production of a commodity, the other stages of its production become converted into
so many independent industries. . . It is not the place, here, to go on to show how
division of labour seizes upon, not only the economic, but every other sphere of
society, and everywhere lays the foundations of that all engrossing system of specializing and sorting men, that development in a man of one single faculty at the expense
of all other faculties . . .' Marx, *Capital*, Vol. 1, pp. 353-4.

between various domains of production that had existed in precapitalist societies, and constantly penetrated into enclaves of simple commodity production and production in pure use-values which had survived from pre-capitalist society into bourgeois society.

If this advancing division of labour was particularly characteristic of industry itself in the age of freely competitive capitalism, from the second technological revolution onwards it also started to exert a direct influence on agriculture. Ever since the emergence of massive demand for agrarian raw materials in industries and for meat products in cities, there had been a growing specialization of agricultural enterprises.[2] Alongside this specialization there now appeared — especially after the great agricultural crisis of the 80's and 90's of the 19th century in Central and Western Europe, with the growth of competition from cheap agrarian imports from overseas — the generalized separation of soil cultivation and stock farming, and the specialization of stock farming itself.

On the whole, however, this whole process of specialization and division of labour developed more slowly in agriculture than in industry until the eve of the Second World War. The mechanization of agriculture and increase in the productivity of agricultural labour lagged far behind that of industry, among other reasons because ground-rent ladelled off a substantial part of the capital needed for such mechanization. But as Marx had predicted a century earlier,[3] the full force of machines and chemicals did belatedly hit agriculture, especially under the impact of the Great Depression of 1929-32 (which had already begun somewhat earlier in agriculture).[4] *The age of late capitalism, at least in its first 'long wave with an undertone of expansion', has been characterized by an even greater increase of labour productivity in agriculture than in industry.*

In West Germany in the period 1950-70 there was a four-fold increase in the gross productivity of labour in agriculture (gross

[2] Karl Kautsky, *Die Agrarfrage*, References here are to the French edition, *La Question Agraire*, Paris, 1900, p. 42 f.

[3] 'Later, productivity advances in both (industry and agriculture), although at an uneven pace. But when industry reaches a certain level the disproportion must diminish, in other words, productivity in agriculture must increase relatively more rapidly than in industry': Marx, *Theories of Surplus-Value*, Vol. 2, p. 110. See also *Capital*, Vol. 3, pp. 761-2.

[4] This agrarian crisis had already become pronounced in the 1920's, and after receding in the years 1926-27 broke out again with renewed force. On this topic see, among others, Eugen Varga, *Die Krise des Kapitalismus und ihre politischen Folgen*, Frankfurt, 1969, pp. 77, 261-74.

output per labour-unit), the net productivity of labour (net output per labour-unit), and the 'effective productivity of labour' (value creation per labour-unit).[5] This rate of growth was far higher than that of industry. In the USA there was an annual growth of 3.8% in production per unit of labour in agriculture in the period 1937-48 (as against 1.9% outside agriculture), a growth of 5.7% (as against 2.6% outside agriculture) in the period 1949-57, and of 6.0% in the period 1955-70. Under capitalist relations of production, the escalation of the productivity of labour in agriculture takes the form of an increasing conversion of agricultural into purely capitalist enterprises — in other words, a radical diminution of the areas of simple commodity production or of individual small peasant enterprises producing use-values. The massive conquest of agriculture by big capital in turn accelerates the social division of labour in agriculture, which now achieves a qualitatively higher stage than in the ages of freely competitive capitalism or classical imperialism. All the features of this complex process of transformation in contemporary agriculture — increasing productivity of labour; penetration of big capital; large-scale enterprise; accelerated division of labour — can be summed up under the rubric of the *growing industrialization of agriculture*.

The significance of this phenomenon is two-fold. In the first place, the growing use of machines and chemicals in agriculture means the conversion of the agricultural production process into a process in every way analogous to that of industrial production,[6]

[5] Information given to the author by Hans Immler, on the basis of a work by Peter Hrubesch, 'Konstruktion eines Input-Output-Index zur Messung der Produktivitätsentwicklung in der westdeutschen Landwirtschaft 1950/51 bis 1964/65', in *Berichte über Landwirtschaft*, 1967, Band 45, Heft/3-4, and information from the Federal Ministry for 'Inter-German' Relations for the period 1965-70.

[6] This is strikingly expressed in the fact that since 1948 the annual expenditure on constant capital, without buildings, in US agriculture has been higher than the 'costs of land capital' (calculated by multiplying the price of land current at the given time in each region by the average interest rates for mortgages). From 1944 onwards the total expenditure of capital exceeded labour income in agriculture, from 1948 onwards the constant capital in annual use alone (i.e., without the 'costs of land capital') was higher than labour income. Hilde Timberlake-Weber, 'Anpassungsprobleme der Landwirtschaft im Wachstumsprozess der amerikanischen Wirtschaft', in *Berichte über Landwirtschaft*, 1963, New Series Vol. 41/3-4, pp. 576-7. While in 1950, US farms consumed $12.7 billion of circulating constant capital and $2.5 billion of fixed constant capital (depreciation), totalling $15.2 billion compared to their net income of $16.9 billion, in 1970 they consumed respectively $24.6 and 6.5 billion of circulating and fixed constant capital, as against a net income of $22.5 billion: *Statistical Abstract of the United States*, 1971, p. 581.

where the constant attempt to reduce production costs under the
pressure of competition finds expression in the release of living
labour and its displacement by machines, and in the improvement of
labour organization and the machines and chemicals which form the
preconditions of production.[7] Agriculture is thus drawn into the
maelstrom of accelerated technological innovation[8] and of the reduced turn-over time of fixed capital spent on agricultural machinery.
For example, the Japanese Institute of Agricultural Machinery
recently developed an automatic 'cultivator-harvester' which 'performs everything from rice-planting to weeding, spraying pesticide,
harvesting and threshing. This work, which normally demands 300
man-hours per hectare, can be completed in 16 hours with this
machine'.[9] Such innovations, in turn, generate new contradictions
between the cycle of the fixed (and the circulating) component of
capital on the one hand, and the cycle of the component spent on
purchase of land, on the other, which in the age of late capitalism
becomes subject to specific laws of land speculation.

In the second place, however, the growing industrialization of
agriculture also means the increasing separation of entire provinces
of production from actual agriculture and their conversion into 'pure'
industrial sectors, in the food industry.[10] Although chicken farming
organized along industrial lines may still be regarded as a transitional form, factories processing and preserving milk and meat,
canning fruit and vegetables and producing frozen or dried foods

[7] F. W. J. Kriellaars, *Landbouwproblematiek bij economische groei*, Leiden, 1965,
p. 21. Between 1950 and 1970, the value of agricultural machinery and equipment
(including farmers' private cars) rose from $12 to $34 billion. Simultaneously, the
farm population declined from 23 to 9.6 million, and persons active in agriculture
from 9.6 to 2.3 million (in 1970, 40% of the so-called active farm population was
employed outside agriculture).

[8] Cochrane estimates that 80% of the increase in agricultural output in the USA
in the period 1940-58 must be ascribed to technological progress (other authors estimate that the percentage is nearer 30%). He further explains: 'The rain of new knowledge across the land, the technological revolution sweeping over agriculture is not a
narrow thing tied to machinery and equipment — it is a broad thing involving improved skills in labour and management, the relocation, recombination and area specialization of commodity enterprises, and the farm adaptation of new techniques.'
W. W. Cochrane, 'Farm Technology, Foreign Surplus Disposal and Domestic Supply
Control', in *Journal of Farm Economics*, December 1959, p. 887.

[9] *The Japan Times*, August 13, 1974.

[10] The share of the total value of foodstuffs represented by the values added to agricultural commodities in their industrial processing can be higher than 50% (Kriellaars, op. cit., p. 15). S. J. Hiemstra, 'How much is being spent in the U.S. this year
for food?', in *Agricultural Situation*, September, 1963, p. 11 f., points out that in the
period 1950-62 the processors and distributors of foodstuffs received a constant 12%

correspond exactly to large-scale enterprises producing stockings or furniture.

This separation of entire provinces of production from actual agriculture explains why the share of agriculture in the working population has fallen much further than the share of food in average consumption. While the later still fluctuates between 20% and 30% in most advanced industrial countries, the proportion of those occupied in agriculture has in most cases fallen to less than 10% of the working population, and in some countries, such as Great Britain or the USA, to as little as 5% and below. If, however, we were to include the employees of the food industry (which is one of the most important industries in all the industrial states) among those occupied in 'agriculture', this percentage would be more than doubled.[11]

Persons Active in Agriculture as % of Total Civilian Employment

	1950	1960	1970
USA	13.5%	8.3%	4.4%
Japan	46.7%	30.2%	17.4%
U.K.	5.6%	4.1%	2.9%
West Germany	24.7%	14.0%	9.0%
France[12]	36.0%(∘)	22.4%	14.0%

(∘)1946

The rapid growth of the productivity of labour in agriculture, combined with a much slower growth in the consumption of food stuffs, and a negative elasticity of demand for certain staple items, has led to a rapid decline in relative agricultural prices, which has radically overturned the classical value- and price-structure of these commodities in the imperialist countries. If international competition were maintained, the absolute as well as the differential ground-rent of agricultural land in a large part of Western Europe would

---

of the disposable income in the average US household budget, while the share of the actual farmers in this income dropped from 8% to 5%. The total share of expenditure on food in disposable income fell from 25% to 19%. In 1970, US farmers received the equivalent of only 19% of consumer's expenditure for flour and bakery products, 25% of their expenditure for vegetables and fruits, and 39% of their overall expenditure for agricultural products.

[11] *OECD Economic Survey of Australia*, December 1972, p. 11; for Japan 1950, Masayoshi Namiki, *The Farm Population in Japan 1872-1965*, p. 40.

[12] For France in 1946, see Commission Economique pour l'Europe des Nations-Unies, *Etude sur la Situation Economique de l'Europe en 1954*, Geneva, 1955, p. 207.

disappear, as has already happened in a not insignificant part of North American agricultural acreage.[13]

The persistence of often major price fluctuations on the world market reflects the oscillation of *stocks* and the shortages which can suddenly appear in key commodities. In terms of value, these fluctuations determine whether or not the production prices of large areas of less fertile soil in North America, Australia or Argentina will suddenly determine the market price. Since production cannot immediately adjust to these sudden fluctuations, and farmers live in fear of chronic overproduction, while state intervention in the imperialist countries more often puts a premium on limiting than on extending output, production is not in fact rapidly extended to these less fertile areas, and land with a higher yield (whether because of natural fertility or greater capital investment, or a combination of the two) only exceptionally provides its owners with a genuine ground-rent.[14] This is why the constraint towards direct cultivation on a big capitalist scale becomes predominant in such countries as the USA, for in contemporary capitalist agriculture there is no longer any surplus-profit over and above the average profit (which is, in addition, also the average profit of the non-monopolized[15] sectors), while even this average profit can only be achieved with a high employment of constant capital. The fact that in many of these big capitalist agricultural enterprises the organic composition of

[13]The number of farms in the USA, which fluctuated about the 6 million mark between 1920 and 1945, had fallen to 2.9 million by 1970. Of these 1.8 million are subsistence and share-cropping farms; in other words, only 1.1 million farms produce for the market. 870,000 farms accounted for 84.4% of total agricultural sales in 1964, with an average turnover of $34,000 per farm (the others never even reached this average). 2,000,000 farms had sales of $4,000 or less. Only 142,000 farms attained a turnover over $40,000. It is no exaggeration to assert that ground rent had practically disappeared on 90% of American farms.

[14]Sudden major price increases in raw materials are accompanied by no less sudden increases in differential rents. This is true, for example, of South African gold mines, after the huge rise in the price of gold on the free market, or of Middle Eastern oilfields. In mid 1974, the necessary investment for producing one barrel of oil a day varied between £100 in the Middle East, £1,200-£1,300 in the North Sea and £3,000-£4,000 for the asphalt sands and bituminous schist layers in the USA. There is no need to emphasize the consequent scale of oil rents in the Middle East.

[15]See Kriellaars, op. cit., pp. 28-31, for the structurally weaker position of farmers vis-à-vis the monopolistic companies. Between 1950 and 1960 the production of agricultural machines in the USA fluctuated between indices of 60 and 100; their price rose by 30%. The production of steel fluctuated between indices of 90 and 120; prices rose by 50%. In agriculture, production fluctuated between indices of 100 and 125; the prices paid to farmers fell by contrast some 20%.

capital is equal or near to that of the average industry similarly explains the tendency for capitalist ground-rent to disappear. Interestingly, this tendency is not necessarily accompanied by a drop in land prices (except in the case of depopulated villages or fields which have been turned into meadows). For one thing, land continues to be a fundamental element in the process of agricultural production, and if it is private property it has a corresponding price — so that rent does not disappear entirely. Secondly, land prices rise to the extent that areas are converted from agricultural to residential or road purposes, and in this roundabout manner they are thus drawn into land speculation, which in turn is both a consequence and a motor of permanent inflation.

The fall of relative agricultural prices does not, however, lead automatically to the disappearance of the small farmer. Even in late capitalism too, a 'return to the land' is temporarily possible in periods of high unemployment or food shortages. On the other hand, if a rapid fall in the relative income of farmers coincides with a growing demand for labour-power in the cities and an increasing gap between agricultural and industrial prices, and between the incomes of peasants and industrial *wage-labourers*,[16] the flight from the soil will assume land-slide proportions, as happened in both Western Europe and North America in the 'long wave with an undertone of expansion' from 1945-48 till 1965.

Under conditions of increasing objective socialization of labour, yet generalized commodity production, a growing division of labour can only be realized if tendencies towards centralization prevail over tendencies towards atomization. In capitalism, this process of centralization is two-fold in character: it is both technical and economic. *Technically*, a growing division of labour can only be combined with growing objective socialization of the labour process by an extension of *intermediate functions*: hence the unprecedented expansion of the sectors of commerce, transport and services generally.[17] *Economically* the process of centralization can only find

[16] In the USA the income per working hour in agriculture, which was still 75% of the average hourly wage of the industrial worker in 1948, had sunk to less than 30% of this wage in 1957. Timberlake-Weber, op. cit., p. 576.

[17] We analyze further below the great variations in the economic structure of the so-called services sector. The function of middle-men, which expands in the course of the growing social division of labour and which can be ascribed in capitalism to enterprises dealing with trade, transport, storage, credit, banks and insurance, only constitutes a part of this sector, which sociologists and bourgeois political economists

expression in a growing centralization of capital, among other things, in the form of vertical integration of big companies, multinational firms and conglomerates.

The separation of previously unified productive activities makes the extension of intermediate functions indispensable. If handicrafts become separate from agriculture, peasants must be guaranteed the mediation of work-tools and consumer goods which they previously made by hand, and artisans must be assured of the mediation of previously self-produced foodstuffs through trade. The extension of these intermediate functions tends to result in their *growing independence*. The separation of agriculture and handicrafts leads ultimately to the insertion of independent trade between the two. The more generalized the production of commodities and the more advanced division of labour becomes, the more do these intermediate functions have to be systematized and rationalized in order to ensure continuous production and continuous sales. The tendency towards a reduced turnover-time of capital, inherent in the capitalist mode of production, can only become a reality if capital (commercial- and money-capital) increasingly gains mastery of these intermediate functions.

In the ages of freely competitive capitalism and classical imperialism such penetration of capital into intermediate spheres was restricted mainly to the circulation process: commercial, transport and bank capital mediated and abbreviated the exchange between Departments I and II (the delivery of raw materials and machines to the consumer goods industry and agriculture), between different enterprises and branches of industry in Department I (the mutual supply of raw materials and machines to the industry manufacturing means of production) and between Department II and the mass of consumers (sale of foodstuffs, industrial consumer goods and luxury goods to wage earners and capitalists).[18] The more advanced the international division of labour and the objective international socialization of labour became, the greater was the importance of the transport system and the intermediate functions in the realm of international trade and the international credit system. In both these epochs of capitalism the penetration of the credit system into the sphere of actual private consumption was limited to cases of misery

---

make into a pot-pourri of the most various activities, stretching from pure commodity producers (gas, water and power production) to pure parasites and crooks.

[18] Marx, *Capital*, Vol. 2, Chapter 6.

(pawning, usury); only in the 20's of our own century was it seriously extended to the area of down-payments for the purchase of durable consumer goods in the USA (in Europe and Japan this new extension of the credit system into the realm of private consumption did not become typical before the advent of late capitalism).[19]

In the age of late capitalism the process of capitalization, and hence the division of labour, acquires a new dimension in this sphere of mediation as well. Here too, rather later than in agriculture, mechanization triumphs promoted above all by electronics and cybernetics. Electronic calculating and accounting machines replace a multitude of office workers, clerks and book-keepers in banks and insurance companies. Self-service shops and automatic dispensing machines take the place of salesmen and shop-girls. The independent general medical practitioner is replaced by a polyclinic with affiliated specialists or by works doctors in big companies; the independent lawyer makes way for the firm of solicitors or legal advisers of banks, enterprises and public administrations. The *private* relationship between the seller of specifically qualified labour power and the spender of private revenues, which still predominated in the 19th century and was thoroughly analysed by Marx,[20] becomes increasingly converted into a *capitalist*, but at the same time becomes objectively socialized, service business. The private tailor is replaced by the ready-made clothes industry, the cobbler by the repairs division of big department stores, shoe shops and factories, the cook by the mass production of pre-cooked meals in self-service restaurants or the branch of industry specializing in them, the housemaid or charwoman by the mechanization of their functions in the shape of the vacuum cleaner, washing machines, dishwasher, and so on.

This objective socialization of services is particularly evident where the slightest degree of rationalization is needed in the infrastructure as a result of high fixed costs and building expences. In the mid-19th century short-distance transport, domestic heating, lighting, water and general power supply were still purely private. In the technically backward colonial areas they even provided one of the main sources for the despotic subordination of the natives, who were obliged to perform private services to their colonial

[19] For the significance of consumer credit as a temporary solution to difficulties of realization and as one of the main sources of inflation, see Chapter 13.

[20] Marx, *Theories of Surplus Value*, Vol. 1, pp. 157-61.

masters, who disposed over 'hewers of wood and drawers of water' in much the same way as the Roman slave-owners. The penetration of capital into this domain, above all through electrification, meant enormous outlays on fixed capital and a corresponding fall in the profitability of private ventures; this change led increasingly to public trains and suburban railways, power stations, and gas and water mains, which today are the rule in most of the imperialist countries. The personal and living domestic slave was replaced by the socialized and dead mechanical slave.

This development should not, of course, be exaggerated. In a commodity-producing society suffused with the acquisitive impulse, it constantly creates its own negation as a secondary current. The thousands of small enterprises trading in coal and wood are replaced by fewer multinational oil and natural gas companies. But in order to be able to reach hundreds of millions of consumers, these corporations must in turn encourage the establishment of innumerable petrol stations and garages. The electricity, water and gas services, centralized and reorganized into public plants, directly service millions of consumers. But the countless apparatuses which mediate these sources of energy to the final consumer in turn demand individual repairmen, plumbers, electricians and tradesmen to fulfil their functions. The cheaper the commodity, i.e., the shorter the labour time in which it is produced, the greater become the costs of supervision and repairs as compared with the costs of production, and the dearer in relative terms the qualified labour-power needed to perform this function.[21] Yet this negation must remain secondary in character, for as soon as any substantial gap in the enormous process of centralization appears to have become 'profitable', it will immediately attract capital, which will seek to achieve at least the average profit there and may progressively eliminate small private concerns. Large repair enterprises tend to displace the individual plumber, just as big department stores push out the small shop-keeper and large banks the private money-changer. The inter-

---

[21] The higher income of those employed in the repairs sector derives from two main sources: (1) the higher value of the commodity of labour-power in this sphere, which depends among other things on the longer time of apprenticeship determined by the growing complexity of appliances; (2) the fact that the price of this labour-power can remain above its value for a long time because of a disproportionately high increase in demand. The sudden introduction of millions of electrical appliances has created a demand for repairmen which can only be met gradually, among other things because of the need for a long apprenticeship and the relative sluggishness of the occupational structure.

mediate links and agents of the process of objective centralization
are centralized in their turn.

Far from representing a 'post-industrial society', late capitalism
thus constitutes *generalized universal industrialization* for the
first time in history. Mechanization, standardization, over-specialization and parcellization of labour, which in the past determined
only the realm of commodity production in actual industry, now
penetrate into all sectors of social life.[22] It is a characteristic of late
capitalism that agriculture is step by step becoming just as industrialized as industry,[23] the sphere of circulation just as much as
the sphere of production, and recreation just as much as the organization of work. The industrialization of the sphere of reproduction
constitutes the apex of this development. Computers calculate the
'ideal' share-package for the private capitalist rentier and the 'ideal'
location for the large company's new plant. Television mechanizes
the school, i.e., the reproduction of the commodity of labour-power.[24]
Television films and documentaries take the place of books and
newspapers. The 'profitability' of universities, music academies and
museums starts to be calculated in the same way as that of brick
works or screw factories.[25]

In the final analysis all these tendencies correspond to the basic
halmark of late capitalism: the phenomenon of *over-capitalization*,
or non-invested surplus capitals, set in motion by the secular fall
of the rate of profit and accelerating the transition to monopoly
capitalism. As long as 'capital' was relatively scarce, it normally
concentrated on the direct production of surplus-value in the traditional domains of commodity production. But if capital is gradually
accumulated in increasingly abundant quantities, and a substantial

[22] Typical examples of this further specialization and sub-division: the all-round
electrician is replaced by the radio and television repairmen, the all-round plumber
by the special repairman for central heating systems, and so on and so forth. Here
too, however, a 'centralized' reconstitution of a new 'uniform' labour may occur, as
for example, in the case of the 'general handyman' for large mansion blocks.

[23] By the turn of the century Kautsky had already analysed the beginnings of the
industrialization of agriculture in *La Question Agraire*, pp. 442-3.

[24] With the rise of the video-cassette the repenetration of capitalist commodity
production into the educational sector has become possible on a grand scale.

[25] Big companies which started off producing photostating machines are taking
over publishing houses, and starting to produce educational material as in the case
of Xerox, Bell, 3M and Bell and Howell. North American Aviation (sic) is involved
in the production of pure drinking water. General Electric is participating in the
creation of a company called General Learning, to prepare for the production of
'educational goods'. Leasco-Pergamon are planning a giant data bank, in order to
sell 'systematized scientific information'.

part of social capital no longer achieves valorization at all, the new mass of capital will penetrate more and more into areas which are non-productive in the sense that they do not create surplus-value, where it will displace private labour and small enterprise just as inexorably as it did in industrial production 200 or 100 years before.

This vast penetration of capital into the spheres of circulation, services and reproduction can in turn lead to an increase in the mass of surplus-value:

1. by partially taking over productive functions from industrial capital proper, as is the case, for example in the transport sector;[26]

2. by accelerating the turnover-time of circulating productive capital, as in the case of commerce and credit;

3. by reducing the indirect costs of production, as in the infrastructure;[27]

4. by extending the boundaries of commodity production — in other words, replacing the exchange of individual services and private revenues with the sale of commodities containing surplus-value.

The housemaid, private cook and private tailor do not produce any surplus-value; but the production of vacuum cleaners, central heating systems, electricity for private consumption and industrially produced pre-cooked meals are a form of directly capitalist production of commodities and surplus-value, like any other kind of capitalist industrial production. Monopoly capital is therefore by no means opposed to the penetration of capital into the so-called services sector, even though this undoubtedly reduces the average rate of profit because an increased mass of surplus-value has to be shared out amongst a mass of invested social capital that has increased yet more than it. Moreover, the collection of a steadily growing mass of idle capital threatens giant companies with the prospect that in the long-run this capital may no longer rest content with the average interest and may forcibly try to break into monopolized sectors once again, thereby reactivating competition and

---

[26] Here too a source of additional commodity production can emerge in late capitalism, as for example in the production of containers.

[27] Although Elmar Altvater's *Gesellschaftliche Produktion und ökonomische Rationalität*, Frankfurt, 1969, is dedicated to the problems of a socialist planned economy, it contains some useful starting points for a Marxist theory of external effects and indirect costs in capitalism.

menacing the surplus-profits of the monopolies. The diversion of excess capital into the services sector helps to avert this change.

Finally, monopoly capital has no reason to be hostile to the whole development of the intensive capitalization and industrialization of all sectors of society because it participates itself in this process — at least as soon as 'new' capital has successfully performed its historical role of opening up new fields for investment and experimenting in new products, so that the profitability of these novel realms is guaranteed. The concentration and centralization of capital in the areas of nutrition and distribution enable large companies to emerge which are a match for steel or electricity trusts (Unilever, Nestlés, General Food). Big companies take over the distribution units (hotels dominated by breweries, petrol stations by oil trusts, and so on) or take large-scale initiatives in the sphere of department stores or transport systems (airline companies, shipping companies, the holiday business). The conglomerates indiscriminately combine steel production, airlines, margarine production, electric machine construction, insurance companies, land speculation and large department stores, in order to secure the average rate of profit for the largest possible volume of capital, to minimize the risks of specialized investment, and even, by exploiting the growing possibilities of rationalized administration and marginal speculation, to bag surplus profits for the whole of this conglomerated capital.[28]

If the availability of large quantities of capital which can no longer be valorized in industry proper is a precondition for the extension of the so-called services sector, an advanced differentiation of consumption, and especially of the consumption of wage earners and the working class, is a complementary precondition for these new forms and domains of capital accumulation. This tendency was already discernible in embryo in the epoch of freely competitive capitalism, and Marx depicted it as follows in the *Grundrisse*: 'In

[28]Thus the Ling-Temco-Vought conglomerate combines among other things an airline, a steel trust, an electronics works, a bank, an insurance society, a sports goods enterprise, and a chemicals plant . . . a genuine symbol of late capitalism. But in other conglomerates too, service enterprises (or delivery enterprises) play a substantial role. Thus we find in the notorious ITT: international communications apparatus, rent-a-car (Avis), hotels (Sheraton), consumer credit, pension fund administration, and so on. Even an enormous bakery belongs to this conglomerate. The Xerox-CIT conglomerate was built up on the production and maintenance of photo-copying machines, consumer credit, X-ray apparatus, office furniture and greetings cards.

production based on capital, consumption is mediated at all points by exchange, and labour never has a direct use-value for those who are working. Its entire basis is labour as exchange value and as the creation of exchange value. The wage-worker, as distinct from the slave, is himself an independent centre of circulation, someone who exchanges, posits exchange-value, and maintains exchange-value through exchange. Firstly: in the exchange between that part of capital which is specified as wages, and living labour capacity, the exchange-value of this part of the capital is posited immediately, before capital again emerges from the production process to enter into circulation, or this can be conceived as itself still an act of circulation. Secondly: to each capitalist, the total mass of all workers, with the exception of his own workers, appear not as workers, but as consumers, possessors of exchange-values (wages), money, which they exchange for his commodity. They are so many centres of circulation with whom the act of exchange begins and by whom the exchange-value of capital is maintained. They form a proportionately very great part — although not quite so great as is generally imagined, if one focuses on the industrial worker proper — of all consumers. The greater their number — the number of the industrial population — and the mass of money at their disposal, the greater the sphere of exchange for capital.'[29]

Marx here, as it were, anticipated the 'consumer society'. Historically, the extension of the capitalist mode of production means a massive extension of money wages and an equally enormous extension of the so-called 'internal market' for industrial consumer goods, called forth by the accumulation of capital itself. How then should we regard this extension of the sphere of commodity circulation to include the wage-earners themselves, in terms of the needs (the standard of living) of the proletariat and the problems of the valorisation and realization of capital? The differentiation in the monetarily effective demand of the proletariat in the industrialized countries, which has gradually developed since the middle of the 19th century, when the industrial reserve army in the West started to undergo a secular decline, derives from the following main sources:

1. The secular decline of the share of 'pure' means of subsistence

---

[29] Karl Marx, *Grundrisse*, p. 419. In the same work see also pp. 282-7, which have already been quoted in Chapter 5 of this book.

in the real wages of the working class. This corresponds to the tendency, indicated by Marx, for a value component in the commodity of labour-power which is historically and socially determined to take its place alongside the component which has a purely physiological determination. When this tendency accelerates — as was the case particularly after the Second World War — the growing differentiation of workers' consumption is accompanied by a permanent crisis in agriculture. The demand for agrarian goods appears to be saturated; in the case of some foodstuffs there is even a negative elasticity of demand. The increase in the workers' consumption of commodities other than food is accompanied by a rapid decline in agricultural employment and the ruin of small peasant enterprise.[30]

2. The increasing displacement of the proletarian family as a unit of production, and the tendency for it to be displaced even as a unit of consumption. The growing market for pre-cooked meals and tinned foods, ready-made clothes and vacuum cleaners, and the increasing demand for all kinds of electrical household appliances, corresponds to the rapid decline of the production of immediate use-values within the family, previously cared for by the worker's wife, mother or daughter: meals, clothes and direct services for the entire household, i.e., heating, cleaning, washing, and so on. Since the reproduction of the commodity of labour-power is increasingly achieved by means of capitalistically produced commodities and capitalistically organized and supplied services, the material basis of the individual family disappears in the sphere of consumption as well.[31]

This development in turn corresponds to an economic constraint: namely the growing occupational activity of women on the one hand (this is the long-term tendency in late capitalism, although in the medium term it is possible to discern different fluctuations, which

[30] One must admittedly take into account the fact that the steep rise in the individual trading prices of many luxury foodstuffs, as a result of the growth of distribution and selling costs, artificially restricts the consumption of the wage-earners. Saturation is only absolute in the case of staple foods. The dietary optimum is naturally by no means guaranteed in the nutrition of the proletariat in the 'rich' countries.

[31] Witness of this is provided by the rise of a pronounced 'teenager' market, the growing consumption of working class youth outside the working-class family, the increasingly sharp separation of the generation of pensioners from the generation of adults, and so on. There is no need to stress the serious psychic damage resulting from such atomization (neglected children, lonely adults, old people wasting away).

correspond among other things to the oscillations of the actual business cycle), and the increasing length of the schooling of the working-class on the other (the social process of reproducing labour qualifications). This economic compulsion corresponds to the contradictory inner logic of capitalist development. On the one hand, capital is obliged to reduce the value of individual commodities by its constant expansion of commodity production as such, and its growing mechanization, which necessitate mass production and sales of these commodities. Hence its endeavours to stimulate ever new consumer needs in the population, including the working-class. On the other hand, production of surplus-value, realization of profit and accumulation of capital remain the ultimate goals of all its efforts; hence the permanent compulsion to limit wages, and to keep them below the level necessary to cover all the new needs of consumption generated by capitalist production itself. The increasing discrepancy between the needs of family consumption and the wages of the individual male worker leads to increased employment of married women and so guarantees an overall expansion of wage-labour.[32]

It can also be concluded that while capital had an obvious interest in integrating the patriarchal nuclear family into bourgeois society, its long-term development tends to disintegrate this type of family by incorporating married women into the wage-labour force and by transforming duties performed by women in the household into capitalistically organized services, or by replacing them with capitalistically produced commodities. Proletarian housewives perform unpaid labour which was for a long period indispensable for the reproduction of the worker's labour-power. But this unpaid labour is not exchanged against capital, and does not directly produce surplus-value. It takes the form of an input *in natura,* compensated by a fraction of the wages which the worker has received in exchange for the sale of his labour-power.[33] In the extreme case, it might be said that if the proletarian housewife's unpaid labour were to disappear suddenly and completely, social surplus-value would probably decrease, because the minimum wage necessary for the reproduction of labour-power would then have to go up. More commodities would have to be bought with wages, and more

[32] For the effects of this phenomenon on the volume and fluctuation of the industrial reserve army of labour, see Chapter 5 of the present book.

[33] See the interesting essay by Wally Seccombe, 'Housework under Capitalism', *New Left Review* No. 83, January-February 1973.

services purchased by the worker outside the household. But when the former housewife joins the mass of wage labourers, she increases the mass of social surplus-value produced, and thereby expands the field of commodity production and capital accumulation. If part of these additionally produced commodities are bought with her additional wages, to replace the formerly unpaid labour services she performed in the household, this is all to the advantage for capitalism, as it facilitates profit realization and expanded reproduction.

3. The cultural achievements of the proletariat won by the ascent and struggle of the modern working class (books, papers, self-education, sport, organization, and so on) lose those features of voluntary self-activity and autonomy from the processes of capitalist commodity production and circulation, which defined them in the period of classical imperialism (particularly notable in Germany in the period 1890-1933), and become drawn into capitalist production and circulation to an increasing extent. Books are produced by commercial publishers instead of by workers' cooperatives; the bourgeois press and television take the place of a socialist press; commercialized holidays, excursions and sport replace the recreational activities organized by young workers' associations, and so on. The reabsorption of cultural needs achieved by the proletariat into the capitalist process of commodity production and circulation leads to a far-ranging *reprivatization of the recreational sphere* of the working class.[34] This represents a sharp break with the tendency typical of the epochs of freely competitive capitalism and classical imperialism, towards a constant extension of the spheres of collective action and solidarity of the proletariat.

4. The direct economic compulsion to purchase certain additional commodities and services, without which it becomes physically impossible to sell the commodity of labour-power and to buy the means for its reproduction (this must be strictly distinguished from indirect socially manipulative compulsions such as,

[34] Sociological works such as those of D. Dumazedier, *Vers une Civilisation du Loisir?*, Paris, 1962, or J. Fourastie, *Les 40,000 Heures*, Paris, 1965, certainly stress the inter-relationship of average labour productivity and the possibility of extended free-time, but they typically make two analytical errors: (1) they conceive of a so-called 'dynamic of mass consumption' independent of the specific social structure of capitalism, and regard the former rather than the latter as the determinant of the quantitative and qualitative configuration of the recreational sphere; (2) they do not understand that social behaviour in free time depends crucially on the relations of

for example, advertising). Thus it is no longer economically possible today for the average wage-earner to go to work on foot, not to enrol in a health insurance scheme, to use privately produced charcoal for heating instead of briquettes, oil, gas or electricity. A distinction must be made between two aspects of this economic constraint. On the one hand, the substantial increase in the intensity of labour makes a higher level of consumption necessary (among other things, better quality food, greater meat consumption, and so on) if labour-power is to be reconstituted at all. On the other hand, the increasing extension of the capitalist conurbations lengthens the circulation time between home and work to such an extent that time-saving consumer goods likewise become a condition for the actual reconstitution of this labour power. This is even true of private cars, where the collective public transport network is non-existent or under-developed (as in many regions of the USA, for example).

5. The differentiation of consumption or the extension of the commodities consumed as a result of *social* pressure (advertisements, conformity). A significant proportion of such commodities can be regarded as largely useless (kitsch in the living room), if not damaging to health (cigarettes). The conversion of many former luxury goods into mass consumer goods generally leads to a systematic reduction in the quality of these commodities.[35] Difficulties in the realization of surplus-value induce a growing trend for the monopolies to alter the form of commodities perpetually, often in a senseless way from the point of view of rational consumption [36] Kay speaks in this context of a shortening of the 'period of consumption' of commodities which, in the case of durable or semi-durable consumer goods, is accompanied by a deterioration in their quality.[37]

6. The genuine extension of the needs (living standards) of the wage-earner, which represents a raising of his level of culture and civilization. In the end this can be traced back virtually completely to the conquest of longer time for recreation, both quantitatively

production; the mass of those condemned to alienated labour cannot suddenly develop creative initiatives in their free time.

[35] See the already copious literature published or inspired by Ralph Nader.

[36] See André Gorz, *Critique de la Division du Travail*, Paris, 1973, p. 258. For the drug industry, the Kefauver Report in the USA estimated actual production costs as only 32% of wholesale prices. Levinson reckons actual production costs at 39% of wholesale prices and less than 20% of retail prices: *The Multinational Pharmaceutical Industry*, p. 29.

[37] Kay, op. cit., pp. 165-6.

(a shorter working week, free weekends, paid holidays, earlier pensionable age, and longer education) and qualitatively (the actual extension of cultural needs, to the extent to which they are not trivialized or deprived of their human content by capitalist commercialization). This genuine extension of needs is a corollary of the necessary civilizing function of capital. Any rejection of the so-called 'consumer society' which moves beyond justified condemnation of the commercialization and dehumanization of consumption by capitalism to attack the historical extension of needs and consumption in general (i.e., moves from social criticism to a critique of civilization), turns back the clock from scientific to utopian socialism and from historical materialism to idealism. Marx fully appreciated and stressed the civilizing function of capital, [38] which he saw as the necessary preparation of the material basis for a 'rich individuality'. The following passage from the *Grundrisse* makes this view very clear: 'Capital's ceaseless striving towards the general form of wealth drives labour beyond the limits of its natural paltriness, and thus creates the material elements for the development of the rich individuality which is as all-sided in its production as in its consumption, and whose labour also therefore appears no longer as labour, but as the full development of activity itself, in which natural necessity in its direct form has disappeared; because a historically created need has taken the place of the natural one.'[39]

For socialists, rejection of capitalist 'consumer society' can therefore never imply rejection of the extension and differentiation of needs as a whole, or any return to the primitive natural state of these needs; their aim is necessarily the development of a 'rich individuality' for the whole of mankind. In this rational Marxist sense, rejection of capitalist 'consumer society' can only mean: rejection of all those forms of consumption and of production which continue to restrict man's development, making it narrow and one-sided. This rational rejection seeks to reverse the relationship between the production of goods and human labour, which is determined by the commodity form under capitalism, so that henceforth the main goal of economic activity is not the maximum production of things and the maximum private profit for each individual unit of production (factory or company), but the optimum

---

[38] Marx, *Grundrisse*, pp. 409-10.
[39] Ibid., p. 325.

self-activity of the individual person.[40] The production of goods must be subordinated to this goal, which means the elimination of forms of production and labour which damage human health and man's natural environment, even if they are 'profitable' in isolation. At the same time, it must be remembered that man as a material being with material needs cannot achieve the full development of a 'rich individuality' through asceticism, self-castigation and artificial self-limitation, but only through the rational *development* of his consumption, consciously controlled and consciously (i.e., democratically) subordinated to his collective interests.

Marx himself deliberately pointed out the need to work out a *system of needs*, which has nothing to do with the neo-asceticism peddled in some circles as Marxist orthodoxy. In the *Grundrisse* Marx says: 'The exploration of the earth in all directions, to discover new things of use as well as new useful qualities of the old; such as new qualities of them as raw materials; the development, hence, of the natural sciences to their highest point; likewise the discovery, creation and satisfaction of new needs arising from society itself; the cultivation of all the qualities of the social human being, production of the same in a form as rich as possible in needs, because rich in qualities and relations — production of this being as the most total and universal possible social product, for, in order to take gratification in a many-sided way, he must be capable of many pleasures, hence cultured to a high degree — is likewise a condition of production founded on capital. This creation of new branches of production, i.e., the creation of qualitatively new surplus time, is not merely the division of labour, but is rather the creation, separate from a given production, of labour with a new use-value; the development of a constantly extending and more comprehensive system of different kinds of labour, different kinds of production, to which a constantly expanding and enriched system of needs corresponds. Thus just as production founded on capital creates universal industriousness on one side — i.e., surplus labour, value-creating labour — so does it create on the other side a system of general exploitation of natural and human qualities, a system of general utility, utilizing science itself just as much as all the physical and mental qualities, while there appears nothing *higher in itself*, nothing legitimate for itself, outside this circle of social production and exchange.'[41] Marx further

[40] Marx and Engels, *The German Ideology*, pp. 67-8.
[41] Marx, *Grundrisse*, p. 409.

wrote: '*Luxury* is the opposite of the *naturally necessary*. Necessary needs are those of the individual himself reduced to a natural subject. The development of industry suspends this natural necessity as well as this former luxury — in bourgeois society, it is true, it does so only in *antithetical form*, in that it itself only posits another social standard as necessary, opposite luxury. These questions about the system of needs and the system of labours — at what point is this to be dealt with? will be seen in due course.'[42]

There is no need to demonstrate here that the possibilities of developing and differentiating material consumption cannot be unlimited; that the concept of 'abundance' is thus a genuine material and historical category and not an idealistic or utopian notion; and that the disappearance of scarcity and an economy based on scarcity is both possible and necessary, as a precondition for a communist mode of distribution. There is equally little need here to attempt a Marxist definition of a rational pattern of development of consumption or of the distinction between creative-productive activity and passive consumption of goods (one does not 'consume' a piano, a scientific book, a friendship or a landscape in the same way as an ice-cream or a shirt).[43]

The more the actual consumption of *goods* is satiated, the more its quantitative extension becomes irrational and indifferent to mankind, and degenerates into pure extravagance, boredom and disgust of life (compare the ruling class of the Roman Empire, in the 1st to the 3rd century and the decadent court aristocracy of the 18th).[44] In this context, it is necessary to grasp the two-fold nature of the development of the material consumption as consumption of mass-produced *commodities*. In his critique of capitalist commodity production Marx stressed that while capitalism creates large-scale production it simultaneously determines the unilateral and massified nature of the product, 'which forces upon it a social character strictly tied to the social context, while its immediate relation to the

[42] Marx, *Grundrisse*, p. 528.
[43] Marx expressly emphasized this relation between consumption and creative activity in his early writtings. See also the explicit rejection of asceticism in *Theories of Surplus Value*, Vol. 3, pp. 260-1; see also pp. 256-7 in the same volume.
[44] In the *Economic and Philosophical Manuscripts* Marx describes the enjoyment of the ruling classes as that of 'mere ephemeral individual(s) frantically spending (themselves) to no purpose' and stresses that 'extravagant wealth' is linked with 'contempt of man'. Karl Marx, *Economic and Philosophical Manuscripts of 1844*, ed. D. J. Struik, London, 1970, p. 156.

use-value which is supposed to satisfy the need of the producer, is made to appear as something contingent, indifferent and inessential'.[45] This dimension of consumption seems completely to have escaped such admirers of the capitalist market economy as Zahn, who see nothing problematical in the universal commercialization of such 'goods' and 'services' as 'cultural goods' and services of 'civilization', naïvely forgetting (but are they really so naïve?) that production of these goods is subordinated to the *profit motive* of capitalist business.[46] Such apologists claim, on the one hand, that the 'mass of buyers' is now sovereign, but concede on the other that the salient characteristics of the 'new advertising' is that these 'sovereign consumers' first have to be persuaded of their new needs.

Despite the considerable extension of the consumption of the proletariat in the highly industrialized countries, however, what the capitalist mode of production cannot do is to increase this consumption at the same rate as the productivity of labour. The constraint to valorize and accumulate capital — in other words, competition and private ownership of the means of production — forbids this. If in the long term, therefore, consumption develops more slowly in terms of value than productivity — which is after all expressed in the law of the growing organic composition of capital (for if there is a secular decline in the variable share of total capital, the demand for commodities from Department II cannot grow at the same rate as that for goods from Department I) — then it will become increasingly difficult to realize the surplus-value contained in consumer goods or to utilize the full social production capacity for consumer goods. What may seem quite realistic for the individual capitalist — namely to regard all proletarians other than his own workers as potential customers with a purchasing power that could grow without limit — is void of meaning for the capitalist class as a whole. The logic of the capitalist mode of production forbids the apportionment of an even greater share of the national income to the proletariat. Since, as Marx explains in the *Grundrisse*, 'the mass of products grows in a similar proportion (to the productivity of labour) . . . so grows the difficulty of realizing the labour-time contained in them — because the demands made on consumption increase.'[47] This is the explanation of the enormous development

[45] Marx, *Resultate des unmittelbaren Produktionsprozesses*, p. 186.
[46] Ernest Zahn, *Soziologie der Prosperität*, Munich, 1964, pp. 35-6, 64-71, 85.
[47] Karl Marx, *Grundrisse*, p. 422.

of two specific services — advertising and market research on the one hand, and consumer credit on the other — whose function is to sound out and break through these limits. The extension of capitalist commodity production and circulation in the sphere of consumption under late capitalism is accompanied by a greater than average expansion of these two sectors.

The large increase in the costs of sales, distribution and administration (in the USA these already absorb more than 50% of national income) is an unmistakable expression of the growing difficulties of realization in late capitalism. At the same time it is striking evidence of the wasteful character of this mode of production in the phase of its historical decline.[48] Although some of these costs can be regarded as socially justified — namely those which facilitate the actual consumption of beneficial use-values — and could not be reduced even after the overthrow of capitalism without wasting the time and energies of the producers-consumers (irregular supply; incomplete stocks; insufficient knowledge of new products), it can be accepted without further ado that the majority of these expenses are not determined by the interests of consumers but by the specific conditions and contradictions of the capitalist mode or production (the constraints of valorization of capital and competition, i.e., private property of the means of production).

The exact effect of the enormous increase in selling expenses on the mass of surplus-value or the rate of profit can only be calculated if a whole series of complex relationships is taken into account. In the first place, a feature of commercial capital in general is also partly characteristic of the capital invested in this area of the services sector: its aim is to reduce the turnover time of circulating productive capital, thereby enabling it to augment the mass of surplus-value produced each year. Its share in the total social surplus-value — the fact that capital invested in the services sector obtains the average profit — thus corresponds to the increase in the production of surplus-value due to its entry into it. In the second place, the cost expenditures of the services sector (buildings, apparatuses, cars, wages and salaries), are not met from ongoing output of surplus-value, but from social capital (i.e., surplus-value accumulated in the past). These costs are repaid by a reconstruction of part of aggregate social

---

[48] See the excellent passages on this subject in Baran and Sweezy's *Monopoly Capital*.

capital and not by tapping ongoing output of social surplus-value. Only the *profit* of the services sector forms a part of this ongoing output of surplus-value. The very high level of selling costs does not restrict the volume of profit accruing to the big companies, or the rate of profit, as decisively as Gillmann mistakenly assumes.[49] What is parasitic about this massive growth is the unproductive squandering of social capital, not the wastage of a substantial part of the ongoing output of surplus-value. The non-productive expenditure of surplus capital naturally means that the total social mass of surplus-value is smaller than it would be if this capital was spent productively. But the fact that it is spent unproductively does not mean that a major part of the surplus-value actually produced is subtracted from the large industrial companies.

The private services sector of the 19th century basically consisted of the exchange between private sellers of a specific labour-power and capitalist revenues; this made no difference to the determination of the total mass of surplus-value, since all that occurred in these conditions was a redistribution of values which had already been created. In 20th century capitalism, the services sector in the sphere of circulation basically consists of the exchange between the owner of a particular part of the aggregate social capital which is unproductively spent and the owner of revenues (both capitalists and wage-earners). This exchange does not enter into the direct determination of the total mass of surplus-value, but it nevertheless has an important indirect bearing on it, for it helps to increase the mass of surplus-value by reducing the turnover-time of circulating capital. The effect on the accumulation of capital, is to release a part of idle capital for participation in the distribution of the aggregate social surplus-value. Ultimately, however, this participation can only tap two sources: it must occur either at the expense of that part of the surplus-value which is distributed amongst the owners of productive capital (thus lowering the average rate of profit by increasing the total capital within which the total surplus value must be divided),[50] or at the expense of wages — in other words, by increasing the rate of surplus-value (among other things via a relative contraction of real wages as a result of price increases in consumer goods).

The substantial extension of consumer credit in the age of late

[49] Joseph Gillman, *The Falling Rate of Profit.*
[50] The drive of the monopolies to secure surplus-profits and the corresponding formation of two average rates of profits — one for the non-monopolized and one for the monopolized sectors — corresponds among other things to the need of big

capitalism provides similar evidence of the growing difficulties of realizing surplus-value. The enormous volume of private indebtedness in the USA not only forms the economic basis for the expansion of the sector of durable consumer goods and the massive expansion, since the Second World War, of building activity. It is also the main basis of permanent inflation. The phenomenon of this indebtedness proves that despite accelerated technological innovation, increased investment and permanent armaments, late capitalism is no more capable of resolving one of the fundamental contradictions of the capitalist mode of production than early capitalism or classical monopoly capitalism — the contradiction between the tendency for forces of production to develop without limitation, and the tendency towards limitation of the demand and consumption of the 'final consumers' (increasingly consisting of wage earners). This contradiction, of course, corresponds to the laws of the valorization of capital itself.

The apparently homogeneous notion of the expansion of the services sector, that is typical of late capitalism, must therefore be reduced to its contradictory constitutive elements. This expansion involves:

1. The tendency towards a general extension of intermediate functions, as a result of the counterposition of a growing division of labour with a growing objective socialization of labour. Part of this expansion is technically determined, and will therefore outlive the capitalist mode of production itself (extension of the transport and distribution network, the maintenance and repair facilities for machines at the disposal of the consumer, and so on).

2. The tendency towards an enormous expansion both of selling costs (advertising, marketing, to some extent expensive packaging and similar unproductive expenses) and of consumer credit. This aspect of the expansion of the services sector is for the most part socially, and not technically determined; it stems from the growing difficulties of realization and will disappear along with the capitalist mode of production or generalized commodity production.

3. The possibilities for developing the cultural and civilizing needs of the working population (education, health care, recreational activity), as distinct from the pure consumption of commodities, created by the growing productivity of labour and the

capital to unload the loss of profit due to the increase of unproductive capital onto the non-monopolized sectors.

corresponding limitation of necessary labour time (with growing differentiation of consumption). The services which correspond to these needs are not exclusively tied to the specific form of capitalist production and exchange, and will not in fact be able to develop fully before the capitalist mode of production has been overthrown. Admittedly, both the commercial nature of these services, which are geared to make a private profit, and their content, will undergo a fundamental change: instead of manipulating and alienating real human needs, they will be subordinated to them. In accordance with this tendency, the independent performance of these 'services' will wither away in socialist society as all men and women themselves gradually become capable of performing them. Forms of individual specialization will remain, but society will no longer be divided into 'productive' performers and passive consumers of cultural and civilizing services.

4. The extension of *commodity* production which is not a part of the so-called 'services sector' at all, but is a result of the growing centralization of certain forms of production which were previously largely private. Electricity, gas, water, ready-made meals and electrical household appliances are material goods and their production is commodity production in the real sense and in no way sale of services.[51]

5. The growth in the number of unproductively employed wage-earners, since the massive penetration of capital into the sphere of circulation and services affords capitals which can no longer be invested productively the opportunity of receiving at least the average profit of the non-monopolized sectors instead of obtaining only the average interest. This growth is consequently a result of the tendency towards over-capitalization in late capitalism.[52]

The expansion of the capitalist services sector which typifies late capitalism thus in its own way sums up all the principal contradictions of the capitalist mode of production. It reflects the enormous expansion of social-technical and scientific forces of production and

[51] The production of films, television broadcasts and means of communication too, is material commodity production in capitalism. If it is performed by wage labourers, it is productive in the capitalist sense, i.e., creative of surplus-value. The 'distribution' of television broadcasts to millions of spectators is not commodity production but a socialized service. Hence it produces no additional surplus-value.

[52] Pierre Naville was the first to point out the basic tendency towards the universalization of wage labour which lies at the root of the extension of the services sector in late capitalism.

the corresponding growth in the cultural and civilizing needs of the producers, just as it reflects the antagonistic form in which this expansion is realized under capitalism: for it is accompanied by increasing over-capitalization (difficulties of valorization of capital), growing difficulties of realization, increasing wastage of material values, and growing alienation and deformation of workers in their productive activity and their sphere of consumption.

Is the capital invested in the services sector productive or not? Is the labour performed by wage-earners in this sector productive or unproductive? As long as capital investment in services was marginal in character,[53] the answer to these questions was of only secondary importance for an analysis of the movement of the capitalist mode of production as a whole. However, once the services sector of late capitalism expands to such an extent that it absorbs a considerable part of aggregate social capital, a correct definition of the precise limits of productive capital assumes the greatest importance. The formula 'in capitalism productive labour is labour which creates surplus-value' is inadequate for such a definition. Although it is correct in itself, it remains a tautology. It does not answer the question of the boundaries of productive labour but merely recasts it in another form. The difficulty exists in Marx's own writings, where there is a certain discrepancy between the *Theories of Surplus Value* and the Second Volume of *Capital*.

In the *Theories of Surplus Value*, in which Marx stresses the positive role of Adam Smith in the development of the labour theory of value and of our understanding of the capital relationship, he still oscillates between the hypothesis that only labour which participates *directly* in *commodity* production — and hence in the production of value and surplus-value — is productive,[54] and the hypothesis that any labour can be counted productive which is bought with capital (exchanged with capital as opposed to revenue).[55] In the section on the 'Concept of Productive Labour', which Kautsky published as an appendix to the First Volume of the *Theories of Surplus Value*, these two definitions are still mixed up with one another.[56] The extent to

---

[53]See Marx, *Theories of Surplus Value*, Vol. 1, pp. 160-1, 410.
[54]Marx, *Theories of Surplus Value*, Vol. 1, pp. 172-3, 185.
[55]Ibid., pp. 157, 166, 185-6, 200.
[56]Ibid., p. 410: "It can then be said to be a characteristic of *productive labourers*, that is, labourers producing capital, that their labour realizes itself in *commodities*, in material wealth." See the contrasting passages on pp. 406, 411.

which a real *indeterminacy* persists in his conception of productive labour is clear from the passage where Marx here — in complete contrast to *Capital* — includes commercial middle-men in the category of productive workers if they perform wage-labour.[57]

In the Second Volume of *Capital* Marx defined the productive labourer as a worker who participates in the production of material commodities and thus of value and surplus-value. He now makes it clear that not all labour which is exchanged for capital is necessarily productive — beginning with wage labour engaged in the sphere of circulation (commercial and bank capital).[58] Marx's polemic against the way in which Adam Smith lumped together the spheres of production and circulation in his consideration of the creation of value and surplus-value is thus developed well beyond his criticisms of Smith in the *Theories of Surplus Value*. In *Capital* Marx provides a consistent formulation of the general law determining the frontiers of productive labour in capitalism: 'If by a division of labour a function, unproductive in itself although a necessary element of reproduction, is transformed from an incidental occupation of many into the exclusive occupation of a few, into their special business, the nature of this function itself is not changed.'[59]

If, therefore, wage labour remains unproductive in function, even though it constitutes a necessary element of reproduction, then this rule presumably applies *a fortiori* to types of labour which do not even play a direct role in reproduction. There is no conceivable reason why the exchange of personal services for revenues, as long as it does not lead to the production of commodities, should suddenly become productive merely because it is organized as a capitalist business and performed with wage-labour. Even in the *Theories of Surplus Value* Marx distinguished within the transport industry between the expedition of people — which involves the unproductive exchange between a personal service and revenue — and the expedition of goods, which increases their exchange value and is therefore productive.[60] If even capitalistically organized traffic in

[57] Ibid., p. 218-9.　　[58] Marx, *Capital*, Vol. 2, p. 127.
[59] Ibid., p. 131. By contrast, see the passages on capitalistic non-material production in *Resultate des unmittelbaren Produktionsprozesses*, pp. 144-6. It is evident that before writing the Second Volume of *Capital* Marx hesitated in his demarcation of the frontiers between productive and unproductive wage-labour performed for capitalists.
[60] Marx, *Theories of Surplus Value*, Vol. 1, pp. 412-413.

human transport is unproductive, then presumably capitalistically organized laundries, concerts, circuses, medical and legal assistance societies are even less so.

In the Second Volume of *Capital* Marx uses the following formula for the often subtle dividing-line between productive capital and circulation capital: 'Costs of circulation, which originate in a mere change of form of value, in circulation, ideally considered, do not enter into the value of commodities.'[61] 'Although in the case submitted the costs of forming a supply (which is here done involuntarily) arises only from a delay in the change of form and from its necessity, still these costs differ from those mentioned under I, in that their purpose is not a change in the form of the value, but the preservation of the value existing in the commodity as a product, a utility, *and which cannot be preserved in any other way than by preserving the product, the use-value itself.* The use-value is neither raised nor increased here; on the contrary, it diminishes. But its diminution is restricted and it is preserved. Neither is the advanced value contained in the commodity increased here; but new labour, materialized and living, is added.'[62] Finally: 'Quantities of products are not increased by transportation. Nor, with a few exceptions, is the possible alteration of their natural qualities, brought about by transportation, an intentional useful effect; it is rather an unavoidable evil. *But the use value of things is materialized only in their consumption, and their consumption may necessitate a change of location of these things, hence may require an additional process of production, in the transport industry.* The productive capital invested in this industry imparts value to the transported products, partly by adding value through the labour performed in transport.'[63]

The frontier between productive capital and circulation capital thus runs between wage-labour which increases, changes, or preserves a use-value, or is indispensable for its realization — and wage-labour which makes no difference to a use-value, i.e., to the *bodily form* of a commodity, but merely arises from the specific needs involved, i.e., *altering* (as opposed to *creating*) the form of an

[61] Marx, *Capital*, Vol. 2, p. 139. See also p. 152. By 'change of form of the value' Marx understands the metamorphosis from commodity into money and from money into commodity outside the process of production.

[62] Ibid., p. 141.

[63] Ibid., p. 153 (Our italics).

exchange value.[64] Extending this definition by Marx, we may therefore conclude that actual service capital—so long as it is not mistakenly confused with capital which produces commodities—is no
more productive than circulation capital.[65]

An important consequence follows. From the standpoint of the
overall interests of the capitalist class, the extension of the services
sector in late capitalism is at best a lesser evil. It is preferable to the
existence of idle surplus capitals, but remains an evil to the extent
that it does nothing whatever directly to increase the total mass of
surplus-value and indirectly contributes to it only in a modest degree,
by shortening of the turnover-time of capital. *The logic of late
capitalism is therefore necessarily to convert idle capital into service
capital and simultaneously to replace service capital with productive
capital, in other words, services with commodities:* transport services
with private cars; theatre and film services with private television
sets; tomorrow, television programmes and educational instruction
with video-cassettes.[63] There is no need to have to stress the dangers
to the environment from the immeasurable growth of this mountain
of commodities.

Capital cannot survive saturation with material goods any more
than it can survive the elimination of living labour-power from

[64]We wrote in our *Marxist Economic Theory* that 'In general, one can say that
all labour which creates, modifies or conserves use-values or which is *technically
indispensable* for realizing them is productive labour, that is, it increases their exchange value.' (p.191.) This was to draw a line between productive labour and
labour performed in the sphere of circulation, always with reference to the production and circulation of commodities. This definition fully corresponds to Marx's own
in the Second Volume of *Capital*, as can be seen from the passages cited above (except that 'increases their exchange-value' would have to read adds exchange-value'
or better still, 'adds value'). Altvater is thus wrong when he declares: 'The concept
of productive labour as defined by Mandel by no means corresponds to Marx's concept' and 'even regresses behind the complexities of the concept in Adam Smith',
Altvater and Huisken, op. cit., p. 249. He does not seem to have understood the
nature of the question we were attempting to answer with reference to Marx: that
of the precise line of division between the productive sphere on the one hand and
the sphere of circulation and services on the other.

[65]The most comprehensive treatment so far of this problem is to be found in Jacques
Nagels, *Travail Collectif et Travail Productif dans L'Evolution de la Pensée Marxiste*,
Brussels 1974. For the *individual capitalist* all wage-labour — even in the sector of
circulation and the services — is obviously productive, since it enables him to appropriate a part of the overall social surplus-value.

[66]This is the rational nucleus of Galbraith's discussion of the dichotomy between
'private affluence' and 'public squalor' in *The Affluent Society* which he cannot
however fully understand because of his rejection of Marx's theory of value and
surplus-value.

material production. This is why the extension of social and cultural services in late capitalism, made possibly by the progress of science and technology, is confined within limits which are just as narrow as those imposed on the extension of automation. At a certain point of development, both would explode the whole process of valorization of capital, and with it the capitalist mode of production.

For all these reasons, the further development of the service sector cannot lower the average social organic composition of capital, and thereby engender a tendency for the average rate of profit to increase. On the contrary, the fraction of the overall social surplus-value which accrues to the capitalist services sector is a deduction from, rather than an addition to, the surplus-value created by productive capital. It is self-evident that with the complete automation of the whole sphere of production of goods, an enormous mass of social revenues would disappear. A society consisting only of service trades, in which the entire proletariat had become unproductive wage-earners (no longer producing commodities), would nonetheless be faced with the problem that these wage-earners could not use their wages solely to buy 'capitalist services', for they would first have to eat, drink, clothe themselves, obtain homes and guarantee their sources of energy before they could go to the doctor, have their shoes mended [67] or take a holiday trip. The capital invested in 'service enterprises' would hence hardly be able to achieve 'valorization'. If the goods which were completely produced by an automatic process were no longer sold but distributed free, then it is difficult to see any reason why masses who were assured of their living standards in this manner should hire out their labour-power to 'service enterprises'. Such a scenario, in other words, would no longer have anything to do with capitalism.

---

[67] Nagels, op. cit., p. 256, includes repair shops for durable consumer goods organized on a capitalist basis, i.e., employing wage-labour, in the productive rather than "service" or distribution sectors of the economy, because such repairs are indispensable for the realization of the use-value of these goods.

13

Permanent Inflation

Money expresses a social relationship, in which social labour potential has been fragmented into private labours performed independently of each other, producers thereby only enter into social
contact through the exchange of the products of their labours,
these products take the form of commodities, these commodities
possess exchange value, and generalized commodity production
is only possible if this exchange value confronts them independently
as money.[1] Money thus lies at the root both of the social nature of the
private labour of commodity-producers and of the fact that this
social character can only prevail by the roundabout route of the
exchange of commodities, the market, and private appropriation
of the value product (in the capitalist mode of production: appropriation of surplus-value by capital). 'Money is in reality nothing but a
particular expression of the social character of labour and its products,
which, however, as antithetical to the basis of private production,
must always appear in the last analysis as a thing, a special commodity, alongside other commodities.'[2]

The fact that the social character of commodity-producing labour
is not given as an *a priori* datum creates the necessity for money
material, in other words, for value to be incorporated in the value
of a specific commodity — a universal equivalent.[3] Marx explained

[1] Marx, *Grundrisse*, pp. 140-1, 143-4, 165.
[2] Marx, *Capital*, Vol. 3, p. 593.
[3] Marx: 'The very necessity of first transforming individual products or activities
into *exchange value*, into *money*, so that they obtain and demonstrate their social

why 'labour money', which would merely express a particular number of working hours ('value'), could not function as a universal equivalent for commodities in a commodity-producing society.[4] Precisely because he thereby overcame the traditional dualism — still visible in Ricardo — between the labour theory of value determining commodity value,[5] and the quantity theory determining 'monetary value', Marx was able to develop a coherent and uniform economic theory on the basis of the labour theory of value.

Any attempt to ascribe the determination of 'monetary value' to some source other than the commodity value of the money commodity (gold, or gold and silver), i.e., by 'convention',[6] state compulsion or mere 'reflection of commodity values' must lead to very serious contradictions. This is evident from the example, among others, of Rudolf Hilferding, who in his *Finanzkapital* advanced a theory of 'socially necessary circulation value' derived directly from the total commodity product (the sum of the values of all the commodities in circulation).[7] Even before the First World War,[8] Kautsky had analysed the basic error of this theory of money, although he did not pursue his critique through to its logical conclusions.[9]

By starting from an unmediated 'sum of the values of all the commodities in circulation', Hilferding overlooked the basis of Marx's theory of money, namely: 'The difference between price and value, between the commodity measured by the labour time whose produce it is, and the product of the labour time against which it is exchanged — this difference calls for a third commodity to act as a measure in which the real exchange value of the commodities is expressed. Because price is not equal to value, therefore the value-determining element — labour time — cannot be the element in

---

power only in this objective form, proves two things: 1) that individuals now produce only for society and in society; 2) that production is not *directly* social, not the "offspring of association", which distributes labour internally.' *Grundrisse*, p. 58. See also, *Capital*, Vol. 3, pp. 503-4.

[4] Marx, *Grundrisse*, pp. 136-40, 153-6. *Critique of Political Economy*, pp. 83-6.

[5] Marx, *Critique of Political Economy*, pp. 171-9.

[6] Marx: 'Money does not arise by conventions, any more than the State does. It arises out of exchange': *Grundrisse*, p. 165.

[7] Hilferding, *Das Finanzkapital*, pp. 29-30.

[8] Lenin used a single word for his verdict on Hilferding's theory of money: false. *Collected Works,* Vol. 39, p. 334.

[9] Karl Kautsky, 'Gold, Papier und Ware', in *Die Neue Zeit,* Vol. 31/31, No. 24, p. 837. For another pertinent critique of Hilferding's theory of money see Suzanne de Brunhoff: *L'Offre de Monnaie*, Paris, 1971, p. 83 f, which, however, does not mention the crucial element in Marx's theory of money any more than did Kautsky.

410 Late Capitalism

which the prices are expressed, because labour time would then have to express itself simultaneously as the determining and the non-determining element, as the equivalent and non-equivalent of itself.'[10]

Hilferding's formula, 'the sum of the values of all commodities' divided by the velocity of the circulation of money, is thus meaningless in a two-fold sense: firstly, because the 'sum of the values of all commodities' represents the sum of non-homogeneous quantities of labour, which can only be reduced to socially necessary labour time by means of exchange and different particular proportions; secondly, because such a quantity of labour cannot possibly be divided by the velocity of the circulation of money': five million working hours divided by gold coins or bank notes which circulate 25 times a year is a vacuous formula.

Admittedly, if the 'sum of the values of all commodities' is replaced by the 'sum of the prices of all commodities',[11] and if it is accepted that price is the *monetary expression* (monetary form) *of value*, then the sum of prices can be seen to be a *relation,* namely between the changing value of the commodities and the changing value of the money commodity, the money material. Any Marxist analysis of the problem of money must start from an analysis of this *relation.*[12] Marx in this sense distinguished between three different forms of money corresponding to three different laws of development:

1. Pure metallic money. Since pure metallic money — and to simplify our analysis we shall consider only gold money as metallic money — here possesses an immanent value (the quantity of socially necessary labour contained in it), the volume of it in circulation is determined by the dynamic of the commodity values in circulation and by the payments to be realized. If the sum of the commodity

---

[10] Marx, *Grundrisse*, pp. 139-40. The last sentence is underlined in Marx.

[11] Marx drew the important conclusion from his general definition of money that commodities *can only enter into circulation* if they have already been provided with an ideal price: *Grundrisse*, p. 193. Hilferding's error was closely connected with his failure to understand the antagonism between use value and exchange value, already criticized here in Chapter 1, which led him to the mistaken hypothesis of a universal cartel, whose proportional production would make it proof against crises. Bukharin to some extent followed him in this direction.

[12] 'Gold must be in principle a *variable* value, if it is to serve as a measure of value, because only as reification of labour-time can it become the equivalent of other com-

values falls (because of an increase in the productivity of labour or a decline in production) while the value of gold remains constant, the circulation of gold money will be reduced or the prices of commodities will fall, and gold money will be withdrawn by an increase in hoarding. If the sum of commodity values rises (because of an increase or stabilization of production or a fall in the productivity of labour) while the value of gold remains constant, the circulation of gold money will increase (hoarded gold will be injected into circulation). Conversely: if the value of gold drops because of a sudden increase in the labour productivity of gold mining, the prices of other commodities will rise, if there is no change in the sum of commodity values. If the value of gold goes up because of a sudden drop in the labour productivity of gold mining, prices will fall if the sum of commodity values remains constant.[13] These examples are, however, exceptional and marginal. The key point is the determination of the volume of money in circulation by the prices of commodities (ultimately determined by the relationship between the sum of all commodity values and the value of gold), divided by the velocity of the circulation of gold money. The autonomous variable is always the circulation and value of the commodities; the flow of gold money into or out of circulation is a function of the needs of capitalist reproduction.

2. Money-tokens, i.e., convertible paper money (or small silver coins), which take the place of pure gold money to economize means of circulation and to extend credit. The same law applies here as to gold money, the only proviso being that such tokens must not be issued in excessive quantities. If this condition if respected, such money is 'as good as gold', and just like gold it can be withdrawn from circulation at any time and later be injected back into it. However, if it is issued in greater quantities than the corresponding quantity of gold, convertible paper money automatically becomes devalued. For example, the equation 1 ounce of gold = 1 ton of steel compares

---

modities, but as a result of changes in the concrete productivity of labour, the same amount of labour-time is embodied in unequal volumes of the same type of use-values.' *Critique of Political Economy*, p. 67.

[13] Strictly speaking this only applies to simple commodity production. In the capitalist mode of production the mediation must take place via the equalization of the rate of profit as between capital invested in gold mines and the rest of capital. On this question, see Otto Bauer, 'Goldproduktion und Teuerung', in *Die Neue Zeit*, Vol. 30/2, No. 27, p. 4 f.

given quantities of labour; thus if 1 ounce of gold is represented by RM 160 instead of by RM 80, this in no way alters the value of gold or steel. But the additional token issue means that every RM 10 bank-note now represents half the previous quantity of gold. Its value has consequently fallen by half — in other words, the price of steel (in paper money) has doubled.[14]

3. Unconvertible paper money with a compulsory rate of exchange. One the whole, this conforms to the same law as convertible paper money, but with one important difference: since the relation between the commodity value and the value of gold is here no longer directly given, it can only be established *post festum* how much gold is objectively represented by this paper money, which will be shown by the rate of exchange of this paper money *for gold* (on a 'free' or 'black' market) *and for foreign currencies*.

Inflation is therefore a meaningful concept only in the case of paper money.[15] The term 'gold inflation' has as little sense as 'iron inflation': the correct concept here is not inflation but a decline in the value of the commodity. It is true that a sudden and massive drop in the value of precious metals, such as occurred in the 16th Century, after 1849 or after 1890 (the Transvaal and the application of the cyanide process to gold production), leads to price increases which are analogous to a massive inflation of paper money. But a significant difference immediately strikes the eye. When gold loses value it can still be used for hoarding; devalued paper money, by contrast, is typically kept in circulation and becomes increasingly useless for the formation of hoards.[16] Hence one can at most apply the term 'inflation' to metallic money only when the gold content of coins is reduced, i.e., if the coinage is adulterated. But this case

---

[14] To repeat: in the capitalist mode of production — as distinct from simple commodity production — the connections are not so simple because, among other things, the distribution of monetarily effective demand over different sectors of production, the dynamics of the prices of production and the development of the accumulation of capital, following the fluctuations of the rate of profit, must each be investigated in these sectors.

[15] Inflationary issues of convertible paper money become inconvertible in the long run, because there would otherwise be the danger of a total collapse of foreign payments through the disappearance of gold reserves. This is exactly what has now happened with the dollar, in practice since 1969, officially since August 1971.

[16] With different national rates of inflation, however, paper money which loses some of its purchasing power, but is not devalued as much as other paper currencies, can be used for hoarding. This was true of the dollar from the end of the Second World War until the mid-60's.

precisely confirms the rule that 'inflationary coins' cease to be hoardable and remain in circulation in line with Gresham's well-known law. Hofmann is therefore wrong to claim that the rising cost of living, which coincided with the predominance of monopolies from the 1890's onwards, marked the onset of 'secular inflation'.[17] The rising prices of that epoch can be explained by other factors, including particularly the fall in the value of gold as a result of declining costs of production.[18] The earliest one can speak of 'secular inflation' is after the First World War, and more accurately only after the Great Depression of 1929-32 had been overcome.

In the developed capitalist countries with a gold currency, paper money inflation first made its appearance with the hypertrophy of state expenditure caused by rearmament and war (when budgetary deficits started to be covered by use of the printing press).[19] Inflation as a mechanism to extend credit facilities within the framework of the actual process of the production and circulation of commodities was rejected as irresponsible by both bourgeois political economists and capitalist politicians.[20] The reasoning behind this view was that only the immanent laws of the market economy could restore normal equilibrium and any attempt to intervene in this process 'artifically' would in the long-run endanger the recovery of the economy and multiply the contradictions and causes of crisis.[21]

This 'orthodox' conception of money undoubtedly contained a grain of truth. Capitalist crises of overproduction among other things fulfil the objective function of facilitating the valorization of total capital (despite the higher organic composition of capital), by a

[17]Werner Hofmann, *Die säkulare Inflation*, Berlin, 1962, pp. 10-11.

[18]For this point see, for example, Karl Kautsky, 'Die Wandlungen der Goldproduktion und der Wechselnde Charakter der Teuerung', Supplement no. 16 to *Die Neue Zeit*, 1912-1913, published on 24 January 1913. Later in this Chapter we shall return to the interesting discussion that developed on this subject before the First World War between Eugen Varga, Karl Kautsky and Otto Bauer.

[19]On this point, see, for example, Eugen Varga, 'Gold und Kapital in der Kriegswirtschaft', in *Die Neue Zeit*, Vol. 34/1, p. 815; by the same author, *Die Wirtschaftspolitischen Probleme der proletarischen Diktatur*, Vienna, 1920: and, also by Varga; *Die Krise der kapitalistischen Weltwirtschaft*, 2nd Edition, Hamburg, 1922, pp. 11, 16, 23-5, etc.

[20]For example, Alfred Marshall, *Principles of Economics*, London 1921, pp. 594-5 and 709-10.

[21]The classical figure in this respect was the well-meaning A. C. Pigou, the father of 'Welfare Economics', who on the eve of the Great Depression seriously argued the thesis that the crisis could be averted by lowering wages, for in this way entrepreneurs would be encouraged to increase their investments.

massive devalorization of particular capitals. This devalorization of productive and fictitious capitals does not take place evenly and in proportion to the capital investment of each individual enterprise. It is a selective process, in which technically advanced enterprises survive, while backward and bogus concerns are completely eliminated. Plants with medium productivity are hit more severely than leaders, although they escape bankruptcy. A crisis of overproduction is thus the appropriate mechanism within the capitalist mode of production for achieving an increased productivity of labour, as the socially necessary labour time in commodity production that determines commodity value, and for eliminating those firms which objectively waste social labour by a wave of bankruptcies, enabling expanded reproduction to proceed again despite the decreased value of commodities. Prices that have increased in the phase of prosperity and 'over-heating' are now adjusted to the decrease in the value of the commodities, and surplus-profits are for the most part eliminated. At the same time a crisis of overproduction is (as we noted above) also the mechanism which periodically makes possible a renewed rise in the average rate of profit by a devalorization of capital, and an increase in the rate of surplus-value. This, in turn, permits an intensification of labour productivity in the 'leading' firms, and therewith a reappearance of surplus-profits for individual capitals.

If swelling credit and inflation prevent such a 'sanitation' of the capitalist economy — in other words, if a periodic plunge in prices, a periodic adjustment of market prices to commodity values (production prices), is artificially forestalled — a whole series of capitalist enterprises which have already fallen below the average productivity of labour in their sector may escape the devalorization of their capital, or bankruptcy, for a longer period. It then becomes difficult to distinguish 'healthy' enterprises from sick or purely bogus ones at all.[22] However, this situation can only increase the disequilibrium between production capacity and monetarily effective demand in the long-run: it therefore contains the danger of a

[22] Marx had already discerned this in his own epoch, when he wrote: 'The entire artificial system of forced expansion of the reproduction process cannot, of course, be remedied by having some bank, like the Bank of England, give to all the swindlers the deficient capital by means of its paper and having it buy up all the depreciated commodities at their old nominal values.' *Capital*, Vol. 3, p. 490. See also, ibid., pp. 503-4. Since the 60's, we are manifestly witnessing just such a situation, with the bankruptcy of Penn Central in the USA, the sudden collapse into insolvency of such giant auto firms as British Leyland, Citroen and Toyo Kogyo, which have only been saved

mere postponement of the crash.[23] The impact, scope and duration of the Great Depression 1929-32 inevitably led to a revision of dominant economic ideology: for there was now a shift in the priorities of bourgeois economic policy. The long-term threat of monetary instability was now considered less menacing than the short and medium-term dangers of permanent unemployment and stagnant production. From the standpoint of the valorization of capital this change was undoubtedly justified. Grave social and political considerations also lay behind the new attitude of the bourgeois class in the USA even before the Second World War and in the remaining imperialist states particularly in the post-War period. For the change in the international relationship of social forces meant that a recurrence of mass unemployment would now be tantamount to a catastrophic social crisis for late capitalism.

For all these reasons, the most important groups of monopoly capital and imperialist governments one after another opted for permanent institutionalized inflation, as a device for overcoming or preventing cataclysmic economic crises of the kind experienced in 1929-32. The 'revolution' in bourgeois political economy inaugurated by Keynes was a conscious ideological expression of this change of priorities. Many statements of the time can be cited to show it is quite proper to speak of a conscious turn in the economic policy of imperialism.[24] We need quote only one such declaration here, made by Keynes himself: 'There is no effective means of raising world

---

by huge government or bank salvaging operations (whether Chrysler will escape a similar fate is not yet certain). Without the inflationary boom of the previous years, the unprofitability of such firms would have become evident much sooner.

[23] A good summary of the 'orthodox-neoclassical' critique of Keynes and Keynesianism can be found in Sudha R. Shenoy's anthology of writings by F. A. Von Hayek, *A Tiger by the Tail — The Keynesian Legacy of Inflation*, London, 1972. The thesis that Keynesianism will ultimately provoke a serious economic crisis by inflation, which this author has put forward with exemplary obstinacy for forty years, seems to be unchallengeable in the long-run. The only point is that for Hayek this leads to the familiar alternative, between the devil and the deep blue sea: to prevent a serious economic crisis in the long-run, this political economist has consistently advocated an economic policy which would have unleashed the same economic crisis in the short-run. A retrospective look at the world of 1945-50 is all that is needed to understand why the governments of the victorious imperialist powers could not have regarded such an alternative as realistic, even with the best will in the world. Keynes's classic answer to his critics: 'In the long-run we are all dead' is an echo of the French nobility's famous maxim 'Après nous le Déluge'. It was the outlook of a class condemned by history, not of one confident in its historical future.

[24] Hofmann, op. cit., pp. 26-9, lists several sources for the doctrinal origins or justifications of 'permanent inflation'.

prices except by increasing loan-expenditure throughout the world. . . . Thus the first step has to be taken on the initiative of public authority; and it probably has to be on a large scale and organized with determination, if it is to be sufficient to break the vicious circle and to stem the progressive deterioration. . . . Some cynics, who have followed the arguments thus far, conclude that nothing except a war can bring a major slump to its conclusion. For hitherto war has been the only object of government loan-expenditure on a large scale. . . . I hope that our government will show that this country can be energetic even in the tasks of peace.'[25]

Technically, permanent inflation started to appear with the extension of *bank money* from the end of the 19th century onwards. Convertible paper money (gold-tokens) was issued as a means of guaranteeing *circulation credit* in the last century. The volume of this issue of paper money varied largely with the volume of the drafts to be discounted, i.e., it was closely adapted to the immediate needs of capitalist commodity circulation. Such paper money could only be created as a means of *expanding* credit through speculation: it was above all commercial capital which took the initiative in this respect. When the practice of granting overdrafts on current accounts became more widespread, the situation changed.[26] The creation of credit by banks now became much more emancipated from the actual circulation of commodities; the initiative moved from commercial capital to the big companies in the sphere of production. These could now obtain credit for production by means of an overdraft on their current account, i.e., by means of bank money.[27] The volume of money thus became an inverted pyramid with three instead of two parts: a base of gold, above which extended a wider layer of paper money, above which in turn extended a still wider layer of bank money.

[25] J. M. Keynes, *The Means to Prosperity*, London, 1933, pp. 19, 22.

[26] Bank capital had a particular interest in this change, which afforded the opportunity of larger profits for it. In this connection, see R. S. Sayers, *Modern Banking*, Oxford, 1967, pp. 267-70.

[27] See for example, the observation which Joseph Schumpeter made as early as 1912: 'In so far as credit (Schumpeter here means production or enterpreneurial credit, as distinct from circulation credit – E.M.) cannot be given out of the results of past enterprise or in general out of reservoirs or purchasing power created by past development, it can only consist of credit means of payment created *ad hoc*, which can be backed neither by money in the strict sense nor by products already in existence . . . . Credit in the one case in which it is essential (i.e., entrepreneurial credit – E.M.) can only be granted from . . . . newly created means of payment.' *The Theory of Economic Development*, New York, 1961, p. 106.

So long as the control of the central banking authorities over the total quantity of money continued to obey the rules of financial orthodoxy on the basis of the gold standard, however, the extension of the methods of creating money remained a purely technical process designed to economize the *faux frais* of circulation. The 'Keynesian revolution', however, transformed not only the form but also the content of money creation. Bank money, or deposits plus overdrafts on current bank accounts, henceforward became the main source of inflation.

Initially, the bourgeois state took the initiative in this transformation, as it was urged to do both by Keynes and by German monetary theorists with similar views. Deficit financing — in other words, the use of budgetary deficits to create additional 'monetarily effective demand' — was the long-term strategy adopted by the State. The role of public expenditure as the main source of inflation became even more pronounced in the Second World War. After the War, however, in the new 'long wave with an undertone of expansion', actual state expenditure, although still substantial, ultimately became of secondary importance in the dynamic of permanent inflation. *Henceforward the main souce of inflation became the expansion of overdrafts on current accounts granted by banks to the private sector, and covered by central banks and governments —* in other words, production credit to capitalist companies and consumer credit to households (above all for the purchase of houses and durable consumer goods). *Thus permanent inflation today is permanent inflation of credit money, or the form of money creation appropriate to late capitalism for the long-term facilitation of extended reproduction* (additional means for realizing surplus-value and accumulating capital).

This explanation of the origin and nature of contemporary permanent inflation continues to be rejected in many circles invoking Marxism. They stubbornly cling to the notion that military outlays constitute the sole, or at least the principal, source of inflation. Nevertheless, the figures speak for themselves. It is sufficient to compare the following series of different aggregates in the US economy since the end of the Second World War:[28] (*See* p. 418)

To round off the picture it is enough to add that total private

[28] GNP and private indebtedness given in *Economic Report of the President*, February 1970, and *Survey of Current Business*, May 1970, cited in *Monthly Review*, September 1970, p. 5. National debt, 1969: see the statistical data published by the EEC.

Year	A Gross National Product (in billions of dollars)	B Public Debt	C Private In- debtedness	B as % of A	C as% of A
1946	208.5	269.4	153.4	129.4	73.6
1950	284.8	239.4	276.8	84.0	97.2
1955	398.0	269.8	392.2	67.8	98.5
1960	503.7	301.0	566.1	59.7	112.4
1965	684.9	367.6	870.4	53.7	127.1
1969	932.1	380.0	1,247.3	40.8	133.8
1973	1,294.9	600.0	1,700.0	46.3	131.2
1974	1,395.0	700.0	2,000.0	50.0	140.0

indebtedness in the USA remained practically stationary between 1925 and 1945 ($ 131.2 billion in 1925; $ 139.7 billion in 1945); its enormous expansion dates only from the period after the Second World War. In West Germany, paper money circulation rose from 14 billion DM in 1955 to 47.5 billion in 1973, but bank loans to home firms and private persons rose in the same period from 63 to 631 billion DM. In Japan paper money circulation rose from 422 billion yen in 1950 to 5,556 billion yen in 1970, but bank loans increased from 2,500 yen in 1952 to 39,500 billion yen in 1970. The case of Belgium — a country with relatively small military commitments — also deserves mention. In the period 1962-71 bank credits to the public sector rose to 210 Belgian billion francs, i.e., almost doubled, while bank credits to the private economy increased from 72 to 340 billion Belgian francs, or nearly five-fold. In the same period, however, the Gross National Product, at constant prices, rose by about 55%. The inflationary nature of this credit creation is obvious.

Contemporary awareness of the phenomenon of permanent inflation began to grow when, by contrast with the traditional pattern, prices ceased to fall in times of obvious over-production — recession — and indeed even continued to rise. The Great Depression, of course, had led to an enormous crash of prices, on a scale beyond anything previously known in capitalist crises of overproduction. The crisis of 1938 similarly led to an abrupt fall in prices.

After the general price increases of the years 1940-46, a contradictory development set in: contrary to all expectations, prices rose steeply in the initial post-war years, except in the USA, where they declined — even if only slightly — in the recession of 1949. The 'Korean War Boom' then gave prices a fresh boost. The effect of 'permanent inflation' became visible when the US recessions of the years 1953, 1957 and 1960 were in every case accompanied by a further rise in retail prices (in 1953 wholesale prices declined slightly once more). In the recession of 1970-71, the continued increase in prices was particularly pronounced, and became even more so in the recession year of 1974.

A whole new terminology to describe 'creeping inflation' thus came into being, reflecting the belated realization that late capitalism has in fact lived under conditions of permanent inflation for more than thirty years. Galbraith had remarked as early as 1958: 'We are impelled by present attitudes and goals to seek to operate the economy at a capacity where, we have seen, inflation must be regarded not as an abnormal but as a normal prospect'.[29]

How can it be proved that the expansion of credit, or credit money (bank money), has an inflationary effect? How can this inflation be measured? At first glance it would be simple to reply: by the increase in the prices of commodities. Such a simplification, however, runs the risk of falling into the circular reasoning of Hilferding. Since prices are the monetary expression of the values of the commodities, money inflation cannot automatically be deduced from rising prices. Commodity prices always express a relation between the value of two commodities — the particular commodity and gold. The development and correlation of *both* sides of this relationship must form the basis of our analysis. A further important factor should be borne in mind, which has to some extent been correctly pointed out by the Keynesian school. Money as purchasing power of monetarily effective demand should not be compared exclusively with the ongoing *flow* of commodity production; for it also has a *mobilising* effect — in other words, it can itself restore fluidity to a given *stock* of commodities.[30] This function is especially important in a crisis of over production. If the system of banks or central banks is used to create additional means of exchange while large stocks of unsold commodities are still on hand, the effect of this additional amount of money may increase prices, yet need not necessarily be inflationary.[31] For it not only assists the exchange of the ongoing

[29] *The Affluent Society*, p. 204. For this whole question see, among others, Gilles Jourdain and Jacques Valier, 'L'Echec des explications bourgeoises de l'inflation', in *Critiques de l'Economie Politique*, No. 1, September-December 1970, pp. 56-8.
[30] John Maynard Keynes, *The General Theory of Employment, Interest and Money*, London, 1936, pp. 117-19, 126-8, 300-3.
[31] Marx was very sarcastic about Peel's Bank Act of 1844, which prevented a

output of commodities; it can also facilitate the settlement of payments which are due and thus reinject into circulation commodities which had been previously withdrawn from it because they could not be sold. The Keynesian and neo-Keynesian school has consequently advanced the general thesis that creation of additional means of circulation or payment only has an inflationary effect if all 'factors of production' are fully utilized.[32]

It is indisputable that additional quantities of paper and bank money have totally different effects, when there are large stocks of unsaleable goods and unutilized productive capacities, and when the productive apparatus is working at full load. Yet the Keynesian thesis is only partially correct. Its basic weakness lies in its insufficiently differentiated use of aggregates, and its belief in automatic and unmediated reactions. It is true that an increase in the quantity of money in periods of recession and crisis can increase the sale of consumer goods (although even so not necessarily in a particular fixed proportion). It will only lead to a growth in productive investments, however, if there are also expectations of a long-term expansion of the market and the rate of profit is increased (especially if capitalists regarded it as too low at the beginning of the recession). If this does not occur, or not to the extent sought by entrepreneurs, private investments will not ensue, or not in the volume expected.[33] The multiplier effect of different forms of state expenditure, budgetary deficits, tax reliefs and so on, may therefore vary very greatly in different conjunctures. Productive investments — i.e., investments leading to an increase in the value produced — have a much higher multiplier effect than unproductive investments. Under certain circumstances the multiplier effect of economic transactions which really represent no more than the conversion of one form of idle capital into another — for example, the sale of securities, in order to use the proceeds to buy up vacant lots for purposes of speculation, or vice-versa — may be so small as

---

temporary extension of the quantity of money in times of crisis. *Capital*, Vol. 3, pp. 513-33, 537. See also, *Critique of Political Economy*, p. 185.

[32] The thesis of the 'inflationary gap' was first formulated by Keynes at the beginning of the Second World War in *How to Pay for the War*, New York, 1940. The elements of it are already present in his *General Theory*, pp. 302-3.

[33] This was the reason for the partial failure of Roosevelt's New Deal and also for the fact that in the Third Reich productive civilian investments were not stimulated significantly in the phase 1933-38, despite a massive increase in state expenditure (see Chapter 5).

to increase the total turnover of the economy only slightly, if at all. It is therefore necessary to correlate three tendencies in order to define the inflationary effect of credit expansion more exactly:

1. The development of the productivity of labour in the gold industry as compared to that of commodity production in the capitalist world, and therefore the long-term tendencies of commodity prices as expressed in gold;

2. The development of the quantity of money as compared with the total value product (i.e., the volume of production multiplied by the average commodity value), taking into account the velocity of the circulation of money;

3. The structural problems of price development, i.e., the divergent development of wholesale and retail prices, of prices of raw materials and agricultural goods and prices of industrial finished goods, of prices on the external market and export prices in the world market, and so on.

The latter should tell us whether the inflation of credit money is the outcome of *specific* needs of the late capitalist monopolies or only of the general difficulties of realizing surplus-value and valorizing capital. This much can be anticipated here: from the standpoint of the theory of money and value, the thesis of 'cost-push-inflation' has no justification.[34] Only if there is a liquidity surplus can companies, under conditions of monopoly capitalism, automatically transfer increases in costs to selling prices, i.e., to consumers.[35] If, by contrast, the quantity of money remains constant while wages rise, or merely adjusts to increases in production, then *even without competition* in certain industries increased costs cannot lead to a rise in prices. Under conditions of stable currency, Marx's theorem that an increase in wages at a given output and value of commodities merely diminishes profits and does not push up prices, is absolutely valid.[36] What lurks behind the thesis of 'cost-push-inflation' is not

[34] For the 'theory of cost inflation' see for example F. W. Paish, 'The Limits of Income Policies', in F. W. Paish and J. Hennessy, *Policy for Incomes*, Institute of Economic Affairs, London, 1968, p. 13 f; F. S. Brooman, *Macro-Economics*, London, 1963, pp. 234-7.

[35] There are many other arguments which demonstrate the weakness of this theory. Analogous price increases can be registered in branches of industry where wage costs constitute 35% and where they constitute 1% of the total costs of production; in general, higher wage increases are caused by previous increases in the cost of living. See the refutation of the theory of 'cost-push-inflation' in Gilles Jourdain and Jacques Valier, op. cit., pp. 58-67.

[36] Marx, *Wages, Price and Profit*, in *Selected Works*, p. 218.

an analysis of the objective effects of wage increases in a capitalist market economy, but the observation that in late capitalism companies are *guaranteed* the quantity of money needed automatically to transfer increased production costs to the consumer, by the system of bank money.[37] This means that it is not 'excessive' wage demands but the specific adaptation of the banking system and creation of money to the interests of monopoly capital which constitutes the technical cause of price increases. *Permanent inflation is the mechanism specific to late capitalism for braking a rapid downturn of the rate of surplus-value and of profit under conjunctural conditions of relatively rapid capital accumulation and relatively high levels of employment.*[38]

The development of the productivity of labour in the gold industry can only be calculated indirectly. Before the First World War, 'working costs' made up about 85% of the 'mining costs' (production costs) of the South African gold industry. These figures do not correspond exactly to Marx's categories of variable capital and costs of production, for the category of 'working costs' undoubtedly concealed a portion of surplus-value in the form of the high salaries of the white overseers and directors. Thus, for example, in 1907 the 17,697 white office workers of these mines received a total salary of £5.94 million, while the 165,000 coloured labourers received a total of only £9.8 million in wages in money and kind as the price for the sale of their labour-power. Production amounted to approximately 234,000 kg of fine gold. The number of working years (total

[37] Inflation thus obviously has a two-fold function: it permits an increase in the rate of surplus-value and simultaneously conceals the fall in the relative share of wages by an increase in money wages. Rising money wages can then be blamed for inflation. For an example, see the study by the 'liberal' English economic journalist Samuel Brittan, *The Treasury under the Tories 1951-1964*, who in one breath declares himself a fervent supporter of money-wage stability (p. 150) and in the other, advises workers not to confuse the cost of living with the standard of life. How living standards are supposed to rise if money wages do not even compensate for growing costs of living is not explained. Brittan is manifestly arguing for faster growth at the expense of the wages bill, in other words, by compulsory saving at the expense of the working class and thereby an increase in the rate of surplus-value.

[38] Jacob Morris writes: 'Inflation provided for a time. . . as substitute for the industrial reserve army as capitalism's way of maintaining its power of exploitation': 'Inflation', *Monthly Review*, September 1973, Vol., 25, No. 4. This is only true to a limited extent. We have tried to demonstrate in Chapter 5 and 14 of this book that during the 'long wave of expansion', and under conditions for permanent inflation, fluctuations in the reserve army of labour exercised, as in the past, a powerful influence on the evolution of real wages and hence on the rates of surplus-value and profit. But it remains true that these repercussions would have been much more brutal without the presence of permanent inflation.

quantity of labour input per year of total manpower) was approximately 183,000. In 1940 the number of working years had risen to 400,000, while production had reached 400,000 kg of fine gold. Compared to 1907, there had thus been a slight increase in the input of living labour per kg of fine gold. The information available does not give the input of dead labour (constant capital), but this certainly also increased. Between the two World Wars, therefore, the average productivity of labour in gold production at best stagnated, and most probably declined slightly.[39]

In 1967 the same labour-units of 400,000 produced more than twice as much as in 1940; 950,000 kg of fine gold. In the meantime, the total costs of production per ton, which were valued at $6.14 per ton of ore in 1907 and in 1940 amounted to $5.15, had risen to $8.36 (devalued dollars).[40] For the year 1973 the corresponding figures were: 852,000 kg of gold produced by 400,000 workers and supervisors, at production costs of $14.7 devalued 1973 dollars per ton of ore, which correspond approximately to $4.05 dollars at 1940 values. Since there had likewise been a decline in the number of working hours per week, a realistic estimate would be that *the value of a gram of gold had halved* between 1907 and 1967; since the working week was further shortened in 1973, it may be assumed that this value still remained about half that of 1907. This 50% reduction in the value of gold produced in South Africa can be traced back among other things to the closing-down of the poorest and the opening up of new, rich mines in the Orange Free State, Klerksdorp, Ewander and Farwestrand, which increased the average

[39] This is not surprising, since in mining the law of diminishing returns for a given ore deposit obtains, as deeper and deeper layers have to be drilled. Consider the following statement by someone with an interest in the matter, which reveals something about the dynamic of the differential yields of gold mines: 'At the 75th annual meeting of the Chamber (Transvaal and Orange Free State Chamber of Mines — E.M.) held in Johannesburg in June 1965, C. B. Anderson, retiring president, said in part with reference to rising costs: . . . . 'I would again stress that every cent increase in working costs per ton milled transfers a quantity of ore in every mine — be the mine old or new, a low-grade or a high-grade producer — from the payable to the unpayable category. . . . This ore will be left unmined, possibly forever. . . . Furthermore, the lives of individual mines are progressively shortened and the day of the decline of the gold mining industry as a whole is brought appreciably nearer.' Bureau of Mines/U.S. Department of the Interior, *Area Reports: International, Mineral Yearbook 1965,* Vol. 4, Washington, 1966.

[40] Data on the South African gold mines, for the year 1907, A. Mill, (ed.), *The Mining Industry,* Vol. XIX New York, 1910-1911. For 1940, *Engineering and Mining Journal,* Vol. 142 (1941), No. 2, p. 68. For 1967, Bureau of the Mines/U.S. Department of the Interior, *Minerals Yearbook 1967,* Washington, 1968, p. 544.

yield of gold per ton of ore in South African mining from 6.67 g in 1955 to 10.78 g in 1965. In addition, some substantial technical improvements had been introduced into gold mining.[41]

The steep increase in the 'price of gold' on the free market (i.e., the sharp fall in the value of the dollar and other currencies) since 1967 had induced important structural changes in the South African gold industry. Less productive mines have been reopened or have increased their production. The output of the richest mines has been curtailed. The gold content per mined ore has fallen to 10.11 g and will decrease still further. At the same time, the net income per ton of ore increased from 3.9 rand in 1970 to 20.7 rand in the first 9 months of 1972 (1 rand was worth 1.4-1.5 dollars in autumn 1974). The wages of the African miners have been increased above starvation levels as a result of the chronic manpower shortage which the latter had previously caused (in 1974, only 22.5% of the miners were recruited within the Union of South Africa; the rest of the labour-force in the mines was immigrant). Wages per shift increased from 0.3 rand in 1970 to 1.6 rand at the end of 1974. Simultaneously, however, the productivity of labour is now starting to increase, as mechanization is introduced on a wider scale; within a few years, the mine-owners hope to produce more gold than at present with only half the labour-force. In short, the value of 1 gr of gold is now starting to glide downwards, as is that of all capitalistically produced commodities.[42]

It is easier to calculate the increase in the productivity of labour within the total imperialist production of commodities during the same period 1907-67. In manufacturing industry in the USA the number of working hours rose by 71% between 1907 and 1967; the increase in the production index, in contrast, was more than 900% (from an index figure of 80 to 738). This suggests a 520% increase in the productivity of labour. In agriculture, the number of working hours declined by about two thirds between 1907 and 1967 (falling from index 95 to 32), while production increased by 77%.[43] In these sixty years, therefore, agricultural labour productivity increased by 540%, practically the same percentage as that of industry.

[41] See Bureau of Mines/U.S. Department of the Interior, *Minerals Yearbook 1967*, Vols. I-II, Washington, 1968, p. 536.

[42] Statistics from *Neue Zürcher Zeitung*, November 30 — December 1, 1974.

[43] The information for the period 1907-65 is taken from US Department of Commerce/Bureau of the Census, *Long Term Economic Growth*. With the aid of the annual official data in the Statistical Abstract of the USA we have extended them up to the year 1967.

In the other imperialist countries the increase in the productivity of labour in the period 1907-14 equalled that of the USA, was much smaller in the period 1914-40, but was then much greater in the period 1947-67.[44] There ought not therefore to be any major differences between the development of the productivity of labour in the USA and in the total commodity production of the imperialist world. This means that the value of the average commodity produced in the imperialist countries is today five to six times lower than before the First World War. Given the fact that the value of gold has dropped by about 50% since that time, the gold prices of commodities ought on average to be three times as low as in 1907.[45] In fact, however, commodity prices, as expressed in paper dollars, are three times as high as in 1907. *This ninefold devaluation of money thus fulfilled a precise objective function: to conceal the substantial fall in the value of commodities as expressed in gold quantities, because a rapid and unbroken drop in the prices of commodities could in the long-run have rendered the capitalist economy incapable of functioning, in the absence of possibilities for geographical expansion.*[46]

A problem arises here which led to an interesting discussion between Varga, Bauer and Kautsky on the eve of the First World War: does an increase in the production of gold in itself produce a rise in the (gold) prices of commodities?[47] In our opinion, the arguments advanced on both sides of this discussion were false from the point of view of a rigorous application of the labour theory of value. Varga's thesis that, by fixing the 'gold price', the central banks could prevent

[44] For the last phase, see the data in current OECD publications, cited in Neusüss, Blande and Altvater, 'Kapitalistischer Weltmarkt und Weltwährungskrise' in *Probleme des Klassenkampfes*, November 1971.

[45] This estimate — which is anyway only a crude one — naturally only makes sense for an identical package of commodities. It is meaningless to calculate the long-term development of the value of commodities not produced, or only produced on a small scale and of a completely different quality, in 1907. For the *global* production of commodities, however, such an estimate makes very good sense.

[46] A durable and rapid decline of commodity prices would cause, among other things, a paralysis of the credit system; because even with a low nominal rate of interest, the real interest would thereby have to be increased by the annual increase in the value of gold. Loan and bank capital would as a whole make a greater profit than industrial and commercial capital. The ongoing depreciation of commodity stocks would hinder the function of commercial capital enormously. Since the resistance of workers to a fall in nominal wages is notoriously much quicker and stronger than their reaction to a rise in the cost of living, mass pressure would develop—to the horror of capital — for a permanent increase in real wages which could only be neutralized by mass unemployment.

[47] Eugen Varga, 'Goldproduktion und Teuerung' in *Die Neue Zeit*, Vol. XXX/I, no. 7, p. 212 f. Eugen Varga, 'Goldproduktion und Teuerung', in *Die Neue Zeit*,

426   *Late Capitalism*

gold production from increasing prices is indefensible and was convincingly refuted by Kautsky and Bauer.[48] Kautsky insisted on the peculiarity of gold for the purposes of demonstrating that an increase in the production of gold represents an additional overall demand — in other words, an extension of the market for capitalist commodity production. The production of gold is the production of the 'universal equivalent' which, as an individual commodity, not only possesses a particular use-value (for jewellers and others), but in addition has the very special use value of being exchangeable for *all* commodities. As such, gold can never become 'unsaleable' in capitalism. This is true and needs no further elaboration. Kautsky, however, overlooked the fact that an increase in the *volume* of gold production leads only to an increase in *money* capital,[49] and that the distinctive characteristic of gold is precisely that it does not have to be injected into circulation, but can also be hoarded in the form of treasure. There is hence no automatic certainty — as Kautsky assumed — that the annual production of gold will raise the total demand for commodities along with its own value. This depends on whether or not the additional quantity of gold is integrated into circulation, i.e., on the given conjuncture of the capitalist economy, the volume of commodity production, the velocity of the circulation of money, the volume of credit (the payments, besides the exchanges functions, which have to be met by this money) and so on.

Between 1929 and 1939 gold production nearly doubled without significantly increasing total demand in the capitalist world. The

Vol. XXXI/I, no. 16, p. 557 f. Otto Bauer, 'Goldproduktion und Teuerung', in *Die Neue Zeit*, Vol. XXX/2, pp. 4 f and 49 f. Karl Kautsky, 'Gold, Papier und Ware,' and 'Die Wandlungen der Goldproduktion and der Wechselnde Charakter der Teuerung' (see above).

[48] The whole notion of the 'price of gold', as used in contemporary economic literature, is meaningless from the point of view of Marx's theory of value. The price of commodities expresses their value in money, i.e., gold, which is not only the measure of values but also the standard of prices. The 'price of gold' would thus be the expression of the value of gold in gold. What is really meant by this expression is the 'value' of currencies, i.e., the quantity of gold which a currency unit represents. The formula 'the price of gold is $35.00 an ounce' really means 'one dollar represents 1/35th of an ounce of gold'.

[49] See Marx: 'We will consider here the accumulation of money capital, in so far as it is not an expression either of a stoppage in the flow of commercial credit or of an economy — whether it be an economy in the actual circulating medium or in the reserve capital of the agents engaged in reproduction. Aside from these two cases, an accumulation of money capital can arise through an unusual inflow of gold, as in 1852 and 1853 as a result of the new Australian and Californian gold mines.' *Capital*, Vol. 3, p. 501.

additional gold flowed into the currency reserves of the USA and *was hoarded*. Only a reduction in the *value* of gold automatically leads to an increase in the prices of commodities expressed in gold. It is precisely the reduction in the *value* of gold since the 1890's and not the increase in the *production* of gold, which played a central role in the rise in the cost of living in the 'heyday' of imperialism from 1893-1914.

The development of the means of circulation and payment (quantity of money) from the epoch immediately preceding the First World War to the end of the 1960's can be established with reasonable accuracy (we shall confine ourselves henceforward to the US economy as the most typical sector of late capitalism). According to the well-known Friedman-Schwartz series,[50] the quantity of money (excluding long-term bank accounts) rose from index 100 in 1915 to index 215 in 1929, i.e., by 115%. In the same period industrial output increased by 70% while agricultural production was constant. According to Friedman and Schwartz there was also a slight acceleration in the velocity of the circulation of money during this period. The latter declined, however, by more than 30% in the years of crisis after 1929, while the volume of gold increased once more by 25%.[51] Corresponding to these figures, we find that the level of wholesale prices was only 10% higher in 1939 than in 1915 (the retail price level, which always shows a certain time-lag in reflecting gold prices, was 10% higher in 1939 than in 1916). Naturally, one can hardly speak of long-term inflation when paper money currency only lost approximately 10% of its purchasing power in 24 years (less than 0.4% per annum).

The picture changes completely if we compare the development since the end of the Second World War with that from 1915 to 1939. Between 1945 and 1967 the quantity of money rose by approximately 90%;[52] by 1967 it was seven times higher than in 1929, and nine times higher than in 1907. The velocity of the circulation of money doubled between 1945 and 1967, reaching the rhythm of the

[50] Milton Friedman and Anna Jacobson Schwartz, *Monetary Statistics of the United States*, New York, 1970.
[51] A handsome refutation of the orthodox 'pure' quantity theory of money! Contrary to its tenets, the velocity of the circulation of money cannot be taken as given: a significant increase in the quantity of money may be neutralized by a deceleration of its velocity, if the needs of commodity circulation and capital accumulation, determined by the business cycle, cannot 'absorb' this additional quantity of money at the old velocity.   [52] Friedman and Schwartz, op. cit.

428 Late Capitalism

year 1929 once again. The total industrial output of 1967, however, was only four times as high as in 1929, while agricultural production was approximately 45% higher. Here an inflationary mass of money, not corresponding to any proportionate increase in the production of commodities, is unmistakable. Consequently, the average price level in 1967 was twice as high as in 1929 and three times as high as in 1907. The increase in the quantity of money, i.e., of paper and bank money, was thus the unequivocal and direct technical cause of dollar inflation. The quantity of money grew much more rapidly than the volume of physical production — moving in the opposite direction to the steep fall in the values (gold prices) of the sum of commodities.

A final comparison of the different dynamics of different price series will afford an insight into the concrete mechanisms of permanent inflation in late capitalism. In 1967, the wholesale price index in the USA was 106.2, as compared with 52.1 in 1929 and 57.9 in 1945; the retail (consumer price) index was 115.4 in 1967 as compared to 59.7 in 1929 and 62.7 in 1945. The corresponding index figures were 142.3 and 152.9 in 1973. There thus seems to be a fairly parallel development in both series. This apparent parallelism changes, however, if the following facts are taken into account:

1. Between 1958 and 1964 wholesale prices in the USA remained practically stable (index 100.4 in 1958, 100.5 in 1964). Even for the period from 1957-64 there was only a 3.5% increase, i.e., less than 0.5% per annum. Between 1951 and 1956, too, the stability of wholesale prices was absolute. *For the entire period 1951-64 the wholesale price index of the USA only rose substantially in a single year, the 'boom' year of 1956.*

2. By contrast, there was an uninterrupted increase in consumer prices during the same period. Only from 1952-55 was this rise insignificant; in all other years it exceeded 1% annually. For the total period 1951-64 retail prices rose by 17.6 points, while wholesale prices increased by only 3.8.

3. In 1967 the wholesale price index for foods directly supplied from farms, as well as for chemicals and rubber goods, was *lower* than in 1957-59. Textile goods, paper goods, furniture and electrical household appliance either showed a below-average increase in wholesale prices in these ten years or remained constant. By contrast, machines, metal goods and timber underwent a wholesale price increase above the average.

4. Starting in 1968, an uninterrupted increase in all the main categories of wholesale prices occurred, i.e., inflation became cumu-

lative and accelerated. But even after that year individual wholesale prices fluctuated. For example, in 1969-70, lumber prices declined considerably, and prices for domestic electrical equipment decreased slightly. Wholesale prices for these last commodities were in 1970 30% below the 1950 and 25% below the 1960 level.

A similar picture emerges from consumer prices. In the period 1957-67 the retail prices of foods, textiles, furniture and electrical household appliances rose less than the average cost of living index (although much more than the wholesale prices in these branches). The costs of services (above all for health and recreation, but also so-called 'mixed goods'), by contrast, registered more than the average increase.

If the virtually uninterrupted tendency for the prices of raw materials to fall on the world market in the same period, which was reversed only in 1973, is further added to these series, then the *structure of monetary devaluation* can be set out like this:

1. The transition from a gold currency to a monetary system which ensures monopoly capital the quantity of money adequate for its needs by the creation of bank money, allows the big capitalist companies, under conditions of relative market control (oligopolistic competition, price leadership), to increase the prices of the commodities they sell slightly in boom periods, and to stabilize them during recessions.[53] Given the major increase in the productivity of labour attendant on the third technological revolution, this means an extension of their profit margins (an increase in the rate of surplus-value) which leads to 'administered prices' and a relatively high rate of self-financing.[54] One of the main goals of the policy underlying these 'administered prices' is the preemption of market fluctuations, i.e., the planning for projects during the recessions which the large

[53] On this subject see among others Gardiner C. Means, *Pricing Power and the Public Interest*, New York, 1962; D. Schwartzman, 'The Effect of Monopoly on Price', in *Journal of Political Economy*, August 1959. According to Means 85% of price increases between 1953 and 1962 can be traced back to the products of heavily concentrated branches of production. Stigler and Kindahl have questioned the importance of 'administered prices' by quoting figures for price fluctuations even in monopolized sectors: *The Behaviour of Industrial Prices*, New York 1970. Means, however, never denied this. He was able to show convincingly, on the basis of Stigler's own statistics, that in the 18 sectors characterized by free competition, price fluctuations were much greater than in the 50 monopolized sectors, and that most of the latter were counter-cyclical: 'The Administered Price Thesis Confirmed', *American Economic Review*, June 1972.
[54] Under these conditions Levinson's distinction (op.cit., p. 30) between price increases *made possible* by monopolization and price increases *made necessary* by the needs of increased capital accumulation has no meaning. The fact that the mono-

companies themselves (as opposed to their ideologues) regard as inevitable. Thus Means has calculated that the above-average price increases introduced by the US Steel Corporation in the 1950's brought down the 'break-even point' (i.e., the minimum utilisation of capacity needed to pass the profitability threshold) to such an extent that in the second half-year of 1960 this company, with a utilisation of capacity of only 47% (!) as a result of the recession, obtained nearly the same net profit as it had in the boom year of 1953, when 98% of its capacity was in use.[55]

2. The substantial increase in the mass of use values, which rises even more rapidly than the productivity of labour underlying it, creates increasing difficulties of realization in late capitalism. These find expression in a steep climb of selling costs and consumer credit. Under conditions of monopoly capitalism, as long as there is no significant foreign competition in the sphere of retail trade, these substantial increases in the costs of circulation (always given an adequate increase in the quantity of money) can be off-loaded onto the consumers. Here is a comparison of the development of consumer prices on the domestic market and export prices (index 100 = 1970 in each case), which also shows which national capitalist classes have successfully increased their export shares of the world market:[56]

| | Consumer Prices | | Export Prices | |
	1969	1973	1969	1973
USA	94	123	95	124
West Germany	93	119	98	104
Japan	93	124	95	107
UK	94	128	94	125
France	95	120	91	118
Italy	95	123	95	108 (1972)
Belgium	96	118	95	99 (1972)
Netherlands	96	126	96	107

polies can achieve above-average profit margins (technological surplus-profits), which ensure the high rate of self-financing needed by accelerated technological innovation, constitutes a single 'structural' complex along with the inflationary policy of money creation pursued by the banks or central banking system. They merely form different dimensions of the same specific structure of late capitalism.

[55] Means, *Pricing Power and the Public Interest*, p. 148. For a similar performance by the big chemical monopolies of West Germany in the 60's, see Aike Blechschmidt, Gerhard Hoffmann, Reinhold von der Marwitz, *Das Zusammenwirken von Konzentration, Weltmarktentwicklung und Staatsintervention am Beispiel der BRD*, Lampertheim, 1974, p 23.

[56] Sachverständigenrat, *Jahresgutachten 1974*, pp. 220-1; the OECD Report *Inflation*, 1970, p. 22, provides a similar survey of the 1961-69 period.

3. A greater degree of monopolization will allow marginally greater price increases. In the sphere of wholesale prices, these increases will be larger in Department I than in Department II. Conversely: the relative growth of the productivity of labour (decline of the values of commodities and their gold prices) will correspondingly restrict the scope of price increases. They will thus be lower in sectors which, since the start of the late capitalist epoch, have been distinguished by a particularly rapid increase in productivity (agriculture, chemicals, electrical appliances), than in sectors with a lesser degree of mechanization (construction and services).[57] But the relative stability of prices in sectors with a higher than average rate of increase in the productivity of labour, is itself just as much an expression of permanent inflation as the faster rise in the prices of sectors whose productivity of labour has registered a slower increase.

It is thus clear that permanent inflation in no way invalidates the law of value. This law now merely operates under particular conditions in which the value (purchasing-power) of paper money, freed from its basis in gold, constantly diminishes. As long as permanent 'creeping inflation' does not turn into 'galloping inflation', intensifying structural overproduction can perfectly well lead to price reductions in certain sectors; even a general fall in wholesale prices cannot be excluded as possibility from the future. The rapid increase in raw materials during 1973-74 — which played only a secondary role in the acceleration of inflation in that period — was then succeeded by a considerable fall in these prices because of the world recession.[58]

Two related problems arise here which demand an answer. Is the hypertrophy of the services sector (and beyond it, the hypertrophy of all activities not directly creative of value, i.e., those of the state apparatus and the circulation sphere as well) a cause of permanent inflation? What is the difference between our explanation of permanent inflation and the conventional quantity theory of Friedman or Rueff?

Analysis of the question of the inflationary effect of the services

---

[57] According to François Perroux ('Inflations importées et structures sectorielles', in François Perroux, Jean Denizet and Henri Bourguinat, *Inflation, Dollar, Euro-Dollar*, Paris, 1971, p. 108), depending on the Western country under consideration, some 70% to 90% of the price increases analysable for the decade 1958-68, can be traced back to increases in the price of services and the building industry.

[58] This is manifest for the USA, whose imports account for only 5% of its GNP. Other obvious cases are those of Japan, Canada and France, whose average import

sector (or of all unproductive outlays) may be helped by an arithmetic example. Let us suppose that the annual value product of a capitalist society has the following structure:

I: $10,000c + 5,000v + 5,000s = 20,000$ means of production
II: $5,000c + 3,000v + 3,000s = 11,000$ means of consumption

Of the 5,000 units of surplus-value created in Department I, 3,750 are accumulated and 1,250 are consumed unproductively. In Department II, 2,250 of the 3,000 units of surplus value are accumulated. With a total output of 11,000 means of consumption, therefore, 10,000 are currently consumed (8,000 by the workers and 2,000 by the capitalists and their servitors) and 1,000 are left over for extended reproduction in the following year (for the employment of additional labour-power). There are 5,000 means of production available for the extended reproduction of constant capital.

Let us now suppose that besides these two sectors there is a third — services — which has come into being in this base year, and that it had sold services for a total price of 3,600 units of value. Assuming that the services sector does not buy any machinery, buildings and so on (a hypothesis introduced merely to simplify the calculation, but which could easily be suspended by an exchange between services and commodities from Department I), the system is in equilibrium — in other words, nothing disturbs the proportion between the commodity value produced and the purchasing power arising from production for the realization of this value — if 2,700 units of consumer purchasing power are used to purchase services instead of consumer goods, if 900 service units are exchanged among those employed in the services sector, and if the consumer goods which thereby become available are bought by those employed in the services sector and used to reproduce their labour-power.

The balance between supply and demand now obtains the following form:

Supply	Demand
20,000 means of production	⎡ 10,000 replacement c I 5,000 replacement c II 3,125 extended reproduction c I ⎣ 1,875 extended reproduction c II

prices in 1973 increased respectively 6%, 12% and 13% above their 1970 levels, while the cost of living increased 24%, 16% and 20% compared with 1970.

11,000 means of consumption
- 3,750 workers Department I
- 2,250 workers Department II
- 812.5 capitalists Department I
- 487.5 capitalists Department II
- 625 reserves for extended reproduction I
- 375 reserves for extended reproduction II [59]
- 2,700 employees in the services sector

3,600 services
- 1,250 workers Department I
- 750 workers Department II
- 437.5 capitalists Department I
- 262.5 capitalists Department II
- 900 services, which are exchanged within this sector.

The hypothesis here is that the workers spend 25% of their real income, and the capitalists 35% of the surplus-value unproductively consumed, on services instead of consumer goods, and that those engaged in the services sector similarly spend 25% of their real income on services. What, then, does this condition of equilibrium economically mean? It shows that a substantial services sector is not necessarily inflationary in a capitalist economy, so long as the purchasing power of the employees in this sector is exactly equal to the portion of the purchasing power of the productive workers plus the fraction of the surplus-value spent unproductively which is exchanged for services instead of commodities. If the second part of this equation is described as the 'consumer income' which has arisen in the production of commodities, and if we presuppose the hypothesis that the per capita income of employees in the services sector is equal to that of those employed in production, we obtain the following formula, which although a simplification, is important for the historical *tendency* of late capitalism. *The system can remain in equilibrium with an extensive services sector — that is, avoid permanent inflation — if the share of services in consumer spending is equal to the*

[59] Since services cannot be 'produced' for stock, the quantity of consumer goods needed for accumulation contains both the value of consumer goods necessary to employ additional 'productive' labourers and the equivalent value of that part of the additional variable capital which has been exchanged for services.

share of the employees of the services sector in the working popula-tion. To get closer to reality, the second part of the equation would have to be multiplied by a coefficient expressing the relation of the average income in the services sector to the average income in the sphere of production.

By this detour, the notion of the 'productivity of the services sector' can be introduced into the analysis (a strict application of the labour theory of value, of course, precludes any use of such a notion without quotation marks, since, as we have shown in Chapter 12, the services sector is no more 'productive' in the real sense of the word, i.e., creative of value and productive of surplus-value, than the circulation sphere).[60] If the equation is voided by a hypertrophy of the services sector and if the share of the employees of this sector in the total working population, multiplied by an income coefficient of 1.1, amounts to approximately 50, while the share of services in consumer spending only comes to 40, an excess income will be left over in the Services Department, which will either lead to an increase in the market price of consumer goods (if it is spent exclusively on such goods) or have an inflationary effect on the economy as a whole because a part of this income also tries to purchase means of produc-tion. *Under these particular conditions the effects of a hypertrophy of the services sector are therefore inflationary.*[61] This is merely a special case of a more general rule, namely that any sectoral disequi-librium in late capitalism has inflationary effects if the increase in

[60] 'The growing importance of the service industries represents a major structural change in the economy. It is a sector in which productivity rises least rapidly because it is difficult to automate and in which more capital investment and labour force . . . . will be employed in turning out non-durable, subjective services, few of which will figure in cost-of-living indices.' Charles Levinson, op.cit., p. 28. According to the OECD report *Inflation*, the annual average rate of price increases in the services sector in the period 1958-68 was twice as high as it was for industrial goods in the USA, West Germany, Great Britain, France and Italy.

[61] The same rule would also apply, *mutatis mutandis*, to the way in which unproduc-tive outlays are covered, such as armaments through taxes. The extent to which this rule helps to understand permanent inflation in late capitalism can be measured by the fact that the number of workers and office workers employed in the sphere of services (excepting transport communications and public utilities) in the USA, rose between 1950 and 1970 from 50.3% to 60.6% of the total mass of wage-earning employees, while the share of services in the average consumption of American citizens only increased from 32.7% to 42.6% in the same period (this includes gas, water and electricity and so on; without these goods, the figure would be approxi-mately 29.5% and 38.5%). In other important imperialist countries, the fraction of gainfully employed civilians active in the service sector increased between 1950 and 1970 from 33.2% to 46.9% in Japan, from 42% to 50.6% in Britain and from 32.5% to 40.7% in West Germany.

the volume of money slows down or curbs the rapid adjustment of the economic resources (quantities of expended labour) of specific sectors to an altered pattern of monetarily effective demand.[62]

Is our explanation of the permanent inflation characteristic of late capitalism, identical or similar to the contemporary versions of the quantity theory of money? It cannot be denied that a certain similarity does exist; but it is already present in Marx's monetary theory, when applied to paper money.[63] In *The Critique of Political Economy* we read : 'The number of pieces of paper is thus determined by the quantity of gold currency which they represent in circulation, and as they are tokens of value only in so far as they take the place of gold currency, their value is simply determined by their *quantity*. Whereas, therefore, the quantity of gold in circulation depends on the prices of commodities, the value of the paper in circulation, on the other hand, depends solely on its own quantity. The intervention of the State which issues paper money with a legal rate of exchange — and we speak only of this type of paper money — seems to invalidate the economic law. The State, whose mint price merely provided a definite weight of gold with a name and whose mint price merely imprinted its stamp on the gold, seems now to transfer paper into gold by the magic of its imprint. Because the pieces of paper have a legal rate of exchange, it is impossible to prevent the State from thrusting any arbitrarily chosen number of them into circulation and to imprint them at will with any monetary denomination. . . . Once the notes are in circulation it is impossible to drive them out, for the frontiers of the country limit their movement, on the one hand, and on the other hand they lose all value, both use-value and exchange-value, *outside* the sphere of circulation. Apart from their function they are useless scraps of paper. But this power of the State

---

[62] Perroux, op.cit., p. 117 ff. In this connection note the interesting thesis advanced by Schultze that price increases in certain sectors in response to a shift in demand, are not accompanied by price reductions in other sectors marked by a relative decline in demand, because of monopoly conditions: Charles C. Schultze, *Recent Inflation in the United States*, US Congress Joint Economic Committee, Study Paper 1, Washington, 1959. This could equally, to some extent, apply to above-average price increases in the services sphere. Although we cannot discuss the problem of permanent inflation in the semi-colonial countries further here, an important determinant of it is the uninterrupted increase in monopolistic import prices. On this subject see Hector Malavé Mata, *Dialectica de la Inflación*, Venezuela, 1972 (with an extensive bibliography), which records, among other things, that between 1956 and 1970 the price index for local goods in Venezuela increased by only 19.4%, while that of imported goods rose by 62.1% (p. 279). On the same subject, more generally, see Anibal Pinto, *Inflación: Raices Estructurales*, Mexico, 1973.

[63] *Critique of Political Economy*, pp. 119-20 (Our italics).

is mere illusion. It may throw any number of paper notes of any denomination into circulation but its control ceases with this mechanical act. As soon as the token of value or paper money enters the sphere of circulation it is subject to the inherent laws of this sphere. Let us assume that £ 14 million is the amount of gold required for the circulation of commodities and that the State throws 210 million notes each called £ 1 into circulation: these 210 million would then stand for a total gold of £ 14 million. . . . As the name pound sterling would now indicate one-fifteenth of the previous quantity of gold, all commodity prices would be fifteen times higher . . .'

The fundamental distinction between Marx's monetary theory, as applied to paper money, and the classical or modern quantity theory of money,[64] is that although Marx attributes a certain degree of autonomy to the sphere of circulation, for him the basic magnitude is the sphere of production or the objective need for means of payment and exchange determined by the law of value, and any increase in the quantity of money can determine a loss in the value of the currency unit *only by comparison with this magnitude.*

This has two crucial implications. Firstly, the socially necessary quantity of money is not fixed but fluctuates during the industrial cycle. It is much larger in times of disturbance in circulation than it is in times when circulation is brisk, because of the increase in immediate payments due. At such moments even a fairly substantial increase in the quantity of money need not lead to a rise in prices.[65] Secondly, it is the activity of productive capital, i.e. the actual and the expected rate of profit, and not the quantity of money, which is the principal determinant of the business cycle. This means that even an additional mass of money in times of recession or depression does not automatically stimulate production, employment and especially investments, as Friedman and his school found out to

[64] Besides this fundamental difference there are a number of secondary ones, for example, the axiom of the stability of the velocity of the circulation of money, which must be rejected from a Marxist point of view. If this velocity is regarded as a variable rather than a constant magnitude, however, then the quantity of money ceases to be the only variable in Fischer's famous formula $\frac{M \cdot V}{T} = P$. and such a formula with two variables then merely expresses an arithmetical tautology. The more refined versions of the quantity theory, such as those of the Chicago School, have discarded this thesis of the constant velocity of the circulation of money. See, for example, Milton Friedman, op.cit., p. 51 f.

[65] The Chicago School confidently proclaimed the opposite until very recently: Milton Friedman, op.cit., p. 235. Friedman's entire essay 'Money and Business Cycles', ibid., pp. 189-235, is devoted to this topic.

their (and to US capital's) cost in the first half of 1971, when production and employment continued to stagnate despite a 6% increase in the quantity of money.[66] The same phenomenon occurred in Great Britain in 1971-72, when the Heath Government's removal of restrictions on credit to the private sector by no means led to an increase in productive investments. In mid-November 1971, the total sum of bank credits to manufacturing industry was at the same level as the average for 1970 — which, taking price inflation into account, was equivalent to a significant decline in 'real credit' (the purchasing power of this sum). These examples clearly show that it is wrong to see the chief cause of permanent inflation in the *ability* of banks to grant an expansion of credit money. The main drive behind it comes from large companies, and their capacity to use the expansion of credit money to obtain at short notice the volume of money adequate for their projections of accumulation and realisation. The role of the permanent inflation of late capitalism in concealing the decline of commodity values, facilitating the accumulation of capital, disguising the rise in the rate of surplus-value and temporarily solving the difficulties of realization by its extension of credit, thus ultimately encounters impassible limits. Creeping inflation then ceases to be functional, or turns into galloping inflation. We shall analyse these limits in the next chapter in the context of the specific forms of the industrial cycle in late capitalism.

[66]Yet more primitive are the views of Jacques Rueff, who still believes in the self-regulation of the gold standard: 'This is an absolute and irresistible mechanism, since it only ceases to function when it has achieved its necessary effect.' *L'Age de l'Inflation*, Paris,1967, p. 54. The claim that in the age of the gold standard economic crises were of only short duration, is contradicted among other things by the long depression of 1873-93.

14

The Industrial Cycle in Late Capitalism

It is well known that ever since capitalist large industry achieved domination of the world market, its development has assumed a cyclical character, peculiar only to this mode of production, with successive phases of recession, upswing, boom, overheating, crash, depression and so on.[1] Although Marx left no finished theory of the industrial cycle and crises of over-production,[2] it is possible to derive the broad outlines of such a theory from his most important writings.[3] We have already cited in Chapter 1 the passage in which Marx explicitly rejects any monocausal explanation of crises, insisting that they are a combination of *all* the contradictions of the capitalist mode of production. In this sense the cyclical movement of capitalist production undoubtedly finds its clearest expression in the cyclical movement of the average rate of profit, which after all sums up the contradictory development of all the moments of the process of production and reproduction.

[1] We have undertaken a specific analysis and explanation of the capitalist economic cycle in Chapter Eleven of our *Marxist Economic Theory* (p. 342f), and do not wish to repeat here what we have said there.

[2] The reason for this is that his analysis of over-production was scheduled, according to the original plan of *Capital*, for inclusion in the unwritten Sixth Part on competition and the world market. There are various indications that even in writing the Third Volume of *Capital* Marx still adhered to this plan: see pp. 261, 363.

[3] The most important passages in this respect are *Theories of Surplus Value*, Vol. 2, Part 2, pp. 492-546; *Capital*, Vol. 2, pp. 185-6, 315-18, 480-1, 467-9; *Capital*, Vol. 3, pp. 236-61, 431-2, 471-2, 477-82.

An economic upswing is possible only with a rising rate of profit, which in its turn creates the conditions for a fresh extension of the market and an accentuation of the upswing. At a certain point in this development, however, the increased organic composition of capital and the limit to the number of commodities that can be sold to the 'final consumers' must both lower the rate of profit and also induce a relative contraction of the market. These contradictions then spill over into a crisis of over-production. The falling rate of profit leads to a curtailment of investments which turns the downswing into a depression. The devalorization of capital and increasing rationalization and unemployment (which lift the rate of surplus-value) permit the rate of profit to rise once more. The decline in output and depletion of stock permit a new expansion of the market, which combines with the recovery of the rate of profit to restimulate entrepreneurial investments, and hence to launch an upswing in production.

The cyclical movement of the rate of profit is undoubtedly linked to the *uneven development* of the various elements of the overall process of production and reproduction. In an upswing, the rate of profit grows more rapidly in Department I than in Department II, thus causing a drain of capital to the former, a substantial increase in investment activity and hence a boom. Conversely: whereas over-production (or over-capacity) makes its first appearance in Department II before becoming manifest in Department I, it will assume its most acute forms in Department I rather than Department II. The re-stimulation of production during the depression following the crash thus mostly proceeds from Department II, where the rate of profit declines less than in Department I.

The fact that Department I develops more powerfully than Department II is merely an overall social expression of an increase in the organic composition of capital. Conversely, the fact that the production of Department I declines more steeply than that of Department II during recessions is ultimately an expression of a fall in the rate of profit and devalorization of capital. It would be superfluous to pursue here this uneven development between the different components of total capital and each of its value-parts. *The important point is that this uneven development — disproportionality — is not merely due to the anarchy of production and the absence of agreements between the capitalists, as was assumed by*

Hilferding and Bukharin,[4] *but is rooted in the inherent laws of development and contradictions of the capitalist mode of produ-ction.* It stems among other things from the antagonism between use-value and exchange-value, from the impossibility of increasing the consumption of the 'final consumers' in equal proportion to social production capacity without a substantial reduction in the rate of profit,[5] and from the impossibility of eliminating capitalist competition altogether — in other words, of throttling investments at the first sign of over-capacity, since firms with a technological lead continue to seek surplus-profits and larger shares of the market. To eliminate the cyclical movement of production there would have to be not only stable growth, and hence a stable rate of investment — in other words, not only a general cartel, but also a general cartel secure for all time, which would mean the abolition of private owner-ship and any independence whatever in accumulation and invest-ment activity — but also a complete adjustment of the distribution of the purchasing power of each individual consumer to the dynamic of the production and value of each individual product. Such condi-tions would involve the abolition of capitalism and commodity productions themselves.[6]

[4] Let us recall the famous passage from the Third Volume of *Capital*: 'The ulti-mate reason for all real crises always remains the poverty and restricted consump-tion of the masses as opposed to the drive of capitalist production to develop the productive forces as though only the absolute consuming power of society constitut-ed their limit.' (p. 484)

[5] Also from the antagonism between the extension of production and the valoriza-tion of capital: 'The contradiction, to put it in a very general way, consists in that the capitalist mode of production involves a tendency towards absolute development of the productive forces, regardless of the value and surplus-value it contains, and regardless of the social conditions under which capitalist production takes place; while, on the other hand, its aim is to preserve the value of the existing capital and promote its self-expansion to the highest limit (i.e., to promote an ever more rapid growth of this value).' Marx, *Capital*, Vol. 3, p. 244.

[6] In the *Grundrisse* Marx makes it clear that general regulation of the economy not based on social ownership and social labour would represent a type of 'despotism' but would no longer be capitalist commodity production: 'The bank would thus be the general buyer and seller . . . . A second attribute of the bank would be neces-sary: it would have the power to establish the exchange value of all commodities, i.e., the labour-time materialized in them in an authentic manner. But its functions could not end there. It would have to determine the labour time in which commodi-ties could be produced, with the average means of production available in a given industry, i.e., the time in which they would have to be produced. But that also would not be sufficient. It would not only have to determine the time in which a certain quantity of products had to be produced, and place the producers in condi-tions which made their labour equally productive (i.e., it would have to balance

So long as capitalism exists, production will continue to follow a cyclical pattern. It is easy to show empirically that this is still the case in late capitalism. The recessions of the US economy in 1949, 1953, 1957, 1960 and 1969-71, and 1974-75 are well-known. Since the end of the Second World War similar downswings have occurred in all the imperialist countries. It was long believed that West Germany was an exception,[7] but the 1966-67 recession provided a striking evidence to the contrary, in the winter of 1971-72 a second recession followed, and in 1974-75 a third recession. Nonetheless, economic cycles have assumed a specific character in each phase of the capitalist mode of production. The economic crises of 1920, 1929 and 1938 reveal many traits different from those of the epoch before the First World War, not least because the geographical expansion of capitalism had ended with the incorporation of China into the world market, while the victorious Russian Revolution had even contributed to its diminution. In the same way, it is necessary to examine specific features of the late capitalist production cycle.

The thesis advanced by the Hungarian Marxist Janossy that a long-term average rate of growth exists, which only war-destruction can disrupt (leading to a subsequent 'reconstruction' period with an above-average rate of growth) is in no way satisfactory.[8] Disregarding the fact that the above-average rates of growth registered in West Germany and Japan during the 1960's can hardly be explained by the destruction wreaked by World War Two, there

---

and to arrange the distribution of the means of labour), but it would also have to determine the amounts of labour-time to be employed in the different branches of production. . . . Nor is this all. The biggest exchange process is not that between commodities, but that between commodities and labour. . . . The workers would not be selling their labour to the bank, but they would receive the exchange value for the entire product of their labour. Precisely seen, then, the bank would be not only the general buyer and seller; but also the general producer. In fact, either it would be a despotic ruler of production and trustee of distribution, or it would indeed be nothing more than a board which keeps the books and accounts for a society producing in common.' *Grundrisse*, pp. 155-6.

[7] In fact, there were several conjunctural fluctuations even before the 1966-67 recession in Germany (with a cyclical peak in the years 1957 and 1960 and a cyclical trough in the years 1959 and 1963.) But before the recession of 1966-67 these oscillations found expression in variations of the rate of growth rather than an absolute decline in production. Nevertheless, it must be remembered that in the 'cyclical trough' of 1962-63 there was an absolute drop in the output of the machine-tool industry, and the total volume of industrial investments also fell back for the first time since the end of the War.

[8] Janossy, op.cit., p. 16 f.

remains the fundamental reality of the accelerated rate of growth of the US economy in the 60's, which naturally had nothing to do with any kind of 'reconstruction'.

In the course of our analysis we have singled out two decisive factors which, in our view, explain the 'long wave with an undertone of expansion' from 1940(45)-66. In the first place, the historical defeats of the working class enabled fascism and war to raise the rate of surplus-value. In the second place, the resultant increase in the accumulation of capital (investment activity), together with an accelerated rhythm of technological innovation and a reduced turnover-time of the fixed capital, led in the third technological revolution, to a long-term expansion of the market for the extended reproduction of capital on an international scale, despite its geographical limitation.

How is permanent inflation connected with this 'long wave with an undertone of expansion'? To what extent does it help late capitalism to mitigate the effects of its internal contradictions? Can it do this for an unlimited period? Money, as the universal equivalent of the values of the commodities, is the counter-value of quantities of socially necessary labour. At the same time, therefore, it is a claim over a fraction of the present or future overall labour resources of society.[9] In the context of the labour theory of value, this definition of money immediately shows that a devaluation of money (i.e., an increase of the money-tokens corresponding to a given quantity of labour) cannot have any direct influence on the total sum of labour quantities to be distributed; it can only determine their *redistribution*. More quantities of labour cannot be distributed than there are to distribute. However, since a crisis of over-production is characterized precisely by the fact that important forces of production (labour-power and machines) are laid idle, the inflationary creation of money can in certain conditions stimulate the accumulation of capital, *if it leads to an increase in production, namely in the production of surplus-value*. It can thus also lead to a growth in the mass of the quantities of labour to be distributed.[10] Under capitalist conditions this will only occur if it promotes an increase in the rate of profit — in

[9] Jourdain and Valier, 'L'Echec des Explications Bourgeoises de l'Inflation', p. 40.
[10] Mattick is wrong, therefore, when, in his otherwise justified critique of Baran and Sweezy's *Monopoly Capital*, he excludes the possibility that capital accumulation can be stimulated by state creation of money — a phenomenon which he reduces merely to a problem of distribution — by confining government intervention to the 'production of non-marketable goods'. Paul Mattick, 'Marxismus und Monopolkapital', in Federico Hermann, Karin Monte and Claus Rolshausen (eds),

other words, reduces the share of wages in the national income. Keynes, more intelligent and cynical than his 'reformist' disciples, was quite frank about this.

Because monetary devaluation and credit can to some extent conceal this state of affairs by an uninterrupted increase in prices (which may well correspond to a reduction in values), they make it necessary to take a searching look at the relationship between inflation, the rate of profit, the real income of wage earners and the accumulation of capital. As we have seen in the previous chapter, one of the main functions of permanent inflation is that it provides the large companies with the means for accelerating the accumulation of their capital. This involves a conversion of idle capital into productive capital in so far as the money capital lent stems from actual deposits in banks. It becomes a conversion of credit money into money capital as soon as the volume of overdrafts exceeds that of the deposits which have autonomously come into being.[11] The discussion as to whether this credit money represents 'pure' money capital, credit money or 'fictitious capital' seems somewhat byzantine: it is actually money capital advanced and (with the rate of inflation) partly devalued. So long as this money capital is used to purchase labour power and means of production, and is thereby converted into productive capital, an actual increase in the production of value and surplus-value takes place — in other words, a real enrichment of capitalist society.

We earlier concluded that armaments production — as commodity production — can raise the mass of surplus-value if idle capital is converted into capital producing surplus-value; the same holds *a fortiori*, of course, for idle capital converted to production not of arms but of use-values entering the process of reproduction. The illusion that creeping inflation can only lead to a redistribution of the *existing* sum of wages and prices arises once it is tacitly assumed that labour-power and the means of production are being fully utilized and that total social capital is reconverted into capital obtaining the average profit. If we drop this unhistorical hypothesis — which does not correspond to the situation of world capitalism either in 1930-40 or after 1945-48 — the mystery is easily solved.

Monopolkapital — Thesen zu dem Buch von Paul A. Baran und Paul M. Sweezy, Frankfurt, 1969, p. 52 f.
[11] In the paragraphs inserted by Engels in his own edition of the Third Volume of *Capital* he defines overdrafts (i.e., the creation of bank money) on several occasions: *Capital*, Vol. 3, pp. 419, 445-7.

Let us suppose an annual social production with the following value structure:

I: $10,000c + 5,000v + 5,000s = 20,000$ means of production.

II: $8,000c + 4,000v + 4,000s = 16,000$ means of consumption.

We are in a recession. Substantial amounts of machinery and raw materials are unused and unemployment is widespread in the working class. The state (or the banking system) now injects 4,500 units of paper money into circulation by giving credit to consumers and enterprises.[12] For some reason, which need not be specified here (e.g., because the stock of consumer goods has already been depleted in the protracted course of the crisis) this initially leads to an increase in the price of the means of consumption. The result is a reduction of, let us say, 15% in the real income of the workers (if commodities worth 36,000 units of value confront 40,500 units of paper money there occurs a 12.5% devaluation of the average unit of paper money. Naturally however, this does not mean that all commodity prices in the devalued paper money rise by the same percentage). An increase in the rate of surplus-value and the rate of profit thereby occurs, which persuades capital to invest the additional quantities of money (quantities of money capital) which are gathering in its hands — in other words, to use it to set in motion idle machines and to purchase unemployed labour power. If the workers now succeed, thanks to a higher level of employment, in making good the loss in the purchasing power of their wages, and if the additional 4,500 units of money capital are distributed in the same proportion as the original productive capital, then after a certain time,[13] there would arise a value product with the following structure:

[12] Or distributes paper money produced by inflationary *deficit financing* to the unemployed. The *technical* mechanism for the creation of additional money is unimportant.

[13] In order not to complicate the calculations unduly, we have deliberately avoided inserting intermediate phases here: for instance, a second phase, in which a certain fraction, say 50%, of the surplus-value produced in the first phase — now increased through the redistribution of revenues in the sphere of circulation — is accumulated, and hence is characterized by a rate of surplus-value over 100%; or a third phase, in which the appearance of new commodities on the market supersedes the devaluation of paper money and coincides with the re-establishment of the original rate of surplus-value as a result of the struggle of the working class, so that we are thence led to a fourth phase which is equivalent to the starting position on an extended scale.

I: $11,667c + 5,833v + 5,833s = 23,333$ means of production
II: $9,333c + 4,677v + 4,677s = 18,677$ means of consumption

What has occurred since the initial situation, therefore, is not a redistribution but an expansion of the value product (and of surplus-value), which was merely set in motion by the creation of additional money. The difficulty existing at the end of this expansion would thus be the same as at the moment of recession, only on a higher plane. Where reserve forces of production are available, the inflationary creation of money performs the same function as the credit system as a whole. It allows the development of the forces of production to proceed beyond the limits of private property, while simultaneously reproducing the inherent contradictions between the two on an extended scale, *but only after a certain period of time*: 'The credit system appears as the main lever of over-production and over-speculation in commerce solely because the reproduction process, which is elastic by nature, is here forced to its extreme limits, and is so forced because a large part of the social capital is employed by people who do not own it and who consequently tackle things quite differently than the owner, who anxiously weighs the limitations of his private capital in so far as he handles it himself. This simply demonstrates the fact that the self-expansion of capital based on the contradictory nature of capitalist production permits an actual free development only up to a certain point, so that in fact it constitutes an immanent fetter and barrier to production, which is continually broken through by the credit system. Hence the credit system accelerates the material development of the productive forces and the establishment of the world market. It is the historical mission of the capitalist system of production to raise these material foundations of the new mode of production to a certain degree of perfection. At the same time credit accelerates the violent eruptions of this contradiction — crises — and thereby the elements of disintegration of the old mode of production.'[14]

We have stressed that the development of overdraft credit to capitalist enterprises represents the most important source of the inflationary creation of money and hence the most important source of permanent inflation itself. This effects a change in the main form of 'production credit'.[15] Whereas in the classical imperialist age

[14] Marx, *Capital*, Vol. 3, p. 441.
[15] For the difference between circulation and production credit, see Hilferding, *Das Finanzkapital*, pp. 77-9. Hilferding called production credit 'bank credit' and

it took the form of shares sold on the capital market and mediated or bought up by the banks, in the recent 'long wave with an undertone of expansion' it was principally overdraft credit. Permanent inflation assured the large companies the means of self-financing through 'administered prices', by supplying an abundance of bank money. This thereupon temporarily altered the relationship between these large companies and bank capital in at least some of the decisive imperialist countries (USA, Japan, Italy, France). The explosive increase in the rates of profit and surplus-value, in which we have discerned the main stimulus for the 'long wave with an undertone of expansion', was not caused by permanent inflation, although it was mediated and prolonged by it. Conceptually the role of inflationary money creation in mitigating crises must be separated into two distinct processes: on the one hand, the possibility of using it to brake the cumulative character of a crisis of overproduction at a certain level; on the other, the possibility of limiting the plunge in the volume of private investments by means of state contracts.

If the state does not intervene in the economy at all, the decline in monetarily effective demand will be more than proportional to the decline in employment. An unemployment ratio of 6% or 10% will then mean a reduction in the sale of consumer goods by the same percentage,[16] which will lead in turn to the curtailment of production in Department II, the curtailment of orders from Department II to Department I, and then to the consequent dismissals in Department I, thus assuming the cumulative character of an avalanche. If, however, the State distributes additional income to the unemployed by means of inflation, to the order of — say — 60% of the average wage of the workers, then an unemployment ratio of 6%

'capital credit'. We believe that the formulation 'production credit' is less ambiguous and have therefore used it in our *Marxist Economic Theory*. Entrepreneurial credit would similarly be used to express this. Renner distinguished between 'company credit' which gave firms additional circulating capital, and 'investment credit', which gave them additional fixed capital (op.cit., pp. 228-32). Although this distinction was valid for classical' imperialism, it loses its force when the expansion of overdraft credit continually allows large monopolies to transform short-term loans into medium-term or even disguised long-term loans.

[16] Naturally this does not mean that there is a uniform decline in the sale of all consumer goods. Since expenditure on basic foods, rent, and so on, can hardly be compressed, any decline in the nominal income of wage-earners leads to a disproportionately high fall in the sales of durable consumer goods. These introduce an element into consumer spending which is more determined by the business cycle than was the case in earlier epochs of capitalism.

will only cause a 2.4% decline in the monetarily effective demand for consumer goods, and a 10% unemployment ratio a decline of only 4%. The drop in the output of Department II will thus be much smaller than it was in the 'classical' cycle,[17] and hence also the decline in orders from Department II to Department I. The cumulative process of the classical crises of over-production crisis will thereby have been curbed.

The effect of the creation of additional income on the purchase of means of consumption in times of over-production and recession is more or less automatic, but the same is by no means true of the effect of increased state investments on the sale of means of production.

If a decline of 5% in the output of consumer goods results in a drop of 20% in the orders for means of production, then an increase in State contracts will not lead automatically to a rise in private investments. These investments have been curtailed not only as a result of a fall in the orders and sales of Department I, but also and above all because of the falling rate of profit and the existence of over-capacity. Growing State contracts to certain branches of industry in this Department will not necessarily lure them into a new wave of investment. The same also holds true of the more limited stagnation of sales in Department II. The only effect of the inflationary creation of credit money is to brake the *decline* of sales in Department II. Braking a decline in sales, however, is by no means the same thing as expanding sales. Department II will only seek to increase its productive capacity — in other words, give orders to the branches of Department I which produce fixed capital — if it can rely on an expansion of sales. The increase of investments by the State thus cannot curb the decline in the output of Department I as effectively as that of Department II. The differential effects of the inflationary creation of money on Departments I and II in times of crises are of great importance because they reveal the limitations of so-called anticyclical policy — even under 'ideal' conditions for late capitalism. No late capitalist government has succeeded in overcoming these limitations.

[17] See the figures given in *Marxist Economic Theory* (pp. 531-2), which compare the decline in sectoral turnover, sale of consumer durables and industrial production in the first nine months of the post-war recessions in the USA (1948-49, 1953-54, 1957-58) with the fall in the final two crises before the War. These figures show unmistakeably that the *start* of the crisis is fully analogous to the typical 'classical' crisis. It is the cumulative development of crises which has changed.

We now come to an analytical difficulty, however. How can a crisis of over-production be postponed or mitigated by inflationary creation of money if, on the one hand, the over-production was itself among other things a result of the relatively limited nature of the demand of the 'final consumers', while on the other, inflation lowers the relative share of the wage-earners (the great mass of the consumers) in the national income even more? This difficulty, which is closely linked to the economic development of the imperialist countries over the past 25 years, can be resolved into four processes:

1. If the extension of the 'unsaleable residue' of means of consumption[18] created by permanent inflation threatens to lower the rate of accumulation, there may occur an expansion of consumer credit, i.e. consumer commodities may increasingly be exchanged in their turn for credit money instead of for genuine revenue created in the production process. This technique, which was very seldom used in the ages of freely competitive capitalism and 'classical' imperialism, has been employed very widely since the Second World War, above all in the USA[19]— but also in other imperialist countries — as can be seen from the following figures on the growth of consumer indebtedness in the USA:[20]

(In Billion Dollars)	1946	1955	1969	1973	1974
A. Disposable income of the households	160.0	275.3	629.6	903.7	860 ±
B. Mortgage debts for freehold homes	23.0	88.2	266.8	465.9	600 ±
C. Consumer debts	8.4	38.8	122.5	173.5	200 ±
D. Total private debt of the households	31.4	127.0	389.3	649.4	800 ±
D as a % of A	19.6%	46.1%	61.8%	71.8%	93%

2. Another reaction to the difficulties of realization resulting from permanent inflation may be an increase in the export ratio — in

[18] This unsaleable residue need not necessarily be produced; it can also take the form of over-capacity. On the other hand, the monopolies may also react to a rise in demand by postponing delivery dates, instead of raising prices. See Zarnowitz, 'Unfilled Orders, Price Changes and Business Fluctuations', in *Review of Economics and Statistics*, November 1962.

[19] This is why the post-war boom in the USA is sometimes called the 'construction boom': the 'mortgage boom' would be a more accurate description.

[20] 'The Long Run Decline in Liquidity', in *Monthly Review*, Vol. 22, No. 4, September 1970, p. 6. For 1973, see *Statistical Abstract of the United States 1973*.

other words, an attempt to overcome the relative stagnation of sales on the domestic market by greater expansion on the world market. Undoubtedly the substantial expansion of world trade since the beginning of the 50's, which exceeded the growth rate of industrial production in certain important imperialist states and eventually made good the long-term stagnation of international trade between the two World Wars,[21] has also helped to dampen crises. In the 1953-63 period, industrial output at fixed prices increased in the capitalist countries as a whole by 62%, while their exports at fixed prices rose by 82%; in the 1963-72 period, industrial production grew by 65% and exports by 111%.[22] Obviously this expansion has taken the form of an *uneven development of the export shares* of particular imperialist countries or branches of production; for if the import share of all countries or branches of industry was the same, they would only lose on the domestic market what they had won by exports. This is by no means the case, however. In 1969, the capitalist countries of Europe imported 26.6% of all the machines and equipment bought within them. But the percentage was only 15.8% in Great Britain, 18% in West Germany, and 20.2% in France, while it rose to 49.7% in the other EEC countries and 45% in the other countries in the European free trade area. In the case of durable consumer goods, the respective import shares were 12.2% for Great Britain, 20.8% for France, 22.1% for West Germany, 52.1% for the remaining EEC countries, and 59.1% for the rest of the EFTA countries. The relation between the increase of imports of manufactured goods and the growth of the Gross National Product between 1959 and 1969 was 2.83 in France, 2.51 in Great Britain, 2 in Italy, and 1.86 in the USA, compared with only 1.45 in West Germany and 1.23 in Japan. These figures show unmistakably which imperialist powers stand to benefit most from the extension of the world market (world exports).[23] Bearing in mind the catastrophic decline of the share of colonial and semi-colonial countries in world trade, and the no less pronounced decline of the share of foodstuffs and raw materials in international commerce, we can con-

---

[21] An interesting example is the production of chemical fibres in the six largest imperialist states (USA, Japan, West Germany, Great Britain, France, Italy) which increased from 2,250,000 tons to 5,565,000 tons in the decade 1959-69; while the export of chemical fibres from these countries rose from 336,000 tons to 1,239,000 tons. In other words, the export share grew from 14.9% to 22.3%. All the competitors increased their share of exports with the exception of the USA.

[22] Blechschmidt-Hoffmann-von der Marwitz, op.cit., p. 45.

[23] OECD, *Inflation*, pp. 109, 98.

clude that this increase in the share of exports in the ongoing industrial production of the most dynamic imperialist powers is equivalent to a *redistribution of the world market* and a long-term, relative *substitution of purchasing power* to the advantage of the products of the imperialist manufacturing industry (especially of countries and branches of production with the most developed technology), and to the prejudice of the products of simple commodity production, agriculture and traditional raw materials and 'light' consumer goods industries.

3. The above average rate of expansion of world trade in the 'long wave with an undertone of expansion' following the Second World War was only made possible by an increase in the volume of international currency over and above the increase in gold production. The Gold-Exchange Standard (really the Gold-Dollar Standard), based on the balance of payments deficits of the USA, served as a device for the constant expansion of international means of payment, at a rate of 4% a year from 1958. *The Gold-Dollar Standard created a system of international inflation of credit money, which simultaneously protected and extended the system of 'national' inflations of credit money.*[24]

4. The effects of permanent inflation on the evolution of prices of ongoing production are limited in the imperialist countries by the existence of considerable reserves of real wealth. Devaluation of paper money leads to 'mobilization' of reserves of material values such as well-situated building sites,[25] art objects,[26] gold, precious

[24] Jean Denizet, 'Chronique d'une Décennie', in Perroux, Denizet and Bourguinat, op.cit., p. 55.
[25] Between 1963 and 1971 the prices for building sites in England and Wales increased by more than 140%: *Financial Times*, 8 January 1972. In France, the price per building site sold (*valeur moyenne des transactions*) rose by 4½ times between 1956 and 1968: *Le Monde*, 20 April 1971.
[26] Arthur Höner-Van Gogh has written an interesting and ironical article on the work of art as a commodity: 'Der Umsatz geht um in der Kunst', in *Information der Internationalen Treuhand AG*, No. 37, Basle, November 1971. The annual increase in value of art works is on average at least 10%. In the purely speculative field (purchase of paintings as an investment for re-sale) price increases of up to 5,000% have been known to occur within the space of 30 years. In the USA and West Germany 'art investment societies' have already come into being. One such fund also deals in postage stamps and vintage wines as a side-line. For the 'self-service stores' of the art trade (Cologne and Basle fairs) and the growing industrialization of art, see *Le Monde*, 30 June 1971. According to an article in the *Times* of 21 February 1970, prices of works of art multiplied as follows in the period 1951-70: modern paintings, 29 times; Old Master drawings, 22 times; Impressionist paintings, 18 times; Old Master paintings, 7 times; 18th Century Italian furniture, 7 times; Dutch furniture of the same period, 5½ times.

metals and antiques, which are increasingly injected into circulation in addition to ongoing production. The speculative character of this 'mobilization of material values' is, of course, further reinforced by the inflationary revaluation of fictitious capital,[27] especially of shares. The greater these reserves, the slower will be the change from cumulative to galloping inflation. The more, however, these reserves are injected into circulation, the greater will be the increase in speculation, hence the rise in prices, and therewith the tendency for cumulative inflation to accelerate — in other words, the greater will be the danger of galloping inflation.

Especially during the inflationary boom of 1972-1973, a qualitatively greater wave of speculation occurred[28] — encompassing not merely the real values enumerated above, but many primary commodities and currencies as well. This speculation inevitably led to the collapse of a whole series of finance corporations, property companies and secondary banks (Franklin Bank in the USA, Herstadt Bank in West Germany, Sindona group in Italy), which marked the start of the 1974-75 recession. But the fact there was simultaneously a sharp fall in stock market prices, of many raw material prices,

Annual Rates of Increase of Consumer Prices

	Average 1960-65	1968	1969	1970	1971
U.S.A.	1.3%	4.2%	5.4%	5.9%	4.3%
Japan	6.2%	5.5%	5.2%	7.6%	6.3%
U.K.	3.6%	4.8%	5.4%	6.4%	9.5%
W. Germany	2.8%	1.6%	1.9%	3.4%	5.3%
France	3.8%	4.8%	6.4%	5.3%	5.5%
Italy	4.9%	1.3%	2.6%	5.0%	5.0%

	1972	1973	1974 (first half)	1974 (third quarter)
U.S.A.	3.3%	6.2%	10.2%	11.6%
Japan	4.3%	11.7%	23.0%	23.4%
U.K.	7.0%	9.2%	14.2%	17.0%
W. Germany	5.5%	6.9%	7.3%	7.0%
France	5.9%	7.3%	12.5%	14.6%
Italy	5.5%	10.8%	14.8%	20.8%

[27] For the notion of ficititious capital, see Marx, *Capital*, Vol. 3, pp. 454-60, 466, 467.
[28] For the case of Japan, see the interesting study by Tasuku Noguchi, 'Recent Japanese Speculation', in *Kapitalistate*, No. 2, 1973.

of building land prices (which in Britain declined by 40% in the twelve months up to mid 1974) and of certain types of paintings, is evidence that inflation is not yet galloping in character. The table above is a survey of the acceleration of inflation.[29]

The inherently contradictory nature of these four possibilities of evasion thus becomes clearly apparent. Both disproportionately great expansion of consumer credit, and speculative price increases of material values [30] or shares, inevitably tend to create inflation, and after a certain period to turn it first into a cumulative and then into a galloping process. The transition from creeping to galloping inflation, however, marks the conversion of excess money from a limited stimulus into a fetter on production: under conditions of galloping inflation capital ceases to perform the metamorphosis of commodity capital into money capital. It increasingly flees from the sphere of circulation, while more and more commodities are hoarded. This in turn means that production declines, and the accumulation of capital rapidly shrinks (even if it is true in itself that in times of galloping inflation variable capital is devalorized much more swiftly than constant, so that the effect on the rate of surplus-value is advantageous to capital).

If the acceleration of inflation as such represents a danger for the accumulation of capital, then it constitutes an even more glaring contradiction to the second solution to difficulties of realization. The more that inflation accelerates in an imperialist country, the smaller will be that country's chances of retaining — let alone increasing — its current share of the world market. After a certain point rising prices, with all the resultant consequences for the domestic market, must have an effect on export prices.[31]

[29] Glyn-Sutcliffe, op.cit., p. 95; Sachverständigenrat, *Jahresgutachten 1974*, p. 16.

[30] There are various connecting threads between the material values integrated into circulation and the commodities sold for the reproduction of capital. Thus speculative price increases in the former sphere must eventually affect the whole mirror of prices, as long as the inflationist expansion of the money supply continues. One of the most important of these connecting links is the price of building sites and land and its effect on building costs or the cost of houses and rents. For example, in West Germany the cost of living increased by 44.3% between 1962 and 1973, producers' prices of industrial materials by 28%, but the prices of private housing by 87.1%, those of industrial buildings by 93.6% and those of building lots even by 171.3%: *Jahresgutachten 1974*, pp. 280-1. In Japan, building site prices in urban areas in 1974 attained a level 22.9 times above that of 1955, whereas the consumer price index was only 2.1 times above the level of 1955.

[31] For the intermeshing of alterations in the rate of exchange, rate of inflation and competitive ability, see Neusüss, Altvater and Blanke, op.cit.

If the rate of profit is threatened — which usually occurs before actual full employment is achieved [32] — monetary devaluation begins to cause structural changes in the distribution of social capital among the various sectors of the economy. Generally speaking, an inflationary atmosphere promotes a cumulative expansion of credit because the devaluation of money, counted on by every capitalist, makes it lucrative to buy on credit today and repay with devalued money tomorrow. This is the explanation of the seeming paradox that in times of growing inflation, when the banks are lending an increasing amount of money, it is sometimes possible for there to be a 'shortage of money' which drives up interest. Inflation itself constantly feeds the demand for money capital and makes the closure of the tap creating credit and money all the more dangerous for business: it always means a sharp turn towards recession. On the other hand, there is no contradiction whatever between this growing demand for money capital and the over-capitalization underlying late capitalism (as also 'classical' imperialism).

A considerable portion of bank credits do not come from 'pure' creation of money, but stem from the accumulation of deposits which have come into being outside the banking system.[33] The no less impressive growth of long-term bank deposits shows how high actual over-capitalization really is.[34] The double role of overdraft credit (not only as the inflationary creation of money, but also as the classical mediation for converting idle capital into productive capital) must never be overlooked.

Permanent inflation, however, not only drives up the rate of interest in the short-run; it also has long-term effects. Just as owners and lenders of money capital get increasingly accustomed to devaluation of money, and start to distinguish between nominal and real interest, so too sellers of the commodity of labour-power learn, in

[32] In the entire post-war history of the US economy, despite occasional 'overheating', the utilization of capacity in manufacturing industry never rose above 94%, and in the period 1948-71 the rate was 90% or over in only six years out of twenty-four.

[33] The inflationary creation of bank money can be reduced to the distinction between the total credits granted by banks and their total deposits (simply called 'money capital formation' in West Germany). In the period 1963-70 the difference between the two came to a total of 33 billion DM net in West Germany (in 1968 money capital formation exceeded credits granted).

[34] In the USA, long-term bank deposits — 'Time Deposits' — which do not come out of overdraft credit, rose from $4 billion in 1915 and $20 billion in 1929 to $32 billion in 1946, $50 billion in 1956, $106 billion in 1963 and nearly $180 billion in 1967.

times of permanent inflation, to differentiate between nominal and real wages. With a currency losing 5% of its purchasing power annually, an annual interest of 4% would make inroads into capital itself; it would become 'negative real interest'. Loans of money capital would dry up completely under such circumstances. If, therefore, the nominal interest is equal to the sum of the average rate of inflation and the real interest, it will have a tendency to rise in conditions of long-term prices increases.[35] If the rate of interest rises over the long run,[36] however, while the rate of profit fluctuates, entrepreneurial profits may suddenly dwindle. The ongoing increase in the nominal rate of interest combined with permanent inflation may forbid long-term investment projects altogether, i.e., both reinforce the reduction in the turnover-time of fixed capital due to the acceleration of technological innovation, and postpone indefinitely certain projects which are too risky because of the long duration of turnover involved in them.

The combination of inflationary creation of money to mitigate crises and growing competition on the world market give the industrial cycle in the first 'expansionary' phase of late capitalism the particular form of a movement interlocked with the credit cycle. In the epoch of freely competitive capitalism, when there was a gold standard and the central banks only intervened marginally in the development of credit, the credit cycle was completely dependent on the industrial cycle. In late capitalism, when institutionalised inflation makes the monetary sphere much more autonomous and capable of independent action — running counter to the industrial

---

[35] Orthodox Keynesians dispute this, because they see the rate of interest as a function of liquidity preference, and cash is naturally devalued just as much as loans are by inflation. (R.F. Harrod, *Money*, London, 1969, pp. 179-81). But this merely demonstrates the weakness of the theory of liquidity preference, which corresponds to the mentality of rentiers (characteristic of a part of the British bourgeoisie in Keynes' time), but in no sense to the attitude of normal, average capitalists. The latter ponder on the *form in which to invest* their idle capital, not whether to invest it at all. Given the various possibilities for investment, it is precisely in times of permanent inflation, that the devaluation of money furnishes an important motive for 'preference' of material values, shares, and so on, which those capitalists who embody the demand for money capital must neutralise by offering a higher rate of interest.

[36] The average rate of interest for short-term business loans in the USA has more than trebled in the past 30 years. In the large industrial cities of the North and East it was about 2% in 1940; 2.7% in 1950; 5.2% in 1960; 6.4% in the first half of 1967. In 1967, however, a nominal interest of 6.4% corresponded to a real interest of approximately only 2.5%.

cycle — to moderate conjunctural fluctuations, a credit cycle temporarily distinct from the industrial cycle comes into being. The expansion of credit money can now stimulate the domestic economy up to the point beyond which it risks jeopardizing the share of the world market controlled by the country in question. Once this threshold is reached, it must be halted as hurriedly as possible. The 'Stop-Go' pattern of the British economy in the first post-war Tory era is the classical example of such a relatively autonomous credit cycle.[37] But the US economy — and to a lesser extent the West German economy — have also been characterized in the past 20 to 25 years by a similar interlocking of industrial and credit cycles.[38] Naturally, even regarded as a separate movement, the credit cycle has no complete autonomy from the actual industrial cycle. It is determined by the credit *policy* of the central banking system and the government, which takes the option between short-term credit expansion or credit restriction. But the decisions of the central banks are in turn not applied without mediation by the private deposit banks — they are modified among other things by the private profit interests of the latter (in France the nationalized banks operate on the same principle). This sets in motion a complicated mechanism, in which the development of bank deposits and the quotation and yield of public funds play a substantial role. The credit restrictions supposed to be enforced by an increase in the liquidity ratio, for example, can be circumvented by the banks via a reshuffling of their assets.[39] The way in which American banks circumvented the US Government's policy of restricting credit by exploiting the Euro-Dollar market is now well-known. Effective credit restriction by a government means a radical limitation of the freedom of action — and hence the pursuit of profit — of the private banks. Such a policy is impossible in the long-run without the imposition of currency controls — in other words,

[37] See, for example, Brittan, *The Treasury under the Tories 1954-1964*, pp. 289-92. It should, however, be added that the credit cycle was ineffective in Great Britain, or did not genuinely run counter to the actual industrial cycle. In this connection see Dow, *The Management of the British Economy*, London, 1964.

[38] Thus the policy of limiting inflation under the Eisenhower Administration led to a lower than average rate of growth. In the Kennedy-Johnson era accelerated growth was provoked by accelerated inflation. Nixon's attempt to limit inflation led to a recession, which then had to be promptly countered by a record amount of 'deficit spending'.

[39] On this problem see Suzanne de Brunhoff, '*L'Offre de Monnaie*', pp. 132-47; S.M. Goldfeld, *Commercial Bank Behaviour and Economic Activity*, Amsterdam, 1966.

without restrictions on the international movement of capital, and hence the abolition of free currency convertibility.[40] Thereby a new contradiction arises, between an effective credit cycle, whose goals must include the maintenance or expansion of a country's share of the world market, and the growth of the same world market on the basis of currency convertibility and the inflation of international credit money. In the long-run the two are incompatible. The credit cycle cannot be isolated from its repercussions on the rate of surplus-value — in other words, its effects on class contradictions and class struggle. Credit expansion that leads to a rapid increase in production depresses the reserve army of labour and, after a certain point, thereby facilitates a rise in real wages. Inflation will impede, but not prevent this rise. If capital seeks to defend the rate of surplus-value, let alone increase it, it must therefore somehow reconstitute a reserve army of labour. This is not possible without restrictions in credit and in the rate of growth of the money supply. Boddy and Crotty have confirmed this rule by a study of the relation between profits and wages (including white-collar workers' salaries) in non-financial corporations of the USA.[41] In the first part of successive business cycles (from the trough of the recession to mid-expansion) 1953-57, 1957-61, 1961-70, this fraction tended to increase sharply — from 10% to 16% in 1953-57; from 9.8% to 14.3% in 1957-59; from 10% to 16.7% in 1961-65. In the second part of this cycle, it declined no less sharply — well before the subsequent recessions. For example, it decreased from 16.7% in 1965 to 9% in 1969, while a recession started only in 1970. While the Boddy-Crotty fraction is not identical with the rate of surplus-value, it is an approximate guide to it.

The basic problematic of the capitalist laws of motion continued to operate unremittingly beneath the surface of the 'long wave with an undertone of expansion' from 1940 onwards. The third technological revolution, by effecting above-average reductions in the cost of important elements of constant capital, led to a further increase in the organic composition of capital, even if not so much as the catchword 'automation' might suggest. The bound upwards of the rate of surplus-value made possible by the great defeats of the international working class in the 30's and 40's could not be repeated in the 50's

---

[40] Jean Denizet, in Perroux, Denizet and Bourguinat, op. cit., p. 62. See also the 1971 annual report of the German Bundesbank.

[41] R. Boddy and J. Crotty, 'Class Conflict, Keynesian Politics and the Business Cycle', *Monthly Review*, October 1974.

and 60's. On the contrary, the long-term diminution of the industrial reserve army, which was the corollary of the substantial growth in the accumulation of capital, enabled the working class periodically to chip away at the rate of surplus-value somewhat. Thus beside the short-term conjunctural fluctuations just discussed, a long-term erosion of the average rate of profit set in, which persisted right through the 'normal' abridged industrial cycle. The strain on the credit cycle therefore increased. More and more autonomous creation of money became necessary to protect the system from the threat of crises of over-production and capital expansion. The rate of inflation started to accelerate.

Simultaneously, the law of uneven development has continued to prevail, shifting the international relationship of forces in inter-imperialist competition. American imperialism is slowly losing its productivity lead over its European and Japanese rivals. Its share in the world market is falling. It is currently attempting to reverse this secular development by stepping up capital exports to its imperialist rivals and increasing the international centralization of capital by acquiring substantial capital ownership within the economies of its competitors. But the long-run faster accumulation of capital in Western Europe and Japan inevitably means—in conditions of accelerated dollar devaluation—greater opportunities for West European and Japanese capital exports to the USA than for American capital exports in the opposite direction. American imperialism has tried to rescue itself from its dilemmas by hitherto successful pressure on its rivals to revalue their currencies, but this in the end can only lead to a further acceleration of European and Japanese capital exports as compared with American.

How little the credit cycle, despite its relative autonomy and the 'political' nature of many of the decisions governing it, can ultimately correct the decisive weight of the industrial cycle, may be seen from the cyclical movement of capacity utilization, which in late monopoly capitalism provides a clearer expression of the tendencies towards over-production inherent in the system than the proliferation of unsaleable goods. The cyclical character of over-capacity is manifest in both the USA and West Germany, as can be seen from the following estimates (*See* table on the next page).

This movement, however, sets an insuperable limit to the credit system. If substantial over-capacity already exists, even the most abundant injections of credit money by the bank system and (or) the

USA: Annual utilization of capacity in manufacturing industry [42]

Cyclical High	Cyclical Low
1952: 94%	1953: 76%
1955: 90%	1958: 74%
1959: 82%	1961: 79%
1966: 91%	1970: 75%
Summer 1973: 87.5%	March 1975: 65%

West Germany: utilization of capacity in manufacturing industry [43]

Cyclical High	Cyclical Low
Autumn 1960: 93%	Beginning of 1959: 87%
Beginning of 1965: 88%	Beginning of 1963: 81%
Beginning of 1970: 95%	Beginning of 1967: 77%
Mid 1973: 93%	End 1971: 88%
	End 1974: 88%

state will not lead to a stimulation of private investments in these sectors.[44] A conjunctural decline of private investments therewith becomes inevitable, and with it a recession. Thenceforth inflation can at most limit the scope of the recession or prevent its cumulative development.

If long-term structural over-capacities are then added to periodic conjunctural over-capacities — a clear indication that the stimulating effect of the third technological revolution is coming to an end — the ability of the credit cycle to smooth over the industrial cycle will be still further reduced. There is little doubt that precisely such structural over-capacities exist today in the steel industry, coal mining, the

[42] *Economic Report of the President, Transmitted to the Congress, January 1962*, Washington, 1962. *Statistical Abstract of the United States, 1968*, p. 719. *Survey of Current Business*.

[43] Sachverständigenrat zur Begutachtung der gesamtwirtschaftlichen Entwicklung, *Jahresgutachten 1969*, Drucksache VI/100, Deutscher Bundestag, 6, Wahlperiode; *Jahresgutachten 1971/1972*, Stuttgart 1971; *Jahresgutachten 1974*.

[44] One could ask: how can inflation be simultaneously combined with substantial unutilized capacities? Such a combination is unthinkable only in the context of a primitive quantity theory of money fixated by abstract aggregates. Once the specific structure of the money supply is grasped, including the structure of the creation of money, then it becomes plain why additional consumer income, for example, cannot assure an increase in the demand for aeroplanes or certain machines. With major price increases and uncertainty about employment, additional consumer income does not necessarily even promote the sale and production of consumer durables.

textile industry, the electrical household appliances industry, the automobile industry and probably also the electronic apparatus and petro-chemical industries.[45]

All this evidence thus points towards a decline in the relative autonomy of the credit cycle, and hence the ability of creeping inflation to restrict the cumulative effect of crises of over-production. This is merely another expression of the fact that the turning point between a 'long wave with an undertone of expansion' and a 'long wave with an undertone of stagnation' of late capitalism is now behind us.

We can observe the signs of this sea-change today in two domains. Firstly, the stimulating impact of inflationary creation of credit ceases to be effective when a rising debt-burden begins to restrict current purchasing power. This phenomenon is already visible both within the US economy and outside it, especially in the semi-colonies of the capitalist world.

In the USA the point will soon be reached where the accumulated burden of debts poses a direct threat both to the disposable income of households (purchasing power for consumer goods) and the liquidity of companies. Annual payments for the interest and repayment of mortgages, and for consumer credit and its repayment, constituted 5.9% of the disposable income of American households in the year 1946, 11.8% of this income in 1950, 18.6% in 1965 and 22.8% in 1969. The creation of credit is here clearly approaching its nemesis. Like a serpent swallowing its own tail, the totality of current additional credit only just covers the annual debt-burden from past credit—in other words, disposable income for ongoing purchase of goods and services is little higher now than it would be without credit expansion. Between 1965 and 1969 mortgage and consumer debts grew by $88 billion, while interest and repayments to be met by consumers increased by $55 billion. In 1969 the difference between the two sums was little more than 5% of disposable household income.[46]

---

[45] At the start of 1972, 20% of Western Europe's production capacity of PVC plastic was unutilised: *Financial Times*, 16 February 1972. The same percentage obtained for the world aluminium industry: *Neue Zürcher Zeitung*, 20 May 1972. After a short boom, every sign suggested a new world-wide over-capacity in synthetic fibres at the end of 1974, this time also seriously affecting the Japanese monopolies. See *Business Week*, October 5, 1974; *Far Eastern Economic Review*, November 29, 1974.

[46] 'The Long-Run Decline in Liquidity', in *Monthly Review*, Vol. 22, No. 4, September 1970, p. 6.

Still more ominous has been the development of company liquidity. The proportion of cash assets (including bank deposits) and public bonds to debts dropped from 73.4% in 1946 to 54.8% in 1951, 38.4% in 1961, 19.3% in 1969, and less than 18% in early 1974 for non-financial companies in the USA. This means that in 1974 debts were more than five times cash or quasi-cash assets. Whereas at the end of the Second World War the liquidity of the large corporations (at more than $100 million worth of assets per company) was superior to that of their smaller rivals, the reverse is now true. On 31 March 1970 the rate of liquidity was 31% for companies with assets of less than $1 million, 24% for those with assets of between $1 and $2 million, 22% for companies with assets of between $5 and $100 million and 19% for those with assets of over $100 million.[47] It is clear that the inflationary screw cannot be turned much further without immediately negative repercussions on the process of production and reproduction — i.e., without producing galloping inflation.

Other imperialist countries witnessed a similar trend towards a declining liquidity of joint-stock companies. In Great Britain, the volume of bank loans to industrial and commercial firms quadrupled between 1958 and 1967, while these companies' gross assets rose only by 30%. As a result of this divergence, net assets sank from £3.1 billion to £975 million.[48] Decreasing corporation liquidity is likewise revealed in declining ratios of self-financing — already cited for France. In Japan, the ratio of non-distributed profits to total capital engaged fell from 15.7% in 1959 to 10.7% in 1962, 9.1% in 1964 and 8.6% in 1970.[49]

Secondly, the relative national autonomy of the credit cycles of the various imperialist states has become a direct threat to the further expansion of the world market, disrupting and undermining the international currency system set up at Bretton Woods and increasingly hindering its replacement by a coherent successor system.

In the epoch of the gold standard, the yellow metal could simultaneously and consistently fulfill a three-fold function as measure of values, standard of prices and world currency. The mechanism of

[47] Ibid., p. 6.

[48] A. D. Bain, *The Control of the Money Supply*, London, 1971, pp. 109-10.

[49] T. Adams and I. Hoshi, *A Financial History of the new Japan*, Tokyo 1972, p. 345.

the gold standard made the industrial cycle virtually immune to the influence of the bourgeois State or to deliberate 'attempts at regulation' by agencies representing the overall interests of capital. Only the law of the uneven development of the capitalist mode of production, and the relative immobility of capital, to some extent limited the repercussions of periodical crises in the major countries of capital (first Great Britain, then the USA) on the total capitalist world market, in certain conjunctures. The apparently smooth operation of the Gold Standard before the First World War, however, was not due to any 'automatic process': it was based on the superior productivity and long-term historical stability of British industry, British capital and British sterling. Because capitalists all over the world had faith in the pound sterling (i.e., in the stability of British capitalism), because pound-notes could buy sought-after British goods, and because government bonds expressed in pounds gave their owners a claim on the secure future surplus-value of British capital, the pound was 'as good as gold' and the capitalist world economy was really based on a gold-pound standard at this time, even though the actual gold reserves of the Bank of England were inconsiderable.[50]

When the ruling strata of the bourgeois class in the most important imperialist states opted for active and massive intervention in the industrial cycle to mitigate crises by use of credit creation, the initial result was a further disruption of world trade because of the contraction of international liquidity.[51] The major paper currencies, now set free from gold, were no longer accepted as international means of payment. The world market broke up into autarkic economic blocs, between which direct exchange of commodities began to

[50] See the interesting book by Marcello De Cecco, *Economia e Finanza Internazionale dal 1890 al 1914,* Bari, 1971, pp. 145-9, 163-74. De Cecco rightly describes the world monetary system of the period 1890-1914 as a *Gold Exchange Standard* rather than a 'pure' gold standard.

[51] Triffin advances the following explanation for the collapse of currency convertibility and the abrupt decline of world trade in the 30's: '1. The extensive use of the issue power of central banks to underwrite the State's own deficits and, in addition, the credit expansion of other banks whenever such expansion conforms to the wishes, or even merely to the existing regulations, of the national monetary authorities; 2. The unwillingness to subordinate fully such credit policies to the preservation or restoration of a competitive price and cost pattern and of an overall external pattern, at current prices and exchange rates, compatible with the amount of gold and foreign exchange resources available to the monetary authorities.' Robert Triffin, *Gold and the Dollar Crisis,* New Haven, 1961, p. 29.

increase, thus eliminating the possibility (among other things) of expanding credit to enlarge world trade.[52] The result was that the restimulation of domestic markets by creation of money was not accompanied by an equivalent expansion of world trade. Indeed, the latter even threatened to decline.[53]

At Bretton Woods the victorious imperialist powers of World War Two established an international monetary system which was designed to provide the basis for an international version of the inflationary credit expansion which had by now gained acceptance on the national scale. Both bourgeois economists and politicians believed that the crucial problem was the expansion of liquidity — the continuous creation of additional means of payment.[54] Since the supply of gold was increasing too slowly and was distributed too unequally to solve the problem of international liquidity, a system was created, *which elevated a specific paper currency to the rank of world money alongside gold*; the concrete historical situation at the end of the Second World War was such, of course, that only the dollar could play the role.[55]

The new system was built on two foundations; firstly, the convertibility of the dollar into gold (facilitated among other things by the substantial over-valuation of gold in the dollar devaluation of 1934), which enabled the central banks of the capitalist world to use dollars alongside gold to cover their national currencies; secondly, the vast production reserves (and productivity lead) of the US economy, which meant that the accumulation of dollar claims in the hands of foreign governments and capitalists was not only unproblematic but downright desirable for them. The central problem of the international capitalist economy in the first years after the

[52] Between 1928 and 1938 the relation of gold reserves to annual world imports rose from 35% to 110%. The expanded gold output was hoarded because it could not be absorbed by the declining commodity circulation on the world market.

[53] The German case was the clearest. Whilst the index of industrial production rose 90% between 1933 and 1938, the exports of the Reich (without Austria) were barely 10% higher in 1938 than in 1933. In the years 1935, 1936 and 1937 they even declined absolutely. But in the USA too, industrial output had surpassed the level of 1929 in 1937, while exports were still less than 60% of the 1929 level.

[54] For Keynes's convictions in this respect, see Harrod, *Money*, pp. 178-9.

[55] Gold production fell by 40% between 1940 and 1945 and stagnated between 1945 and 1949. In 1945 the USA alone possessed 75% of the world's entire gold reserves. Significant participants in world trade, such as Germany, Japan, Italy, and India possessed practically no gold at all. For the reasons why the decision to let sterling also play the role of a reserve currency inevitably failed, see Elmar Altvater, *Die Weltwährungskrise*, Frankfurt, 1969, pp. 49-50.

Second World War was not the abundance but the shortage of dollars.[56]

Thus the Marshall Plan and similar 'Dollar-Aid' programmes of the US government had much the same effect in the context of the capitalist world economy as Keynesian policy in the national context: a large quantity of additional purchasing power was injected into the international area which — given a great deal of unutilized capacity — inevitably led to a major expansion of world trade.[57] The intensification of the extended reproduction of capital on an international scale, together with the steep increase in the rate of surplus-value and the impact of the third technological revolution, then generated a cumulative process of growth, on which national industrial cycles (mitigated by local credit cycles) could have a restrictive, but not a catastrophic effect. Conversely: since the industrial cycle was now modified by the cycle of credit creation — hence by the *political* decisions of national governments, it henceforward became internationally desynchronized.[58] The result was to enable the movement of the industrial cycle in one country to further mitigate the industrial cycles of other imperialist countries. A recession in one imperialist power now typically coincided with a boom in others, and increased exports to the expanding markets of the latter limited the repercussions of the decline in demand on the internal market of the former.[59]

[56] As late as 1952 the Annual Report of the Bank for International Payments contained the following definition of the major difficulty in the way of a further expansion of world trade: "Convertibility must necessarily require a sufficient amount of dollars and, while the first condition for this is that the countries of Europe should have goods to sell in sufficient quantities and at competitive prices, a further condition is that it should be possible to sell these commodities in ways which will permit them to earn the dollars and other currencies they need.' *Twenty-Second Annual Report*, Basle, 9 June 1952, p. 264. With greater dialectical insight, Triffin warned four years later that the growing deficit in the US balance of payments would lead the US Government to take measures which could endanger a further expansion of international liquidity.

[57] The fact that this was also in the interest of the USA can be seen from the very substantial expansion of US exports; which grew from $9.5 billion in 1945 to $15.7 billion in 1953, i.e., by 66%, while in the same period the gross national product increased by less than 20% and industrial output by 30%.

[58] We must note self-critically in this respect that in *Marxist Economic Theory* we underestimated the significance of this absence of simultaneity: p. 529. However, we made the necessary correction of this error in the mid-60's, predicting the serious consequences of a general recession affecting most or all of the imperialist states at the same time.

[59] The classical example in this respect is the recession in West Germany in 1966-67. But the repercussions of the 1970-71 recession in Great Britain were also attenuated

The whole rationale of the international monetary system created at Bretton Woods for promoting the expansion of world trade was reversed, however, as soon as the mainstays of the system began to disintegrate. The decomposition of these mainstays was not the result of accidents or mistakes, moreover; it was an inevitable outcome of the same inherent logic which had originally produced the international expansion of credit money.

We have already seen that a marginal acceleration of dollar inflation was a central precondition for the avoidance of serious crises of over-production in the American economy. Accelerated dollar inflation, however, meant an aggravation of the US balance of payments deficit and a growing threat to the gold-dollar parity at a fixed rate of exchange. From both sides, the dollar's convertibility into gold was increasingly undermined. Eventually, its official abolition became only a question of time.

Moreover, the law of uneven development led to an increasing decline in the ability of American commodities to compete with those of the USA's most important imperialist rivals.[60] The capitalists of other industrial powers consequently became less and less interested in possessing notes for the purchase of current and future American goods.[61] These paper dollars only remained useful for the purchase of American *capital*. The result was the threat of a retreat to gold. Such a retreat, however, would mean a return to the same problems that haunted the 20's and 30's but under social and political conditions much less propitious to world capital.

The foundering of the Bretton Woods system shows that the whole international credit expansion based on the use of the paper dollar as a world currency,[62] could collapse like a house of cards. It is a

by the upswing in exports, facilitated among other things by the devaluation of the pound.

[60] It is important to point out that this was not provoked by phenomena in the spheres of currency or circulation, but by radical changes in the sphere of production. The rate of inflation of the dollar between 1960 and 1965 was much smaller than the relative devaluation of the Deutsch Mark or the Yen. In this period the dollar suffered a 6.8% loss of purchasing power, as against 15.1% for the Mark and 34% for the Yen. In spite of this, the USA's balance of trade with Japan ran a deficit as early as 1964, and with West Germany as early as 1965. For labour productivity rose by 100% in West German industry in the period 1953-65, while it increased by only 50% in American industry.

[61] This does not apply to the capitalists of the semi-colonies, who obviously continue to suffer from a shortage rather than an excess of dollars.

[62] The Euro-Dollar system which arose in the second half of the 60's further considerably extended this international system of credit money. As a result of credit restrictions in the USA, American companies began short-term borrowing at fairly

sign of the growing insecurity of national credit expansion. There is a manifest and profound connection between the two phenomena. The nexus between them obviously lies in the contradiction between the role of the dollar as the buffer of the US industrial cycle and its role as a world currency. Its first role implies permanent inflation; its second role maximum stability. It was possible for the system to survive so long as dollar inflation was very mild and American labour productivity unchallenged. But both conditions were gradually eliminated precisely by the 'long wave with an undertone of expansion'. This left the capitalists in the rest of the world with no further alternative: to buy dollar stability at the cost of a crisis of over-production in the USA — the most important section of the world market — would have been equivalent to cutting off the branch on which they were sitting.

The present monetary crisis lies in the fact that the influence of all the mechanisms curbing the long-term post-war boom necessarily increased difficulties of sales and capital valorization in domestic markets, and hence intensified international rivalry. The result was to make the use of national trade, customs and currency policies more and more unavoidable for the advancement of particular imperialist interests in the inter-capitalist competitive struggle, and thereby more and more to condemn the special role accorded to the currency of a single imperialist power as an international medium of exchange. The insecurity of the world economy today finds expression in intensified international competition, which in turn corresponds to the relative decline in the preponderance of the USA.

---

high interest, of dollars in the possession of European companies (including European branches of American companies) and also of central banks. These dollars increased the expansion of credit in the USA, hence the deficit of the American balance of payments, hence the drain of dollars to Europe, where they led both to an extension of the circulation of paper and credit money in the European currencies and to a renewed expansion of Euro-dollars. For this whole merry-go-round, see, among others, Paul Einzig, *The Euro-Dollar System*, London, 1967. The Euro-dollar system was an attempt to create an international short-term money capital market with a uniform rate of interest. It corresponded both to the growing internationalization of capital and to the contradiction between this internationalization and national credit money cycles. This became particularly clear in the years 1968-69 when the USA, in order to improve its balance of payments, raised its domestic interest rate, which led to a worldwide increase in rates of interest without any improvement in the US balance of payments. (For the problem of the Euro-dollar market, Euro-loans, international companies, the international money and capital market and its disjuncture with national credit cycles, see also the first Chapter of Charles P. Kindleberger, *Europe and the Dollar*, Cambridge, USA, 1966, who, however, tried to minimize the crisis of the dollar).

A paradoxical situation, which is nonetheless typical of the history of capitalism, has thus come into being, in which international credit expansion threatens to dry up at the very moment when it is needed most. So long as production expanded at a rapid rate in the capitalist world, the burgeoning of international means of payment, which was a function of the inflation of the dollar and the deficit in the US balance of payments, could be kept within certain bounds. But as soon as there is a fall in the rate of growth and overcapacity increases in the manufacturing industries of the capitalist world, then the expansion of international means of payment ought to be accelerated to mobilise reserves of production. But precisely at this point the expansion of international credit threatens to seize up, because in the long-run none of the other imperialist powers is likely to accept the 'devalued dollar' as the arbiter of the international monetary system.[63] A partial solution of this contradiction has been sought in 'paper gold', i.e., international credit money which only circulates between the central banks and is completely freed from any national currency. A genuine long-term solution to the problem of 'international liquidity' along these lines, however, is obstructed by inter-imperialist rivalry, which makes the distribution of 'paper gold' itself a function of the international relationship of forces, and by the detour of this distribution brings the inflation of national currencies back once more into the domain of international means of exchange and payment. In the last analysis, inconvertible paper money can only be imposed upon commodity owners and holders of monetary

---

[63] In this connection the three phases of the history of the Euro-dollar analysed by Denizet are particularly characteristic. In the first phase, European banks, in competition with US banks, sought to grant higher interest on their deposits and to impose lower interest on their debtors than the US banks. In the second phase, the US banks, and especially foreign branches of US multinational companies, turned to this international money market to circumvent the restrictions on credit and capital exports imposed by the US Government. The dollar holdings of the European and Japanese central banks were 'reprivatised' by means of the Euro-Dollar market. In the third phase, however, there was a rapid fall in the rate of interest and Euro-Dollar capital flowed back into the central banks (especially the German Bundesbank). For private owners, European and Japanese private banks and multinational companies had no good reason to retain paper dollar deposits which obtained a low interest and were currently being devalued. From the end of 1967 to the end of 1969 the dollar holdings of non-American central banks declined from $15.6 to $11.9 billion dollars, while private ownership of Euro-Dollars rose from $15.7 to $28.2 billion. From the end of 1969 to the end of January 1972, however, the dollar assets of European and Japanese central banks increased by nearly $36 billion. Denizet, *op. cit.*, pp. 70-8. *Neue Zürcher Zeitung,* 20 April 1972.

claims within the framework of a State. World paper money would necessitate a single world government. Inter-imperialist rivalry and the role of the State as an instrument of self-defense of specific capitalist groups against each other—in other words, capitalist competition and private property or the phenomenon of 'many capitals' — render the emergence of such a world impossible for the foreseeable future, as we have indicated in Chapter 10.

It is important to point out here that the present situation differs critically from the world currency system before 1914, in a way which indicates the profound structural crisis of contemporary capitalism. At that time, the Bank of England could afford to hold gold reserves at a level no higher than 5% of annual imports. If the Bank wished to increase its gold supply, it could at any time sell English government bonds or shares to buy gold.[64] It was only during crises of over-production that gold had to be thrown into circulation, for a short space of time and for a negligible fraction of the total payments due. Such is no longer the case today: central banks now always have to hold a much higher ratio of gold and foreign-currency reserves to national imports.[65] This change reflects the fact that the self-confidence of world capital has been *permanently* shaken, in spite (or more correctly because) of the long-term expansion of international credit money.[66]

[64] Triffin, *Gold and the Dollar Crisis*, p. 31.

[65] H. G. Johnson claims that the crisis of the world currency system is built into the nature of the gold-exchange-standard itself — in other words, is independent of the development of the business cycle and the inter-imperialist relationship of forces. Even if the non-American central banks were to keep the gold-dollar relation of their currency reserves unaltered, they would absorb an increasing percentage of ongoing gold output and thus in the long term threaten the convertibility of the dollar. 'Theoretical Problems of the International Monetary System', in R. N. Cooper (ed.), *International Finance*, London 1969, pp. 323-6. Johnson himself, however, shows an obvious solution to this dilemma by pointing out that it is possible for the USA to use other imperialist currencies alongside gold to cover the dollar. If this does not happen, then it is because the distrust among the imperialist states concerning the future of their currencies is mutual. This distrust is in turn not purely subjective, but is closely connected with world-wide permanent inflation and the growing instability of the monetary system.

[66] See Marx: 'But it is precisely the development of the credit and banking system, which tends, on the one hand, to press all money-capital into the service of production (or what amounts to the same thing, to transform all money income into capital) and which, on the other hand, reduces the metal reserve to a minimum in a certain phase of the cycle, so that it can no longer perform the functions for which it is intended—it is the developed credit and banking system which creates this over-sensitiveness of the whole organism . . . . The central bank is the pivot of the credit system. The metal reserve, in turn, is the pivot of the bank. The change-over

The deeper and more generalized recessions become, the greater
is the injection of credit and the expansion of bank money supply
necessary to prevent these recessions from deteriorating into full-
scale depressions — and therewith the more acute grows the danger
that inflation and speculation will escape the control of the bourgeois
State in a runaway rush towards a bank panic and collapse of the
whole financial system.[67] Already in 1974, the failure of a few secondary banks brought the international bourgeoisie to the brink of such a
panic, when generalized withdrawals of deposits from the large banks
could have provoked a collapse of this type. This was avoided by the
collective and conscious decision of the key central banks and the
largest deposit banks to come to the immediate assistance of all financial institutions in jeopardy. The reserves of these banking centres
were obviously more than sufficient to conduct such a rescue operation successfully. But this would cease to be the case if several of the
largest banks themselves were struck by problems of solvency, especially if this were to occur simultaneously or within a short period
of time. Hence the pressure on international capital to improve the
liquidity of the world banking system and to take measures to ensure
long-term recovery, which imply the need to put a brake on any
further expansion of the menacing debt pyramid. Hence the compulsion to simultaneous credit restrictions in all the major imperialist
countries. Hence the unavoidable prospect of a succession of generalized recessions. How relative the restrictions in credit expansion

---

from the credit system to the monetary system is necessary, as I have already shown
in Book I (Ch. III, pp. 137-8) in discussing means of payment. That the greatest
sacrifices of real wealth are necessary to maintain the metallic basis in a critical
moment has been admitted by both Tooke and Loyd-Overstone. The controversy
revolves merely round a plus or a minus, and round the more or less rational treatment of the inevitable. A certain quantity of metal, insignificant compared with the
total production, is admitted to be the pivotal point of the system . . . . But how are
gold and silver distinguished from other forms of wealth? Not by the magnitude of
their value, for this is determined by the quantity of labour incorporated in them;
but by the fact that they represent independent incarnations, expressions of the
social character of wealth.' *Capital*, Vol. 3, p: 572 f.
   [67]On the fears concerning this in the USA, see the article *Are the Banks Over-
extended?*, in: *Business Week* September 21, 1974. Between 1967 and 1974 the
ratio between the banks' own capital — reserves and their total assets sank from 7%
to 5%. The ratio between bank loans and total deposits rose in the same period from
65% to 75% (it is now nearing 80%). Above all, the banks have growing fears about
the solvency of their main debtors: 'Corporate working capital and current assets
are each up about 30% over the past four years, but commercial and industrial
loans by the banks are up 60%. Personal income has climbed by less than 50% in the
past four years, but instalment credit debt held by the banks is up 70%'.

and the growth of money supply have been till now can be seen from the following figures:

March-June 1974 changes compared with the previous year in %

	Money Supply M_1°	M_1 + time deposits under 4 years	Bank loans	Real GNP (First Semester 1974)
West Germany	+44.4%	+ 8.8%	+ 8.3%	+1.5%
U.K.	+ 1.2%	+21.8%	+31.4%	−1.5%
France	+ 9.9%	+15.8%	+19.9%	+5.0%
Italy	+20.6%	+22.6%	n.a.	+7.5%
U.S.A.	+ 5.3%	+ 8.4%	+18.4%	−0.5%
Japan	+ 5.3%	+ 3.1%	+ 3.0%	−3.0%

°Paper money + demand deposits

Both the constraint on capital to curb the development of creeping into galloping inflation, and the impossibility of consolidating the expansion of international credit money any further, express the fact that the contradiction between an enormously enlarged productive capacity, and limited possibilities of sales and capital valorization on the world market, is starting to assume increasingly exposive forms. They are clear indications that the 'long wave with an undertone of expansion' is coming to an end. Despite its enormous unproductive outlays, especially on armaments, despite the hypertrophy of its sales apparatus, despite its enormous increase in indebtedness and permanent inflation, late capitalism has been and remains unable to overcome the fundamental contradictions of the capitalist mode of production. It has only temporarily moderated and dammed them, thereby in certain respects even augmenting the explosive pressure welling up within the system.

The perilous logic of inverting the relation between the credit cycle and the industrial cycle can now be seen in the multiplication of recent signs of an increasing international synchronization of the industrial cycle. The crisis of the international currency system is

[68] Given the conditions of increasingly uneven regional development within the enlarged EEC, an actual European currency union would either result in pressure for a very substantial transfer of income to the relatively peripheral and declining regions, or lead to serious social crises in these regions. At present it is still uncertain whether capital would be prepared to pay the price (or rather, a part of the price) of such a transfer of income.

steadily eroding the autonomy of national economic decisions — unless there is a hazardous reversion to autarkic isolation from the world market such as occurred in the 30's. The attempts to introduce a currency union [68] in the enlarged EEC will likewise significantly reduce the monetary autonomy of the most important West European imperialist countries. The constant increase in the power of multinational companies is working in the same direction.

It has been estimated that the multinational corporations which in 1970-71 controlled 20% of the industrial output of the capitalist world and 30% of world trade, possessed some $30-35 billion of liquid assets (paper money and demand deposits) in 1970 — i.e., thrice as much as the gold and currency reserves of the US State. In early 1972 they were responsible for 50% of the Eurodollar movements, which had increased at that time to a volume of $60 billion.[69] By the end of 1974, Eurodollar lending had reached $185 billion; and while the proportion held by multinational corporations had declined somewhat, as a result of the influx of government-owned petrodollars, the total assets of those corporations has registered a further notable increase compared with 1972. It is thus not surprising that multi-national corporations urgently need the formation of an internationally-organized money market. Nor is it any wonder that they try to protect themselves against sudden exchange losses, threats of reintroduction of currency or capital controls, or increases in customs duties.[70] Their conduct simply corresponds to the logic of a mode of production based upon private property and competition, and not upon a 'national sovereignty' which in the last resort must be subordinated to the overall interests of capital. But this same logic tends not only towards avoidance of losses but also towards maximization of profit — in other words, towards currency speculation to realize quick financial gains, and hence constant international transfers of huge sums of money capital. The collapse of the Bretton Woods systems with its fixed exchange rates, and the general introduction of floating exchanges with their great amplitude of variations (in Zurich the dollar fluctuated between 3.76 and 2.67 Swiss francs — i.e., by more than 25% between January 1973 and November 1974), have greatly increased such currency speculation,

[69] Tugendhat, op. cit., p. 161; *Le Monde*, March 21, 1972.
[70] The Hoover corporation has stated that it incurred losses of £68 million because of the devaluations of the British, Danish and Finnish currencies in 1967. See Tugendhat, op cit., p. 164. This claim seems exaggerated.

which was previously oriented to the occurrence of abrupt modifications (devaluations and revaluations) in official exchanges. 'In 1964 and 1965, when the devaluation of the £ seemed imminent . . . 30% of the 115 foreign-owned subsidiaries in Britain covered by the (Brooke-Remmer) survey, which had not paid dividends during the previous 3 or 4 years did so. 25 of the 115 remitted over 100% of their earnings, which meant dipping into their accumulated profits. A few sent home virtually all their retained earnings, and one, whose profits had been running at about £700,000 a year, paid a dividend of £3 million to its parent in 1964 alone. In 1967, when the devaluation of sterling finally occurred, there was another wave of high dividend payments in the months leading up to the crisis in November. The same thing happened in France in 1968 and 1969.'[71]

The most important determinant of this growing synchronization of the industrial cycles of the imperialist powers is the increasing objective socialization of labour on an international level. The antagonism between this internationalization on the one hand, and private appropriation under conditions of increasing international centralization of capital and the persistence of different imperialist states on the other — in other words, the contradiction between the international socialization of labour and the national property-competition and state-system of capital — becomes increasingly blatant. The development of valorization of capital, productive forces and technology, which was both cause and effect of the 'long wave with an undertone of expansion' 1940(45)-65, has accelerated this objective socialization of labour on the international level at an unprecedented tempo. The development of the international division of labour in manufacturing industry, as shown in Chapter 10, has advanced far beyond that achieved by capital before the First World War. The tendency towards uniformity of world market prices has likewise been extended beyond the traditional framework of raw materials, semi-manufactured goods, a few foodstuffs and the mass-produced consumer products of light industry (such as textiles). There is an unmistakable trend today for the prices of consumer durables, means of transport and some machines and elements of equipment

---

[71] Tugendhat, op. cit., p. 166. For the currency speculations of the multinational corporations, see ibidem pp. 167-76, and Vernon, op. cit., pp. 166-7. The ability of these corporations to manipulate transfer prices between parent companies and their subsidiaries often enables them to evade even the strictest government regulations.

to become uniform, even if there is still significant resistance to this process.[72] Under such conditions the spreading phenomena of structural over-capacity must occur simultaneously; it becomes increasingly difficult for an industry to escape from falling sales and flagging competitive ability at home by turning to exports abroad; while the use of currency manipulations to gain short-term export advantages threatens to turn into a general trade war.

Analysis of the industrial cycle thus confirms the central conclusions reached in our preceding chapters. The major economic expansion of late capitalism after the Second World War has solved none of the fundamental internal contradictions of the capitalist mode of production. The periodical oscillation of investments, determined by the periodical oscillation of the average rate of profit, remains the rule. The use of an interlocked credit cycle to mitigate the industrial cycle could only be effective for a limited period, under the favourable conditions of accelerated expansion induced by the third technological revolution, and at the expense of a permanent devaluation of money and growing disruption of the international currency system.

The more limited the efficacy of anti-cyclical monetary creation on the national level, and the greater the difficulties of assuring steady creation of international credit money (adequate international liquidity), the more will the desynchronized cycles of the 40's and 50's converge into a new synchronization of the industrial cycle on a world-wide scale, leading to graver and graver generalized recessions. The greater the slow-down in the average rate of growth of capitalist world production, the shorter the phases of boom and the longer the phases of recession and relative stagnation will threaten to become.

The transition from a 'long wave with an undertone of expansion' to a 'long wave with an undertone of stagnation' is today intensifying the international class struggle. The main objective of bourgeois economic policy is no longer to dismantle social antagonisms but to unload the costs of improving the competitive struggle of each national capitalist industry onto the wage earners employed in it. The myth of permanent full employment fades away. What political integration and seduction have failed to achieve is now to be accomplished by the reconstruction of the industrial reserve army, and the

---

[72] Manipulations of currency parity and dumping practices play a not significant role in this resistance.

cancellation of the democratic freedoms of the workers' movement (among other things, state repression of strikes and the right to strike). The struggle over the rate of surplus-value moves into the centre of the dynamic of economy and society, as it did in the period from the turn of the 20th century to the 30's. Therefore, a theory of late capitalism must also include a critical analysis of the role played by the late bourgeois state and late bourgeois ideology in contemporary class struggle.

15

The State in the Age of
Late Capitalism

The State is a product of the social division of labour. It aroṣe from
the growing autonomy of certain superstructural activities, mediated
to material production, whose role was to sustain a class structure
and relations of production. The starting-point of Marx's theory
of the State is its fundamental distinction between State and society [1] — in other words, the insight that the functions performed
by a State need not necessarily be transferred to an apparatus separated from the mass of the members of a society, but only become
so in historically determinate and specific conditions. It is this
thesis which sets it apart from all other theories of the origin,
function and future of the State. Not all functions of the superstructure fall within the province of the State, let alone those which
correspond to the interests of subordinate classes (for example,
erstwhile ruling classes or oppressed revolutionary classes). The
superstructural functions which pertain to the domain of the state can
generically be summarized as the protection and reproduction of the
social structure (the fundamental relations of production), in so far
as this is not achieved by the automatic processes of the economy.

---

[1] The outline of a theory of the state is the weakest part of the otherwise excellent
book by Leo Koflèr, *Technologische Rationalität im Spätkapitalismus*, Frankfurt,
1971. Kofler underestimates this element of growing autonomy, with the result that
although he condemns a simple identification of state and society, he tends to reintro-
duce it by the back door.

Hence not all functions of the State are 'purely' superstructural today; nor was this the case in pre-capitalist social formations. This aspect of the State is of particular importance in the capitalist mode of production, for reasons that will be discussed below.

The main functions of the State can be classified as follows:

i) Provision of those general conditions of production which cannot be assured by the private activities of the members of the dominant class.[2]

ii) Repression of any threat to the prevailing mode of production from the dominated classes or particular sections of the dominant classes, by means of army, police, judiciary and prison-system.

iii) Integration of the dominated classes, to ensure that the ruling ideology of the society remains that of the ruling class, and that consequently the exploited classes accept their own exploitation without the immediate exercise of repression against them (because they believe it to be inevitable, or the 'lesser evil', or 'superior might', or fail even to perceive it as exploitation).

The repressive function of enforcing the rule of the dominant class by coercion (army, police, law, penal system) was the dimension of the State most closely examined in classical Marxism. Later, Lukács and Gramsci laid greater emphasis on its integrative function, which they ascribed essentially to the ideology of the ruling class. It is obvious, of course, that class domination based solely on repression would be tantamount to an untenable state of permanent civil war.[3] In different modes of production or concrete socio-economic formations, the integrative function is predominantly exercised through different ideologies:[4] magic and ritual, philosophy and morality, law and politics; although to a certain extent each of these different superstructural practices performs such a role in every class society. The reproduction and evolution of these

[2] Well-known examples are the great irrigation systems in the so-called Asiatic mode of production; and the transport of vast supplies of corn to Rome and other large cities in late antiquity. The formula of 'the general conditions of production' is to be found in the *Grundrisse*, p. 533. See also Engels: 'The modern State, again, is only the organization that bourgeois society takes on in order to support the general external conditions of the capitalist mode of production, against the encroachments as well of the workers as of individual capitalists.' *Anti-Dühring*, p. 386.

[3] It was Napoleon, an expert in the matter, who coined the adage that one can do anything with bayonets except sit on them.

[4] Nicos Poulantzas, *Political Power and Social Classes*, London, 1973, pp. 211-13.

integrative functions is achieved through instruction, education, culture and means of communication — but above all the predominant categories of thought[5] peculiar to the class structure of every society.

Whereas Marxist theory has already provided a fairly thorough survey of the way in which the repressive and integrative functions of the State are both distinct and interlocking mechanisms,[6] analysis of the function comprised under the rubric of the 'provision of the general conditions of production' is much less developed. The latter differs from the other two main functions of the State in that it is immediately related to the sphere of production, and so ensures a direct mediation between the infrastructure and superstructure.[7] This functional domain of the State includes essentially: the as-asurance of the *general-technical* preconditions of the actual process of production (means of transport or communications, the postal service, and so on); the provision of the *general-social* preconditions of this same process of production (for example, under capitalism: stable law and order, a national market and territorial State, a currency system); and the continuous reproduction of those forms of intellectual labour which are indispensable for economic production, although they do not themselves belong to the immediate labour-process (the development of astronomy, geometry, hydraulics and other applied natural sciences in the Asiatic mode of production, and to some extent in Antiquity; the maintenance of an educational system adequate to the needs of economic expansion in the capitalist mode of production, and so on).

The origin of the State coincides with the origin of private property, and is therefore to some extent linked to the separation between private and public spheres of society that is inherent in simple commodity production, with its fragmentation of social labour

---

[5] In the case of societies founded on the capitalist mode of production it is above all the law of commodity fetishism discovered by Marx that prevails, through which social relations between men assume the appearance of relations between things: *Capital*, Vol. 1, p. 72.

[6] See among other things the crtique of Gramsci's concept of hegemony in Poulantzas, op.cit., pp. 204-6.

[7] On these questions, see the interesting contributions by Wolfgang Müller and Christel Neusüss, 'Die Sozialstaatillusion und der Widerspruch von Lohnarbeit und Kapital', *Sozialistische Politik*, No. 6/7, June 1970, and by Elmar Altvater, 'Zu einigen Problemen der Staatsinterventionismus', *Probleme des Klassenkampfes*, No. 3.

capacity into independent private work-processes.[8] But this relationship should not be exaggerated. The State is older than capital, and its functions cannot be immediately derived from those of commodity production and circulation. Specific forms of State in precapitalist societies perform quite other functions than those involved in ensuring the type of legal security necessary for the development of commodity production. Private property in these societies takes the form of the private appropriation of land and soil, not of commodities. In these cases, the State guarantees the inter-relationships between landowners, and their union against both internal and external enemies (for example, against the 'domestic' exploited classes, that do not belong to the community: first subjugated tribes, then slaves, and so on).[9] Such a State is wholly inadequate, if not actually often inimical, to the logic of simple commodity production, let alone primitive accumulation of capital. Its despotic power may often long dam up the development of commodity production, for example by systematic confiscations. The first onset of private rights that corresponded to the interests of commodity-owners thus frequently coexisted with communal rights designed to protect the stability of tribes or villages against the dissolvent effects of a monetary economy.

It was not until the primitive accumulation of usury and merchant capital had reached a certain degree of maturity, fundamentally altering the relationships between old and new possessing classes and undermining traditional forms of political domination by the expansion of money capital, that the State itself increasingly became an instrument of progressive capital accumulation, and a midwife of the capitalist mode of production. Marx's analysis of the role played by national debts, government contracts during dynastic wars, naval and colonial expansion, mercantilism, statutory prolongation of the normal working day and limitation of the normal wage, and state sponsorship of manufacturing enterprises, is classic in this respect.[10] It is thus incorrect to seek to deduce the character and function of

[8] See E. H. Pashukanis, *La Théorie Générale du Droit et Le Marxisme*, Paris, 1970, which develops the thesis that law is merely the mystified form of conflicts between private commodity-owners, and that therefore without private property and its contracts, in other words without simple commodity production, there is no law.
[9] See Marx's account of the emergence of the State of early antiquity: *Grundrisse*, pp. 475-6.
[10] See Marx, *Capital*, Vol. 1, p. 751.

the State immediately from the nature of commodity production and circulation.[11]

The bourgeois State is a direct product of the absolutist State, generated by the seizure of political power and its institutional machinery by the bourgeois class.[12] But it is also the negation of the latter. For the classical bourgeois State in the epoch of the victorious ascent of industrial capital was a 'weak State' *par excellence* — because it was accompanied by the systematic demolition of the economic interventionism of the absolutist States, which had impeded the free development of capitalist production as such. The rule of capital was now distinguished from all pre-capitalist forms of class rule by the fact that it was not based on extra-economic relations of coercion and dependence, but on 'free' relations of exchange[13] which concealed the economic dependence and subjection of the proletariat (separation from the means of production and subsistence) and lent it the appearance of freedom and equality. Since these relations of exchange became generally internalized by the immediate producers,[14] especially under the conditions of ascendant capitalism, the more untrammelled the economic domination and expansion of capital, the more the bourgeoisie could abstain from the direct use of armed coercion against the working-class and permit a reduction of State power to a minimum of security functions. This was above all true of those bourgeois states which were 'weakest' in internal

---

[11] A too immediate derivation of the bourgeois State from the imperatives of commodity production, without an adequate study of its relationship to the concrete class struggles and competitive conflicts of the ascendant bourgeoisie, is the main limitation of the otherwise very interesting and useful work by Dieter Läpple, *Staat und allgemeine Produktionsbedingungen*, West Berlin, 1973.

[12] See Marx's famous discussion of the French State in *The Eighteenth Brumaire of Louis Bonaparte*, Marx-Engels, *Selected Works*, p. 170.

[13] Marx: 'The organization of the capitalist mode of production, once fully developed, breaks down all resistance. The constant generation of a relative surplus-population keeps the law of supply and demand of labour, and therefore keeps wages in a rut that corresponds with the wants of capital. The dull compulsion of economic relations completes the subjection of the labourer to the capitalist. Direct force, outside economic relations, is of course still used, but only exceptionally.' *Capital*, Vol. I, p. 737.

[14] Georg Lukács, *History and Class Consciousness*, London 1971, p. 173, at least concedes that it is *possible* for the worker to liberate himself from this process of internalization of exchange relations. Kofler notes with regard to late capitalism: 'In this tension between enjoyment and asceticism, ideological reconciliation with existing social conditions needs a powerful psychic support. This is provided by the process of internalization, achieved by a manipulation of consciousness.' Op. cit., p. 85.

machinery in the epoch of competitive capitalism, such as England, USA, Belgium and Holland. Where, on the contrary, the bourgeois state possessed a more powerful administrative apparatus at home, as for example in France after Napoleon I, this was a sign not of the strength but of the relative weakness of the local bourgeoisie, both economically and politically.[15]

The bourgeois State is, however, distinguished from all previous forms of class rule by a peculiarity of bourgeois society that is inherent in the capitalist mode of production itself: the isolation of public and private spheres of society that is a consequence of its unique generalization of commodity production, private property and competition of all against all. Thus any representation of the general interests of capital by individually operative capitalists is normally extremely difficult, if not altogether impossible, in a bourgeois society — by contrast, for instance, with a feudal State that could be constituted simply by the most powerful single lord, the king. 'The capitalist class rules, but it does not govern. It is content to give orders to the government.'[16] Capitalist competition thus inevitably determines a tendency towards an autonomization of the State apparatus, so that it can function as an 'ideal total capitalist'[17] serving the interests of the protection, consolidation and expansion of the capitalist mode of production as a whole, over and against the conflicting interests of the 'real total capitalist' that is composed of 'many capitals' in the actual world. 'Capital is itself incapable of producing the social nature of its existence in its actions; it needs a separate institution, based on itself, but not subject to its limitations, whose actions are thus not determined by the need to produce (its own) surplus-value. This separate institution "beside and outside bourgeois society" can, on the unaffected basis of capital, comply with the immanent necessities neglected by capital. . . . The State should thus be seen neither as a mere political instrument nor as

[15] See Marx's analysis of the manner in which classical Bonapartism rested on the French small peasantry, and thereby corresponded to a retarded development of capitalism in agriculture, in *The Eighteenth Brumaire*. In the same work, Marx explicitly wrote: 'It was a feeling of weakness that caused them to recoil from the pure conditions of their own class rule and to yearn for the former more incomplete, more undeveloped and precisely on that account less dangerous forms of this rule.' Marx-Engels, *Selected Works*, p. 120.

[16] This was Kautsky's formulation 70 years ago.

[17] 'The modern State, no matter what its form, is essentially a capitalist machine, the State of the capitalists, the ideal personification of the total national capital': Engels, *Anti-Dühring*, p. 386.

a superseded institution of capital. It can only be regarded as a special form for preserving the social existence of capital "beside and outside competition".'[18]

The economic functions assured by this 'preservation of the social existence of capital' include the maintenance of universally valid legal relations, the issue of fiduciary currency, the expansion of a market of more than local or regional size, and the creation of an instrument of defense of the specific competitive interests of indigenous capital against foreign capitalists — in other words, the establishment of a national law, currency, market, army and customs system. The cost of these unavoidable functions nevertheless has to be kept to a minimum. To the triumphant bourgeoisie the taxes needed for the maintenance for the State seemed a pure waste of a portion of surplus-value which could otherwise have been used productively. The ascendant industrial bourgeoisie thus always sought to control State expenditure very strictly and to question or reject any increase in them.

The autonomization of State power in bourgeois society is a result of the predominance of private property and capitalist competition; but the same predominance also prevents it from ever being more than relative. The reason for this is that the decisions of the 'ideal total capitalist', while they transcend the conflicting competitive interests of specific capitalists, are neither 'value-free' nor neutral in their effect on them. Every decision of the State concerning tariffs, taxes, railways or budgetary allocations affects competition and influences the overall social redistribution of surplus-value, to the advantage of one or other group of capitalists. All groups of capital are therefore obliged to become politically active, not just to articulate their own views on collective class interests but also to defend their particular interests.[19] For this reason the 'classical' function of parliament in the epoch of competitive capitalism was to embody common class interests in a form which gave each group of capitalists an equal chance of defending its sectional interests —

---

[18] Altvater, 'Zu Einigen Problemen des Staatsinterventionismus'.

[19] There is always, of course, an interconnection between these two aspects of 'political activity', although it is not mechanical or unilateral. For example, the American banker Bray Hammond has demonstrated that the disputes over the US banking system in the first half of the 19th century were to some extent linked to very definite conflicts of material interest between groups of capitalists in New York and Philadelphia. See *Banks and Politics in America from the Revolution to the Civil War*, Princeton, 1957.

in other words, to prevent such class interests from being felt as extra-economic coercion or pure dictation. From this point of view the bourgeois parliamentary republic is indisputably the 'ideal form' of the bourgeois State, because it best reflects the dialectical unity and struggle of the contradiction between the 'competition of many capitals' and the 'social interest and nature of capital in its totality'. [20]

The transition from competitive capitalism to imperialism and monopoly capitalism necessarily altered both the bourgeoisie's subjective attitude towards the State and the objective function fulfilled by the State in the performance of its central tasks.[21] The emergence of monopolies generated a tendency to permanent over-accumulation in the metropolitan countries and a corresponding trend to the export of capital and the division of the world into colonial dominions and spheres of influence under the control of the imperialist powers. This produced a sharp increase in arms expenditure and a growth of militarism. These in turn led to a major growth in the State apparatus, involving an increased diversion of social revenues to the State.[22] Arms expenditure, of course, had a dual function, to defend the special interests of each metropolitan power against imperialist rivals (and colonial peoples), and to provide a source of additional capital accumulation.

At the same time, in Western Europe at least, the rise of monopoly capitalism coincided with a growth in the political influence of the working-class movement, reflected notably in the gradual acquisition of universal suffrage and its use by classical social democracy. This

[20] Marx: 'The parliamentary republic was more than the neutral territory on which the two factions of the French bourgeoisie, Legitimists and Orleanists, large landed property and industry, could dwell side by side with equality of rights. It was the unavoidable condition of their *common* rule, the sole form of state in which their general class interest subjected to itself at the same time the claims of their particular factions and all the remaining classes of society.' *Selected Works*, p. 153.

[21] Marx: 'As long as capital is weak, it still itself relies on the crutches of past modes of production, or of those which will pass with its rise. As soon as it feels strong, it throws away its crutches, and moves in accordance with its own laws. As soon as it begins to sense itself and becomes conscious of itself as a barrier to development, it seeks refuge in forms which, by restricting free competition, seem to make the rule of capital more perfect, but are at the same time the heralds of its dissolution and of the dissolution of the mode of production resting on it.' *Grundrisse*, p. 651.

[22] Hilferding and Luxemburg had already perceived this before the First World War, as can be seen from the citations earlier in this work, while Bernstein was the first of the 'revisionists' to foster the illusion that the political power of the bourgeoisie could be gradually replaced by a democracy based on 'the equal rights of all members of the community' (op. cit., p. 177), neutral between classes or guarantor of compromises between them.

development had contradictory effects on the evolution of the bourgeois State in its imperialist phase. On one hand, the appearance of powerful working-class parties lent a further urgency and scale to the integrative role of the State. For the wage-earner the illusion of formal equality as a seller of the commodity of labour-power was now increasingly reinforced by the illusion of formal equality as a citizen or voter — concealing the fundamentally unequal access to political power that is a consequence of the massive inequality of economic power between classes in bourgeois society. The bourgeoisie could therefore derive considerable advantage from this form of integration of mass working-class parties into bourgeois parliamentary democracy, so long as economic and social crises did not yet immediately threaten its position as the dominant class.[23]

On the other hand, however, the large-scale entry of social-democratic and later also communist deputies into bourgeois parliaments meant that these assemblies increasingly lost their role as arbiter between competing interests *within* the bourgeois class. The task of ensuring the continued political domination of capital was thus gradually transferred from parliament to the upper levels of the State administration.[24] The tendency for political power henceforward to be increasingly centralized in the State apparatus was a response to these developments. It was also a reversal of the situation which had existed under competitive capitalism. Whereas previously autonomous action by the State apparatus to preserve the economic power of the bourgeoisie by a *political* expropriation of it as a class [25] was exceptional, it now steadily became more frequent in the form of military dictatorships, bonapartism and fascism.

Another characteristic of this epoch was a general extension of social legislation, which gained particular impetus in the period of imperialism. In one sense this was a concession to increasing class

---

[23] This, however, in no way corresponded to the 'natural' development of bourgeois society, which tended much more towards the identification of 'positive' political rights with ownership of private property, in other words towards the exclusion of wage-labour from the suffrage. This was not merely the prevalent state of affairs for more than a century after the industrial revolution, but the declared conviction of virtually all, including the boldest, bourgeois ideologues from Locke to Kant. See Leo Kofler: *Zur Geschichte der burgerlichen Gesellschaft*, Hall, 1948, pp. 437, 443-4, 462.

[24] On this question see the analysis and extensive bibliography in Joachim Hirsch, *Wissenschaftlich-technischer Fortschritt und politisches System*, Frankfurt, 1971, p. 242f.

[25] See Marx's comments on Bonapartism, *Selected Works*, p. 132.

struggle by the proletariat, designed to safeguard the domination of capital against more radical attacks on it by labour. At the same time, however, it also corresponded to the general interests of expanded reproduction under the capitalist mode of production, in assuring the physical reconstitution of its labour-force where it was endangered by super-exploitation. The trend towards an extension of social legislation for its part determined a significant redistribution of socially created value towards the public budget, which had to absorb a growing share of social revenues to provide an adequate material basis for the enlarged scale of the monopoly capitalist State.

All subsequent delusions about a 'social state' were based on an arbitrary extrapolation of this tendency, into the false belief in a growing redistribution of national income towards labour and away from capital.[26] In fact, of course, the fall in the average rate of profit resulting from any such redistribution in a capitalist mode of production would jeopardise not only expanded but also simple reproduction; it would detonate an investors' strike, a flight of capital and mass unemployment. Illusions in the possibility of 'socialization through redistribution'[27] are typically no more than preliminary stages in the development of a reformism whose logical end is an outright programme for the actual stabilization of the capitalist economy and its levels of profit. Such a programme will usually include periodic restrictions on working-class consumption in order to increase the rate of profit and so 'stimulate investment'.

A further extension of the functions of the State takes place in the late capitalism stage of monopoly capitalism. It is a consequence of three main features of late capitalism: the shortening of the turnover-time of fixed capital, the acceleration of technological innovation, and the enormous increase in the cost of major projects of capital accumulation due to the third technological revolution, with

---

[26] Among other things, this involves an incomprehension of the structural unity of capitalist relations of production and distribution. An interesting early criticism of illusions in a 'social state', and their causes in the class collaboration of the war economies during the First World War, may be found in P. Lapinski, 'Der "Sozialstaat" —Etappen und Tendenzen seiner Entwicklung', *Unter dem Banner des Marxismus*, No. 4, November 1928, p. 377.

[27] Karl Renner defined 'circulation as the point of departure for socialization' as early as 1924, in *Die Wirtschaft als Gesamtprozess und die Sozialisierung*, pp. 348, 379. The British reformist literature of the 30's, 40's and 50's was all based on similar illusions.

its corresponding increase in the risks of any delay or failure in the valorization of the enormous volumes of capital needed for them. The results of these pressures is a tendency in late capitalism towards an increase not only in State economic planning, but also in State socialization of costs (risks) and losses in a steadily growing number of productive processes. There is thus an *inherent trend under late capitalism for the State to incorporate an ever greater number of productive and reproductive sectors into the 'general conditions of production' which it finances.* Without such a socialization of costs, these sectors would no longer be even remotely capable of answering the needs of the capitalist labour process.

This extension of the sphere of the 'general conditions of production' is a perfect reflection of an inherent tendency of capital as Marx described it in the *Grundrisse*: 'The smaller the direct fruits borne by *fixed capital*, the less it intervenes in the *direct production process*, the greater must be this relative *surplus population and surplus production*; thus, more to build railways, canals, aqueducts telegraphs than to build the machinery directly active in the production process.' [28] Direct examples of this tendency are the increasing use of State budgets to cover research and development costs, and of State expenditure to finance or subsidize nuclear power stations, jet aircraft and large industrial projects of every sort. Indirect examples are the provision of cheap raw materials by the nationalisation of the particular industries producing them, which thereby make concealed subvention to the private sector. State capital thus acts as a prop for private capital (and in particular for monopoly capital). [29] The table below shows how the nationalization of the electricity industry has worked to the advantage of the monopolies by guaranteeing large industrial consumers supplies of power at lower prices [30] (*See* table on page 485).

Late capitalism is characterised by increasing difficulties in the valorization of capital (over-capitalization, over-accumulation). The State overcomes these difficulties, at least in part, by *providing additional opportunities on an unprecedented scale for 'profitable'*

[28] Marx, *Grundrisse*, pp. 707-8.

[29] Marx uses the notion of 'state capital' only in the sense of capital achieving valorization from wage-labour that is in the possession of the State: 'so far as governments employ productive wage-labour in mines, railways and so on, perform the function of industrial capitalists'. *Capital*, Vol. 2, p. 97.

[30] *National Utility Services*, cited in the *Neue Zürcher Zeitung*, 25/7/1974.

Average Electricity Prices in Selected Countries, 1973
US cents per kWh*

	Artisan	Artisan + Small Industry	Large Industry	Large Industry with Above-average Use
France (Nord/Pas de Calais and Paris)	3.01	2.38	2.19	1.75
Great Britain NE Elec. Board	2.36	2.24		
NW Elec. Board			1.85	1.72
Italy	2.33	2.00	1.77	1.56
USA Tennessee Valley	1.67	1.37	1.09	0.92

* The four classes of purchasers =
   I: 50kw/12,500 kWh low voltage
  II: 150kW/45,000 kWh low voltage
 III: 500 kW/180,000 kWh high voltage
 IV: 1000 kW/450,000 kWh high voltage

investments of this capital in the armaments industry, the 'environment industry', overseas 'aid', and infrastructural works (where 'profitable' means made profitable by a State guarantee or subsidy).

Another hallmark of late capitalism is the increasing liability of the social system to explosive economic and political crises which directly threaten the whole capitalist mode of production. Consequently, *'crisis management'* is just as vital a function of the late capitalist State as its responsibility for a greatly increased range of 'general conditions of production' or its efforts to ensure a more rapid valorization of surplus-capital. Economically, this 'crisis management' includes the whole arsenal of government counter-cyclical policies, designed to prevent, or at least postpone for as long as possible, the return of catastrophic slumps on the scale of 1929-32. Socially, it involves a permanent effort to avert the growing cirsis of capitalist relations of production by a systematic attack on proletarian class consciousness. The State thus deploys a huge machinery of ideological manipulation to 'integrate' the worker into late capitalist society as a consumer, 'social partner' or 'citizen' (and ipso facto supporter of the existing social order), and so on. It constantly seeks to divert any rebellion into reforms containable within the system, and to undermine working-class solidarity in factory and economy (for example by the introduction of new methods for calculating and paying wages, the promotion of tension between indigenous and immigrant workers, the fabrication of a variety of participatory and consultative boards, the proclamation of incomes policies or 'social contracts', and so on). The general pressure for increased control of all the elements of the productive and reproductive process, either directly by monopoly capital or indirectly by the late capitalist State, is an inevitable consequence of the combined need to prevent social crises from menacing the system, and to provide economic guarantees for the process of valorization and accumulation in late capitalism.

The growing hypertrophy and growing autonomy of the late capitalist State are historically a corollary of the increasing difficulties of a smooth valorization of capital and realization of surplus-value. They reflect capital's increasing lack of confidence in its ability to extend or consolidate its rule by automatic economic processes.[31] They are also linked to the intensification of class struggle between capital and labour—in other words, to the growing emancipation of the working-class from complete and passive subordination to the ideology of the bourgeoisie, and its periodic emergence as an independent force in political conflicts. They correspond to the aggravation of social contradictions both within and between the metropolitan imperialist countries, between the imperialist system as a whole and the non-capitalist States, and between the ruling and exploited classes in the semi-colonies. The greater the intervention of the State in the capitalist economic system, the clearer does it become that this system is afflicted with an incurable malady.

In this connection, the notion recently advanced by Poulantzas that in the present phase of capitalism the main function of the bourgeois State is political, while the main form of bourgeois ideology is 'economist', is a scholastic and artificial attempt to separate closely interdependent class mechanisms.[32] Late capitalism is characterized by the *simultaneous* combination of the directly economic role of the

---

[31] This fully corresponds to the logic of Marx's analysis of capital, which explicitly emphasises that 'the highest development of capital exists when the general conditions of the process of social production are not paid out of deductions from the social revenue': *Grundrisse*, p. 532.

[32] Poulantzas, op. cit., p. 211.

bourgeois State, the drive to depoliticize the working-class and the myth of a technologically determined, omnipotent economy which can allegedly overcome class antagonisms, ensure uninterrupted growth, steadily raise consumption and thereby bring forth a 'pluralistic' society. The objective function of 'economist' ideology is undoubtedly to try to dismantle proletarian *class* struggle. But the objective necessity of this ideology corresponds exactly to the increasing compulsion for the State to intervene in the late capitalist economy, and to the danger that this intervention will educate the working-class in the overall economic and social shape of the society whose wealth it produces—potentially an enormous threat to late capitalism. To isolate one element out of this total complex and declare it the 'principal' aspect is intellectually a futile pastime. [33]

The growth of the direct role of the late capitalist State in the economy gives it greater control over social revenues. In other words, the fraction of total capital which is redistributed, spent and invested by the State steadily increases.

State Expenditure as a Proportion of the US GNP [34]

1913	7.1%
1929	8.1%
1940	12.4%
1950	24.6%
1955	27.8%
1960	28.1%
1965	30.0%
1970	33.2%

[33] Poulantzas' book, like Kofler's is marked by a general underestimation of directly economic connections and material interests. Kofler's thesis that managers are tied to the large bourgeoisie mainly, if not exclusively, by ideological bonds (op. cit., pp. 76, 83) overlooks a crucial point: that in the capitalist mode of production ultimate security of existence can never be guaranteed by status or income, but only by *ownership of capital*; managers are therefore also driven to acquire such ownership, and thereby come to possess common material interests with the big bourgeoisie in maintaining a social order which defends this property.

[34] For the USA, see US Department of Commerce, *Long-Term Economic Growth*, for the pre-war data, and *Statistical Abstract of the United States, 1971*, for post-war data. The two series are not fully comparable, since the pre-war estimates are of the share of state purchases of goods and services (thus including the salaries of state employees) in the gross national product, while the post-war estimates are of the share of total expenditures by the State in the gross national product. For West Germany, see *Elemente einer materialistischen Staatstheorie*, Frankfurt, 1973.

Total Public Expenditure (including National Insurance) as a Proportion of GDP, Germany (after 1948 Federal Republic only)

1913	15.7%
1928	27.6%
1950	37.5%
1959	39.5%
1961	40.0%
1969	42.5%

The hypertrophy of the State in late capitalism is inevitable and necessary for total capital, but nevertheless creates new contradictions for it. The nationalization of a portion of capital only makes sense from the point of view of the bourgeois class if it leads, not to a fall, but to a stabilization, and if possible to an increase, in the profits of private capital. Likewise, the redistribution of social revenues towards the national budget must not be allowed to lead to a long-term reduction in the rate of surplus-value or to threaten the valorization of capital; from the point of view of the bourgeois class, the ideal budget is one that generates an increase in the rate of surplus-value and of profit.

All that can ultimately occur, therefore, is a 'horizontal' redistribution by a centralization of fractions of surplus-value and wages ('indirect wages') — whose effect is to ensure that certain expenditures important for the preservation of bourgeois society, but which the private outlays of the two main income groups do not cover, are in fact realized.

The limits of this 'redistribution' are fully confirmed by Parkin's study of the evolution of income differentials and the incidence of the tax burden on the population of the Western countries between 1935 and 1960, despite the existence of particularly advanced social security systems in these countries.[35] The possibility of even such a merely 'horizontal' redistribution of national income by the State nevertheless depends on objective conditions such as the general rate of growth of production, the development of the rate of profit, the relationship of forces between the classes, the range of functions performed by the State and the degree of interference with the private interests necessitated by them. If these conditions register gradual

[35] Frank Parkin, *Class Inequality and Political Order*, London, 1971, p. 117. For earlier estimates of the situation in France, Britain, Denmark and the USA, see Chapter 10 of our *Marxist Economic Theory*.

(let alone sudden) changes, such as have unquestionably occurred since the end of the 'long wave of rapid growth', the result is an endemic financial crisis of the late capitalist State.[36] Once this sets in, the specific functions of the State listed above can no longer all be performed simultaneously. Permanent 'crisis-management' by the State therewith turns into a permanent crisis of the State.

On the other hand, the growing economic role of the late capitalist State in centralising and redistributing portions of the social surplus makes it an increasingly immediate object of concern to all groups of capitalists, and even individual capitals, to influence its decisions. In many cases success or failure in this respect can determine the prosperity or ruin of an individual capital: most obviously in cases where the State is the sole customer, and output is a function of State contracts. Thus the actual articulation of bourgeois class interests — the concrete process by which the 'ideal total capitalist' establishes determinate priorities among its range of diverse functions — becomes of more fateful importance to many (in the long run to all) groups of capitalists, than in any previous phase of the capitalist mode of production. Two sets of problems arise directly from a survey of the general functions of the bourgeois State and of their specific mutations in late capitalism. First, how and where are capitalist class interests formulated and embodied in political goals under late capitalism? Second, how are economic power and ideological domination translated into control over the State apparatus? In other words, given that conditions are formally 'disadvantageous', because the organised working-class makes widespread use of bourgeois-democratic freedoms, how far is the bourgeois State apparatus an adequate instrument for implementing the economic and socio-political policies of the capitalist class?

The transition from competitive capitalism to monopoly capitalism means a qualitative jump in the concentration and centralisation of capital, which necessarily determines a displacement of the articulation of bourgeois class interests from the political arena of parliament into other spheres. The increased importance of the upper levels of the bourgeois State apparatus ('Ministers come and go; the police and the permanent secretaries remain') is only one manifestation of this shift. The enormous extension of the range of the State's

---

[36] See the fundamental work by James O'Connor, *The Fiscal Crisis of the State,* New York, 1973.

interventions in economic and social life, and geometric progression of laws, decrees, orders and regulations of every sort, mean that professional politicians are in practice unable to understand the full significance and effect of much new legislation, let alone to formulate it. The result is that 'government', in the sense of 'administration', itself becomes a profession obeying the rules of the division of labour.

In this situation the private lobbies of the capitalist class acquire a greatly enhanced importance. They are often the source of ideas for new governmental measures or amendments to them, and in practice they nearly always have the last word. The result is that real negotiations more often take place between these pressure groups and the State administration (perhaps with the government as mediator) than between political parties.[37] In this respect, a distinction should be made between lobbies, employers' organisations and true monopolies. Lobbies represent the sectional interests of particular groups of capitalists, individual branches of trade and industry, banking capital, export-firms versus domestic producers). Employers' organizations in many countries represent the interests of small and medium firms rather than those of large companies. Monopolies proper command such massive financial and economic power that they can intervene directly in their own right in the shaping and making of political decisions at State and government level.[38] In concrete cases, it is always necessary to establish how these various forms of private influence exerted by capital on the State connect, intersect and conflict. The result is not always necessarily a consensus, but it will be a decision which reflects the class interests of the bourgeoisie in the sense of promoting or consolidating the general conditions for the valorization of capital, though it may simultaneously

[37] One example among many: while political campaigns were raging in the parliament, press and public for or against the tax reform sponsored by the Social-Democrat/Christian-Democrat coalition government of Théo Lefèvre in Belgium in 1961-62, the great financial groups of the country were using backstage negotiations to settle the amended plan that was finally passed, with the civil servants and technocrats of the relevant ministries. A much diminished tax reform was 'exchanged' against new banking regulations, which permitted an explosive development of bank credits to the private and therewith of bank profits.

[38] See, for example, Anthony Sampson, *The Sovereign State — the Secret History of ITT*, London, 1973. Among the countless political decisions determined by the intervention of this company may be singled out the official regulations of the Plans of the 'anti-American' Fifth Republic in France, which ensured that telephone costs per line in 1970-75 were twice as high in France as in Britain or West Germany — to the greater profit of ITT.

endanger particular interests of even important sections of the bourgeois class.

This unofficial 'reprivatization', so to speak, of the articulation of bourgeois class interests is a counterpart to the increasing concentration and centralisation of capital. It is an inseparable shadow of the growing autonomy and hypertrophy of the late bourgeois State. If reaches its highest point when the decisions which it affects are no longer subsidiary, but strategic and historic options of the bourgeois class as a whole. Domhoff has made an extensive study of the way in which the big bourgeoisie in the USA takes its overall strategic decisions and formulates its class interests.[39] Most frequently the whole process unfolds outside the sphere of official State institutions altogether (though leading politicians will be involved), and is mediated by foundations, 'policy planning groups', 'think-tanks' and so on, up to specific 'task forces' which propose' or 'suggest' these decisions to particular branches of the State apparatus or the government.

The juxtaposition of a private articulation of bourgeois class interests and an increasing centralisation of political decisions in the technical administrative apparatus of the State leads to a 'synthesis' in the personal union between large firms and high (highest) government offices which has now become the rule in many countries. The claim that big capitalists have largely withdrawn from the direct exercise of political rule can be accepted only with serious qualifications, and for a few imperialist countries.[40] In the USA, Great Britain and Japan the connivance between leaders of the State apparatus and prominent representatives of the major companies has been overwhelmingly documented since the Second World War (in Great Britain, the exceptions have been Labour Cabinets, but here too the trend towards 'integration' with the top management of the economy is unmistakable).[41] If this personal union is less marked in France,

[39] G. William Domhoff, 'State and Ruling Class in Corporate America', in F. Harris (ed), *In the Pockets of a Few: The Distribution of Wealth in America*, New York, 1974. In the field of foreign policy, Domhoff discusses the determinant role played by 'unofficial' entities like the Foreign Policy Association, the World Affairs Council and Council on Foreign Relations in forming bourgeois 'public opinion' in the USA, and their relation to the largest corporations and financial groups.

[40] See, for example, Kofler, op. cit., p. 55.

[41] Numerous examples of this personal union—recently exemplified by the nomination of Nelson Rockefeller to the Vice-Presidency of the United States—are cited in Chapter 14 of *Marxist Economic Theory*. Barnet estimates that of 91 persons occupying the highest positions in the US government in the period 1940-1967, 70

Italy and West Germany,[42] the reason is that big capital is quite willing to leave routine everyday administration (as in large firms themselves) to experts and managers—in this case, professional politicians—the better to concentrate on fundamental *strategic decisions*.

What are the concrete mechanisms which mediate the control of the bourgeois class over the State apparatus of late capitalism? Direct financial and economic domination of the State machine—in accordance with the Marxist axiom that the social class which controls the social surplus product will also control the superstructure financed by it—continues to obtain to a large extent, even it is decreasingly stressed in the most recent Marxist writting on the subject. The dependence of the State apparatus on short-term bank credit, greater today than ever before, and the impotence of even the 'strong' Gaullist State or US Government to deal with sudden, short-term international movements of capital, are a graphic enough reminder that the 'golden chains' binding the State to monopoly capital have by no means disappeared, where capitalist relations of production have not been abolished. It remains true, however, that any account of the political domination of big capital which is confined to direct and obvious leverage over the State of this type, is an evident vulgarization of Marxism. The following elements must also be integrated into any consideration of the complexity of the political rule of capital. Although the class origins of the individual members of the State apparatus should not be identified with the class nature of the State, the capitalist State machine nevertheless possesses a *hierarchical organization* correspondent to the order of capitalist society itself,[43] whose top functionaries virtually without exception either come from bourgeois backgrounds or are integrated into the bourgeoisie.[44] Brittan has provided some telling figures for the British State apparatus: out of 630,000 officials in the English civil service, only 2,500 actually have decision-making powers. They are the 'administrative

---

were from the world of high finance and large industry. Conversely, innumerable former diplomats and ministers assume high positions in private firms after retirement. See *The Roots of War*, pp. 179, 200.

[42] However, it is necessary to remember the personal links between Pompidou and the Rothschild group and Giscard d'Estaing and the Schneider-Creusot group, and the interconnections of various factions within the Italian Christian-Democratic Party with Fiat, Montedison, ENI and so on.

[43] N. Bukharin, *Theorie des historischen Materialismus*, pp. 169-70.

[44] Because the size of their salary permits them to accumulate capital.

civil servants' described by the American analyst Kingsley as 'permanent politicians',[45] and the majority of them are recruited from specific strata of the capitalist class.[46] In France, Meynaud has shown that in 1962 80% of the students admitted to the *Ecole Nationale d'Administration*, which trains personnel for the top posts in the French State apparatus, belonged to 'the most privileged section of the population'.[47]

But it is not only its hierarchical organization which determines the role of the capitalist State as an instrument of bourgeois rule. It is its total structure which ensures that the State—even where it is most 'democratic'—can play this and only this role.[48] For this structure is twice over-determined by the bourgeois class. Firstly, promotion to the executive positions in the State apparatus is filtered by a long selection process, in which it is not so much professional competence as conformity to the general norms of bourgeois conduct[49] which assure success—if not, as in many imperialist countries, outright membership of one of the large 'governing' parties. Since this selection itself involves ruthless elimination and inculcates both a competitive spirit and empathy with the ruling ideology, it is inconceivable that anyone rejecting or resisting the existing social order and its norms of thought and action could in the ordinary course of events advance to the top of the bourgeois State apparatus. Convinced and active pacifists do not normally become generals, and it is absolutely certain that they do not become Chiefs of General Staff. To imagine that the bourgeois State apparatus could be used

[45] J. Donald Kingsley, *Representative Democracy*, Ohio, 1944, cited in Samuel Brittan, *The Treasury under the Tories*, London, 1964, pp. 19-20.

[46] Brittan, op. cit., pp. 20, 23. This author describes their background as that of the 'non-commercial middle classes', who 'tend to have small private incomes invested in government stock or other fixed interest securities'. But in the same breath he states: 'They were not the capitalist bourgeoisie, whom Marx wrongly believed had captured the state machine'. The bourgeoisie is the class of capital owners—and the families of top civil servants described by Brittan undoubtedly belong to this class. He clearly confuses the bourgeoisie as a whole with its economically dominant upper stratum. We have already explained why this upper stratum generally does not exercise its power directly.

[47] Jean Meynaud, *La Technocratie*, Paris, 1964, p. 51.

[48] Failure to understand the structural character of the bourgeois state and capitalist relations of production is the main error of all reformists and neo-reformists, including those with the 'best intentions': the proponents of reforms 'transcending the system' and adherents to the notion of an 'anti-monopolist alliance'.

[49] Brittan, op. cit., pp. 33, 58, 76. Ralph Miliband, *The State in Capitalist Society*, London, 1969, pp. 120-9.

for a socialist transformation of capitalist society is as illusory as to suppose that an army could be dissolved with the aid of 'pacifist generals'.

In general of course, it must always be recalled that the dominant ideology of any society is the ideology of the dominant class and that the class which appropriates the social surplus product will control the superstructures constructed upon it.[50] The function of the bourgeois State in institutionally protecting and juridically legitimating private property is one that necessarily pervades the typical structure of belief and behaviour of the great majority of the whole population in 'normal' times. It must, therefore, exercise an all the more powerful influence on those members of society who are vocationally employed within the State apparatus itself.[51] For the general ideology of the bourgeoisie inevitably remains massively predominant over the working-class during 'quiet periods', within the framework of the division of labour, atomized work and fetishized merchandise of generalized commodity production. A swarm of 'basic myths' are in these conditions accepted as self-evident by the majority of the population for the very reason that they form an ideological reflection of existing social relations. The vast integrative power of the bourgeois state system is thus readily comprehensible. Symbiosis with the capitalist State apparatus via numerous joint committees typically draws leading cadres of mass working-class parties and trade-unions into conformity with the system, if not into outright collusion with late capitalism.[52] The rigorous instrumentalization of the bourgeois State as a weapon of capitalist class interests, is concealed from both the actors and from the observers and victims of this tragi-comedy by the mystifying image of the State as an

[50] Marx and Engels: 'The ideas of the ruling class are in every epoch the ruling ideas: the class, which is the ruling material force of society, is at the same time its ruling *intellectual* force. The class which has the means of material production at its disposal, has control at the same time over the means of mental production' *The German Ideology*, 1960, p. 39.

[51] A good exception that confirms the rule is provided by the labour inspectors created by social legislation, whose official activity is necessarily always restricted, in so far as their function does not defend the interests of private property and profit, but encroaches on them.

[52] On this problem, see the whole of the Seventh Chapter of Miliband's book, which includes the following exemplary comment by the American Professor Heilbroner: "The striking characteristic of our contemporary ideological climate is that the "dissident" groups labour, government, or academica, all seek to accommodate their proposals for social change to the limits of adaptability of the prevailing business order.' (op. cit., p. 214.)

arbiter *between* classes, a representative of the 'national interest', a neutral and benevolent judge of the merits of all 'pluralist forces'.[53]

The way this instrumentalization works in practice can be illustrated by an account of the origins of economic programming in Great Britain provided by a leading liberal-bourgeois journalist, and naively presented by this commentator as proof of the 'conversion' of capitalism into a 'mixed economy' in England: 'When Selwyn Lloyd (Conservative Chancellor of the Exchequer) entered the Treasury, he already thought that long-term planning of government expenditure was, like other things he believed in, 'common sense'. He was converted to the belief that planning has something to offer for the private sector as well by a conference of the Federation of British Industries, held in Brighton at the end of November 1960, to consider 'The Next Five Years'[54].... The Brighton Conference was attended by 121 leading businessmen and 31 guests, including the heads of government departments and of the nationalized industries, and a few economists[55].... During the course of 1960, some of the more active minds in the Treasury had, quite independently of the FBI, become interested in new ideas for adding some zip to British industry.... There were a very small number of officials who thought that it was worth putting together the forecasts and plans on which individual industries were already working, to see if they fitted together.'[56] It would be difficult to find a more obvious confirmation of the Marxist account of the functions of the late bourgeois State than this candid report of strategic decisions suggested by 'leading businessmen', empathized by high civil servants, and implemented by bourgeois politicians.

Secondly, the structure of the bourgeois State is determined by the principles of the separation of powers and of a professional bureaucracy — in other words, the permanent prevention of any direct exercise of power (self-administration) by the mass of the working-class. This structure could at best constitute an *indirect* democracy — rule by the people's representatives rather than rule by the people themselves;[57] but in fact even this is purely formal in

[53] Galbraith's *American Capitalism: The Concept of Countervailing Power*, London 1956, was a good example of such mystifying theses.
[54] Samuel Brittan, op. cit., p. 216. [55] Ibid., p. 217. [56] Ibid., p. 219.
[57] The extent to which this purely formal character of representative democracy is today openly and cynically admitted by 'experts'—as opposed to 'pure' ideologists—is shown by the development of the technique of 'computer simulation' in American elections. Pollock sums up the significance of the latter as follows: 'The

character because of the economic impotence of the majority of wage-earners to acquire the material means for the actual exercise of their democratic liberties. This impotence is not only a direct consequence of the inequality of property under capitalism, but also of the alienation and fragmentation of labour, which constantly conditions the consciousness of the workers condemned to it. Proletarian class consciousness can only be achieved and exercised *collectively*, whereas each worker is admitted to the ballot-booth only as an isolated and atomized individual. A State apparatus constructed on these foundations is designed to administer the existing social system — or at best to modify it by 'acceptable', in other words assimilable, reforms. It is inherently conservative in function. A State apparatus that did not preserve the social and political order would be as unthinkable as a fire-extinguisher that spread flames rather than quenched them. A conservative institution of this sort is naturally completely incapable of conceiving, let alone effecting, any radical alteration of the existing social system. In late capitalism, departmental officials can become experts and vice-versa. But bourgeois ideology confines them strictly to 'rational' solutions of partial problems; they must remain imprisoned in this ideology in order to exercise their functions in a socially (not technically) competent manner. One of the most telling confirmations of this rule is the fate of anti-monopoly measures, often introduced in various branches of a capitalist economy 'to protect the public' (the 'general interests of capital', if not the 'general interests of society'). For these are typically converted in practice into measures *advantageous* to the monopolies, or specific groups of capital: 'Even the best-run agencies with the best intentions are continually dependent on the industry they regulate. Regulators must rely on the regulated simply for the basic information they need to make decisions. Once decisions are made, enforcement through-

---

electorate will always be supplied with the image of the candidate and the solution of current problems which seems most desirable to itself at that point, however little it may accord with the principles or interests of society. It is as if the tricks of the demagogue, based on intuition and the ability to empathize, and hence so to speak still at the stage of handicrafts, are now to be replaced by highly rationalized methods of automatic procedure. *It is assumed that the great majority of the electors reach their position on individual problems in a merely schematic manner and are incapable of judging whether a candidate also really deserves the confidence which they express in him through their vote.* They are manipulated like consumers, whose freedom to buy what they want . . . may exist in an individual case, but only applies to a very limited degree to consumers as a group.' (op. cit., pp. 345-6) (Our italics).

out an industry's operations typically would overwhelm the industry's staff if it were taken seriously — which it usually is not'.[58]

The structurally and fundamentally conservative character of the bourgeois State apparatus, which makes it an efficacious instrument for maintaining and defending capitalist relations of production, finds its clearest demonstration when these relations of production are directly threatened in pre-revolutionary and revolutionary crises. In these situations, the proletariat *periodically* breaks out of the normal massive predominance of bourgeois ideology over it. It then characteristically and instinctively makes a radical transformation of existing relations of production into the goal of large-scale mass actions, or even the main issue of electoral campaigns. In such conjunctures the free development of its political struggles may present a direct challenge to the capitalist mode of production.

When confronted with such a danger, the bourgeois class may still continue to manoeuvre. It may promise or enact reforms, to create a temporary impression of fundamental change rather than allow a real social revolution to develop.[59] In the end, however, it will be forced back to the *ultima ratio* of brute violence. The true nature of the capitalist State apparatus is then suddenly and unambiguously revealed. Fundamentally it remains what it always was, a 'group of armed men' arrayed to maintain the political domination of a social class. If necessary, it will proclaim a 'state of internal war', as in Chile in 1973, when its actions explicitly became an assault on the working-class of its own country, and its machinery an instrument of civil war. The transition from conscription to a professional army, justified on purely techincal groups, and the expansion of repressive institutions and of punitive legislation in most imperialist states, is further confirmation that everywhere in the epoch of late capitalism the bourgeois class is preparing and arming for such 'exceptional cases', and will not slide helplessly into explosive social crises.[60]

[58] *The New York Review of Books*, June 28, 1973. Many examples may be found in Kolko's book on the US railways, and in Mark Green, *The Monopoly Makers*, New York, 1973. For earlier examples of these widespread practices, see Chapter 14 of *Marxist Economic Theory*.

[59] An example is the notorious slogan of the SPD in Germany 'Socialization is advancing', designed to persuade workers at the time of the Weimar Assembly to accept the suppression of the councils that alone were capable of achieving this socialization, in December 1918-January 1919.

[60] The ideal exercise-grounds for such preparation are the colonial wars of 'democratic governments', such as that of France in Algeria, Britain in Malaya or Northern Ireland, and the USA in Vietnam.

The propensity of late capitalism to develop extreme forms of violent dictatorship has hitherto on the whole emerged in exceptional situations, when it has produced fascist States, or quasi-fascist regimes like the Spanish or Chilean military systems, which also seek to wipe out the organized workers' movement and atomize the proletariat as a class. But it is nevertheless from the tendencies visible in the economic and social development of the present stage of monopoly capitalism that conclusions about the general political evolution of the late capitalist State should be drawn. Today, the movement is clearly towards a 'strong State', imposing increasing restrictions on the democratic liberties which have existed in the past when conditions were most propitious for the organised working-class movement.

The basic reasons for this development have been explained in Chapters 5 and 7 of this work. We are at present in a 'long wave dominated by stagnation'. Major struggles over the rate of surplus-value had already flared up at the end of the preceding 'long wave of expansion', and the current deceleration of the rate of economic growth can only make these more explosive. They are, in fact, intensified still further by the whole characteristic mode of operation of late capitalism itself, whose techniques of economic programming and public subsidies to private industry, provide the proletariat with a permanent education in overall economic and social — in other words, *political* — class struggle.

The working class can now potentially use its organised power, by direct popular actions and mass strikes, to solve the profound social problems created by the internal contradictions of late capitalism. [61] But the exercise of this proletarian power increasingly collides with another tendency inherent in late capitalism, the subordination of all the elements of the productive and reproductive process to the direct control of monopoly capital and its State. Wage-struggles by trade-unions and unrestricted rights to strike, 'normal' liberal freedoms of press, assembly and organisation, rights of demonstration — all these are becoming increasingly intolerable to late capitalism. They must therefore be legally restricted, undermined, and abolished by the State. The struggle to preserve and extend these rights not

[61] In the last decade, there has been ascendant graph of semi-political and political mass strikes and general strikes in Western Europe, from the Belgian General Strike of 1960/1961 to the French General Strike of May 1968, to the Italian mass strikes of 1969, and the two British miners' strikes of 1972 and 1974.

only develops a deeper understanding of the true class nature of the late capitalist State and bourgeois parliamentary democracy, and conversely of the superiority of the proletarian democracy of workers' councils as a social form of genuine liberty, it also provides further mass energy for the decisive struggle for power between capital and labour, by a constant demonstration that the working-class cannot break the domination of capital in each factory separately, but only in society as a whole. The precondition of this emancipation is the conquest of political power and the demolition of the bourgeois State apparatus, by the associated producers.

16

Ideology in the Age of Late Capitalism

Just as the triumphal march of ascendant capitalism was accompanied
by a spreading conviction of the omnipotence and beneficence of
competition, so the rearguard action of declining capitalism is accompanied by a generalized proclamation of the advantages of
organization.[1] The most obvious expression of this 'belief in organization' is the late capitalist ideal of a 'regimented society', in which
everyone has (and keeps) his place, while visible (and invisible)
regulators ensure the steady and continuous growth of the economy,
divide the benefits of this growth more or less 'evenly' among all
the social classes, and buffer more and more sectors of the economic
and social system from the repercussions of a 'pure' market
economy. The 'robustly individualistic industrial pioneer' is replaced by the 'team of experts',[2] and 'financial giants' by anony-

---

[1] The fact that those processes were by no means 'self-evident' and spontaneously
accepted can even be demonstrated by linguistic history. Subordination of use-
values to exchange-values no more corresponds to the 'nature of man' than does
subordination to the apparatus of domination controlled by big capital. The outraged
cry of the peasant still engaged in natural economy echoed far into the 19th century:
commodity trade is synonymous with theft and fraud. Like traders at that time, the
organizer or planner today is popularly seen as a swindler. Since the First World
War the identification (which originated in the war economy and the prison camps)
between 'organizing' and 'stealing' has stubbornly persisted in popular usage, in
which 'planning' is still equated with 'wasting'. See, for example, Zahn, op. cit.,
p. 72f.

[2] Galbraith's *The New Industrial State*, with its belief in the omnipotence of a
'technostructure', is an archetype of this conception.

mous boards of directors (in symbiosis with bureaucratic functionaries, or sometimes even with trade union leaders). *Belief in the*
omnipotence of technology is the specific form of bourgeois
ideology in late capitalism. This ideology proclaims the ability of
the existing social order gradually to eliminate all chance of crises,
to find a 'technical' solution to all its contradictions, to integrate
rebellious social classes and to avoid political explosions. The notion
of 'post-industrial society',[3] whose social structure is supposed to
be dominated by norms of 'functional rationality', corresponds to
the same ideological trend. In the 'higher' intellectual regions it
finds expression in a static structuralism which has inherited the
category of totality from Hegel, but not that of movement, and has
adopted the category of the organic reproduction of all social
formations from dialectical materialism, but not that of their
inevitable decomposition. It is no accident that the events of May
1968 dealt such theories a devastating blow in France, from which
they have never since recovered.

Although there are many versions of this ideology, the following
theses itemized by Kofler are common to most, if not all, the proponents of 'technological rationality':

'1. Scientific and technical development has condensed into
an autonomous power of invincible force.

2. Traditional views of the world, man and history which form
"value systems" beyond the realms of functional thought and action,
are repressed as meaningless or no longer play any significant role
in the public consciousness. This process of "de-ideologization"
is a result of technological rationalization, foreseen by Weber in
his paradigm of the "disenchantment of the world".

3. The existing social system cannot be challenged because of
its technical rationalization; emergent problems can only be solved
by specialist functional treatment; the masses therefore willingly
assent to the existing social order.

4. The progressive satisfaction of needs by the technological
mechanisms of production and consumption increases popular
consent to incorporation and subordination.

5. Traditional class rule has given way to the anonymous rule
of technology, or at least a bureaucratic state that is neutral between
groups or classes and is organized on technical principles; party

[3] See Daniel Bell, *The Coming of Post-Industrial Society*, New York, 1973.

politics becomes superficial shadow-boxing, a thesis especially stressed by Schelsky.'[4]

The ideology of organization is a direct reflection of late capitalism, in which bourgeois society cannot survive without the regulative function of the state. But it is also rooted at a deeper — and more mediated — level in the trend towards industrialization of super-structural activities analyzed earlier.[5] Many of these activities are today already organized along industrial lines: they produce for the market and aim at maximization of profit. Pop-art, television films and the record industry are in this respect typical phenomena of late capitalist culture.

To the captive individual, whose entire life is subordinated to the laws of the market — not only (as in the 19th century) in the sphere of production, but also in the sphere of consumption, re-creation, culture, art, education, and personal relations, it appears impossible to break out of the social prison. 'Every-day experience' reinforces and internalizes the neo-fatalist ideology of the immutable nature of the late capitalist social order. All that is left is the dream of escape — through sex and drugs, which in their turn are promptly industrialized. The fate of the one-dimensional man seems to be wholly predetermined.[6] In reality, however, late capitalism is not a completely organized society at all. It is merely a hybrid and bastardized *combination* of organization and anarchy. Exchange value and capitalist competition have in no way been abolished. The economy is in no sense based on planned production of use-values for the needs of mankind. The quest for profit and the valorization of capital remain the motor of the whole economic process, with all the unresolved contradictions which they inexorably generate. In the framework of this private capitalist economic order, state direction and guidance of the economy are only make-shifts to patch up fissures and postpone explosions. But behind the façade the decay is spreading.

The thesis of the abolition, reconciliation or repression of all contradictions — the end of all ideologies[7] — is itself merely an

---

[4] Kofler, op. cit., p. 74.

[5] See Chapter 12 of the present work.

[6] See Herbert Marcuse, *One Dimensional Man*, London, 1964, especially Chapters Six and Seven.

[7] Daniel Bell, *The End of Ideology*, Glencoe, 1960, seems to have been the first to have coined this concept.

ideology, or false consciousness. Its objective function is simply to convince the victims of alienated labour that it is senseless to rebel against it. It is thus naturally unable to explain periodic new flare-ups of rebellion except by psychological commonplaces. Like any ideology, however, it is not simply a 'deception', but a specific and socially determined reflection of the reality which it mystifies.

The ideology of 'technological rationalism' can be exposed as a mystification which conceals social reality and its contradictions, at four successive levels. *Firstly*, it represents a typical example of reification, as Kofler has commented. All bourgeois and many self-styled Marxist theorists of the omnipotence of technology elevate it into a mechanism completely independent of all human objectives and decisions, which proceeds independently of class structure and class rule in the automatic manner of a natural law.[8] The distinction between natural and human history, essential to historical materialism, in effect disappears. Thus Habermas, endorsing Gehlen's thesis that means of labour supplement man's inadequate physical capacities, draws the mistaken conclusion that: 'so long as the organization of human nature does not change, and we have to sustain our existence by social labour and tools that are labour-substitutes, it is impossible to see how we can ever discard technology, indeed *our* technology, for a qualitatively different one.'[9] Behind this sentiment lies the naive or apologetic belief that only the technology developed by capitalism is capable of superseding the inadequacy of simple manual labour. The vast wastage of late capitalism makes a mockery of any such view, and Habermas is naturally unable to offer any proof for it. It remains a mystery why men and women under different social conditions, increasingly liberated from mechanical labour and progressively unfolding their creative capacities, should be unable to develop a technology answering to the needs of a 'rich individuality'. Commoner, in contrast to Habermas, has persuasively shown from the examples of misuse of chemical fertilizers, spread of detergents, and air

[8] The germs of such a false, reified conception of technology can be found in Bukharin (*Theorie des historischen Materialismus*, pp. 126, 131, 148-50) and were early criticized by Lukács. In *One Dimensional Man*, Marcuse comes very close to an analogous reification of science.

[9] Jürgen Habermas, *Technik und Wissenschaft als 'Ideologie'*, Frankfurt, 1969, pp. 56-7.

pollution, that threats to the environment are not due to any 'technical necessity' but to harmful technological decisions determined by private interests — harmful from the standpoint of the interests of humanity. He comes to the following conclusion: 'The earth is polluted neither because man is some kind of especially dirty animal nor because there are too mány of us. The fault lies with human society — with the ways in which society has elected to win, distribute and use the wealth that has been extracted by human labour from the planet's resources. Once the social origins of the crisis become clear, we can begin to design appropriate social actions to resolve it.'[10] Class interests and the economic laws of development of the *existing* social order (including the laws of competition, the sum of whose 'accidents' produces the strongest competitor at any particular point in time in a particular market) govern basic technological decisions today. An additional example of their operation will suffice here.

The blatant deformation of urban development since the industrial revolution, has been the unequivocal product of social conditions: private ownership of land; real-estate speculation; systematic subordination of town planning to the development of 'growth sectors' of private industry; general underdevelopment of socialized services. These societal conditions, far from being suspended or neutralized by any technical logic, in their turn determined technological underdevelopment — for example, the backwardness of industrial methods in the construction industry — and aberrant development (high-rise blocks, dormitory cities, and so on).[11]

Secondly, the ideology of 'technical rationality' is incomplete and therefore internally incoherent. It completely fails to account for the spread of irrationalism, and the regression to superstition, mysticism and misanthropy which accompany the alleged victory of 'technological rationality' in late capitalism.[12] The contradiction between the increased skill and culture of the mass of the working-

[10] Barry Commoner, *The Closing Circle: Nature, Man and Technology*, London, 1972, p. 178.

[11] This is why Marxist sociologists such as Henri Lefebvre, who have made a thorough investigation of the problems of town planning, are passionate opponents of the technocracy and blind faith in partial expertise. See his works, *Vers le Cybernanthrope*, Paris, 1971; Casterman *La Pensée Marxiste et La Ville*, Paris, 1972.

[12] Kofler provides an excellent analysis of this question too (op. cit., pp. 64-5 and elsewhere). By contrast, he does not discuss the other two mystifying aspects of the ideology of 'technological rationality' with which we deal below.

class on the one hand, and the petrified hierarchical structure of command in the factory, economy and state on the other, generates a pragmatic and apologetic ideology which combines idealization of 'experts' with scepticism towards 'education' and 'culture'. This ideology replaces the naive faith in the perfectibility of man, characteristic of the rising bourgeoisie of the 18th and 19th centuries, with a 'certainty' of the incorrigibly evil and aggressive 'nature' of man. Crude neo-Darwinism (Lorenz), profound cultural and civilizational pessimism and fundamental misanthropy serve as auxiliary supports of the ideology of 'technical rationality' in its overall justification of the existing social order.[13]

The germs of the 'destruction of reason' — which first appeared at the outset of the monopoly-capitalist or imperialist age — bore their fruit in the fascist or crypto-fascist ideologies of the inter-war period.[14] Despite the contemporary adulation of the exact sciences, the aura of experts and the cult of space travel, irrationalism has continued to flourish in different forms since the Second World War. Suggestively it has now spread on a wide scale to the Anglo-Saxon countries, which before the Second World War were still largely dominated by bourgeois-rationalist pragmatism. 'Lower' ideological phenomena, such as the vast extension of commercial astrology, fortune-telling, and narcotism should be viewed in the same light.[15] Late capitalist social structure and ideology further inculcate compulsive striving for success and mechanical submission to 'technological authority', which generate frequent neurotic stress. Such modes of behaviour, with their elimination of critical thought or conscience, and their training towards blind conformity and obedience, potentially create perilous preconditions for semi-fascist acceptance of inhuman orders, for reasons of convenience or habit.[16]

Thirdly, the ideology of 'technological rationality' mystifies the

[13] Obviously life under the shadow of atomic annihilation, to which mankind is condemned today, provides particularly fertile soil for this spreading fatalistic irrationalism.

[14] See Georg Lukács, *Die Zerstörung der Vernunft*, Neuwied, 1962.

[15] The massive psychological frustrations induced by late capitalism, among other things by the systematic inculcation of consumer dissatisfaction with consumption — without which a durable rise in consumption would be impossible — plays an important role here.

[16] See the terrifying experiments of Prof. Milgram: *Obedience to Authority*, London, 1974.

reality of late capitalism by claiming that the system is capable
of overcoming all the fundamental socio-economic contradictions
of the capitalist mode of production. The present work has sought
to show that late capitalism has not, and cannot, accomplish this.
In fact, the alleged 'integration' of the working-class into late capitalist society inevitably encountered an insuperable barrier — the
inability of capital to 'integrate' the worker as producer at his place
of work and to provide him with creative rather than alienated
labour as a means of 'self-realization'. Events in Europe and outside
it since the French revolt of May 1968 have amply demonstrated
this.[17] When thinkers sincerely and profoundly hostile to capitalism
proclaim the impotence of the proletariat in the imperialist countries
to challenge the existing social order, their own tragic misjudgement make them unwitting cogs in the vast ideological machine
constructed by the ruling class to achieve the vital objective of
convincing the working-class that it is helpless to change society.
The source of this misjudgement lies less in the 'successes' of late
capitalism than in disappointment with the bureaucratic degenera-
tion of the first victorious socialist revolutions [18] and in mistaken
estimates of the conjunctural and transient character of the decline
of proletarian class consciousness. It was a tragic misreading of the
facts when Adorno wrote: 'The pseudo-revolutionary gesture is
the complement of the technical military impossibility of a spontaneous revolution, pointed out years ago by Jürgen von Kempski.
Against those who control the bomb, barricades are ridiculous;
one therefore plays at barricades, and the masters temporarily
let the players have their way.'[19] Adorno failed to understand that
'military technology' cannot be applied independently of living
people engaged into social activity. In the final analysis Auschwitz
and Hiroshima were not products of technology but of *relationships of social forces* — in other words, they were the (provisional)
terminus of the great historical defeats of the international proletariat after 1917. After the end of the Second World War annihilation so total in form and vast in scale ceased to be possible for an

[17] This problem is further discussed in the last chapter of the present work.
[18] The ruling ideology swings to and fro between the 'theory of totalitarianism' and
the 'theory of convergence' in its assessment of the Eastern bloc, pragmatically adapting itself to the predominant 'needs' of 'Cold War' or 'Détente'—the needs, in other
words, of capital.
[19] Theodor Adorno, 'Marginalien zu Theorie und Praxis', in *Stichworte—Kritische
Modelle 2*, Frankfurt, 1969, p. 181.

entire historical epoch. The Vietnamese War has shown that it is not 'military technology' but the growing resistance of the American population to the war which has set limits to the type of weapons that the 'masters' can deploy. Simultaneously, the barricades at which French students allegedly 'played' in May 1968 unleashed a mass strike of 10 million workers, employees and technicians, and proved in its turn that given a certain political and social balance of forces the use of murderous means of repression becomes impossible or inoperative on the streets. To assert, after these experiences, that mass resistance or rebellion by the ruled can only occur because of the temporary tolerance of the rulers is not merely to absolutize the power of the latter unhistorically: it objectively aids them to convince the ruled of their powerlessness and hence of the futility of radical revolt. It is this conviction — rather than weapons of mass destruction — which is today the most effective instrument of domination commanded by capital.[20]

Philosophers who fall prey to the fetishism of technology and overestimate the ability of late capitalism to achieve the integration of the masses, typically forget the fundamental contradiction between use-value and exchange-value by which capitalism is riven, when they seek to prove the hopelessness of popular resistance to the existing social order. They make a great stir out of the fact that capital succeeds in converting 'everything' into a commodity, including revolutionary Marxist literature. It is undoubtedly true that publishers 'insensitive' to the specific use-value of their commodities saw the chance of good business in the growing interest of a wide public for Marxist literature. Whoever deems this phenomenon an 'integration' of Marxism into the 'world of commodities', however, refuses to see that the bourgeois social order and the individual consumer by no means have a 'value-free' or 'neutral' attitude to the specific use-value of 'Marxist literature'. Mass distribution of Marxist literature — even via the market — ultimately means the mass formation (or heightening) of anti-capitalist

---

[20] The dead end in which the Frankfurt School contrived to land itself (and in which Herbert Marcuse also found himself before the French May) was a direct consequence of its thesis that the 'integrated' working-class is ultimately incapable of socialist consciousness and action. We have investigated this question further in 'Lenin and the Problem of Proletarian Class Consciousness', which appeared in the collection, *Lenin, Revolution und Politik*, Frankfurt, 1970.

consciousness. Ideological production that becomes a commodity in this way threatens to lose its objective function of consolidating the capitalist mode of production, because of the nature of the use-value sold.

A very recent example of the contradictory nature of the 'process of ideological integration' is furnished by the rapidly increasing awareness of industrial dangers to the environment in the imperialist countries. From the standpoint of the production of commodities and of value this development can undoubtedly open up new markets for the late capitalist economy: a whole 'ecology industry' is now in the process of emerging. [21] But merely to perceive this immediate aspect of the problem, without also seeing that systematic explanation of the nature of the threat to the environment, as an effect of the capitalist mode of production itself which cannot be overcome within it, can be a powerful weapon against capitalism (not just in the sphere of 'abstract theory' but also as a 'stimulus to action' and mass mobilizations), is to be blind to the complexity of the social crisis of late capitalism.

This brings us to the *fourth* and most important level at which the ideology of 'technological rationality' can be shown to be a mystification. The notion of capitalist rationality developed by Lukács,[22] following Weber, is in fact a *contradictory combination of partial rationality and overall irrationality*. [23] For the pressure towards exact calculation and quantification of economic processes, generated by the universalization of commodity production, comes up against the insuperable barrier of capitalist private ownership, competition and the resultant *impossibility of exactly determining the socially necessary quantities of labour* actually contained in the commodities produced.

This contradiction finds expression in the fact that the micro-economic measures taken by entrepreneurs on the basis of 'rational calculations' inevitably lead to macro-economic consequences which conflict with them. Every investment boom leads to over-capacity

[21] See James Ridgeway, *The Politics of Ecology*, New York, 1970.

[22] Georg Lukács, *History and Class Consciousness*, p. 88 ff.

[23] Lukács himself certainly understood this, in contrast to many of his disciples. 'It is evident that the whole structure of capitalist production rests on the interaction between a necessity subject to strict laws in all isolated phenomena and the relative irrationality of the total process': *History and Class Consciousness*, p. 102. Occasionally, however, he reduces this 'relative irrationality' mainly to crises of overproduction.

and over-production. Any acceleration in the accumulation of capital ultimately leads to the devalorization of capital. Every attempt by an entrepreneur to increase 'his' rate of profit by forcing down the costs of production eventually leads to a fall in the average rate of profit. If economic rationality is ultimately regarded as economy of labour-time [24] — as saving of human labour — then the inherent contradiction in capitalism between partial rationality and overall irrationality re-emerges in the paradox that the compulsion to *save* the maximum amount of human labour in the factory or the company leads to increasing *waste* of human labour in the society as a whole. *The real idol of late capitalism is therefore the 'specialist' who is blind to any overall context*; the philosophical counterpart of such technical expertise is neo-positivism.

Godelier is certainly right to criticize Lange and other writers for absolutizing the notion of 'economic rationality' derived from Weber and for postulating universally valid rules of 'rational behaviour' abstracted from the concrete structure of economy and society. [25] He is wrong, however, to evade the whole problem of economic rationality by substituting for the notion of 'overall social rationality' — distinct in each social order and determined by its specific structure. [26] The criterion of the productivity of labour, related to the satisfaction of rational human needs and the optimal self-development of individuals, provides a perfectly adequate yardstick for comparing different social systems; without it, indeed, the notion of human progress loses any materialist basis. Ultimately the contradiction between the partial rationality and the overall irrationality of capitalism neglects the contradiction between the maximum valorization of capital and the optimum self-realization of men and women. This contradiction, masterfully developed by Marx in the *Grundrisse*, undoubtedly involves a teleological dimension, for human action is always goal-oriented. [27] The opposition between

[24] 'Real economy — saving — consists of the saving of labour time (minimum and minimization of production costs); but this saving [is] identical with the development of the productive force. Hence in no way abstinence from consumption, but rather the development of power, of capabilities of production, and hence of the capabilities as well as the means of consumption.' Marx, *Grundrisse*, p. 711.

[25] Maurice Godelier, *Rationality and Irrationality in Economics*, London, 1972, pp. 15-24. Godelier's polemic is directed against Oskar Lange, *Political Economy*, Oxford, 1963.

[26] Godelier, op. cit., p. 291.

[27] See for example Karl Marx, *Grundrisse*, pp. 487-8.

partial rationality and overall irrationality is anchored in the contradiction between two types of calculation — of the maximum
economy of means and the achievement of optimum ends. The
reified autonomy of the means — of exchange values — is triumphant
today. Partial rationality always consists of the best combination
of paid-up economic resources for the profitability of the individual
firm. Hence it excludes anything that has 'no (or only a very low)
price'. Even in purely economic terms, of course, it is far inferior
to a social 'globalization' of 'costs' and 'returns'. [28] There is no more
dramatic expression of the contradiction between partial rationality
and overall irrationality in late capitalism, than the notion of 'growing
economic and weapons efficiency' in American arms production —
in other words, the effort to organize the collective nuclear suicide
of mankind with the greatest possible 'economy of human labour'.
An American economist entrusted with this task, Frederic Scherer,
has made this pathetic confession: 'I am troubled more directly by
a basic policy premise of this book: that efficiency is a desirable
objective in the conduct of advanced weapons development and
production programs. It is by no means certain that this is true.
The weapons acquisition progress may be too efficient already. To
be sure, there are gross inefficiencies. But despite them, the process
has given mankind all too much power for its own annihilation. . . .
I believe that continuation of this arms race will not reduce and
probably will increase the already grave risk of nuclear war due to
accident, escalation, miscalculation or madness. . . . Increasing the
efficiency of the weapons acquisition process certainly will not help,
and by dulling our appreciation of the economic sacrifices weapons
programs require, may well impair the development among decision
makers and the average citizen of a more farsighted perspective.' [29]

[28] As early as 1936 Ernst Bloch anticipated much of the contemporary discussion of
'technological rationality' when he wrote: 'Just as the proof of the pudding is in the
eating, and the proof of the theory lies in practice, the technical practice made possible by mathematical science has indeed done much to justify bourgeois calculation
in this field. But bourgeois technology has also increased the number of accidents,
and methodologically a technological accident is comparable to an economic crisis —
that is to say, mathematical calculation, too, relates to its object in an abstract manner
rather than by concrete material mediation with it.' *Das Materialismusproblem,
seine Geschichte und Substanz*, Frankfurt, 1972, pp. 433-4. See also *Das Prinzip
Hoffnung*, Frankfurt, 1959, p. 811, where technological accidents and economic
crises are traced back to the 'ill-mediated, abstract relationship of men to the material substance of their action.'
[29] Frederic M. Scherer, *The Weapons Acquisition Process: Economic Incentives*,
Boston 1964, pp. IX, X.

Having said this, the same author goes on to write four hundred pages on 'economic efficiency' in the production and procurement of weapons of mass destruction.

The ideologies of technical fetishism by definition cannot confront the growing overall social irrationality of late capitalism. The hybrid combination of market anarchy and state interventionism typical of it tends, indeed, to erode some of the main foundations of traditional bourgeois ideology, without replacing them with any groundwork of comparable strength. A society based on private commodity ownership and exchange made the economic contract between equals the centrepiece of its whole legal system.[30] Political and cultural conceptions derived from the formal equality of the contract affected every domain of bourgeois and petty bourgeois ideology. Relations regulated by economic contracts between private commodity owners were also combined with earlier *status-bound* relations derived from pre-capitalist class societies (from feudal or asiatic modes of production). The ideologies corresponding to the latter were based on the principle of 'special rights' for special groups of people rather than that of formal equality. Imperialist colonialism characteristically juxtaposed 'purely' capitalist commodity relations and pre-capitalist master-servant relations: a notorious example was the transformation of Protestant doctrines by the *Nederlandse Hervormde Kerk* of South Africa into an entire ideology of 'special rights' for whites, in keeping with the material system of exploitation ensured by *Apartheid*.

In late capitalism, the scale of intervention of the bourgeois State and monopolies in economic life renders the formal equality of commodity owners increasingly hollow. 'Special rights' for special groups of possessors thus acquire legal status, secured by contracts or tolerated in practice.[31] The system of state subsidies and guarantees of profit assume the appearance of formal and partial analogy to the welfare measures won through struggle by the working class. The legal norms which were traditionally characteristic of bourgeois society have thus gradually been inverted. Whereas the average capitalist in the 19th century respected the law as a matter of course, in the interests of the orderly peace and quiet and his own business, the average capitalist of the 20th century lives more and more on the

---

[30] E. B. Pasukanis, *La Théorie générale du droit et le Marxisme*, Paris, 1970, pp. 110-11.
[31] Hilferding discerned this development as early as 1914, in 'Organisationsmacht und Staatsgewalt', *Die Neue Zeit*, Vol. 32/2, p. 140f.

margin of the law, if not in actual contravention of it. This is now believed unalterable.[32] The sheer quantitative increase in the number of legal regulations in the economy has rendered this evolution virtually inevitable.[33]

The hypertrophy of the late capitalist state today leads to a heavy tax burden on the individual citizen (the individual commodity owner), for whom the category of 'gross income' loses any practical significance. What capitalists or capitalist firms pay out in taxes cannot be directly accumulated as capital by them, even if a substantial part of the state's fiscal income 'ultimately' flows back to them in the form of state contracts or subsidies, thus giving them back more than they had to give. Tax avoidance and tax evasion become fine arts for capitalist companies. Academic economists henceforward take the 'right' of fiscal evasion for granted: learned treatises on public finances repeatedly argue that excessive rates of direct taxation are counter-productive because they are neutralized by more or less automatic increases in tax evasion.[34] The peculiar combination of market anarchy and state interventionism is thus faithfully reflected in the practices of late capitalist corporations: they both seek to keep their own taxes as low as possible, and expect the state to supply higher contracts, subsidies and guaranteed profits, which presuppose a rapid growth in state revenues. This

[32] '*A business that defined "right" and "wrong" in terms that would satisfy a well-developed contemporary conscience could not survive.* No company can be expected to serve the social interest unless its self-interest is also served, either by the expectation of profit or by the avoidance of punishment. . . . Even the compulsion of the law is often regarded in corporate thinking as an element in a contest between government and the corporation, rather than as a description of "right" and "wrong". The files of the Federal Trade Commission, the Food and Drug Administration and other government agencies are filled with records of respectable (!) companies that have not hesitated to break or stretch the law when they believed they could get away with it. *It is not unusual for company managements to break a law, even when they expect to be caught,* if they calculate that the fine they eventually must pay represents only a fraction of the profits that the violation will enable them to collect in the meantime.' Albert Z. Carr, 'Can an Executive Afford a Conscience?', in *Harvard Business Review*, July-August 1970, p. 63. (Our italics). See also Louis Finkelstein, 'The Businessman's Moral Failure', *Fortune*, September 1958.

[33] In its issue of 18 March 1972, *Business Week* published an article showing why the vast growth of legislative activity by the State, and the increasing differentiation of production in companies, makes it indispensible for *each* of the great corporations to influence the state *directly*. The same article also stresses that this influence is not exercised merely through professional lobbying, but also by the direct intervention of the head of the company himself.

[34] See among others C. Wright Mills, op. cit., p. 343f. See also Fred J. Cook, *The Corrupted Land*, London 1967.

ambivalent relationship to the state permeates the whole of late capitalist society. It reproduces forms of conduct, thought and morality typical of a pre- or early capitalist society, to bolster the valorization of capital in an over-ripe society of commodity production. Both in the mental conceptions and practical relations of commodity owners of varying economic power, there develops a mixture of formal legal equality and juridical or practical inequality (status-bound privileges), that reveals the alterations undergone by classical bourgeois ideology to adapt it to the new epoch. The new extension and generalization in the most advanced industrial countries of extreme forms of corruption among top politicians, revealed by the Watergate and Tanaka Affairs—phenomena once associated with the early epoch of capitalism or with 'underdeveloped countries'—bears clear testimony to this transformation. Much of it is even bureaucratically sanctioned as inevitable or legitimate. For example, the US Internal Revenue Service has permitted companies to deduct bribes paid to foreign officials as an 'ordinary and necessary business expense'.[35]

The essential traits of late capitalist ideology can accordingly be deduced from the particular features of the late capitalist infrastructure. The origin and specificity of these ideologies in intellectual history must not be denied. But when these have been explored, it still remains to be explained why these ideologies have acquired a significance in the age of late capitalism which they never knew in the age of liberal 19th century capitalism or even to some extent the age of 'classical' imperialism.

*   *   *

Like the most perceptive bourgeois authors, the various representatives of the theory of so-called 'state monopoly capitalism' fail to understand the dynamic of late capitalism *as a whole*. They therefore likewise come to the mistaken conclusion that the inner contradictions of late capitalism have diminished. More so than in the case of Baran and Sweezy, it is a question with the writers of this school of an ideological operation rather than a simple theoretical error. For the main intention of these theorists—who all belong to the 'official' Communist Parties—is to defend the thesis that the main

[35] Robert Engler, *The Politics of Oil*, p. 457.

contradiction in the contemporary world is not the contradiction between capital and labour (between capital and all anti-capitalist forces), but the contradiction between the 'world camps' of 'capitalism' and 'socialism'. The function of this 'chief contradiction' is then to weaken the inner contradictions of the 'capitalist world camp' (by forcing monopoly capital to 'adapt itself') until the great day comes when the average productivity of labour (or the average standard of living, or production per capita) of the 'socialist camp' exceeds that of the 'capitalist camp' and the popular masses of the West become converted to socialism under the influence of this achievement.[36]

The ideological origin of this conception is not hard to trace: it is the theory of socialism in one country, the negation of Lenin's conception of the relationship between socialist world revolution and the beginnings of the construction of a socialist economy in isolated countries.[37] The ideological function of this conception is equally plain: it is designed to justify the subordination of working-class struggle in the imperialist states to the diplomatic manoeuvres of the Soviet bureaucracy, and to replace the struggle for anti-capitalist transitional demands with a struggle limited to democratic demands

[36] The Party Programme adopted by the CPSU at its XXII Congress declares: 'Our effort, whose main content is the transition from capitalism to socialism, is an effort and struggle between the two opposing social systems, an effort of Socialist and national liberation revolutions, of the breakdown of imperialism and the abolition of the colonial system, an effort of the transition of more and more people to the Socialist path, of the triumph of socialism and communism on a world-wide scale. The central factor of the present effort is the international working class and its main creation, the world Socialist system.' 'The New Program of the Communist Party of the Soviet Union', in Arthur P. Mendel (ed.), *Essential Works of Marxism*, New York, 1965, pp. 372-3. Further: 'The international revolutionary movement of the working class has achieved epochmaking victories. Its chief gain is the world Socialist system. The example of victorious socialism has a revolutionizing effect on the minds of the working people of the capitalist world; it inspires them to fight against imperialism and greatly facilitates their struggle.' Ibid., p. 397. Finally: 'In the current decade (1961-1970), the Soviet Union, in creating the material and technical basis of communism, will surpass the strongest and richest capitalist country, the USA, in production per head of population' (Ibid., p. 422). 'The Soviet Union will thus have the world's shortest and, concurrently, the most productive and highest-paid working day' (Ibid., p. 97).

[37] Lenin's many statements on the subject: 'It is not the Great Power status of Russia that we are defending. . . nor is it national interests, for we assert that the interests of socialism, of world socialism are higher than national interests, higher than the interests of the State' (*Collected Works*, Vol. 27, p. 378); 'We knew at the time that our victory would be a lasting one only when our cause had triumphed the world over, and so when we began working for our cause we counted exclusively on the world revolution' (*Collected Works*, Vol. 31, p. 397).

by an 'anti-monopolist alliance'.[38] In the age of imperialism, which for Lenin was 'overripe' for a socialist revolution, the only justification for such a policy could be that this 'overripeness' has since been superseded by the gradual ability of 'state monopoly capitalism' to *dismantle* its contradictions. The function of the theory of 'state monopoly capitalism' is to prove that this is so.

The formula itself stems from Lenin and was used by him essentially to describe the war economy of Imperial Germany in a number of writings in the years 1917-18. In Lenin's lifetime it was not used in the programmatic documents of the Communist International, although it does appear in his second draft of the 1919 Programme for the Communist Party of Russia (Bolsheviks).[39] The objections to it are of two kinds. In the first place, contemporary usage of this notion, originally coined by Lenin to describe monopoly capitalism in the years 1914-19, implies that there has been no new stage in the development of the capitalist mode of production ever since. But it is precisely the new stage of development since the Second World War (or at the earliest since the Great Depression 1929-32) which it is necessary to explain. In the second place, the formula 'state monopoly capitalism' lays exaggerated emphasis on the relative autonomy of the state, whereas the essential features of the present stage of development of the capitalist mode of production should be explained by the inner logic of capital itself rather than by the role of the state.

These objections would, of course, be secondary if the formula 'state monopoly' capitalism' was backed by a correct Marxist analysis of late capitalist tendencies of development. It would be pointless to dispute over different formulae if their basic content were the same. It is necessary to criticize the theory of 'state monopoly capitalism' here, not because of its name, but because of its substance. Such

[38] This is not the place for a discussion of the relation between democratic and transitional demands in the imperialist countries in the age of imperialism. Revolutionary Marxists oppose any curtailment of democratic liberties and demand their extension. But they also make it clear to workers that a genuine and meaningful democracy is impossible without the abolition of capitalist relations of production and the bourgeois State, and can only be achieved within the framework of a socialist democracy based on workers' councils. They will especially combat any tendency to hold workers back from the struggle for anti-capitalist *class objectives* under the pretext that such a struggle is 'premature' and 'jumps over' the 'democratic stage' or 'endangers' the 'anti-monopolist alliance'. Such a tendency demobilizes the working class and weakens its fighting capacity.
[39] Lenin, *Collected Works*, Vol. 29. p. 122.

a criticism is not made any easier by the fact that there are numerous variants of this theory. We will limit ourselves here to three of them: the recent Soviet, German and French versions.[40]

Victor Cheprakov's book *State Monopoly Capitalism* is only the last in a long succession of official disquisitions produced in the U.S.S.R. since the '50s, inspired by a theme originally derived from Varga.[41] Its lack of scientific accuracy and theoretical haziness are the price of its abandonment of any materialist dialectic. Cheprakov freely declares that every tendency produces its counter-tendency, but at the same time completely ignores the existence of any *main direction of development* (determined by the inner logic of the contradictions of the process in question). Thus while on the one hand Cheprakov sees state monopoly capitalism as the product of the inherent contradictions of the capitalist mode of production, on the other, he regards it as the reaction of monopoly capitalism to a 'new relationship of forces' (the international and domestic weakening of the bourgeoisie and the strengthening of anti-capitalist forces).[42] Similarly, on the one hand monopoly capitalism implies an organic fusion between the state apparatus and the monopolies, but it should not be denied, on the other hand, that this same apparatus possesses 'a certain degree of autonomy' and that there are 'contradictions' between it and groups of monopoly capitalists.[43] Sometimes, the judicious eclecticism of 'on the one hand—on the other hand' is to be found within a single sentence: 'State monopoly capitalism is imperialist capitalism in the epoch of its general crisis and collapse, when the fusion of the monopolies and the state has become necessary for the extended reproduction of monopoly capital and hence for the achievement of new monopoly surplus-profits'.[44] The *collapse* of imperialism, which finds expression in its *extended* reproduction and the achievement of *new surplus-profits* is a small masterpiece of sophistry.

Cheprakov's basic thesis that in the epoch of state monopoly capitalism the state assumes the function of accumulation or extended

---

[40] Werner Petrowsky provides an interesting analysis of the successive variants of this theory in his article 'Zur Entwicklung der Theorie des staatsmonopolitischen Kapitalismus', *Probleme des Klassenkampfs*, No. 1, November 1971, pp. 125ff.

[41] Victor Cheprakov, *La Capitalisme Monopoliste d'Etat*, Moscow, 1969; V. Kuusinen (ed.), *Les Principes du Marxisme-Leninisme*, Moscow, 1961, pp. 321f.

[42] Cheprakov, op. cit., pp. 15, 16-18.

[43] Ibid., pp. 16, 96, 119, 120, 428.

[44] Ibid., p. 17.

reproduction[45] cannot be reconciled with his numerous incidental remarks that competition between the monopolies is 'greater than ever', without being voided of content. Ultimately this thesis is little more than a repetition, cast in pseudo-Marxist terminology, of the claim of bourgeois economists that State intervention and planning 'by and large' eliminate competition in late capitalism. There is a world of difference between registering that the late capitalist state is an increasingly indispensible instrument (accelerator) for the private accumulation of big monopolistic companies, and claiming that it is the State itself, rather than these monopolies, which actually performs the principal function of capital accumulation.

The contradictions of Cheprakov's eclecticism find distilled expression in the strategic conclusions which he draws from his analysis of state monopoly capitalism. On the one hand he declares: 'Contemporary imperialism confronts the great mass of the proletariat not merely with isolated entrepreneurs, but increasingly with the capitalist class and its state apparatus as a whole; the working-class comes into direct conflict with the State apparatus, which implements the policy of the monopolies'.[46] Elsewhere, however, he calmly writes: 'The conversion of monopoly capitalism into state monopoly capitalism leads increasingly to the isolation of the monopolies from the non-monopolized strata of the bourgeoisie'.[47] Further: 'The democratic forces set themselves the task of wresting the administration (of the economy), the levers of state regulation, from the hands of the monopolies, and after they have been transformed, of using them against the monopolies.'[48] The argument culminates in this stirring call: 'The democratic programmes demand state intervention to limit (!) monopoly capital's free right of disposal over the means of production and to ensure working class participation (!) in the administration of enterprises.'[49]

Cheprakov's revisionism is here unequivocally spelt out. How can the bourgeois state apparatus which has allegedly 'fused' with the monopolies, suddenly 'deprive the monopolies of their power'? How can state regulation of the economy, whose aim is to ensure monopoly surplus-profits, 'limit' the capitalists' power of disposal over the means of production? How can an economy simultaneously be 'guided'

[45] Ibid., p. 15.   [46] Ibid., p. 427.   [47] Ibid., p. 427.
[48] Ibid., p. 460.
[49] Ibid., p. 460.

by the satisfaction of needs and the drive for profit? Where are the mysterious 'non-monopolized' strata of the bourgeoisie, prepared to sacrifice their private quest for profit? [50] Or is the aim perhaps to subordinate the working class, on the pretext of a 'united anti-monopolist alliance', to the profit-making of 'good' capitalists?

By contrast with Cheprakov, who merely echoes commonplaces, the East German authors Gündel, Heininger, Hess and Zieschang, in their *Zur Theorie des staatsmonopolistischen Kapitalismus*, provide some valuable factual information. Among other things, they consider the forms of *mobilization* of capital (which Cheprakov confuses with the *accumulation* and *valorization* of capital) employed by the State in our epoch, and the repercussions of permanent armaments and economic programming on competition and the rate of profit. [51] But at the same time the revisionist bent of the theory of 'state monopoly capitalism' is more clearly developed and more plainly expressed by these theorists than by Cheprakov. It will suffice to cite three passages:

'For the anti-monopolist forces, influence over the form that (state outlays) take is one of the most important objectives in the struggle against the economic and political aims(?) of the mono-polies. Although state expenditure helps the monopolies to maintain their power, reality at the same time demonstrates that the growth of this expenditure may drive them into the position of Goethe's sorcerer's apprentice, who was finally unable to get rid of the spirits he had invoked'.[52] Further: 'This reinforcement of the power of the financial oligarchy by State intervention at the same time provides the anti-monopolist forces with new possibilities of influencing production (!), distribution, and economic power. . . . The State—and here lies the weakness of this new form of monopoliza-tion by the financial oligarchy—is not simply an organ tied to and governed by capital in the same way as, for example, a monopoly. As the instrument of the political superstructure of society, the imperialist state also includes overall social aspects (which must necessarily receive greater attention (*sic*) as the socialization of

[50] The contradiction of Cheprakov's argument becomes even more blatant when it is remembered that the same author emphasises elsewhere that 'these non-monopolist strata, which cling to "laissez faire" more than the monopolies, are basically reactionary'.

[51] Rudi Gündel, Horst Heininger, Peter Hess and Kurt Zieschang, *Zur Theorie des staatsmonopolistischen Kapitalismus*; Berlin, 1967, p. 17f.

[52] Ibid., p. 40.

production develops) and is thus not simply and exclusively an organ of the power of the monopolies. Just as different interests, political and economic constellations and groupings of forces find expression in its activity . . . so state monopolist capitalism also creates new possibilities for the anti-monopolist forces to influence state monopoly policy'. Finally: 'At the same time, since state expenditure represents gigantic state capital (?) or the highest and ultimate form of social capital, the working class with its numerous allies and organizations possesses real and objective opportunities to influence State expenditure and the form it takes, according to its own standpoint.'[53]

The fact that state expenditures cannot be described *in toto* as capital (and certainly not as state capital) is self-evident. If the state covers the losses of private entrepreneurs or grants them allowances to achieve monopoly profits, then it has not valorized any 'state capital' but has spent some of its revenues to valorize private capital. To present total state outlays as capital (whereas in reality they are for the most part redistributed surplus-value, of which a not insignificant portion is expended as revenues) is an error similar to the mistake made by Baran and Sweezy when they calculate their 'surplus'. But how can the working class obtain influence over the 'form taken' by 'capital' (even if it is state capital) according to 'its own standpoint'? Does not this standpoint consist precisely in making the valorization of capital more difficult by forcing down the rate of surplus-value? Is it possible for a capitalist economy to function otherwise than according to the laws of the valorization of capital? How can it be said in the same breath that the monopolies demand State regulation to guarantee them their profits, and that the working class can nonetheless use the same State-monopolist regulation (with the same state apparatus, i.e., without previously demolishing and replacing it with a workers' state) for goals which are the diametric opposite to monopoly profits? The entire structure of the capitalist mode of production and of capitalist relations of production vanishes in this theory — as it does in that of 'vulgar' reformists.

These East German writers formulate the central problem to be solved quite correctly in the final chapter of their book: 'The immediate question which arises is the effect of the new economic

[53] Ibid., p. 50.

relations, new manifestations and connections described in these investigations on the operation of the economic laws of capitalism and the development of its contradictions. To pose this question is naturally to raise a host of problems, of which the most basic is the nature of the overall system of contemporary capitalism and the way in which it functions.'[54] But after correctly asking the question, they fail to give any answer to it. Indeed, they do not even risk the conclusion that the 'development' of the internal contradictions of the capitalist mode of production may be intensifying them, a finding which Cheprakov repeatedly announces, without adducing any evidence for it. How could they formulate any such conclusions, when they limit themselves to such impressionistic comments as this: 'Above all, with the development of the technical revolution, we can reckon on a relatively rapid increase in national income'?[55] (In the long run? Forever? Independent of the difficulties of valorization and realization?). Alfred Lemnitz, another East German economist, writes even more clearly: 'With the growth of State monopoly regulation there is a tendency for *certain changes to occur in the operation of economic laws (for example, the law of value).'* [56] He adds: 'State monopolist regulation, whose principal aim is to stabilize the capitalist system internally, (guaranteeing rapid extended reproduction while maintaining a high level of employment, and simultaneously accelerating the structural changes in the economy emerging in the course of the technical revolution, made necessary by the increasing intensity of competition) becomes an important factor in the increasing unevenness of development between individual countries.' [57] But the whole question is precisely whether the State — 'state monopolist regulation' — *can* guarantee a high level of employment and accelerate structural changes in the economy *in the long-run*. This question receives no answer.

The volume of essays entitled *Le Capitalisme Monopoliste d'Etat*, written by a number of French Communist economists under the editorship of Paul Boccara, is not only the most comprehensive, but also by far the most theoretically refined and serious of the

[54] Ibid., p. 317.
[55] Ibid., p. 326.
[56] Alfred Lemnitz, 'Die westdeutsche Bundesrepublik — ein Staat der Monopole', *Einheit*, Vol. 11, 1964, p. 91.
[57] Ibid., p. 351.

works devoted to this theme. [58] At the same time, the apologetic function of the theory of 'state monopoly capitalism' becomes even more patent in this French volume than in its East German or Russian counterparts: here it is designed to justify the policy of the PCF, which advocates a transitional stage of 'advanced democracy' between the final phase of capitalism and the socialist revolution.[59]

The French Communist authors of this volume provide many interesting analyses, among other things, of automation, over-accumulation, inflation, the ideological implications of planning techniques, and the internationalization of the productive forces. But they completely ignore the central hallmark of late capitalism — the *crisis of capitalist relations of production* unleashed by the development of all the contradictions inherent in the capitalist mode of production. Since they regard 'state monopoly capitalism' as an 'objective adaptation' of the relations of production to the ongoing advance of the forces of production,[60] and since they hope to turn this 'adaptation' to the advantage of the working-class in the phase of 'advanced democracy', they lose any real awareness of the fact that the exploitation of labour-power is *rooted* precisely in these relations of production.[61] It remains a mystery how this exploitation can be conjured away without abolishing capitalist relations of production themselves.[62]

It should also be stressed that Boccara and his colleagues appear to lose sight of the whole basis of Marx's theory of value and surplus-value: namely, that capitalism (be it 'liberal' or 'monopoly', early or

---

[58] Paul Boccara (ed.), *Le Capitalisme monopoliste d'Etat* (2 Vols.), Paris, 1969.

[59] Ibid., Vol. 1, pp. 185-92. Vol. 2, pp. 388-440.

[60] Ibid., Vol. 1, pp. 157-9, 183. Roger Garaudy, *The Turning Point of Socialism*, London, 1970, presents a similar view.

[61] Boccara and his fellow writers speak of 'heterogeneous' (*sic*) relations of production (Vol. 1, p. 191, Vol. 2, pp. 342, 363-7), apparently without being aware of the fact that from the standpoint of Marx's theory of the capitalist mode of production, this is not only a revisionist but also a meaningless notion. The economy cannot function simultaneously according to the laws of competition and the compulsion to accumulate which arises from it, and according to the qualitatively different laws generated by the satisfaction of needs.

[62] Cheprakov is more honest in this respect. He candidly states that 'the general democratic transformations do not destroy the exploitation of man by man' (op. cit., p. 456). Boccara and his comrades for their part admit that: 'At the present time, capitalist relations of production, in their modern form of state monopoly capitalism, envelop the whole of society in a network in which everything is interconnected. " (op. cit., Vol. 1, p. 181). It is totally inexplicable how the monopolies can be 'deprived of their power' in such conditions — without the abolition of the capitalist relations of production.

late capitalism) is founded on the *generalized production of commodities*. In this large volume of essays the contradictions of commodity production play a completely secondary role: they are not even mentioned in the section devoted to the theme of 'Depriving the Monopolies of their Power'. [63] This is no accident, for the phase of 'advanced democracy' remains fully within the limits of the capitalist mode of production. Moreover, a thorough Marxist critique of commodity production would anyway sit uncomfortably on the PCF authors, since the notion of 'socialist commodity production' has of course been elevated into one of the apologetic mainstays of the rule of the Soviet bureaucracy.

[63] The problem of the commodity economy is analysed only in connection with the problem of money and inflation (op. cit., Vol. 1, pp. 390-401). In the discussion of 'advanced democracy', it is not mentioned. Indeed a 'rational organization of production' is simply declared possible through nationalizations in the context of a capitalist commodity economy (Ibid., Vol. 2, pp. 362 f.).

17

Late Capitalism as a Whole

The problem which now arises is as follows. How are the increasing attempts at private and state regulation of the economy to be explained by the laws of development of capital itself? How can the ultimate limits of such regulation — its inability to overcome the inherent contradictions of the capitalist mode of production — be demonstrated? Put another way: how should the *interlinkage* between 'organized capitalism' and generalized commodity production be conceived and analysed?

The general failure of attempts — both Marxist and non-Marxist — to explain late capitalism hitherto can be attributed to neglect of this interlinkage — in other words, to incomprehension of the famous formula applied to joint-stock companies by Marx in *Capital*: '*It is the abolition of the capitalist mode of production within the capitalist mode of production itself*, and hence a self-dissolving contradiction, which *prima facie* represents a mere phase of transition to a new form of production. It manifests itself as such a contradiction in its effects. It establishes a monopoly in certain spheres and thereby requires state interference. It reproduces a new financial aristocracy, a new variety of parasites in the shape of promoters, speculators and simply nominal directors; a whole system of swindling and cheating by means of corporation promotion, state issuance, and stock speculation. It is private production without the control of private property.'[1] Likewise: 'The credit system appears

[1] Marx, *Capital*, Vol. 3, p. 438 (Our italics).

as the main lever of over-production and over-speculation in commerce solely because the reproduction process, which is elastic by nature, is here forced to its extreme limits, and is so forced because *a large part of the social capital is employed by people who do not own it and who consequently tackle things quite differently than the owner, who anxiously weighs the limitations of his private capital in so far as he handles it himself* This simply demonstrates the fact that the self-expansion of capital based on the contradictory nature of capitalist production permits an actual free development only up to a certain point, so that in fact it constitutes an immanent fetter and barrier to production, which are continually broken through by the credit system.'[2]

With the exception of those dogmatists who content themselves with declaring that there has been no change in the international capitalist economy since the Second World War (if not since the Great Depression 1929-32), virtually all Marxist and non-Marxist attempts to explain the late capitalist economy show one common denominator: the assumption that private and state regulation of the economy have managed to eliminate or suspend the internal economic contradictions of this mode of production. Variations of this thesis — from the theories of the 'mixed economy' to those of the 'industrial society' — reappear again and again in the political economy of late capitalism. Whatever their other divergences, they debouch onto a common conclusion.

In this sense the 'official' political economy of late capitalism, both avowedly non-Marxist and ostensibly Marxist, can trace a continuous ancestry back to the original theorists of the gradual mitigation of capitalist contradictions and self-dissolution of the capitalist mode of production into a 'mixed economy'. The most important representative of this school was Eduard Bernstein. The German Social-Democrat Richard Löwenthal and the English Social-Democrats of the 40's and 50's — above all, Strachey and Crosland — relayed its tradition to the current political economy of the 60's and 70's of our century.[3] The 'official' theory of late capitalism is itself, of course,

[2] Ibid., p. 441 (Our italics).

[3] 'Rather a third question arises, already to some extent implicit in the previous one. Namely, whether the vast geographic expansion of the world market, in combination with the extraordinary reduction in the time needed for communications and transport, have not so increased the possibility of *evening out disturbances*, and whether the enormous growth in the wealth of the European industrial states, in

an expression of late capitalism. The technocratic ideology generally predominant in this stage of bourgeois society, which proclaims the ability of experts to overcome all explosive conflicts and integrate antagonistic social classes into the existing social order, corresponds to the specific role of technology and economic programming in late capitalism. The political economy of late capitalism is thus a keystone of the general ideology of late capitalism discussed above. In this sense it is a constitutive precondition of the capitalist mode of production in the present epoch. It is therefore not surprising to find that its various attempts at an interpretation of economy and society are very similar, if not identical, in character. Products of the same social class or stratum (the late capitalist technocratic intelligentsia), their authors loyally reflect the mental structures of their background, and time and again display the same type of bias or blindness. In the case of self-styled Marxist authors, comparable errors should be attributed either to a partial failure to understand historical materialism or to a common outlook with privileged sections of the working class interested in maintaining the international social status quo (the Communist bureaucracies in the East, the Social-Democratic and trade-union bureaucracies in the West and Japan).

No arbitrary separation of the social or socio-political sphere from the economic sphere can provide a satisfactory answer to the question of the overall nature of late capitalism.[4] To reduce the capital relationship merely to the hierarchical structure of the factory is to ignore a decisive aspect of the totality of this mode of production. Capitalism has its roots in the generalization of commodity

---

combination with the elasticity of the modern credit system and the rise of industrial cartels, have not so reduced the *repercussions* of local or particular disturbances on the general business situation, that at least for a long period ahead general economic crises of the earlier kind can be regarded as altogether improbable.' Eduard Bernstein, *Die Voraussetzungen des Sozialismus und die Aufgaben der Sozialdemokratie*, Stuttgart, 1921, pp. 113-14. See also Richard Löwenthal (Paul Sering), *Jenseits des Kapitalismus*, 3rd edition, Nürnberg, 1948 (the first edition appeared in 1946); John Strachey, *Contemporary Capitalism*, London, 1956, pp. 278-9, 289-90 ; C. A. R. Crosland, *The Future of Socialism*, London, 1956, pp. 1-42. Joseph Schumpeter's *Capitalism, Socialism and Democracy*, New York, 1962, also deserves to be mentioned. On pp. 131-4 of this book (which first appeared in 1942) Schumpeter anticipated Galbraith's thesis that the capitalist entrepreneur and the capitalist profit motive would disappear.

⁴ This separation is evident in those theorists who proclaim late capitalism's ability to solve its economic difficulties, but at the same time acknowledge its susceptibility to crises in the social sphere generated by the insuperable contradiction between the producers of surplus-value and those who extort it from them.

production and in competition. Private ownership — i.e., a situation in which the power to dispose of the means of production is split up between many autonomous centres, resulting in *private organization of labour* — is the root cause of the competitive constraint to constant accumulation of capital in order to reduce costs of production, and hence also to constant elevation of the productivity of labour.[5] This is the peculiar socio-economic matrix of the capitalist mode of production, from which all its laws of motion derive.

Exploitation has existed in all social formations and modes of production based on class divisions. The specifically *capitalist* form of exploitation is defined by the universalization of commodity production — which, of course, involves the transformation of labour-power into a commodity and of the means of production into capital.

Is late capitalism, therefore, a new phase in the development of the capitalist mode of production, or merely its monopoly capitalist stage, or a rival system that has left behind the laws of development of capitalism altogether? The answer to this question can be gauged by one central criterion. Can government regulation of the economy, or the 'power of the monopolies', or both, ultimately or durably cancel the workings of the law of value?

To say that this is possible is to say that contemporary society has ceased to be capitalist. If this is so, then the course of the economy is no longer determined by the objective laws of development of capitalist production working themselves out behind men's backs, but by the conscious, planned or arbitrary[6] decisions of the monopolies and the state. If economic crises and recessions still occur,

---

[5] This problem is of especial importance for Marxist analysis of the relations of production in the transitional society between capitalism and socialism, or an understanding of the social nature of the USSR, the People's Republic of China, and so on. Our next book will be devoted to this subject. Accusations that we support the theory of 'convergence', levelled against us by the German Communist Party and the DDR, are the products either of ignorance or deliberate falsification. Along with all our like-minded comrades, we have always stressed the fundamentally different social character of the late capitalist and the Soviet or Eastern Bloc economies. It would need a social revolution in the former, or a social counter-revolution in the latter, to make them similar.

[6] An extensive literature upholding this view exists. See, for example, Carl Kaysen: The managers of giant corporations (whom he calls irresponsible oligarchs) possess great scope for decision making unconstrained by market forces. . . so that what management takes into account is what management decides to take into account.' 'The Social Significance of the Modern Corporation', in *American Economic Review*, May 1957, p. 316. Berle's theory of the 'social conscience of the monopolies' and

then this can no longer be due to forces inherent in the system but merely to the subjective mistakes or inadequate knowledge of those who 'guide the economy'. It should then only be a matter of time before such errors in economic regulation are ironed out and an 'industrial society' emerges that is genuinely free of crises. If the 'regulation of the economy' by government and monopolies, on the other hand, is simply an attempt to deflect and temporarily attenuate (i.e., ultimately merely postpone) the effects of the law of value, then the operations of this law must inevitably prevail in the end. If this is the case, crises remain inherent in the system. The long-term development of Western 'industrial society' will continue to be governed by the laws of motion of the capitalist mode of production discovered by Marx. The contemporary economic and social order remains indisputably *capitalist* in nature.

The present work has been devoted to the verification of the latter thesis. We shall now try to synthesize the separate and successive themes of the foregoing analysis, and to *demonstrate the ways in which the law of value prevails in late capitalism as a whole.*

In a commodity-producing society the law of value has a two-fold role. 1) It provides an objective standard which regulates the distribution of economic resources (forces of production) over the various branches of the capitalist economy so that periodic equilibrium and more or less continuous production and reproduction can be assured;[7] 2) it ensures that this distribution corresponds at least approximately to the structure of demand (structure of consumption)

Galbraith's *The New Industrial State* are based on similar illusions. For contrast, see the sober British study by C. F. Carter and B. R. Williams: 'It appears that in the post-war period which we have studied the extent of grave uncertainty, involving serious efforts of prediction (of the success of innovatory investments — *E.M.*) was usually small. . . . The main reason for the "unimportance of uncertainty" was the extent to which firms were drawn into innovation *by excess demand or short supply*, or the enterprise of suppliers of plant and machinery. . . . The period was, in fact, one of optimism, in which innovation moved forward *under the pressure* of immediate demand or of generally-held hopes about the future.' *Investment in Innovation*, London, 1969, p. 99 (Our italics). The same can obviously be said of every 'long wave with an undertone of expansion', such as the phase from 1893 to 1913, for example.

[7] Paul Mattick rightly criticizes Hilferding's view that this role of the law of value corresponds to ahistorical 'objective conditions' rather than to a *specific* distribution of economic resources over various branches of production corresponding to the logic of the *capitalist* mode of production and distribution: *Marx and Keynes*, London, 1969, pp. 32-5.

of the 'final consumers' (individuals, families; and broader consumer units — local, regional, national, and already marginally international communities — for so-called 'social services').[8]

As we know, the law of value works directly through the exchange-value of commodities only in the context of simple commodity production. In the capitalist mode of production it is mediated by the equalization of the rates of profit — in other words, by competition between capitals. Profits are not divided between rival capitals in proportion to the surplus-value produced by each variable capital, but in proportion to the *total* mass of capital set in motion by each autonomous firm. For this reason capital that increases the average productivity of labour by the application of more machinery appropriates a part of the surplus-value produced by capitals which are 'backward' in terms of labour productivity. Capital will flow from sectors with a below-average rate of profit into sectors with an above-average rate of profit. This leads to a redistribution of economic resources to the advantage of the latter sectors until such time as the expansion of production there reduces market prices and profits, and the decline in production in the former sectors increases their prices and profits. This redistribution of exchange-values, however, must be congruent with the structure of demand for use-values determined by capitalism. Here two cases can be separated for consideration.

If the commodities produced at a below-average profit on the whole retain their share in the demand structure of the 'final consumers', then there will only be a *temporary* outflow of capital from this branch of production. The reduction in the productive forces used in this branch means that output will fall below demand. Rising prices will then lead to an increase in the rate of profit, which will once more attract capital with a 'more modern' composition into this sector. The upshot of the whole process will ultimately be simply an adaptation of the structure of productivity, or the organic composition of capital, to an average social level which has in the meantime risen.

If, however, the process of capital-outflow from a branch of production coincides with an alteration in the structure of the consumption of the 'final users' at the expense of the use-values produced

[8] Marx, *Capital*, Vol. 3, p. 183 ff.

by this branch of production,[9] then the outflow of capital from this sector will be *final*. At the end of the period of disequilibrium — or adjustment — a smaller share of social labour resources will be invested in this branch of production than before the outflow of capital. (Needless to say, if there has been a significant growth in total production, this smaller *share* may well correspond to a growth in its absolute mass of capital and will always be accompanied in the long-run by a higher organic composition of capital.) The outflow of capital results from the fact that the rate of profit in this sector has fallen below the social average, and this in turn is merely an expression of the fact that because of an alteration in the structure of consumer demand bourgeois society now allots to the branch of production in question a smaller part of the total economic resources at its disposal.

This general theoretical analysis immediately reveals both the function of monopolies, or of monopoly surplus-profits, and the limitations to which they are subject. The function of a monopoly is to prevent (or postpone indefinitely) the equalization of the rate of profit by making it difficult for capital to flow in and out of certain branches of production. Monopolies find their limits at the point where such equalization *cannot be prevented in the long run*, where the methods designed to prevent this equalization fail to achieve their goal.

The validity of the concept of monopoly capitalism (as distinct from that of freely competitive capitalism) does not imply that no monopolies existed before the monopoly capitalism, nor that competition is absent under monopoly capitalism. It denotes the *novel and specific* combination of competition and monopoly[10] which stems from a *qualitative* increase in the concentration and centralization of capital. Under freely competitive capitalism, the relatively small

---

[9] Irrespective of whether the alteration in the structure of consumption precedes the capital outflow (as in bituminous coal mining), occurs at the same time (as in cotton) or succeeds it (as in the copper industry).

[10] See Marx: 'Monopoly produces competition, competition produces monopoly. Monopolists are made from competition; competitors become monopolists. If the monopolists restrict their mutual competitition by means of partial associations, competition increases among the workers; and the more the mass of the proletarians grows as against the monopolists of one nation, the more desperate competition becomes between the monopolists of different nations. The synthesis is of such a character that the monopoly can only maintain itself by constantly entering into the struggle of competition.' *The Poverty of Philosophy*, Moscow, 1956, p. 152.

value of its 'many capitals' rendered the preservation of surplus-profits for extended periods nearly impossible—with the institutional exception of monopoly landownership Barriers of entry into branches of production were negligible. Under monopoly capitalism — of which late capitalism itself is no more than a phase — it is the gigantic size of the 'monopolies', in other words the accumulation of certain of its 'many capitals' to astronomic dimensions,[11] which presents a formidable barrier to entry into monopolized sectors and thereby extends the duration of surplus-profit appropriation.

This approach to the problem of monopoly emphasises less the market side of the problem than the production side. Of course, monopoly always means in the first instance ability to eliminate price competition — i.e., to control markets for a given length of time. But in the last analysis market control is determined by what happens in the domain of production, not in that of the market or in conspiratorial gatherings of financiers and managers. If and when the surplus profits achieved by means of monopolistic market controls attract enough competitors into the same branch of industry, the monopoly situation will tend to disappear, and with it the surplus-profits. 'Extra-economic coercion' cannot prevent such a reemergence of competition in a given branch of production or sector of the market for any reasonable length of time (although one should not underestimate the guile of the legislators and politicians who often seek to ensure just this, at the behest of the monopolies). An immensely greater barrier is represented by the simple fact that, if another capital needs one billion dollars to compete with a monopolist, it will not find such a sum easily and will normally not be loaned it by the big banks that are linked to the monopolies either. The monopoly will therefore tend to be stabilized by economic facts of life, not by 'extra-economic' means. However, it will not remain stable for an unlimited period of time. Monopolies cannot emancipate themselves from the operation of the law of value. Competition must in the long run reassert itself, although not necessarily price

[11] The 100 largest manufacturing corporations in the USA owned 39.7% of all assets of manufacturing firms in 1950, and 48.9% in 1970. Seven hundred giant corporations with more than 100 million dollars assets form only 0.1% of all companies; they possessed half of all assets in 1950, and two-thirds of all assets in 1970. 115 manufacturing corporations owned assets of 1 billion dollars or more in 1972: they controlled 51% of all assets and received 56% of all profits.

competition. Monopoly surplus-profits are always subject to erosion.

Let us first consider the problem from the standpoint of exchange-value. One of the foundations of Marx's theory of value and surplus-value was the thesis that the total quantity of new value (income) at the disposal of society in the process of production is fixed or predetermined by the total quantity of labour expended. This quantity can be redistributed in the process of circulation, but it cannot be increased or reduced. The sum of the prices of production remains equal to that of values. [12] If monopolies secure lasting monopoly surplus-profits for themselves, then these can only come from two sources, or from a combination of them: they either derive from a reduction in the amount of profit at the disposal of the non-monopolized branches of production, i.e., a reduction of their rate of profit below the social average; or they come from an increase in the social rate of surplus-value (a reduction in the value of the commodity of labour-power which need not, of course, necessarily be accompanied by a drop in real wages). Both processes, however, result in medium — and long-term — effects which inevitably undermine or reduce monopoly profits.

An increase in the social average rate of surplus-value has two contradictory consequences, which must ultimately generate a reduction of the social rate of profit — in other words, of the relation between the total social capital and the total quantity of social surplus-value. It leads, on the one hand, to a growth in the accumulation of capital; on the other, to a fall in the share of living labour in the total social expenditure of labour. Since only living labour produces surplus-value, however, it is only a matter of time before the increase in the organic composition of capital caused by accelerated accumulation surpasses the increase in the rate of surplus-value. At that point, the rate of profit — including that of the monopolies — begins to fall once more.

Is it possible to restrict this fall in the rate of profit exclusively to the non-monopolized spheres of production? This question brings us to the second possible source of monopoly surplus-profits: the redistribution of the socially produced surplus-value to the advantage of the monopolies. For the sake of simplicity we shall start from the hypothesis that Department I is entirely composed of monopolies,

---

[12] 'Consequently, the sum of the profits in all spheres of production must equal the sum of the surplus-values, and the sum of the prices of production of the total social product equal the sum of its value.' Karl Marx, *Capital*, Vol. 3, p. 173.

while free competition still predominates in the whole of Department II. Let us suppose, further, that production initially has the following value-structure, with the rate of surplus-value constant at 100% and an increasing organic composition of capital:

$$\text{I}:\ 4{,}000c + 1{,}500v + 1{,}500s = 7{,}000\ \text{I}$$
$$\text{II}:\ 2{,}000c + 1{,}200v + 1{,}200s = 4{,}400\ \text{II}$$

Under conditions of free competition, the equalization of the rate of profit between the two sectors would result in the following prices of production in successive cycles:

First Cycle

I: $4{,}000c + 1{,}500v + 1{,}750$ profit $= 7{,}205$ means of production.
II: $2{,}000c + 1{,}200v + \ \ 995$ profit $= 4{,}195$ means of consumption.

Second Cycle

I: $4{,}905c + 1{,}800v + 2{,}060$ profit $= 8{,}765$ means of production.
II: $2{,}300c + 1{,}400v + 1{,}140$ profit $= 4{,}840$ means of consumption.

Third Cycle

I: $6{,}005c + 2{,}160v + 2{,}450$ profit $= 10{,}615$ means of production.
II: $2{,}760c + 1{,}600v + 1{,}310$ profit $= \ \ 5{,}670$ means of consumption.[13]

Now if, instead of an equalization of the rate of profit to 31% in the first cycle, 30.7% in the second cycle, 30% in the third cycle, and so on, Department I sought to secure a steady monopoly rate of 40%, then the redistribution of values would be structured as follows:

First Cycle

I: $4{,}000c + 1{,}500v + 2{,}200$ profit $= 7{,}700$ means of production.
II: $2{,}000c + 1{,}200v + \ \ 500$ profit $= 3{,}700$ means of consumption.

---

[13] In the first cycle 500 units of profit in Department I, and 495 units in Department II, are consumed unproductively. In the second cycle, 600 units in Department I and 480 in Department II are so consumed.

Second Cycle

I: $5,350c + 1,850v + 2,880$ profit $= 10,080$ means of production.
II: $2,350c + 1,250v + 220$ profit $= 3,820$ means of consumption.[14]

Third Cycle

I: $7,610c + 2,070v + 3,370$ profit $= 13,050$ means of production.
II: $2,460c + 1,300v + 0$ profit $= 3,760$ means of consumption.[15]

Already in the third cycle it would have become impossible to achieve the monopoly rate of 40%. Even if the non-monopolized sector made no profit at all — i.e., if production there came to a halt — the monopolized sector's rate of profit would have dropped to 3370/9680, or to below 35%.

If we discard the hypothesis of a monopoly profit well above the average rate — 40% as compared with 31% — and instead take a monopoly rate of profit that is closer to the average social rate, e.g., 35%, then the fact that this rate too cannot be sustained becomes apparent in the sixth instead of the third cycle, as is shown by the following series: [16]

First Cycle

I: $4,000c + 1,500v + 1,925$ profit $= 7,425$ means of production.
II: $2,000c + 1,200v + 775$ profit $= 3,975$ means of consumption.

---

[14] In the first cycle the profit in Department I is distributed as follows: 500 units consumed unproductively, 1,350 invested in c and 350 in v; in Department II, 100 units consumed unproductively, 350 accumulated in c and 50 in v.

[15] In the second cycle the distribution of profit is as follows: Department I, 400 consumed unproductively, 2,260 accumulated in c and 220 in v; Department II, 50 consumed unproductively, 120 accumulated in c and 50 in v.

[16] In the first cycle the distribution of profit is as follows: Department I, 400 consumed unproductively, 1,025 accumulated in c and 500 in v; Department II, 150 consumed unproductively, 400 accumulated in c and 225 in v. In the second cycle: Department I, 500 consumed unproductively, 1,424 accumulated in c and 500 in v; Department II, 200 consumed unproductively, 500 accumulated in c and 201 in v. In the third cycle: Department I, 300 consumed unproductively, 1,968 accumulated in c and 529 in v; in Department II, 200 consumed unproductively, 529 accumulated in c and 200 in v. In the fourth cycle: Department I, 500 consumed unproductively, 2,971 accumulated in c and 500 in v; Department II, 100 consumed unproductively,

Second Cycle

I: $5,025c+1,900v+2,424$ profit $= 9,349$ means of production.
II: $2,400c+1,425v+$ 901 profit $= 4,726$ means of consumption.

Third Cycle

I: $6,449c+2,400v+3,097$ profit $= 11,846$ means of production.
II: $2,900c+1,626v+$ 929 profit $= 5,455$ means of consumption.

Fourth Cycle

I: $8,417c+2,929v+3,971$ profit $= 15,317$ means of production.
II: $3,429c+1,826v+$ 784 profit $= 6,039$ means of consumption.

Fifth Cycle

I: $11,388c+3,429v+5,186$ profit $= 20,003$ means of production.
II: $3,929c+2,010v+$ 253 profit $= 6,192$ means of consumption.

Sixth Cycle

I: $15,924c+3,779v+5,842$ profit
II: $4,079c+2,063v+$ 0 profit

Even if the valorization of capital ceased altogether in the non-monopolized sector in the sixth cycle — which would mean that production in this sector closed down — the monopolized sector would no longer be able to obtain the monopoly rate of profit of 35%: the rate of profit would even have dropped below the initial average profit of 31% — to 29.6%, to be precise.

Let us now abandon one of our initial simplifying assumptions, namely a constant rate of surplus-value. With an increasing rate of surplus-value, the impossibility of maintaining the monopoly rate of profit would be postponed until the seventh, eighth or ninth cycle, depending on the rhythm of increase. In the same way, the tempo of the fall of the monopoly rate would change if the initial proportions

---

500 accumulated in c and 184 in v. In fifth cycle: Department I, 300 consumed unproductively, 4,536 accumulated in c and 350 in v; Department II, 50 consumed unproductively, 150 accumulated in c and 53 in v.

in the distribution of the social capital (between the two Departments, between c and v, and so on) were altered. All these considerations would enable us to formulate a more exact definition of the law of development, but not to abolish it; *the higher the monopoly profit over the average profit, and the larger the monopolized sector, the faster must the monopoly profit drop to the level of the average social profit operative at the start, or decline together with it*. The increase in the rate of surplus-value can merely retard this law, not abolish it.

To put it another way: the monopoly profit can only rise high above the average profit if the monopolized sector still dominates only a fairly small sphere of production. The more the monopolized sector expands, so the less becomes the margin between the monopoly profit and the average profit.

This explains why it is not in the interests of the monopolized sectors to absorb all those sectors where 'free competition' remains. Indeed, they even stand to gain from the creation of new non-monopolized sectors in the economy. The classic examples in this connection are the so-called sub-contracts granted to medium and small enterprises that have been spared. The classical example is the automobile industry. But the system of sub-contracting has been extended to most monopolized sectors today. In 1965, West German monopolies dominated the following number of sub-contracted firms: AEG — 30,000; Siemens — 30,000; Krupp — 23,000; Daimler-Benz — 18,000; Bayer — 17,500; BASF — 10,000; Opel — 7,800. [17]

Baran and Sweezy's main error in *Monopoly Capital* is that they fail to grasp the limits imposed on monopoly profits by the finite quantity of overall social surplus-value. Their mistake derives from an eclectic attempt to combine Marx's labour theory of value with a neo-classical theory based on Keynes' concept of 'total demand'. [18]

[17] J. Huffschmid, *Die Politik des Kapitals, Konzentration und Wirtschaftspolitik in der Bundesrepublik*, Frankfurt, 1969, p. 70. Three Italian authors have used the example of the metal-processing industry of the Italian province of Emilia-Romagna to show that the survival of artisan and small industrial enterprises, which still employ half of the total number of workers in this branch, depend in the overwhelming majority of cases on the policy of the large corporations, and can be explained exclusively by the more intensive exploitation — the greater production of surplus value — achieved in these enterprises. See Garibaldi, Rinaldini and Zappelli, 'Un' Analisi sull' Impresa Minore in Emilia – Ristrutturazione Capitalistica e Sfruttamento Operaio', *Fabbrica e Stato*, Vol. 1, No. 2, March-April, 1972, p. 29f.

[18] We have already analyzed the weaknesses and contradictions of this concept of 'surplus' in Chapters 12, 13 and 14. A more extensive critique of Baran and Sweezy's book can be found in two articles written by us, which appeared along with criticism

Baran and Sweezy's 'surplus' includes all the revenues which correspond to the *redistribution* of the social income twice and even three times over. Their concept thus immediately loses all rigour. It cannot be used to prove an opposition between the alleged 'tendency for the surplus to rise' and Marx's law of the tendency for the *average rate of profit* to fall or his hypothesis of a tendency for the *quantity of surplus-value* to grow. These magnitudes are simply incomparable. Their analysis, moreover, is made even more difficult by the fact that Baran and Sweezy further include surplus *capital* in their notion of 'surplus'.

Baran and Sweezy's assumption that the monopolies are capable of maintaining stable selling prices (while cost prices fall) — the main source of the 'growing surplus' — leads them to conclude that they are permanently overcapitalised. The monopolies thus become largely independent of both the general sales market and the monetary and financial markets. Here Baran and Sweezy clearly extrapolated unduly from a conjunctural phenomenon. In the 'long wave with an undertone of expansion' there was a generally steep rise in the rate of self-financing by the monopolies. But as soon as the average rate of profit began to decline once more, the rate of corporate self-financing inevitably also began to fall. It is remarkable that Sweezy should have perceived and described this phenomenon accurately in his role as the editor of the magazine *Monthly Review*, while stubbornly clinging to the thesis of the complete financial autonomy of the large corporations as the author of *Monopoly Capital*—despite the evidence of the years 1969-71.[19]

Let us now consider the problem from the point of view of use-value. The systematic transfer of surplus-value from the non-monopolized to the monopolized sector cannot continue for any length of time without causing major disruptions, except in a special case: when this transfer is accompanied by an alteration in the structure of consumption — in other words, when monetarily effective demand shifts from the consumption of use-values produced in the non-monopolized sector to those produced in the monopolized sphere in a more or less equal proportion to this transfer. In Chapter 12, we

---

by other authors, in a collection entitled *Monopolkapital — Thesen zu dem Buch von Paul A. Baran und Paul M. Sweezy*, Frankfurt, 1969.

[19] Baran and Sweezy, *Monopoly Capital*, pp. 15-20. *Monthly Review*, Vol. 22, No. 4, September 1970; Sweezy's article in *Monthly Review*, Vol. 23, No. 6, November 1971.

have demonstrated that such a shift has in fact taken place in the age of late capitalism, among other things at the expense of agriculture, textiles, shoes, timber and similar branches. [20] But although such a tendency undoubtedly exists, the very terms of the problem reveals the difficulties confronting monopoly capital. For the monopolies must after all not only secure a *durable relative decline* in the demand for goods produced by the non-monopoly sectors — which is physiologically impossible, since consumption of food, or clothing in temperate countries, cannot drop to zero — but also ensure that this decline occurs in an *exactly correspondent proportion* to the process of redistribution of the social surplus-value. There is no need to emphasize here that this is impossible to achieve under conditions of private ownership and the market economy. [21]

If monopoly capital reacts to the increasing inelasticity of a part of the total monetarily effective demand by seeking to annex formerly non-monopolized branches of production, [22] this automatically leads to an expansion of the monopolized sector as compared with the non-monopolized one, which means a reduction in the volume of surplus-profits in comparison to the total mass of profits. The result will be a tendency for the monopoly rate of profit to decline further towards the average rate of profit.

If, by contrast, the transfers of surplus-value to the advantage of the monopolized sectors do not correspond to a specific shift in the structure of consumption, then the resultant retardation of accumulation in the non-monopolized sectors will lead to a relative shortage of the use-values produced by them. The market prices of these commodities will go up, not only absolutely, but also relatively to the goods produced by the monopolies, and there will thus be a periodic decline in the transfer of surplus-value. In this case, the pressure of demand

[20] See for example Anne P. Carter, *Structural Change in the American Economy*.

[21] See our criticisms of the notion of a crisis-resistant 'general cartel' and the relevant quotation from Marx in Chapter 1 and 14 of this work. One of the main reasons for Bukharin's mistaken belief that finance capital could eliminate the anarchy of production, at least within a single imperialist state (*Ökonomik der Transformationsperiode*, p. 5) was his failure to understand the contradiction between exchange-value and use-value — in other words, the inability of capital to 'organize' a proportionate distribution of hundreds of different use-values among millions of independent consumers, endowed with individual incomes, under conditions of commodity production.

[22] This has increasingly occurred in the USA in the past twenty years — in Western Europe and Japan in the last 10 to 15 years — in the textile and clothing industries, the food industry, and the small retail trade.

determines an equalisation of the rate of profit, if necessary accompanied by an acceleration of accumulation in the non-monopolized sectors — in other words, by an adjustment of the organic composition of capital in them to that of the monopolies. Precisely this process does periodically occur in certain spheres of non-monopolized raw materials production or agriculture.

The monopolies' long-run ability to secure stable monopoly surplus-profits — i.e., to withdraw from the effect of the law of value and from the competition between capitals which mediates this law in capitalism — therefore stands or falls with their ability to obtain a constant market for their commodities, exactly proportionate both to the total monetarily effective demand and to the increased productive capacity for the output of use-values in the monopolized sector due to the accumulation of monopoly capital. The immense development of advertising, market research and sales activity can be seen, as Galbraith points out, as an *attempt to secure this specific demand* in precise quantities. [23] The rationality of such efforts is dubious to say the least. The end result is unmistakable, however: not a single monopoly in a single branch of production has succeeded in withdrawing itself from the law of value in the long-run. After an initial phase in which substantial monopoly profits were obtained, all have sooner or later gone through phases of a cyclical decline in sales. They are thus all threatened by the danger of permanent over-capacity or a relative structural decline in sales, if these have not already set in. The ability of the monopolies to secure long-term stability of profits, proclaimed by several bourgeois authors and others who claim to be Marxists, is a myth.[24]

If the monopolies cannot secure durable growth in sales for their

[23] See Galbraith, *The New Industrial State*, Chapter 18.

[24] Baran and Sweezy likewise argue that the large corporations have in the long-run largely withdrawn from any kind of competition (*Monopoly Capital* pp. 47, 51, 74-5). In reality, a comparison of the list of corporations before the Second World War with the roll thirty years later reveals that the third technological revolution, and the major variations in the rates of growth of different branches of the economy and of individual corporations, have often increased the relative vulnerability of huge companies and reduced their ability to compete. A good recent example is provided by the massive surplus-profits (mainly technological rents) which the American corporation Texas Instruments initially obtained from its micro-circuits — which it then promptly lost when the inflow of capital into this branch led to an abrupt fall in prices. The same setback befell the Control Data Corporation, which produces large computers. For the crisis in the US electronics industry in 1970-71, see *Le Monde*, September 12, 1972.

particular commodities, then competition comes fully back into its own even between the monopolies. The threat of a fall in monopoly surplus-profits — i.e., the approximation of the monopoly rate of profit to the average rate, which is subject to a falling tendency — can only be averted by the constant expansion both of markets and of product differentiation. Product differentiation is also greatly promoted by the fact that monopolistic firms tend to limit output while their capital and productive capacity tend to grow faster than the average, precisely as a result of their appropriation of surplus-profits. They are therefore confronted with a problem of under-utilization of productive capacity — which can be temporarily solved by diversification of output.' With a given demand, it is irrational for a monopolistic firm to invest in the expansion of capacity of its original product if average cost remains unchanged, except as a measure to forestall entry or to initiate a struggle for a bigger market share . . . . Given an unchanged demand curve, and ignoring investment in cost-reducing improvements which only raise the same problem at a later stage, there remains only investment in new products. . . . The tendency towards diversification is likely to be stronger, the lower the elasticity of demand in the original product, the greater the excess capacity, and the lower the degree of specialization of the firm's productive facilities.' [25]

This is the reason for the tendency towards the massive growth of Research and Development, the acceleration of technological innovation, the incessant search for technological 'rents' and the efforts to avert the dangers of conjunctural, and particularly structural, relative decline in the demand for specific commodities by international centralization of capital — the multinational corporations — and formation of conglomerates. The more this process advances, and the nearer the package of goods produced by the monopolies comes to comprise the whole range of social production, the smaller monopoly surplus-profits will tend to become and the closer the monopoly rate of profit will have to adjust to the average rate of profit. The monopolies will thus increasingly be dragged into the maelstrom of the tendency for this average rate of profit to fall.

Sweezy argues that under monopoly capitalist conditions, monopoly capital can also flow from spheres with a higher rate of profit into spheres with a lower rate; the critical consideration is for a

[25] Merhav, op. cit., pp. 88-9.

large corporation the *additional* profit of the *additional* capital invested.[26] It is obvious that the monopolies enjoy a greater autonomy in their choice of fields for investment of new capital than was the case with companies in the 19th century. But Sweezy fails to see that this autonomy has certain *limits*. If additional capital is *systematically* invested in spheres with below-average rates of profit or even only at the average rate of interest, the total profit of these monopolies will fall. A corporation that takes this course will suffer a decline in its self-financing ability and ultimately also in its growth rate, as compared with its rivals. Its whole competitive position would thereby be undermined. It is precisely when we define the limits to the autonomy of the large corporations and the wide-ranging uncertainty under which they have to operate in the long term, that we rediscover the effects of the law of value.[27]

The fact that monopoly corporations are on the whole able to withdraw from classical price competition is of course itself not a new discovery; it was one of the mainstays of Lenin's theory of monopoly capitalism. Galbraith's thesis, however, that the 'liberation' of the corporations from the pressure of price competition is equivalent to their 'emancipation' from the market and its laws[28] is based on a two-fold confusion. In the first place, it confuses *short-term* and *long-term* profit maximisation; secondly, it confuses price competition with competition as a whole.

Empirically, price behaviour in a late capitalist economy could be reduced to a two-sector schema: the area of administered prices and

[26] Paul Sweezy, 'On the Theory of Monopoly Capitalism', *Monthly Review*, Vol. 23, No. 11, April 1972. The Xerox Corporation offers a fine example of this. Its photocopying division provides large profits, its educational equipment division provides average profits, while its computer division operates at a loss and is no longer viable in such a situation. Nubuo Kanayama, 'Encounter with Inscrutability', *The Oriental Economist*, Vol. 40, No. 740, June 1972.

[27] Means describes the limits of the decision-making autonomy of the corporations in the American steel industry in the following sober sentences: 'That the price leader in steel has an area of discretion in setting steel prices does not mean that it can set any price it chooses. Obviously, the price must cover its costs and yield a profit if the enterprise is to remain healthy and continue to serve its productive function in our society. Likewise, the leader cannot set and maintain a price which its major followers find too high. In a sellers' market, the smaller companies may charge a premium over the leader's price; and in a buyer's market they may set prices below those of the leader. Geographical or other differentials are likely to develop. But in the main, there is an area of discretion between two limits of necessary profits and followership by competition, within which the price leader exercises judgment.' *Pricing Power and the Public Interest*, New York, 1962, p. 44.

[28] Galbraith, *The New Industrial State*, pp. 123-8, 268-9, etc.

the area of competitive prices. [29] However the interaction between the two is considerable. Competition within the monopolized sector, aiming for maximization of growth (assets) constantly seeks for technological innovation to lower costs and product diversification to expand outlets; it thus always tends to threaten the frontiers between adjacent and rival monopolies. If demand for a specific product collapses, price reductions have to be conceded even by monopolies. In the competitive sector, conversely, price agreements among a large number of competitors can seek to compensate temporarily for poor market situations. Such agreements will not remain effective over time; but they can be successful in the short run.

Galbraith rightly starts from the primacy of growth for the monopoly corporations. But what produces the *compulsion* to growth, if not competition? Galbraith's attempt to explain this compulsion by attributing it to the moral or patriotic convictions of those who command the 'technostructure', cannot be taken seriously. [30] Competition between monopoly corporations does, of course, assume different forms from those which obtained between rival cloth manufacturers in the 19th century or vegetable merchants in the early 20th century. What else but this monopoly competition, however, forces corporations constantly to reduce their costs of production, incessantly to pursue technical innovation, uninterruptedly to produce 'new' products, tirelessly to expand their spheres of operation? Does not the compulsion to

[29] For the debate on 'administered prices', see Chapter 13.

[30] Galbraith's claim that the leading experts are extremely secure in their positions, i.e., 'emancipated' from cyclical oscillations and the effects of the falling rate of profit, cannot be proved either empirically or theoretically. It is no more than an extrapolation of a particular conjunctural trend, the product of an illusion created by a particularly long period of economic prosperity (the U. S. economy did not experience any real recession between 1961 and 1969). In reality no employee in a capitalist firm, however highly placed, has a security of income equivalent to that of a senior civil servant. Not only may he lose his position if returns drop too sharply; he may also do so if his firm has to proceed to mass dismissals or goes bankrupt. At the time of writing, 65,000 scientists and technologists were unemployed in the USA, with high percentages in some fields. (*Le Monde*, 28 July 1971). Strange 'masters' of the 'new industrial state', who take their own daily bread from themselves. If all salary earners are characterized by this fundamental insecurity of tenure, then their only means of obtaining genuine economic security consists in the acquisition of *private property*, i.e., *capital* (in shares and real estate, and so on). In other words, the behaviour of the 'technostructure' is basically determined by the principal feature of the capitalist mode of production, rather than by any socio-political — let alone aesthetic — motives.

growth involve a compulsion to maximise self-financing? How can this in turn be achieved except by long-term maximisation of profits?[31]

If the compulsion for monopolies to grow is due to the compulsion for them to remain competitive — in other words, to their inability to withdraw from the effects of the law of value — then the problem of the 'dual rate of profit' which we raised in our *Marxist Economic Theory*,[32] becomes explicable. This term has come under sharp attack from some circles.[33] It can very easily be verified empirically, however, for the whole of the age of monopoly capitalism, including the period of 'classical' imperialism from 1890 to 1940. The origin and function of this 'dual rate of profit' derive from the very nature of monopolies, which in the last resort always make it qualitatively more difficult for capital to flow into certain sectors and thereby prevent surplus-profits from entering into the general equalization of profits.

The blockage of capital inflow into a certain sector is always merely relative, however, and never absolute. For one thing, the achievement of surplus-profits through monopoly prices typically leads to relative or absolute market stagnation, and eventually brings substitute products into play.[34] For another, rival capitals can-

---

[31] Ultimately the notion of the 'technostructure' is merely a somewhat refined version of Burnham's 'managerial revolution'. The following passage from Sering (Löwenthal), *Jenseits des Kapitalismus*, shows how little originality Galbraith's concept really possesses: 'The increasingly scientific nature of production has resulted in increased specialization and a higher demand for personnel with many years of special training. The organizational tasks of modern mass production, and the state administration which accompanies it, have been complicated rather than simplified by the enlargement of the sphere of organization. . . . The tendency towards the formation of a career hierarchy is hence just as much inherent in modern production as in the modern state. We have seen how the skeleton of such a hierarchy emerges beneath the disguise of the capitalist market economy itself, as most capitalist proprietors lose their function as enterpreneurs and many also lose their executive functions.' Op. cit., pp. 67-8.

[32] Ernest Mandel, *Marxist Economic Theory*, pp. 423-6.

[33] For example the article by a writer's collective, 'Marxistische Wirtschaftstheorie — ein Lehrbuch der Politischen Oekonomie?', *Das Argument*, Vol. 12, No. 57, May 1970, pp. 223-4.

[34] 'On the remoter horizon there are the threats of new competitions, substitute products, wholly new techniques. Even the biggest of businessmen probably feel much less secure in their oligopoly positions than the theorist often assumes they should.' Professor Shorey Patterson, 'Corporate Control and Capitalism', *The Quarterly Journal of Economics*, February 1965, p. 10. The systematically excessive steel prices sustained over 30 years in the USA led in the 1950's to the increasing substitution of steel by light metals and plastics as materials in industry and construction. Carter, *Structural Change in the American Economy*, p. 84f.

not resist the attraction of high surplus-profits. Competition in the monopolized sector may therefore be limited, *but it cannot be eliminated*. In practice both of these forces lead to the convergence of surplus-profits — in other words, they generate a tendency towards the equalization of the monopoly rate of profit. If certain monopolies exceed this average rate of profit of all the monopolies, then capital will flow into the sector dominated by them despite all difficulties and will thus lower the surplus-profits there (the US electronics industry of the 1960's is a good case in point). [35] If the surplus-profits of certain monopolies fall below the average, then they can bring them up to par by raising monopoly prices, without this provoking any major resistance.

However, since capitals continue at the same time to flow freely back and forth in the non-monopolized spheres, there must also be a tendency for the rate of profit to be equalized in these spheres. In monopoly capitalism, therefore, there arise two different average rates of profit, separated from each other by the average rate of surplus-profit: one in the monopolized and the other in the non-monopolized sector.

Bain has shown that in the period 1936-40 major enterprises engaged in branches of industry where the eight largest firms produced over 70% of total output, showed a rate of profit which was considerably higher than that of corporations operating in less monopolized branches of industry (an average of 12.1% compared with 6.9%). The following estimates leaves no doubt that two average rates of profit really existed, and that they were consolidated in the long-run (*See* p. 544).

Two comments should be made on these statistics. On the one hand, if we eliminate special cases like the aircraft industry (much influenced by fluctuations in military expenditure), the long-term similarities within each branch are obvious. The case of the oil refining industry in 1972 is an obvious exception; but this industry achieved above-average rates of profit for every single year of the period 1968-72 except 1972, and compensated on a sensational scale in 1973-74 for its exceptionally low rate of profit in the previous

[35] The critical role played by the 'difficulties of entry' into certain branches of the economy in the consolidation of monopoly prices and profits, and the fact that these difficulties are always merely *relative*, is confirmed by numerous empirical investigations in the USA. See among others Joe S. Bain, *Barriers to New Competition;* Richard R. Nelson, Merton J. Peck and D. Kalachek, *Technology, Economic Growth and Public Policy*, pp. 70-1; Gardiner C. Means, *Pricing Power and the Public Interest*, p. 230 f.

Branch of Industry [36]	1958	1968	1972
Overall average of the rate of profit in manufacturing industry:	10.9%	12.1%	10.6%
Above-average rates of profit:			
Aviation	17.8%	14.2%	7.4%
Chemicals	13.2%	13.3%	12.9%
Electrical machinery	12.6%	12.2%	10.8%
Automobiles	12.5%	15.1%	14.5%
Oil	12.4%	12.3%	8.6%
Scientific apparatuses	12.0%	16.6%	14.3%
Below-average rates of profit:			
Metal processing	9.3%	11.7%	11.0%
Paper and printing	8.9%	9.7%	9.0%
Foodstuffs	8.6%	10.8%	11.2%
Textiles and clothing	4.8%	8.8%	7.5%

year. On the other hand, the rate of surplus-profits tends to decrease in the very long run. This may be seen from the fact that the differences between the average rate of profit for all industrial branches and the average rate of profit in the most competitive branches has declined: for example, in the textile industry, the discrepancy was −6.1% in 1958, −3.3% in 1968 and −3.1% in 1972, and in the printing industry it was −2% in 1958, −2.4% in 1968 and −1.16% in 1972.[37]

We have already seen that the tendency for the monopolies to expand their sphere of operations must *in the long run* reduce the volume of surplus-profits. The emergence of two 'average rates of profit' in monopoly capitalism ultimately results in the *retardation rather than the abolition of the process of formation of the overall social average rate of profit.* In the age of free competition it generally took a cycle of seven or ten years for the rate of profits to average

[36] Joe S. Bain, 'Relation of Profit Rate to Industrial Concentration: American Manufacturing 1936-1940', *The Quarterly Journal of Economics*, August 1951; Joe S. Bain, *Barriers to New Competition*, Harvard, 1965, p. 195. *Statistical Abstract of the United States, 1961,* 1971. For 1972, see *Statistical Abstract of the United States 1973.*

[37] The question has been asked: is it correct to use branch rates of profit as evidence of the presence or absence of monopoly? Strictly speaking, a combination of two criteria is necessary to determine monopoly surplus-profits: branch distinctions and size distinctions. Size by itself is no guarantee of monopoly conditions. In competitive sectors, even huge firms cannot achieve monopoly controls, if their fraction of total sales is too small, or if the total number of firms is too large; price competition cannot then be eliminated. The ideal combination for monopolization is that of the auto industry: a small number of firms, each of vast size.

out, but the relative economic power of the monopolies now creates substantial obstacles to this process of equalization. It hence takes longer for it to be completed.

It would be in keeping with one of the basic hypotheses of this work if the 'long wave' of economic development after 1893 was the period needed to equalise the rate of profit between the monopolized and the non-monopolized sectors. Each 'long wave with an undertone of expansion' is by its very nature (as an expansionary phase) marked by a temporary extension of the non-monopolized sectors, i.e., by the possibility of growing surplus-profits. In the closing phase of such a wave, and especially in the 'long wave with an undertone of stagnation' which succeeds it, there is by contrast an increase in the tempo of concentration and centralization of capital. The sphere of activity of the non-monopolized sectors contracts. There is hence a reduction in the mass of surplus-value produced in these sectors and a corresponding decline in the source of surplus-profits. The monopoly profit thus comes nearer to the average profit. We do not wish to develop this hypothesis further detail, however; it will have to be the subject of another investigation.

Everything points to the fact that the average rate of monopoly profit is not an empty abstraction, but is very much present in the minds of the corporations. Thus the heads of some corporations have stated quite frankly that they regard a certain rate of profit as 'normal' and gear their price-calculations (in a monopoly market!) to it. Gardiner Means speaks in this sense of a 'target rate of return of investment', which Lanzillotti has studied in US manufacturing industry. For the period 1947-55 it is said to have been 20% for General Motors, Du Pont de Nemours and General Electric, 18% for Union Carbide and 16% for Standard Oil of New Jersey (in this case, the average rate of profit actually realised). The big corporations can of course also make miscalculations. Growing overcapacity can render their expected average monopoly rate of profit unattainable in the long-run, whereupon there will be an equalization of the average rate of profit. The highly concentrated synthetic-fibres industry offers an example. In this sector, 14 concerns are responsible for 80% of the entire output of the capitalist world (Du Pont, Celanese and Monsanto in the USA; ICI and Courtaulds in Great Britain; Toray, Toyobo and Asahi in Japan; Rhône-Poulenc in France; Montedison and Snia Viscosa in Italy; AKZO in Benelux-West Germany and Switzerland, and Hoechst and Bayer in West Germany). The price for a kilo of polyster thread fell from S1.25

546   *Late Capitalism*

in 1970 to S0.80 in 1972. There was consequently a precipitous fall in the rate of profit. [38]

Elmar Altvater has sharply criticized the thesis of two average rates of profit under monopoly capitalism: the average rate of profit in the non-monopolized sectors, and the average rate of profit in the monopolized sectors. In considering his arguments, it is necessary to distinguish between his criticism of the justifications given by authors like Dobb or Varga for the duality of these averages, and his conclusion that these two averages are non-existent because the law of value permits of only one average rate of profit, which is realized under monopoly capitalism, as it was under competitive capitalism, but at a slower tempo and after a longer interval. Altvater starts his refutation by claiming that the existence of two movements of equalization of the rate of profit in a single capitalist society implies the possibility of 'eternal' monopolies, and thereby dissolves the capitalist economy into two 'societies' and not merely into two sectors. [39] This, however, is an unwarranted inference.

The emergence of two average rates of profit, in monopolized and non-monopolized sectors, is the outcome of a *single movement of equalization* determined by the operation of a single law of value. Capital continues to flow out of the sectors in which profit is below-average, and to flow into sectors where profits are above-average. The emergence of two average rates of profit simultaneously expresses this single movement of equalization, and the obstacles posed to its completion by 'barriers to entry' which are above all *barriers of size*. To identify the process of equalization under monopoly capitalism with that under 'freely competitive capitalism' is to minimize these barriers and to eliminate monopoly from Marxist analysis. To deny the operation of this process of equalization, because of the existence of monopolies, is to assume that the latter can indefinitely evade the law of value by means of extra-economic coercion, manipulation, fraud or state intervention, and thereby also to abandon Marxist analysis. In fact, it is the *combination* of an immanent thrust towards equalization of the rate of profit, and formidable barriers posed by monopolies to this equalization, that precisely results in the emergence of two average rates of profit side by side with each other for a lengthy period of time, which tend to

[38] Means, op. cit., p. 240. *Manager-Magazin*, June 1972.
[39] Elmar Altvater, *Monopolprofit und Durchschnittsprofit* (Manuscript), pp. 2-4.

converge only in the very long run. We entirely agree with Altvater that 'eternal monopolies' do not and cannot exist, under conditions of commodity production, private property, and 'many capitals'. The emergence of an average rate of monopolistic surplus-profit in the monopolized sectors does not contradict, but on the contrary corresponds to the operation of the law of value, as we have emphasised earlier. If capital invested in a monopolized sector — for example, the automobile industry — implements constant price increases in spite of cost reductions and thereby achieves a monopolistic surplus-profit above the average surplus-profit of other monopolized sectors, the law of value will exercise a double adverse pressure on it.

a) Additional capital will flow in the automobile industry, attracted by these huge super-profits. This will create relative over-capacity (or over-production) and thus reduce somewhat the rate of surplus-profit. But as hundreds of millions of dollars are needed in order to create a new automobile firm, *only the capital of other monopolies will be able to participate in this movement of equalization.* Small businessmen cannot collect enough capital to create a new automobile corporation and thereby profit from the surplus-profits of that sector. [40] This is the main mechanism for the emergence of an average rate of monopolistic surplus-profit.

b) The sale of these overpriced commodities will either decline absolutely, or at least relatively compared to their levels without overpricing (or to the expectations of the selling firm). For the law of value also bears down on 'excessive' surplus-profits by the mediation of social demand. This is, in fact, what actually occurred on a large scale in the international automobile industry in 1974. In the case of monopolies which sell primary or semi-fabricated products to manufacturers — for example, the large American steel corporations — the possibilities of technological substitution to counter over-pricing are obvious, again resulting in a decrease of demand and an equalization of the average rate of monopolistic surplus-profit. The same is potentially true even in the field of manufactured products.

---

[40] Capital here designates the operative organizational form of a company or corporation, not a title to ownership of shares. A petty manufacturer or even a grocer can of course buy stocks in an automobile firm. For that he does not need hundreds of millions of dollars. But in return, he will not receive monopoly surplus-profits, merely the average rate of interest on the current value of his stock, and often not even that.

Altvater provides no answer to these concrete arguments for the existence of two average rates of profit under monopoly capitalism. The contradictions in his position appear most evidently when he passes from criticism of other writers to formulation of his own solution to the problem of monopoly surplus-profits. 'Modification of the law of value can only mean that the tendencies inherent in movements of value impose themselves during the course, not of a single cycle, but over several cycles.' [41] Altvater himself correctly states that the duration of the business cycle has decreased under 'highly developed capitalism' from 7-11 to 4-6 years. 'Several cycles' thereby implies at the very least a period of 8-12, probably of 12-18, if not indeed of 16-24 years. For Altvater, the 'modification' of the workings of the law of value is that surplus-profits remain 'fixed' for a lengthy period of this order. But what actually happens to monopolistic surplus-profits during this span of time? Can they operate without trammels — in other words, can they *grow* from year to year and from cycle to cycle? If Altvater were to adopt such a position (which he does not), it would imply a reversion to the notion which he rightly combats — that the monopolies can emancipate themselves for a quarter of a century or so from any influence of the law of value. Are their movements then completely fortuitous or random, so to speak? Again, such a thesis would deny any objective regulation of surplus-profits by the law of value. There is only one way to avoid these untenable conclusions, and to maintain the basic position that *the monopolies cannot emancipate themselves from the operation of the law of value, even while they continue to appropriate surplus-profits*, during a number of successive trade cycles: that is to accept the thesis that first two different average rates of profit are formed, in the monopolized and non-monopolized sectors, before they merge — in the very long run — into a single average rate of profit.

We believe that the reason for Altvater's error is his undue identification of the phenomenon of monopoly with obstacles to free movements of capital due to technical (patent) and market factors and inadequate awareness of the obstacles to equalization of rates of profit due to the *size* of the monopolies — in other words, to the degree of concentration and centralization of capital. If genuine competition in a given branch necessitates a concentration of 1 or

[41] Altvater, op. cit., pp. 16, 21-2.

1.5 billion dollars, this fact in itself becomes by far the biggest barrier to capital moving in and out of that branch, and thus to an effective equalization of the rate of profit. [42] The size of the capital involved explains at one and the same time why competition can be effectively restricted for longer periods in these branches, why it can suddenly ignite again (sometimes very violently) when adequate capitals of similar size confront each other, and why such competition is necessarily confined to capitals of this size. Occasionally, a smaller 'outsider' can gain entry into a monopolized branch. But the exception promptly confirms the rule: it will then be absorbed by the monopolies.

It should not be forgotten that Marx said that the average rate of profit is an economic 'fact of life' which enters the consciousness of capitalists and forms the basis of their calculations.[43] It is therefore necessary to ask: which 'average rate of profit' forms the basis of the monopolists' calculations? An abstract 'general average' which .becomes a reality only every 16 or 24 years? Or the average rate of monopolistic surplus-profit, which we have seen to be nothing but the 15-20% 'expected rate of return' which the monopolies add to their production costs? Marx himself posed the problem of the equalization of the rate of surplus-profit, albeit in relation to the question of landed rent. 'If the equalization of the values of commodities into prices of production does not meet any obstacles, then the rent resolves itself into differential rent, i.e., it is limited to the equalization of the surplus-profits which would be given to some

[42] It could be said that the violent shocks to the markets of the imperialist countries in 1973-74 due to the huge increase in oil prices, resulted in a massive influx of capital into the oil (and subsequently the whole energy-producing) sector, and a progressive outflow of capital from the automobile sector. But the very size of the automobile industry, and the disastrous implications of any massive outflow of capital from it for employment, brought no less massive state subsidies into play to limit this outflow — limitations not present on the same scale in the competitive sector of the economy.

[43] 'Average profit is the basic conception, the conception that capitals of equal magnitude must yield equal profits to equal time spans. This, again, is based on the conception that the capital in each sphere of production must share *pro rata* to its magnitude in the total surplus-value squeezed out of the labourers by the total social capital; or that every individual capital should be regarded merely as a part of the total social capital, and every capitalist actually as a share-holder in the total social enterprise, each sharing in the total profit *pro rata* to the magnitude of his share of capital. This conception serves as the basis for the capitalist's calculations, for instance, that a capital whose turnover is slower than another's, because its commodities take longer to be produced, or because they are sold in remoter markets, nevertheless charges the profit it loses in this way, and compensates itself by raising the price.' Marx, *Capital*, Vol. 3, pp. 205-6.

capitalists by the regulating prices of production and which are now appropriated by the landlord. Here, then, rent has its definite limit of value in the deviations of the individual rates of profit, which are caused by the regulation of prices of production by the general rate of profit. . . . Finally, if equalization of surplus-value into average profit meets with obstacles in the various spheres of production in the form of artificial or natural monopolies, and particularly monopoly in landed property, so that a monopoly price becomes possible, which rises above the price of production and above the value of the commodities affected by such a monopoly, then the limits imposed by the value of the commodities would not thereby be removed. The monopoly price of certain commodities would merely transfer a portion of the profit of the other commodity-producers to the commodities having the monopoly price. A local disturbance in the distribution of the surplus-value among the various spheres of production would indirectly occur, but it would leave the limit of his surplus-value itself unaltered.' [44]

What is true of the private attempts by monopolies to regulate the economy applies equally to the State regulation. There is no need to analyze the social function of this regulation here. We have already tried to show in Chapter 15 that the State in late capitalism continues to be what it was in the 19th century — a bourgeois State which can ultimately only represent interests of the bourgeois class ('capital as a whole'), above all its dominant socio-economic stratum. We are here concerned with the economic function of State regulation, in other words, its alleged ability to emancipate the late capitalist economy once and for all from the operation of the law of value and the laws of motion of the capitalist mode of production. State intervention in the late capitalist economy can be summarized in three rubrics: stimulation, inflation, and subvention. We have already discussed, in Chapters 13 and 14 of this study, the attempt to moderate the industrial cycle by creating money or credit. In the optimum case, where state action is limited to government intervention to increase employment or to encourage the utilization of capacity without inflation of the means of circulation and bank money, it is undoubtedly effective to some extent, as we have shown. Its effect is temporarily limited, however, for two reasons. In the first place, it can only have a stimulating influence if it simultaneously increases the rate of surplus-value — and thereby automatically increases the difficulties of realization, to the very extent that it improves the conditions of capital expansion. (For capital in general this would be equivalent to 'missing out' one cycle in a series of cycles of extended reproduction). In the second place, the temporary restriction of the range of cyclical fluctuations also reduces the positive effect of the crisis for capital as a whole. Many enterprises operating below the social average productivity of labour or profitability are kept above water longer than they would have been without government intervention. This slows down the devalorization of total capital, but at the same time retards the stepping up of the average rate of profit which results from such a devalorization. Even in this optimum case of non-inflationary state intervention in the economy, therefore, the outcome clearly fails to diminish, let alone abolish, the contradictions of the capitalist mode of production: it merely postpones the hour at which they will break out. Historically speaking, this type of stimulating intervention by the State in the economy has a similar effect to that of the classical monetary and credit system of the 19th century.

For the reasons outlined further above, however, the 20th century has virtually never witnessed an example of a government inducing an economic upswing in this 'optimum' manner, after the outbreak of a crisis of over-production. Every one of the existing examples of such stimulation of the economy has hitherto been inflationary. The basic reason for this has already been discussed, and Keynes himself was quite familiar with it. [45] Mere stimulation of consumer demand is doubly ineffective under capitalist conditions: firstly, it lowers the rate of surplus-value and hence also the rate of profit, and secondly it does not increase entrepreneurial investment activity — with the possible exception of a limited rise in outlays in Department II. But if the State wishes not to increase the monetarily effective demand of the 'final consumers', but also to raise the global volume of investments, it can only do so by ensuring that its investments do not compete with those of private capitalist enterprises — in other words, do not deprive the latter of their already restricted markets. State investments will thus only promote an upswing if they create 'additional markets'. Historically

---

[45] J. M. Keynes, *The General Theory of Employment, Interest and Money*, p. 131, which contains the famous passage: 'Two pyramids, two masses for the dead, are twice as good as one; but not so two railways from London to York.'

speaking, arms production and public works have fulfilled this role.

The promotion of the production of new use-values or 'services' by the State is not the end of the matter, however. The problem now arises of the distribution of surplus-value or the valorization of capital. If such state outlays are wholly financed by taxation, then once again there will be no change in global demand and state investments will simply lead to a relative — if not even an absolute — decline in the sales of the private sector. Only if these investments at least to some extent result in a direct nominal increase in purchasing power — i.e., bring additional means of payment into circulation — will they have a stimulating effect on the economy (deficit financing). But since such investments do not increase the quantity of commodities in circulation to the same extent as they create additional means of payment, they inevitably contain an inflationary bias.

In concrete terms, therefore, State intervention to stimulate an upswing in the economy (to overcome or limit a crisis) has regularly led to inflation. There is no need to return to this topic, which has already been discussed in Chapter 13 here. We have, moreover, demonstrated in an analysis of the effect of arms production on the laws of motion of the capitalist mode of production in Chapter 9, that inflation is incapable of either weakening or of abolishing these laws of motion. Thus here too, the effects of State regulation to postpone the outbreak of the contradictions of capitalism gradually merge with effects that intensify these contradictions.

The subventionary activity of the State is already embryonically present in the bourgeois State's function as the guarantor of the general conditions of capitalist production, explored in Chapter 15. Any government activity in the sphere of public works or the infrastructure creates 'free goods' and services which facilitate the valorization of total capital. By passing the responsibility for the *indirect costs of the production and realization of surplus-value* over to the State, the capitalist class as a whole also gains in terms of value, if the means to finance this activity do not derive exclusively from the profits of capitalist enterprises. Taxation of the incomes of small independent producers and the petty bourgeoisie as a whole, as well as of the gross wages of the proletariat, thus accomplishes a redistribution of social income by the roundabout route of the expansion of social (state) capital, which leads to an increase in the production of surplus-value. In this sense, the growing infrastructural activity of the bourgeois State is in itself equivalent to an increasing subsidization of private capital. It is thus a manifestation of the intensifying structural crisis of the capitalist mode of production — for in the heyday of rising capitalism capital sought to limit State activity, even in respect of its role of creating the general conditions for capitalist production, rather than to extend it. The more acute this structural crisis becomes in the age of monopoly capitalism and particularly in its late capitalist phase, the greater the scale on which the subventionary activity of the State develops. This activity is, of course, interlocked with the phases of the industrial cycle: in times of a deterioration in valorization of capital it increases by leaps and bounds,[46] while in periods of a temporary upswing in the average rate of profit it is correspondingly curtailed. The State's activity in expanding the infrastructure is thus determined by both structural and cyclical factors. This generates a typical opposition in late capitalism between the interests of those sections of the bourgeoisie as a whole which depend on the anti-cyclical employment of this expenditure and the interests of those capitalist enterprises (including individual monopolies) which specialise in major State contracts, which seek to plan such projects several years in advance and therefore prefer a permanent infrastructural policy to ensure the continuous utilization of their own productive capacity.[47]

It is necessary to distinguish here between two different forms of government subvention — indirect and direct.[48] Indirect state subvention to capital can be combined with the direct production of surplus-value, namely when the nationalization of certain branches of industry producing raw materials, energy or semi-finished goods leads to the sale of the commodities produced by this public sector at a below-average rate of profit, if not at a loss,

[46] For examples of the forced cartelization which took place under State pressure in the period of the Great Depression, see Chapter 14 of our *Marxist Economic Theory*, pp. 496-9; and for cases of the nationalization of unprofitable factories and their re-sale to private capitalists as soon as the profitability threshold had been crossed once more, see this same work, pp. 502-6.

[47] See among others Duccio Cavalieri, 'La Politica dei Lavori Publicci: Sviluppi Teorici e Indirizzi Programmatici', in *Pianificazione*, Vol. 3, No. 3, September-December 1966, which includes a considerable bibliography.

[48] In an interesting essay James O'Connor distinguishes between 'complementary' and 'discretionary' state investments. The former create establishments which are indispensible for the profitable production of the private sector (e.g., investments in the infrastructure), while the latter represent investments abandoned or never undertaken by the private sector because of their lack of profitability. 'The Fiscal Crisis of the State', in *Socialist Revolution*, January-February, 1970.

to private enterprise. In this case, a part of the surplus-value produced by workers in the nationalized sector is transferred to private capital, which has the same effect as a general subvention to capitalist private enterprise or a general increase in the mass of profit appropriated by private capital.[49]

Let *A* be the nationalized sector (say of Great Britain, France or Italy) and *B* the private sector. The creation of value in the two assumes the following proportions:

$A: 2,000c + 1,000v + 1,000s = 4,000$
$B: 6,000c + 3,000v + 3,000s = 12,000$

Now if the goods produced in *A* (which are all taken to be elements in the constant capital of *B*) are sold to *B* for 3,000 then *B* will appropriate the 1,000 units of surplus-value produced in *A*; and this subvention will increase the rate of profit of private capital from 33.3% to 44.4%.

Even in the interests of private capital, however, the nationalized branches of industry must be able to achieve extended reproduction (although not necessarily all of them, and not necessarily at the same rate as the private sectors of the economy).[50] Deductions from the mass of surplus-value produced in them must therefore at least partly be made good by other means, if the system of indirect subventions is not to lead to the systematic disappearance of profitability in the nationalized sector. The quantities of labour needed for this purpose can in turn ultimately only be obtained at the expense of wages (through heavier taxation of the gross income of wage-earners), or at the expense of small independent producers, or at the expense of surplus-value produced elsewhere. In the final analysis, therefore, the system of indirect subventions leads either to an increase in the social rate of surplus-value or to a redistribution of the social surplus-value to the advantage of certain groups of capitalists and to the disadvantage of others. Indirect subsidization can also take the form of excessive profits on State contracts. These profits may be achieved through a transfer of surplus-value at the expense of private firms not working for the state, or through an

---

[49] This increase in the total mass of profit appropriated by private capital, obviously does not benefit every individual capital in equal proportion: it corresponds rather to a redistribution of surplus-value between individual capitals.

[50] In branches of industry with a falling relative or even absolute demand, nationalization can obviously be accompanied by a massive devalorization of the nationalized capital. But this state of affairs, too, is perfectly compatible with the constraint to modernise or make new investments. See in this respect the example of the coal industry.

increase in the taxation of the proletariat and the petty bourgeois, or through a combination of all these variants.

Direct subventions usually take the form of State coverage of the losses of capitalist enterprises or guarantees of additional profits, or financing of certain costs of production, such as expenditure on research and development. [51] Such direct subsidies also result either in an increase in the social rate of surplus-value or a redistribution of the social surplus-value. The inherent contradictions of the system cannot be overcome in this way. On the contrary, these contradictions will prevail on the other side of any increase in the rate of surplus-value — which must always remain socially and economically limited — and will be left unaffected by the distribution of profits over the various branches of productive capital.

Naturally, this does not mean that State intervention in the economy — which can be classified as stimulation, inflationary creation of credit money, and subsidization of private capital — is inconsequential or insignificant. In a two-fold sense, it is an essential feature of late capitalism. In the first place, the role of a general clearing house for total capital in guiding the distribution of the total social surplus-value over the various branches of industry, which was mainly fulfilled by the banks and finance capital in the age of classical monopoly capitalism, is now increasingly fulfilled by the joint action of the State and the big monopolies. In the second place, the growing intervention of the State in the economy is ultimately merely a manifestation of the fact that the present degree of the objectives socializations of labour and of the forces of production not only clashes epochally with private ownership of the means of production, but has become directly incompatible with it here and now in a growing number of spheres. There is thus a tendency for the State to intervene in more and more originally productive spheres of the economy in order to create pre-conditions of production which can no longer be guaranteed by private capital. These extend from the actual infrastructure and the sphere of education and administration, to certain branches of raw materials production, the transport system and even branches of production which have 'leapt ahead' too far technologically (for example, nuclear power stations).

The specificity of State regulation of the late capitalist economy,

[51] This problem, like that of the social significance of selective investment guidance, is dealt with in Chapter 15.

and its adopted role as the central clearing house for the expansion, investment and distribution of available capital, lies in the inter-linkage of this intervention with the laws of motion of the capitalist mode of production. The economy remains based on the production and realisation of surplus-value, it is still subject to the remote control of the law of value, and it continues to be governed by the compulsion to valorize capital and the resultant compulsion to growth. Within this framework, the State cannot in the long run diminish, let alone abolish, any of the contradictions or laws of motion of this mode of production. Still less can it do so since in the last resort it remains an instrument of bourgeois class domination. Although it will often defend the particular interests of the monopolies, it cannot pursue these beyond the point where they would endanger the survival of the system. In no sense does the State 'produce monopoly profits' or even assume responsibility for extended reproduction as such.

In the long run, the State cannot simultaneously improve the conditions of valorization of capital and reduce the difficulties of realisation. If the rate of profit declines, there will also be a fall in the accumulation of capital even if the market is expanding. If the rate of profit is high or rising, the accumulation of capital will still slow down if there is simultaneously a relative contraction of the market or the utilisation of capacity decreases. No combination of private and State regulation of the economy has managed to achieve in the long-run the miracle of a rising rate of profit *and* an expanding market (a high utilization of capacity in both Departments). Mattick too has recently concluded that the State cannot in the long-run successfully overcome the contradictions inherent in the capitalist mode of production.[52] He reaches this correct conclusion with a false argument, however, for he claims that State expenditures involve a deduction from the mass of surplus-value and hence a retardation of the accumulation of capital. This is wrong for two reasons. We have shown that State expenditures can in fact increase the rate of surplus-value and thus speed up rather than slow down the accumulation of capital. Mattick's critical mistake, however, is that of neo-classical bourgeois economists: he starts from the tacit hypothesis that full employment obtains and that therefore all capital is invested and obtain the average rate of profit. This assumption is inapplicable to the age of monopoly capitalism. If one assumes that a part of the over-accumulated capital only obtains the average interest, i.e., that it is idle from the point of view of the *production* of surplus-value then its use to produce armaments or infrastructural facilities bought by the State can perfectly well increase the mass of surplus value and hence also accelerate the accumulation of capital, even if the State pays for its purchases partly by means of deficit financing and partly through taxation. A claim on a portion of future surplus-value is in no way incompatible with an increase in current surplus-value as long as extended reproduction does actually occur. Even the production of commodities which do not enter into the process of reproduction can increase the mass of surplus-value produced.

At the outset of this work, in Chapters 2, 3 and 4, we sketched an anticipatory outline of the place of late capitalism in the history of the capitalist mode of production, and of the way in which the law of value governs its inherent contradictions. We can now, in conclusion, elucidate and summarize our main findings. The late capitalist phase began when fascism and the Second World War generated a significant increase in the rate of surplus-value, which was prolonged by a substantial reduction in the price of important elements of constant capital. This allowed 'capital in general' to overcome the long-term decline or stagnation of the average rate of profit. The result was an acceleration in the accumulation of capital (further favoured by the permanent arms economy), which now seized on the discoveries and innovations that had been maturing over the previous decade, and thereby unleashed a third technological revolution.

Under these specific conditions, the accelerated accumulation of capital promoted the rate of profit in a two-fold sense. Firstly, labour-power was steadily released, so that the rate of surplus-value could be maintained at a high level. Secondly, there was a further reduction in the cost of elements of constant capital, so that the growth in the organic composition of capital was much slower and more moderate than appeared at first glance. The rate of profit therefore remained relatively high for a lengthy period; late capitalism has consequently been distinguished by a major long-term growth of the forces of production. This general development, however, was not equally distributed over all portions of the world's capital. A section of the capitalist class, even if a less important one, was completely expropriated in this period.[53] In the imperialist metropolitan countries, a series of monopolies established themselves in the so-called 'growth-sectors' and secured substantial technological surplus-profits for themselves, to some extent magnified by unequal exchange with the colonies and semi-colonies. The accelerated accumulation of capital predominantly occurred in these sectors — which were the real 'bearers' of the expansionary 'long wave' — and this led to an alteration in the structure of demand, whereby a number of spheres of production suffered a relative or absolute decline in profits: bituminous coal mining, agriculture, the traditional textile industry (and partly even the clothing industry), small retailers, and so on. Rapid expansion, however, allowed the labour employed in these branches be transferred to the growth sectors of late capitalism (industry and services) and the 'expansionary long wave' therefore assumed the character of a new tide of industrialization (in breadth, especially in such countries as France, Italy, Japan, the Netherlands, Scandinavia, the Southern States of the USA, Spain, and a few semi-colonies like Brazil, Mexico, Hong Kong and Singapore; and in depth, by the 'industrialization' of agriculture, accounting, the banking system, certain sectors of services and building). But precisely because of the substantial monopoly surplus profits obtained in this manner, the growth sectors were marked by a rate of capital accumulation surpassing the development of demand on the part of the 'final consumers' or the modification of the overall structure of social demand. A growing over-capacity thus emerged in the branches principally responsible for the long 'boom', similar to that which had already become evident in stagnating or declining branches of production in the mid 1960's.

The expansion of credit, the 'industrialization' of wholesale and

[53] We refer here to the owners of enterprises expropriated without compensation in Central and Eastern Europe, China, Korea, Vietnam and Cuba, or the section of the capitalist class of these countries which fled after the victory of the socialist revolution. This does not mean that these one-time owners ceased to function as capitalists. In many cases they managed to take some of their capital with them and set up new capitalist enterprises in West Germany, the USA, Canada, Australia, Hong Kong, Singapore and elsewhere. This phenomenon was naturally even more marked among owners of nationalized enterprises in countries where capitalism was not overthrown. The *Compagnie du Canal de Suez*, the Bolivian tin magnate Patiño or the Union Minière possess more capital today than they did before the nationalization of their original enterprises.

retail trade, the extension of the service sector, and the innovations of the third technological revolution in the transport and tele-communication sector as well as in such activities as inventory control, permitted a considerable acceleration of the rotation of circulating capital, which further contributed to the rise in the rate of profit after the Second World War. [54] Subsequently, however, the increasing expense of fixed capital investment projects, the lengthening of the time necessary to build new factories and productive complexes, the declining rate of self-financing and the growing trend towards credit contraction, restricted the shortening of the turnover-cycle of fixed capital and of circulating capital, and tended to immobilize more and more capital in conditions where it could no longer operate productively, and thus in turn depressed the rate of profit again.

In the more important imperialist countries the long duration of above-average growth simultaneously meant the absorption of the industrial reserve army — despite immense imports of foreign workers from the semi-capitalist periphery to the centres of late capitalism. The rate of profit thus also became threatened by the decline in the rate of surplus-value, while the long-term increase, however slow, in the organic composition of capital inevitably had a further disadvantageous effect upon it. The third technological revolution, the reduced turnover-time of fixed capital, the increasing importance of the reproduction of labour-power at a higher level of intellectual and technical qualification, the growing significance of research and development, itself increasingly financed by the state, all combined to generate a compulsion towards greater economic planning within companies and economic programming in society as a whole. The greater sensitivity and vulnerability of the complex system of production created a growing need for private and public economic regulation and social control. The limits of the efficacy of such regulation, however, are set by the insuperable barrier of the commodity character of production and the compulsion towards valorization of capital. In the long run, monopoly

[54] See the interesting calculations by Helmut Zschocke (op.cit., p. 88), who estimates that the number of annual turnover cycles of circulating capital in West German industry increased from 3.86 in 1950 to 5.10 in 1968. For the importance of computerized control of inventories, see Stephen Bodington, *Computers and Socialism*, Nottingham 1973, pp. 101-2.

surplus-profits and the average rate of profit, the market for specific commodities and the growth rate of specific enterprises, remain uncertain and subordinate to the law of value.

The increasing attempts to regulate the industrial cycle have hitherto only succeeded because of the relative autonomy of the various national currency zones of the large imperialist powers. This relative autonomy was only compatible with a steady expansion of the world market,[55] as long as the currency of the strongest imperialist power, the US dollar, could function alongside gold as a world money. The steady erosion of the purchasing power of the dollar, itself induced by increasing difficulties in the realization of surplus-value and the valorization of capital within the USA, has now undermined the dollars function as a world currency. This in turn endangers the whole system of nationally manipulated currencies and makes it increasingly necessary to return to a generally accepted universal equivalent on the world market, free from the interference of national sections of 'capital in general'. The role of 'national' monetary and credit policy in moderating the business cycle thus threatens to be decisively curtailed. This threat is also becoming a reality to the extent that the 'long wave' of accelerated expansion, under conditions of a new technological revolution, has led to a new phase of accelerated concentration and centralization of capital, which has made the multinational corporation into the decisive organisational form of the late capitalist enterprise. The late bourgeois State has much less influence over this organisational form than over the 'national' trusts and monopolies of yesteryear and before. As the forces of production outgrow the national state, they likewise gradually outgrow the State's role in controlling the industrial cycle and promoting economic upswing and growth. *The more the monopolies think they have withdrawn from the law of value nationally, the more they become subject to it internationally.*

Finally, the whole economic process unleashed by the search for technological surplus-profits and their appropriation has accumulated vast explosive material at both poles of the capitalist

[55] The dialectic of this development is such that a geographic reduction of the world market may perfectly well be accompanied by its extension in terms of value and of physical quantities of use-values sold. Admittedly, this kind of expansion only became significant in the 1960's, if we compare world trade per head of population, or the export share of the most important products of the finished goods industry, of this period with that of 1913 or 1929.

world economy. International capital movements are more than ever today determined by the imperialist monopolies, while no uniformity exists on the international capital market (nor any homogenization of the relations of production on a world-wide scale). The result is that the productivity, income and prosperity differential between the inhabitants of the metropolitan countries, and those of the colonies and semi-colonies, is steadily increasing and hence steadily multiplying revolutionary movements of liberation among the latter. The third technological revolution has brought about profound changes in the needs of the working masses in the metropolitan countries — including the need for qualitative changes in the form and content of work; but late capitalism is unable to fulfil these needs. Still less can it do so today as the outbreak of a *universal struggle over the rate of surplus-value* has even forced it in practice to deny 'rights' (especially full employment and autonomy in wage negotiations) previously conceded to the proletariat. Social contradictions and tensions are thus intensifying in the metropolitan countries. Their roots lie in the growing universalization of a social crisis whose origins will be discussed in our final chapter.

18

The Crisis of Capitalist Relations of Production.

Late capitalism is the epoch in history of the development of the capitalist mode of production in which the contradiction between the growth of the forces of production and the survival of the capitalist relations of production assumes an explosive form. This contradiction leads to a spreading crisis of these relations of production.

We must first define the essence of capitalist relations of production more closely. For Marx, the relations of production include *all* the fundamental relations between 'men and women in the production of their material life.[1] It is thus incorrect to reduce these relations merely to a single aspect of the relations of capital, such as, for example, the subordination of living to dead labour, or the relations of the producers to their means of production within a unit of production. The specific nature of capitalist relations of production lies in generalized commodity production. The latter determines the particular form of the separation of the producers from the means of production, which is distinct from that of the period of slave labour; the particular form of appropriation of the surplus product, which is distinct from that under feudalism; the

---

[1] Marx: 'In the social production of their existence, men inevitably enter into different relations, which are independent of their will, namely relations of production appropriate to a given stage of their material forces of production. The *totality* of these relations of production constitutes the economic structure of society.' *Critique of Political Economy*, p. 20 (Our italics).

particular form of the reconstitution of social labour, the inter-connection between units of production, and so on. Generalized commodity production implies that labour-power and the means of labour have themselves become commodities. Capitalist relations, therefore, cannot simply be derived from the subordination of the producers to 'administrators' or 'accumulators', who have existed in every class society. They entail the *sale* of the commodity of labour power to the *owners* of the means of production; the splitting of these owners into different capitals in competition with one another,[2] who must *exchange* for money the quantities of value they have appropriated in order to realize the surplus-value contained in them and to continue production on an extended scale; and the *accumulation* of this additional capital in separate units in a process determined by the constraint of competition.

Material production would be just as unthinkable without a regular supply of raw materials, machines and other instruments of labour, auxiliary materials and sources of energy, as it would without a particular relationship between the workers and the means of labour. Thus when Marx defines capital as a specific relationship between men — i.e., as a specific type of relations of production — he simultaneously defines commodity production in the same way as a specific relationship between men.[3]

The fact that enterprises buy means of production, raw materials or energy from each other as exchange values therefore similarly constitutes a specific feature of the relations of production characteristic of the capitalist mode of production. If the relation between

---

[2] 'Since value forms the foundation of capital, and since it therefore necessarily exists only through exchange for *counter-value*, it thus necessarily repels itself from itself. A *universal* capital, one without alien capitals confronting it, with which it exchanges — and from the present standpoint, nothing confronts it but wage-labourers or itself — is therefore a non-thing. The reciprocal repulsion between capitals is already contained in capital as realized exchange value.' Marx, *Grundrisse*, p. 421. See also the statement already quoted: 'Capital exists and can only exist as many capitals, and its self-determination therefore appears as their reciprocal inter-action with one another.' *Grundrisse*, p. 414.

[3] Marx: 'In capital-profit, or better still capital-interest, land-rent, labour-wages, in this economic trinity represented as the connection between the component parts of value and wealth in general and its sources, we have the complete mystification of the capitalist mode of production, the conversion of social relations into things, the direct coalescence of the material production relations with their historical and social determination. It is an enchanted, perverted, topsy-turvy world, in which Monsieur le Capital and Madame la Terre do their ghost-walking as social characters and at the same time directly as mere things.' *Capital*, Vol. 3, p. 808.

capital and labour were completely abolished *within* the enterprise (say through their transformation into productive cooperatives), but generalized commodity exchange was still allowed to prevail between these cooperatives (i.e., reciprocal purchase or sale of the means of production as commodities), then it would only be a matter of time before the separation of the producers from their means of production would itself be reproduced by the persistence of this element of capitalist relations of production.[4]

Men produce commodities because the social labour at their disposal has *previously* been divided into 'private tasks carried out independently of each other'.[5] This characteristic form taken by labour in turn depends on a particular dialectic determined by the development of the social division of labour and the social instruments of labour. So long as social labour is undertaken in small units of production which are more or less self-sufficient (tribal, kinship or village communities), the directly social nature of labour is ensured without great difficulties by a simple *a priori* rule based on custom, ritual and elementary organization. The development of the division of labour, exchange, private property and simple commodity production gradually fragments this social labour-capacity into private tasks, whose social nature is acknowledged completely, only partially or not at all, *a posteriori* via the detour of commodity relations on the market, and only after passing the critical test of the realization of the value of the commodity (in capitalism: of the average profit).

While, on the other hand, this long historical process of the atomization of social labour into private tasks carried out independently of each other reaches its highpoint in the stage preceding

[4] Marx: 'But it was left to M. Proudhon and his school to declare seriously that the degradation of *money* and the exaltation of *commodities* was the essence of socialism and thereby to reduce socialism to an elementary misunderstanding of the inevitable correlation existing between commodities and money.' *Critique of Political Economy*, London, 1971, p. 86.

[5] Marx: 'As a general rule, articles of utility become commodities, only because they are products of the labour of private individuals or groups of individuals who carry on their work independently of each other. The sum total of the labour of all these private individuals forms the aggregate labour of society. Since the producers do not come into social contact with each other until they exchange their products, the specific social character of each producer's labour does not show itself except in the act of exchange. In other words, the labour of the individual asserts itself as a part of the labour of society, only by means of the relations which the act of exchange establishes directly between the products, and indirectly, through them, between the producers.' *Capital*, Vol. 1. pp. 72-73.

the capitalist mode of production, on the other hand a contrary tendency sets in with the development of this mode of production and the technology which corresponds to it. Capital assembles a constantly increasing number of workers together in a consciously organized labour process. It combines larger and larger sections of mankind in processes of production which are objectively socialized and connected to each other by thousands of threads of reciprocal dependence. The fundamental contradiction of the capitalist mode of production — the contradiction between the increasing objective socialisation of labour and the further continuance of private appropriation[6] — thus corresponds to the contradiction between the increasing disappearance of private labour (not only in the context of individual factories, but also of large or world-wide companies) on the one hand, and the survival of the commodity form of exchange value or profit as the goal of production on the other, which is based on private labour.

The capitalist mode of production only becomes possible at a particular stage of the development of the forces of production — once the material preconditions exist, first for the formal, and then for the actual, subsumption of labour under capital. These material premises are naturally preceded and overlaid by the social preconditions already described. The capitalist mode of production thus presupposes a particular level of development of the socialization of labour, which is both real and contradictory. When the elementary division of labour is arrested at the stage of complete private labour, where use values for small units of consumers are produced with virtually unchanged instruments of labour, and the mutual dependence of the producers is reduced to only partial dependence on the labour of others for the satisfaction of a few needs, it is certainly possible for simple commodity production to develop, but not capitalist commodity production. The level of the socialization of labour, the productivity of labour, and the

---

[6] Engels: 'The means of production, and production itself, had become in essence socialized. But they were subjected to a form of appropriation which presupposes the private production of individuals, under which, therefore, everyone owns his own product and brings it to market. The mode of production is subjected to this form of appropriation, although it abolishes the conditions upon which the latter rests. This contradiction, which gives to the new mode of production its capitalist character, *contains the germ of the whole* of the social antagonism of today.' *Socialism, Utopian and Scientific,* in Marx and Engels, *Selected Works*, p. 420. See also the pages following this passage.

development of the social surplus product, are all still too low at this stage to permit generalized capitalist commodity production.[7]

For this to emerge, the socialization of labour must begin to supersede the individual character of labour. Division of labour in manufactures and large enterprises must be added to the division of labour between various occupations. The majority of producers must cease to produce for their own needs altogether and satisfy these needs primarily by way of the market. This demands developed machinery, i.e., a much larger social surplus product, without which additional, vastly extended machinery cannot be produced at all. The production of machinery, the development of the material productivity of labour, the constant acceleration of the process of the objective socialization of labour — these constitute the historically progressive achievements of the capitalist mode of production.[8]

The antagonistic character of this socialization of labour by capital consists in the fact that the worker now confronts both his product and his means of labour as something alien, hostile and separated from him, in a mysterious way inherent in capital. Marx has stressed that this form of the objective socialization of labour in capitalism, which is so oppressive to the worker, can be attributed among other things to the fact that the worker must engage himself *individually*, and the mass of workers must engage themselves in an *atomized* fashion, in a process of production in which their own common productive force becomes a *thing* separated from them:

'In actual fact the *communal* unity in cooperation, combination in the division of labour, in the application of natural forces and sciences, of the products of labour as *machinery* — all this confronts the individual worker independently, without and often against his intervention, as something *alien, material, pre-given*, as the bare form of existence of the *means of labour* which are independent of him and *govern* him in so far as they are material; and insight and will of the whole workshop incarnate in the capitalist and his understrappers, insofar as this is formed by their own combination — as *functions* of capital which live in the capitalist. The social forms of their own labour — subjective and objective — or the form of their own social labour are relations formed completely independently of the individual worker; the workers, as

[7] Marx, *Grundrisse*, pp. 397-8.
[8] Ibid., pp. 309, 699-700.

subsumed under capital, become elements in these social formations, but these social formations do not belong to them. They
therefore confront them as *forms* of capital itself, as belonging
to capital as distinct from their own isolated labour capacity, as
combinations stemming from capital and incorporated in it. This
assumes forms that are all the more real the more, on the one hand
that their labour capacity itself is so modified by these forms that
it becomes powerless as an independent force, hence *outside* the
capitalist context, so that its independent ability to produce is
broken, and the more, on the other hand, that with the development of machinery the conditions of labour appear to govern labour
technologically as well, and at the same time replace, suppress and
make it redundant in its independent forms. In this process, in
which the *social* character of their labour in a certain sense confronts them in a capitalized form — as, for example, when in
machinery the visible products of labour appear to govern labour
— the same thing naturally happens to natural forces and science,
the product of general historical development in its abstract
quintessence — they confront the worker as *powers* of capital.
They in fact become separated from the skill and knowledge of the
individual worker and — even if, considered at their source, they
are again the product of labour — they appear to be *incorporated*
in capital wherever they appear in the process of labour.'[9] Marx
added: 'The social natural force of labour does not develop in the
process of capital expansion as such; but in the actual *process of
labour*. It therefore presents itself as properties which adhere to
capital as a *thing*, as its use-value. Productive labour — as producing
value — confronts capital as the labour of *isolated* workers, whatever social combinations these workers may enter into in the process of production. While to the workers, therefore, capital represents the social productive force of labour, to capital productive
labour always merely represents the labour of isolated workers.'[10]

This is why Marx always describes socialist society as a society
of *associated producers*; for once this isolation in the process of
production and labour is completely abolished once and for all,
and if the producers henceforth organize, plan,[11] discuss and realize

---

[9] Marx, *Resultate.* . . . pp. 158, 160.
[10] Ibid., p. 162.
[11] Marx: 'Let us now picture to ourselves by way of a change, a community of free
individuals, carrying on their work with the means of production in common, in

their process of labour in common, in *voluntary* association, then naturally the mystery of the *social* force of production disappears, and the latter no longer seems to adhere to things, as a collective force 'external' to the producers, but is seen to be the result of the common, commonly planned and commonly organized labour capacity of all workers.

The objective socialization of labour is a process which the development of technology, science and the forces of production has made irreversible. But the concrete form of its combination with the social structure differs fundamentally in a capitalist and a non-capitalist economic order. Within the limits of the capitalist mode of production, the socialization of labour only prevails indirectly. It is still the law of value which determines the distribution of economic resources among various branches of the economy, corresponding to the fluctuations of the average rate of profit and the deviations from it (capital flows primarily into sectors where surplus-profits can be realized). If, by contrast, the capitalist mode of production — i.e., generalized commodity production — has been abolished, then the associated producers can apprehend *a priori* the objective socialization of their labour. Economic resources will be distributed among the various branches of the economy in a planned manner according to *socially* determined priorities. It is then that the character of labour becomes immediately social, and the category of 'socially necessary labour-time' (the socially necessary quantity of labour) ceases to have any more meaning than that of the valorization of capital.[12]

At this point there commonly arises a second misunderstanding of Marx's concept of the relations of production: the attempt to

---

which the labour power of all the individuals is consciously applied as the combined labour power of the community . . . . Labour time would . . . play a double part. Its apportionment in accordance with a definite social plan maintains the proper proportion between the different kinds of work to be done and the various wants of the community.' *Capital*, Vol. 1, pp. 78-9.

[12] Naturally this does not mean that economic calculation and comparison of labour costs — with the aim of saving labour — likewise disappear. On the contrary: they become even more important than previously. For they can now be assessed more exactly, on the overall social level, taking into account all the costs which are not calculated in commodity production, but are 'socialized' behind the back of society. Moreover, they can be gauged by exact book-keeping of all quantities of labour actually expended (irrespective of whether these are now expressed in hours of work or in money of account). For since society itself henceforward distributes its economic resources over the different branches of its production, it cannot abdicate responsibility for the directly social character of any part of the labour collectively organized.

divide these into 'technical' and 'social' relations.[13] There are, of course, technical *preconditions* for particular relations of production. It is just as impossible to achieve the real subsumption of labour under capital without the existence of modern machinery as it is effectively to socialize small enterprises based on artisanal methods of labour without a transformation of their technology.[14] But to conclude from this that so long as 'technical relations of production' do not permit a 'complete socialization' of labour or a 'complete appropriation of products' by society, there must be a continuation of commodity production,[15] is to reduce Marx's conception, which defines relations of production as relations between men, to relations between men and things — in other words, to introduce a new fetishism of technology.

The character of labour is not determined *directly* by technology, nor the stage of development reached by the forces of production. It is certainly in no way so determined within each isolated production unit.[16] Nor is it even so determined in society as a whole. Two fundamentally different social structures can correspond to one particular level of technology. This will always be the case in epochs of social revolution.[17] In such epochs, the development of new technology, whose tendency is to overshoot existing relations of production, will become increasingly incomplete, contradictory and destructive within the traditional social order, while at the same time the introduction elsewhere of new, revolutionary relations of production — which, like all such structures, cannot be introduced 'step by step' — will tend to race ahead of the existing state of technology (thus precisely creating the necessary space for a dynamic development of new forces of production). The parallel but distinct problems of late capitalism and contemporary

[13] See among others Poulantzas, op.cit., pp. 64-7.

[14] Such socialization can nevertheless accelerate the development of productive forces if it enables labour to be saved by simple co-operation on a broad basis, as appears to be the case in the Chinese communes.

[15] This thesis is advanced at length by Charles Bettelheim in his book *La Transition vers l'Economie socialiste*, Paris, 1968.

[16] See the claim by Bettelheim in his book just cited.

[17] 'At a certain stage of development, the material productive forces of society come into conflict with the existing relations of production or — this merely expresses the same thing in legal terms — with the property relations within the framework of which they have operated hitherto. From forms of development of the productive forces these relations turn into their fetters. Then begins an era of social revolution.' Marx, Preface to *Critique of Political Economy*, p. 21.

transitional societies between capitalism and socialism can be traced back to this particular dialectic of the forces and relations of production.[18]

In a period of increasing *contradiction* between productive forces and social relations of production, it is therefore not to be expected that all the innovations made possible by science and technology will be completed before the social relations of production can be transformed. This contradiction, after all, is expressed precisely in the fact that a *potential* technical and scientific revolution can only find *partial* realization within the framework of existing social relations of production. General automation in large industry is impossible in late capitalism. To await such generalized automation before overthrowing capitalist relations of production is thus just as incorrect as to hope for the abolition of capitalist relations of production through the mere advance of automation.[19]

The crisis of capitalist relations of production must be seen as an overall social crisis — that is, the historical decline of an entire social system and mode of production, operative throughout the whole epoch of late capitalism. This is neither identical with classical crises of over-production, nor does it exclude them. The highest peaks of this social crisis are pre-revolutionary and revolutionary situations of class struggle, when it culminates in an outright political crisis of bourgeois State power, in which the proletariat objectively poses the threat of overthrowing capitalism and inaugurating the transition towards socialism. Such peaks are powerfully prepared by all those episodes of the crisis of capitalist relations of production which impel workers to establish provisional organs of dual power at factory, industry, local, regional and national level. Whether this occurs under conditions in which there is no economic recession, as in France in May 1968 and Italy

[18] To do full justice to this dialectic one would have to add: 1. that the maturity of existing forces of production for new socialized relations of production obtains at the level of the imperialist *world* economy; 2. that the social crisis provoked by this maturity, determined by the law of uneven and combined development, does not develop simultaneously but discontinuously in time and space, creating the possibility and necessity of socialist revolutions which are initially victorious only within national limits. 3. that a further contradiction then arises between the international development of forces of production and national attempts to revolutionize relations of production.

[19] It is this kind of hope which underlies the views of Roger Garaudy's *The Turning Point of Socialism*, London, 1970, and partly also the Richta Report, *Politische Oekonomie des 20. Jahrhunderte*, Frankfurt, 1970.

in 1969, or in which there is such a recession, as in Spain in 1974-75, depends on conjunctural factors that are extrinsic to the nature of the epoch. The essential and intrinsic consequence of the end of the long wave of post-war expansion, and the intensified struggle over the rate of surplus-value unleashed from the second half of the 60's onwards, is a world-wide tendency towards qualitatively sharpened class conflicts, which will bring the endemic crisis of capitalist relations of production to explosion point.

The crisis of capitalist relations of production hence appears as the crisis of a system of relations between men, within and between units of production (enterprises), which corresponds less and less to the technical basis of labour in either present or potential form. We can define this crisis as a crisis not only of capitalist conditions of appropriation, valorization and accumulation, but also of commodity production, the capitalist division of labour, the capitalist structure of the enterprise, the bourgeois national state, and the subsumption of labour under capital as a whole. All these multiple crises are only different facets of a *single* reality, of one socio-economic totality: the capitalist mode of production.[20]

The crisis of capitalist relations of production appears as a crisis of capitalist conditions of appropriation, valorization and accumulation. We have already emphasised in our discussion of permanent inflation that the system is now unable to utilize a substantial part of its productive capacity under 'normal' conditions of stable gold values — in other words, without permanent inflation of credit and money. The fundamental difficulties of realization have never been so obvious, for a theoretical analysis penetrating beneath the surface of economic phenomena, as in the phase of the 'long wave with an undertone of expansion' following the Second World War.

---

[20] Marx: 'Capitalist production is distinguished from the outset by two characteristic features. *First*. It produces its products as commodities. The fact that it produces commodities does not differentiate it from other modes of production; but rather the fact that being a commodity is the dominant and determining characteristic of its products . . . . The *second* distinctive feature of the capitalist mode of production is the production of surplus-value as the direct aim and determing motive of production. Capital produces essentially capital, and does so only to the extent that it produces surplus-value. We have seen in our discussion of relative surplus-value, and further in considering the transformation of surplus-value into profit, how a mode of production peculiar to the capitalist period is founded hereon — a special form of development of the social productive powers of labour, but confronting the labourer as powers of capital rendered independent, and abanding in direct opposition therefore to the labourers' own development.' *Capital*, Vol. 3. pp. 857-8.

The permanent competitive pressure to reduce cost prices, increase the productivity of labour, socialize labour, improve machinery and raise the organic composition of capital inevitably finds expression in a *disproportionate growth in the mound of use-values*. The 'many capitals' are thus compelled towards a permanent artificial expansion of the market, and extension of the needs of the masses.[21] While every individual capitalist would like to restrict the consumption of his 'own' workers, the capitalist class as a whole must widen the market for consumer goods, and at the same time ensure the valorization of capital. It can *partially* bridge this contradiction in number of ways. Firstly, it can render the production of consumer goods increasingly 'indirect', so that a growing portion of the total product consists of means of production rather than consumer goods.[22] Secondly, it can sell a substantial part of the consumer goods produced to social classes other than the proletariat (peasants and artisans at home and abroad), or shift purchasing power to the disadvantage of simple commodity producers or other capitalists (including 'foreign' capitalists, by a re-division of the world market). Thirdly, it can sell an increasing portion of consumer goods on credit rather than in exchange for income (increase in private indebtedness). Finally, it can ensure that the growth of mass consumption (including that of its 'own' workers) is proportionately less than that of total commodity values, so that the production of relative surplus-value increases.

None of these remedies, however, can suppress the fact that the difficulty of simultaneously realizing surplus-value, and raising the rate of surplus-value, is anchored in the capitalist mode of production as such, for the process of the reproduction of capital represents a unity of the process of labour and valorization of capital on the one

[21] 'If valuable machinery were employed to supply a small quantity of products, then it would not act as a force of production, but rather make the product infinitely more expensive than if the work had been done without machinery. It creates value not in so far as it has value — for the latter is simply replaced — but rather only in so far as it increases relative surplus time, or decreases necessary labour time. In the same proportion, then, as that in which its scope grows, the mass of products must increase, and the living labour employed relatively decrease. *The less the value of the fixed capital in relation to its effectiveness, the more does it correspond to its purpose.*' *Grundrisse*, p. 739.

[22] According to official figures, the production of consumer goods as a share of the total industrial output of the USA fell from 39% in 1939 to 28% in 1969. *Federal Reserve Bulletin*, July 1971.

hand, and the process of circulation and realization on the other, such that capital can only assure the first by means which in the long run increase the uncertainty of the second, and vice versa.

Trade and credit (including the specifically late capitalist form of the permanent inflation of credit money) are the two fundamental means of temporarily averting the difficulties of realizing surplus-value. The growing autonomy of commercial and bank capital and the development of an independent sphere of commodity and money circulation are the price paid by industrial capital for a provisional and partial relaxation of the permanent difficulties of realization. The resultant acceleration of the turnover of circulating capital enables the mass of surplus-value annually produced to be increased, so that this autonomy does not *necessarily* diminish the profit appropriated by industrial capital. But alongside the general pressure to raise the organic composition of capital, there thus develops a further pressure to diminish the share of circulating capital in total productive capital, and to convert all capital into fixed capital, which increases the organic composition of capital still further and in the long-run must depress the rate of profit.

The burgeoning of the spheres of circulation and services in the capitalist mode of production fulfills yet another function, however. It is an indispensible instrument for the steady expansion of the money and commodity economy, and the constant extension of money-commodity relations to domains hitherto immune from them: 'The more production as a whole develops into the production of commodities, the more each man must and wants to become a *dealer in commodities*, making money either from his own product or from his *services*, if his product only exists in the natural form of a service; and this *money-making* then appears as the ultimate goal of all activity (see Aristotle). In capitalist production, the production of products as commodities on the one hand, and the form of labour as *wage-labour* on the other, now become absolute. A multitude of functions and activities which had an aura of sanctity about them, counted as an end in themselves, were performed free of charge or were paid for in a roundabout way (like the role of all professionals, doctors, barristers and so on, in England, where the barrister and physician could not and cannot sue for payment), are on the one hand transformed directly into *wage-labour*, however different their content and *payment*. On the other hand, they become subject —

574   *Late Capitalism*

in terms of their value, of the *price* of these different *activities*, from that of a whore to that of a king — *to the laws that regulate the price of wage labour.*'[23]

Independent handicrafts, cottage industry, small agricultural enterprise (subsistence farming), small trade, research, private services and the production of 'cultural goods' succumb one after another to 'money-making as an organized business'. This process reaches its apogee in the age of late capitalism, as we have seen, with the generalized commercialization of art, teaching, scientific research and individual 'free vocations'. On the one hand permanent inflation alone permits the realization and appropriation of the surplus-value contained in the total output of commodities, while on the other hand there develops increasing over-capitalization, or a growing mass of non-valorizable capital which can only achieve temporary valorization by direct intervention of the late bourgeois State in the economy. More and more branches of industry depend solely on State contracts for their survival.

In our discussion of the permanent arms economy, we have emphasised the significance of military contracts for the US economy after the Second World War (there is no need to stress the role played *internationally* by the arms economy in eventually overcoming the Great Depression of the 30's). More and more research projects are financed directly by society. Spokesmen of the British employers' federations have even demanded the complete socialization of virtually all research costs.[24] More and more investments are rendered possible only by direct or indirect State subventions, not because the bourgeois class is short of capital in an absolute sense, but because the conditions of valorization of capital have deteriorated to such an extent that the entrepreneurial risk will not be taken without guarantee of profitability from the bourgeois State. The rapid development of the forces of production in the age of late capitalism in the course of the third technological revolution has historically begun to shatter even the primary foundation of the capitalist mode of production, namely generalized commodity production. It does so from two sides at once.[25] On the one hand, the progress of technology

[23] Marx, *Resultate* . . ., p. 132.
[24] *The Times*, 26 July 1968.
[25] Another example of the crisis of the market economy; the Professional Association of the West German Nitrogen Industry is considering 'whether one could not

in the industrialized countries produces increasing phenomena of saturation, which take the market economy to the absurd. The most striking example here is that of agriculture. In the USA and Canada an artificial system for throttling production has existed for decades, which since the establishment of the European Economic Community has increasingly spread to Western Europe, and is now also beginning to develop in Japan. Since the products of agrarian labour, now massively cheapened, cannot shed this commodity form within the framework of the capitalist mode of production, the growing excess of these products cannot simply be distributed among the large number of those in need who still exist in the 'rich' countries — nor, above all, among the famished populations of the underdeveloped countries. Instead, an irrational system of subsidies has had to be created, which involves the curtailment of food production and the destruction of stocks, artificially restricts possible consumption and yet still fails to assure the agricultural producers their expected return per hour of performed work. It is a logical consequence of this absurd and inhuman order that the systematic reduction of output and contraction of cultivated area in the agriculturally richest countries in the world 1968-70 finally led to the menace of terrible famine in Asia and Africa in 1973-74.

On the other hand, the objective opposition between partial rationality and overall irrationality, which is rooted in the contradiction between the growing socialization of labour and private appropriation and is a hallmark of the capitalist mode of production,[26] acquires such explosive potential that the overall irrationality of late capitalism threatens in the medium term not only the existing form of society, but human civilization altogether. The fact that it would be not only irrational and senseless, but suicidally dangerous to permit the 'free sale and purchase' of atom bombs or poisonous gases can be understood by any child. A growing volume of research has demonstrated that the 'free production' and 'free sale' of poisoned foods, pharmaceuticals and drugs injurious to health, unsafe cars and chemicals destructive of the environment — all of which are entrusted to private initiative driven by the profit motive — may even-

---

save on freight costs by supplying the consumer only from the nearest factory, irrespective of which proprietor owns this factory.' *Frankfurter Allgemeine Zeitung*, July 1971.
[26] See Chapter 16 of the present work.

tually threaten human life.[27] The experts who have exposed these processes, have, however, generally refused to draw the necessary social conclusions from their analysis.[28] The root of these evils lies in the survival of commodity production — in other words, the reconstruction of the total social labour-power fragmented into private labours via the detour of the laws of the market, with its reification of all human relations and its conversion of all economic activities, from means to the end of satisfying rational human needs and extending the possibilities of human life, into ends in themselves.[29] Only the direct socialization of production and its conscious subordination to the democratically determined needs of the masses, can lead to a new development of technology and science promoting the self-development, and not the self-destruction, of individuals and of mankind.[30]

[27] Apart from Commoner's book cited earlier, see among others Max Nicholson, *The Environmental Revolution*, London, 1969, John Esposito, *Vanishing Air*, Washington, 1965, and H. Nicol, *The Limits of Man*, London, 1967. The literature on this subject is growing at an exponential rate — like the problem itself. So far the best Marxist work to deal with the overall problem of the capitalist threat to the environment and the possible measures to counter it has been written by our friend Harry Rothman, *Murderous Providence — a Study of Pollution in Industrial Societies*, London, 1972.

[28] Examples are works by E. J. Mishan (*The Costs of Economic Growth*, London 1969) and the recent Nobel Prize Winner Dennis Gabor, which deal with many of the problems briefly summarized here, but do so only in partial fields, either not raising the question 'Why?' at all or answering it with banalities such as 'human aggression' or 'ignorance'. Such writers refuse to expose the nexus between commodity production, positivist partial rationality and overall social irrationality. They therefore themselves remain prisoners of the complex of specialized partial rationality and overall irrationality. A good critique of both books appeared in the magazine *Contemporary Issues*. Vol. 14, No. 55, April 1971: Andrew Maxwell, 'On the Notion of "Wealth" '.

[29] Herbert Gintis, in his intelligent treatment of commodity fetishism (a hitherto unpublished manuscript), rightly emphasizes the misleading nature of the basic axiom of bourgeois political economy, namely that any consumption which is realized through monetarily effective demand is *ipso facto* rational. If they were consistent, the protagonists of this doctrine would have to declare the distribution of hard drugs to be rational as well, since after all these also find buyers. Marx always emphasized that consumption is to a large extent determined by production, and that its tendencies of development consequently depend on the relations of production. After Galbraith and Mishan, no-one today any longer believes in the fairy-tale of 'consumer sovereignty'.

[30] An extension of the contemporary American structure of production to the entire world would destroy all sources of raw materials before the end of the century, indeed endanger the world's hydrogen belt, write Donella H. Meadows, Dennis L. Meadows, Jorgen Randers, William Randers and William W. Behrens III in *The Limits of Growth*, New York, 1972. They are possibly right, although they undoubtedly make exaggerat-

In purely economic terms, the objective overall irrationality of the capitalist mode of production can be reduced to the opposition between the calculation of 'privately paid' production costs at the level of the factory (or company) and the overall social, direct and indirect costs of production — in other words, the opposition between the profitability of individual firms and the social balance-sheet of costs and benefits.[31] Bourgeois economics merely mystifies this opposition with the terminology of 'returns' yielded in part by 'free goods'.[32] The growing threat to environment from contemporary technology is thus attributed to an increasing shortage of such 'free goods', or is reckoned as 'negative commodities' or 'negative returns'.[33] By this detour, the future of commodity production and eternal scarcity is assured. There is no need to expatiate on the brutal logic of market fanaticism here. Because companies pollute the atmosphere to maximize their profits, the simple right to fresh air is abolished: 'access' to this 'scarce commodity' must be purchased by a 'tax'.[34] The real task, of course, is precisely to emancipate pro-

---

ed use of extrapolations from current tendencies of development. It is clear that a radical alteration of the social system and hence of the distribution of material resources and social priorities could achieve a qualitative improvement in techniques for fighting pollution and protecting the environment, and a qualitative increase in substitutes for scarce raw materials. It goes without saying that the world-wide extension of American capitalism would be a nightmare for mankind. It naturally does not follow that economic growth should be halted, imprisoning among others the masses of the underdeveloped countries in their misery. The only logical conclusion to be drawn is that anarchic and destructive growth must be replaced by growth that is consciously planned and takes all 'indirect social costs' into account.

[31] Although the technique so-called of Cost Benefit Analysis (see among others E. J. Mishan, *Cost-Benefit Analysis*, London, 1971) permits the inclusion of 'indirect social costs' in the choice of different investment projects, it is forced to express damage to health and even human life in 'money values', which can only be done on the basis of capitalising . . . the proceeds. The implicit inhumanity of this way of treating the problem, and the reactionary results to which it leads, are obvious (see a good critique in Rothman, op.cit., pp. 312-16). Cost-benefit analysis merely reveals the limits of partial economic rationality, even when generalised to take account of 'indirect costs'.

[32] See for example Robert Dorfman, *Prices*, New Jersey, 1964, pp. 119-210.

[33] Tibor Scitovsky, *Welfare and Competition*, London, 1952, p. 187. This argument stems originally from A. C. Pigou, *The Economics of Welfare*, here cited from the Fourth Edition, London, 1960, pp. 134-5, 183-7.

[34] See Weiss's comment: 'The fundamentally impermissible premise (of efforts to turn human life and health into money values) is a reinterpretation of primary physical needs for the rest, clean air, unpolluted water, and bodily health, as needs for monetary income. It so happens that precisely these needs should not be articulated and satisfied through the mechanism of the market.' Dieter Weiss, 'Infrastrukturplanung', in *Ziele, Kriterien und Bewertung von Alternativen*, Berlin, 1971, p. 46.

duction from calculations of profitability related to either factory or company, from private ownership and commodity production, and to satisfy needs rationally, without gigantic wastage[35] Once these conditions are achieved, conscious and democratic planning will naturally ensure that neither 'population explosion' nor the 'commodity avalanche' threaten air, water, earth or man. For it is not science and contemporary technology 'in themselves' but their capitalist organization and application which endanger the survival of humanity. The pursuit of technological rents creates conditions which collide directly with the protection of human health. For example, it obliges the chemical industry to throw new synthetic products onto the market every four or five years, before it has had time for any responsible study of the biological and ecological risks potentially involved in them. Marx foresaw this development over a century ago, when he wrote that capital could only develop itself (and the forces of production) by simultaneously pillaging both the sources of human wealth, earth and labour.

In the age of late capitalism, this pillage has reached immeasurable proportions. The opposition between exchange-value and use-value, which in the heyday of capitalism surfaced only exceptionally and suddenly in times of economic crises, is permanently visible in late capitalism. This opposition has found its most dramatic expression in the mass production of means of destruction (not only of military weapons, but also of all the other instruments for the physical, psychological and moral destruction of man): it may be seen, too, in those sectors of the economy no longer determined by calculations of company-profitability but by 'public' priorities[36] The forces of production, the interests of humanity, the 'immanent' evolution of science, tend more and more in this direction. Within the framework of the capitalist mode of production, however, such

[35] See for example the frightening refuse production which characterizes late capitalism: 1.25 kg. per capita per day in the USA in 1920; 2.5 kg. in 1970 (in Belgium it was still only 250g. per capita per day in 1960), i.e. more than 180 millions of tons of refuse per annum.

[36] An example was the US moon programme. At the same time, however, the intermeshing of arbitrarily chosen 'social priorities' (ultimately determined by the arms race and 'political competition' with the USSR) and private capitalist relations of production was of such a kind that the enterprise became a gigantic source of monopoly surplus profits and squandered resources. See the study by the *Sunday Times* reporters Hugo Young, Bryan Silcock and Peter Dunn.

projects must always remain marginal. The setting of public priorities by small cliques of the ruling class threatens merely to create additional wastage of material resources and damage to human existence (military exploitation of space travel, biological experiments by state apparatuses and private interests).[37] Likewise, the project of an individual 'card index' for every citizen, summarily coding all the 'incidents' of his private and public life, with obvious uses for potential political surveillance, is yet another example of the inhuman application of contemporary technology for the conservation of the social system.[38] The combination of private appropriation and state economic intervention has a further economic effect, which must be investigated more closely. Capitalist private property, competition between the 'many capitals', leads to precise calculation within enterprises and to partial rationality in the reduction of production costs. The governing principle here is the strictest economy of resources.[39] Yet the State sector, by contrast, in which there is no objective social mechanism for the constant reduction of costs, is governed by the principle of an *allocation economy*, which involves a permanent wastage of resources to the extent that the individuals active in it have a material interest in increasing these allocations,[40] since they remain dominated by the private urge for self-enrichment which is generalized in a commodity-producing economy.[41]

This contradiction is further intensified by the fact that increased allocations from the state sector can constitute a source of increased private profit for companies and capitalists or enhance their capacity

[37] For the dangers connected with the 'biological time bomb' see among others G. Rattray Taylor, *The Biological Time Bomb*, London, 1969, and David Fishlock, *Man Modified*, London, 1971.

[38] See Gerald Messadié, *La Fin de la Vie Privée*, Paris, 1974.

[39] This is naturally much less true of monopoly capitalism than of the capitalism of the age of free competition.

[40] In an allocation economy saving on expenditure leads to a reduction in allocations. Those concerned, whose interest lies in an increase in allocations — and not a capitalist maximization of profits — are thus constantly and automatically impelled to increase their expenditure. This principle governs all public administration in a commodity-producing society.

[41] Insofar as the state and economic bureaucracy in the transitional societies of the East has subtracted itself from any political control by the mass of producers, whose basic interest lies in economizing on their labour time, and exhibits a drive for personal enrichment in a money economy, the same principle applies to this social stratum too.

to compete against other capitals.[42] The interlocking of nationalized sectors of the economy and the private appropriation of surplus-value thus heightens the irrationality of the overall system — generating, among other things, a greater wastage of economic resources. This irrationality cannot be overcome even by the simulation of profitability in the public sector.[43]

The decline of the capitalist mode of production which underlies this interlocking of the private economy and State intervention emerges even more clearly in a historical perspective. At one time, capital — spurred by the compulsion to compete and accumulate, to achieve valorization on an extended scale — sped well ahead of technical progress, initiated it, guided it into productive channels and kept it firmly within its power. The centralization of capital (say in the banks) was far superior to that of the actual labour process. Therein lay the basis of the 'economic autonomy' of capital in the 19th century. Today, the development of technology has sped past the centralization of 'many capitals', once and for all. The objective socialization of labour, the most up-to-date production methods, repeatedly overshoot the most advanced forms of the concentration and centralization of capital. Capitalist private property, the private appropriation of surplus-value and private accumulation increasingly becomes an obstacle to the further development of the forces of production. *State (and supra-national) centralization of part of the social surplus product has once again* — as in numerous pre-capitalist societies — *increasingly become a material precondition for the further development of the forces of production.* But although growing State centralization of the social surplus-value in late capitalism is more adapted than private capitalist competition to the objective socialization of labour, it too increasingly lags behind the most advanced technology. This lag finds its clearest expression in the phenomenon of the *multi-national corporations* and all the tendencies inherent in them.

The strengthening of the State in late capitalism is thus an expression of capital's attempt to overcome its increasingly explosive

[42] For example, the combination of a free government health service and a private pharmaceutical industry becomes a vast mechanism for the constant expansion of the profits of this branch of industry, significantly increasing its ability to compete with other sectors of the chemical industry.

[43] The attempt at this kind of simulation was introduced on a major scale into the Pentagon by Ford-technocrat MacNamara.

inner contradictions, and at the same time an expression of the necessary failure of this attempt. Today only a world-wide association of producers is congruent with the contemporary state of the forces of production and the objective socialization of labour. Any 'intermediate solution' that abolishes competition (i.e., anarchy) on one level, only reproduces it with all the more destructive force on a higher level. This is true of the late bourgeois State just as much as it is of the late capitalist multinational monopolies.

The further growth of productive forces not only clashes ever more frontally with the commodity form of *production*, its private appropriation and determination by the individual profitability of the large companies; it likewise collides directly against the commodity form of *labour-power*. The freezing of the division of labour and the qualification of labour, which corresponds to this commodity form, is taken to the absurd by the acceleration of technological innovation — just as the commodity form of butter or apples is taken to the absurd by permanent 'over-production' in Western Europe. The necessity of periodic 'retraining', due to the increasingly rapid change of basic labour skills, now spreads to the domain of intellectual labour; it even creates within the framework of capitalist reforms of the university, marginal tendencies towards permanent part-time study, thereby fulfilling one of Marx's prophecies. But within the limits of the capitalist mode of production, this potential tendency naturally cannot prevail. It is accompanied and stifled by a neutralizing and repressive counter-tendency to make the university and the teaching system as a whole directly 'profitable'. The objective constraint towards prolongation of learning activity over the greater part of life, however, necessarily undermines the 'private' character of labour qualifications. The latter made sense so long as individual qualifications were principally a function of individual effort — and were also paid for by individual families (or the individual himself). Today, however, the production costs of individual qualification have for the most part been socialized. The overwhelming majority of inventors, researchers, scientists and doctors could never perform their functions if hundreds of thousands, indeed millions of workers had not produced the laboratories, buildings, machines, apparatuses, instruments and materials with which they operate; if the social surplus product, produced by the total mass of the producers, had not ensured them the necessary working-time free from the constraint of reproducing their immediate existence, without which they

could not pursue their scientific work; if past and present generations of other inventors, researchers, scientists and doctors had not
performed the necessary antecedent and concomitant labour, without which individual scientific activity would in most cases be
impossible. Every contemporary can thus only realize his private
talents as part of social labour capacity. It is precisely in the sphere
of intellectual production that the belated socialization of the labour
process is now most manifest, eliminating any justification for the
existence of a social-hierarchical division of labour between 'producers' and 'administrators', or between lower-paid 'material' and
higher-paid 'intellectual' creators.[44]

But the objective challenge gathering within late bourgeois
society to the capitalist division of labour and its specific phenomenal form, the commodity character of labour-power, also assumes
another, unexpected form. Here again, Marx's analyses have, however, been confirmed.[45] The productive force of the individual
becomes more and more emancipated from physical and nervous
effort (alienation of energy) and increasingly becomes a function
of technical or scientific equipment, and scientific or technical qualification. The consequence is that the frontiers between working-
time and free-time start to become fluid. The objective result of
labour in the technically most developed enterprises and branches
of industry becomes a function of the attention and interest accorded
by the employee to his activity. These have an inverse relationship
to the length of his working-time and the degree of alienation of his
labour, and are a direct function of the possibility of self-confirma-
tion and self-determination by the immediate labour collective.[46]
Indeed, the situation is nearing *where the productivity of labour
depends more and more on the growth of free-time*, both in the

[44] Bourgeois sociologists still cling to the myth of the 'ignorance' of workers, or
their 'feeling of ignorance', to justify or eternalize the social hierarchy, whose class
character they usually deny. See for example, Irving Louis Horowitz, 'La conduite
de la classe ouvriere aux Etats-Unis', in *Sociologie du Travail*, no. 3, 1971.

[45] See the well-known passage in the *Grundrisse*, which we have already cited:
'The saving of labour time (is) equal to an increase of free time, i.e., time for the full
development of the individual, which in turn reacts back upon the productive power
of labour as itself the greatest productive power': p. 711.

[46] Attempts to introduce the four-day week in the USA, and 'sliding day work'
in the USA and Switzerland, have raised the productivity of labour. Such schemes,
however, are always determined by the pressure to increase profitability (otherwise
they would not be introduced) or by particular monopoly conditions: see for example
Lou Gomolak: 'Quattro Giorni di Lavoro e tre di Festa' in *Espansione*, April 1971.

sense of free-time as learning-time, and in the sense of free-time as the development of individual talents, wishes, desires which alone can stimulate interest and potentially *creative* labour. The reduction of mechanically repetitive labour by thorough automation will in turn doom strictly quantitative measurement of labour-time — the historical means of exorting the maximum amount of surplus-value from each producer — to disappear.

The characteristic taylorist organization of work based on conveyor belts and parcellization of labour inside the factory, corresponded neither to any absolute technical or scientific necessity, nor to an attempt at any maximum economy of living labour. It was consonant only with the *capitalist* goal of combining a sharp decrease in costs of production with a maximum increase in surplus-value or profit accruing to the firms using these techniques. This implied the need for total control and regulation of the labour-process of every single producer, and its reduction to a near-mechanical and easily quantifiable part of a global machine system.[47] But in semi-automatic or automatic factories, the capital-conserving function of living labour becomes more important than its surplus-value producing function, since these factories (firms) essentially appropriate fractions of social surplus-value actually generated in other firms. The immensely complex and expensive machinery which has to be maintained and repaired by living labour in these plants necessitates great attention and skill, which cannot be so mechanically and rapidly acquired. Therefore, high turnover of labour and pervasive indifference towards work and machinery become a threat to capital in such plants — as also in precision factories which demand the utmost attention for the quality of their output. In these circumstances, it is not only with the aim of 'decreasing social tensions' and thereby lowering the explosion-points of the overall crisis of capitalist relations of production, but also with the much more direct objective of profit maximization, that employers have started to experiment with techniques of 'job enrichment', greater mobility of labour inside the factory, suppression of conveyor-belts, and so on.[48] But, of course, the extortion of surplus-value and surplus-labour can never wither away under capitalist relations of reproduction, no matter how camouflaged under late capitalism.

[47] Andre Gorz is correct to emphasise this, in his essay, 'Technique, Techniciens et Lutte de Classe', in *Critique de la Division du Travail*, Paris 1973.
[48] See the interesting analysis of the organization of the labour process in the Italian

The social division of labour characteristic of the capitalist mode of production — the division between producers of surplus-value and all those who extend or ensure the process of capital-expansion — determines a hierarchical structure within each enterprise based on the strict enforcement of partial rationality and the principle of achievement. The objective tendencies towards the socialization and higher qualification of labour inherent in the third technological revolution inevitably clash especially sharply with this hierarchy.

Furthermore, social labour capacity today is not the activity of freely associated producers, self-administered and consciously directed, i.e., democratically and centrally planned; it falls, on the contrary, more than ever before under the central power of a vertical chain of command. This contradiction, however, is an Achilles Heel of late capitalism, even in times of the 'most favourable upswing', 'fastest' growth, and 'broadest' mass consumption. For the more that labour becomes objectively socialized and dependent on conscious cooperation, the more that immediate shortages disappear, and the higher are the educational level and average qualification of the typical producer — all the more intolerable will the direct organizational and technical subsumption of labour under capital become to the mass of wage-earners, and with it their social and economic subordination.

The crisis of capitalist relations of production thus finds logical expression in a crisis of the authority of the entrepreneur and of the structure of the enterprise. Although capital constantly attempts to halt or limit this crisis,[49] a new trend in daily class struggles emerges, capable of turning the conflicts over it into the starting point of mass anti-capitalist movements. The emphasis of class struggle increasingly shifts from the issue of the division of the values newly created by labour between wages and surplus-value, to the issue of the right of control over machines and labour-power. The number of immediate labour disputes detonated by revolts against

---

IBM factory in *Per La Critica della Organizzazione del Lavoro*, February 1973; for the experiences at Norsk Hydro and Volvo respectively, see *Le Monde*, 5 April 1972 and *Neue Zürcher Zeitung*, 16 June 1974.

[49] Hence the spreading attempts of big capital to neutralise the revolutionary potential of this new development of 'spontaneous' class struggle, by schemes for 'participation' or 'co-determination' designed to convert it into a positive instrument of late capitalist economic programming. Revolutionary Marxists, of course, struggle for workers' control as a power of *veto* without any responsibility for profit ('Not company profitability, but class solidarity').

the structure of the enterprise is constantly growing: workers today are increasingly rejecting the right of employers to reduce the number of employees, to shift machines and orders, to set the rhythm of the assembly belt, to alter the organization of labour, to revise the system of wage-payment, to widen the span between the highest and lowest (or average) earnings in the factory, or to close factories.[50]

But the capitalist mode of production does not consist of production units which are loosely and only occasionally combined with one another. The degree of the objective socialization of labour which it has created, makes it economically and socially impossible for the working class to win back the means of production which it has set in motion in the enterprise alone.[51] The action of the late capitalist State as the representative of the collective interests of capital in repeatedly intervening to control the labour situation and income levels of the working-class (taxes and inflation, employment and credit policy, foreign trade or agricultural decisions, and so on) is a permanent source of political education for the proletariat. State intervention, in effect, trains the working-class for the highest forms of class struggle: for the conquest of political power and control over the means of production, for the abolition of the capitalist mode of production and gradual dissolution of the commodity and money economy and the social division of labour. The growing contradiction between objectively socialized labour and private appropriation is determined not only by the third technological revolution, the increasing necessity of highly qualified labour and the widening cultural and political horizon of the working-class, but also by the gulf between potential abundance on the one hand, and actual alienation and reification on the other. Whereas in the age of classical capitalism the main impulse for workers' struggles came from the tension between the present and the past, today it lies in the tension between the actual and the possible.

Set against potential abundance and possible development of the creative powers of the individual, the growing fatigue with

[50] This trend is manifest in the strike statistics of recent years in Great Britain, France, Italy and Belgium. It is interesting to note that the same tendency is slowly but surely emerging in the USA. See for example Emma Rothschild's penetrating analysis of the revolt of the automobile workers in the ultra-modern General Motors plant in Lordstown (Ohio), *New York Review of Books*, 23 March 1972.

[51] See our introduction to the anthology, *Controle Ouvrier, Conseils Ouvriers, Autogestion*, Paris, 1970.

senseless production of inferior goods,[52] the widespread sentiments of anxiety among workers and capitalists alike, resulting from the suppression of spontaneous self-activity and the spread of generalized insecurity, with the compulsion to 'conform' and to 'succeed' characteristic of bourgeois society, the increasing solitude of social life and frustration with advertising and product differentiation, the deteriorating state of mass transport, the decay of housing conditions and the strangulation of large cities are becoming increasingly unbearable. At the very moment when the self-development of the social individual would be incomparably easier to achieve than ever before, its realization seems to be receding ever further away.

For Marx, alienation is an objective, not merely a subjective category. Even an individual alienated from consciousness of his alienation remains alienated. This objective condition is in the long run a more powerful reality than all the attempts at manipulation or integration of the industrial working-class; in late capitalism it drives wage-earners towards collective awareness of the unremitting alienation to which they are subjected, and so creates the conditions for socialist self-liberation. Even under conditions of maximum 'prosperity' these fundamental contradictions of capitalism have proved insoluble and irreducible in our age. In the long-run, the worker will never be satisfied with hours of work which seem a loss of life, with a labour process which appears forced labour, and with an enterprise whose structure accords him no more than subject status.

A profound crisis of capitalist relations of production is evident when workers challenge the authority of employers in enterprises with direct factory struggle. Today, however, the mass of wage-earners are increasingly contesting the fundamental values and priorities of the capitalist mode of production on a social level too. This global 'process of contestation', directed against capitalist relations of production as a whole, has hitherto taken three main forms, as we enter a new epoch of social revolution:

1. Critical attack on the contradiction between the growing abundance of consumer *goods* and the massive underdevelopment

---

[52] Each year, 20 million Americans are injured badly enough in production-related accidents to need medical treatment. Some 110,000 are permanently disabled, and 30,000 die from them. The cost to the economy is more than 5.5 billion dollars annually.

of social consumption (*collective services*). The acute contrast between the two, now admitted even by liberals,[53] contributes to the increasing insecurity of bourgeois and petty bourgeois ideologies based on the glorification of the 'free market economy' and the 'social welfare state'. The rising level of needs determined by the development of the forces of production and the long wage of expansion since the Second World War, have conferred increasing importance on certain services — health, housing, education, local transport, holidays — not only in the 'objective' structure of consumption, but also in the subjective consciousness of workers. By their very nature these needs can only marginally be satisfied by capitalist *commodity production:* it is, of course, for this reason they are systematically 'underdeveloped' by the private capitalist economy. But this underdevelopment in turn intensifies mass pressure for their common-economic satisfaction and potentially raises the demand for the complete socialization of the costs of satisfying these needs. A struggle thus tends to arise for a new form of distribution profoundly antagonistic to the capitalist mode of production, based on optimum satisfaction of needs and complete elimination of the market (free health service, local transport, housing, and so on). The declarations of the British politician Powell that needs for medical care are 'unlimited' and that therefore their price should be determined by a 'free market economy',[54] are already felt to be barbaric by a majority of the population of many, if not most, of the industrialized countries.

2. Frontal challenging of the mechanisms which determine investments. In the capitalist mode of production, capital theoretically flows out of sectors realizing less than the average rate of profit into such sectors which realize more than the average. Since technological advantage (and positions of technological monopoly) facilitate

[53]Galbraith's *Affluent Society*, as well as the efforts of the Nader circle in the USA, have had a major influence in this respect.

[54]This argument merely exposes the absurdity of 'orthodox' bourgeois economic ideology. Are we really to believe that people take 'more and more' medicines and remain in hospital 'longer and longer' simply because these goods and services are distributed cash-free on the basis of need? Would such over-consumption not be damaging to health? Could not its irrational character be impressed on the population by mass-scale education? Is it not precisely the logic of profit maximization and the market economy whose advertisements and media systems (not to speak of unconscious escapism) create the very notion of such over-consumption in capitalism?

surplus-profits, official doctrine claims that the pattern of sectoral investments generally promotes the efficiency and rationality of the total economy. In practice, as we have seen, the strategically decisive investments of large companies have increasingly deviated from such norms of allocation. Monopolistic and oligopolistic market situations have long since ended the relative approximation between market success and labour productivity. State subvention, State guarantee of monopoly profits and permanent inflation exercise a direct influence on the investment decisions of large firms, very often in a sense directly counter to economic rationality. The logic of 'monopolistic competition' and the 'competitive game' has very little to do with the systematic lowering of production costs today. Under these conditions it has become more and more unacceptable to great masses of wage earners that investment decisions taken by a tiny handful of directors on the boards of large companies, should determine the employment, income and even the domicile of hundreds of thousands of families. The socialization of investment decisions — and the public presentation of the social priorities underlying such decisions — will soon become another proletarian demand tending to explode capitalist relations of production.

3. Popular denunciation of the contradiction between the repeated dependence of large companies on State subventions, contracts and aid during recessions, and the jealous preservation of business and banking secrecy by these companies.[55] The demand for the abolition of banking secrecy, the publication of accounts, workers' control over production in the workshop, the plant and society as a whole, is today gathering strength. It too directly menaces capitalist relations of production, putting in radical question private property, competition and the control of capital over labour-power and the means of production. At the same time, the late capitalist tendency towards the integration of the trade-unions with the State apparatus, and the restriction or abolition of the freedom of wage-bargaining, determined by corporate cost and investment planning and economic programming for total capital, is encountering growing resistance.

The contemporary crisis of the bourgeois nation state, finally, is

---

[55] See for example the popular indignation in France after the devaluation of the franc in 1969: a proposal from *bourgeois* circles that speculators who had despatched their capital abroad before the devaluation should be prosecuted, was rejected by a small parliamentary majority.

indivisible from the crisis of capitalist relations of production. The increasing internationalization of forces of production, the vast and unsatisfied needs of the semi-colonial masses, and the global spread of the threat to the environment render conscious planning of basic economic resources on a world-wide scale imperative. But the survival of the national state is inseparable from imperialist competition and capitalist commodity production. It can no more be superseded within the framework of the capitalist mode of production than can the manufacture of useless or harmful commodities, the laying idle of gigantic economic resources, the recurrence of unemployment or the systematic under-utilization of machines and other means of production.

All these searing problems will remain insoluble so long as control over the forces of production is not wrested from the hands of the capital. The appropriation of the means of production by the associated producers, their planned application to priorities determined democratically by the mass of the workers, the radical reduction of working time as a precondition of active self-administration in economy and society, and the demise of commodity production and money relations are the indispensable steps to their solution. The final abolition of capitalist relations of production will be the central objective of the mass revolutionary movement of the international working-class that is now approaching.

Glossary

ABSOLUTE LAND RENT: specific form of surplus-profit originating from a monopoly of landownership by a special class of agrarian proprietors, who prevent the sum-total of surplus-value produced in agriculture from being redistributed among all capitalists, by appropriating part of that surplus-value as a prior condition of access to the land which they own.

ACCUMULATION OF CAPITAL: increase in the value of capital by the transformation of part of surplus-value into additional capital. That part of surplus-value which is not accumulated will be unproductively consumed by capitalists or their dependents.

AVERAGE SOCIAL PRODUCTIVITY OF LABOUR: the level of productivity of labour at which the average commodity is produced in each important branch of production. A minority of goods will be produced below this average in 'backward' firms, and another minority at a higher level of productivity in 'advanced' firms.

CAPITAL: exchange-value which seeks a further accretion of value. Capital first appears in a society of petty commodity producers in the form of owners of money (merchants or usurers) who intervene in the market with the aim of buying goods in order to resell them at a profit.

CAPITALIST MODE OF PRODUCTION: generalized commodity production, in which the direct producers have been dispossessed of their means of production, and therefore have to sell their labour-power (the only commodity which they still possess) to those who own the means of production. Labour-power and means of production alike have become commodities. Means of production in turn become capital — accruing further exchange value by the surplus-value created by the direct producers and appropriated by the owners of capital. A society dominated by the capitalist mode of production is basically divided into two classes: the capitalist class which monopolizes the means of production, and the proletariat which is economically compelled to sell its labour-power.

CENTRALIZATION OF CAPITAL: the fusion of different capitals under a single common command.

CIRCULATING CAPITAL: that part of constant capital used to purchase raw materials, energy and auxiliary products; plus variable capital needed to purchase labour-power.

COLLECTIVE LABOUR CAPACITY: the sum total of all manual and intellectual labour indispensable in a modern capitalist factory for the process of physical production to occur. By extension: social collective labour capacity is the sum total of manual and intellectual labour at the disposal of society as a whole for organizing its economic life. Commodity production and operation of the law of value arise out of the fragmentation of this social collective capacity into private labours, expended independently of each other. Under a system of use-value production (for example, primitive communism, or future communism), the associated producers consciously divide this social collective labour capacity between different spheres of production and communal activities.

COMPRADOR BOURGEOISIE: that section of the ruling-class in colonial and semi-colonial countries which, although owning and accumulating capital, is closely tied to foreign imperialism, especially via the intermediary functions of merchant capital (import-export businesses), and normally does not engage in industrial investment.

CONCENTRATION OF CAPITAL: the growth in the value of capital in each major capitalist firm as a result of accumulation and competition (elimination of smaller and weaker firms).

CONSTANT CAPITAL: that part of capital which is used to purchase buildings, machinery, raw materials or energy, and whose value remains constant because it is incorporated into the value of final commodities and conserved by the activity of labour-power.

CRISES OF OVER-PRODUCTION: periodic interruptions in the process of expanded reproduction, classically occurring every seven or ten years, induced by a fall in the rate of profit, determining a decline in investment and employment: during such a crisis, the capital engaged in the production of commodities cannot be wholly recuperated, because some of these commodities can no longer be sold, or can only be sold at a loss. Crises of over-production are a necessary phase in the normal pattern of capitalist production, which successively passes through industrial upswing, boom, overheating, crisis and depression.

DEPARTMENT I: branches of capitalist production producing means of production (raw materials, energy, machinery and tools, buildings).

DEPARTMENT II: branches of capitalist production producing means of consumption (consumer goods), which reconstitute the labour-force of the direct producers and contribute to the livelihood of the capitalists and their dependents.

DEPARTMENT III: branches of capitalist production which do not enter the process of reproduction – i.e., which renew neither constant nor variable capital: for example, production of luxury goods exclusively consumed by capitalists, or production of weapons.

DEVALORIZATION (ENTWERTUNG): the process whereby capital loses part of its value, which takes two main forms during a capitalist crisis. Firstly, as a result of the decline in value (price of production) of commodities, especially means of production, the capital invested in these commodities is devalorized. Secondly, as a result of commercial bankruptcies and firms going out of business, much of the value of their capital is destroyed. This capital was part of total social capital, which thereby loses part of its aggregate value.

DIFFERENTIAL LAND RENT: specific form of surplus-profit originating from the differential productivity of specific agricultural or mining land (or successive investments in these lands), so long as the value and market price of the agricultural or mining products in question are regulated by less productive land.

EXCHANGE-VALUE: value for which a commodity is exchanged on the market. According to Marx's (perfected) labour theory of value, the exchange-value of a commodity is determined by the socially necessary quantity of unskilled labour needed for its reproduction at a given social average productivity of labour, and measured by the length of labour-time (hours or days) needed to produce it.

FIXED CAPITAL: that part of constant capital used to purchase buildings and machinery.

INCREASE OF ABSOLUTE SURPLUS-VALUE: obtained by a lengthening of the working day (or week) without any commensurate increase in wages for the direct producers.

INCREASE IN RELATIVE SURPLUS VALUE: obtained by a shortening of that part of working-day (or week) during which the worker reproduces the equivalent of his wage, without any overall reduction of the working-day (or week), via an increase in the productivity of labour in agriculture and those branches of industry which produce consumer goods for the working-class.

INTERNATIONAL INTERPENETRATION OF CAPITAL: centralization of capital on an international scale.

LAW OF VALUE: the economic mechanism in a society of private producers which distributes the total labour-power at the disposal of society (and thereby all material resources necessary for production) between its various branches of production, via the mediation of the exchange of all commodities at their values (in the capitalist mode of production: at their prices of production). Under capitalism, this law determines the pattern of investment — i.e., the inflow and outflow of capital in different branches of production, according to the deviation of their specific rate of profit from the average rate of profit.

MONEY: the specific commodity in whose exchange-value the exchange-value of all other commodities is expressed. Money is the general equivalent for the value of all commodities.

MONOPOLY CAPITALISM (IMPERIALISM): that phase in the development of the capitalist mode of production in which a qualitative increase in the concentration and centralization of capital leads to the elimination of price competition from a series of key branches of industry, monopolistic agreements are formed, a few firms completely dominate successive markets, banking-capital increasingly merges with industrial capital into finance capital, a few very large financial groups dominate the economy of each capitalist country, these giant, monopolies divide the world markets of key commodities between themselves, and the imperialist powers divide the globe into colonial empires or semi-colonial spheres of influence. A trend to 'regulate' (i.e., limit) investment and production in monopolized sectors henceforward prevails, in spite of the emergence of monopolistic surplus-profits, so that over-accumulation leads to a frantic search for new fields of capital investment and hence to a growth of capital exports.

MONOPOLY SURPLUS-PROFITS: specific forms of surplus-profit originating from obstacles to entry into special branches of production.

OBJECTIVE SOCIALIZATION OF PRODUCTION: the growth of technical coordination, interdependence and integration in production, by which capitalism increasingly generates the negation of the private labour and private production from which it is born — first inside single factories, then within a number of production units and branches of industry, and finally between countries.

ORGANIC COMPOSITION OF CAPITAL: the technical or physical relationship between the mass of machinery, raw materials and labour necessary to produce commodities at a given level of productivity, and the *value* relationship between constant and variable capital determined by these physical proportions.

OVER-ACCUMULATION: a state in which there is a significant mass of excess capital in the economy, which cannot be invested at the average rate of profit normally expected by owners of capital.

PRICE (MARKET PRICE): the monetary expression of the exchange-value of a commodity, which oscillates about this value according to the laws of supply and demand.

PRICES OF PRODUCTION: transformation of values of commodities by means of competition between capitals, which tends to equalize the rate of profit for each capital. The result of this process of equalization is that each capital does not appropriate the sum-total of the surplus-value produced by 'its own' workers, but a part of total social surplus-value proportionate to the fraction of total social capital which it represents. The sum total of prices of production is equal to the sum total of values, because in the process of competition and equalization of the rate of profit, no additional surplus-value can be created nor any portion of socially produced surplus-value be destroyed.

PRODUCTIVE CAPITAL: that part of social capital invested in sectors where surplus-value is directly produced. Unproductive capital, like commercial capital or banking capital, can acquire part of total social surplus-value because it helps to reduce the turnover-time of capital, or to enlarge the scope of production by credit beyond the operative limits of productive capital itself, and thereby indirectly countributes to an expansion of surplus-value.

PRODUCTIVE LABOUR: in a capitalist society, only that labour which directly produces surplus-value. This notion has nothing to do with that of socially useful labour, in a socialist society.

PROFIT: that part of social surplus-value which is appropriated by each particular capital (each capitalist firm).

RATE OF ACCUMULATION: the relationship between the accumulated portion of surplus-value and the value of the capital which this surplus-value increases.

RATE OF INTEREST: interest is in the first instance that portion of surplus-value which productive capitalists pay to owners of money capital, in order to increase the scope of their productive operations beyond the limits of the capital which they themselves possess. The rate of interest therefore normally and in the long-run remains lower than the average rate of profit. In a capitalist society, any sum of money can obtain the average rate of interest by being deposited in the banking system, which centralizes available savings and transforms them into money capital.

RATE OF PROFIT: the relationship between surplus-value and the sum-total of constant and variable capital engaged in the production of this surplus-value.

RATE OF SURPLUS-VALUE: the relationship between the surplus-value produced by variable capital, and the variable capital that has produced it: also called, rate of exploitation of wage-labour.

REALIZATION OF SURPLUS-VALUE: surplus-value, produced by workers in the process of production, and therefore contained in the commodities as soon as this production is completed, can only be appropriated by capitalists in money-form — in other words, after the commodities in question have been sold. Realization of surplus-value thus involves sale of commodities at such a market price that part or whole of the surplus-value which they contain can be appropriated by their owners.

RECESSION: a crisis of over-production abbreviated and mitigated by deliberate State intervention in the form of credit expansion, inflation, public works and so on.

REPRODUCTION: the process by which, after production and sale of commodities, a new cycle of production is undertaken by a given capital. Simple reproduction means that capital starts a new cycle with the same value as at the outset of the previous cycle (accumulation is zero: total surplus-value has been unproductively consumed). Expanded reproduction means that capital starts a new cycle with an increase of value over the previous cycle (accumulation is positive: part of surplus-value has been productively invested). Contracted reproduction means that capital starts a new cycle with a lower value than in the previous cycle (not only has all surplus-value been unproductively consumed, but the sale of commodities has not reconstituted the total value of the capital initially engaged in their production).

SEMI-COLONIAL COUNTRIES: those capitalist nations which are politically (formally) independent, but whose economies continue to be dominated by international imperialist capital.

SIMPLE COMMODITY PRODUCTION: economic system in which producers sell the products of their labour on the market, but remain proprietors of, or have direct access to, their own means of production and livelihood (essentially: small farmers and independent artisans). The general purpose of such commodity-owners is to sell their own products in order to buy goods necessary for their livelihood which they do not produce themselves, because of the social division of labour.

SOCIAL SURPLUS PRODUCT: that part of the annual product of any society which is neither consumed by the direct producers nor used for the reproduction of the stock of means of production available at the start of the year. In a class-divided society, the social surplus product is always appropriated by the ruling class.

SOCIALLY AVERAGE RATE OF PROFIT: the relationship between the sum-total of surplus-value produced in a given capitalist society, and the sum-total of capital.

SURPLUS-PROFITS: all profits over and above the socially average rate of profit.

SURPLUS-VALUE: the monetary form assumed by the social surplus product in a commodity-producing society. In a capitalist society, surplus-value is produced by wage-labourers and appropriated by capitalists: in other words, it is the difference between the new value produced by labour in the process of production and the cost of reproducing labour-power (or the value of labour-power). In the final analysis, it represents unpaid labour appropriated by the capitalist class.

TECHNOLOGICAL RENTS: those monopoly surplus-profits originating from technical advances protected by monopolistic practices.

TURNOVER-TIME OF CAPITAL: the time during which the value of a capital is reconstituted. Normally, one cycle of production and circulation (sale of commodities) reconstitutes circulating capital, whereas fixed capital is only reconstituted after several cycles of production and circulation of commodities.

UNPRODUCTIVE LABOUR: all those forms of wage-labour which do not increase the social mass of surplus-value, but which help specific groups of capitalists to appropriate parts of this surplus-value, or indirectly increase surplus-value — for example, wage-labour in commerce, banking or administration.

USE-VALUE: utility of a commodity for the fulfillment of a specific need of its purchaser. Goods without use-value for anyone cannot be exchanged or sold. By extension, production of use-values pure and simple, as opposed to production of commodities, is production of goods for the consumption of their direct producers, or collective units of such producers.

VALORIZATION (VERWERTUNG): the process whereby capital increases its own value by the production of surplus-value. Marx presents the process of commodity production as a unity of two distinct processes — the labour process through which labour-power produces use-values, and the valorization process through which labour-power produces additional value over and above its own value. This surplus-value, although created during the process of production, has first to be realized through the sale of commodities before capital can appropriate it and therewith actually increase its own value. The traditional translation of this notion (*Verwertung*) in *Capital* as the 'self-expansion' of capital is misleading, because it abstracts from the labour-process which materially creates value and from the process of realization which is necessary for capital to achieve its 'expansion': it is therefore not used in *Late Capitalism*.

VALUE OF LABOUR-POWER: the sum total of the exchange-values of all those commodities necessary to reproduce the labour-power of the direct producer and his family. This contains a purely physiological element, and a moral-historical element. The latter is a function of those workers' needs that are formed by a specific level of civilization and a given relationship of forces between social classes, which have become acknowledged as integral to a normal standard of living.

VALUE OF SKILLED LABOUR-POWER: a multiple of the value of simple labour-power, incorporating into it the costs of producing the skills in question.

VARIABLE CAPITAL: that part of capital which is used to purchase labour-power (to hire workers) and whose value accrues with the surplus-value extracted from this labour-power by the owners of capital.

WAGE: price of the commodity of labour-power, or monetary expression of its exchange value, which oscillates about the value of labour-power via the operation of the law of supply and demand, and especially via the regulation of the reserve army of labour, or volume of unemployment.

Index of Subjects

'absolute immiseration', thesis of, 155–7, 302
advertising, 393–4, 398, 399, 401, 538
Afghanistan, 372
AFL–CIO, 179
Africa, 72, 131, 189, 325, 348, 353, 375, 376n, 575
agriculture, 74, 363, 391; crisis of European, 61, 378; curtailment of production, 575; and handicrafts, 384; industrialization of, 379–83, 387, 558; organic composition of capital, 98–9, 343, 382–3; penetration of capital, 80, 92, 186, 379; plantation economy, 58–9; prices, 381–2, 383; productivity of labour, 79, 80–1, 89, 375–6, 378–9, 381, 424; rent, 381–3; specialization, 378–9
Algeria, 311, 363–4
amortization, tendency towards planned, 230–1
'anti-monopoly alliance', theory of, 515–22
arms production, 10, 12, 38, 62, 178, 190, 193, 251, 443, 481, 578; in history of capitalism, 274–5; permanence in late capitalism, 275–6, 294, 300–9, 469, 552; and problem of realization, 277–83,

288; resistance of sections of capitalists, 303; wages and surplus-value 280–3, 285–7, 296–9; see also department III, 'permanent arms economy'
arms race, 223, 301, 578n
art objects, 450–1, 452
Argentina, 55n, 66n, 68, 259, 347, 349, 369, 372, 382
Asiatic production, 45, 475n, 476
Australia, 89n, 123n, 138n, 145, 202, 259, 333, 362, 363–4, 382, 558n
Austro-Hungarian Empire, 88
automation, 120n, 121, 175–9, 182–3, 190–2, 193, 250–1, 258, 583; and competitiveness, 197, 228, 230; division of labour, 208, 215–6, 249, 268–9, 319; enterprise planning, 228; four types, 193–4; impossibility of capitalist generalization, 206–11, 214–5, 407, 570; organic composition of capital, 200, 456; partial and total, 198–9, 204, 206; production of automatic machines, 206; unemployment, 216

banks, 225, 339, 416–7, 419–20, 422, 428, 429, 443, 445–6, 453, 455; solvency of, 451, 468
bankruptcies, 414

of, 38–43, 107; 'monocausal' ex-
planations of laws of motion, 34–9,
77, 438; and non-capitalist sectors, 23, 26, 43,. 44, 47, 73, 84,
90, 311, 363, 377–8; 'organized'
capitalism, 32–5, 500, 526–7;
and relations of exploitation,
521–2, 526; social crisis, 570–
89; sharpening of contradictions, 197, 267–8, 341–2, 401,
469, 472, 520–2, 524, 537n, 562,
570–89; theories of inevitable collapse, 34–7; uneven and combined
development, 22–3, 42, 70, 75,
85–103, 311, 325, 352, 439, 464;
see also late capitalism
Ceylon, 59n, 163
Chile, 46n, 66n, 347, 372, 497–8;
and world market, 57
circulation process, 390; capital
penetration, 384, 388, 402, 573;
and commodity value, 404–5; and
ideal price, 410n
Colombia, 202, 347, 349, 354
colonial surplus profits, 345, 348,
350, 355
Communist International, 218, 515
Communist Party of the Soviet
Union, 514
company planning; and administration, 243; and automation, 228,
232; and economic programming,
233–4, 236–7, 246–7, 508–10,
559, 579; and profitability 244;
and military programming, 251
competition, 23, 27, 30–1, 34–5, 75,
76, 104, 230, 440, 517; and
equalization of rate of profit, 92–3,
98n, 538–9, 543–50; and interests
of capital in its totality, 480–1;
internationalization of, 311–2,
317–8, 324, 331, 332, 449–50,
454, 465, 467
consumer credit, 385n, 399, 400–1,
417–8, 430, 448, 452, 572
consumer goods; in early capitalist
accumulation, 184–8; and purchasing power of the masses, 301,
398; quality of, 394; sector of
durable, 190, 385, 401; and social
consumption, 586–7; unsaleable
residue, 278–9, 281, 447–8, 572
'consumer society', scientific and
utopian critique of, 395–8, 407
consumption, development and dif-

ferentiation of working-class,
390–8, 401–2
corruption, 513
credit system, 84, 225, 246, 384–5,
388, 414, 415, 445; and commodity prices, 425; and contradictions of capitalism, 445, 524
crises, 37, 108, 414, 418, 438, 440–2,
447, 501, 526–7; and consumption, 35–6, 301–2
Cuba, 131, 351n, 367, 558n
currency system; instability, 320,
328, 415, 460–7, 560; currency
controls, 455–6, 458, 467, 471,
472, 560
cycle, 108–9, 392; credit and industrial, 454–66, 469–70, 472, 550–1,
560; and anti-cyclical measures,
446–7, 455, 461, 463, 472, 485,
550–1; determination of length,
110, 436; in building industry,
133n, 452; impossibility of capitalist elimination, 440–2; international synchronization of, 469–
72; and overcapacity, 457–9, 466

data-processing, 193, 194, 228–9,
538n
deficit-financing, 417
demand; barriers to expansion, 85,
281, 301–2, 401, 440; and supply
in determination of market price,
98, 99, 102; changed structure,
536–8, 587; and law of value,
527—9
Denmark, 202
department III ('means of destruction'); and average organic composition of capital, 283–4, 285–6,
287, 289, 292, 303; and departments I and II, 296–9, 303, 304,
307; and extended reproduction,
167–8, 285, 289, 297, 443; and
rate of surplus value, 284–7, 293
dollar, 412; fall in value, 424, 428,
457, 464–6, 470, 560; and international monetary system, 462,
464–5

East India Company, 54
econometrics, 37
economic programming, 233–4, 264,
327–8, 342, 495, 498, 525; capitalist limits of, 234–8, 246–7

81; and technological revolution, 120, 258, 456, 557; and turnover time, 225; 'value' and 'technical' composition, 111; variations from social average, 77

Pakistan, 372
parliament, 482, 489, 495, 499
peasantry, 383; in E. and S. Europe, 80
'permanent arms economy', theory of, 37–8, 287–9, 301–3
Peru, 57, 347, 373
petro-chemical industry, 193, 195n, 197, 226, 253
Phillipines, 373
Poland, 52
Portugal, 44, 325, 363–4
'post-capitalist society', notion of, 191, 501
post-war boom (1945–65), 8, 163; end of, 180, 258, 459, 469, 489, 571; market expansion in, 168–9, 170–1, 442; and rate of surplus-value, 147ff., 258, 442, 559; sub-periods of, 194; and weakening of working-class, 169, 178–9, 442
prices of production, 289–90; deviation of market prices from, 97; and surplus profits, 72; transformation of values during circulation process, 12, 99, 290, 291, 293, 531; uniformity only in national market, 71, 83, 91, 351–2
productivity of labour, 40, 41–2, 76, 102, 111, 145, 172, 178, 179, 223, 398, 414, 528; and determination of value, 100–2, 203; equalization in late capitalism, 191–2; and free time, 393, 401–2, 582–3; growth in post-war boom, 191, 200, 378, 424, 429; and human progress, 509; internal differentiation, 86, 431; international differentiation, 60–2, 66, 69, 71–4, 82n, 83, 85, 192, 214, 341–2, 343, 351, 354n, 361, 364–5, 376, 561; and prices, 431
production process, shortening of, 196
profit, mass of; and cycle, 108–9; long-term maximization, 232, 235, 262, 303, 318, 540–2, and internationalization of production,

318–9; *see also*, rate of profit, surplus-profit
Puerto Rico, 369

rate of profit; and arms production, 283–93; and crises of overproduction, 108–10, 113, 151, 414, 436, 438–9, 442–3; determination of, 40, 68, 76n, 272, 290–3, 557; and devalorization, 93–4, 114; equalization of, 12, 45, 92–3, 101, 187, 307, 411n, 528, 532, 543, 544–50, obstacles to, 75, 77, 78, 83–4, 351, 529; fluctuations, 39, 133, 136, 137, 145, 568; and investment, 114–6, 120, 144–5, 164, 168, 295, 439, 444, 447, 483, 528–9, 587; and luxury production, 290–2; 'dual rate' in monopoly and non-monopoly sectors, 95, 531–50; and nationalizations, 488; periods of rise, 83, 116, 130–2, 146, 559; and rate of interest, 189, 294, 388, 402, 453–4, 547n; and services sector, 388, 399–400, 407; and surplus-profits, 94, 531–5, 537, 539; tendency to fall, 20, 43, 62, 76, 78, 81, 94, 120, 189, 212, 341, 457, 536, 539, 546, 557, 559; in 1972–4 inflationary boom, 70
rate of surplus-value, 39–41, 42, 43, 67, 100, 116, 145, 147–50, 160, 164, 165–6, 168, 170–2, 290–1, 422; and arms expenditure, 281–3, 284–7, 297–9; and class struggle, 40, 115, 116, 131, 150–1, 153, 155, 158–9, 162, 180, 183, 211, 219, 341–2, 442, 456–7, 473, 498, 519, 571, 584; and credit cycle, 456; deviation from average, 78; evolution in late capitalism, 147ff., 190, 224, 272, 281, 306, 456–7, 557, 559; and productivity of labour, 82n, 147–8, 168, 208–11, 284; in underdeveloped countries, 81, 354
raw materials, 201, 449, 576n; and export of capital, 57–62, 64–5, 82, 146, 188, 189, 343, 349; decline in relative price, 64–5, 69, 78, 82, 85, 116, 146, 190, 381, 429; earlier rise in relative price, 58–9, 62, 81; inflationary boom (1972–4), 371–2, 429, 431, 451; and rate of profit, 69, 545–6; search for, 57–8,

wages, 40, 280; of commercial employees, 165; international differentials, 51, 77–8, 79, 85, 92, 183, 344, 352–3, 359–64, 367, 373; planning of wage costs, 238–42; post-war rise in real, 171–4, 179, 304, 344, 391; and price rises, 421–2, 425, 447–8; and profits, 150, 421, 443, 456; reductions in real, 76, 79, 148–9, 151, 158–62, 168, 363; in 'settler' colonies, 362–4; *see also*, labour-power surplus-value
wars, 147, 149, 178, 416; in late

capitalism, 302, 303, 333, 506–7, 510–1
women, and wage-labour, 171, 181, 182, 391–2
workers' control, 584–5, 586
working-day, length of, 147, 158, 161
world market, 9, 10, 39, 43; and autarky, 461–2, 470; expansion of, 310, 449, 456, 524n, 560; formation of prices on, 70–4, 83, 471–2; lack of homogeneity, 84, 91–2; specialization on, 74, 318–9, 357, 363

Yugoslavia, 325

Index of Names

Kumps, Anne-Marie, 318n
Kuznets, Simon, 133n, 137, 139, 142n, 143n, 324n

Laclau Ernesto, 55n, 365n
Landes, David, 119n, 141n, 185n, 187n, 188n, 313n
Lange, Oskar, 120n, 140n, 509
Lapinski, P., 483n
Läpple, Dieter, 478n
Lassalle, Ferdinand, 155
Lattes, Robert, 337
Lefebvre, Henri, 504n
Lefèvre, Théo, 490n
Leiman, Melvin, 88n
Lemnitz, Alfred, 520
Lenin, Vladimir Ilyich, 10, 14–15, 38, 56n, 82, 214–5, 218, 220, 222, 225, 309, 312n, 332–4, 366, 409n, 514–5, 540
Leontief, Vassili, 105n, 200, 234n, 252, 307n
Lessure, J., 123n
Lettieri, Antonio, 241n
Levinson, Charles, 192n, 195n, 197, 223n, 254n, 257n, 320n, 328n, 330, 332, 338n, 339, 394n, 429n, 434n
Lévy-Leboyer, Maurice, 51n
Lewis, Bernard, 313n
Lewis, W. Arthur, 154, 172n, 177
Lilley, S., 250n
Lipson, E., 91n
Löbl, Eugen, 267
Locke, John, 482n
Lockwood, W. W., 53n, 275n
Lohmann, M., 231n
Lorenz, Konrad, 505n
Löwenthal, Richard, 524, 542n
Ludwig, Helmut, 196n
Lukács, Georg, 475, 478n, 505n, 508
Lundberg, Ferdinand, 245n
Luxemburg, Rosa, 24n, 25, 26n, 28, 29–32, 34, 35, 44, 48n, 103, 150n, 153n, 155, 181, 207, 282–3, 285n, 299–300, 307, 481n
Lynn, Frank, 227n

MacArthur, Douglas, 303n
MacRae, Norman, 322n
Magdoff, Harry, 322, 335n, 349n
Mage, Shane, 176–7, 202
Mairesse, Jacques, 227n, 237n
Mansfield, Edwin, 223n, 227n, 251n, 252n

Marcuse, Herbert, 502–3, 507n
Marini, Ruy Mauro, 68n
Marshall, Alfred, 413n
Marx, Karl, 10–12, 13–34, 37, 38–9, 40, 42–3, 44–5, 46, 47n, 49n, 50n, 51n, 58n, 66, 71, 73n, 74n, 75n, 76n, 77n, 78n, 79n, 81n, 83, 84n, 85, 86–7, 90, 91n, 95, 96n, 97–102, 104, 105n, 106, 109n, 110, 111–2, 116–9, 123, 129, 133, 137, 138n, 144, 147, 148n, 149–52, 153n, 154–6, 160n, 165, 176–7, 178n, 185n, 188, 195, 199, 202–3, 207–8, 210, 214n, 215, 216–7, 221–2, 224n, 226, 244, 247, 248–9, 252, 255, 259n, 262, 266n, 270–1, 274n, 275n, 277n, 279, 283n, 287, 289–92, 301, 310n, 311n, 342, 344n, 351–4, 356, 358, 359, 361, 362, 377n, 378, 384n, 385, 389–91, 395–8, 403–6, 408–10, 414n, 419n, 421, 422, 426n, 435–6, 438, 451n, 467n, 474, 476n, 477, 478n, 479n, 481n, 482n, 484n, 486n, 493n, 494n, 509, 521, 523–4, 528n, 529n, 531, 536, 537n, 549–50, 562–9, 571–2, 574, 576n, 578, 581, 582, 586
Massé, Pierre, 234n
Mata, Hector Malavé, 435n
Mattick, Paul, 19n, 300n, 442n, 527n, 556–7
Mattison, Alan C., 225
Maxwell, Andrew, 576n
Means, Gardiner C., 429n, 430, 543n, 545
Meier, Bernard, 241n
Meldolesi, Luca, 181–2
Melman, Seymour, 307n, 308n
Merrett, A. J., 233n, 244n, 246n
Messadié, Gerald, 579n
Meynaud, Jean, 493
Milgram, Prof., 505n
Miliband, Ralph, 493n, 494n
Minas, Bagicha Singh, 202n
Mishan, E. J., 576n, 577n
Mitchell, B. R., 59n, 141n
Mola, Aldo Alessandro, 88n
Morf, Otto, 15
Morris, Jacob, 422n
Moszkowska, Natalie, 34n, 301–4
Muller, Ron, 350n, 353, 371n, 372n
Müller, Wolfgang, 476n
Müller-Plantenberg, Urs, 68n
Munk, Bernard, 369n
Murray, Robin, 329n